MEASURES OF RELIGIOSITY

MEASURES OF RELIGIOSITY

edited by
Peter C. Hill and Ralph W. Hood Jr.

Religious Education Press
Birmingham, Alabama

The paper in this book meets the guidelines for permanence and durability
of the Committee on Production Guidelines of the Council for Library Resources.

Library of Congress Cataloging-in-Publication Data

Measures of religiosity / edited by Peter C. Hill and Ralph W. Hood Jr.
     p.   cm.
  Includes bibliographical references and index.
  ISBN 0-89135-106-X (alk. paper)
  1. Religiousness—Testing. 2. Christianity—Psychology.
I. Hill, Peter C., 1953–   . II. Hood, Ralph W., 1942–
BR110.M43   1999
291.4—dc21   99-10330
                                                    CIP

Religious Education Press
5316 Meadow Brook Road
Birmingham, Alabama 35242-3315
10 9 8 7 6 5 4 3

Contents

Introduction

The idea for this book can be traced back to a fall 1986 conference in upstate New York sponsored by the Eastern Region of the Christian Association for Psychological Studies. Over coffee one evening at that conference, seven or eight researchers were lamenting the fact that so much effort in the psychology of religion is being spent in constructing new measures when others already exist, probably because many earlier measures have been lost over the years in the research shuffle. During that discussion the researchers expressed appreciation for the 1973 volume *Measures of Social Psychological Attitudes*, authored by John Robinson and Phillip Shaver and published by the Institute for Social Research at the University of Michigan. That book is a compendium of reviews of attitudinal scales developed by that time on such social-psychological constructs as life satisfaction, values, locus of control, and authoritarianism. One of the eleven chapters in Robinson and Shaver's book reviews seventeen measures of religious attitudes.

As helpful to the psychology of religion that the single chapter in the Robinson and Shaver book has been, the measures reviewed there are but a small fraction of the many dozens of measures that have been developed, even to that time. Unfortunately, the revised edition of their book, published in 1991, did not include a chapter on religious attitudes. Most of the handful of researchers in that 1986 discussion committed themselves to locate measures in the psychology of religion and to provide a review of each. We soon discovered, however, that there were too many measures for our group to review, so we enlisted others to help provide reviews. This volume is the product of those efforts. It goes without saying that any credit that this book receives is due to the reviewers' excellent work.

Much of the work on this book has been supported by a grant from the John Templeton Foundation. Sincere thanks go to Sir John Templeton and the staff at the foundation for helping bring this book to fruition. Thanks also go to the many fine people at the National Institute for Healthcare Research (NIHR), especially David Larson, NIHR president, and Mike McCullough, for their backing of this project. The major impetus to complete this book came from a series of conferences on scientific progress in spiritual research sponsored by NIHR and funded by the Templeton Foundation. Leading authorities from major universities in the United States and abroad on the relationship between religion, spirituality, and health care were invited to convene at three different locations over a twelve-month period. Those attending the conference repeatedly expressed a need for this book and a companion volume on measures of spirituality, which is in progress. Both authors sensed great encouragement and support as they worked to complete this project.

The authors recognize the vision of James Michael Lee, publisher of Religious Education Press, in appreciating the value of a substitute reference book like this and are grateful for the patience and encouragement of him and his staff at Religious Education Press. We also wish to express thanks to key individuals at our institutions for their backing. President John Moore and Deans Garth Runion and Bill Anderson of Grove City College have shown great interest in this volume. The support of Rich Metzger at the University of Tennessee at Cattanooga is gratefully acknowledged. Two professional colleagues deserve mention for their helpful editorial work: Richard Butman and Michael Donahue. Of the many students who provided help over the years, the work of seven demand special recognition and thanks: Jennifer Bailey, Toby Basalla, Emily Griffin, Kelly Hetrick, Sandi Kamerman, Susan Sheffer and Kathy Stokes.

Of course, it is those closest to us who bear the brunt of the demands that a project such as this makes. So the most heartfelt thanks of all go to Carol, Rob, Jon, Sarah, and Dan.

Peter C. Hill
Ralph W. Hood Jr.

A Preliminary Note on Measurement and Scales in the Psychology of Religion

For some time the authors have felt a need for a book that would provide a ready reference source for existing measures in the psychology of religion. We believe that many researchers would include religious variables in their studies if they knew that measures were readily available. This text is meant to relieve researchers of the unnecessary task of creating scales for which adequate measures already exist. The unnecessary duplication of scales hampers the advancement of psychology of religion in two ways. First, it proliferates a variety of measures for constructs, such as fundamentalism or religious orthodoxy, when a single existing measure would suffice. Second, it hampers the accumulation of knowledge when identically titled scales, whose correlations with each other are not established, are used in research projects. One then cannot be certain of different findings regarding a construct such as "fundamentalism." Gorsuch (1990; p. 84) has persuasively argued that researchers should *not* develop new scales until they can establish a definite need. This book is intended as a guide for determining whether or not such a need exists.

Before attempting to construct a measure, the investigator should check for an existing measure, which should be used so that a body of empirical research can be established derived from the uniform of measurement of theoretically meaningful constructs. The need for a new measure must be justified on one of three bases: (a) existing measures are not psychometrically adequate to the task, (b) conceptual or theoretical issues demand modification of existing measures, and (c) there are no measures available for particular constructs. Although we do not oppose the development of new measures, we are confident that existing measures have been underutilized and that the researcher is unlikely to be interested in a construct for which a measure is not already available. It is in this sense that Gorsuch (1984) has argued that a common paradigm has emerged, at least in the American approach to the psychology of religion since its reemergence during the 1970s. The paradigm is measurement itself and the operationalism of variables of interest to the researcher in questionnaires or scales. This text is a testament to the existence of a wide variety of scales and affirms Gorsuch's description of what amounts to the new paradigm in the American psychology of religion. Furthermore, it supports what Gorsuch aptly titles the "boon" of psychology. As he states the case, *"We are ready to go beyond measurement to basic enduring issues,* and thus our measurement success should be a boon to the area" (Gorsuch, 1984 p. 235, emphasis in original). The measurement success is represented in this text, in which the scales reviewed collectively represent measurement sophistication that is as good as in most specialty areas in psychology (Gorsuch, 1984; 1990). However, it must be emphasized that specialty areas in psychology seldom have measures that come up to the standards of standardized tests widely used in psychological assessment. One should not expect tests in specialty areas of research to match the statistical and psychometric sophistication of standardized tests used in personality, intelligence, and clinical assessment (American Psychological Association, 1985). Measurement success in research terms is more limited in scope.

If this text is indicative of the measurement success of the area, it is not uncritically so. While it is true that the variety of scales reviewed here measure many constructs of interest to investigators in the psychology of religion, the scales in this text collectively have obvious limits and deficiencies. Some of the more serious limitations deserve at least a brief discussion.

SCALES LIMITATIONS

First, while this book is intended to service researchers in the psychology of religion (among others), the phrase "psychology of religion" is somewhat misleading. Since the psychology of religion in America has largely been dominated by convenience sampling of college students, an American Protestant orientation is overrepresented (Gorsuch, 1988, 1990; Hood, Spilka, Hunsberger, & Gorsuch, 1996). This deficiency is obvious and the researcher is cautioned to recognize that scales to measure non-Protestant religion are less common; in terms of non-Western faith traditions, relevant scales are virtually nonexistent. Somewhat related is the subtle problem that measures of religion are likely to reflect Christian religious biases, even when not explicitly identified as measures of *Christian* religion (Heelas, 1985). In this sense our text reflects both the interest and the deficiency of the area. Indeed, it is our hope that this text will stimulate interest in determining the usefulness of current measures of religion with samples of diverse faith traditions for which the scales in this text nevertheless appear to have some applicability.

Second, while the reliability of the scales in this text are generally adequate and as impressive as the dominant scales in most areas of empirical research, validity issues remain more complex. A major problem in the area has been the failure to develop sustained research programs using standardized measures. While notable examples exist, such as Batson's (Batson, Schoenrade, & Ventis, 1993) extensive research program with his Quest Scale, Hood's (1995, 1997) research with his Mysticism Scale, Pargament's (1997) programmatic use of his coping measures, and perhaps most notably the extensive and diverse tradition of research with varieties of Intrinsic/Extrinsic Scales (see Hood et al., 1996, for review), many measures have been utilized in only a limited number of research studies and hence issues of validity are more difficult to assess. One purpose of this text is to encourage investigators to contribute to the validity of studies by utilizing established measures in programmatic research. As Gorsuch (1984, p. 235) states, measurement can be a bane to the area if investigators focus upon measurement of religion at the expense of using established measures of religion to study religion itself.

Third, we initially were interested in having measures associated with selection for religious training or for employment in religious organizations included in this text. However, virtually no measures for selection purposes specific to religion have been developed. Organizations that do use selection criteria based upon measurement tend to use some form of existing standardized personality measures or clinical scales (such as the MMPI) that are beyond the scope of this text. Such scales are reviewed in many standard sources (Newmark, 1985). Hence we do not have a section on selection or screening of religious professionals. It is likely that scales measuring specific characteristics and relevant aptitudes (as well as the screening out of inappropriate persons) for religious training and professional work are worthy of development.

Fourth, our text reflects "measures of religion"—a term that has come under intense scrutiny among investigators in this area. Perhaps most significant are the efforts to investigate the relationship between "religion" and concepts that are closely related such as "spirituality" (see Wulff, 1997, chap. 1). While we do not want to discuss the complexities of such distinctions, suffice it to say that most of the measures in this text assess *religious* phenomena that include some relevance to traditional institutionalized searches to acknowledge and maintain some relationship with the transcendent. Given the sampling bias characteristic of the field, measures in this text typically conceptualize institutionalization in terms of churches or synagogues, and the transcendent is typically referenced as God. While there are some exceptions (especially measures included in chap.10, "Scales of Spirituality and Mysticism"), it is apparent that a second text devoted to the exploding area of spirituality measures is needed. This text focuses on established measures of *religion*. How measures of spirituality might relate to religion conceptually and theoretically is an intriguing issue. However, any empirically documented relationship between these constructs presupposes the use of religious measures that are likely to be in this text.

CHAPTER ORGANIZATION

The chapters in this volume clearly are not mutually exclusive. In many instances a measure properly belongs under several chapter headings. The assignment of measures to chapters is basically determined by five factors. First, measures on specific topics that may overlap with general psychology but are of particular interest in the psychology of religion are clustered together: religious beliefs/practices (chap. 1), religious attitudes/identity (chap. 2), religious development (chap. 4), religious involvement (chap. 5), religious and moral values (chap. 7), and institutional religion (chap. 16). Second, measures that have generated a reasonably consistent programmatic research tradition are clustered together: religious orientation (chap. 3), religious coping and problem solving (chap. 9), and spirituality/mysticism (chap. 10). Third, measures that have commanded extensive investigation within the psychology of religion and are essentially specialty topics within the discipline are assigned to separate chapters: God concept (chap. 11) and religious fundamentalism (chap. 12). Fourth, topics common to general psychology but expressed in specific religious measures are clustered into chapters: religious experience (chap. 6), death and views of afterlife (chap. 13), divine intervention/religious attributions (chap. 14), and forgiveness (chap. 15). Multidimensional scales are in a separate chapter (chap. 8), given the fact that most scales in the area are unidimensional. Finally, related constructs are clustered in a separate chapter (chap. 17).

Our clustering of measures ignores the distinction between substantive and functional definitions of religion as well as the extent to which any given measure is substantive or functional. Substantive measures define religion by content, whereas functional measures focus upon processes regardless of content. In some cases, such as religious beliefs, substantive measures dominate for obvious reasons, but in others, such as religious orientation, functional measures dominate. In many instances, as in psychology of religion in general, the distinction itself is problematic, as are the measures involved (See Hood, 1994).

We asked contributors to this volume to provide basic descriptions of each scale, introduced by a brief discussion of the construct the scale is designed to measure, along with descriptive information regarding reliability and validity. In addition, normative data on the original sample (and subsequent samples if reported in other research) and bibliographic references of recent research using the scale are included. No effort is made to identify the best measures, and reviewers were instructed *not* to provide critical evaluations of the scales; such evaluations are left up to the reader. Obviously, some standard guidelines in evaluating scales ought to be considered; the novice can consult any standard source on test and measurement (e.g., Anastasi & Urbana, 1997; Bohrnstedt & Borgatta, 1981; Cronbach & Glesser, 1965). Here we mention only a few fairly obvious guidelines that have particular relevance to religious measures.

GUIDELINES FOR SCALE SELECTION

First, selection of any scale should be guided primarily by one's theoretical orientation. Measures that do not effectively operationalize theoretical concepts are unlikely to generate meaningful results. As in other specialty areas of psychological research, scale selection should be based as much as possible on what Robinson, Shaver, and Wrightsman (1991, p. 2) call "decision theoretic criteria."

Closely related to the theoretical basis of scale selection is the basic methodological postulate that researchers should select measurement of variables aggregated at similar levels of abstraction (Fishbein & Ajzen, 1974). Someone who wants to predict specific denominational beliefs or behaviors should *not* use a generalized measure of religiosity. Conversely, general measures of religiosity may not be expected to predict specific religious phenomena very well. Any exceptions that are made to this general methodological postulate should have a strong theoretical justification.

Third, selection of scales must consider reliability. Most basic is some measure of internal consistency. Cronbach's alpha is most common (Cronbach, 1951). Test-retest reliabilities are not common in this area, despite their obvious value in identifying stable scores over time. None of the measures in this text have been sufficiently established to have parallel forms, a factor to be noted in any proposed research strategy.

While we propose no hard and fast criteria for adequate reliability, it is generally true that less reliable scales make significant correlations between measures less likely. The researcher must consider whether or not the reliability of any scale permits the likelihood of significant findings being obtained even in adequately designed studies. Most measures in this book have at least acceptable internal consistency reliabilities (coefficient alpha), but few are in the excellent range (>.90).

Fourth, questions of validity need to be carefully considered. It is our view that issues of face validity are of particular relevance in psychology of religion. Investigators familiar with a particular religious tradition can easily identify measures likely to give, at best, biased assessments. In this sense, if a measure appears unsuitable on the surface, it probably is. Investigators less familiar with the traditions they propose to study might be at a disadvantage in selecting measures if they ignore face validity. For instance, among more evangelical or fundamentalist Protestant groups, measures of orthodoxy are likely to use terms such as "inerrant" or "authoritative" or "infallible" with reference to the

Bible. It behooves the investigator to note that each of these terms has different implications; among some religious groups they are hardly interchangeable.

Additional issues of validity are immensely complicated. Given the lack of programmatic research in some areas, construct and/or convergent validity are often difficult to assess. Many measures have been used only a few times and their validity in terms of meaningful coherence within a systematic theoretic framework are inferred at best. Other measures, particularly religious orientation measures, have generated a controversial literature in which firmly established empirical findings are open to a wide range of interpretations (Kirkpatrick & Hood, 1990). In other instances, programmatic research with particular measures has been associated with a small number of researchers and lack replication by truly independent research teams. The interested researcher is urged to be informed about the range and scope of empirical findings, their limitations, and the conceptual and theoretical debates engendered before deciding whether or how to use a particular measure in terms of a given strategy. This text is intended to provide the basis for at least a preliminary assessment of such measures with appropriate references so that the researcher can explore issues more in depth.

Fifth, for most of the scales in this volume, basic statistical data typically found with established assessment tests are not available. Few tests have standardized norms. Often the literature lacks even basic descriptive data, such as means and standard deviations, for research samples. Few tests have been developed based on truly representative sampling. As already noted, most tests are based on convenience samples of American Protestant college students. Though the established measures remain useful, these limitations, as severe as they are, must be kept clearly in mind. In particular, generalization from such tests to general theories of "religion" are not simply suspect but are unwarranted.

Sixth, issues of response set are complex and have generated some debate within the area. Social acquiescence—the tendency to agree or disagree with items—is not a controversial issue and is readily handled by reversed scored items or negatively wording some scale items. However, social desirability is a controversial issue in the area of research on religion (Batson, Schoenrade, & Ventis, 1995; Watson, Morris, Foster, & Hood, 1986). The researcher who selects a technique to control for this possible confound must be sensitive to the theoretical issues in this area as it applies to religion, as well as to the methodological issues involved in controlling for social desirability as a general issue in measurement (Paulhus, 1991, chap. 2).

A final caveat involves considerations of standardization of test administration. Few tests have clear guidelines of how they are to be administered. Most researchers simply obtain a copy of a test, reproduce it, and administer it in their own way. What effects such ad hoc procedures have on empirical results is open to question. Again, the researcher should at least consult a standard text on psychological testing of test procedures to employ some constancy in administration and to be assured that she or he is sensitive to experimenter effects that can be involved in the way tests are administered.

Without claiming to provide an exhaustive list of all measures of religion, the text does represent the major scales that have been developed and typically dispersed across a wide variety of journals. Here in one volume are the major scales, reproduced and described, for ready access and use by investigators. We hope that readers who find significant scales missing from this text will write us with reprints of such scales so that they can be included in subsequent editions.

References

American Educational Research Association, American Psychological Association, and National Council on Measures in Education (1985). *Standards for Educational and Psychological Tests*. Washington, D.C.: American Psychological Association.

Anastasi, A., & Urbana, S. (1997). *Psychological testing* (7th. ed.) Upper Saddle River, NJ.

Batson, C. D., Schoenrade, P., & Ventis, W. L. (1993). *Religion and the individual: A social-psychological perspective* (Rev. ed.). New York: Oxford University Press.

Bohrnstedt, G., & Borgatta, E. (Eds.). (1981). *Social measurement: Issues*. Newbury Park, CA: Sage.

Cronbach, L. (1951). Coefficient alpha and the internal structure of tests. *Psychometrika, 31*, 93–96.

Cronbach, L., & Glesser, G. (1965). *Psychological tests and personnel decisions* (2nd ed.). Urbana: University of Illinois Press.

Fishbein, M., & Ajzen, I. (1974). Attitudes toward objects as predictors of single and multiple behavioral criteria. *Psychological Review, 81*, 59–74.

Gorsuch, R. L. (1984). Measurement: The boon and bane of investigating religion. *American Psychologist, 39*, 228–236.

Gorsuch, R. L. (1988). Psychology of religion. *Annual Review of Psychology, 39*, 201–221.

Gorsuch, R. L. (1990). Measurement in psychology of religion revisited. *Journal of Psychology and Christianity, 9*, 82–92.

Heelas, P. (1985). Social anthropology and the psychology of religion. In L. B. Brown (Ed). *Advances in the psychology of religion* (pp. 34–51). Oxford: Pergamon Press.

Hood, R. W., Jr. (1994). Psychology and religion. In U.S. Ramachdran (Ed.). *Encyclopedia of human behavior*, 3 vols. (pp. 619–629). New York: Academic Press.

Hood, R. W., Jr. (1995). The facilitation of religious experience. In R. W. Hood Jr. (Ed.), *Handbook of religious experience* (pp. 568–597). Birmingham, AL: Religious Education Press.

Hood, R. W., Jr. (1997). The empirical study of mysticism. In B. Spilka & D. N. McIntosh (Eds), *The psychology of religion: Theoretical approaches* (pp. 222–232). Boulder, CO: Westview Press.

Hood, R. W., Jr., Spilka, B., Hunsberger, B., & Gorsuch, R. L. (1996). *The psychology of religion: An empirical approach* (2nd. ed.). New York: Guilford.

Kirkpatrick, L., & Hood, R. W., Jr. (1990). Intrinsic-extrinsic religious orientations: The boon or bane of contemporary psychology of religion? *Journal for the Scientific Study of Religion, 29*, 442–462.

Newmark, C. S. (1985). *Major psychological assessment instruments* (2nd. ed.). Needham Heights, MA: Allyn & Bacon.

Pargament, K. (1997). *The psychology of religion and coping*. New York: Guilford.

Paulhus, D. L. (1991). Measurement and control of response bias. In J. P. Robinson, P. R. Shaver, & L. S. Wrightsman (Eds.), *Measurement of personality and social psychological attitudes* (pp. 17–59). New York: Academic Press.

Robinson, J. P., Shaver, P. R., & Wrightsman, L. S. (1991). *Measures of personality and social psychological attitudes*. New York: Academic Press.

Watson, P. J., Morris, R. J., Foster, J., & Hood, R. W. Jr. (1986). Religiosity and social desirability. *Journal for the Scientific Study of Religion, 25*, 215–232.

Wulff, D. M. (1997). *Psychology of religion: Classic and contemporary* (2nd ed.). New York: Wiley.

Chapter 1

Scales of
Religious Beliefs and Practices

The focus of the scales included in chapter 1 centers around religious belief and practice. These scales are useful in that they help researchers investigate substantive understandings and definitions of religion and religious experience. By taking a substantive approach to the psychology of religion, the researcher is investigating *what* it is that a person believes or practices, not *why* a person holds particular beliefs. A substantive understanding of religion often places supreme importance on the belief, doctrine, or creed in relation to a person's understanding of the sacred or divine. Frequently the beliefs themselves are about religious practices.

In one sense, religious belief is involved in virtually every measure throughout this book. For example, measures of divine intervention (chap. 14) or religious values (chap. 7) or almost any other chapter category necessarily involve religious belief. In fact, it may be hard to distinguish between measures of religious belief in chapter 1 and the attitudinal measures of religion in chapter 2. The measures of religious belief or practice chosen for chapter 1 assess a specific set of beliefs, perhaps doctrines or creeds in some cases, that may tap fundamental elements of a substantive understanding of religious experience.

Substantive definitions of religion can range from the quite broad to the rather specific. Substantive measures of religion, as operationalizations, obviously tend to be more specific than the definitions themselves. Most of the scales measure specific aspects of conservative Christian religious belief. Examples of such scales include the Certainty in Religious Belief Scale (1.1), the Christian Conservatism Scale (1.2), the Christian Orthodoxy Scale (1.4), the Inventory of Religious Belief Scale (1.6), the Religious Belief Inventory (1.12), the Religious Belief Scale (1.13), the Religious World View Scale (1.15), and the Scriptural Literalism Scale (1.18). Some scales, such as Panton's Religious Identification Scale (1.14) and Bassett and colleagues' Shepherd Scale (1.16) mix items of Christian belief with Christian practice while Katz's Student Religiosity Questionnaire (1.20) measures Jewish beliefs and practices.

Scales designed to measure less conservative Christian beliefs include Stellway's Christian Liberalism Scale (1.3), Kaldestad's Humanistic Morality/Liberal Belief Scale Scales (1.5) and the Religious Orientation Scale of the Omnibus Personality Inventory (1.10) by Heist and Yonge. Other scales such as Dunkel's Inventory of Religious Concepts (1.7), Armstrong and colleagues' Religious Attitude Scale (1.11), and the Salvation Opinionnaire (1.17) attempt to measure multiple orientations (e.g., conservatism, liberalism, orthodoxy, radical belief, etc.) within the Christian tradition.

Meanwhile, the What I Believe Scale (1.21) by Gill and Thornton measures Judeo-

Christian beliefs in contrast to two other belief systems: spiritism/occult and atheism/secular humanism. Yinger's Nondoctrinal Religion Scales (1.9) attempt to measure religious belief that is outside of the context of a particular faith system.

Finally, two other scales are included in this chapter, though they do not fit any of the categories already described. Hunt's LAM Scales (1.8) were designed to measure an individual's characteristic belief *style* as literal, antiliteral, or mythological. Therefore, while this is in one sense a substantive measure of religious belief, it also recognizes that religious belief may be expressed in a literal or nonliteral fashion. Also, Luckow and colleagues' Structure of Prayer Scales (1.19) is one of the few attempts to measure specifically one aspect of religious practice.

The psychology of religion has a definite Western, primarily Christian, bias. These measures of religious belief, by representing the field as a whole, also represent that bias. The extent to which some of these measures may be modified or expanded to measure religion more broadly conceived is a question that awaits empirical investigation.

1.1
CERTAINTY IN RELIGIOUS BELIEF SCALE (Thouless, 1935)
Reviewed by Peter C. Hill

Variable: The Certainty in Religious Belief Scale was designed to measure a tendency toward certainty with regard to religious belief. Religious beliefs and attitudes, like all beliefs or attitudes, can be held with surety and passion or can be tentative and superficial. Although the certainty of belief is important, it represents only one aspect of religiousness.

Description: The scale includes 40 items, 25 of which are religious. The other items are either nonreligious factual statements, political viewpoints, or philosophical statements that have little or no relation to religion. Because many of these other statements reflect the culture and time period in which the scale was written (e.g., "The total national debt of Great Britain is more than a thousand million pounds."), it is recommended that the nonreligious items be dropped from the scale. Hence, what is reproduced in this volume are only the 25 religious items. It should be noted that Thouless's intent was to measure the degree of certainty held with religious versus nonreligious beliefs, and hence he included both types of belief in his measure. With the particular items used, Thouless found that religious beliefs maintained greater certainty.

The respondents are asked to indicate the degree of certainty with which they believe or disbelieve statements on a 7-point Likert-type scale ranging from "complete certainty" that the item is true (+3) to "complete certainty" that the item is false (–3). Ratings of 2 indicate a strong conviction, but not amounting to certainty, that the item is true (+2) or false (–2). Ratings of 1 (positive or negative) indicate greater tentativeness about the truthfulness or falseness of the item, and a rating of 0 demonstrates total uncertainty. The average degree of certainty was determined by summing the scores on the items (disregarding signs) and dividing by the number of items. The possible range was therefore 0 to 3. Thus, this scale measures neither belief content nor direction, but the degree of certainty with which a religious belief is held.

Practical Considerations: This brief, self-administered scale requires no special considerations for administration.

Norms/Standardization: Thouless's original sample consisted of 138 students at the University of Glasgow, Scotland, during the early 1930s. The students were a "heterogeneous collection of subjects of various occupations and of both sexes and of all ages from twenty upwards" (p. 17). The mean degree of certainty of the religious items was 2.13 with a standard deviation of .32.

Reliability: No measure of the scale's reliability was reported.

Validity: No direct measure of the scale's validity was reported. Thouless did report a number of research findings that provided, at best, mixed support for the validity of the scale. Thouless had available intelligence scores from a portion of his sample. Contrary to his expectations, he found no considerable decrease (in fact, a slight increase) in the tendency to certainty among those who scored higher on the intelligence tests.

Thouless also devised a measure of orthodoxy among the scale's items and found that certitude among the unorthodox was just as strong as among the orthodox. Thouless discovered no gender differences in the tendency to certainty. These findings may shed light on the scale but should not be interpreted as conclusive tests of validity.

Location:
Thouless, R. (1935). The tendency to certainty in religious belief. *British Journal of Psychology, 26,* 16–31.

Subsequent Research:
Brown, L. B. (1962). A study of religious belief. *British Journal of Psychology, 53*(3), 259–272.

Appendix

The 'Beliefs' Test

Please rate each item below using the following rating scale:

+3 — I am completely certain that this statement is true.
+2 — I am almost certain that this statement is true.
+1 — I think that this statement is true, but I am not at all certain.
  0 — I am completely uncertain about this statement.
–1 — I think this statement is false, but I am not at all certain.
–2 — I am almost certain that this statement is false.
–3 — I am completely certain that this statement is false.

_____ 1. There is a personal God.
_____ 2. Jesus Christ was God the Son.
_____ 3. There are spiritual realities of some kind.
_____ 4. The world was created by God.
_____ 5. There is a personal Devil.
_____ 6. Matter is the sole reality.
_____ 7. There is a God who is all-powerful.
_____ 8. There is a God who is altogether good.
_____ 9. There are such spiritual beings as angels.
_____ 10. Jonah was swallowed by a great fish and afterwards emerged alive.
_____ 11. Man has been evolved from lower forms of life.
_____ 12. There is an impersonal God.
_____ 13. Evil is a reality.
_____ 14. The spirits of human beings continue to exist after the death of their bodies.
_____ 15. Religion is the opium of the people.
_____ 16. There is no God (personal or impersonal).

____ 17. Attendance at church is a better way of spending Sunday than taking a walk in the country.
____ 18. Moses was the author of the first five books of the Bible.
____ 19. Christianity is a better religion than Buddhism.
____ 20. The Bible is literally true in all its parts.
____ 21. Man is, in some degree, responsible for his actions.
____ 22. There is a Hell in which the wicked will be everlastingly punished.
____ 23. The spirits of persons who have died can sometimes communicate with the living.
____ 24. Right will triumph.
____ 25. Belief in evolution is compatible with belief in a Creator.

Thouless, R. (1935). The tendency to certainty in religious belief. *British Journal of Psychology, 26,* 16–31. Copyright © 1935. The British Psychological Society. Reprinted with permission.

1.2
CHRISTIAN CONSERVATISM SCALE (Stellway, 1973)
Reviewed by P. J. Watson

Variable: Stellway (1973) created the Christian Conservatism Scale to measure commitments to the theological, anthropological, and epistemological assumptions of conservative Christianity. As described by Stellway, conservative Christians view God as an all-wise, personal, and morally pure supernatural power. In contrast, such Christians view human beings as relatively ignorant and tainted by sin. Because of these and other imperfections, humans cannot rely on reason and science to solve their most important problems. True solutions must come from the Bible and church authorities. Ultimately, a person must accept divine forgiveness, and social life must reflect biblical standards.

Description: Stellway operationalized Christian conservatism as part of his effort to test the hypothesis that religious and sociopolitical conservatism covary directly. His scale consisted of one negatively worded statement and six positively worded statements. Individuals responded to each statement on a 5-point strongly disagree (1) to strongly agree (5) continuum. Stellway examined the average rating per item, but all seven responses could be added together to create a total Christian Conservatism score, ranging from 7 to 35.

Practical Considerations: In Stellway's investigation, all data were obtained through interviews. His scale, nevertheless, could be employed as a simple paper-and-pencil test. Standard instructions would have to preface the items. Such an instrument would offer a usefully brief and face valid assessment of Christian conservatism as defined by Stellway. Subjects could probably complete this scale within five minutes. The reading level should not be too demanding.

Norms/Standardization: All 322 of Stellway's subjects were 25- to 50-year-old white male heads of households. They came from rural areas and a small town in west-central Illinois. Stellway failed to report the mean and standard deviation of his Christian Conservatism scores. Thus, there is little useful normative data for this scale.

Reliability: No reliability data were supplied by Stellway.

Validity: Stellway presented a number of findings supporting the validity of his scale. As would be expected, Christian Conservatism correlated inversely with a measure of Christian liberalism (−.48). Other data involved an examination of partial correlations controlling for education and occupational status. In these analyses, the Christian Conservatism Scale yielded expected linkages with a commitment to maintaining the status quo in American society (.21) and with a personally expressed conservative political preference (.26).

Considerations within the sociological literature led Stellway to hypothesize that partial correlations would be more robust in individuals who had unfulfilled occupational aspirations. When the relevant subsample was explored, Christian Conservativism did indeed correlate more strongly with a status quo orientation (.36) and with a self-professed political conservatism (.40).

Location:

Stellway, R. J. (1973). The correspondence between religious orientation and sociopolitical liberalism and conservatism. *Sociological Quarterly, 14*, 430–439.

Recent Research: Since its publication, Stellway's study has been cited on numerous occasions, but his Christian Conservatism Scale has seen little use. Hunter (1981) criticized the instrument for "subtle" inadequacies as an operationalization of evangelicalism. This scale, he argued, insufficiently records traditional Christian beliefs about sin and forgiveness. Boivin, Darling, and Darling (1987), nevertheless, found that this instrument had at least some validity when used with Christian samples. They also obtained a coefficient alpha of .86, thereby documenting its internal reliability as well.

Boivin, M. J., Darling, H. W., & Darling, T. W. (1987). Racial prejudice among Christian and non-Christian collge students. *Journal of Psychology and Theology, 15*, 47–56.

Reference

Hunter, J. D. (1981). Operationalizing evangelicalism: A review, critique and proposal. *Sociological Analysis, 42*, 363–372.

Appendix

Christian Conservatism Scale[1]

[The items below should be preceded by standard questionnaire instructions. Subjects react to each statement using the following response options: "strongly agree" (5), "agree" (4), "neutral or no opinion" (3), "disagree" (2), and "strongly disagree" (1).]

1. All Biblical miracles happened just as the Bible says they did.
2. A man must seek God's forgiveness to enjoy fellowship with Him.
3. Jesus was more than a great prophet; he was God's only son.
*4. Biblical miracles did not happen as the Bible says they did but have been used as examples.
5. If they stay true to God, people who suffer in this life are sure to be rewarded in the next.
6. Religious truth is higher than any other form of truth.
7. The Bible is God's message to man and all that it says is true.

---

[1] An asterisk (*) identifies a negatively scored item for which 5 = 1, 4 = 2, 3 = 3, 2 = 4, and 1 = 5.

1.3
CHRISTIAN LIBERALISM SCALE (Stellway, 1973)
Reviewed by P. J. Watson

Variable: This scale measures a personal commitment to the theological, anthropological, and epistemological assumptions of liberal Christianity. Stellway (1973) argues that within a liberal Christian framework, God is described more in natural than in supernatural terms. Orthodox notions about sin receive little attention, emphasis being placed instead on the dignity and creative potential of human beings. Associated with these beliefs is a confidence in reason and empiricism rather than revelation as the most reliable means for obtaining trustworthy knowledge.

Description: Stellway created his instrument to test the prediction that religious and sociopolitical liberalism would be positively correlated. Researchers had explored this question previously but typically had assumed that religious liberalism was made apparent in an absence of fundamentalism, orthodoxy, or conservatism. Stellway's position was that "Christian liberalism constitutes more than a residual category" and that it "must be measured as precisely as possible" (p. 431).

This operationalization of Christian liberalism includes six positively scored statements. Reactions to each are made along a 5-point strongly disagree (1) to strongly agree (5) scale. Stellway analyzed the average reaction to each statement, but total scores could be computed by summing across all six responses. In this latter instance, scale values would range from 6 to 30.

Practical Consideration: Stellway used interviews to obtain his data, but these items could be combined in a simple self-report questionnaire that utilizes standard instructions and typical administration procedures. Subjects should be able to complete such an instrument in five minutes or less. The six items seem fairly easy to read, and such a scale represents a reasonable and usefully brief operationalization of Christian liberalism as defined by Stellway (see appendix).

Norms/Standardization: Residents of a small town and rural areas of west-central Illinois served as Stellway's subjects. All 322 were white male heads-of-households between the ages of 25 and 50. Stellway did not report the mean and standard deviation of his Christian liberalism scores. However, given the nature of his sample, these data would not have served as acceptable norms for most research purposes.

Reliability: Stellway supplied no reliability data.

Validity: A number of findings supported the validity of this scale. Most important, perhaps, Christian liberalism correlated $-.48$ with a measure of Christian conservatism. After education and occupational status were partialed out, Christian liberalism also displayed predicted relationships with a belief that free enterprise should be controlled (.22), a commitment to the use of law to improve the living conditions of disadvantaged groups (.19), and a personally expressed liberal sociopolitical preference (.18).

Based on the sociological literature, Stellway further hypothesized that partial correlations would be more robust in subjects who had unfulfilled occupational aspirations. With these participants, Christian liberalism did indeed correlate more strongly with a belief in controlling free enterprise (.49) and with a liberal sociopolitical preference (.35). An inverse relationship also appeared with a conservative defense of the status quo in American society ($-.34$).

Location:
Stellway, R. J. (1973). The correspondence between religious orientation and sociopolitical liberalism and conservatism. *Sociological Quarterly*, 14, 430–439.

Recent Research: Researchers periodically reference Stellway's study, but the Christian

Liberalism Scale has attracted little or no research attention. A greater social scientific concern with conservative Christian commitments (e.g., Hunter, 1981) perhaps serves as one factor that explains the apparent disinterest. Still, the effects of Christian liberalism remain an important empirical issue (e.g., Pyle, 1993), and Stellway's operationalization of this variable could prove useful in future investigations.

References

Hunter, J. D. (1981). Operationalizing evangelicalism: A review, critique and proposal. *Sociological Analysis, 42,* 363–372.

Pyle, R. E. (1993). Faith and commitment to the poor: Theological orientation and support for government assistance measures. *Sociology of Religion, 54,* 385–401.

Appendix

Christian Liberalism Scale

[The items below should be preceded by standard questionnaire instructions. Subjects respond to each statement using the following response options: "strongly agree" (5), "agree" (4), "neutral or no opinion" (3), "disagree" (2), and "strongly disagree" (1).]

1. Science and religion are both equally good ways to find truth.
2. Biblical miracles did not happen as the Bible says they did but have been used as examples.
3. "God" and "Nature" are in some ways the same thing.
4. It is more important that we believe that Jesus was a great prophet than that he was God's only son.
5. Some Biblical miracles really happened as the Bible says they did but others can be explained by natural causes.
6. If a man does good for others, he will enjoy fellowship with God.

1.4
THE CHRISTIAN ORTHODOXY SCALE
(Fullerton & Hunsberger, 1982; Hunsberger, 1989)
Reviewed by Raymond F. Paloutzian

Variable: The Christian Orthodoxy (CO) Scale is a relatively unidimensional measure of the degree to which someone accepts beliefs central to Christianity. Although, over the centuries, different Christian groups have varied somewhat in particular aspects of their beliefs, there are certain beliefs that are common to all who would use the name "Christian." These are the "bedrock" statements that define the faith and are expressed in the Apostles' Creed and the Nicene Creed. It is the degree of acceptance of the content of such statements that this scale is designed to assess.

Description: The CO Scale taps beliefs that fall into the following categories: the existence of God, the nature of the Trinity, God as creator, Jesus as divine, the virgin birth of Jesus, Jesus' mission to save humankind, Jesus' death and resurrection, Jesus' imminent return to Earth, God's judgment of people after death, life after death, the inspiration of the Bible, miracles, and the efficacy of prayer. The various items that make up the scale represent one or more of these elements. A tenet of the scale is that they are knit together to define Christian orthodoxy.

Two versions of the CO Scale are available. The first, longer version (Fullerton & Hunsberger, 1982) is highlighted in this review. The second, shorter version (Hunsberger, 1989) is composed of only six items; yet, for its brevity, its statistical properties are comparable to those of the longer scale. The two scales correlate highly with each other.

The CO Scale comprises 24 items and takes 10 to15 minutes to complete. Half of the items are negatively worded so that disagreement with the item is scored in the orthodox belief direction. Each item is answered on a 7-point Likert scale ranging from -3 (strongly disagree) to $+3$ (strongly agree), with 0 as a neutral point. A constant of 4 is added to each raw score, and these numbers are then summed to yield the total CO score. CO scores can range from a low of 24 to a high of 168.

Practical Considerations: No special instructions or training are needed. The rationale stated in the instructions for taking the scale is clear. The resulting CO score can be meaningfully compared across a variety of religious denominations.

Norms/Standardization: Subject samples on which item selection was based included several hundred students from Manitoba high schools and the University of Manitoba. The subjects came from predominantly Christian (both Protestant and Catholic) backgrounds and a cross-section of the socioeconomic strata.

Fullerton and Hunsberger (1982) published means and standard deviations for 2,297 subjects in the following (mostly Canadian) samples: urban high school students, rural high school students, university students, university students identified as apostates or as denominational switchers, matched control groups for the apostates and switchers, Australian university students, and parents of Canadian university students. In addition to reporting the overall scores for each sample, scores for males and females are reported separately. Some differences in CO scores between males and females seem apparent; for 7 of the 10 believer groups (discounting the apostates), the women scored higher than the men.

As expected, the apostates had, by far, the lowest CO score. Their overall mean was 61.8; *all* other groups averaged between 111.9 and 130.4. These are sufficient comparison data for future research purposes.

Reliability: The CO Scale has strong statistical reliability properties. In the several samples mentioned above, mean interitem correlation coefficients range from .57 to .70. Internal consistency reliability coefficients for the same samples are all .98, except for one that is .97. Factor analysis showed that there was one factor that runs through the set of items and that all of the items load on this factor. These findings suggest that the CO Scale items "hang together" well to form a unidimensional measure of orthodox belief.

Validity: Similarly impressive validity coefficients are documented. The CO Scale shows the following correlations with a variety of measures that it ought to predict: attendance at religious services (.62), frequency of prayer (.70), scriptural-devotional reading (.57), overall religious behavior (.75), and extent of trust in the religious guidance of the Bible (.77) and the church (.68).

Furthermore, mean CO scores for various "known groups" emerge the way they should. For example, people who were raised in a particular religion but then rejected religion had a mean of 61.8, whereas people who merely switch from one denomination to another had a mean of 130.4. Overall, these data and the face validity of the items on the scale suggest that it measures what it is intended to measure.

Location:
Fullerton, J. T., & Hunsberger, B. (1982). A unidimensional measure of Christian orthodoxy. *Jour-*

nal for the Scientific Study of Religion, 21, 317–326.

Hunsberger, B. (1989). A short version of the Christian orthodoxy scale. *Journal for the Scientific Study of Religion, 28,* 360–365.

Subsequent Research:

Altemeyer, B., & Hunsberger, B. (1992). Authoritarianism, religious fundamentalism, quest, and prejudice. *The International Journal for the Psychology of Religion, 2,* 113–133.

Kirkpatrick, L. A. (1993). Fundamentalism, Christian orthodoxy, and intrinsic religious orientation as predictors of discriminatory attitudes. *Journal for the Scientific Study of Religion, 32,* 256–268.

Pratt, M. W., Hunsberger, B., Pancer, S. M., & Roth, D. (1992). Reflections on religion: Aging, belief orthodoxy, and interpersonal conflict in the complexity of adult thinking about religious issues. *Journal for the Scientific Study of Religion, 31,* 514–522.

Hunsberger, B., Pratt, M., & Pancer, S. M. (1994). Religious fundamentalism and integrative complexity of thought: A relationship for existential content only? *Journal for the Scientific Study of Religion, 33,* 335–346.

Pancer, S. M., Jackson, L. M., Hunsberger, B., Pratt, M. W., & Lea, J. (1995). Religious orthodoxy and the complexity of thought about religious and nonreligious issues. *Journal of Personality, 63,* 213–232.

Appendix

Christian Orthodoxy Scale

ATTITUDE SURVEY

This survey includes a number of statements related to specific religious beliefs. You will probably find that you *agree* with some of the statements and *disagree* with others, to varying extents. Please mark your opinion on the line to the left of each statement, according to the amount of your agreement or disagreement, by using the following scale:

Write down a – 3 in the space provided if you *strongly disagree* with the statement,
– 2 in the space provided if you *moderately disagree* with the statement,
– 1 in the space provided if you *slightly disagree* with the statement.

Write down a + 1 in the space provided if you *slightly agree* with the statement,
+ 2 in the space provided if you *moderately agree* with the statement,
+ 3 in the space provided if you *strongly agree* with the statement.

If you feel exactly and precisely *neutral* about a statement, write down a "0" in the space provided.

1. _____ God exists as Father, Son, and Holy Spirit.

2.* _____ Man is *not* a special creature made in the image of God; he is simply a recent development in the process of animal evolution.

3. _____ **Jesus Christ was the divine Son of God.**

4. _____ The Bible is the word of God given to guide man to grace and salvation.

5.* _____ Those who feel that God answers prayers are just deceiving themselves.

6.* _____ It is ridiculous to believe that Jesus Christ could be both human and divine.

7. _____ Jesus was born of a virgin.

8.*_____ **The Bible may be an important book of moral teachings, but it was no more inspired by God than were many other such books in the history of Man.**

9.*_____ **The concept of God is an old superstition that is no longer needed to explain things in the modern era.**

10. _____ Christ will return to the earth someday.

11.*_____ Most of the religions in the world have miracle stories in their traditions; but there is no reason to believe any of them are true, including those found in the Bible.

12. _____ God hears all of our prayers.

13.*_____ Jesus Christ may have been a great ethical teacher, as other men have been in history. But he was not the divine Son of God.

14. _____ God made man of dust in His own image and breathed life into him.

15. _____ **Through the life, death, and resurrection of Jesus, God provided a way for the forgiveness of man's sins.**

16.*_____ **Despite what many people believe, there is no such thing as a God who is aware of Man's actions.**

17. _____ **Jesus was crucified, died, and was buried but on the third day He arose from the dead.**

18.*_____ In all likelihood there is no such things as a God-given immortal soul in Man which lives on after death.

19.*_____ If there ever was such a person as Jesus of Nazareth, he is dead now and will never walk the earth again.

20. _____ Jesus miraculously changed real water into real wine.

21. _____ There is a God who is concerned with everyone's actions.

22.*_____ Jesus' death on the cross, if it actually occurred, did nothing in and of itself to save Mankind.

23.*_____ There is really no reason to hold to the idea that Jesus was born of a virgin. Jesus' life showed better than anything else that he was exceptional, so why rely on old myths that don't make sense.

24. _____ The Resurrection proves beyond a doubt that Jesus was the Christ or Messiah of God.

Note: No response is scored a "0" on the (–3 to +3) response scale for each item. It is suggested that a participant's data be discarded if he or she does not answer 10 or more items. Data can easily be prepared for analysis rescaling responses such that –3 = 1, –2 = 2, –1 = 3, 0 (or no response) = 4, + 1 = 5, +2 = 6, and +3 = 7. The keying of all negatively worded items—indicated above by an asterisk (*)—is reversed so that for all items a low score indicates an unorthodox belief and a high score indicates an orthodox belief. The CO score is then computed for each subject by summing over the 24 items.

Note 1: The scale authors also use a –4 (very strongly disagree) to +4 (very strongly agree) response format. Procedures for using this format are similar to those for the –3 to +3 format noted above.

Note 2: Those items printed in bold face are the six items for the short form of the scale.

Fullerton, J. T., & Hunsberger, B. (1982). A unidimensional measure of Christian orthodoxy. *Journal for the Scientific Study of Religion, 21,* 317–326.

Hunsberger, B. (1989). A short version of the Christian orthodoxy scale. *Journal for the Scientific Study of Religion, 28,* 360–365.

1.5
HUMANISTIC MORALITY / LIBERAL BELIEF SCALE SCALE
(Kaldestad, 1992; Kaldestad & Stifoss-Hanssen, 1993)
Reviewed by David M. Wulff

Variable: The Humanistic Morality and Liberal Belief Scales were developed by Norwegian psychiatrist Eystein Kaldestad as part of a larger effort to create a battery of measures usable with Norwegian subjects in studies of the relation of religiosity to personality and mental health. Several of the scales he employed are translations of religiosity measures prominent in the English-language literature (e.g., the Allport-Ross Intrinsic and Extrinsic Scales and Batson's Quest Scale; see Kaldestad, 1991). Concluding that these established scales do not adequately assess the increasingly liberal religious views found today among Norwegians, 92% of whom are at least nominal members of the Norwegian Lutheran State Church, Kaldestad developed his Liberal Belief and Humanistic Morality Scales. Available now in English translation, they should be serviceable in other countries as well.

Description: Kaldestad's Liberal Belief Scale takes its inspiration from Andrew Weigert's (1988) delineation of liberal and fundamentalist types of Christian eschatology. The scale consists of eight items, all of which are positive expressions of the liberal point of view. Responses to each item are made on a 5-point Likert scale, ranging from "strongly agree" (5) through "do not know" (3) to "strongly disagree" (1). Total scale scores are calculated by finding the mean rating that was given the eight items.

Kaldestad's Humanistic Morality Scale, which was designed to give expression to the more permissive and relativistic moral-

ity that emerged in Norway following World War II, started out as a five-item scale but was expanded to eight items to raise its reliability. Once again, all statements are written as positive expressions of a liberal perspective. Subject responses are made on the same 5-point scale, and total scale scores are calculated as above. The Humanistic Morality Scale correlates about .70 with the Liberal Belief Scale, which indicates that they have virtually half of their variance in common.

Practical Considerations: These two scales are brief enough that researchers could easily include them with other religiosity measures. Kaldestad suggests, however, that new versions of these scales might first be in order, especially to eliminate one of the two potentially conflicting elements in each of the first three items of the Liberal Belief Scale as well as to make the scales more internally homogeneous. Given the relatively high correlation between the two scales, researchers could also consider combining them into a single liberalism scale.

Norms/Standardization: Like many other scales of their type, these two are intended for use strictly as research instruments. Thus no norms have been made available for interpreting individual scores. Kaldestad's (1992) original report on these scales does contain some means and standard deviations that could be use for comparative purposes.

Reliability: Internal consistency reliabilities were calculated by means of Cronbach's coefficient alpha. Kaldestad's first sample, consisting of 78 staff members of a psychiatric hospital, yielded alphas of .77 for the Liberal Belief Scale and .34 for the original five-item Humanistic Morality Scale. For a second sample, likewise consisting of staff members, the expanded eight-item version of the Humanistic Morality Scale had a far more satisfactory alpha of .72. A third sample, which consisted of 70 staff members and 88 nonpsychotic psychiatric inpatients, yielded alphas of .73 for the Liberal Belief Scale and .80 for the Humanistic Morality Scale. Thus the reliabilities are more than sufficient for research purposes.

Validity: Content validity of the scales was assessed by asking, on two occasions, a total of 15 theologians to sort the randomly arranged statements into their respective scales. On both occasions, all of the theologians sorted the Humanistic Morality Scale items without error. There was similar unanimity for six of the eight items on the Liberal Belief Scale and the great majority concurred on the remaining two.

Convergent validity—the tendency of a scale to correlate appropriately with similar or related measures—was first demonstrated by comparing the mean scale values of a group of persons who said that they "strongly agree" with the statement "I am a believing Christian" with the means of all those who gave a less confident answer (but did not strongly disagree). For both scales, the more hesitant believers scored significantly higher, on the average, than the firm believers. Much as we might expect, the Liberal Belief Scale correlated −.59 with Batson and Ventis's Doctrinal Orthodoxy Scale and −.48 with Woodrum's Moral Conservatism Index. It also correlated .37 with Batson's Quest scale, and −.43 and .49 with the Allport-Ross Intrinsic and Extrinsic scales, respectively. The Humanistic Morality Scale correlated −.50 with the Moral Conservatism Index, −.58 with the Doctrinal Orthodoxy Scale, .48 with the Quest Scale, −.46 with the Intrinsic Scale, and .56 with the Extrinsic Scale. The correlations with the Allport-Ross Scales, which are consis-

tent with findings in earlier studies, suggest that these widely used scales incorporate more of the liberal/conservative dimension than they were originally intended to have.

The factorial validity of Kaldestad's scales, finally, was examined by factor-analyzing each of the scales separately and then in combination with the Moral Conservatism Index and the Doctrinal Orthodoxy Scale. Factor-analyzed separately, the Liberal Belief Scale yielded two factors, accounting for 37.0 and 16.8 percent of the variance, respectively. The first of these factors, which includes items 1, 2, 4, and 5, would seem to be a biblical literalism factor. Factor analysis of the Humanistic Morality Scale likewise yielded two factors, explaining 42.5 and 14.3 percent of the variance, respectively. When these two scales were factor-analyzed with the other two, their items tended to be scattered among four or five of the resulting seven factors, suggesting to Kaldestad that the scales may not be sufficiently homogeneous. As Anastasi (1988) points out, however, scale homogeneity is not a virtue when the criterion is itself heterogeneous, as is likely in this case.

Location:

Kaldestad, E. (1992). Questionnaires for belief and morality. *Journal of Empirical Theology, 5,* 70–84.

Slightly revised versions of several of the statements, along with further discussion of the scales' reliability and validity, can be found in

Kaldestad, E., & Stifoss-Hanssen, H. (1993). Standardizing measures of religiosity for Norwegians. *International Journal for the Psychology of Religion, 3,* 111–124.

Subsequent Research: In his continuing investigations of the relation of religiosity to personality and mental health, Kalkestad has found that nonpsychotic psychiatric patients tended to score higher than nonpatients on both the Liberal Belief Scale and the Humanistic Morality Scale. Furthermore, the two scales showed low but significant positive correlations with the Obsessive and Hysterical scales of the Basic Character Inventory.

The Humanistic Morality Scale also showed a low positive correlation with the SCL-90 Global Symptom Index.

Kaldestad, E. (1992). Religious orientation, personality, mental health, and religious activity. *Nordic Journal of Psychiatry, 46*, 321–328.

Kaldestad, E. (1993). Letter to the editor [correction]. *Nordic Journal of Psychiatry, 47,* 305–306.

References

Anastasi, A. (1988). *Psychological testing* (6th ed.). New York: Macmillan.

Kaldestad, E. (1991). Intrinsic, extrinsic and quest scales: Development of Norwegian versions. In O. Wikström (Ed.), *Klinisk religionspsykologi* (pp. 85–101). Uppsala: Teologiska institutionen, Uppsala Universitet.

Weigert, A. (1988). Christian eschatological identities and the nuclear context. *Journal for the Scientific Study of Religion, 27,* 175–191.

Appendix

(Items are worded according to Kaldestad & Stifoss-Hanssen, 1993)

Kaldestad's Liberal Belief Scale

Please use the following scale to indicate your level of agreement with each of the following statements.

> 1 = strong disagree   4 = partly agree
> 2 = partly disagree   5 = strongly agree
> 3 = neutral

1. The Bible cannot be understood literally, and it can be interpreted in different ways.
2. The Bible contains both true and some historically incorrect information.
3. There is a lot of evil in the world, but I doubt whether the devil exists or not.
4. On the basis of the Bible we cannot prophesy the future history of the world.
5. We human beings know little or nothing about the end of the world.
6. People's life on earth is just as important as a possible life after death.
7. God at last will reconcile to Himself even those people who stand up against Him.
8. I believe that all human beings are good, if they do their best and are sincere.

Kaldestad's Humanistic Morality Scale

Please use the following scale to indicate your level of agreement with each of the following statements.

> 1 = strong disagree   4 = partly agree
> 2 = partly disagree   5 = strongly agree
> 3 = neutral

1. Practical love for my neighbor is more important to me than to obey the Ten Commandments.
2. People can from their own life experiences develop their own values for good and evil behaviors.
3. When I need to decide if something is wrong, I consider first of all whether the behavior can hurt anyone.
4. Living together without being married ought to be morally accepted just like marriage.
5. A sexual relationship before marriage ought to be morally accepted if the couple uses

contraception or takes the full responsibility for the possible offspring.

6. I do not believe in religiously founded, absolute moral norms.
7. It is better to evaluate each situation and use reasonable judgment than to obey absolute moral norms.
8. Knowledge, insight, and reason ought to guide people's behaviors more than religious, moral norms.

Kaldestad, E., & Stifoss-Hanssen, H. (1993). Standardizing measures of religosity for Norwegians. *International Journal for the Psychology of Religion, 3,* 111–124. Copyright © 1993, Lawrence Erlbaum Associates, Inc. Reprinted with permission.

1.6
INVENTORY OF RELIGIOUS BELIEF (Brown & Lowe, 1951)
Reviewed by Rodney L. Bassett

Variable: The Inventory of Religious Belief Scale measures belief in traditional Christian dogma. The authors acknowledge that several factors establish Christian identity and their instrument measures one—belief. Fifteen items in a Likert-like format measure beliefs about such issues as the inspiration of Scripture, the nature of human beings, life after death, the Trinity, the virgin birth of Jesus Christ, the implications of believing in Jesus, and the eventual return of Jesus Christ. Brown and Lowe included a variety of belief items, anticipating that people would vary in the degree to which they embrace all of traditional Christian dogma.

Description: Of the 15 items that make up the Inventory of Religious Belief, 8 of the items are aimed in a fundamental or traditional direction. The other 7 items are worded in a more liberal direction. Often, a concept is captured in 2 items, with one being traditionally worded and the other liberally worded.

Participants respond to the items on a 5-point scale. These response options include (a) strongly agree, (b) agree, (c) not sure, (d) disagree, and (e) strongly disagree. The instrument does a good job of measuring beliefs that have traditionally been identified with the conservative branch of the Christian church. However, there are a few items that tap divisive issues within the church, issues on which Christians in good conscience have disagreed. For example, there

are items that measure belief in the inerrancy of Scripture and belief in the uniqueness of humans from the animal kingdom. Thus, as acknowledged by the authors, the instrument is mainly aimed at conservative Christianity and does not capture the entire Christian spectrum.

Practical Considerations: Liberally worded items are reverse scored and a score ranging from 1 to 5 is given to all the items. The lowest score is given to responses that indicate liberalism, or nonbelief, and the highest score is given to responses that indicate conservatism. The scores for the individual items are then summed to produce an overall score that can range from a high of 75 to a low of 15. The hypothetical midpoint is 45. The instructions for using the instrument are clear enough that researchers should have no problems using it in their own work.

Norms/Standardization: In the study by Brown and Lowe, the inventory was given to 887 male and female university students. Of these students, 622 were members of Protestant churches or were not church members but had Protestant backgrounds. Overall, the mean score for these individuals was 47.16 and the standard deviation was 12.33. When these students were divided into denominational groups, the sample sizes, means, and standard deviations were the following: (a) Baptists ($n = 38$, mean = 59.76, $SD = 10.5$), (b) Lutherans

($n = 27$, mean $= 53.43$, $SD = 11.82$), (c) Presbyterians ($n = 70$, mean $= 51.99$, $SD = 11.91$), (d) Congregationalists ($n = 21$, mean $= 49.44$, $SD = 11.58$), (e) Methodists ($n = 126$, mean $= 49.11$, $SD = 10.02$), (f) Episcopalians ($n = 47$, mean $= 44.82$, $SD = 9.63$), and (f) nonchurch members ($n = 209$, mean $= 40.8$, $SD = 10.65$).

Within this same group of university students, there were also 122 Catholics and 44 other students who were raised in a Catholic background. For those students who were members of the Catholic Church, the average score was 58.20 and the standard deviation was 8.61. For those students who were raised in a Catholic background but were not members of the church, the average score was 39.82 and the standard deviation was 8.74.

Reliability: Brown and Lowe estimated the reliability of the inventory by looking at the responses of 100 students randomly selected from the first 300 university students they surveyed. Using a split-half procedure, responses for half the items (randomly chosen) were correlated with the other half of the items to produce a reliability coefficient of .77. When the Spearman-Brown formula was used, the reliability coefficient changed to .87.

Validity: Brown and Lowe reported several attempts to assure the validity of their inventory. First, the items were reviewed by the dean of a Bible college. Second, the inventory was given to 35 students at a Bible college and 21 students at a liberal theological seminary. The mean score for the Bible college students was 73.8, whereas the mean score for the students at the liberal seminary was 48.6. Further, there was no overlap between the distributions of scores for these two groups of students. And, finally, when the inventory was given to over 887 university students, scores on the inventory correlated positively with frequency of prayer, Bible reading, church attendance, and contributions to the church.

Virkler (1979) surveyed 54 active Christian pastors from northern and southern American cities. In the process of collecting these surveys, Virkler had the pastors indicate their theological orientation (from liberal to conservative) and respond to the Inventory of Religious Belief. The correlation between self-defined theological orientation (with conservative self-labels given higher scores) and the inventory was .74.

Location:

Brown, D. G., & Lowe, W. L. (1951). Religious beliefs and personality characteristics of college students. *Journal of Social Psychology, 33*, 103–129.

Subsequent Research:

Virkler, H. A. (1979). Counseling demands, procedures, and preparation of parish ministers: A descriptive study. *Journal of Psychology and Theology, 7*, 271–280.

Virkler, H. A. (1980). The facilitativeness of parish ministers: A descriptive study. *Journal of Psychology and Theology, 8*, 140–146.

Appendix

Inventory of Religious Belief

Please indicate the extent to which you (1) strong agree, (2) agree, (3) are not sure, (4) disagree, or (5) strongly disagree with each of the following items.

1. It makes no difference whether one is a Christian or not as long as one has good will for others. (reverse scored)
2. I believe the Bible is the inspired Word of God.
3. God created man separate and distinct from animals.
4. The idea of God is unnecessary in our enlightened age. (reverse scored)
5. There is no life after death. (reverse scored)

6. I believe Jesus was born of a virgin.
7. God exists as: Father, Son and Holy Spirit.
8. The Bible is full of errors, misconceptions and contradictions. (reverse scored)
9. The gospel of Christ is the only way for mankind to be saved.
10. I think there have been many men in history just as great as Jesus. (reverse scored)
11. I believe there is a heaven and a hell.
12. Eternal life is the gift of God only to those who believe in Jesus Christ as Savior and Lord.
13. I think a person can be happy and enjoy life without believing in God. (reverse scored)
14. In many ways the Bible has held back and retarded human progress. (reverse scored)
15. I believe in the personal, visible return of Christ to the earth.

Brown, D. E., & Lowe, W. L. (1951). Religious beliefs and personality characteristics of college students. *Journal of Social Psychology, 33,* 103–29. Reprinted with permission.

1.7
INVENTORY OF RELIGIOUS CONCEPTS (Dunkel, 1947)
Reviewed by Peter C. Hill

***Variable*:** The Inventory of Religious Concepts was established as the result of a joint effort among several colleges, many church related, to identify what contribution religion was making to students' philosophy of life. The measure was created within the context of a broader inventory (the Inventory of General Life Goals) designed to help the colleges improve their programs of general education. Specific areas of belief, intended for use with Protestant students (the study was found to be less useful with Catholics and inapplicable to belief systems other than Christian), are covered.

***Description*:** One hundred twenty items were developed to assess 10 general areas of Christian belief. An additional ten miscellaneous items are included in the scale but are not used to assess the 10 general areas of Christian belief. The respondent may answer each item by accepting the statement, expressing uncertainty, rejecting the statement, or providing no opinion (i.e., the statement has no meaning, seems ambiguous, or implies unacceptable assumptions).

Care was taken to avoid misleading classifications such as liberal/conservative, Christian/non-Christian, etc., by simply labeling responses as either *x* or *y*. The meaning of *x* and *y* for each of the 10 belief areas is as follows:

1. The Hebrew-Christian concept of God (10 items)
   x scores: the position of those who accept the poetic and anthropomorphic language of the Hebrew-Christian tradition referring to God
   y scores: the position of those to whom the *x* point of view is untenable
2. Theism and nontheism (10 items)
   x scores: the position of those for whom reference to a personal God and the supernatural have little or no meaning; the nontheistic position
   y scores: the position of those believing in some form of theism
3. Historic Christian doctrines and practices (20 items)
   x scores: the position of those accepting the orthodox Protestant view of Christianity
   y scores: the position of those rejecting the *x* point of view
4. Nontraditional statement of religious values (10 items)
   x scores: the position of those accepting nontraditional statements of religious values
   y scores: the position of those to whom these statements are not acceptable
5. The Bible (20 items)
   x scores: the position of those who believe that the integrity of the Christian faith is dependent on belief in biblical prophesy, miracles, and the trustwor-

thiness of the biblical record

y scores: the position of those who accept the findings of biblical higher criticism

6. Support of the church (10 items)

x scores: the position of those who believe in the work of the church and are likely to support it

y scores: the position of those who are critical of the church and are unlikely to support it

7. The economic order (10 items)

x scores: the position of those who believe that the competitive system of free enterprise should be supported

y scores: the position of those who believe we should move in the direction of a more socialized economy

8. War and the use of force (10 items)

x scores: the position of those who believe that participation in war can be reconciled with the Christian way of life

y scores: the position of the Society Friends or Christian pacifists

9. One's sense of worth or purpose (10 items)

x scores: the position of those who feel that their life has significance and purpose

y scores: the position of those who feel that their life has little or no meaning

10. Freedom and determinism (10 items)

x scores: the position of those who feel that their life is determined by various forces (pp. 81–82)

y scores: the position of those who believe in free will and individual responsibility

"No opinion" (n) and "uncertain" (u) alternatives were provided in addition to the *x* and *y* scores just defined.

Practical Considerations: No special skills are needed to administer, score, or interpret this measure, though the scoring and interpretation system proposed by Dunkel (1947) is somewhat unusual. Dunkel has, for example, provided lengthy case studies of the religious beliefs of three students based on frequency analysis of their *x*, *y*, *n*, and *u* scores for all ten content areas. Profiles are identified and then discussed on the

basis of simple frequency counts of individual items for each of the ten content areas. There are no other recommended scoring procedures, although one possible measure indicated is to assign *x* scores a value of 3, *n* and *u* scores a value of 2, and *y* scores a value of 1. However, given that little psychometric data is available, other rating scales (such as a Likert scale) may be tested. Some items are reversed scored.

Norms/Standardization: The Inventory of Religious Concepts is a subset of a more inclusive measure called the Inventory of General Life Goals, which includes multiple measures of attitudes toward the humanities. Though not planned to form a battery, a question or hypothesis raised in one inventory was frequently investigated in light of responses found in the other measures. The inventory on religion was developed to assess what impact religion was making on life philosophy. The sponsors of this large study, the American Council of Education, selected 22 colleges, which represented the following categories: a landgrant college, a municipal university, a state teachers college, an independent liberal arts college, a Catholic college, a Protestant church-related college, a black college, a women's four-year college, a women's two-year college, and a two-year coeducational college. No normative data were reported.

Reliability: Reliabilities within categories (based on the sample of 700 students), estimated by Kuder-Richardson Formula 21, are identified in parentheses next to each category in the appendix. The reliability coefficients range from .44 (economic order and sense of worth) to .86 (historic doctrines and practices).

Validity: The more commonplace quantitative measures of validity (e.g., construct validity, predictive validity, concurrent validity, etc.) were not reported. Rather, a few lengthy case studies were reported to indicate in "some small way" the validity of the instrument. The case studies are, at face value, supportive of the instrument's validity.

It should be noted that the individual responsible for assessing the instrument's validity (as well as some other psychometric properties) was unable, because of factors beyond his control, to complete his work by the time Dunkel's 1947 report was published. A brief footnote in the report was provided, however, which indicated high correlation between the Thurstone Attitude Scales and the inventory scores in the categories on God and on the church.

Given the extensiveness of this inventory and given that few psychometric properties are reported and few scoring procedures are suggested, this instrument is a good candidate for further investigation.

Location:

Dunkel, H. B. (1947). *General education in the humanities*. Washington, D.C.: American Council on Education.

Subsequent Research: A computer search found no research using this instrument.

Appendix

Inventory of Religious Concepts (listed by categories)

Please indicate how you rate each of the statements below by using one of the following labels:

x - you agree with the statement
y - you disagree with the statement
n - you have no opinion about the statement
u - you are uncertain about the statement

Hebrew-Christian Conceptions of God (.81)

1. Man is ultimately responsible to God.
2. God is like a father, longsuffering, merciful, just, and infinitely kind.
3. God is the Great Companion who shares with us the travail and tragedy of the world.
4. God knows our thoughts before we utter them; He is acquainted with all our ways.
5. There is a spark of God in every man to which His Spirit can speak directly.
6. We were made to have fellowship with God and our hearts will be restless until they rest in Him.
7. There is a divine purpose which directs all events for the ultimate good of mankind.
8. The chief end of man is to glorify God and enjoy Him forever.
9. "I believe in God the Father Almighty, maker of heaven and earth."
10. I humbly bow before the glory and majesty of God.

Attitudes toward God (Theism and Nontheism) (.63)

11. I believe that men working and thinking together can build a just society *without* any supernatural help.
12. Belief that in the end God's purposes will be achieved tends to destroy man's sense of social responsibility.
13. The idea of a personal God is an outworn concept.
14. We live in a universe which, in so far as we have any reliable evidence, is indifferent to human values.
15. Belief in God as a personal force, or being, in the universe is not consistent with a scientific view of the world.
16. "God" is *only* a symbol of man's ideals.

17. I can make sense of the world without thinking of any mind higher than man.
18. The term "God" is a symbol no longer helpful in man's quest for the good life.
19. Whether there is or is not a God is a matter of indifference to me.
20. The attempt to believe in God is sign of a person's failure to accept responsibility for his own life.

Nontraditional Expressions of Religious Values (.59)

21. I believe a mature person should feel a sense of guilt when he fails to serve the needs of men.
22. There is a fundamental process at work in the world, often symbolized as God, which, though it is related to human purposes, far transcends the mind of man.
23. God is the symbol of man's assurance that the universe supports his struggle for the larger social values.
24. God is the personality-producing force in the world.
25. God is the name given to the underlying, integrating reality of life.
26. God is that power in the world which works for righteousness.
27. Whatever obstructs or perverts the growth of quality or meaning in the world is "sin."
28. I believe that what is most needed today is a spiritual discipline—a way of sensitizing our inner lives to the work of God in the world.
29. We are all members of one another—Russian, German, American; rich and poor; black and white.
30. A person developing the quality of life seen in Jesus is realizing the essential purpose of Christianity regardless of his conception of the Bible or the "nature" of Jesus.

Historic Christian Doctrines and Practices (.86)

31. I believe God sent His Son Jesus Christ to be the Saviour of the world.
32. Man by nature is prone to evil rather than good.
33. I believe the sacrament of baptism is an essential part of the Christian life.
34. God is triune: Father, Son, and Holy Spirit.
35. Man by nature is lost and in need of a saviour.
36. The Christian church is a divine-human society which God has ordained for the redemption of mankind.
37. Our hope of immortality rests upon our belief in the Lord Jesus Christ.
38. Man is saved by the free gift of God's grace.
39. Regular participation in the Lord's Supper or Holy Communion is to me essential.
40. I believe in the guidance of the Holy Spirit.
41. We need to believe in the Lord Jesus Christ to be saved.
42. Jesus Christ is seated "at the right hand of God the Father Almighty: from thence He shall come to judge the quick and the dead."
43. Jesus was born of the Virgin Mary in a manner different from all other human beings.
44. There is a personal Satan.
45. All who have not accepted Jesus Christ as their personal Saviour are eternally lost.
46. Hell, in addition to being a description of experiences in this life, is *also* a form of existence in a future life.
47. "On the third day Jesus Christ rose from the dead"; after appearing to various persons and groups, "He ascended into heaven."
48. I believe the theory of evolution tends to destroy a true religious faith.
49. We will be able to know our friends in the future life.
50. Christ offered himself a perfect sacrifice upon the Cross to take away the sins of the world.

Attitudes toward the Bible (.81)

51. Jesus walked on water and raised the dead.
*52. One's interpretation of any part of the Bible should be made in the light of the findings of Biblical or literary criticism.
*53. The Biblical story of creation is probably based on one of the early Babylonian myths.
54. All the miraculous deeds of Jesus recorded in the Gospels are reliable history.
55. The actual time, place, and circumstances of Jesus' birth were predicted in the Old Testament.
56. The Biblical story of creation is a divine revelation of what actually occurred.
57. The Biblical writers were endowed with a divine wisdom that enabled them to foretell specific events in the distant future.
*58. We may be reasonably certain today that man evolved from the lower forms of animal life.
59. All the miracles in the Bible are true.
*60. The Bible contains some books which are definitely inferior from a religious standpoint to some contemporary religious writing.
61. Man has no right to question the truth of God's Word, which is clearly revealed in the Bible.
*62. The writings of Plato, Aristotle, Dante, and Shakespeare are as inspired as the writings of Moses and Paul.
63. The Bible in the original manuscript was infallible, i.e., without error.
*64. The "fall of man" in the story of the Garden of Eden is a myth symbolizing the problem of good and evil in the world.
*65. We should attempt to understand and explain, rather than accept on faith, all biblical "miracles."
66. If I believed that any part of the Biblical record was unreliable, I could no longer have confidence in its moral and spiritual teaching.
*67. The story of Moses contains legendary material.
*68. Many of the sayings in the Gospel of John are interpretations reflecting the mind of the early church rather than reports of what Jesus actually said.
*69. The four Gospels (Matthew, Mark, Luke, and John) contain some legendary material.
70. The entire account of Jesus' teachings as recorded in the Gospels presents what he actually said.

Support of the Church (.62)

*71. The work of the church could be just as effectively done by the schools and social agencies.
*72. In general, I consider church attendance a waste of time.
*73. I believe that most people can grow spiritually just as well without going to church.
74. To me, the church is the greatest single agency for good in the world.
75. I feel that the work of the church deserves my time and money.
*76. The church deals with platitudes and is afraid to follow the truth.
*77. It is difficult for a person to be honest and still endorse what the church teaches.
78. I believe the foreign missionary enterprise is one of the most effective means we have for developing a world brotherhood.
79. In so far as I find it possible, I intend to be actively interested in the work of the church.
80. I believe the church should engage in evangelistic work.

Attitudes toward the Economic Order (.44)

81. An employer has a right to hire and fire men as he sees best.
82. In the long run the competitive principle in business works for the good of all men.
83. A man has a right to do what he wants to with his own money.
84. The government should keep out of business and confine its operations to safeguarding the public, compelling fair observances of the rules of the game, and serving its citizens in the realms of education and culture.
*85. All property and money that affect the welfare of large numbers of people should be controlled by groups responsible to the people, not by individuals or groups who are legally responsible only to themselves as owners.
86. A competitive or free enterprise system in the long run tends to serve the interests of the common man more effectively than does a more socialized economy.
*87. I believe that socialism under democratic control should be encouraged.
88. I want the church to become more actively interested in social and economic questions.
89. I believe that any movement that encourages a more socialized economy is contrary to the true American way of life.
*90. The socialization of medicine should be encouraged.

Attitudes of Christians toward War (.70)

91. I believe that there are situations in which Christians should use not only reasonable persuasion but also physical force in the defense of their ideals.
*92. All war is contrary to the teachings of Jesus.
*93. As a Christian, I cannot reconcile war with the principle of the Cross.
*94. As Christians, we should refuse to kill our enemies.
95. When our nation is at war, it is the duty of a Christian to work for a military victory.
96. The way of nonviolence or Christian pacifism is an impractical philosophy of life.
97. In a country having required military training, it is the duty of Christians to support this program.
*98. I believe that the way of nonviolence—soul force—when practiced, is the most effective means we have for overcoming tyranny and injustice.
99. If the people, through their duly elected representative, decide to go to war, it is a Christian's duty to support his government.
*100. I refuse to support or participate in any kind of war.

One's Sense of Worth (.44)

*101. Life is more or less drab and meaningless to me.
102. I believe I can achieve some significant purpose in the world.
*103. I often wonder why I was born.
*104. I am inclined to feel that my life is unimportant.
105. I feel that God has placed me in the world to make some significant contribution to the welfare of mankind.
*106. There may be some purpose in life, but I have yet to discover it.
*107. The idea of a goal or purpose in life has little or no meaning to me at the present time.
*108. I believe our main purpose in life is to reproduce ourselves to maintain the human race.
*109. There does not seem to be any real purpose for living.
110. I believe that God has a plan for my life.

Freedom and Determinism-Man (.67)

111. There is no real freedom of choice, since all of our actions are determined by past experiences.
112. Man cannot be held responsible for his own acts since he did not choose his parents or the conditions under which he has been reared.
113. All of our actions may be explained in terms of the way we have been conditioned.
114. Freedom of will is only an illusion.
115. Psychology proves, or tends to show, that there is no such thing as "choice" between "right" and "wrong."
116. I am inclined to feel that our lives are completely controlled by "natural law."
117. I believe that we are more or less puppets of social and economic forces beyond our control.
118. We are parts of a mechanistic universe which controls every action of man.
119. Since man is determined by his heredity and his environment, human freedom is illusory.
120. Our lives are completely controlled by subconscious processes.

Miscellaneous Identifying Items

121. It is possible to talk with the departed dead.
122. There is probably some relationship between the course of a person's life and the combination of starts and planets at the time of his birth.
123. Our soul existed in another form before it entered this life.
124. Numbers and signs have divine or mystical significance.
125. It is possible to read a person's character by studying phrenology—a science based on the relation of mental powers and abilities to the shape of the head.
126. The world will continue to get worse until Christ returns for the final judgment.
127. We are living in the "last days"; the end of the world is at hand.
128. The good is the only reality; evil is illusory or unreal.
129. Healing is brought to pass when a belief of disease which has been entertained in thought is dispelled and destroyed by the law and power of God.
130. A good Christian goes to confession and attends Mass.

*These items are reversed scored (x=y; y=x)

Dunkel, H.B. (1947). *General education in the humanities.* Washington D.C.: American Council on Education. Reprinted with permission.

1.8
THE LAM SCALES (Hunt, 1972a)

Reviewed by Christopher T. Burris

Variable: The LAM scales attempt to measure an individual's characteristic interpretive style with respect to biblical or theological assertions. Three styles (on which the LAM acrostic is based) are represented: (1) the literal (L) style, which involves straightforward, face-value endorsement of an assertion; (2) the antiliteral (A) style, embodied in straightforward, face-value rejection of an assertion; and (3) the mythological (M) style, characterized by neither straightforward endorsement nor rejection but by reinterpretation of an assertion in nonliteral or symbolic terms.

Description: Hunt's (1972a) stated rationale for developing the LAM scales was to address what he perceived to be a fundamentalistic bias inherent in contemporary approaches to measuring religiosity. Specifically, he argued that the wording of such measures seemed to equate religiosity with wholehearted assent to the literal truth of a given set of (typically Christian) theological statements. As a result, religious persons who interpreted such statements in a more symbolic, nonliteral fashion might—owing to a lack of alternatives—errantly misclassify themselves as "nonreligious" by rejecting the statements' literal endorsement. Thus, in the LAM scales, Hunt attempted to tap not only the customary literal and antiliteral response styles but also a third, symbolic style that he labeled "mythological."

The LAM scales themselves consist of 17 (out of an original 25) theological statements, each followed by 3 (occasionally 4) interpretive responses. Each response, in turn, begins with either "agree" or "disagree," followed by a brief justification based on literal, antiliteral, or symbolic grounds. Hunt (1972a) offered two scoring methods; both are ipsative, i.e., scores on the 3 scales are not independent of each other. The first method involves assigning either 2, 1, or 0 points to a response based whether the respondent ranked it as first, second, or third (fourth) closest to his or her own position (the "2-1-0" method). The second option involves assigning a score of 1 to the top-ranked response to each item, and 0 to all other responses (the "1-0-0" method). Classification as L, A, or M is based on the highest of the respondent's 3 scores. Hunt himself recommended the second scoring method on the basis of minimal interscale correlations (but in the absence of clear theoretical justification; see discussion under "Validity").

Other item formats and scoring approaches have also been used. Poythress (1975; see also Orlowski, 1979), for example, combined each of the 17 theological statements with its respective interpretive responses to create items to which responses could be recorded using a -2 (*strongly disagree*) to +2 (*strongly agree*) Likert-type response format. Classification is again determined on the basis of the highest score (or a combination of scores; see Poythress, 1975).

Practical Considerations: The LAM scales are relatively short and easy to administer in a paper-and-pencil format. Explicit instructions are not provided, although Hunt (1972a) stated that "subjects were asked to respond by ranking each set of three [four] alternatives according to the extent to which each expresses his [sic] personal opinion" (p. 44). Because responses are keyed, scoring presents no difficulty via the Likert or either of the ipsative methods. Statistical analyses based on the ipsative scoring methods are a bit complex and difficult to interpret for the nonspecialist, however. Hunt (1972a) noted that the lack of independence among the LAM scales' scores alters the meaning of interscale correlation coefficients, for example. An additional concern is that the LAM scales assume not only a relatively high reading level but also sophistication with a rather specialized (i.e., liberal Protestant) theological tradition (see Greeley, 1972). Removal of sexist language present in several items should also be considered prior to administration.

Norms/Standardization: The original sample consisted of 88 female and 85 male undergraduates at Southern Methodist University. Hunt (1972a), using his preferred 1-0-0 scoring method, reported means of 3.1, 3.3, and 10.0 for women, and 3.6, 4.7, and 8.1 for men on the L, A, and M scales, respectively. (None of the apparent sex differences was significant; mean scores summed across the 3 scales cannot exceed approximately 17 due to their nonindependence.) Poythress (1975) did not report means. Orlowski (1979) reported Likert-based means of 3.74 (L), 1.71 (A), and 3.62 (M) among 82 members of a Roman Catholic religious order; he did not, however, specify scale ranges.

Reliability: Hunt (1972a) reported reliability coefficients of .87 (L), .92 (A), and .77 (M) via Gullikson's variance-covariance procedure. Poythress's (1975) Likert-type items yielded Spearman-Brown corrected split-half reliability coefficients of .94 (L), .95 (A), and .76 (M); Orlowski (1979) reported somewhat lower coefficients using the same method (i.e., .83 for L, .71 for A, and .67 for M). Thus, reliabilities appear adequate, although consistently lower for M.

Validity: Deficiencies with respect to support for the validity of the LAM scales have begun to be addressed only recently. In his original report, Hunt (1972a) found a strong positive and a strong negative correlation, respectively, between the L and A scales and McLean's (1952) Religious Worldviews Scale, offering some evidence of convergent validity. The obtained correlations are hardly surprising, however, in that the stems used to construct the LAM scales' items are based on items from McLean's scale. Of somewhat greater value, however, the M scale was found to be unrelated to McLean's scale, which is consistent with Hunt's claim that the M scale taps an interpretive style not addressed in traditional measures of religiosity (although this does not help to establish what the M scale in fact measures).

Orlowski (1979) provided some support for the convergent validity of the LAM scales: In his Franciscan sample, L and M self-ratings were reliably positively correlated with peer-observers' respective L and M ratings of the same individuals. Ratings on the A scale were not reliably related, however, which Orlowski attributes, in part, to the restricted variance associated with these ratings. Another possible explanation is that the explicitly religious social surround—a Roman Catholic religious order—may have suppressed behavioral expression of any antiliteral tendencies among sample respondents, resulting in a discrepancy between privately held and publicly endorsed (i.e., peer-observable) interpretive styles.

More recently, using a substantially revised instrument, van der Lans (1991) found some support for the predictive validity of the L and M ("metaphorical") scales. Specifically, structured interviews of extreme L and M scorers revealed that the latter tended to approach religious language and symbols in a less concrete, more flexible manner than did the former. Nonetheless, a number of validity issues warrant further attention.

The first issue concerns the dimensionality of the LAM scales. Hunt's (1972a) stated rationale for developing his scales was to disentangle the "literal-symbolic" and the "conservative-liberal" (or "religious-nonreligious," see Hunt, 1993) interpretive dimensions, which he believed to be confounded in traditional measures of religiosity. It is unclear whether Hunt regarded these dimensions as orthogonal (i.e., independent of each other); if so, the extant scales seem to represent only the literal-religious (L), literal-nonreligious (A), and symbolic-religious (M) alternatives—missing is a symbolic-nonreligious alternative. Northover, Montoro-Gonzalez, and Hunt (1993) dealt with this omission by assuming a different dimensional structure, wherein literal and antiliteral interpretive styles represent endpoints of a single bipolar dimension, with the mythological style representing a sort of neutral or noncommittal position.

Uncertainties regarding the dimensional structure of the LAM fuel questions concerning what exactly the M scale measures. The recent validation studies by van der Lans (1991) are somewhat helpful here, but other questions have yet to be adequately addressed. For example, is the mythological interpretive style in fact the most "mature" style, as Hunt (1972a) claimed? To illustrate, it can be argued that the M scale measures, at least in part, a sort of theological latitudinarianism regarded as socially respectable in mainstream religious denominations, i.e., that it taps the tendency to adopt a truce-like stance with respect to the clashing stances of the hardcore religiously and scientifically orthodox (as respectively represented in the L and A scales) . Establishing the truth or falsehood of this interpretation of the M scale is a matter for future research.

A final issue concerns the representativeness of M scale response alternatives. As Greeley (1972) noted, M-scored responses on the LAM scales have a decidedly humanistic, liberal Protestant tone that is not exhaustive of possible symbolic reinterpretations, a point that Hunt (1972b, 1993) has conceded. Thus, an individual whose predominant interpretive style is mythological may agree with the spirit but not the letter of M scale responses, and may therefore respond somewhat inconsistently. This may partially explain the lower reliability of the M scale as compared to the L and A scales (see "Reliability").

Location:

Hunt, R. A. (1972). Mythological-symbolic religious commitment: The LAM scales. *Journal for the Scientific Study of Religion*, *11*, 42–52. (Note that only the 17 final items are shown in the appendix of this review, not the entire 25 as declared in the text.)

Recent Research:

Jablonski, P., Grzymala-Moszczynska, H., & van der Lans, J. (1994). Interpretation of religious language among Poles and the Dutch: Cognitive competence or cultural construction? *Polish Psychological Bulletin*, *25*, 283–302.

Kalecinska-Adamczyk, E. (1995). Religion and anti-Semitism: The influence of the social approval of prejudices on the tendency to manifest them in behavior. *Polish Psychological Bulletin*, *26*, 158–160.

References

Greeley, A. M. (1972). Comment on Hunt's "Mythological-symbolic religious commitment: The LAM scales." *Journal for the Scientific Study of Religion*, *11*, 287–289.

Hunt, R. A. (1972a). Mythological-symbolic religious commitment: The LAM scales. *Journal for the Scientific Study of Religion*, *11*, 42–52.

Hunt, R. A. (1972b). Reply to Greely. *Journal for the Scientific Study of Religion*, *11*, 290–292.

Hunt, R. A. (1993). Response to Northover and Gonzalez. *International Journal for the Psychology of Religion*, *3*, 201–204.

McLean, M. (1952). Religious world views. *Motive*, *12*, 22–26.

Northover, W. E., Montoro-Gonzalez, L., & Hunt, R. A. (1993). A cross-cultural comparison of religious belief: Canadian and Spanish students' responses to the Hunt scale. *International Journal for the Psychology of Religion*, *3*, 187–199.

Orlowski, C. D. (1979). Linguistic dimension of religious measurement. *Journal for the Scientific Study of Religion*, *18*, 306–311.

Poythress, N. G. (1975). Literal, antiliteral, and mythological religious orientations. *Journal for the Scientific Study of Religion*, *14*, 271–284.

van der Lans, J. M. (1991). Interpretation of religious language and cognitive style: A pilot study with the LAM scale. *International Journal for the Psychology of Religion*, *1*, 107–123.

Appendix

The LAM Scales

Please rank each set of alternatives according to the extent that alternative expresses your personal opinion. Place a "1" next to the alternative that best matches your opinion, a "2" next to the alternative that next best matches your opinion, etc.

1. I believe in God the Father Almighty, maker of heaven and earth.

   L 1. Agree, since available evidence proves God made everything.

   A 2. Disagree, since available evidence suggests some type of spontaneous creation for which it is unnecessary to assume a God to create.

   M 3. Agree, but only in the sense that this is an anthropomorphic way of talking about whatever Process, Being, or Ultimate Concern stands behind the creative process.

2. I believe that men working and thinking together can build a just society without supernatural help.

L 1. Disagree, since man without God's help can do very little that is good.

A 2. Agree, since men have and are increasing the ability and technical knowledge to improve society if they will apply this knowledge to the problems of society.

M 3. Disagree, although men's ability and technical knowledge is increasing, they must build on the ultimate power within oneself [sic] to understand and accomplish the full implications of justice and a good society.

3. The writings of such commentators on human life as Plato, Aristotle, Dante, and Shakespeare are as much inspired as are the writings of Moses and Paul.

L 1. Disagree, because the writings of Moses and Paul contain a special inspiration from God which other human writings do not have.

A 2. Agree, since there is really little difference in these writings. In fact, Plato and Aristotle may be even more important for us than Moses or Paul.

M 3. Disagree, although any writing may be inspired, the writings of Moses and Paul are especially significant because they form part of the revelation of God in history.

4. All miracles in the Bible are true.

L 1. Agree, because the Bible cannot contain any false report of God's work.

A 2. Disagree, since "miracles" can be explained by our modern understanding of the principles by which nature and human society operate.

M 3. Agree, but only in the sense that "miracles" are a dramatic report and interpretation of a natural process, with the literary purpose of pointing to the sovereignty of God. They are probably not factually accurate.

M 4. Perhaps, since there is considerable evidence for extra-physical power used by a few persons in every major cultural tradition, though there is no clear scientific proof.

5. Jesus was born of a virgin in a manner different from human beings.

A 1. Disagree, although most religions claim a virgin birth for their founder, we know that such an event is physically impossible.

M 2. Agree, but only in the sense that this is an ancient mythological way of talking about the Ultimate Reality as manifested in Jesus.

L 3. Agree, since God conceived Jesus in Mary's womb before she had sexual relationship with her Joseph, her husband.

6. The attempt to believe in a supernatural being is a sign of a person's failure to accept responsibility for his own life.

A 1. Agree, since belief in God is usually an escape from the problems of everyday life. Such belief does nothing to help solve one's problem.

L 2. Disagree, because belief in God is really the only way in which man can be saved and make his life worthwhile.

M 3. Disagree, since belief in God is basically man's way of talking about his full acceptance of personal responsibility in the face of ultimate and sometimes uncertain reality.

7. I believe in the guidance of the Holy Spirit.

   L 1. Agree, since God has said that he will be with us always. Prayer thus is an effective way of listening to God's guidance.
   A 2. Disagree, since the supernatural, if it exists at all, is in no way directly involved in telling man what to do.
   M 3. Agree, because this is one way of describing the involvement of God with his creation and man.

8. The chief end of man is to glorify God and enjoy him forever.

   L 1. Agree, since God created man and expects man to do God's will at all times.
   A 2. Disagree, since man must find his own purposes in life. There are probably no purposes for man which are apparent in nature.
   M 3. Agree, because the essential purpose of God is that man achieve his own maximum fulfillment through personal development and service to others.
   M 4. Agree, since the individual who enjoys God's creation and serves his fellow man is at the same time glorifying God.

9. I believe Hell is a form of existence in a future life.

   M 1. Disagree, since Hell is not a future life existence, but rather a present state in this life which occurs when man disregards his own code of ethics and/or rights of other individuals.
   A 2. Disagree, since there is little, if any, evidence for any type of existence after this life.
   L 3. Agree, since there is ample evidence in the Bible and other authoritative sources for Hell as a form of future existence.

10. The four gospels, Matthew, Mark, Luke, and John, contain some legendary materials.

    A 1. Agree, since most of the material in the gospels cannot be supported by other historical sources or is not relevant to life in today's world.
    L 2. Disagree, since nothing in the four gospels could be legendary or in error, because these are part of the Bible and therefore infallible.
    M 3. Agree, but this does not deny the basic purpose of the gospels, which is to use written language (however inadequate) to announce God's revelation of himself to man.

11. We are made for fellowship with God and our hearts are restless until they rest in him.

    M 1. Agree, although this is merely a way of talking about the ultimate nature of man's activities as being in some way related to God's purposes.
    A 2. Disagree, since man's restlessness results from his inability to identify with a group of persons and enjoy people about him, not in a supposed relation to some God.
    L 3. Agree, since God's basic purpose in creating man is so that man can be a companion to God.

12. Man is saved by the free gift of God's grace.

    L 1. Agree, since the Bible clearly states that salvation is by man's faith in God and his grace.
    A 2. Disagree, since whatever salvation there is must come through man's work in the world about him.
    M 3. Agree, since this is a traditional expression which really refers to the unconditional nature of God's grace toward man.

13. The biblical writers were endowed with a divine wisdom which enabled them to foretell specific events in the distant future.

   M 1. Disagree, since the basic purpose of prophecy in the Bible was to announce God's judgment of the ways in which that present generation failed to act in harmony with God's purposes for man.
   L 2. Agree, since many of these prophecies either came true in earlier history, in the Bible, or are coming true in the world today.
   A 3. Disagree, since biblical writers had no greater wisdom than other men of their day. Any prophecies which may have come true were the result of a knowledge of cause and effect which any man could achieve.

14. Man is ultimately responsible to God.

   A 1. Disagree, because man is finally responsible only to himself and his society.
   M 2. Agree, because this is a way of describing the basic assumption upon which all other concepts of responsibility depend.
   L 3. Agree, because God has created man in his image and expects man to do God's will.

15. God is only a symbol of man's ideals.

   M 1. Disagree, although man's experiences may be symbolized in the image of God, the reality of God always transcends man's symbols for that reality.
   A 2. Agree, since religious men tend to ascribe to God their own highest ideals.
   L 3. Disagree, since there is clear evidence for a real God who is much more than just the result of man's rational powers.

16. Jesus walked on water and raised the dead.

   A 1. Disagree, since these are probably exaggerated reports of events which could be explained through our knowledge of nature.
   L 2. Agree, since there are several accounts in which Jesus actually brought a physically dead person back to life. These accounts provide evidence for God's power over nature.
   M 3. Agree, but only in the sense that these are figurative ways of describing man's awareness of the meaning of life in relation to the revelation of God.

17. The biblical story of creation is probably based on one of the early Babylonian myths.

   M 1. Agree, but the basic purpose of the creation story is to symbolize God's creative and redemptive relation to the universe and to man.
   L 2. Disagree, since the biblical story of creation has not been duplicated in any way at any time. It refers to God's creation of the world and man.
   A 3. Agree, since most religions provide such a creation story. Modern scientific theories of the origin of the universe have replaced these ancient accounts.

Hunt, R. A. (1972). Mythological-symbolic religious commitment: The LAM Scales. *Journal for the Scientific Study of Religion, 11,* 42–52. Copyright © 1972 Journal for the Scientific Study of Religion. Reprinted with permission.

1.9
NONDOCTRINAL RELIGION SCALES (Yinger, 1969; Yinger, 1977)

Reviewed by Caro E. Courtenay and Lee A. Kirkpatrick[1]

Variable: The Nondoctrinal Religion Scales are designed to measure cross-cultural, nondoctrinal aspects of religion regarding ultimate concerns of universal human interest, such as questions of meaninglessness, suffering, and injustice. The 1969 scale contains 7 items; the 1977 scale contains 20 items.

The nondoctrinal religious measure created by Yinger (1969) was rooted in an assumption that interest in existential questions is a structural foundation for much belief and behavior that is not traditionally defined as "religious," as well as for all religious belief and behavior. Yinger (1969, p. 90) described these as the "ephemeral, the emergent, the poorly institutionalized expressions of ultimate concern." Although he cites the writings of Clifford Geertz as an influence on his thinking, Yinger unfortunately was rather vague in both papers concerning the basis on which he created and selected his particular questions, or how "years of research" (Yinger, 1977, p. 68) led him to hypothesize suffering, meaning, and injustice to be humanity's most essential issues.

Description: The 1969 scale consists of seven statements to be rated on a Likert-type scale with respect to agreement-disagreement. For each question he identified certain responses (either agreement or disagreement, depending on the wording of the item) as "religious" responses. Yinger (1969) did not advocate summing the items to form a scale (although subsequent researchers attempted to do so; see "Reliability" and "Validity" below) but simply presented tabular data for each question separately.

In addition, Yinger (1969) asked respondents to write answers to four open-ended questions regarding their idea of the "most important issue" for humanity, the responses to which he classified "informally" into such categories as major social issues (e.g., peace, poverty); interpersonal relations; individual creativity and happiness; and meaning, purpose, and relationship of humans to God. Because these items do not represent a "scale" per se, we do not include them here.

Yinger's approach to the subject in 1977 included soliciting more respondents and sampling from a variety of cultures by translating the scale into several other languages (including Japanese, Korean, and Thai). The 20-item measure presented in 1977 was designed specifically to measure respondents' concerns about (1) worldwide human suffering, (2) injustice, and (3) meaninglessness. In addition, he included separate sets of items concerned respectively with (4) "religion generally" and (5) politics. Respondents rated their agreement with each statement on a 5-point scale. However, despite his conceptual grouping of the items into these five categories, Yinger again analyzed the data separately by item instead of summing items to create composite scale scores. In his large sample of international students he examined the degree to which responses to individual questions varied as a function of national citizenship, religious identity, and sex.

Practical Considerations: Both the 7-item 1969 scale and the 20-item 1977 scale are easy to administer. Each item is rated on a 5 point Likert-type scale ranging from *fully agree* to *fully disagree*. Yinger (1969, p. 93) emphasized that respondents "were given a minimum of instructions" and that the term "religion" was avoided in the introduction to the scale in order to minimize potential biases on the part of responses. As Yinger did not discuss any procedures for combining items into total or subscale scores, no further scoring is necessary.

[1]Preparation of this review was facilitated by a Charles Center Research Fellowship to Caro Courtenay and a Summer Research Grant to Lee Kirkpatrick from the College of William & Mary.

On the 1969 scale Yinger scored "disagree" responses on items 1, 3, and 5, as well as "agree" responses on the remaining items, as "religious" responses. He did not explicitly classify items on the 1977 scale as "religious" or "nonreligious."

On the 1977 scale, items 1–4 (as listed in the appendix) compose the *meaninglessness* cluster, items 5–8 compose the *suffering* cluster, items 9–12 compose the *injustice* cluster, items 13–18 compose the *religion* cluster, and items 19 and 20 compose the *politics* cluster.

Norms/Standardization: Yinger (1969) presented frequencies of responses to each of the seven items separately for two samples: a "pretest" sample of 96 students from an unspecified college and a larger sample of 1,325 students drawn from 10 different colleges. In total, 69% of all responses were classified as "religious" when scored in the manner described above.

The 1977 analysis was based primarily on responses from 751 college students from Korea, Japan, Thailand, New Zealand, and Australia, although some analyses included (a) 124 additional respondents from 11 different countries and/or (b) 151 U.S. students from an unspecified earlier sample. Samples were drawn from a variety of academic courses, but some courses were overrepresented and the data from the non-American students were obtained while they were in residence at an American research center, so in several ways the samples cannot be generalized to any well-defined population. Again, simple raw frequencies were presented for each of the questions separately.

Reliability: Because Yinger never suggested that the seven items on the 1969 scale should be summed to create a single or total scale, he did not report any measure of internal consistency reliability. However, Nelsen, Everett, Mader, and Hamby (1976) examined the items from this perspective and reported poor internal consistency: an alpha coefficient of only .34 and interitem correlations ranging from .19 to .28. Their factor analysis suggested the presence of two factors, which they referred to as "ac-ceptance of belief and order" and "acceptance of the value of suffering." However, the internal consistency reliabilities of these scales were also poor (alphas = .45 and .37, respectively). Roof, Hadaway, Hewitt, McGaw, and Morse (1977) replicated the finding of poor internal consistency for the 7-item scale, and found three factors in a factor analysis ("value of religious efforts," "value of difficult experience," and "the basic human condition").

In short, there seems to be little basis for summing the 1969 items into total or subscale scores, although it should be noted that both the Nelsen et al. (1976) and Roof et al. (1977) studies employed relatively small samples for psychometric purposes (ns = 217 and 113, respectively). No other measures of reliability of the scale have been reported, and no reliability data of any kind have been published for the 1977 scale.

Validity: The factor analyses reported by Nelsen et al. (1976) and Roof et al. (1977) suggest that the 1969 items are multidimensional and do not well represent a unitary dimension of any kind; however, there is little agreement between these two sets of results in terms of what the scales *do* measure. In both cases, however, the authors concluded that the "nondoctrinal" measures were significantly correlated with traditional religiosity (e.g., orthodoxy, prayer, and "self-rated religiosity"), and therefore questioned the degree to which Yinger's measures tap anything distinct from more conventional definitions of religiousness.

Based on a factor analysis of the 1977 scale, Brown (1981) raised several questions about the factor structure and validity of the items. However, these results are of little value given his very small sample (n = 80) and inclusion of nine additional fundamentalism items in the analysis.

Location:

Yinger, J. M. (1969). A structural examination of religion. *Journal for the Scientific Study of Religion, 8,* 88–99.

Yinger, J. M. (1977). A comparative study of the substructures of religion. *Journal for the Scientific Study of Religion, 16,* 67–86.

Subsequent Research:

Brown, L. B. (1981). Another test of Yinger's measure of nondoctrinal religion. *The Journal of Psychology, 107,* 3–5.

References

Nelsen, H. M., Everett, R. F., Mader, P. D., & Hamby, W. C. (1976). A test of Yinger's measure of nondoctrinal religion: Implications for invisible religion as a belief system. *Journal for the Scientific Study of Religion, 15,* 263–267.

Roof, W. C., Hadaway, C. K., Hewitt, D., & Morse, R. (1977). Yinger's measure of non-doctrinal religion: A Northeastern test. *Journal for the Scientific Study of Religion, 19,* 403–408.

Appendix

Nondoctrinal Religion

Please use the following scale to indicate the extent to which you agree with each item below.

1 = fully agree	4 = partly disagree
2 = partly agree	5 = fully disagree
3 = uncertain	

Items from Yinger (1969)

1. Efforts to deal with the human situation by religious means, whatever the content of the beliefs and practices, seem to me to be misplaced, a waste of time and resources. (higher score is religious response)
2. Suffering, injustice, and finally death are the lot of man; but they need not be negative experiences; their significance and effects can be shaped by our beliefs. (lower score is religious response)
3. In face of the almost continuous conflict and violence in life, I cannot see how men are going to learn to live in mutual respect and peace with one another. (higher score is religious response)
4. There are many aspects of the beliefs and practices of the world's religions with which I do not agree; nevertheless, I consider them to be valuable efforts to deal with man's situation. (lower score is religious response)
5. Somehow, I cannot get very interested in the talk about "the basic human condition" and "man's ultimate problems." (higher score is religious response)
6. Man's most difficult and destructive experiences are often the source of increased understanding and powers of endurance. (lower score is religious response)
7. Despite the often chaotic conditions of human life, I believe that there is order and pattern to existence that someday we'll come to understand. (lower score is religious response)

Items from Yinger (1977)

1. I am not very interested in discussion of the question of the meaning or meaninglessness of life.
2. Despite the often chaotic conditions of human life, I believe there is an order to existence that someday we will come to understand.
3. I often wonder what life is all about.
4. Although mankind understands the world around him better, the basic meaning of life is beyond our understanding.

5. In recent generations, there has been a significant reduction in the amount of human suffering.
6. It is a mistake to believe that the reduction of suffering on earth is the critically important question for mankind.
7. The types of human suffering may have changed, and continue to change, but mankind is not likely to reduce the extent of suffering.
8. In recent generations, suffering has increased in the world.
9. The types of injustice may have changed, and may continue to change, but mankind is not likely to reduce the extent of injustice.
10. In recent generations injustice has increased in the world.
11. In recent generations there has been a significant reduction in the amount of injustice in human life.
12. It is a mistake to believe that the reduction of injustice on earth is the critically important question for mankind.
13. Mankind's most difficult and destructive experiences are often the source of increased understanding and powers of endurance.
14. In the long run, undeserving persons seem to be the ones who win the most advantages.
15. In the face of the almost continuous conflict and violence in life, I cannot see how men are going to learn to live in mutual respect and peace with one another.
16. Suffering, injustice, and finally death need not be negative experiences; their significance can be shaped by our religious beliefs.
17. Efforts to deal with man's most difficult problems by religious means seems to me to be a waste of time and resources.
18. There are many aspects of the beliefs and practices of the world's religions with which I might not agree; nevertheless, I consider them to be valuable efforts to deal with man's most important questions.
19. Efforts to deal with man's most difficult problems by political means seem to me to be a waste of time and resources.
20. In the long run, mankind will be able to reduce injustice and suffering by wise political action.

1.10
OMNIBUS PERSONALITY INVENTORY—
RELIGIOUS ORIENTATION SCALE (Heist & Yonge, 1968)

Reviewed by W. Brad Johnson

Variable: The Religious Orientation Scale (RO) is one of 14 scales that constitute the Omnibus Personality Inventory (OPI: Heist & Yonge, 1968). The RO measures individual attitudes, opinions, and values with respect to religious belief and practice. The authors conceptualized religious orientation as a bipolar dimension with liberal versus fundamental religious commitment indicated by high versus low scores respectively (Heist & Yonge, 1968). High RO scores suggest a skeptical, rejecting attitude toward conventional religious beliefs and practices, especially if they are orthodox or fundamentalist (Dellas & Jernigan, 1990). Low RO scores suggest a strong commitment to Orthodox belief and practice as well as more general conservatism and dogmatism. Such persons believe God exists and hears prayers, strongly prefer to be with others who are religious, and never want to be considered skeptical or agnostic in religious matters (Heist & Yonge, 1968).

Description: The OPI (Heist & Yonge, 1968) was developed to assess selected attitudes, values, and interests related to academic activity and readiness among college students. Described by the authors as "eclectic," the OPI was not rooted in a particular personality theory and was intended primarily for use in educational research. Development of the OPI began with a pool of items borrowed from existing personality inventories. Rational-intuitive analysis reduced the pool to the 385 items contained in the standard OPI form (Form F). Each item belongs to one or more of the 14 OPI scales.

The Religious Orientation Scale (RO) (initially termed the "Religious Liberalism Scale"), consists of 26 true-false items designed to assess religious beliefs and related attitudes as well as degree of commitment to fundamentalistic or dogmatic thinking (Heist & Yonge, 1968). The RO scale is highly correlated with the Autonomy Scale (Au), which measures personal autonomy and independence of thought. Together, these scales tap a dimension the authors described as "freedom to learn" or more simply "authoritarianism versus nonauthoritarianism" (Heist & Yonge, 1968).

One point is obtained for each item answered in the scored direction (see appendix) resulting in a raw score range of 0 to 26 with high scores indicative of low religiosity or liberalism and low scores indicative of high religiosity or conservatism. Norms are provided in the form of raw scores, whereas subsequent research has reported RO results as standard scores with a mean of 50 and standard deviation of 10. Heist and Yonge (1968) offer a standard score conversion table in the OPI manual (p. 11).

Practical Considerations: Normative data regarding the OPI-RO is based on standard administration of the full OPI. Given the paucity of data regarding effects on the scale's psychometric properties, separate administration of the RO items is not recommended. The OPI is easy to administer to individuals and groups. The 385 true-false statements typically require 45 minutes to complete and there is no time limit.

Norms/Standardization: OPI norms (Heist & Yonge, 1968) were based on a substantial sample of 7,283 college freshmen (3,540 men, 3,743 women) from 37 diverse colleges and universities across 14 states. The OPI was administered to all subjects in group format early their freshman year. Institutions were selected to be representative of schools in various categories of higher education. RO scores ranged from 0 to 26 with a mean for this sample of 11.8 (standard score equivalent = 50) and a standard deviation of 6.2. The mean for men was 12.6 (*SD* = 6.2), while the mean for women was 11.1 (*SD* = 6.0).

Subsequent research indicates consistent differences between first and fourth year college students on the RO Scale. Across several samples, RO standard scores range from 39 to 46 during the freshman year and from 49 to 51 during the senior year (Baird, 1990; Chickering, 1974; Kuh, 1976). No other specialized norms are available for the RO Scale.

Reliability: Heist and Yonge (1968) utilized two procedures to evaluate the reliability of the RO Scale. Internal consistency in the normative sample (*N* = 7283) was established with a Kuder-Richardson coefficient of .86. In a subsequent study with 400 college freshman, a split-half Spearman Brown coefficient of .91 was reported. Test-retest reliability was reported for two samples. Among 67 female college students, the stability coefficient was .92, while for a sample of 71 upper-class students, the coefficient was .91. Both stability estimates were based on intervals of three to four weeks.

Validity: Heist and Yonge (1968) attempted to ensure content validity of the RO Scale through careful item selection from existing instruments on the basis of congruence with the religious orientation construct. Subsequent research has focused exclusively on establishing the RO Scale's concurrent and construct validity.

Several authors have established a correlation between education and RO scores, suggesting that during the college years, students evidence decreasing levels of religiosity and increased religious tolerance and autonomy. Chickering (1974) found that the mean RO score changed from 46 to 50 from freshman to senior year. Subsequent authors, utilizing both stratified sample and longitudinal designs have confirmed this relationship (Baird, 1990; Kuh, 1976; Lavin & Prull, 1989). Kuh (1976) and Baird (1990), using 5- and 20-year follow-up designs, found significant increases in RO scores from freshman to senior year with either no change or slight decrements in RO scores at follow-up.

Concurrent and construct validity has been further enhanced via correlations between the RO and religious behavior. Heist and Yonge (1968) found that among students who reported attending religious services more than once a week, the RO raw score was 4.9 versus 17.3 for students reporting such attendance once or twice per year. The RO was also positively correlated with verbal (.26) and mathematical (.27) performance on the SAT (Heist & Yonge, 1968), indicating a link between religious orientation and general achievement. The RO was not predictive, however, of psychology doctoral students' subsequent scholarly productivity (Tinsley, Tinsley, Boone, & Shim-Li, 1993).

Evaluating the RO's convergent validity, Heist and Yonge (1968) reported no significant correlation between the RO and the Edwards Personal Preference Schedule or the Minnesota Multiphasic Personality Inventory. Strong positive correlations were reported between the RO and the scales of intellectual quality, social undesirability, and creative personality from the Opinion, Attitude, and Interest Survey. Significant correlations between the RO and the California Personality Inventory were reported for the social presence (.34), socialization (−.34), and achievement via independence (.31) scales. As expected, the RO was significantly correlated with the Study of Values—Religious Scale (−.66), Theoretical Scale (.32), and Aesthetic Scale (.32). Finally, Heist and Yonge, (1968) found significant correlations between the RO and several Strong Vocational Interest Blank professions such as psychologist (.35), office worker (−.31), and banker (−.41). In a sample of 220 college students, RO scale scores were found to be minimally correlated with Social Desirability scores (Heist & Yonge, 1968).

OPI scale intercorrelations reported for the normative sample (Heist and Yonge, 1968) lend considerable support to the construct validity of the RO scale. The RO was negatively correlated with the Practical Outlook Scale (PO = −.40) and positively correlated with scales tapping autonomy (Au = .63), complexity of thought (CO = .46), thinking introversion (TI = .32), and theoretical/scientific interests (TO = .35). Factor analysis of the OPI has shown the RO scale loads significantly on Factor 1 (anti-intellectual authoritarianism, −.41) and Factor 8 (religious orientation, .88). This factor structure is confirmatory of the notion that low scores on the RO are indicative of pragmatic, utilitarian, and dogmatic qualities in belief and behavior. Further, the relationship of the RO to the OPI factor structure is stable over time (Elton & Terry, 1969).

The OPI-RO scale has established moderate reliability and reasonable validity for the purpose of measuring religious liberalism versus religious conservatism among late adolescent and young adult samples in educational research. Nonetheless, the scale's utility is compromised by a restricted definition of religiousness as rigid, dogmatic, and indicative of authoritarianism. The dichotomous nature of the items creates a false polarity between religious (rigid) and nonreligious (flexible). Rather than serving as a useful measure of religiousness or religious belief, the real value of this RO scale for the scientific study of religion may be its usefulness in tapping cognitive style (flexibility) as it relates to religious belief.

Location:

Heist, P., & Yonge, G. (1968). *Omnibus Personality Inventory: Form F manual*. New York: The Psychological Corporation.

Subsequent Research:

Baird, L. L. (1990). A 24-year longitudinal study of the development of religious ideas. *Psychological Reports, 66,* 479–482.

Chickering, A. W. (1974). The impact of various college environments on personality development. *Journal of the American College Health Association, 23,* 82–93.

Dellas, M., & Jernigan, L. P. (1990). Affective personality characteristics associated with undergraduate ego identity formation. *Journal of Adolescent Research, 5,* 306–324.

Elton, C. F., & Terry, T. R. (1969). Factor stability of the Omnibus Personality Inventory. *Journal of Counseling Psychology, 16,* 373–374.

Kuh, G. D. (1976). Persistence of the impact of college on attitudes and values. *Journal of College Student Personnel, 17,* 116–122.

Lavin, T. J., & Prull, R. W. (1989). Student personality traits and values across generations. *Journal of College Student Development, 30,* 407–412.

Tinsley, D. J., Tinsley, H. E. A., Boone, S., & Shim-Li, C. (1993). Prediction of scientist-practitioner behavior using personality scores obtained during graduate school. *Journal of Counseling Psychology, 40,* 511–517.

Appendix

Omnibus Personality Inventory-Religious Orientation Scale

OPI Item Number	Keyed Response	Item
39	False	I pray several times a week.
58	True	In matters of religion it really does not matter what one believes.
69	False	I believe there is a God.
101	True	Each person should interpret the Bible for himself.
109	False	There must be something wrong with a person who is lacking in religious feeling.
150	True	I generally prefer being with people who are not religious.
156	False	I believe in a life hereafter.
161	False	When it comes to differences of opinion in religion, we should bc careful not to compromise with those whose beliefs are different from ours.
169	True	It doesn't matter to me what church a man belongs to, or whether or not he belongs to a church at all.
175	False	Every person should have complete faith in a supernatural power whose decisions are obeyed without question.
208	False	My church, faith, or denomination has the only true approach to God.
211	False	When science contradicts religion, it is because of scientific hypotheses that have not been and cannot be tested.
217	True	I have read little or none of the Bible.
227	False	The prophets of the Old Testament predicted the events that are happening today.
231	False	God hears our prayers.
243	True	In religious matters I believe I would have to be called a skeptic or an agnostic.

OPI Item Number	Keyed Response	Item
252	True	The only meaning to existence is the one man gives to it.
260	False	One needs to be wary of those persons who claim not to believe in God.
272	True	I frequently have serious doubts about my religious beliefs.
286	False	I go to church or temple almost every week.
301	True	Organized religion, while sincere and constructive in its aims, is really an obstacle to human progress.
327	True	Religion should be primarily a social force or institution.
335	True	We cannot know for sure whether or not there is a God.
343	True	I believe in the worth of humanity but not in God.
364	False	I am more religious than most people.
367	True	I expect that ultimately mathematics will prove more important for mankind than will theology.

*Note: the ROS is best administered in the context of the OPI, not as an independent scale.

1.11
RELIGIOUS ATTITUDE SCALE (Armstrong, Larsen, & Mourer, 1962)
Reviewed by Leslie J. Francis

Variable: The Religious Attitude Scale (RAS) was constructed to assess three types of religious response: orthodoxy, conservatism, and liberalism. Orthodoxy is understood to characterize the Roman Catholic position; conservatism is understood to characterize the Protestant position; liberalism is understood to characterize the Unitarian position.

Description: The authors began by identifying 16 religious concepts: God, Jesus, Holy Ghost, Virgin Mary, saints, angels, devil, heaven, hell, soul, sin, salvation, miracles, Bible, prayer, and rituals and sacraments. Twelve judges were asked to define each concept. These definitions were then classified by 15 judges into the three categories of orthodoxy, conservatism, and liberalism. The definitions most consistently selected as representative of the three types of reli-

gious response were used to construct the 16-item multiple choice test.

Subjects are presented with the list of 16 concepts, followed in each case by the three definitions. They are invited to "select and check for each item the one descriptive phrase which would best describe your attitude or behavior."

The first stage in scoring the Religious Attitude Scale is to calculate the number of times each type of religious response (orthodox, conservative, and liberal) has been selected. The authors then propose a scoring key to convert the three separate scores, recorded on each of the dimensions of orthodoxy, conservatism, and liberalism, into one continuous score ranging from 153 (most orthodox) to 1 (most liberal). This conversion is based on a conceptual, rather than an empirical, schema. The scoring key and the conversion scale are reproduced in the appendix.

In addition to the 16 concepts, the Religious Attitude Scale contains four other multiple-choice questions dealing with religious interest, church attendance, valuation placed on religion, and concern about religion. These items do not contribute to the overall scale score.

Practical Considerations: This paper-and-pencil measure requires no special examiner skill to administer or score. Only minimal instructions are necessary and are provided. Interpretation of the scale scores, however, may be more problematic. The face validity of the scale is closely tied to the authors' definitions of orthodoxy, conservatism, and liberalism, which may transfer uneasily to a contemporary religious climate. It is also not clear what precisely is being assessed when the three dimensions are collapsed into a supposedly continuous scale. Moreover, the process of conversion from dimensional scores to a cumulative score is cumbersome, time consuming, and complex to translate into a computer program.

Norms/Standardization: The Religious Attitude Scale was administered to 100 male and 109 female adults, including 88 hospitalized psychiatric patients (31 Catholics, 51 Protestants and 6 without denominational links), and 121 nonpsychiatric persons (38 Catholics, 48 Protestants, and 35 Unitarians).

The mean scores for the normal subjects were as follows: Catholics, 139.50 (*SD*, 13.83); Protestants, 105.95 (*SD*, 28.70); Unitarians, 13.48 (*SD*, 16.46). The mean scores for the hospitalized subjects were as follows: Catholics, 119.97 (*SD*, 21.80); Protestants, 109.72 (*SD*, 25.80).

Reliability: The authors reported a test-retest reliability of .98 among a sample of 71 nonpsychiatric subjects. For the separate religious groups test-retest reliability ranged from .73 among 27 Catholics, .67 among 25 Protestants, and .48 among 19 Unitarians. The authors also reported intertest reliability coefficients (Kuder-Richardson) of .66 among 38 Catholics, .61 among 48 Protestants, and .72 among 37 Unitarians.

Validity: Inspection of the individual items revealed that Catholics tended to agree with eleven of the orthodox definitions but were in disagreement on the items defining Jesus, the Virgin Mary, saints, heaven, and soul. The Unitarians tended to disagree with eleven of the liberal definitions, chose two of the conservative definitions (prayer and rituals and sacraments) and were in disagreement on three items (God, Virgin Mary, and saints). The Protestants tended to agree with only three conservative definitions (Virgin Mary, saints, and soul); they chose four orthodox definitions (salvation, miracles, Bible, and prayer), and were in considerable disagreement on the other nine items. The authors argue that these discrepancies between their operational definitions of orthodoxy, conservatism, and liberalism and the empirical findings may indicate the wide variety of religious concepts among Americans rather "than just a weakness of this test." Nonetheless, the authors reported that the total scale scores differentiated significantly among the three religious groups.

Location:
    Armstrong, R. G., Larsen, G. L., & Mourer, S. A. (1962). Religious attitudes and emotional adjustment. *Journal of Psychological Studies*, *13*, 35–47.

Subsequent Research: The study by Armstrong, Larsen, and Mourer (1962) has been cited in subsequent research, but no published material on the independent use of the scale was found.

Appendix

Religious Attitude Scale

Select and check for each item the one descriptive phrase that would best describe your attitude or behavior.

1. GOD
    a) Spiritual, guiding force (C)
    b) All-powerful creator of the universe (O)
    c) Manmade explanation of the unknown (L)

2. JESUS
    a) Wise prophet and successful crusader (L)
    b) God manifest in man (C)
    c) Son of God (O)

3. HOLY GHOST
    a) Third person of the Blessed Trinity (O)
    b) God revealed in spiritual form (C)
    c) Supposedly a divine being (L)

4. VIRGIN MARY
    a) Mother of Jesus (C)
    b) Supposedly the mother of a prophet (L)
    c) Blessed mother of God (O)

5. SAINTS
    a) Agents effecting communication between God and man (O)
    b) Good people living or having lived Christian lives (C)
    c) Humans falsely elevated to holiness (L)

6. ANGELS
    a) Heavenly beings created in God's likeness (O)
    b) Revelation of God's ways (C)
    c) Manmade symbols of goodness (L)

7. DEVILS
    a) Manmade symbols of evil (L)
    b) Our temptations to do evil (C)
    c) Fallen angels (O)

8. HEAVEN
    a) Peaceful state of mind (L)
    b) The place of eternal happiness for only those who are saved (O)
    c) Future life in the kingdom of God (C)

9. HELL
    a) Threat of future punishment for man's sins (C)
    b) Our earthly suffering (L)
    c) Place of eternal punishment for the damned (O)

10. SOUL
    a) Personality (L)
    b) Spiritual part of man, linking him to God (C)
    c) Immortal, immaterial part of man (O)

11. SIN
    a) Falling short of our best and our misdeeds toward others (L)
    b) Transgression against God's law (O)
    c) Breaking an established moral and religious code (C)

12. SALVATION
    a) Saving one's soul, which is the ultimate end of man's creation (O)
    b) Submitting to God's will (C)
    c) Having fulfilled one's purpose in life (L)

13. MIRACLES
    a) Illustrations explaining God's ways (C)
    b) Unusual occurrences which do have a logical explanation (L)
    c) Unusual acts produced through the power of God (O)

14. BIBLE
    a) Book of history and moral behavior (L)
    b) Book of reverent religious writings (C)
    c) Revealed word of God (O)

15. PRAYER
    a) Attempts at magical wish fulfilment (L)
    b) Religious meditation (C)
    c) Communication with God (O)

16. RITUALS AND SACRAMENTS
    a) Means of achieving grace (O)
    b) Man-made actions for the pleasure of mythical beings (L)
    c) Symbolic actions during worship (C)

17. My interest in religion is:
    a) none
    b) very little
    c) some
    d) great
    e) very great

18. I attend church services:
    a) never
    b) seldom
    c) monthly
    d) weekly
    e) two or more times a week

19. To me religion is:
    a) very harmful
    b) somewhat harmful
    c) indifferent
    d) somewhat helpful
    d) very helpful

20. I worry about religion:
    a) not at all
    b) very little
    c) some
    d) much
    e) very much

Score Conversion Chart

O	C	L	Score	O	C	L	Score
16	0	0	153	9	2	5	120
15	1	0	152	9	1	6	119
15	0	1	151	9	0	7	118
14	2	0	150	8	8	0	117
14	1	1	149	8	7	1	116
14	0	2	148	8	6	2	115
13	3	0	147	8	5	3	114
13	2	1	146	8	4	4	113
13	1	2	145	8	3	5	112
13	0	3	144	8	2	6	111
12	4	0	143	8	1	7	110
12	3	1	142	8	0	8	109
12	2	2	141	7	9	0	108
12	1	3	140	7	8	1	107
12	0	4	139	7	7	2	106
11	5	0	138	7	6	3	105
11	4	1	137	7	5	4	104
11	3	2	136	7	4	5	103
11	2	3	135	7	3	6	102
11	1	4	134	7	2	7	101
11	0	5	133	7	1	8	100
10	6	0	132	7	0	9	99
10	5	1	131	6	10	0	98
10	4	2	130	6	9	1	97
10	3	3	129	6	8	2	96
10	2	4	128	6	7	3	95
10	1	5	127	6	6	4	94
10	0	6	126	6	5	5	93
9	7	0	125	6	4	6	92
9	6	1	124	6	3	7	91
9	5	2	123	6	2	8	90
9	4	3	122	6	1	9	89
9	3	4	121	6	0	10	88

O	C	L	Score	O	C	L	Score
5	11	0	87	2	9	5	43
5	10	1	86	2	8	6	42
5	9	2	85	2	7	7	41
5	8	3	84	2	6	8	40
5	7	4	83	2	5	9	39
5	6	5	82	2	4	10	38
5	5	6	81	2	3	11	37
5	4	7	80	2	2	12	36
5	3	8	79	2	1	13	35
5	2	9	78	2	0	14	34
5	1	10	77	1	15	0	33
5	0	11	76	1	14	1	32
4	12	0	75	1	13	2	31
4	11	1	74	1	12	3	30
4	10	2	73	1	11	4	29
4	9	3	72	1	10	5	28
4	8	4	71	1	9	6	27
4	7	5	70	1	8	7	26
4	6	6	69	1	7	8	25
4	5	7	68	1	6	9	24
4	4	8	67	1	5	10	23
4	3	9	66	1	4	11	22
4	2	10	65	1	3	12	21
4	1	11	64	1	2	13	20
4	0	12	63	1	1	14	19
3	13	0	62	1	0	15	18
3	12	1	61	0	16	0	17
3	11	2	60	0	15	1	16
3	10	3	59	0	14	2	15
3	9	4	58	0	13	3	14
3	8	5	57	0	12	4	13
3	7	6	56	0	11	5	12
3	6	7	55	0	10	6	11
3	5	8	54	0	9	7	10
3	4	9	53	0	8	8	9
3	3	10	52	0	7	9	8
3	2	11	51	0	6	10	7
3	1	12	50	0	5	11	6
3	0	13	49	0	4	12	5
2	14	0	48	0	3	13	4
2	13	1	47	0	2	14	3
2	12	2	46	0	1	15	2
2	11	3	45	0	0	16	1
2	10	4	44				

1.12
RELIGIOUS BELIEF INVENTORY (Lee, 1965)
Reviewed by Nancy Stiehler Thurston

Variable: The Religious Belief Inventory (RBI) measures the extent to which one agrees with various doctrines of religious faith. It was based on the premise that "religious beliefs cluster in homogeneous patterns, as indicated by the existence of theological systems within the history of Christian thought" (Lee, 1965, p. 1). Lee developed this measure primarily to aid him with empirically investigating the relationship between theological belief and personality.

Description: The Religious Belief Inventory (RBI) consists of the following seven scales: Fundamentalism, Orthodoxy, Humanism, Scientism, Puritanism, Pietism, and Liberalism. This multidimensional religious belief inventory was designed to reflect various historical currents within Methodism. However, Lee hoped that the RBI would generalize from Methodists to Protestants in measuring religious trends.

Each of the seven scales of the RBI consists of eight items. In addition, the RBI has four ad hoc items designed to stimulate future research. Thus the entire RBI consists of 60 items.

Each item on the RBI is scored on a 5-point "agree-disagree" continuum. A separate score is obtained for each of the seven scales. Four of the eight items on each scale are reverse scored. Each scale is scored by, first, reverse scoring the appropriate four items and, second, summing across all eight items. Possible scores for each scale range from 0 to 32.

Practical Considerations: This measure is self-administered and takes approximately thirty minutes to complete.

Several caveats are offered for the interpretation of this scale, arising from the present author's experience of administering it to lay church members. First, the negatively worded items confused some people. Second, the use of sophisticated language made

a number of items difficult to comprehend (e.g., "fallible," item 4, and "natural procreation," item 20). Third, obscure scriptural references made some items difficult for people to know how to respond. For example, when the RBI was administered to lay members of fundamentalist churches, a surprising number of them asked if item 47 ("When Joshua commanded the sun to stand still, it did so.") was really in the Bible. They added that if it was, they would score the item "strongly agree" and that if it was not, "strongly disagree." Overall, these three caveats suggest that this measure would be more suitable for a seminary or clerical population than for laypersons.

A fourth caveat regarding this scale involves the lack of gender-neutral language. Future revisions of this scale would be able to rectify this with substitutions such as "people" for "man" (e.g., item 43: "People are not sinful, merely foolish").

Norms/Standardization: Three sets of normative data were gathered for the original RBI, consisting of Garrett Theological Seminary students (United Methodist Church), Northwestern University undergraduate students, and a sample of persons holding atheistic or agnostic beliefs.

The Garrett Theological Seminary sample consisted of 302 students (271 males; 31 females), with an impressive response rate of 85%. Means and standard deviations obtained from this sample were as follows: Fundamentalism ($M = 14.15$; $SD = 5.54$), Orthodoxy ($M = 23.22$; $SD = 5.11$), Humanism ($M = 12.55$; $SD = 4.42$), Scientism ($M = 8.37$; $SD = 3.27$), Puritanism ($M = 12.62$; $SD = 3.84$), Pietism ($M = 18.75$; $SD = 4.08$), and Liberalism ($M = 17.44$; $SD = 3.39$).

The sample of 111 Northwestern University undergraduate students yielded the following means and standard deviations: Fundamentalism ($M = 15.15$; $SD = 7.01$), Orthodoxy ($M = 15.58$; $SD = 6.36$), Humanism ($M = 18.14$; $SD = 4.16$), Scientism ($M =$

12.87; *SD* = 4.35), Puritanism (*M* = 10.59; *SD* = 4.62), Pietism (*M* = 13.45; *SD* = 3.97), and Liberalism (*M* = 18.36; *SD* = 3.94).

While the sample of persons with atheistic or agnostic religious orientations was small (*N* = 26), the normative data obtained was valuable in establishing the validity of several of the scales. Means and standard deviations were as follows: Fundamentalism (*M* = 6.15; *SD* = 3.75), Orthodoxy (*M* = 9.00; *SD* = 3.37), Humanism (*M* = 19.38; *SD* = 4.53), Scientism (*M* = 16.60; *SD* = 3.71), Puritanism (*M* = 8.93; *SD* = 4.28), Pietism (*M* = 11.57; *SD* = 4.09), and Liberalism (*M* = 17.88; *SD* = 4.23).

Reliability: Lee found that only three of the original seven scales were reliable and homogeneous: Fundamentalism, Orthodoxy, and Humanism. As a result, Lee revised the RBI and administered it to a sample of 111 of entering Garrett Theological Seminary students. Reliability statistics on the revised RBI found only Fundamentalism and Orthodoxy Scales to be reliable. Due to this unexpected finding, Lee recommended that future research on the RBI use the revised version of the measure, with the exception of inserting the Humanism Scale from the original RBI. (The "combined" version of the RBI is included in the appendix of this review as Lee recommended, i.e., the revised RBI with the original Humanism Scale). The revised RBI's most effective component was the Puritanism Scale, which was found to be significantly more reliable than the original version of the scale.

Overall, the following four Scales of the combined RBI were found to be sound, reliable, and homogeneous: Fundamentalism, Orthodoxy, Humanism, and Puritanism. Guttman reproducibility coefficients (a measure of homogeneity) were excellent for each of the four scales, respectively: .93, .88, .88, and .94. The Kuder-Richardson reliability coefficients were, respectively: .72, .69, .50, and .62. Split-half reliability coefficients were, respectively: .70, .54, .45, and .60. Of all the scales, the Fundamentalism scale was found to have the strongest psychometric properties.

Validity: The validity of the Fundamentalism, Orthodoxy, Humanism, and Puritanism scales were investigated by administering the RBI to a seminary sample, a secular university sample, and an agnostic/atheistic sample. The Fundamentalism scores were significantly lower for the agnostic sample than for the other two groups. The same pattern was found for scores on the Orthodoxy and Puritanism Scales. On the Humanism Scale, the atheistic/agnostic and secular university students both scored significantly higher than the seminary sample. Thus, the scores obtained from these three samples supported the validity of all four of these scales.

Lee developed the RBI, in part, to aid him in testing the hypothesis that the seven orientations of religious belief were differentially associated with intelligence and personality styles. He tested these hypothesis by correlating RBI scores in his Garrett sample with scores obtained on the Wechsler Adult Intelligence Test, Rorschach InkblotTest, and Crowne-Marlowe Social Desirability Test. While his particular hypotheses were generally not supported, he nevertheless did find other significant results. Thus Lee found that the RBI could be used to glean valuable information on the personality characteristics of various religious orientations. Subsequent research using the RBI has likewise focused on investigatng the relationship between theological beliefs and personality styles.

Location:

Lee, R. R. (1965). *Theological belief as a dimension of personality*. Unpublished doctoral dissertation, Northwestern University, Evanston, IL.

Subsequent Research:

Gorsuch, R. L. & McFarland, S. G. (1972). Single vs. multiple item scales for measuring religious values. *Journal for the Scientific Study of Religion*, *11*, 53–64. Reprinted in H. N. Malony (Ed.), *Current perspectives in the psychology of religion*. Grand Rapids, MI: Eerdmans, 1977.

Smith, C. S. (1983). *Sanctioning and causal attributions to God: A function of theological position and actors' characteristics*. Unpublished doctoral dissertation, Graduate School of Psychology, Fuller Theological Seminary, Pasadena, CA.

Stiehler, N. J. (1991). *Attitudes and personality characteristics of conservative and mainline/liberal church congregations.* Unpublished doctoral dissertation, Central Michigan University, Mount Pleasant, MI.

Appendix

Religious Belief Inventory

This inventory surveys a variety of religious beliefs.

You have five choices for each statement. You can indicate your choice by marking the appropriate column.

     1. You strongly agree with the statement.
     2. You agree somewhat with the statement.
     3. You neither agree nor disagree with the statement.
     4. You disagree somewhat with the statement.
     5. You strongly disagree with the statement.

There is no time limit, but please answer all the questions in the order in which they occur.

There are no right or wrong answers; please feel free to give your own leanings whether or not you feel strongly about the statement.

Please erase completely any answer you may wish to change.

Although you may obtain your own score from the person who administers the test, your opinions will be kept confidential.

By using the back of the answer sheet, you may mark any explanations or raise any objections to the statements. Number the item to which you refer. You may also wish to indicate beliefs that you hold strongly but are not included here.

  1. [P]   Setting aside a portion of each day for family prayer and meditation is a part of Christian living.
  2. [M*]   There is nothing intrinsically wrong with smoking.
  3. [F]   All these modern translations of Scripture present a real threat to the gospel.
  4. [F*]   The Bible is fallible.
  5. [P]   All preaching ought to include an urgent appeal for conversion.
  6. [F*]   Adam and Eve are not historical persons.
  7. [O*]   The Bible is principally a record of man's developing thought about God.
  8. [S]   Man's primary concern ought to be with the laws of nature.
  9. [H*]   An open mind is an appealing but unrealistic goal.
10. [H*]   Authority of the State rests on more than just the consent of the people.
11. [S*]   There are other types of knowledge that outweigh scientific knowledge.
12. [L*]   Our business is to concentrate on both this world and the world to come.
13. [P*]   Small, regular, midweek meetings for prayer, study, and discussion are an appendix to the major purpose of the church.
14. [H*]   All major religions teach different basic beliefs.
15. [M]   Life in this world is a constant struggle against evil and wickedness.
16. [O]   Jesus Christ is the supreme revelation of God; very God of very God.

17. —   No one is foreordained to eternal salvation.
18. [O*]   The doctrine of the Trinity has little relevance for the Christian faith.
19. [F]   We know that God forgives us our sins because Christ gave his life as a substitute for us.
20. [F*]   Jesus Christ was born by natural procreation.
21. [M]   It is a sin to play any sport or do any work on the Sabbath.
22. [O]   We can't be reconciled to God except by Christ's atoning work on the cross.
23. [P]   No one can be a Christian unless he has a personal relationship with Jesus Christ.
24. [S*]   Science is inadequate to ultimately overcome all the problems of society.
25. [L*]   When we attempt to reduce it to modern terms, the Christian message is deprived of its deeper meanings.
26. [M]   Alcohol is a dangerous agent of misery and vice.
27. [P*]   Christianity is more a philosophy or a system of beliefs than a way of living.
28. [H]   The major function of religion is the integration of personality.
29. —   Sin, sickness, and death are unreal.
30. [L*]   The Sermon on the Mount was never intended to be a simple set of rules for living.
31. —   God is a process.
32. [M*]   Card playing is a harmless pastime.
33. [F]   After Jesus arose from the dead He walked, talked, and ate with the disciples.
34. [S]   One day science will supersede religion.
35. [H]   Man has proved adequate as the central concern of society.
36. [P*]   The experience of a new birth is unnecessary for membership in the church.
37. [L]   The Church's task is to build the kingdom of God.
38. [S*]   The trouble with science is that it has structured the world in a cold, depersonalized way.
39. [L]   God created man through evolution.
40. [F*]   At Cana, Jesus did not literally turn water into wine.
41. [S]   What we know can only come to us through the five senses.
42. [M*]   Dancing is a normal, healthy social activity.
43. [H]   Man is not sinful, merely foolish.
44. [P*]   God's ministers are only those who are ordained by the church.
45. [S*]   Science should have little concern for such things as ultimate truth or reality.
46. [L]   Man has within him the capacity for morality, justice, and goodness.
47. [F]   When Joshua commanded the sun to stand still, it did so.
48. [O]   We are saved by God's grace, through faith, without any merit of our own.
49. [L]   History shows us that the modern era is progressing toward the kingdom of God.
50. [M*]   Providing a person stays within his financial means, gambling is harmless.
51. [S]   When compared with the vastness of space and the power of the atom, man fades into insignificance.
52. [O]   Our experience of God's salvation on earth is but a foretaste of heaven.
53. [O*]   Doctrine is relatively unimportant.
54. [P]   A large proportion of the church's mission and money ought to be directed toward the poor, the ill-educated, and underprivileged, both at home and abroad.
55. [M]   The world is full of demonic forces that seek to control our lives.
56. —   Perfect love is impossible.
57. [O*]   Original Sin is an archaic myth.
58. [L*]   Pacifism is unsuitable as a position in Christian ethics.
59. [H*]   Man is quite incapable of setting and achieving his own goals.
60. [H]   The way to build a better society is to appeal to people's reason.

[F]   Fundamentalism
[H]   Humanism
[L]   Liberalism
[M]   Puritanism
[O]   Orthodoxy
[P]   Pietism
[S]   Scientism

* indicates items that are reverse scored

Note: This is a combined version of the RBI, which consists of the Humanism Scale from the original RBI and the remaining six scales from the revised RBI.

Reprinted with permission of the author.

1.13
THE RELIGIOUS BELIEF SCALE (Martin & Nichols, 1962)
Reviewed by W. Brad Johnson

Variable: The Religious Belief Scale (RBS) was developed as a measure of Judeo-Christian religious belief in individuals. The content of the RBS items centers around "belief . . . in the Bible, in the efficacy of prayer, in an afterlife, in a personal God who is near and present, in the divinity of Jesus, and in the church and religion as necessary for a good life" (Martin & Nichols, 1962, p. 4). The RBS measures acceptance of religious teachings and positive valuing of religion (Shaw & Wright, 1967).

Description: Martin and Nichols (1962) borrowed items from several established religious belief scales and wrote additional items for an initial pool of 50 items. The authors specifically developed the RBS to test certain personality and demographic correlates of religiosity. Nine items were discarded due to nonsignificant correlations with the total score in a sample of 80 subjects. The resulting 41-item true-false inventory (see appendix) constitutes the RBS.

Subjects respond "true" or "false" to each item on a separate answer sheet. Eighteen of the 41 RBS items are negative and thus are reverse scored. One point is scored for each positive item marked "true" and one point for each negative item marked "false." Points are summed for the total

RBS score, which can range from 0 to 41. High scores suggest acceptance of religion and religious teaching (Shaw & Wright, 1967).

Practical Considerations: This paper-and-pencil measure requires no special examiner skill to administer, score, or interpret. Instructions are printed on the test form, which directs the subjects to respond either "true" or "false" to every item on the basis of their agreement or disagreement that the item content is true about them.

Norms/Standardization: The only data available regarding the RBS were obtained from a sample of 163 undergraduate college students. Fifty-nine male and 104 female students completed the RBS in a group testing situation. No additional data regarding this sample was reported. Unfortunately, Martin and Nichols (1962) only reported correlations for the RBS with other variables and neglected to report the sample mean and standard deviation. To date, there is no normative data regarding the RBS.

Reliability: Using a subgroup ($N = 83$) of the original sample, Martin and Nichols (1962) reported a Kuder-Richardson reliability coefficient of .95. There has been no subsequent confirmation of the scale's reliability.

Validity: Face validity of the RBS items was paramount in item selection. Review of the scale's items suggests considerable homogeneity in content, which is reinforced by the rather high reliability coefficient. RBS items appear to consistently reflect common Judeo-Christian religious teachings. There is little empirical confirmation of the scale's content or construct validity. Martin and Nichols (1962) reported significant positive correlations between the RBS and demographic variables such as a rural background, female gender, church membership, church attendance, and having experienced positive parental attitudes toward religion. Contrary to prediction, the RBS was also significantly positively correlated with the Authoritarianism Scale and there was no significant relationship between RBS scores and level of religious information. The authors report a curvilinear relationship between RBS scores and level of information about religion, with subjects in the moderate range of information (biblical and general religious) obtaining the highest RBS scores.

Location:

Martin, C., & Nichols, R. C. (1962). Personality and religious belief. *Journal of Social Psychology, 56,* 3–8.

Shaw, M. E., & Wright, J. M. (1967). *Scales for the measurement of attitudes.* New York: McGraw-Hill.

Subsequent Research: A review of the literature revealed no subsequent published research using the RBS.

Appendix

Religious Belief Scale

Instructions: If you agree with a statement or feel that it is true about you or true to the best of your knowledge, answer "true." If you disagree with a statement or feel that it is not true about you or not true to the best of your knowledge, answer "false." Be sure to answer either true or false for every statement, even if you have to guess at some.

1. Religious faith is better than logic for solving life's important problems.
*2. I don't think it makes any difference if one is a Christian as long as he has good will for others.
3. I often think that I couldn't do without my religion.
4. I believe the Bible is the inspired Word of God.
*5. I think there were many men in history as great as Jesus.
6. God is constantly with us.
*7. Christ's simple message of concern for your fellow man has been twisted by superstitious mysticism.
8. I attend church to worship God with devotion and to gain guidance for everyday life.
*9. A person can be happy and enjoy life without believing in God.
10. I believe that eternal life is a gift of God to those who believe in Jesus Christ as Savior and Lord.
*11. Man can solve all his important problems without help from a Supreme Being.
12. It is through the righteousness of Jesus Christ and not because of our own works that we are made righteous before God.
*13. I don't think prayers go above the ceiling of the room in which they are uttered.
14. I am sometimes very conscious of the presence of God.
*15. "God" is an abstract concept roughly equivalent to the concept of "Nature."
*16. I think that the Bible is full of errors, misconceptions, and contradictions.

17. If I were without my religion and my understanding of God, I would have little left in life.
18. I think God is revealed in every person who feels and acts unselfishly.
19. I believe that men working and thinking together can build a just society without superhuman help.
20. I believe that God exists as Father, Son, and Holy Spirit.
*21. The Bible in many ways has held back and retarded human progress.
22. I think of God as present wherever there is genuine beauty.
*23. I am not a religious person.
*24. Science makes me doubt that man has a soul.
25. When in doubt, it is best to stop and ask God what to do.
*26. Christ was not divine, but his teachings and the example set by his life are important.
27. I believe that following the gospel of Christ is the only way for mankind to be saved.
28. God exists in all of us.
29. I think that God's purposes are best shown by Christ.
30. God created man separate and distinct from the animals.
*31. I can take religion or leave it.
32. I think that Jesus was born of a virgin.
*33. I think that God may *possibly* have created the world, but he does not show Himself or interfere in it today.
*34. I think there is no life after death.
*35. As science advances, religion will fade out in importance and eventually no religion will be needed.
36. God is very real to me.
*37. A person should follow his own conscience—not prayer—in deciding right and wrong.
38. I believe there is a Heaven and a Hell.
39. Because of His presence we can know that God exists.
40. Religion gives meaning to my life.
*41. I don't believe that history reveals the working out of God's plan.

* These items are negative and must be reversed for purposes of scoring.

1.14
RELIGIOUS IDENTIFICATION SCALE OF THE MMPI (Panton, 1979)
Reviewed by W. Brad Johnson & Roger Olson

Variable: The Religious Identification Scale (RI) is an item content scale from the Minnesota Multiphasic Personality Inventory (MMPI: Hathaway & McKinley, 1951) developed by Panton (1979). The RI was intended to reflect the individual's "identification with and participation in religious activities irrespective of faith or denomination within a faith" (Panton, 1979, p. 588). High RI scores imply belief in and identification with a religious faith as well as individual or collective participation in the worship tradition of that faith. Low RI scores reflect little or no participation in religious worship, lack of identification with religious principles and/or rejection of religion altogether (Panton, 1979).

Description: Panton, a prison psychologist, had discovered from experience and previous unpublished research that inmates who had identified with and participated in religion prior to incarceration often made a more adequate adjustment to prison confinement than inmates without such a religious identification. Panton reasoned that a measure of religious identification would facilitate prediction of adjustment versus maladjustment among the inmate population.

Hathaway and McKinley's (1940) original MMPI item pool of 550 statements were classified into 26 item categories. Category 15, "religious attitudes," was composed of 19 religious-content items. Panton (1979) subjected these items to rational-intuitive evaluation based on each item's manifest religious content. Five of the 19 items were rejected secondary to their implication of a psychotic illness (i.e., "my soul sometimes leaves my body"). Two additional items that reflected specific fundamentalist beliefs not shared by most faiths were also rejected. The remaining 12 items composed the RI scale (see appendix).

Approximately half the items reflect broad Judeo-Christian content, with the remaining items reflecting nonfaith-specific religious content. These items are spread throughout the MMPI and all items are scored 1 if true, with the exception of items 369 and 491, which are scored 1 if false. The RI shares 10 items in common with the Religious Fundamentalism Scale (REL: Wiggins, 1966) and it is unclear why Panton does not refer to the REL in his development of the RI. Given the significant item overlap between these scales, one must assume the REL and RI tap largely the same construct. However, two items contained in the REL and not the RI reflect more overt fundamentalist beliefs (i.e., "everything is turning out just as the prophets of the Bible said it would") and thus some distinction between scales may be warranted. The RI items appear congruent with the "identification" construct or what may best be described as adherence to religious belief and behavior. Norms are reported in terms of raw scores, which range from 0 to 12 (higher scores indicating greater religious identification). Panton's (1979) article also offered a T-score conversion table for the RI scale.

Practical Considerations: Unfortunately, available normative data is based on standard administrations of the full MMPI. While no norms are available for separate administration of the RI items, research in-

dicates minimal effects on results when single MMPI scales are administered separately (Perkins & Goldberg, 1964). The MMPI contains 566 items, which cover a range of subject matter from physical condition to the subject's moral and social attitudes. Time for administration varies but rarely exceeds 90 minutes. Subjects must have a sixth-grade reading level and are instructed to respond true or false to every item. The MMPI is easily self-administered and requires no extra instruction or supervision. RI scale scores must be obtained by hand scoring the 12 scale items. In contrast to the standard MMPI scales, no K-correction or other internal adjustment procedure is available to correct for self-favorableness versus self-criticalness on the RI scale. Due to their controversial nature, nearly all of the RI items were deleted during development of the MMPI-2 (Butcher, Dahlstrom, Graham, Tellegen, & Kaemmer, 1989), making it impossible to calculate the RI from MMPI-2 data.

Norms/Standardization: The RI scale was normed on an initial sample of 234 male prison inmates (Panton, 1979). Panton did not report demographics such as age, race, education, or crime classification for the sample. One hundred seventeen of the inmates had been referred for evaluation due to difficulty adjusting to the prison environment (maladjusted sample). One hundred seventeen additional inmates were randomly selected from the population of inmates who had adequately adjusted to incarceration (adjusted sample). The mean RI score for the adjusted sample was 8.8 (SD = 1.5; Range = 5–12), whereas the mean for the maladjusted sample was 4.0 (SD = 1.9; Range = 0–8). A second "validation" study was reported by Panton (1979) utilizing similar samples of adjusted (n = 100) and maladjusted (n = 100) prison inmates. In this study, the mean RI scores were 9.1 (SD = 1.5) for the adjusted group and 4.6 (SD = 1.7) for the maladjusted group. The only other study to employ the RI scale (Megargee & Carbonell, 1985) also utilized a prison population. In a sample of 1,214 male offenders, the mean age was 22.2, the mean Beta I.Q. was 100.83, and the mean highest school grade attended was 9.85. Sixty-four percent of the sample were white and 35% were black. The authors reported a mean T score on the RI of 52.89 (SD = 14.21). Additionally, the mean score for black inmates (54.32) was significantly higher than the mean score among white inmates (52.12) at the .01 level of significance.

Reliability: Neither the original development study by Panton (1979) nor the subsequent validation study (Megargee & Carbonell, 1985) offers information regarding the reliability of the RI.

Validity: In developing the Religious Identification scale, Panton (1979) attempted to ensure the scale's content or face validity through careful item selection. Panton's only attempt at empirical validation of the RI involved a demonstration of criterion-related validity using the method of contrasted groups. Utilizing distinct groups of adjusted versus maladjusted prison inmates (described earlier in this review), Panton found that an RI cutting score of 7 successfully identified 89% of the maladjusted and 95% of the adjusted sample. Between-group differences in mean RI scores were significant (t = 21.34, p < .001). A second study with similar prison samples confirmed these findings, with the RI effectively identifying 90% of a maladjusted sample and 94% of an adjusted sample (t = 20.45, p < .001).

Further validity was established by Megargee and Carbonell (1985), who reported negative correlations between the RI and screening measures of prison maladjustment (−.33), recidivism (−.18), escape probability (−.25), and habitual criminalism (−.18). In addition, the RI demonstrated moderate negative correlations with rate of infractions and days in segregation and small positive correlations with adjustment ratings by prison staff and work performance.

Location:
Panton, J. H. (1979). An MMPI item content scale to measure religious identification within a state prison population. *Journal of Clinical Psychology, 35,* 588–591.

Hathaway, S. R., & McKinley, J. C. (1951). *The Minnesota Multiphasic personality inventory manual—revised.* New York: The Psychological Corporation.

Subsequent Research:
Megargee, E. I., & Carbonell, J. L. (1985). Predicting prison adjustment with MMPI correctional scales. *Journal of Consulting and Clinical Psychology, 53,* 874–883.

References

Butcher, J. N., Dahlstrom, W. G., Graham, J. R., Tellegen, A., & Kaemmer, B. (1989). *Minnesota Multiphasic Personality Inventory—2 (MMPI-2): Manual for administration and scoring.* Minneapolis: University of Minnesota Press.

Hathaway, S. R., & McKinley, J. C. (1940). A multiphasic personality schedule (Minnesota): I. Construction of the schedule. *Journal of Psychology, 10,* 249–254.

Perkins, S. R., & Goldberg, L. R. (1964). Contextual effects of the MMPI. *Journal of Consulting Psychology, 28,* 133–140.

Wiggins, J. S. (1966). Substantive dimensions of self-report in the MMPI item pool. *Psychological Monographs: General and Applied, 80,* (22, whole no. 630).

Appendix

MMPI Religious Identification Scale

MMPI Item Number	Keyed Response	Item
95	True	I go to church almost every week.
98	True	I believe in the second coming of Christ.

115	True	I believe in a life hereafter.
232	True	I have been inspired to a program of life based on duty which I have since carefully followed.
249	True	I believe there is a Devil and a Hell in afterlife.
258	True	I believe there is a God.
369	False	Religion gives me no worry.
373	True	I feel sure that there is only one true religion.
483	True	Christ performed miracles such as changing water into wine.
488	True	I pray several times every week.
490	True	I read the Bible several times a week.
491	False	I have no patience with people who believe there is only one true religion.

Source: Minnesota Multiphasic Personality Inventory (MMPI). Copyright © 1942, 1943 (renewed 1970) by the University of Minnesota. Reproduced by permission of the University of Minnesota Press.

1.15
RELIGIOUS WORLD VIEW SCALE (McLean, 1952; Jennings, 1972)
Reviewed by Michael J. Boivin

Variable: The Religious World View Scale assesses the extent to which one agrees with a number of orthodox tenets of the Christian faith. The respondent is asked to respond to various statements pertaining to central aspects of Christianity, including the divinity of Christ, the existence of hell, the occurrence of miracles, the validity of the Bible, and the means of salvation.

Description: This scale was developed to stimulate interest in religious thought and to help students understand and clarify their religious worldview. Twenty-five scale items are presented according to a Likert scale ranging from 5 to 1 (strongly agree to strongly disagree) format. Some of the items are reverse scored. All of the items contribute to a single total score for the instrument.

Practical Considerations: The instrument consists of 25 items presented in a clear manner that can be completed quickly. The instrument evaluates the extent to which one agrees with the orthodox tenets of the Christian faith. It assumes some nominal reli-

gious background or knowledge in that respect. The reverse-scored items are denoted in the Jennings (1972) study, and the responses to all of the items are simply totaled for a final score.

Norms/Standardization: Jennings (1972) studied 364 students in a metropolitan junior college in Dallas, Texas. The sample age range was between 20 and 24 years, 61% male and 48% married. The study subjects were broadly representative of the various types of students attending the school. Jennings's Likert Scale means and standard deviations across all of the items in the scale for males under ($n = 129$) and over ($n = 91$) 25 years of age were 79.7 ($SD = 20.1$) and 86.9 ($SD = 21.2$) respectively. The Likert Scale means and standard deviations for females under ($n = 101$) and over ($n = 37$) 25 years of age were 89.3 ($SD = 19.3$) and 84.1 ($SD = 22.5$) respectively.

Reliability: None given.

Validity: Construct validity is supported by Jennings (1972), who found that females scored significantly higher than males, consistent with findings in religiosity that females tend to be more religious than males. Jennings's (1972) study also found that older males scored significantly higher on the instrument than younger males. Of the various instruments that Jennings used in his study, the strongest pairwise correlation ($r = 0.91$) was for the Religious World View Scale and another measure of orthodoxy of belief, the Scriptural Literalism Scale (Hogge & Friedman, 1967).

Location:

Jennings, F. L. (1972). A note on the reliability of several belief scales. *Journal for the Scientific Study of Religion, 11*, 157–164.

Subsequent Research: None located.

References

Hogge, J., & Friedman, S. T. (1967). The Scriptural Literalism Scale: A preliminary report. *Journal of Psychology, 66*, 275–279.

McLean, M. (1952). Religious world views. *Motive, 12*, 22–26.

Appendix

What Do You Believe?

For each of the following statements, *circle* the choice that best indicates the extent of your agreement or disagreement as it describes your personal experiences:

1 - strongly disagree	4 - agree
2 - moderately disagree	5 - moderately agree
3 - disagree	6 - strongly agree

*1. The work of the church could be just as effectively done by schools and social agencies.   1   2   3   4   5   6

2. I believe in God the Father Almighty, maker of heaven and earth.   1   2   3   4   5   6

*3. I believe that men working and thinking together can build a just society without supernatural help.   1   2   3   4   5   6

*4. The writings of Plato, Aristotle, Dante, and Shakespeare are as much inspired as are the writings of Moses and Paul.   1   2   3   4   5   6

5. All miracles in the Bible are true.   1   2   3   4   5   6

*6. In general, I consider church (or synagogue) attendance a waste of time.   1   2   3   4   5   6

*7. Belief that in the end God's purposes will be achieved tends to destroy man's sense of social responsibility.   1   2   3   4   5   6

8. God is the great companion who shares with us the travail and tragedy of the world.   1   2   3   4   5   6

9. Jesus was born of the Virgin in a manner different from human beings.   1   2   3   4   5   6

10. The revelation of God's word in the Holy Scriptures is man's ultimate authority.   1   2   3   4   5   6

*11. The attempt to believe in a supernatural   1   2   3   4   5   6
being is a sign of a person's failure to accept
responsibility for his own life.

12. I believe in the guidance of the Holy Spirit.   1   2   3   4   5   6

13. The chief end of man is to glorify God and   1   2   3   4   5   6
enjoy Him forever.

14. I believe Hell is a form of existence in a future life.   1   2   3   4   5   6

*15. The four gospels, Matthew, Mark, Luke, and   1   2   3   4   5   6
John, contain some legendary materials.

*16. We live in a universe indifferent to human values   1   2   3   4   5   6

17. We were made for fellowship with God and   1   2   3   4   5   6
our hearts are restless until they rest in Him.

18. Man is saved by the free gift of God's grace.   1   2   3   4   5   6

19. The biblical writers were endowed with a   1   2   3   4   5   6
divine wisdom which enabled them to fore-
tell specific events in the distant future.

*20. The fall of man in the story of the Garden of   1   2   3   4   5   6
Eden is a myth symbolizing the problem of
good and evil in the world.

21. Man is ultimately responsible to God.   1   2   3   4   5   6

*22. God is only a symbol of man's ideal.   1   2   3   4   5   6

23. Jesus walked on water and raised the dead.   1   2   3   4   5   6

*24. The biblical story of creation is probably   1   2   3   4   5   6
based on one of the early Babylonian myths.

*25. If I believed that any part of the Bible were   1   2   3   4   5   6
unreliable I would no longer have confidence
in its moral and spiritual teachings.

(* indicates reversed-scored item)

Jennings, F. L. (1972). A note on the reliability of several belief scales. *Journal for the Scientific Study of Religion, 11,* 157–164. Copyright © 1972 Journal for the Scientific Study of Religion. Reprinted with permission.

1.16
SALVATION OPINIONNAIRE (Wendland, 1949)
Reviewed by James Casebolt

Variable: The Salvation Opinionnaire (SO) is intended to be "a brief measure of religious conservatism, liberalism, and radicalism in the Christian tradition" (Dreger & Adkins, 1991, p. 179). The authors' original intent was to place subjects appropriately along a continuum from conservative to radical.

Description: The SO consists of 25 items, each of which represents an opinion about the nature and purpose of salvation. It is to be completed in a forced-choice agree-or-disagree format. Dreger and Adkins (1991), the only published source containing the complete list of scale items, gives a scoring procedure based on the Thurstone method (Thurstone & Chave, 1929). This method involves summing item weights for endorsed items to get a raw score, then converting this raw score into a percentile score. Although the scale was originally attributed to Wendland (1949), all known research using the scale to date has been done by Dreger (1952; Dreger, 1991; Dreger & Adkins, 1991).

Practical Considerations: The Thurstone scoring method described by Dreger and Adkins (1991) is more complex and involved than the summed scoring method frequently used with Likert scales. However, the process of deriving raw scores from the item weights could be easily automated using any statistical computer package allowing for variables to be created from equations. Automating the process of deriving percentile scores would be much more complex, but it may be more efficient than determining percentiles by hand if a sufficiently large number of subjects is involved.

Norms/Standardization: The initial standardization of the SO is most clearly described in Dreger and Adkins (1991). Starting with a pool of hundreds of potential items, the 145 that seemed most probable were selected. Using methods suggested by Thurstone, these were reduced to 45 items on the basis of expert judges' responses. These items were given to 763 respondents and were reduced to 25 items using Thurstone's method of equal-appearing intervals. A scoring procedure for this 25-item scale was based on the responses of another group of 351 subjects. These results yielded a trimodal distribution, interpreted by Dreger (1952) as corresponding to religious conservatism, liberalism, and radicalism.

The purpose of the Dreger and Adkins (1991) article was to restandardize the scale, using a similar procedure. The initial judges were 48 church professionals and seminarians and another religiously heterogenous sample of 48 laymen. These judges rated each item on a 1 (conservative) to 7 (liberal) scale; these were used to derive scale values for each item. Seven hundred seventy-eight

subjects then completed the SO in the forced-choice format; 485 of these subjects were high school, undergraduate, and graduate students from one southern city, and the remainder were members of churches and church school classes in two southern cities. The overall sample had an average age of 41.1 years, with approximately equal numbers of men and women.

Dreger (1991) examined the latent structure of the SO using the responses from these 778 subjects. Using a combination of exploratory and confirmatory factor analysis on all subjects' responses or those for odd-even halves, he interpreted his results as showing a four-factor structure: Conservative, Liberal: Integration and Growth, Liberal: Freeing Oneself from Insincerity and Conflict, and Radical. However, Dreger does not give a procedure for, or even mention the possibility of, scoring the SO for each of these dimensions.

Reliability: None of the published uses of the SO give any reliability statistics. It is unclear how reliable the scale could be using the unidimensional scoring procedure recommended by Dreger and Adkins (1991), given the multidimensional nature of the scale discovered by Dreger (1991).

Validity: Dreger (1952) did extensive intelligence and personality testing with 60 selected subjects from his sample. These subjects were categorized as liberal or conservative according to denominational membership. Dreger found a significant difference between the conservatives (M = 7.84) and liberals (M = 4.00) on their SO scores (t = 27.33, p < .01). He also found that SO scores were correlated with scores on the Ferguson (1941) Primary Social Attitudes Scale No. 1: Religionism (r (28) = .77, p < .01).

As a part of the SO, subjects are asked to rate themselves on the dimesion of religious liberalism and religious conservatism. Dreger and Adkins (1991) reported that these ratings were virtually uncorrelated (r = .04, p < .22) with SO scores and that similar results were found in the initial standardization (Dreger, 1952). They also reported that when subjects were categorized by denomination ordered by how conservative or liberal the denomination is, these categorizations correlated .26 ($p < .0001$) with SO scores.

Location:

Wendland, L. V. (1949). *The Salvation Opinionnaire.* Unpublished manuscript, Graduate School of Religion, University of Southern California.

Subsequent Research:

Dreger, R. M. (1952). Some personality correlates of religious attitudes, as determined by projective techniques. *Psychological Monographs: General and Applied, 66* (3) (Whole No. 335).

Dreger, R. M. (1991). The latent structure of the Salvation Opinionnaire, a measure of religious attitudes in the American Christian tradition. *Educa-* *tional and Psychological Measurement, 51,* 707–719.

Dreger, R. M., & Adkins, S. A. (1991). A restandardization of a brief scale of religious orthodoxy, religious humanism, and religious radicalism. *International Journal for the Psychology of Religion, 1*(3), 173–181.

References

Ferguson, L. W. (1941). The stability of the primary social attitudes: I. Religionism and II. Humanitarianism. *Journal of Psychology, 12,* 283–288.

Thurstone, L. L., & Chave, E. J. (1929). *The measurement of attitudes.* Chicago: University of Chicago Press.

Appendix

Salvation Opinionnaire

Check (with an *X*) those statements below that describe your understanding and attitude toward "salvation." Leave all other statements blank.

1. Salvation "is a very ambiguous term used by orthodox groups indicating when a person is saved." (IV)
2. Salvation means "saving myself from myself, eliminating the conflict in my personality." (III)
3. Salvation "is a great joy and peace that comes with the knowledge of sins forgiven." (I)
4. Salvation "makes me think of a Southern Revival meeting and uncontrolled emotions." (IV)
5. Salvation is "being saved from sin by the blood of Christ on the cross." (I)
6. Salvation is "a state of spiritual integration." (II)
7. Salvation is "accepting Christ as Savior and putting one's entire trust and faith in Him as a living Savior." (I)
8. Salvation means "to save yourself from yourself." (III)
9. Salvation "is integration of my life around constantly progressive meanings and values." (II)
10. Salvation is "a promise that the church makes to people to keep them under its thumb." (IV)
11. Salvation is "the knowledge of sins forgiven." (I)
12. Salvation is "accepting Christ as Savior." (I)
13. Salvation "means being saved from the guilt and power of sin through faith in Christ." (I)
14. Salvation is "to be saved from eternal condemnation unto eternal life and an eternal home in heaven with God." (I)
15. Salvation is "character development." (II)
16. Salvation is "eternal life hereafter, and peace, joy, and a greater work to do now." (I)
17. Salvation is "a social and psychological orientation toward the realization of worthfulness." (II)

18. Salvation is "being born again, thus letting the Holy Spirit guide my life now and for-ever." (I)
19. Salvation is "living an objective life; that is, being objective about my subjectivity." (II)
20. Salvation is "deliverance from the penalty of sin, the power of sin, and eventually the presence of sin." (I)
21. Salvation is to be "relieved from feelings of insincerity, self-pity, inadequacy." (III)
22. Salvation is "growth toward ultimate reality." (II)
23. Salvation is "a mighty work of grace given to every man and partaken of by a few." (I)
24. Salvation is "the freedom from neurotic conflict and harmonious living." (IV)
25. Salvation "is release from sin and finding peace of mind through living close to God." (I)

I consider myself a: (Mark an X anywhere along the line.)

Religious Liberal   Religious Conservative

Numbers in parentheses after each item represent the factor identified by Dreger (1991) on which that item loads:

I—Conservative
II—Liberal: Integration and Growth
III—Liberal: Freeing Oneself from Insincerity and Conflict
IV—Radical

Dreger, R. M., & Adkins, S. A. (1991). A restandardization of a brief scale of religious orthodoxy, religious humanism, and religious radicalism. *International Journal for the Psychology of Religion, 1(3),* 173–181. Copyright © 1991, Lawrence Erlbaum Associates. Reprinted with permission.

1.17
SCRIPTURAL LITERALISM SCALE (Hogge & Friedman, 1967)
Reviewed by Michael J. Boivin

Variable: The Scriptural Literalism Scale assesses the degree to which an individual believes in a literal, God-inspired interpretation of the Bible—as opposed to viewing the Bible as ordinary literature not necessarily inspired directly by a personal deity. This scale is unidimensional and evaluates the degree of scriptural literalism along a continuum.

Description: Hogge and Friedman (1967) constructed an initial pool of 30 statements concerning the interpretation of Scripture, which they administered to a sample of 43 undergraduate students. The 16 items having the highest correlation with the sum of the other items in the pool were selected for the final version of the instrument, which was administered as part of a comprehensive sur-vey of student samples at several major universities in Texas. Subjects respond to the individual items according to a 5-point Likert Scale format: +1 = slightly agree, +2 = agree, +3 = strongly agree, −1 = slightly disagree, −2 = disagree, −3 = strongly disagree.

The 16 items having the highest correlation with the sum of the other items in the pool were selected for a shorter version of the scale (SLSc). In addition, two 12-item parallel forms of the scale (SLSa and SLSb) were constructed. These items included such statements as "the scriptures contain religious truths," "quotations appearing in the Scriptures are accurate," "the Scriptures are a collection of myths," and "the passage of time is accurately presented in the Scriptures."

The three forms of the SLS were included as part of a longer form (the "attitude survey") and were readministered to university students to develop norms for this instrument.

Practical Considerations: The instrument is worded in a straightforward manner that enables it to be easily administered and scored. Furthermore, it is a brief instrument than can be easily incorporated into a more comprehensive religious assessment battery, as was done in the Jennings (1972) study. It should be noted that some of the items are reverse scored.

Norms/Standardization: Hogge and Friedman (1967) administered this instrument as part of a longer form to 309 University of Texas students, 375 University of Houston students, and 146 students from Southwestern University at Georgetown, Texas. The overall mean for the SLSa scale was 3.83 (*SD* = 16.63). The overall mean for the SLSb scale was –0.61 (*SD* = 15.56). The overall mean for the SLSc version was 4.86 (*SD* = 22.53). Single-classification analysis of variance (with corresponding group means) was used to compare the scores of Unitarians and Baptists, Unitarians and Methodists, freshmen and seniors, and males and females. Hogge and Friedman (1967) report means and standard deviations for these groups as well.

Jennings (1972) used the Scriptural Literalism Scale along with several other religious and personality inventories with a sample of 364 students in a metropolitan junior college in Dallas, Texas. Using a different scoring method from Hogge and Friedman, Jennings' Likert Scale means and standard deviations across all of the 16 items in the scale for males under (*n* = 129) and over (*n* = 91) 25 years of age were 50.1 (SD = 16.0) and 55.3 (SD = 16.6) respectively. The Likert Scale means and standard deviations for females under (*n* = 101) and over (*n* = 37) 25 years of age were 55.7 (*SD* = 14.9) and 53.2 (*SD* = 17.9) respectively.

Reliability: Split-half reliability coefficients are available in both the Hogge and Friedman (1967) and Jennings (1972) studies, with all above 0.90. Jennings also computed a Spearman-Brown coefficient value for reliability (*r* = 0.95) derived from the split-half coefficient. Taken together, these values indicate a high degree on interitem consistency in measurement.

Validity: Scores compared on the Scriptural Literalism Scale for religious groups substantially differ on the extent to which they take a more literal interpretation approach to the Scriptures. In the Hogge and Friedman study, both Baptist and Methodist students scored significantly higher on the scale than Unitarians. Freshmen tended to take a significantly more literal approach than seniors, and females were significantly more literal than males. All of these between-group differences are consistent with previous findings pertaining to descriptive traits that are related to more conservative versus less conservative views of scripture, and support the validity of this measure.

In Jennings (1972) findings, the Scriptural Literalism Scale was strongly correlated with McLean's (1952) Religious World View Scale (*r* = 0.91), moderately correlated with the Cognitive Salience portion of King and Hunt's (1975) Religious Position Scale (*r*= 0.63), and somewhat moderately correlated with the Religious Position Scale's Extrinsic Religious Orientation portion (*r* = 0.35).

Location:
Hogge, J. H., & Friedman, S. T. (1967). The scriptural literalism scale: A preliminary report. *The Journal of Psychology*, 66, 275–279.
Jennings, F. L. (1972). A note on the reliability of several brief scales. *Journal for the Scientific Study of Religion*, 11, 157–164.

Subsequent Research:
Annis, L. V. (1976). Emergency helping and religious behavior. *Psychological Reports*, 39, 151–158.

References
King, M. B., & Hunt, R. A. (1975). Measuring the religious variable: National replication. *Journal for the Scientific Study of Religion*, 14, 13–22.
McLean, M. (1952). Religious world views. *Motives*, 12, 22–26.

Appendix

The Scriptural Literalism Scale

For each of the following statements, *circle* the choice that best indicates the extent of your agreement or disagreement as it describes your personal experiences:

    1 = strongly disagree   4 = agree
    2 = moderately disagree   5 = moderately agree
    3 = disagree   6 = strongly agree

1. Life originated differently than is suggested by the Scriptures. (R)	1	2	3	4	5	6
2. The precise words spoken by God may be found in the Scriptures.	1	2	3	4	5	6
3. The Scriptures contain God's rules for living.	1	2	3	4	5	6
4. The Scriptures are a product of man's imagination. (R)	1	2	3	4	5	6
5. The Scriptures should be taken as divinely-inspired writings.	1	2	3	4	5	6
6. The Scriptures contain religious truths.	1	2	3	4	5	6
7. The Scriptures should be regarded more as beautiful writing than as religious truths. (R)	1	2	3	4	5	6
8. The scriptural account of creation is accurate.	1	2	3	4	5	6
9. Quotations appearing in the Scripture are accurate.	1	2	3	4	5	6
10. We can put our trust in the teachings of the Scriptures.	1	2	3	4	5	6
11. Most of the writing in the Scriptures should be taken literally.	1	2	3	4	5	6
12. The miracles reported in the Scriptures actually occurred.	1	2	3	4	5	6
13. The Scriptures are the ultimate truth.	1	2	3	4	5	6
14. The Scriptures accurately predict future events.	1	2	3	4	5	6
15. The Scriptures are a collection of myths. (R)	1	2	3	4	5	6
16. There are more accurate accounts of history than the Scriptures. (R)	1	2	3	4	5	6

(R) Means the item is reversed-scored.

Jennings, F. L. (1872). A note on the reliability of several belief scales. *Journal for the Scientific Study of Religion, 11,* 157–164. Copyright © 1972 Journal for the Scientific Study of Religioun. Reprinted with permission.

1.18
THE SHEPHERD SCALE (Bassett et al., 1981)
Reviewed by Peter C. Hill

Variable: The Shepherd Scale is designed to assess Christian identity. A unique characteristic of this instrument is that it is based on an explicit biblical operationalization of the Christian faith. The subtitle of the article where the scale is found (Bassett, Sadler, Kobischen, Skiff, Merrill, Atwater, & Livermore, 1981) is "Separating the Sheep from the Goats." Sheep and goats refer to New Testament (Matt. 25:32) terms used by Jesus to distinguish Christians from non-Christians. The authors acknowledge that developing such an instrument is fraught with theological danger and may give the appearance of spiritual arrogance. But the authors also believe that "there is, to some degree, an observable and measurable life pattern which is distinctively Christian" (p. 342). The authors' attempt to measure such a distinctive pattern is thus called the Shepherd Scale.

Description: The scale consists of 38 items presented in a 4-point ("true" to "not true") Likert-type format. The items are conceptually divided into two subscales: a 13-item belief subscale and a 25-item Christian walk subscale. The belief subscale measures beliefs about God in general and about Jesus Christ in particular. The Christian walk subscale measures behaviors, values, and attitudes consistent with a Christian lifestyle.

The items were based on the authors' reading of New Testament passages that describe the qualifications, characteristics, and /or behaviors of a Christian. These passages were grouped according to common themes, and an item was written for each group. The relevant scriptural passages are presented next to each item in the Bassett et al. (1981) article but are not included in this volume and, of course, should not be included in scale adminstration. An effort was made to write the items in a nonsectarian fashion.

This scale is one of the most frequently cited scales from 1985 to 1994 in the *Journal of Psychology and Theology* and the *Journal of Psychology and Christianity*

(Jones, Ripley, Kurusu, & Worthington, 1998), two journals that are explicit in their purpose of integrating psychology with claims of the Christian faith.

Practical Considerations: Administering and scoring of the Shepherd Scale are straightforward. Each item is scored between one ("not true") and four ("true"), and the overall score is computed by simply summing the scores across all items. Thus scores can range from 38 to 152. No specific cutoff is suggested for separating Christians from non-Christians.

Norms/Standardization: Four studies have reported normative data on the Shepherd Scale:

source	Sample	Sample Size	Mean	Range	SD
Bassett et al. (1981)	Christian college students	62	136	111–152	8.7
Bassett et al. (1981)	Adult suburbanites	67	—	63–152	—
Pecnik & Epperson (1985)	State univ. students	238	110	52–149	18.6
Godwin (1986)	State univ. students	204	116	61–149	19.4

Reliability: Bassett et al. (1981) report a test-retest (at a two-week interval) reliability coefficient in their Christian college sample of .82 and found a split-half reliability coefficient of .83 with the same sample. Cronbach's alpha with this sample was .86. A modified Shepherd Scale (using 29 of the 38 items) by Boivin, Darling, and Darling (1987) had a KR-20 reliability coefficient of .73.

Validity: Bassett et al. (1981) reported that among their Christian college sample, the Shepherd Scale correlates .41 with Glock and Stark's (1966) Dimensions of Religious Commitment Scale and .64 with King and

Hunt's (1975) Ten Dimension Religious Variable instrument. In a second sample with suburban adults, Bassett et al. found that self-identified Christians scored significantly higher on the Shepherd Scale than did self-identified non-Christians, t (28) = 6.29, p <.001.

Pecnik and Epperson (1985) found that among state university students, the Shepherd Scale correlated .71 with self-reported importance of religious beliefs, .52 with denominational preference (coded as Christian or non-Christian; the positive correlation showing that Christians score higher than non-Christians) , and .43 with self-reported frequency of participation in religious activities.

Location:

Bassett, R. L., Sadler, R. D., Kobischen, E. E., Skiff, D. M., Merrill, I. J., Atwater, B. J., & Livermore, P. W. (1981). The Shepherd Scale: Separating the sheep from the goats. *Journal of Psychology and Theology, 9*(4), 335–351.

Subsequent Research:

Bassett, R. L., Camplin, W., Humphrey, D., Dorr, C., Biggs, S., Distaffen, R., Doxtator, I., Flaherty, M., Hunsberger, P. J., Poage, R., & Thompson, H. (1991). Measuring Christian maturity: A comparison of several scales. *Journal of Psychology and Theology, 19,* 84–95.

Boivin, M. J., Donkin, A. J., & Darling, H. W. (1990). Religiosity and prejudice: A case study in evaluating the construct validity of Christian measures. *Journal of Psychology and Christianity, 9*(2), 41–55.

Elzerman, J. H., & Boivin, M. J. (1987). The assessment of Christian maturity, personality, and psychopathology among college students. *Journal of Psychology and Christianity, 6*(3), 50–64.

Lupfer, M. B., Tolliver, D., & Jackson, M. (1996). Explaining life altering occurences: A test of the 'God of the gaps' hypothesis. *Journal for the Scientific Study of Religion, 35*(4), 379–391.

Mangis, M. W. (1995). Religious beliefs, dogmatism, and attitudes toward women. *Journal of Psychology and Christianity, 14*(1), 13–25.

References

Boivin, M. J., Darling, H. W., & Darling, T. W. (1987). Racial prejudice among Christian and non-Christian college students. *Journal of Psychology and Theology, 15*(1), 47–56.

Glock, C. & Stark, R. (1966). *Christian beliefs and anti-Semitism.* New York: Harper & Row.

Godwin, T. C. (1986). *Analogue study of expectations for Christian and traditional counseling: A partial replication and extension.* Unpublished master's thesis, Appalachian State University, Boone, NC.

Jones, D. R., Ripley, J. S., Kurusu, T. A., & Worthington, E. L. (1998). Influential sources in the integration of psychology and theology: A decade summary. *Journal of Psychology and Christianity, 17,* 43– 54.

King, M. B., & Hunt, R. A. (1975). Measuring the religious variable: National replication. *Journal for the Scientific Study of Religion, 11,* 53–64.

Pecnik, J. A., & Epperson, D. L. (1985). A factor analysis and further validation of the Shepherd Scale. *Journal of Psychology and Theology, 13*(1), 42–49.

Appendix

The Shepherd Scale

Instructions: These questions consider different aspects of Christian experience. Note that some of the items consider how you think about or act toward Christians. These items should not be thought of as exclusive. In other words, having respect for Christians does not mean that you lack respect for non-Christians.

Please respond to all of the following items using the responses listed below.

1 = not true   2 = generally not true   3 = generally true   4 = true

Belief Component

____   1. I believe that God will bring about certain circumstances that will result in the judgment and destruction of evil.

___ 2. I believe I can have the personal presence of God in my life.

___ 3. I believe that there are certain required duties to maintaining a strong Christian lifestyle (i.e., prayer, doing good deeds, and helping others).

___ 4. I believe that it is possible to have a personal relationship with God through Christ.

___ 5. I believe that by following the teachings of Jesus Christ and incorporating them into my daily life, I receive such things as peace, confidence, and hope.

___ 6. I believe that God raised Jesus from the dead.

___ 7. I believe that God will judge me for all my actions and behaviors.

___ 8. I believe that by submitting myself to Christ, He frees me to obey him in a way I never could before.

___ 9. I believe in miracles as a result of my confidence in God to perform such things.

___ 10. Because of God's favor to us, through Jesus Christ, we are no longer condemned by God's laws.

___ 11. Because of my personal commitment to Jesus Christ, I have eternal life.

___ 12. The only means by which I may know God is through my personal commitment to Jesus Christ.

___ 13. I believe that everyone's life has been twisted by sin and that the only adequate remedy to this problem is Jesus Christ.

The Christian Walk Component

___ 14. I am concerned that my behavior and speech reflect the teachings of Christ.

___ 15. I respond positively (with patience, kindness, self-control) to those people who hold negative feelings toward me.

___ 16. I do kind things regardless of who's watching me.

___ 17. Status and material possessions are not of primary importance to me.

___ 18. I do not accept what I hear in regard to religious beliefs without first questioning the validity of it.

___ 19. I strive to have good relationships with people even though their beliefs and values may be different than mine.

___ 20. It is important to me to conform to the Christian standards of behavior.

___ 21. I am most influenced by people whose beliefs and values are consistent with the teachings of Christ.

___ 22. I respect and obey the rules and regulations of the civil authorities which govern me.

___ 23. I show respect toward Christians.

___ 24. I share things that I own with Christians.

___ 25. I share the same feelings Christians do whether it be happiness or sorrow.

___ 26. I'm concerned about how my behavior affects Christians.

___ 27. I speak the truth with love to Christians.

___ 28. I work for Christians without expecting recognition or acknowledgments.

___ 29. I am concerned about unity among Christians.

___ 30. I enjoy spending time with Christians.

___ 31. My beliefs, trust, and loyalty to God can be seen by other people through my actions and behavior.

___ 32. I can see daily growth in the areas of knowledge of Jesus Christ, self-control, patience, and virtue.

___ 33. Because of my love for God, I obey his commandments.

___ 34. I attribute my accomplishments to God's presence in my life.

___ 35. I realize a need to admit my wrongs to God.

___ 36. I have told others that I serve Jesus Christ.

___ 37. I have turned from my sin and believed in Jesus Christ.

___ 38. I daily use and apply what I have learned by following Jesus Christ.

1.19
STRUCTURE OF PRAYER SCALE
(Luckow, Ladd, Spilka, McIntosh, Parks, & Laforett, unpublished)
Reviewed by James P. David

Variable: The Structure of Prayer Scales measure prayer behavior. The scales were designed to assess several broad, conceptually distinct categories of prayer such as petition and confession.

Description: The measure has 28 items that assess six prayer types: confession, petition, ritual, meditation-improvement, habitual, and compassionate petition. Initially, individual items were generated with the explicit intention of covering a variety of prayer types and habits. Factor analytic procedures were then employed, resulting in the following scales:

Confession (5 items) 3, 4, 7, 14, & 17
Petition (3 items) 13, 15, & 22
Ritual (3 items) 1, 9, & 20
Meditation-improvement (5 items) 2, 16, 23, 26, & 27
Habit (4 items) 10, 12, 25, & 28
Compassionate petition (8 items) 5, 6, 8, 11, 18, 19, 21, & 24

Practical Considerations: This pencil-and-paper measure requires 5 to 10 minutes to complete. Instructions are required but can be altered for specific purposes. For example, researchers may want to assess general prayer practices or prayer behavior within a specific context (e.g., in response to a stressful event).

Norms/Standardization: The authors obtained data from a general university in Colorado (S1, N = 145), a Christian college in Colorado (S2, N = 101), a general university in Indiana (S3 and S4, Ns = 159 and 307, respectively), a conservative evangelical seminary in Colorado (S5, N = 108), and a group of cancer patients (S6, N = 166). The majority of the participants in these samples were Christian (N = 745, 80%). The authors report that the samples represent a broad range of religious perspectives from liberal to conservative. Descriptive statistics for demographic variables and prayer scales are not presented.

Reliability: A principal components analysis was conducted on the data from each of the six samples. In addition, data from the three samples (S1, S2, and S3) where a common response coding system was used were combined for a separate analysis. This allowed for greater response variability and a greater ratio of respondents to items. Multiple solutions employing both orthogonal and nonorthogonal rotations were considered. In choosing a solution, the authors considered eigenvalues (i.e., equal to or greater than one) as well as meaningfulness/conceptual integrity of the factors. A factor loading of .30 was adopted as the item selection criterion. Items that demonstrated the highest factor loadings across the samples were selected for the final scales. The following are Cronbach's alpha reliability coefficients for the scales:

Scale	S1	S2	S3	S4	S5	S6	S1/S2/S3
Confession	.89	.58	.86	.84	.77	.84	.88
Petition	.81	.44	.65	.68	.65	.65	.76
Ritual	.80	.73	.72	.72	.75	.68	.62
Meditate/ imp.	.86	.68	.85	.79	.19	.79	.84
Habitual	.88	.80	.82	.88	.67	.70	.89
Comp. petition	.95	.82	.87	.89	.81	.87	.93

In most cases, the scales demonstrate adequate reliability; however, the coefficients for confession and petition based on the S2 (the Christian college) data and the coefficient for meditation-improvement based on the S5 (seminary) data are particularly low. This may reflect restricted variation within these samples of highly religious individuals.

Validity: In general, the scales have face validity. Intercorrelations of the scales are not presented; however, in previous studies that used many of the same items and yielded a similar factor structure, the intercorrelations suggested that people who pray tend to use a variety of prayer strategies. Another issue concerns the meditation-improvement scale. Several items on this scale (e.g., "when I pray I feel secure") appear to reflect an affective outcome of prayer as much as prayer habits/behavior. Researchers investigating the relations among prayer and positive/negative affect, subjective well-being, and other similar constructs should be aware of this. Finally, with respect to establishing validity, future research may focus on the relations among the present scales and other measures of religious thought and behavior.

Location:
    Luckow, A., Ladd, K. L., Spilka, B., McIntosh, D. N., Parks, C., & LaForett, D. (1997). *The structure of prayer*. Unpublished manuscript, University of Denver, Denver, CO.

Recent Research:
    Beck, J. R., Spilka, B., & Mason, R. (1992, August). *Prayer in religious and social perspective: A study of a seminary sample*. Paper presented at the meeting of the American Psychological Association, Washington, D. C.
    Luckow, A., Ladd, K. L., Spilka, B., McIntosh, D. N., Paloma, M., Parks, C., & LaForett, D. (1996, August). *The structure of prayer: Explorations and confirmations*. Paper presented at the meeting of the American Psychological Association, Toronto, Canada.

Appendix

Instrument

Prayer or meditation is approached in a wide variety of fashions. For the purposes of this study, please think of "pray" and "meditate" as the same sort of practice. We would like you to indicate for each of the following statements the position that most accurately reflects your personal practices. Please use this code for your answers:

    1 = strongly disagree   4 = slightly agree
    2 = moderately disagree   5 = moderately agree
    3 = slightly disagree   6 = strongly agree

___ 1. When I pray alone, I have a ritual that I adhere to strictly.
___ 2. Through deep prayer I am able to know God better.
___ 3. It is important to me to tell God about my sins or faults.
___ 4. When I pray, I want to share my life with God.
___ 5. I usually pray for God to make me a better person.
___ 6. I pray to give thanks for all God has done for me.
___ 7. When I feel guilty about something, it helps to tell God about it.
___ 8. When God has answered my prayers, I usually give thanks.
___ 9. My prayers are like rituals; they have a regular, orderly sequence.
___ 10. I usually say a prayer before each meal.
___ 11. I like to say prayers for people about whom I care very much.
___ 12. I always pray before I go to sleep.
___ 13. I must admit that I usually pray to get something.
___ 14. Confession is important to me because it helps me lead a more respectable life.
___ 15. When I pray, I ask God for special favors.
___ 16. Prayer helps me keep my life balanced and happy.
___ 17. When I pray, I confess to God the things I should not have done.
___ 18. Usually when I feel unable to help my loved ones, I ask God for help.
___ 19. I ask God to help others when I am unable to.
___ 20. When I pray, I have certain words of phrases that I repeat a number of times.
___ 21. In my prayers I like to express my recognition for what God grants me.
___ 22. Most of my prayers are for God to solve problems.
___ 23. When I finish praying, I feel like a better person.
___ 24. I pray for other people.
___ 25. A morning prayer helps me cope with the world during the day.
___ 26. Prayer is a way for me to connect with my inner spirit.
___ 27. When I pray, I feel secure.
___ 28. I pray daily.

Reprinted with permission from the authors.

1.20
STUDENT RELIGIOSITY QUESTIONNAIRE (Katz, 1988)

Reviewed by Duane Kauffmann

Variable: The Student Religiosity Questionnaire (SRQ) was designed to measure general religiosity in student samples. The scale items are focused on beliefs and practices associated with the Jewish religious tradition. Factor analysis of the scale items identified two dimensions labeled by the author as (1) religious principles and (2) religious practices.

Description: The original scale consisted of 20 items written by the author. The 20-item scale used in the first studies was modified to 18 items in later work. Responses to each

question are made using a 5-point continuum, with 1 indicating minimal agreement and 5 showing maximal agreement.

Practical Considerations: The scale as written is useful only for research with samples from the Jewish religious tradition. It is easy to administer, requiring only instructions concerning the meaning of the continuum responses. Scale scores for the two factors are obtained by adding appropriate item scores.

Norms/Standardization: The initial data set was derived from a sample of 110 white

South African teacher trainees. Factor analysis of this data generated two-factors: Religious Principles and Religious Practices. Following translation into Hebrew, data was gathered from a sample of 531 Israeli 11th-grade students attending national-religious comprehensive schools. Factor analysis responses from these students generated the same two-factor solution. A sample of 221 Israeli 11th-grade students from a diverse selection of schools supported the two-factor scale. Ten of the 20 items loaded significantly on the Religious Principles factor and 7 items loaded significantly on the Religious Practices factor.

Reliability: For the South African sample of 110 respondents, an alpha reliability of .89 was reported. For the Israeli student sample of 221, the alpha coefficient was .91. The coefficients were .90 and .83, respectively, for the factors labeled Religious Principles and Religious Practices. A sample of 190 teacher trainees from Bar-Ilan University yielded a Cronbach's alpha of .96 (for the 18-item scale version used in this later study).

Validity: A panel of ten theologians judged each item. An item was included on the scale if at least 7 of the 10 judges indicated that the item had face validity for assessing general religiosity.

Location:
Katz, Y. (1988). The relationship between intelligence and attitudes in a bilingual society: The case of white South Africa. *The Journal of Social Psychology, 128*, 65–74.

Subsequent Research:
Francis, L. & Katz, Y. (1992). The relationship between personality and religiosity in an Israeli sample. *Journal for the Scientific Study of Religion, 31*, 153–12.
Katz, Y., & Schmida, M. (1992). Validation of the student religiosity questionnaire. *Educational and Psychological Measurement, 52*, 353–356.

Appendix

Student Religiosity Questionnaire

Directions: For the following activities, rate your degree of observance from 1 (minimal observance) to 5 (maximal observance).

1	2	3	4	5	Sabbath observance
1	2	3	4	5	Inter sex socializing
1	2	3	4	5	Dietary laws—observance at home
1	2	3	4	5	Dietary laws—observance out of home
1	2	3	4	5	Observance of days of mourning
1	2	3	4	5	Observance of fast days
1	2	3	4	5	Grace before meals on Sabbath
1	2	3	4	5	Sabbath termination prayers
1	2	3	4	5	Tabernacles festival observance
1	2	3	4	5	Giving of tithes

Directions: For the following religious principles, rate your degree of agreement from 1 (minimal agreement) to 5 (maximal agreement).

1	2	3	4	5	Biblical miracles
1	2	3	4	5	Rabbinical authority
1	2	3	4	5	Reward and punishment
1	2	3	4	5	Individual supervision by God
1	2	3	4	5	Resurrection of the dead

1	2	3	4	5	Creation ex nihilo
1	2	3	4	5	Oral law
1	2	3	4	5	Messianic era
1	2	3	4	5	Divine law
1	2	3	4	5	Prophecy

Reprinted with permission from the author.

1.21
WHAT I BELIEVE SCALE (Gill & Thornton, 1989)
Reviewed by Kevin S. Seybold

Variable: The What I Believe (WIB) Scale was developed to differentiate three religious/philosophical belief systems (i.e., Judeo-Christian, Spiritism/Occult, and Atheism/ Secular Humanism) and to measure the extent to which those belief systems are associated with personality factors (e.g., self-esteem) that influence academic performance.

Description: The scale consists of 50 statements to which the respondent answers true or false. Because the questionnaire attempts, in part, to differentiate among three ideologies, some of the 50 statements are more crucial to a particular ideological category than others (the core or foundational statements). Other statements, called satellite responses, are less crucial (Gill & Thornton, 1988). However, the scale's authors state that it is a subject's combination of core and satellite responses that determine category placement. The scale is scored in such a way that the total score reflects the strength of an individual's Judeo-Christian beliefs. In addition to the Judeo-Christian Total score, the WIB provides values for an Atheism Total and a Spiritism/Occult Total.

Practical Considerations: The WIB scale is designed to be administered in groups but can be administered individually and should take 10 to 15 minutes. Scoring is accomplished by determining the number of "correct" responses (correct defined according to a particular ideological category) and converting that number into a percentage of correct responses for a representative category. For example, in the Judeo-Christian category, all 50 items of the questionnaire are used in calculating a person's score. The correct responses are response B for questions 1–8,10,12–14,16–17,20–27,29–34, 36–43, and 48–50; response A for all other questions. A person responding correctly on 33 items would receive a score of 66 on the Judeo-Christian category (2 x number correct). For the Atheism and Spiritism/Occult categories, half of the questions are scored. For the Atheism category, correct responses are: response A for questions 2, 4, 5, 8, 13, 21, 23, 25, 26, 29, 30, 31, 42, and 48; response B for questions 7, 10, 11, 18, 28, 32, 34, 45, 46, 47, and 50. For the Spiritism/Occult category, correct responses are: response A for questions 1, 3, 5, 7, 11, 12, 14, 16, 20, 24, 27, 28, 30, 32, 34, 36, 38, 40, 41, 43, 45, 49, and 50; response B for questions 26 and 44. A person answering correctly on 17 of the items in each of these categories would receive a score of 68 (4 x number correct).

Norms/Standardization: Subjects included 179 high school students selected on the basis of classroom teacher cooperation and a desire on the part of the experimenters to maintain a homogeneous sample. Two comparison groups were created: (a) 92 senior honor students from two public schools and (b) 87 seniors from a Catholic school. The mean age of the public school students was 17.6 and for the parochial school students was 17.0 years. Both genders were represented in the sample. No formal attempt was made by the authors to assess economic similarities between the two groups.

Reliability: Using 17 subjects over a two-week period, test-retest reliability was used and indicated a reliability coefficient of .79; no other attempt to measure reliability was reported.

Validity: Validity of the instrument was obtained through the responses of subjects identified as strongly representing a particular category. The subjects in each instance made near perfect scores in their belief category and scored low on the other belief categories; the authors interpreted this result as supporting the validity of the scale. Intercorrelations among the various scales indicated an inverse relationship between the Judeo-Christian score and the Atheism/Secular Humanism score as would be expected if the measurement has validity.

Location:

Gill, N.T., & Thornton, L.H. (1989, October/November). Religious orientation and self-esteem among high school students. *The High School Journal*, 73(1), 47–60.

Recent Research:

Thornton, L.H., & Gill, N.T. (1989, November). *Consistency of religious beliefs and self-esteem among high school students.* Paper presented at the meeting of the Florida Educational Research Association, Tallahassee, FL.

Thornton, L. H., & Gill, N. T. (1990, November). *Student interest and religious beliefs.* Paper presented at the meeting of the Florida Educational Research Association.

References

Gill, N.T., & Thornton, L.H. (1988, November). *Religious orientation and self-esteem among college students.* Paper presented at the meeting of the Florida Educational Research Association, Sarasota, FL.

Appendix

What I Believe (WIB) Scale

Directions: This is to be an anonymous survey of some of your basic beliefs. Read each statement carefully and indicate in the space provided whether you feel the statement is *true* (A) or *false* (B). Please do *not* discuss the statements with others until everyone has completed the survey. Please respond to all 50 items.

		True (A)	False (B)
1.	A religious faith passionately believed in can act as a catalyst releasing psychic forces.	____	____
2.	Human nature is really neither good nor bad	____	____
3.	Such things as black magic and voodoo interest me	____	____
4.	I tend to believe only in what I can see or can be explained.	____	____
5.	I see no harm in wearing good luck charms	____	____
6.	I believe any unusual powers exhibited by people can be explained scientifically as resulting from an external energy force, such as the sun. In such cases, people are merely acting as channels or conductors.	____	____
7.	Personally, I'm drawn to the psychic approach when details are so specific as to rule out coincidence.	____	____
8.	Discussing spiritual occurrences and supernatural phenomena is foolish and absurd.	____	____
9.	Generally speaking, people can *not* be trusted	____	____

		True (A)	False (B)
10.	Reality exists *only* in the mind.	_____	_____
11.	The supernatural power which exists externally from us is a being or beings with motivation and intent.	_____	_____
12.	Prayer is a psychic phenomena.	_____	_____
13.	Although some things are still not known or understood, some day all will be known by increasing our own human intelligence.	_____	_____
14.	I find the occult interesting.	_____	_____
15.	Life on this planet has deteriorated and will most probably become worse.	_____	_____
16.	The mind has extrasensory powers.	_____	_____
17.	Supernatural explanations lie totally within the human potential or ability.	_____	_____
18.	There are two supernatural spiritual beings of major significance in the universe: a loving and just creator, and an evil force or spirit.	_____	_____
19.	Man's basic or fundamental nature is selfish.	_____	_____
20.	Prayer is merely a material power, like electricity, available to all persons no matter what they believe.	_____	_____
21.	Life on earth is relatively quite good and will probably get much better.	_____	_____
22.	I believe the only supernatural force in the universe is that of a loving God.	_____	_____
23.	There is a natural order to everything and all phenomena can be explained naturally.	_____	_____
24.	Every human being is a member of the cosmos and "God" is the cosmic mind.	_____	_____
25.	People are basically good.	_____	_____
26.	Voodoo deaths are most probably due to mind control.	_____	_____
27.	I see nothing harmful in transcendental meditation or the practice of Yoga.	_____	_____
28.	Some events can only be explained supernaturally and are thus unexplainable through logic or science.	_____	_____
29.	All so called "miracles" are either myths or can be explained scientifically.	_____	_____
30.	The notion of an everlasting hell is a repugnant religious doctrine and completely unacceptable.	_____	_____
31.	We live in an objective world in which what we see is generally the way things really are.	_____	_____
32.	There are many gods and spirits of which some are good and some are evil.	_____	_____

	True (A)	False (B)
33. People are generally honest and in most cases should be trusted.	____	____
34. In some instances, it is possible to communicate with people after death.	____	____
35. There is a universal conspiracy to control and enslave people.	____	____
36. The existing supernatural force is *only* energy or force, not a thinking or feeling being with a personality.	____	____
37. Miracles, such as instant healing and the raising of the dead, may have actually occurred at some point in history, but are certainly not happening today.	____	____
38. Strange occurrences, such as hauntings and ghosts, may be attributed to the restless spirits of people who have died.	____	____
39. The only supernatural force of any consequence in the universe is evil.	____	____
40. Following an individual's death, their spirit may inhabit the body of another living person.	____	____
41. I see no harm in periodically reading one's horoscope.	____	____
42. Any mysterious or unexplained powers exhibited by people today will in time be explained scientifically in terms of human potential or talent.	____	____
43. Supernatural forces or spirits can be controlled and used to one's own advantage if one is clever.	____	____
44. Explanations for the supernatural must lie outside of human potential or ability.	____	____
45. There is both a *spiritual* as well as a *natural* side to reality.	____	____
46. The supernatural spirit or force is a being with a personality and a close intimate or personal relationship is possible.	____	____
47. It is foolish to believe there is no God.	____	____
48. Humility and meekness, for the most part, are human characteristics of individual weakness.	____	____
49. I enjoy tales of the supernatural, horror and the macabre.	____	____
50. Halloween is a very important time of the year.	____	____

This instrument was developed by Newell T. Gill, Ed.D., at Florida Atlantic University, Boca Raton, Florida, and is not to be used without the prior consent of the author.

From the *High School Journal, 73* (1). Copyright © 1989 by the University of North Carolina Press. Used by permission of the publisher and the author.

Chapter 2

Scales of Religious Attitudes

Attitudes toward religion are the focus of the scales included in this chapter. Attitudes are understood as evaluative reactions, in this case, toward religion or religious experience. A religious attitude necessarily includes religious beliefs, but it also involves the positive or negative feelings associated with those beliefs. The measures in this chapter, therefore, frequently include a number of belief items. Each scale, as a whole, also incorporates an evaluative component. The researcher searching for a measure of religious attitude may also want to consider some of the religious belief and practice scales in chapter 1.

A number of the scales included in this chapter provide a general attitudinal measure toward Christianity. Examples of such scales include Francis and Stubb's Attitude toward Christianity Scale (2.1), Bardis's Religion Scale (2.6), Ausubel and Schpoont's Religious Attitude Inventory (2.7), and Poppleton and Pilkington's Religious Attitude Scale (2.8). Virtually all of these scales include a number of belief items (e.g., belief about the value of religion to society, the role of the church, whether God intervenes in the world or not, etc.) as part of their attitudinal assessment. The Rejection of Christianity Scale (2.5) authored by Greer and Francis takes an opposite approach by measuring negative attitudes toward the Christian faith. Another general attitudinal measure, but one not specific to Christianity, is Katz's Social-Religious-Political Scale (2.12). As the name of the scale indicates, this is not just a measure of religion, but considers social and political attitudes as well.

Other scales measure more specific aspects of Christianity. For example, Seyfarth and his colleagues have provided a measure of attitude toward evangelism (2.2). Postovoit's Attitude toward Christian Women Scale (2.3) measures patriarchal beliefs by assessing how adult women see their roles in light of Christian belief. Coursey has provided a measure of attitude toward the Catholic Church (2.4).

Altemeyer provides a series of three measures that assess the extent to which people experience doubt about their religion (2.9). These measures of religious doubt are accompanied by Altemeyer's Religious Pressures Scale (2.10), which is designed to ascertain how much pressure one feels to affirm religious faith in face of doubts. Morrow and his colleagues have developed the Religious Values Scale, which measures the degree of tolerance held by people of faith (whether Christian or otherwise) toward other religious beliefs. Finally, Silber and Reilly developed a religious and spiritual attitudinal index (2.13) for a specific population of adolescents following hospitalization in a psychiatric inpatient unit.

Given that the attitudinal construct is so broad, there is obvious overlap between the measures reviewed in this chapter and measures included not only in chapter 1 but also chapters 3, 6, 7, 8, and 12. The interested researcher is encouraged to consider the scales reviewed in those chapters also.

2.1
ATTITUDE TOWARD CHRISTIANITY SCALE
(Francis, 1978; Francis & Stubb, 1987)

Reviewed by Timothy J. Aycock

Variable: The attitude toward Christianity Scale focuses solely on people's perception of the Christian religion. References to Jesus, the Bible, and prayer prevent it from being used as a generic measure of interest in religion.

Francis (1993) conceptualizes attitude as an "underlying, deep seated and relatively stable evaluative predisposition" (p. 4). While some researchers conclude that persons' attitudes are unrelated to their behavior, the author positions himself with those who conclude that attitudes can predict behaviors when the two are measured in similar manners and in similar degrees of specificity.

Description: This scale measures attitudes toward Christianity for both children and adults. It examines persons' self-evaluation of their personal prayer life, church attendance, and beliefs about Jesus, God, and the Bible. Because these variables clearly belong to the religious domain, they are likely to reflect one's general view of Christianity.

Form ASC4B of the child and adult version consists of 24 (Likert-type) items to which subjects respond on a 5-point scale ranging from "agree strongly" to "disagree strongly." Eight questions are reverse scored because they are negatively phrased. Higher scores indicate more favorable attitudes toward Christianity. The child and adult versions differ by two questions. The item "I like school lessons about God very much" was altered in the adult version to "I like to learn about God very much"; the item "saying prayers in school does no good" was altered to "I think saying prayers does no good." A short form of this scale also has been developed. Preliminary findings suggest that it strongly correlates to its parent version.

Practical Considerations: This scale requires no special administration skills and can easily be administered to individuals or groups. It is brief and takes less than five minutes to complete. Because some of the items are negatively phrased, children under age 8 may have difficulty understanding their meaning. Their scores should be interpreted cautiously (Francis, 1988).

Norms/Standardization: Normative data are provided in several research studies cited by Francis (1993). Specialized norms are provided for the following groups: 12- to 18-year-old Roman Catholic school pupils in England; 11- to 16-year-old Roman Catholic school pupils in Northern Ireland; 11- to 16-year-old Protestant school pupils in Northern Ireland; 11- to 16-year-old nondenominational school pupils in England; 8- to 16-year-old nonchurch-related school pupils in England; and 11- to 16-year-old Roman Catholic school pupils in Scotland. The sample sizes in these studies were large, ranging from 935 subjects to 4,405 subjects.

Normative data for the adult version is presently less extensive, but several studies have provided means and standard deviations for the following groups: a British sample of 185 adults with ages ranging from 18 to 64 (Francis & Stubbs, 1987); a sample of 126 undergraduate students in the United Kingdom (Francis, 1993); a sample of U. S. adults with ages unreported and the mean and standard deviations reported only by gender (Lewis, 1995; Maltby, 1994).

Reliability: In the original sample for the children's version of the ASC4B, Cronbach's alpha coefficients ranged from .954 to .971 for ages 8–16. Subsequent samples have yielded Cronbach's alpha coefficients between .91 and .97. In the adult version, Cronbach alpha coefficients have ranged from .95 to .98. These coefficients are exceptionally high and suggest that this scale is highly reliable. In the child's version, item-to-rest-of-test correlation coefficients ranged from .40 to .87 (for ages 8–16) and in the adult version ranged from .42 to .92, which supports this instrument's unidimensionality and homogeneity.

Short versions of this instrument have been developed for both the child and adult versions. Preliminary studies have yielded samples with reliability statistics similar to the parent scales (Francis 1993).

Validity: Subjects completing the ASC4B are likely to be aware that they are answering questions related to their views of Christianity, which supports the face validity of this instrument. Because no specific relationship can be assumed between attitude and behavior, the author argues that the support for this instrument's construct validity is inferred by determining the extent to which attitude scores predict different aspects of religious behavior and beliefs. Research studies (Francis, 1988, 1993) utilizing the child version of this instrument have yielded outcomes predicting the following: gender attitudes toward religion, decline of interest in religion with age among adolescents, personal practice of religion versus public expression, parental religious behavior and children's attitude toward religion, and personality variables and attitudes toward religion.

Research with the adult version of the ASC4B is less extensive but generally supportive of its construct validity. Several studies have yielded results demonstrating strong relationships between religious atti-

tudes and the following: religious practices, religious beliefs, psychoticism, and other personality variables. Some studies have yielded findings differing from previous research with the child's version. Gender, for example, has been significantly correlated to attitudes toward Christianity with children, but this relationship has produced mixed results with adults. Scores on lie scales, extraversion, and neuroticism also have produced unanticipated relationships to the ASC4B. These disparate findings may reflect the actual differences between child and adult populations as opposed to reflecting the ASC4B's inability to measure religious attitudes.

Location:

Child's version: Francis, L. J. (1978). Attitude and longitude; A study in measurement. *Character Potential, 8,* 119–130.

Adult Version: Francis, L. J. & Stubbs, M. T. (1987). Measuring attitudes towards Christianity: From childhood to adulthood. *Personality and Individual Differences, 8,* 741–743.

Recent Research:

Francis, L. J. (1992). Reliability and validity of the Francis Scale of attitude towards Christianity (adult). *Journal of Comparative Religious Education and Values, 4,* 17–19.

Francis, L. J. (1993). Attitudes towards Christianity during childhood and adolescence: Assembling the jigsaw. *Journal of Beliefs and Values, 14*(2), 4–6.

References

Francis, L. J. (1988). Measuring attitude towards Christianity during childhood and adolescence. *Personality and Individual Differences, 10,* 695–698.

Lewis, C. A. (1995). Religiosity and personality among US adults. *Personality and Individual Differences, 18,* 293–295.

Maltby, J. (1994). The reliability and validity of the Francis scale of attitude towards Christianity among Republic of Ireland adults. *Irish Journal of Psychology, 15,* 595–598.

Appendix

Attitude toward Christianity, Form ASC4B (Child Version)

INSTRUCTIONS

Read the sentence carefully and think, "Do I agree with it?"

If you *agree strongly*, put a ring round.	(AS)	A	NC	D	DS
If you *agree*, put a ring round	As	(A)	NC	D	DS
If you are *not certain*, put a ring round	AS	A	(NC)	D	DS
If you *disagree*, put a ring round	AS	A	NC	(D)	DS
If you *strongly disagree*, put a ring round	AS	A	NC	D	(DS)

1. I find it boring to listen to the Bible.*.	AS	A	NC	D	DS
2. I know that Jesus helps me.	AS	A	NC	D	DS
3. Saying my prayers helps me a lot.	AS	A	NC	D	DS
4. The church is very important to me.	AS	A	NC	D	DS
5. I think going to Church is a waste of my time.*. .	AS	A	NC	D	DS
6. I want to love Jesus.	AS	A	NC	D	DS
7. I think church services are boring.*.	AS	A	NC	D	DS
8. I think people who pray are stupid.*.	AS	A	NC	D	DS
9. God helps me to lead a better life.	AS	A	NC	D	DS
10. I like school lessons about God very much.	AS	A	NC	D	DS
(10. I like to learn about God very much.[1]).˜.	AS	A	NC	D	DS
11. God means a lot to me.	AS	A	NC	D	DS
12. I believe that God helps people.	AS	A	NC	D	DS
13. Prayer helps me a lot.	AS	A	NC	D	DS
14. I know that Jesus is very close to me	AS	A	NC	D	DS
15. I think praying is a good thing.	AS	A	NC	D	DS
16. I think the Bible is out of date.*.	AS	A	NC	D	DS
17. I believe that God listens to prayers	AS	A	NC	D	DS
18. Jesus doesn't mean anything to me.*.	AS	A	NC	D	DS
19. God is very real to me.	AS	A	NC	D	DS
20. I think saying prayers in school does no good.*. .	AS	A	NC	D	DS
(20. I think saying prayers does no good.*[1]).	AS	A	NC	D	DS
21. The idea of God means much to me.	AS	A	NC	D	DS
22. I believe that Jesus still helps people.	AS	A	NC	D	DS
23. I know that God helps me	AS	A	NC	D	DS
24. I find it hard to believe in God.*.	AS	A	NC	D	DS

*Negative items are reverse scored.
[1] Adult version

Reprinted with permission of the author.

2.2
ATTITUDE TOWARD EVANGELISM SCALE (Seyfarth et al., 1984)
Reviewed by Peter C. Hill

Variable: The Attitude toward Evangelism Scale measures the degree to which people are open to the rights of religious groups to evangelize. The authors define evangelism as "the employment of religious ideology in intensive direct contacts with prospective recruits" (p. 56). The conceptual basis of this instrument is the public (i.e., the promulgation of faith in public places or media to recruit converts) and visitation (i.e., securing conversions through direct visitation with individuals or families) components of evangelism.

Description: The scale consists of 21 items to which people respond in a standard 5-point Likert format ranging from "strongly disagree" (1) to "strongly agree" (5). These items were selected from a total of 80 items on the basis of showing the largest differences between the 10% of an original sample of introductory psychology students who scored highest on the 80-item scale and the 10% who scored lowest on the 80-item scale. Seven of the 21 items are reverse scored.

The concept of attitude toward evangelism is multidimensional. Four factors with item loadings of at least .30 were identified (with items listed in decreasing correlational order):

Factor 1: Respect for the courage to stand up for one's beliefs (items 9, 4, 7, 18, 3, 13, 10, 1, 16, 8, and 17)
Factor 2: Interpersonal approach (items 19, 20, 14, 12, 2, and 5)
Factor 3: Not identified (items 5 and 15)
Factor 4: Not identified (item 11)

Practical Considerations: The scale is straightforward and requires no special considerations for administration. It should take no more than 10 minutes to complete.

Norms/Standardization: The initial sample of students for the item-selection phase of the study consisted of 130 introductory psychology students at Oregon State University in fall, 1980. The age range was 18 to 37 years, with the mean age of 19.58. The sample was equally divided between males and females. No descriptive statistical data (means, standard deviations, etc.) were reported.

A similar second sample of introductory psychology students during the same semester at the same institution (55% male; mean age of 20.65) was selected to test the scale's reliability and validity. Again, no descriptive data were reported.

Reliability: The scale demonstrates high internal reliability. The uncorrected split-half reliability coefficient was .83. The corrected split-half reliability coefficient (using the Spearman-Brown prophecy formula) was .91.

Validity: A construct validity correlation coefficient of .76 was calculated between this scale and the Fanaticism scale of Putney and Middleton's (1961) Dimensions of Religious Ideology Scale (see chap. 8). Higher evangelism scores were reported by the authors for Protestants versus non-Protestants, for those who claim a religious identity versus those who claim no religious identity and for those "active in religion" versus those "inactive in religion." On the basis of "generally known denominational belief, policy, and practice" (p. 59), Protestants from "high-outreach" denominations scored higher than Protestants from "low-outreach" denominations.

Location:
   Seyfarth, L. H., Larsen, K. S., Lamont, K., Haasch, C., Hale, T., & Haskin, D. (1984). Attitude toward evangelism: Scale development and validity. *Journal of Social Psychology, 123*, 55–61.

Recent Research: No subsequent research using this scale was found.

Reference

Putney, S., & Middleton, R. (1961). Dimensions and correlates of religious ideologies. *Social Forces*, 39, 285–290.

Appendix

Instrument

Please respond to each of the 21 items below by using the following rating scale.

> 1 = strongly disagree
> 2 = disagree
> 3 = neutral
> 4 = agree
> 5 = strongly agree

1. I like to listen to a religious evangelist.
2. Religious soliciting is an infringement on my right to privacy. (R)
3. There is a strong need for more people to openly attempt to convert others.
4. People testifying to their faith are an inspiration to me.
5. People who wish to spread their beliefs should be restricted to a designated area. (R)
6. Religion shouldn't be pushed. (R)
7. It is time that more people listen to religious spokesmen.
8. Freedom to seek religious converts is important to me.
9. I am thrilled when someone approaches me with the story of what God has done for him and can do for me.
10. If a person believes he knows the word of God, it is his duty to spread it.
11. I don't like it when people push their religion on me in public places. (R)
12. Door-to-door evangelists deserve at least two minutes of listening time.
13. I love it when someone speaks in public of his faith.
14. Religious solicitors who go door-to-door are often helpful.
15. I'm annoyed at people who feel it is necessary that the rest of the world must conform to their beliefs and standards. (R)
16. I hate it when I am approached on matters of religion. (R)
17. If people who "sell" religion could convert everyone, we would have a much better society.
18. When someone publicly shares his testimony with me, I take it as a great gift.
19. It doesn't bother me to see religious evangelists going door-to-door.
20. Religious evangelizing is an invasion of privacy. (R)
21. I like people who come door-to-door to bring God to me.

From *Journal of Social Psychology, 123,* 55–61, 1984. Reprinted with permission of the Helen Dwight Reid Educational Foundation. Published by Heldref Publications, 1319 Eighteenth St., N.W., Washington, D.C. 20036-1802. Copyright © 1984.

2.3
ATTITUDES TOWARD CHRISTIAN WOMEN SCALE (Postovoit, 1990)
Reviewed by Katheryn Rhoads Meek and Mark R. McMinn

***Variable*:** The Attitudes Toward Christian Women Scale (ACWS) is designed to measure patriarchal Christian beliefs held by adult women. One assumption is that it may be helpful in illuminating the relationship between patriarchal beliefs and domestic violence. It contains five subscales: female physical and emotional independence, female submissiveness and guilt, female innate and demonstrated efficacy, martyrdom, and God's nature.

Description: It is assumed that patriarchal beliefs are multidimensional. The scale consists of 34 items, which are scored on a 6-point Likert continuum. The items were derived from historical and modern theological views concerning the role of women in the family, church, and community.

Interitem correlation coefficients were used to group items together into the five subscales. A minimum correlation coefficient of 0.6 was required before grouping items together.

Because no item is represented in more than one subscale, the five subscales are independent and can be scored separately. The score of each subscale is determined by summing the scores of the items. Only 23 of the 34 items are included in the subscales. An overall score can also be obtained by totaling the responses of all 34 items.

Practical Considerations: This scale does not require special training to administer or score. Each statement is clearly identified with either a patriarchal or an egalitarian view of women's roles in the family, church, and society.

Norms/Standardization: Those fifty subjects were personally recruited from the great Los Angeles area by a member of the research team. All subjects spoke English, ranged in age from 18 to 65, and came from diverse ethnic educational, occupational, and Christian denominational backgrounds. In order to be included in the sample, each participant needed to be currently involved in a heterosexual relationship for at least one year.

Reliability: Pearson product-moment intercorrelations were calculated among all the items to create subscales. A minimum correlation of .6 between items was used to select items for inclusion, resulting in five subscales' using 23 of the 34 original statements.

Internal consistency reliability coefficients were not reported.

Validity: The scale has high face validity with each item clearly identified as an egalitarian or patriarchal view toward women. Several steps were taken to establish validity for this scale. First, the author attempted to demonstrate content validity by having three doctoral students familiar with both theology of women and domestic violence review the initial pool of statements drawn from theological materials on Christian womanhood. The items were then administered to six women who were subsequently interviewed for their impressions of the statements. The statements were then revised to form the final version.

The author hypothesized that there would be a correlation between gender role beliefs and ongoing behavior in heterosexual relationships. She chose to administer an already established scale as well, The Attitudes toward Women Scale (AWS), which is designed to measure conservative, traditional female behavior and liberal, egalitarian female behavior. The AWS short form was used because it has been shown to significantly correlate with the longer version (.97 for college women and .96 for mothers of college students). With one exception (Female Submission and Guilt), all of the subscales of the ACWS correlated significantly with the summed score of the AWS short form. On the basis of these results, the author concluded that religious gender role beliefs are multidimensional and may be indicative of expectations and behavior in heterosexual relationships.

Location:

Postovoit, L. E. (1990). The attitudes toward Christian women scale (ACWS): Initial efforts towards the development of an instrument measuring patriarchal beliefs. *Journal of Psychology and Christianity, 2,* 65–72.

Subsequent Research: There is no further research available on this instrument at this time.

Appendix

The Attitudes Toward Christian Women Scale (ACWS)

1. Males are the correct ministers of God's word because both God and Jesus Christ are men.

2. Wives are commanded to honor their husbands as the head of the family.

3. There may be reasons besides adultery which make divorce the right decision for a Christian wife.

4. When sexual passion gets "out of hand," it's usually the woman's fault.

5. Woman is subservient to man because she came out of his rib.

6. The woman should never desire to teach the man but should always learn from him in subjection and quiet submission.

7. Women were considered as important as men by Jesus Christ during his ministry on earth.

8. Both husband and wife are equals in the family, the community, and the church.

9. Wives and husbands are commanded to treat each other as equals in mutual submission.

10. If a woman is unhappy in her subordinate role, she shows her sinful nature.

11. Man's superior strength and common sense show he's more in the image of God than is woman.

12. If a husband gets angry with his home situation, it is his wife's fault for not preventing the problem.

13. God calls women to be more humble and submissive to their husbands than their husbands are to them.

14. In marriage, both the husband the wife should make the important decisions, with both having the final word.

15. Adam and Eve were made absolutely equal, out of the same substance.

16. The Bible shows that Christian women can be prophets, leaders, wives, and mothers.

17. It is acceptable for a woman to preach in the church.

18. A Christian woman is disgraced if she is divorced because it shows she has failed.

19. In the Old and New Testaments, God is spoken of as having female as well as male characteristics.

20. A woman's salvation will come through her husband.

21. A Christian wife is not responsible for her husband's behavior or feelings.

22. The wife follows her husband's leadership to achieve greater Christian unity in their marriage.

23. Husbands and wives have God-given rights to discipline each other.

24. The Bible uses female symbols for God and Jesus Christ.

25. A Christian woman should be subject even to her non-Christian husband so he will be won over by her meek and quiet spirit.

26. A Christian marriage should be based on equality between the husband and wife.

27. Christian husbands are given the right to discipline their Christian wives as necessary to keep them on the Christian path, but wives are not granted the same rights by God.

28. It is all right for a Christian woman to be divorced.

29. God's image and personality are seen equally in the forms of the female and the male.

30. God grants a special blessing to wives who give up their desires for their husbands because these women are living in accordance with God's plan for the family.

31. Adam and Eve are equally responsible for the origin of sin.

32. God intends for women to be free from the emotional burden which comes from the responsibility of leadership.

33. The Bible states that the equality of males and females is the Christian ideal.

34. A Christian woman should divorce her husband only if he is unfaithful to her.

Subscale 1: Female Physical and Emotional Independence
    Items 2, 3, 14, 22, 25, and 28.
Subscale 2: Female Submissiveness and Guilt
    Items 6, 11, 12, and 13
Subscale 3: Female Efficacy
    Items 7, 8, 9, 15, 16, 17, 18, and 33
Subscale 4: Female Submissiveness and Guilt
    Items 30 and 32
Subscale 5: Female Submissiveness and Guilt
    Items 19 and 24

Note: It is unclear what are the exact 6-point Likert response items. It appears that the responses could be "strongly disagree," "moderately disagree," "slightly disagree," "slightly agree," "moderately agree," and "strong agree."

Postovoit, L. E. (1990). The attitudes toward Christian women scale (ACWS): Initial efforts towards the development of an instrument measuring patriarchal beliefs. *Journal of Psychology and Christianity, 9,* 65–72. Copyright © 1990. Christian Association for Psychological Studies. Reprinted with permission.

2.4
THE LIBERAL-CONSERVATIVE SCALE (Coursey, 1971, 1974)
Reviewed by Susan Sheffer

Variable: The Liberal-Conservative Scale measures attitudes of members of the Roman Catholic Church on two dimensions: liberalism (L) and conservatism (C). Catholics with liberal attitudes are characterized as advocating radical changes in religious practices and beliefs. Conversely, "conservative" Catholics seek to maintain traditional approaches to the Church. Coursey (1974) maintains that liberalism and conservatism are relatively consistent and strong dimensions that characterize members of the Catholic faith. The liberal-conservative religious attitudes held by Catholics are similar to and consistent with liberal-conservative attitudes toward other areas of life.

In addition to the two main dimensions, this scale is broken down further into six subscales that measure the following factors: pious submissiveness, ecumenical attitudes, marriage issues, church rules, styles of worship, and social rights. The piety factor (subscale 1) measures loyalty and obedience to authority and level of zeal for adhering to traditional recommendations for piety from the Church. The ecumenical attitudes factor (subscale 2) refers to the degree to which members see a need to close the church off to other religions. Coursey

(1974) labels this factor the "Catholic ghetto mentality." Marriage issues (subscale 3) are primarily concerned with issues such as birth control, divorce, and celibacy of the clergy. The fourth subscale deals with maintaining or rejecting church regulations of a nontheological nature (e.g., appropriate dress for priests and nuns, and level of involvement of Church authority in Catholic education). Styles of worship (subscale 5) addresses issues involving changes in the Mass implemented as a result of recommendations made by the Second Vatican Council (1962–65), such as the celebration of Mass in English instead of Latin and the types of hymns allowed. The sixth factor, social rights, deals with the Church's involvement in social and political issues.

Description: This scale was designed in response to the conflict within the American Catholic Church that arose following the declarations passed by the Second Vatican Council. Traditional (conservative) Catholics feared that introducing a large number of major changes in to the Church structure and worship format would lead to the downfall of Catholicism. More liberal Catholics welcomed and eagerly embraced the new changes. Coursey (1971, 1974) developed the L-C Scale in order to help psychologists and clergy better serve members of this once very unified denomination by placing their conflicting attitudes within a psychological framework.

This scale consists of 40 forced-choice items in a 4-point Likert-type format. Responses range from "strongly agree" to "strongly disagree." Twenty of the items reflect a liberal (L) attitude, and 20 advocate a conservative (C) stance. The L items are reverse scored. For each item, then, scoring is as follows: 1 = the most liberal response, 3 = no response to the item, and 5 = the most conservative response. A summary score is obtained by summing responses to each item. Scores can range from 40 (an extremely liberal attitude) to 200 (an extremely conservative attitude).

Practical Considerations: This scale is a self-administered paper-and-pencil measure.

The responses are easy to score and interpret. No special skills or instructions are required to administer this scale. It was designed for the average American Catholic layperson, with a ninth-grade education, since the items were pretested for understanding at this level.

One caution for using this scale, over 20 years after its initial development, is that the political climate of the Church has changed markedly since the early 1970s. Many of the issues addressed in the scale items, which were highly controversial immediately following Vatican II (e.g., casual dress for religious leaders, mass celebrated in English, and guitar music at worship), may not distinguish liberal from conservative Catholics today. However, some of the items do reflect ongoing controversial issues (e.g., marriage of priests, use of birth control, and abortion).

Norms/Standardization: The normative sample consisted of adult members of two parishes: a moderately conservative parish (Parish A) and a moderately liberal parish (Parish B). This sample was given the original scale, which consisted of 55 items. The sample from Parish A consisted of 275 individuals with a mean age of 41.4 years ($SD = 14.25$), a mean education level of 12.66 years ($SD = 2.54$), and a mean of 6.24 years ($SD = 5.36$) of Catholic education. The mean summary score for Parish A was 171.04 ($SD = 34.34$). There were 403 respondents from Parish B. They had a mean age of 34.6 years ($SD = 9.00$), a mean education level of 14.88 years ($SD = 2.06$), and a mean of 5.7 years ($SD = 1.42$) of Catholic education. The mean summary score for Parish B was 155.82 ($SD = 31.19$). The total pool of subjects ($N = 678$) was used for the factor analysis. The reliability of the factors was established by factor analyzing each parish separately and then correlating the factor loadings.

Reliability: For both parishes, the average interitem correlation was .19 with a reliability estimate of .93. Individually, the parishes provided reliability estimates of .92. Factor reliability across time was established one year later with three additional factor analyses. L-C summary score correlated .32 with age, .29 with occupational level, and -.40 with education.

Validity: Ninety-eight potential items were originally generated for this scale. These items were examined by 10 judges from the sociology and theology departments at a Catholic college in order to establish face validity. In order for an item to be included in the scale, an 80% agreement among the judges about the item's liberal/conservative nature was required. Fifty-five items remained after this process.

The results of three studies were used to establish construct validity for this scale (Coursey, 1974). Several predictions about the nature of the liberal and conservative constructs were made. In the first study, it was predicted that members of a more conservative parish would score higher on the L-C Scale than members of a more liberal parish. The mean scores for these two parishes (conservative parish: $M = 171.04$, $SD = 34.34$; liberal parish: $M = 155.82$, $SD = 31.19$) were significantly different ($t = 5.85$, $p < .001$) in the predicted direction.

It was predicted in the second study that students exposed to a liberally oriented education would score lower on this scale than students who receive a more conservative education. In addition, it was also predicted that students with a longer exposure to a liberally oriented education would have more liberal scores than students with less exposure to such an education. Two hundred eighty-six 9th and 12th grade students from four Catholic coeducational high schools participated in this study. A shortened high school version of the original 55 item scale was used. Consistent with the predictions, students from the more liberal schools scored lower than students from the less liberal schools. Also, the mean score for the 12th graders was significantly lower than the mean score for the 9th graders.

A third study used 98 matched pairs of individuals (matched on sex, age, vocational status, education, and income) from two samples to cross-validate the L-C Scale. The two samples were drawn from subscribers who read and endorsed either a liberal or a conservative Catholic journal. The 40-item L-C Scale was administered to the respondents. The overall summary score and the scores on the six subscales were all significantly different for the two samples in the predicted direction with $p < .001$.

Location:
Coursey, R. D. (1971). The L-C Scale measuring liberal-conservative religious attitudes among Roman Catholics. *Dissertation Abstracts International, 32*(3-B), 1819.
Coursey, R. D. (1974). Consulting and the Catholic crisis. *Journal of Consulting and Clinical Psychology, 42*, 519–528.

Subsequent Research: No additional studies that used the L-C Scale were located in the published literature since its initial development.

Appendix

Liberal-Conservative Scale

Instructions: For each item below, state whether you "strongly disagree," "disagree," "agree," or "strongly agree."

1. The most important part of a person's action is gaining merit for heaven. (C)[1] [.56]
2. Catholics should try to gain all the indulgences they can. (C)[1] [.62]
3. The celebration of Mass in private homes should be edncouraged. (L)[5] [.52]
4. Nuns should wear modern dress. (L)[4] [.36]
5. Priests should wear a distinctive outfit. (C)[4] [.68]

6. Catholics should support birth control clinics set up by the government. (L)^3 [.73]

7. Sermons at Mass should deal with current social problems. (L)^6 [.45]

8. Catholic children should not be exposed to non-Catholic ways. (C)^2 [.51]

9. The church is losing its hold on its members by relaxing the laws of fasting and abstinence. (C)^5 [.58]

10. There are times when Catholics should criticize Church authorities in the press.(L)^1 [.49]

11. Parts of the Mass should be in Latin. (C)^5 [.55]

12. Catholic magazines that will strongly defend the Church's views are needed. (C)^1 [.57]

13. A priest should run his parish and not get involved in political issues. (C)^6 [.47]

14. Disobedience to Church authority leads to chaos and anarchy. (C)^1 [.59]

15. Catholic colleges and universities should be free from interference from Church authority. (L)^4 [.49]

16. Titles such as "your Excellency" and "Monsignor" should be dropped. (L)^4 [.42]

17. Confirmation should be postponed until the late teens. (L)^1 [.49]

18. Nuns should receive training outside the convent. (L)^2 [.58]

19. Many popular hymns lack the majesty that is fitting for Mass. (C)^5 [.68]

20. Protestant hymns and prayers should be avoided in Catholic services. (C)^5 [.40]

21. Catholic schools should hire Catholic teachers. (C)^2 [.51]

22. Parishes should have guitar Masses. (L)^5 [.55]

23. Seminarians should attend class with other college students. (L)^2 [.63]

24. Catholics should make the nine First Fridays at least once in their lives. (C)^1 [.61]

25. Following one's conscience is a legitimate excuse for disobeying Church authority. (L)^1 [.50]

26. A layman should not criticize the actions of a priest or nun. (C)^1 [.52]

27. More theologians from other faiths should teach at Catholic colleges. (L)^2 [.72]

28. The Church should never grant a divorce to someone validly married. (C)^3 [.50]

29. Sunday Mass should remain obligatory. (C)^4 [.48]

30. Catholic organizations should help blacks obtain jobs and earn better incomes. (L)^6 [.79]

31. Artificial birth control is morally wrong. (C)^3 [.78]

32. Catholics should help disadvantaged groups to secure equal rights. (L)^6 [.76]

33. Priests should change from their traditional clerical garb and wear ordinary clothes. (L)^4 [.70]

34. A good Catholic should say the Rosary often. (C)^1 [.67]

35. Priests should be allowed to marry. (L)^3 [.37]

36. Parochial schools should be closed. (L)^1 [.38]

37. It is a Catholic's duty to defend the Church when someone criticizes it. (C)^1 [.56]

38. Catholics should be allowed to use birth control pills. (L)^3 [.80]

39. Children should be ten years old before going to Confession. (L)^1 [.45]

40. Priests and nuns should devote their time and energy only to activities that are sponsored by Catholic groups. $(C)^2$ [.47]

C = Conservative; L = Liberal; superscript indicates subscale that item belongs to; factor loadings are in [ ].

Coursey, R. D. (1974). Consulting and the Catholic crisis. *Journal of Consulting and Clinical Psychology, 42*, 519–528. Copyright © 1974 by the American Psychological Association. Reprinted with permission.

2.5
REJECTION OF CHRISTIANITY SCALE (Greer & Francis, 1992)
Reviewed by Richard L. Gorsuch

Variable: This scale measures negative attitudes towards Christianity. The scale was developed because the usual scales to measure attitudes towards Christianity in Northern Ireland only measured positive attitudes toward Christianity. The usual scales were therefore open to a tendancy toward acquiescence. The purpose of this scale is to provide a scale that would have a negative valence, to offset possible acquiescence response bias.

Although it has not been previously mentioned, this reviewer feels there are theoretical reasons to have a negatively oriented scale. Learning theory notes that negative reinforcement works somewhat differently than positive reinforcement. Motivation theory notes that negative and positive motivations lead, for example, to different approach/avoidance curves. Measuring motivation toward religion in terms of negatives and positives should lead to better overall theory development.

Description: The scale consists of 20 items on a range of topics about "religion," "church," "clergy," and "God." The word "Christianity" is not used. The original items included 32 negatively worded items "covering 8 somewhat overlapping conceptual areas" of "religion, God, church, belief, religious practice, individual rights, authority and science." Exploratory factor analyses (method unspecified) resulted in selecting 20 items that cohered most "consistently" (Greer & Francis, 1992, p. 1346).

Practical considerations: The scale is easily administered and scored. Some who are anitreligion but pro-Chrisitianity may need some wordings reinterpreted.

Norms/Standardization: The only normative data provided are for Protestant and Catholic male and female adolescents in Northern Ireland.

Reliability: The internal consistency reliabilities were .94 and .90 for 466 Protestants and 409 Catholics (Greer & Francis, 1992) and .93 (N = 1,177; Greer & Francis, 1990). All were Northern Ireland adolescents in forms 4 to 6.

Validity: Content validity appears good except that the term "religion" is used but not "Christianity," although other terms used make Christianity the only religion to which the scale can be applied. Concurrent/construct validity is high in that the scale correlates well with positive measures of Christian faith. Differences found between Protestants and Catholics are consistent with the other data. No differential validity has been tested comparing it with positively worded scales.

Location:
Greer, J., & Francis, L. J. (1992). Measuring "rejection of Christianity" among 14 to 16-year-old adolescents in Catholic and Protestant schools in Northern Ireland. *Personality and Individual Differences, 13*, 1345–1348.

Other Research:
Greer, J. E., & Frances, L. J. (1990). The religious profile of pupils in Northern Ireland. *Journal of Empirical Theology, 3*, 35–50.

Reference
Greer, J. E., Frances, L. J. (1990). The religious profile of pupils in Northern Ireland. *Journal of Empirical Theology, 3*, 35–50.

Appendix

Instrument

Please print a number from 1 to 5 to indicate how you feel about it.

Use the following scale to indicate how you feel about each item:

      1. Strongly disagree
      2. Disagree
      3. Not certain
      4. Agree
      5. Strongly agree

_____ Religion is out of touch with my experience and interests.

_____ I cannot believe in a personal God.

_____ I do not believe that there is any life after death.

_____ The clergy are completely out of touch with young people today.

_____ In the past religion has done more harm than good to mankind.

_____ I see too much innocent suffering to believe in a good God who is all powerful.

_____ The church should not dictate a way of living and a moral code for everyone.

_____ Religious education in school is uninteresting and ineffective.

_____ Sermons in church are a boring waste of time.

_____ Money and enjoyment are more important to me than religion.

_____ If God does exist, I want evidence to help me believe.

_____ I find it hard to accept that the miracles of Jesus really happened.

_____ Going to church is a dull, meaningless ritual.

_____ Most religious people are hypocrites who do not practice what they believe.

_____ I get no satisfaction from going to church on Sundays.

_____ The resurrection is unbelievable because people do not come back from the dead.

_____ God is something which people create for themselves.

_____ The church has not helped me get any satisfactory ideas about God.

_____ The church is out of date and has no attraction for me.

_____ The universe is entirely governed by chance.

Reprinted with permission of the author.

2.6
RELIGION SCALE (Bardis, 1961)

Reviewed by Duane Kauffmann

Variable: The Religion Scale is designed for use in surveys whose goal is to measure attitudes toward religious beliefs and practices. The definition of religion used by Bardis in- volves three components: (1) ideas about di- vinity, (2) doctrines concerning relation- ships between divinity and humanity, and (3) behaviors designed to satisfy God's expectations and achieve future rewards (and avoid punishment).

Description: The scale consists of 25 items. Each question requires a response from a continuum whose end points are represented by 0 ("strongly disagree") and 4 ("strongly agree"). Item scores are summed to yield a religiosity score between 0 and 100. High scores indicate a greater degree of typical religiosity.

Practical Considerations: The scale is very easy to administer and involves minimal instructions. The instructions outline the meanings attached to the 0 to 4 Likert scale and direct those taking the scale to respond with answers reflecting their own beliefs. The scale is easily scored by simply summing the responses to items. No items are reverse scored.

Norms/Standardization: The inital pool of 200 items was taken from religious publications or supplied by persons representing a range of religious faiths. The original 200 items were pretested on 500 postelementary-school Jews and Christians from the Midwest. The 46 items that showed discriminatory power were administered through interview to 100 additional midwesterners. Comparison of the 10 highest and 10 lowest-scoring individuals in this sample of 100 led to the acceptance of 25 items with discrimination power for the final scale.

Reliability: Reliability coefficients are re- ported for a number of diverse samples. Thirty students attending a midwestern Methodist college generated a reliability coefficient of .74 (using the split-half method). (the Spearman-Brown correction raised this reliability to .85). Forty agnostics gave a split-half reliability coefficient of .58 (.73 when corrected). Reliability coefficients from several other samples are also reported: a Methodist college (.81 corrected to .90), a large midwestern university (.98), Jews from a large city (.84), and Greeks born in Greece (.86 corrected to .93).

Validity: Little detail is provided concerning the samples on which the scale was developed, except to note that they represented men and women from a variety of Christian denominations as well as from the Jewish community. The validity of the test is defended by comparison of means from groups that would be expected to differ on a scale of religiosity. The mean for a sample of 30 agnostics was 11.93, significantly different from a sample of Greek Orthodox Church members whose mean was 68.73. Similar studies found agnostics ($M = 10.81$) to be significantly less religious than Catholics ($M = 79.11$) and Methodist students studying for the ministry ($M = 68.83$) to be more religious than Methodist nonministerial students ($M = 57.97$).

Location:
    Bardis, P. (1961). A religion scale. *Social Science*, *36*, 120–123.

Appendix

Religion Scale

Below is a list of issues concerning religion. Please read all statements very *carefully* and respond to *all* of them on the basis of *your own true* beliefs, *without* consulting any other persons. Do this by reading each statement and then writing, in the space provided at its left, *only one* of the following numbers: 0, 1, 2, 3, 4. The meaning of each of these figures is:

    0 = strongly disagree
    1 = disagree
    2 = undecided
    3 = agree
    4 = strong agree

(For research purposes, you must consider all statements as they are without modifying any of them in any way.)

_____ 1. A sound religious faith is the best thing in life.
_____ 2. Every school should encourage its students to attend church.
_____ 3. People should defend their religion above all other things.
_____ 4. People should attend church once a week if possible.
_____ 5. Belief in God makes life more meaningful.
_____ 6. Every person should give 10 percent of his income to his church.
_____ 7. All people are God's children.
_____ 8. People attending church regularly develop a sound philosophy of life.
_____ 9. We should always love our enemies.
_____ 10. God rewards those who live religiously.
_____ 11. Prayer can solve many problems.
_____ 12. Every school should have chapel services for its students.
_____ 13. There is life after death.
_____ 14. People should read the Scriptures at least once a day.
_____ 15. Teachers should stress religious ideals in class.
_____ 16. Young people should attend Sunday School regularly.
_____ 17. People should pray at least once a day.
_____ 18. A religious wedding ceremony is better than a civil one.
_____ 19. Religious people should try to spread the teachings of the Scriptures.
_____ 20. People should say grace at all meals.
_____ 21. When a person is planning to be married, he should consult his minister, priest, or rabbi.
_____ 22. Delinquency is less common among young people attending church regularly.
_____ 23. What is moral today will always be moral.
_____ 24. Children should be brought up religiously.
_____ 25. Every person should participate in at least one church activity.

Reprinted with permission of author.

2.7
RELIGIOUS ATTITUDE INVENTORY (Ausubel & Schpoont, 1957)
Reviewed by Susan Sheffer

Variable: The Religious Attitude Inventory is designed to measure the intensity or extremeness of an individual's religious attitude. Intensity of religious attitude (ranging from extremely orthodox to neutral to extremely nonconformist) is measured toward four issues: God, immortality, religious doctrine, and the church. It is assumed that individuals with very intense attitudes toward a particular topic have a high ego involvement with the issue. High ego involvement attitudes are very important to the individual and are closely intertwined with the very essence of their personalities. These are attitudes that define an individual's self-image. An attitude that is not very ego involving is less important to the characteristics that make up the individual and thus is held less strongly. The Religious Attitude Inventory examines the intensity of the religious attitudes of both orthodox and nonconformist individuals. An orthodox individual holds positive attitudes toward traditional religious doctrines, God, immortality, and the church in general. An individual who holds nonconformist religious attitudes, on the other hand, has negative attitudes toward traditional religious ideals, i.e., the church, God, religious doctrine, and immortality.

Description: The Religious Attitude Inventory consists of 50 statements that measure religious attitudes *in general* and are not specific to any one particular religious affiliation. Individuals respond to the items on a 5-point Likert-type scale (1 = strongly agree; 5 = strongly disagree). Nonconformist items are reverse scored. Higher scores indicate positive/orthodox religious attitudes and lower scores indicate more negative/nonconformist attitudes toward religion. Respondents with moderate or neutral views on an item have the option of choosing "3," indicating "neither agree nor disagree" on the response scale. Scores can range from 50 (extremely negative/nonconformist attitude) to 250 (extremely positive/orthodox attitude). Two features of this scale serve to reduce the possibility of response sets: (a) orthodox and nonconformist statements alternate randomly in the scale and (b) the inclusion of a neutral point on the response scale instead of limiting responses to agree/disagree positions.

Practical Considerations: The Religious Attitude Inventory is a self-administered paper-and-pencil measure that could easily be administered in groups. It takes 15 to 20 minutes to complete. This scale requires no special skills to score and the results are easy to interpret. Since this scale is not specifically tied to one religious affiliation, it is widely applicable to members of diverse religious backgrounds.

Norms/Standardization: An early form of the inventory containing 156 items was administered to 38 education graduate students at the University of Illinois. The graduate students rated each item on a 1 (extremely orthodox) to 5 (extremely nonconformist) scale. From this original sample, the mean rating for each statement was calculated. The final 50-item form consisted of the 25 most extreme orthodox items and the 25 most extreme nonconformist items.

This final 50-item form was then administered to 95 undergraduate students (82 females, 13 males) who were enrolled in in-troductory education classes at the University of Illinois. The mean age of these students was 20.5 years.

Reliability: Reliability was determined by using a split-half coefficient of equivalence (corrected with the Spearman-Brown formula). Total scores for all of the odd-numbered items and for all of the even-numbered items were calculated for each respondent in the sample. The two sets of scores were then correlated. Ausubel and Schpoont (1957) report an "unusually high internal consistency" with a correlation coefficient of .97. This result is consistent with the split-half reliability coefficient of .96 reported independently by Foy, Lowe, Hildman, and Jacobs (1976). Test-retest reliability was not reported.

Validity: A validity study (Ausubel & Schpoont, 1957) was conducted using the original 95-member sample. Participants were categorized as orthodox, neutral, or nonconformist based on their scores on the inventory. Twenty-six students each were in the "orthodox" and "nonconformist" groups. The "neutral" group consisted of the remaining 43 students. Significance tests of the differences between the mean scores for these groups showed statistical significance at $p < .01$ among all three groups. The Religious Attitude Inventory was able to discriminate between individuals who hold extreme religious attitudes.

Another study (Foy et al., 1976) used two different samples to establish validity of the Religious Attitude Inventory. The first sample, consisting of 88 undergraduates from the University of Southern Mississippi, completed both the Religious Attitude Inventory and a 5-item questionnaire developed by the researchers to assess religious background and current religious practices. A correlation coefficient of .73 was obtained for the respondents' scores on these two measures.

The second sample consisted of 195 (80 males and 115 females) South Mississippi residents who completed the Religious Attitude Inventory anonymously. Consistent with other religious measures (cf. Lenski, 1953), scores of males and females differed significantly ($p < .001$), with females' scores reflecting more orthodox attitudes than males.

Location:

Ausubel, D. P., & Schpoont, S. H. (1957). Prediction of group opinion as a function of extremeness of predictor attitudes. *The Journal of Social Psychology, 46,* 19–29.

Shaw, M. E., & Wright, J. M. (1967). *Scales for the measurement of attitudes.* New York: McGraw-Hill.

Recent Research:

Dolby, J. R., Hanson, C., & Strayer, R. (1968). Personality factors and religious attitude change. *Journal for the Scientific Study of Religion, 7,* 283.

Foy, D., Lowe, J. D., Hildman, L. K., & Jacobs, K. W. (1976). Reliability, validity, and factor analysis of the Religious Attitude Inventory. *Southern Journal of Educational Research, 10,* 235–241.

Wyatt, C. S., & Johnson, R. W. (1990). The influence of counselors' religious values on clients' perceptions of the counselor. *Journal of Psychology and Theology, 18,* 158–165.

References

Ausubel, D. P., & Schpoont, S. H. (1957). Prediction of group opinion as a function of extremeness of predictor attitudes. *The Journal of Social Psychology, 46,* 19–29.

Foy, D., Lowe, J. D., Hildman, L. K., & Jacobs, K. W. (1976). Reliability, validity, and factor analysis of the Religious Attitude Inventory. *Southern Journal of Educational Research, 10,* 235–241.

Lenski, G. (1953). Social correlates of religious interest. *American Sociological Review, 18,* 533–544.

Appendix

The Religious Attitude Inventory

Respond to each of these items on a 1 to 5 scale:

1. Means that you strongly agree with a given statement.
2. Means that you tend to agree more than disagree with a given statement.
3. Means that you neither agree nor disagree with a given statement.
4. Means that you tend to disagree more than agree with a given statement.
5. Means that you strongly disagree with a given statement.

1. God made everything—the stars, the animals, and the flowers.
2. The gift of immortality has been revealed by prophets and religious teachers.
3.* The church has acted as an obstruction to the development of social justice.
4. There are many events which cannot be explained except on the basis of divine or supernatural intervention.
5.* The church is a monument to human ignorance.
6.* The idea of God is useless.
7. God hears and answers one's prayers.
8.* The soul is mere suppositions, having no better standing than a myth.
9.* The universe is merely a machine. Man and nature are creatures of cause and effect. All notions of Deity as intelligent Being or as a "spiritual force" are fictions, and prayer is a useless superstition.
10. It is by means of the church that peace and good-will may replace hatred and strife throughout the world.
11. God created man separate and distinct from the animals.

12.* The church is a harmful institution, breeding narrow-mindedness, fanaticism, and intolerance.

13. Christ, as the Gospels state, should be regarded as divine, as the human incarnation of God.

14.* There is no evidence in modern science that the natural universe of human destiny is affected by faith or prayer.

15.* The notion of retribution in a future life is due to wishful thinking.

16.* The good done by the church is not worth the money and energy spent on it.

17. The orderliness of the universe is the result of a divine plan.

18.* The church is a stronghold of much that is unwholesome and dangerous to human welfare. It fosters intolerance, bigotry, and ignorance.

19. The existence of God is proven because He revealed Himself directly to the prophets described in the Old Testament.

20. The church is the greatest influence for good government and right living.

21.* God is only a figment of one's imagination.

22. Man is a creature of faith and to live without faith in some Supreme Power is to suffer a homesickness of the soul.

23. God will, depending on how we behave on earth, reward or punish us in the world to come.

24.* People who advocate Sunday observance are religious fanatics.

25.* It is simple-minded to picture any God in control of the universe.

26. The church is the greatest agency for the uplift of the world.

27.* The idea of God is mere superstition.

28. The world was created in six solar days.

29.* The idea of God is unnecessary in our enlightened age.

30. God has good reason for everything that happens to us, even though we cannot understand it sometimes.

31. The soul lives on after the body dies.

32. The existence of God is shown by the fortunate results through approaching Him in prayer.

33.* The country would be better off if the churches were closed and the ministers were set to some useful work.

34.* The so-called spiritual experience of men cannot be distinguished from the mental and emotional, and thus there can be no transference from this world to a so-called spiritual one.

35. The first writing of the Bible was done under the guidance of God.

36.* The church is hundreds of years behind the times and can not make a dent on modern life.

37. Belief in God makes life on earth worthwhile.

38. God cares whether we repent or not.

39.* Man cannot be honest in his thinking and endorse what the church teaches.

40.* There is no life after death.

41. Since Christ brought the dead to life, He can give eternal life to all who have faith.

42.* The church represents shallowness, hypocrisy, and prejudice.

43. There is an infinitely wise, omnipotent creator of the universe, whose protection and favor may be supplicated through worship and prayer.

44.* The paternal and benevolent attitude of the church is quite distasteful to a mature person.

45.* The church deals in platitudes and is afraid to follow the logic of truth.

46. God protects from harm all those who really trust Him.

47. Immortality is certain because of Christ's sacrifice for all mankind.

48.* There is a far better way of explaining the working of the world than to assume any God.

49.* It seems absurd for a thinking man to be interested in the church.

50. The idea of God is the best explanation for our wonderful world.

*These items are negative, and the weights for their alternatives must be reversed for purposes of scoring (e.g., a response of 4 should be converted to a 2 and vice versa).

Reprinted with permission of the senior author.

2.8
RELIGIOUS ATTITUDE SCALE (Poppleton & Pilkington, 1963)
Reviewed by Anne E. Luckow

Variable: The Religious Attitude Scale was designed to measure British university students' attitudes toward the Christian religion. It assesses the degree of agreement with a series of statements regarding general tenets of Christianity, as well as the necessity of religion for life well-being and moral development. Results are set on a continuum from an overall positive to an overall negative attitude toward religion.

Description: Although the present scale was created specifically to look at the religious attitudes of students at a British university, the authors also aimed to create a measure that could be used in other research on religious attitudes. At the time of its development, other tools existed for assessing similar constructs, such as attitudes toward the church and God (Thurstone & Chave, 1929), social attitudes (Eysenck, 1947), and religious beliefs (Brown & Lowe, 1951). However, none were adequate for the au-

thors' purpose. Previous scales were directed toward a more general population, used only with American students, or were designed to obtain two distinct groups rather than a continuum of religious attitudes. In order to minimize the dimensions of belief that are included, only Christians, agnostics, and atheists were used in the development of the scale.

Construction of the scale began with a pilot study using the same population that was used in the final analyses. Results were obtained using two initial, parallel forms of the questionnaire, Form A and Form B, consisting of 22 items each. Half of the participants received Form A first and the other half Form B, with each receiving the alternate form three weeks later. The items were then analyzed, resulting in the final 21-item scale and corresponding weights for each response. The measure requires participants to indicate their degree of agreement or disagreement with statements concerning religious beliefs by using a 5-point Likert-type scale (strongly agree, agree, uncertain, disagree, strongly disagree). Scores can range from a low of 40, indicating an antireligious attitude, to a high of 130, indicating a proreligious attitude.

Practical Considerations: The Religious Attitude Scale is a brief, self-administered scale and should take approximately 15 minutes to complete. No directions are required for its administration, but scoring involves weighted responses and, therefore, a key is necessary. Because it is directed toward university students with a Christian, atheist, or agnostic background, it would not be appropriate for use with other religious populations.

Norms/Standardization: The normative sample for this scale was derived from a stratified random sample of students from the University of Sheffield. The resulting 463 participants came from all disciplines and ranged from first to fourth year of study. The majority of the sample consisted of Christians, although atheists and agnostics were also included.

Reliability: The authors used two methods to determine reliability. First, the scale was divided into three sections that were then correlated. Results of this analysis showed that the sections were correlated above .95, suggesting good internal consistency. Second, Cronbach's formula for the coefficient

alpha revealed a score of .97, again indicating good reliability for the scale.

Validity: To assess validity of the scale, respondents were divided into two groups based on reported religious activities and beliefs. The proreligious group consisted of those who indicated active church membership, church attendance more than three times in one month, and saying private prayers at least once a week. The antireligious group consisted of those who indicated their beliefs to be either atheist or agnostic. Scores on the Religious Attitude Scale did not overlap between these two groups. Those in the antireligious group had a median score of 60, whereas the proreligious group had a median score of 116, with those reporting more frequent religious activities revealing even higher scores.

Location:
   Poppleton, P., & Pilkington, G. (1963). The measurement of religious attitudes in a university population, *British Journal of Social and Clinical Psychology*, *2*, 20–36.

Subsequent Research:
   Morris, P. A. (1982). The effect of pilgrimage on anxiety, depression and religious attitude. *Psychological Medicine*, *12*, 291–294.
   Pilkington, G. W., Poppleton, P., Gould, J., & McCourt, M. (1976). Changes in religious beliefs, practices and attitudes among university students over an eleven-year period in relation to sex differences, denominational differences between faculties and years of study. *British Journal of Social and Clinical Psychology*, *15*, 1–9.

Appendix

Religious Attitude Scale

Below are 21 statements that concern religious beliefs. Please indicate the extent to which you agree or disagree with each of them. On the right-hand side of the page you will find five alternative answers. Place an "X" opposite each statement in the column that best represents your opinion.

For example:

	strongly agree	agree	undecided	disagree	strongly disagree
More time in broadcasting should be allotted to agnostic speakers.			X		

Please do not leave out any statements even if you find it difficult to make up your mind.

	strongly agree	agree	undecided	disagree	strongly disagree
1. To lead a good life it is necessary to have some religious belief. (3.15)	6	6	5	4	2
2. Jesus Christ was an important and interesting historical figure, but in no way divine. (9.84)	2	2	2	5	7
3. I genuinely do not know whether or not God exists. (5.59)	2	2	4	6	6
4. People without religious beliefs can lead just as moral and useful lives as people with religious beliefs. (6.90)	2	4	5	6	6
5. Religious faith is merely another name for belief which is contrary to reason. (10.05)	2	2	4	5	7
6. The existence of disease, famine and strife in the world makes one doubt some religious doctrines. (7.43)	2	2	4	6	6
7. The miracles recorded in the Bible really happened. (1.22)	6	6	4	2	2
8. It makes no difference to me whether religious beliefs are true or false. (6.20)	3	3	3	4	5
9. Christ atoned for our sins by His sacrifice on the cross. (0.62)	7	6	4	2	1
10. The truth of the Bible diminishes with the advance of science. (9.00)	2	2	3	6	6
11. Without belief in God life is meaningless. (0.73)	7	6	4	2	1
12. The more scientific discoveries are made the more the glory of God is revealed. (1.47)	6	6	3	2	2

	strongly agree	agree	undecided	disagree	strongly disagree
13. Religious education is essential to preserve the morals of our society. (2.64)	6	5	4	2	2
14. The proof that Christ was the Son of God lies in the record of the Gospels. (1.53)	6	6	3	2	2
15. The best explanation of miracles is as an exaggeration of ordinary events into myths and legends. (8.71)	2	2	4	6	6
16. International peace depends on the worldwide adoption of religion. (2.06)	6	6	5	3	2
17. If you lead a good and decent life, it is not necessary to go to church. (7.33)	2	3	4	6	6
18. Parents have a duty to teach elementary Christian truths to their children. (2.70)	6	5	3	2	2
19. There is no survival of any kind after death. (10.37)	1	1	2	5	7
20. The psychiatrist rather than the theologian can best explain the phenomena of religious experience. (8.88)	2	2	3	6	6
21. On the whole, religious beliefs make for better and happier living. (3.32)	6	5	3	2	2

The numbers in parentheses after each statement refer to the Thurstone scale values of the items. Values range from 0 to 11. Low values indicate proreligious and high values antireligious attitudes.

Weights are indicated by the numbers in the ruled columns and should not be included when administering this scale.

2.9
RELIGIOUS DOUBTS SCALES (Altemeyer, 1988; Hunsberger et al., 1993)

Reviewed by Raymond F. Paloutzian

Editors' Note:

The assessment of religious doubt is relatively new to the psychology of religion literature. Recently, three ways of assessing doubt have been presented, including a short religious doubts scale (Altemeyer, 1988), a series of vignettes that assess doubt rooted in a variety of circumstances (Hunsberger, McKenzie, Pratt, & Pancer, 1993), and a method of tapping doubt held in secret (Altemeyer, 1988). Each of these is briefly described below.

RELIGIOUS DOUBTS SCALE
(Altemeyer, 1988)

The Religious Doubts (RD) Scale is designed to measure the degree to which people experience doubts about traditional religious teaching. The scale is composed of ten items. Each item is answered on a six-point scale that asks the subject to indicate the extent to which he or she has had such doubts. The answer options range from 0 (none at all) to 5 (a great deal). The total score is simply the sum of the answers to the 10 items. The statements are designed to assess both intellectual and experience-based hesitations about religious belief and commitment.

In a sample of over 500 University of Manitoba psychology students and a similar-sized sample of their parents, the average interitem correlations were .32 and .36, respectively. The internal consistency reliability coefficients were .84 for the students and .86 for their parents. The mean of the single-item scores for the students was 1.89 (scale mean = 18.9); the mean for their parents was 1.45 (scale mean = 14.5). As would be expected on theoretical grounds, RD scores correlated negatively with belief in Christian orthodoxy, intrinsic religious orientation, church attendance, frequency of prayer, loyalty to beliefs acquired during childhood, belief in a final judgment, control of impulses, obedience to authority, and a belief in Satan. RD scores correlated positively with extrinsic religious orientation and the importance of being good over holding beliefs. These trends occurred in both the parents' and students' samples.

The interitem correlations, internal consistency reliability coefficients, and pattern of relationships attained with other measures suggest that the Religious Doubts Scale has good statistical properties and shows promise for use in subsequent research. It has recently been replaced by a 20-item version (Altemeyer & Hunsberger, 1997) that asks respondents to indicate both (a) the extent to which they have ever had questions about religion because of the issues raised and (b) the extent to which they presently doubt religion because of these matters.

Location:

Altemeyer, B., (1988). *Enemies of freedom: Understanding right-wing authoritarianism*. San Francisco: Jossey-Bass.

Altemeyer, B., & Hunsberger, B. (1997). *Changed lives*. Amherst, NY: Prometheus Press.

Appendix A

The Religious Doubts Scale

Below are listed reasons that people sometimes give for doubting traditional religious teachings. Please indicate the extent to which you have had these doubts.

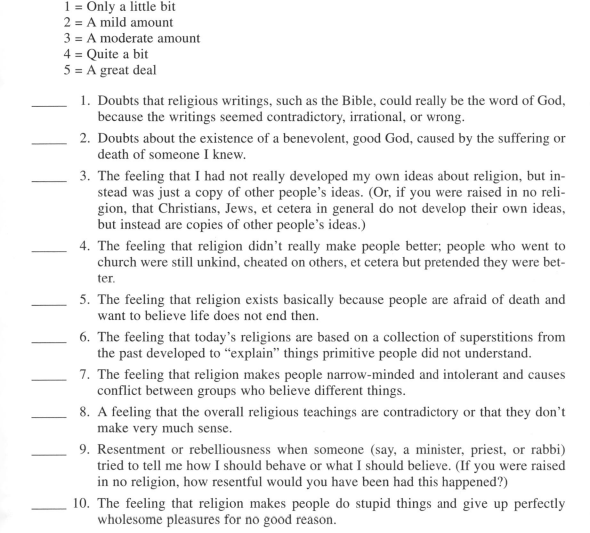

0 = None at all
1 = Only a little bit
2 = A mild amount
3 = A moderate amount
4 = Quite a bit
5 = A great deal

_____ 1. Doubts that religious writings, such as the Bible, could really be the word of God, because the writings seemed contradictory, irrational, or wrong.

_____ 2. Doubts about the existence of a benevolent, good God, caused by the suffering or death of someone I knew.

_____ 3. The feeling that I had not really developed my own ideas about religion, but instead was just a copy of other people's ideas. (Or, if you were raised in no religion, that Christians, Jews, et cetera in general do not develop their own ideas, but instead are copies of other people's ideas.)

_____ 4. The feeling that religion didn't really make people better; people who went to church were still unkind, cheated on others, et cetera but pretended they were better.

_____ 5. The feeling that religion exists basically because people are afraid of death and want to believe life does not end then.

_____ 6. The feeling that today's religions are based on a collection of superstitions from the past developed to "explain" things primitive people did not understand.

_____ 7. The feeling that religion makes people narrow-minded and intolerant and causes conflict between groups who believe different things.

_____ 8. A feeling that the overall religious teachings are contradictory or that they don't make very much sense.

_____ 9. Resentment or rebelliousness when someone (say, a minister, priest, or rabbi) tried to tell me how I should behave or what I should believe. (If you were raised in no religion, how resentful would you have been had this happened?)

_____ 10. The feeling that religion makes people do stupid things and give up perfectly wholesome pleasures for no good reason.

Altemeyer, B. (1988). *Enemies of freedom*. San Francisco: Jossey-Bass. Copyright © 1988 Jossey-Bass, Inc. Reprinted with permission.

DOUBTS VIGNETTES (Hunsberger, McKenzie, Pratt, & Pancer, 1993)

Philosophical discussion and life experience suggest to us that there may be a variety of root causes of religious doubt. For example, one person may doubt because of apparent conflicts between religion and science, while another may doubt as a response to personal tragedy.

In order to assess the degree to which various sources of doubt are germane to a partic-

ular case, Hunsberger, McKenzie, Pratt, and Pancer (1993) wrote a set of short vignettes, each of which is intended to be sensitive to a different reason for doubting. Ten vignettes were prepared. The subject was instructed to read each one and then answer the following question: "How much religious doubt does this type of issue arouse for you?" Response alternatives could range from 0 (no doubt at all) to 10 (a great deal of doubt).

The ten vignettes assessed doubt rooted in the following causes: science versus religion controversy, a specific event such as the death of a close friend, truth claims of other religions, challenges to traditional teachings by scholars of religion, violation of self-interest such as unanswered prayer, shortcomings of organized religion, the idea that God may be a mere human projection, the failure of religious claims such as faith healing, and the perception that there is no need for God in attempts to explain the universe.

Responses to all of the vignettes correlated positively with the response to a single item, "If you were brought up under some religious influence, to what extent have you doubted the religious beliefs taught?" Responses to 8 of the 10 vignettes correlated negatively with religious emphasis during childhood; the remaining 2 correlations were almost 0. The correlations between the scores for all vignettes and present and past church attendance were negative. These trends also held for the total vignette score.

These findings suggest that this methodology for measuring doubt, particularly its ability to pinpoint the particular source of that doubt, has potential for future research.

Location:
Hunsberger, B., McKenzie, B., Pratt, M., & Pancer, S. M. (1993). Religious doubt: A social psychological analysis. In M. Lynn & D. Moberg (Eds.), *Research in the Social Scientific Study of Religion* (Vol. 5, pp. 27–51). Greenwich, CT: JAI Press.

Appendix B

Doubt Vignettes

1. Darwin's theory of evolution has gained a good deal of acceptance in the scientific community. Can Darwin's theory and the Bible's story of creation both be accepted? (*Scientific doubt*)

2. Suppose that a very close friend, an excellent student, who has been enjoying fine health, has been killed in a car accident. How can you explain such an incident relative to God's being a loving God? (*Doubt generated by a specific event*)

3. There are many different world religions, including Hinduism, Judaism, Buddhism, Islam, and Christianity. Many of these are very old and established, having many believers, and all seem to claim having "the truth." How do you deal with this, based on your religious beliefs? (*Religion as self-deception*)

4. The Bible says that "God is love" (John 4:7). Life often seems to make that a lie, especially if God is believed to be all-powerful. Natural disasters occur where thousands and millions die. The famine in Africa is an example of such massive disasters. Has this ever made you doubt that God is all-loving or that He exists at all? (*Doubt generated by specific events*)

5. Many modern biblical scholars believe that many of the recorded sayings of Jesus were spoken by others, not by Jesus. These scholars suggest that many of the events in Jesus' life as recorded in the Gospels were probably myths used by the Gospel writers to increase the believability of what they wrote. Has any of this ever crossed your mind? (*Referential doubt*)

6. If often seems that prayers go unanswered. The words don't go beyond the ceiling; they float into the air and are blown away by the merest breeze. Has this happened to you? (*Violation of self-interest*)

7. The Bible teaches that the second commandment is to "love your neighbor as yourself." History shows that in the name of Christ, many atrocities have been committed. The war between the Protestants and Catholics in Ireland might be an example of Christians' hypocritically practicing their faith. Does this ever cause you to doubt Christianity? (*Shortcomings of organized religion*)

8. Some people question the basis of religious beliefs, considering them to be man's creation to explain how we came to be, rather than the divine inspiration of God as the Bible

would have us believe. To believe in God is thus really just a way of deceiving ourselves. (*God as a projection*)

9. Faith healers become well-known quickly, and reportedly "cure" serious physical illness. Often, however, such healings simply don't occur. The healer is unsuccessful. Has this ever caused you to doubt that God can heal? (*Ritual doubt*)

10. The more that scientists discover about the universe, the more it might seem that God is not present. There seems to be no physical place for heaven or hell, and in fact, science seems to explain the universe without any need to bring up the concept of "God." Has this ever crossed your mind? Have you ever doubted the existence of God? (*Reactive and negativistic doubt*)

Hunsberger, B., McKenzie, B., Pratt, M., & Pancer, S. M. (1993). Religious doubt: A social-psychological analysis. In M. Lynn & D. Moberg (Eds.), *Research in the Social Scientific Study of Religion* (Vol. 5, pp. 27–51). Greenwich, CT: JAI Press. Copyright © 1993 JAI Press. Reprinted with permission.

SECRET DOUBTS (Altemeyer, 1988)

The above two ways of measuring doubt enable us to assess those hesitancies about religion that people can easily admit. But some people may have *secret* doubts about what they have been taught that they have never shared with another person. These would naturally be difficult to access, but Altemeyer (1988, pp. 152–153) developed a clever methodology for getting a glimpse of them.

Over 400 students in his general psychology course had learned about the "Hidden Observer" phenomenon in hypnosis research. The Hidden Observer is a technique used in hypnosis research to see if subjects will reveal experiences that the hypnotist has told them do not exist. For example, your arm may be submerged in a bucket of ice water, which ought to feel very painful, but your hypnotized self feels no conscious pain (due to hypnotic suggestion to feel no pain). However, the Hidden Observer is aware that it hurts and can admit such if asked. With this knowledge about the "Hidden Observer" phenomenon as a background, the students were later given the instructions contained in Appendix C.

Of the 200 subjects for whom Altemeyer reports data, 101 high (top quartile) and 99 low (bottom quartile) in right-wing authoritarianism, one fourth (50) of them said that the Hidden Observer indicated "secret doubts that s/he had kept strictly to her/himself." The high authoritarians are more likely to firmly adhere to conservative religious beliefs. Yet for them, the Hidden Observer expressed secret doubts, ones that had never been shared with another person, at a rate of approximately one third. This method can be adapted in order to explore feelings, opinions, or tendencies that a person or group may not be inclined to openly discuss.

Location:

Altemeyer, B. (1988). *Enemies of freedom: Understanding right-wing authoritarianism*. San Francisco: Jossey-Bass.

Appendix C

Secret Doubts Scale

INSTRUCTIONS

You may recall the lecture on hypnosis dealing with Hilgard's research on the "Hidden Observer." Suppose there is a Hidden Observer in you, which knows your every thought and deed, but which only speaks when it is safe to do so, and when directly spoken to. This question is for your Hidden Observer: Does this person (that is, you) have doubts that (s)he was created by an Almighty God who will judge each person and take some into heaven for eternity while casting others into hell forever?

Choose one of the following answers:

_____   Yes, (s)he has secret doubts which (s)he has kept strictly to herself/himself that this is really true.

_____   Yes, (s)he has such doubts, but others (such as parents and friends) know (s)he has these doubts.

_____   No, (s)he totally believes this, and has *no doubts* whatsoever.

_____   Yes, in fact (s)he openly says (s)he *does not believe* there is a God or an afterlife, but (s)he has some secret worries there might be.

_____   Yes, in fact (s)he openly says (s)he *does not believe* there is a God or an afterlife, and (s)he has no doubts about this whatsoever.

(emphasis in original)

Altemeyer, B. (1988). *Enemies of freedom.* San Francisco: Jossey-Bass. Coyright © 1988 Jossey-Bass, Inc. Reprinted with permission.

2.10
RELIGIOUS PRESSURES SCALE (Altemeyer, 1988)
Reviewed by Bruce Hunsberger

Variable: The Religious Pressures Scale (RPS) measures the extent to which a person might feel pressure to remain religious in the face of doubts about religious teachings. The scale is intended to be a companion to Altemeyer's (1988) Religious Doubts scale, also reviewed in this volume. The RPS was developed in the context of Altemeyer's work on right-wing authoritarianism and its link with religion (Altemeyer's, 1988).

Description: Respondents are asked to indicate the extent to which they have had 10 feelings of pressure about religion, using a 6-point response format. Response alternatives include 0 (none at all), 1 (only a little bit), 2 (a mild amount), 3 (a moderate amount), 4 (quite a bit), and 5 (a great deal). The total scale score is determined by a summation of the 10 item scores.

Practical Considerations: This paper-and-pencil measure is straightforward to use, requiring no special examiner skill to administer, score, or interpret. The test has been used both with university students and their

parents in Canada. It appears to be suitable for adolescent through adult samples in similar cultures.

Norms/Standardization: Two primary samples were used in the initial work with this scale. Four hundred twenty-three introductory psychology students completed the scale as part of a course research bonus credit system. Also, 506 of these students' parents responded to the scale, which was part of a questionnaire package sent and returned by regular mail. Average scores on the scale were 18.1 for the students and 21.1 for the parents; variance was 154 and 218 for students and parents, respectively (Altemeyer, 1988).

Reliability: For the university student sample, the average interitem correlation for these 10 items was .47, with a resulting Cronbach's alpha of .90. For the sample of parents, the mean interitem correlation was .54 and Cronbach's alpha was .92.

Validity: Altemeyer (1988) provided documentation regarding correlations between the RPS and other measures of religion and authoritarianism. These relationships are in the expected directions and are robust and highly significant. For example, correlations between Religious Pressures scores and other measures developed by Altemeyer (1988), for the student and parent samples respectively, were the following: Right-Wing Authoritarianism (.47, .50), Religious Emphasis (in the childhood home) (.59, .43), and Religious Doubts (−.36, −.25). Comparable correlations for other scales included Fullerton and Hunsberger's (1982) Christian Orthodoxy scale (.69, .58), and Allport and Ross' (1967) Intrinsic Religious Orientation (.69, .64) and Extrinsic Religious Orientation (−.23, −.30) scales. The correlations with a single-item measure of church attendance were .60 and .57 for the two groups respectively.

Further, Altemeyer found that highly religious persons reported feeling under considerable pressure to maintain their religious beliefs. This information is indirectly related to validity issues in the sense that one might expect highly religious persons to report relatively strong and specific pressures to maintain their religious beliefs. Item analyses indicated that, among his student sample, the strongest reported pressures for highly religious people were the following: parental disappointment and disapproval (*M* = 4.27, where the highest possible answer was 5.00) and fear of disappointing religious authorities (*M* = 4.15). They were also reportedly afraid that they would feel lost, adrift, having lost their anchor in life (*M* = 3.29), they were ashamed that they had not been strong enough to keep their faith (*M* = 3.12), and they feared punishment from God (*M* = 2.95) if they ceased to believe. Among the highly religious parents, the strongest pressures were disappointment/disapproval by ministers (*M* = 4.34), their children (*M* = 4.22), and their spouses (*M* = 3.97). They also reported that they would feel adrift (*M* = 4.21) and ashamed (*M* = 3.77) and that they would have betrayed the ultimate purpose of their lives (*M* = 3.72).

Location:
Altemeyer, B. (1988). *Enemies of Freedom: Understanding right-wing authoritarianism*. San Francisco: Jossey-Bass.

Subsequent Research: None.

References

Allport, G. W., & Ross, J. M. (1967). Personal religious orientation and prejudice. *Journal of Personality and Social Psychology, 5*, 432–443.

Altemeyer, B. (1988). *Enemies of Freedom: Understanding right-wing authoritarianism*. San Francisco: Jossey-Bass.

Fullerton, J. T., & Hunsberger, B. E. (1982). A unidimensional measure of Christian Orthodoxy. *Journal for the Scientific Study of Religion, 21*, 317–326.

Appendix

The Religious Pressures Scale

What do you suppose it would cost you if you dropped your religion and became an agnostic or atheist? How much of the below do you think you would experience? (If you have dropped your religion and would now say you have "none," answer according to how you felt right at the time you decided to stop believing in that religion.)

    0 = none at all
    1 = only a little bit
    2 = a mild amount
    3 = a moderate amount
    4 = quite a bit
    5 = a great deal

1. Disappointment, disapproval of parents.
2. Disappointment, disapproval of close friends.
3. Disappointment, disapproval of ministers, priests, et cetera.
4. It would threaten a romantic love relationship.
5. I would feel lost, adrift; I'd have lost my "anchor" in life.
6. I would fear punishment from God.
7. I would fear that without my religious beliefs I would become an evil person.
8. I would be ashamed that I had not been strong enough to keep my faith.
9. I would feel I had betrayed the ultimate purpose of my life.
10. I would fear being damned and condemned to everlasting fire in hell.

Note. Item 1 is used with student samples. On the parent sample this item was changed to "Disappointment, disapproval of your children. (How much would your children disapprove of such a change?)"

Altemeyer, B. (1988). *Enemies of freedom.* San Francisco: Jossey-Bass. Coyright © 1988 Jossey-Bass, Inc. Reprinted with permission.

2.11
RELIGIOUS VALUES SCALE (Morrow, Worthington, & McCullough, 1993)
Reviewed by Steven J. Sandage

Variable: The Religious Values Scale (RVS) measures individuals' religious attitudes and beliefs and the degree to which she can tolerate others' holding different religious values. The scale consists of seven subscales: religious commitment, authority afforded sacred writings, authority afforded religious group identification, authority afforded religious leaders, tolerance for others holding different views on Scripture, tolerance for those with different group identification, and tolerance for those with different views regarding the authority of religious leaders.

Description: This scale is based on Worthington's (1988) model for understanding the values of highly religious clients of psychotherapy. In Worthington's model, clients who are highly committed to their religion will evaluate their interpersonal worlds in terms of three primary value dimensions. These value dimensions are the authority afforded to sacred writings, the authority afforded to religious leaders, and the degree of identification with his or her religious group. In addition, Worthington (1988) adds the notion that each person has a "zone of tolerance" handling the inevitable differences of opinion that occur in this diverse society.

The RVS is composed of 62 items that are scored on the same 5-point Likert continuum scale, with 1 indicating "not at all true of me" and 5 indicating "totally true of me." The subscale item totals are as follows: religious commitment (20 items), authority afforded sacred writings (11 items), authority afforded religious leaders (8 items), authority afforded religious group identification (8 items), tolerance for different scriptural beliefs (3 items), tolerance for different views of leadership (3 items), and tolerance for different religious groups (3 items).

Practical Considerations: No special skills are required to administer or score this paper-and-pencil measure. McCullough and Worthington (1995) divided participants into high and low levels on each of Worthington and colleagues' (1988) seven constructs based on the means and standard deviations of their present sample of students. Specific directions for administration and scoring can be found in the set of materials available on request from Dr. Worthington at Virginia Commonwealth University.

Norms/Standardization: Three primary norm samples have been used. All three samples were composed of undergraduate student volunteers at a large southeastern university. The first sample (Worthington et al., 1988) consisted of 257 students with most being of 18 to 25 years old (88%). The racial composition of this sample was 197 Caucasian (78%), 43 African-American (17%), and 11 other ethnicity (5%). African-Americans in this sample were significantly more religious than Caucasians on six of the seven subscales.

The second sample (Worthington et al., 1989) consisted of 252 students. Since the theory is thought to apply only to highly religious people, only the top one third of the sample were selected based on their scores according to religious commitment.

The third sample (McCullough & Worthington, 1995) consisted of 148 students. The racial composition of this sample was 104 Caucasian (70%), 29 African-American (21%), 6 Asian (4%), and 9 other ethnicity (5%). Collectively, these three groups formed the standardization sample.

Reliability: With the first sample (Worthington et al., 1988), estimates of internal consistency using Cronbach's alpha were calculated for the seven empirical factors found through principle components factor analysis with varimax rotation. A factor loading of .45 was considered the minimum for inclusion of an item on a factor. The tolerance for those holding different views of Scripture scale was not supported and was replaced by a factor labeled "preference for a counselor of similar attitudes." Cronbach's alphas for the seven factors ranged from .99 for religious commitment to .47 for preference for a counselor of similar attitudes.

In the second sample (Worthington et al., 1989), estimates of internal consistency were generally higher and were calculated for the six scales corresponding to the original theory (Worthington, 1988). Cronbach's alphas ranged from .84 for authority afforded sacred writings to .64 for tolerance for others holding different views on Scripture. Individual item-to-scale correlation were reported, and

items with low item to total scale correlations were dropped from analysis.

In the third sample (McCullough & Worthington, 1995), estimates of internal consistency were calculated for the seven original subscales. Cronbach's alphas ranged from .92 for the religious commitment subscale to .73 for the authority afforded religious groups and the tolerance for different views of leadership subscales.

Validity: Worthington et al. (1988) examined the construct validity of the RVS by conducting principle components factor analysis using varimax rotation. The principle components analysis found seven factors and generally supported the theoretical factor structure.

Pearson correlations were also calculated between each scale of the RVS and self-reports of church attendance, attendance at other church meetings, participation in religious leadership, and number of leadership positions held. Of the 28 correlations, 25 were significant ($p = .01$).

The RVS scales were correlated with the 11 subscales of the Basic Religiosity Scales (King & Hunt, 1972). Of 77 correlations, 74 were significant ($p = .01$), with most correlations ranging between .4 and .8.

The RVS scales were also correlated with the four subscales of Glock and Stark's (1965) scale. No significant correlations were found between the seven RVS scales and biblical knowledge. Of the religious belief, practice, and experience subscales, 19 of 21 correlations were significant.

Worthington et al. (1989) conducted confirmatory factor analysis of the RVS. The goodness of fit index of .61 was below the acceptable value of .9, so the theoretical model was not supported.

The same data was subjected to exploratory factor analysis. Eight factors were identified. The scale that was thought to measure the authority of Scripture appeared to include two components—a value of Scripture in daily life and a doctrinal belief in the authority of Scripture. The scale thought to measure authority of group identification appeared to include two components, also—personally valuing the group and looking to the group to provide norms for behavior. The scale thought to measure the authority afforded religious leaders was supported. The hypothetical structure of tolerance for people with different religious views was not validated. Instead, the three factors revealed showed a preference for similarly religious people who (1) give advice, (2) give counsel, and (3) provide affiliation. Overall, it is clear that reasonable efforts have been exerted to establish the reliablility and validity of the RVS.

Location: For a copy of the Religious Values Scale, contact

>   Dr. Everett Worthington Jr.
>   Department of Psychology
>   Virginia Commonwealth University
>   808 West Franklin Street
>   Richmond, VA 23284-2018

Subsequent Research:

McCullough, M. E., & Worthington, E. L., Jr. (1995). College students' perceptions of a psychotherapist's treatment of a religious issue: Partial replication and extension. *Journal of Counseling and Development, 73,* 626–34.

References

Glock, C., & Stark, R. (1965). *Religion and society in tension.* Chicago: Rand McNally.

King, M. B., & Hunt, R. A. (1972). Measuring the religious variable: Replication. *Journal for the Scientific Study of Religion, 11,* 240–251.

Morrow, D., Worthington, E. L., & McCullough, M. E. (1993). Observers' perceptions of a counselor's treatment of a religious issue. *Journal of Counseling and Development, 71,* 452–456.

Worthington, E. L., Jr. (1988). Understanding the values of religious clients: A model and its application to counseling. *Journal of Counseling Psychology, 35,* 166–174.

Worthington, E. L., Jr., Hsu, K., Gowda, K. K., & Bleach, E. (1988, November). *Preliminary tests of Worthington's (1988) theory of important values in religious counseling.* Paper presented at the First International Congress on Christian Counseling, Atlanta.

Worthington, E. L., Jr., Berry, J. T., Hsu, K., Gowda, K. K., Bleach, E., & Bursley, K. H. (1989, October). *Measuring religious values: Factor analytic study of the Religious Values Survey.* Paper presented at the meeting of the Virginia Psychological Association, Richmond.

Appendix

Religious Values Scale

Instructions: After each of the following 62 statements circle one of the numbers (1 through 5) that best describes how true the statement is of you.

>   1 = Not at all true of me   4 = Mostly true of me
>   2 = Somewhat true of me   5 = Totally true of me
>   3 = Moderately true of me

1. I am concerned that my behavior and speech reflect the teachings of my religion.

2. I do not accept what I hear in regard to religious beliefs without first questioning the validity of it.

3. It is important to me to conform to my religious standards of behavior.

4. I enjoy spending time with others of my religious affiliation.

5. Religious beliefs influence all my dealings in life.

6. It is important to me to spend periods of time in private religious thought and meditation.

7. I feel there are many more important things in life than religion.

8. I enjoy working in the activities of my religious organization.

9. I keep well informed about my local religious group and I have some influence on its decisions.

10. I make financial contributions to my religious organization.

11. I often read books and magazines about my faith.

12. I spend time trying to grow in understanding of my faith.

13. I have personally tried to convert someone to my faith.

14. I talk about my religion with friends, neighbors, or fellow workers.

15. Religion is especially important to me because it answers many questions about the meaning of life.

16. My religious beliefs lie behind my whole approach to life.

17. I would break fellowship with my local religious group if there were things being said of me that are damaging and untrue.

18. I am willing to be persecuted for my religious beliefs.

19. My living environment (room, apartment, house, office) reflects my religious beliefs (i.e., posters, plaques, bumper stickers).

20. I would publicly defend my religious beliefs.

21. I believe the scriptures of my faith are completely true.

22. I think it is important to obey my faith's scripture.

23. My faith's scriptures have practical value in the modern world.

24. I read my faith's scriptures almost every day.

25. I memorize my faith's scriptures.

26. I depend on my faith's scriptures to help me make decisions in conflict situations.

27. I have experienced the usefulness of my faith's scriptures in my daily life.

28. It is important to understand the historical significance of my faith's scriptures.

29. I understand my faith's scriptures.

30. I like to study my faith's scriptures.

31. I believe that my faith's scriptures are important but other books of wisdom are equally important.

32. I enjoy being with people whose attitudes toward my faith's scriptures are similar to my own.

33. I prefer to take advice from people whose attitude toward my faith's scriptures is similar to my own.

34. If I went to counseling, I would like a counselor whose attitude toward my faith's scriptures is similar to mine.

35. What other members of my religious group expect of me is important.

36. I avoid doing things that members of my local religious group would disapprove of.

37. I feel accepted by the members of my local religious group.

38. I share the goals of the members of my local religious group.

39. The standards of my local religious group guide me in making decisions.
40. If I have a conflict with what my local religious group tells me is right, I go along with the religious group.
41. I couldn't get along without involvement in my local religious group.
42. Being recognized by non-members as a member of my local religious group gives me a good feeling.
43. I can get along with the goals of my local religious group but not with the overall goals of the whole organization (e.g., national or world-wide religious group).
44. I prefer the local chapter of my religious group to the larger overall organization.
45. The goals of my local religious organization are the same as the goals of the entire organization.
46. It is more important to me to belong to a particular part of my religious group than to think of myself as merely Christian or Jewish or Muslim (or other faith).
47. I enjoy being with people in my local religious group more than people who are not in that group.
48. I enjoy being with people who belong to my overall religious organization.
49. I prefer not to take advice from people outside my local religious group.
50. I prefer not to take advice from people outside my overall religious organization.
51. If I went to counseling, I would like a counselor whose faith is similar to mine.
52. It is a religious duty for me to obey governmental authorities.
53. One should follow the guidance of one's pastor, priest, or rabbi without question or complaint.
54. It is a religious obligation for children to obey their parents.
55. Husbands should exercise wise, loving authority over their wives.
56. It is a religious obligation even for adults to obey their parents.
57. When counselors make suggestions, they should be obeyed.
58. When the board of elders (or the leaders of a local religious group) take a stand, the congregation should follow their leading.
59. One should obey the leader(s) of one's organized religion (e.g., Pope, President of denomination, or other leader).
60. I enjoy being with people who share my attitudes toward human authorities.
61. I prefer not to take advice from people whose attitudes toward human authorities differs from my own.
62. If I went in to counseling, I would like a counselor whose attitude toward human authorities is similar to mine.

Reprinted with permission of the authors.

2.12

THE SOCIAL-RELIGIOUS-POLITICAL SCALE (KATZ, 1984, 1988)

Reviewed by Leslie J. Francis

Variable: The Social-Religious-Political Scale was designed to measure social, religious, and political attitudes of adult respondents. The two axes of the scale are defined as liberal and conservative. The fundamental difference between the liberal position and the conservative position concerns the extent to which the respondent is open to individuals from other religious denominations or political persuasions.

Description: The author began by collating approximately 200 items from various attitude scales as well as adding original items pertinent to the constructs under consideration. These items were presented to 10 judges who were requested to judge the face validity of the items. A total of 60 items survived this process: 20 relevant to social attitudes, 20 relevant to political attitudes, and 20 relevant to religious attitudes.

Originally compiled in English, the instrument was translated into Afrikaans. The development of the present instrument emerged from factor analyses of the responses of 210 white South African teacher trainees, 110 of whom were English speakers and 100 Afrikaans speakers, as well as 100 undergraduates, 50 of whom spoke English and 50 Afrikaans. Factor analysis identified two factors, one of which was labeled "religious attitudes" and the other of which was labeled "sociopolitical attitudes."

In its present form the scale contains 20 items. Each item is assessed on a 5-point scale ranging from 1 to 5. The five points are anchored as follows: 1 = strongly agree, 2 = agree, 3 = uncertain, 4 = disagree, 5 = strongly disagree. The first group of 12 items is concerned with the importance of religious affiliation; the second group of 8 items is concerned with the importance of political persuasion. Scale scores are computed as the product of the two separate sets of items. This means that scores on the reli-

gious subscale range between 12 and 60 and scores on the social-political subscale range between 8 and 40. In both cases a low score indicates a conservative attitude and a high score indicates a liberal attitude.

Practical Considerations: This paper-and-pencil measure requires no special examiner skill to administer, score, or interpret. Minimal instructions are provided. Face validity of the scale is high in that items are clearly related to either the religious or the political dimension. The clear assumption of the items is that the individual respondents are both religiously and politically committed. The scale may appear inappropriate when these assumptions are not met.

Norms/Standardization: Using the original sample of 310 white South African students, a principal components analysis with varimax rotation was performed on the data. Salient item loadings were set at the .30 level; factors with an eigenvalue greater than 1.00 and explaining more than 10% of the variance were retained. A scree-test served as an additional criterion. The author has published no normative scores from this sample.

Reliability: The author reports alpha reliability coefficients of .92 for the whole scale, and .94 and .93 for the religious attitudes and sociopolitical attitudes subscales respectively. Individual item-to-subscale correlations were not reported. Factor loadings on the religious attitudes subscale ranged between .30 and .75. Factor loadings on the sociopolitical subscale ranged between .31 and .73. It needs to be stated, however, that these published figures are for a 25-item version of the instrument rather than for the 20-item instrument provided by the author.

Validity: No data have been provided on the validity of the scale in addition to the self-evident face validity suggested by the items themselves.

Location:

Katz, Y. J. (1984). *The influence of some attitudes on intelligence.* Unpublished Ph.D. dissertation, University of the Witwatersrand.

Katz, Y. J. (1988). A validation of the social-religious-political scale. *Educational and Psychological Measurement, 48,* 1025–1028.

Subsequent Research: The instrument has not been employed in any subsequent research. An earlier and shorter version was used by Katz (1976) in the medium of Hebrew.

Katz, Y. J. (1976). *An investigation of social integration after the establishment of junior high schools in the Israeli educational system.* Unpublished M.A. dissertation, Bar-Ilan University, Israel.

Appendix

The Social-Religious-Political Scale

Please use the following scale to answer each item below.

1 = strongly agree	4 = disagree
2 = agree	5 = strongly disagree
3 = uncertain	

1. I am often conscious of my affiliation to a certain religious denomination.

2. My religious denomination is morally superior to other religious denominations.

3. I prefer to work in the company of people belonging to my religious denomination.

4. I like to spend my leisure time with members of my religious denomination only.

5. My family objects to my befriending members of religious denominations different from mine.

6. I have no social relationships with members of religious denominations other than mine.

7. It should be forbidden for members of one religious denomination to marry members of another religious denomination.

8. When I consider forging a friendship with a person I have just met, I always take his religious denomination into consideration.

9. When choosing a home it is important to take the religious denomination of the neighbors into consideration.

10. When considering marriage it is important to take the religious affiliation of one's future spouse into consideration.

11. Praise heaped on a member of my religious denomination gratifies me personally.

12. I generally find a common bond with members of my religious denomination only.

13. My political persuasion is morally superior to other political persuasions.

14. I prefer to work in the company of people belonging to my political persuasion.

15. I would like to spend my leisure time with members of my political persuasion only.

16. I have no social relationships with members of political persuasions other than mine.

17. When I consider forging a friendship with a person I have just met, I always take his political persuasion into consideration.

18. When choosing a home it is important to take the political persuasions of the neighbors into consideration.

19. Praise heaped on someone of my political persuasion gratifies me personally.

20. I generally find a common bond with members of my political persuasion only.

Reprinted with permission of the author.

2.13
SPIRITUAL AND RELIGIOUS CONCERNS QUESTIONNAIRE
(Silber & Reilly, 1985)

Reviewed by Steven J. Sandage

Variable: The Spiritual and Religious Concerns Questionnaire (SRQ) measures the spiritual and religious beliefs, attitudes, needs, and behaviors of adolescents. The scale was designed to assess the spiritual and religious concerns of newly hospitalized patients in an adolescent inpatient unit. The main purpose of the scale is to provide clinically useful information that might prove useful to caregivers in delivering more focused and wholistic services.

Description: The SRQ is not based on any particular theoretical orientation. Silber and Reilly (1985) asserted that the intensity of an adolescent's spiritual and religious concerns would increase following hospitalization in proportion to the severity of his or her illness.

The SRQ consists of 11 items scored on a 9-point Likert continuum scale with 1 indicating low spiritual and/or religious concern and 9 indicating high spiritual and/or religious concern. The Likert response categories are not consistent across items. The overall SRQ score is obtained by averaging all eleven items. The authors included a final item asking patients if they "would like help with any of your spiritual and/or religious concerns." This item was answered yes or no and space was provided to specify the kind of help desired.

Practical Considerations: Silber and Reilly (1985) used trained volunteers to administer the SRQ. No guidelines were offered on required reading level or time of administration. The authors do not describe any spe-cial instructions for administration, but it would seem important that the purpose and rationale for giving the scale should be explained to hospitalized adolescents.

Norms/Standardization: Specialized norms for the SRQ have not been developed. The original sample consisted of 114 newly hospitalized adolescents in an adolescent inpatient unit. The participants ranged in age from 11 to 19 years of age with equal representation in early (11-13 years), middle (14-15 years), and late (16-19 years) adolescence categories. Thirty-nine participants were male and 75 were female. The ethnic composition of the sample consisted of 58 African-American, 54 Caucasian, and 2 Asian participants. The vast majority (92) of the participants attended a public school. Participants were separated into three categories of severity of illness, including (a) severe with high probability of being fatal (24 patients), (b) severe (53 patients), (c) moderate (37 patients).

Mean scores on the SRQ ranged from a low of 2.45 for early adolescents to a high of 2.94 for older adolescents. This trend was not statistically significant. Mean scores for females (2.59) were significantly higher than mean scores for males (2.33). African-Americans had higher mean scores (2.58) than Caucasians (2.41). The most seriously ill participants had higher SRQ scores regardless of gender or ethnicity.

Reliability: No analysis of the reliability of the SRQ was reported.

Validity: Silber and Reilly (1985) were particularly interested in the relationship between changes in adolescent spiritual and/or religious concerns and severity of illness. Item 3 assesses changes in the patient's spiritual and/or religious concerns since his or her illness began, and item 10 assesses changes in frequency of prayer since entering the hospital. There was a significant severity of illness trend for scores on both of these items, with higher scores indicating more serious illness. The wording of item 3 inquires about changes in spiritual and/or religious concerns "since your illness began," not since hospitalization. This presents an inconsistency in that a patient's illness may have begun well before hospital-ization. The measure appears to have fine "face validity."

Location:
   Silber, T. J., & Reilly, M. (1985). Spiritual and religious concerns of the hospitalized adolescent. *Adolescence, 20*, 217–224.

Subsequent Research: Silber indicated through personal communication that he is currently working on further validation of the SRQ. Information about the SRQ can be obtained by contacting
   Tomas J. Silber, M.D.
   Department of Adolescent Medicine
   Children's Medical Center
   10011 Michigan Ave. NW
   Washington, DC 20010

Appendix

Patient Questionnaire on Spiritual and Religious Concerns (SRQ)

1. Sex:
2. Age:
3. Race:
4. School:
5. Religious affiliation:
6. Medical diagnosis:

7. While you are in the hospital, how often do you talk about spiritual and/or religious concerns?

   1   2   3   4   5   6   7   8   9
   Never   Average   Very Often

8. Do you consider yourself a person with spiritual and/or religious concerns?

   1   2   3   4   5   6   7   8   9
   Not religious   Average   Very religious
   and/or spiritual   and/or spiritual
   at all

9. Have you had any changes in your concerns relating to spiritual and/or religious matters since your illness began?

   1   2   3   4   5   6   7   8   9
   Much less   No change   Much more
   interested   interested

10. Do you believe in God (Supreme Being)?

   1   2   3   4   5   6   7   8   9
   I don't   I sometimes   I believe
   believe   believe   firmly

11. If you believe in God (Supreme Being), how do you feel toward God (Supreme Being)?

1	2	3	4	5	6	7	8	9
Angry, abandoned				Indifferent, don't care				Confident, grateful

12. Have your feelings toward God (Supreme Being) changed since your illness began?

1	2	3	4	5	6	7	8	9
I feel negative about God (Supreme Being)				No change				I feel more positive about God (Supreme Being)

13. Mark the numeral you feel relates best to your illness.

1	2	3	4	5	6	7	8	9
God (Supreme Being) has nothing to do with my illness				I don't know if God (Supreme Being) is involved in my illness				God (Supreme Being) willed my illness

14. How often do you pray?

1	2	3	4	5	6	7	8	9
Never				Sometimes				Often

15. Since you have come to the hospital, do you pray?

1	2	3	4	5	6	7	8	9
Less than before				Unchanged				More than before

16. If you pray about illness answer the following question:
Prayer has helped . . .

1	2	3	4	5	6	7	8	9
Not at all				Some				Very much

17. How often do you participate in organized spiritual and/or religious activities?

1	2	3	4	5	6	7	8	9
Never				Average				Very often (at least weekly)

18. Would you like help with any of your spiritual and/or religious concerns?
_____ Yes (If yes, what kind of help?)   _____ No

Silber, T. J., & Reilly, M. (1985). Spiritual and religious concerns of the hospitalized adolescent. *Adolescence, 20,* 217–224. Copyright © 1985 Libro Publications, Inc. Reprinted with permission.

Chapter 3

Scales of Religious Orientation

Note: The editors are indebted to Christopher Burris, who wrote portions of this introduction as background material in his review of the Allport and Ross Religious Orientation Scale (3.9). It was readily apparent that his material should be incorporated into this chapter introduction rather than embedded in the review of the Allport and Ross scale.

The 10 scales selected for inclusion in this chapter all center around the single most dominant research paradigm in the psychology of religion—religious orientation. It was the development of a single scale, the Religious Orientation Scale (3.9) by Allport and Ross, that probably did more that anything else to foster the empirical investigation of how one approaches religion. Religious orientation has dominated the research landscape in the psychology of religion so much that we would be remiss not to devote an entire chapter to a review of its measures.

The conceptual background of the religious orientation scale dates from the post-World War II period. This was the era of the "authoritarian personality" (Adorno, Frenkel-Brunswik, Levinson, & Sanford, 1950), when North American psychologists in particular were engaged in a frenzied search for "markers" that might aid in identifying persons most likely to endorse ethnocentric ideologies akin to Nazism. One such marker implicated in early research by Gordon Allport (e.g., Allport & Kramer, 1946)—a devout Episcopalian and an extremely influential figure in contemporary personality and social psychology (Wulff, 1997)—was religious involvement. That is, data indicated that belonging to and/or attending a church rather consistently predicted greater self-reported endorsement of more prejudiced attitudes than the absence of such religious participation (at least among white North American Christians; see Batson, Schoenrade, & Ventis, 1993, chap. 9, for a review). Perhaps as an attempt to temper the implications of this disturbing finding, Allport (1950), in his landmark *The Individual and His Religion*, asserted that not all religion is created equal; that is, although any two individuals might engage in similar religious behaviors, such as church attendance, their underlying motives may differ, depending on the "maturity" of their respective "religious sentiments." Conceptual differentiation of the clearly value-laden "mature" and "immature" religious sentiments eventually gave way to discussion of the less judgmentally labeled "intrinsic" (religion as master motive whereby one "lives" his or her religion) and "extrinsic" (religion as convenience whereby one "uses" his or her religion) religious orientations, which were subjected to a succession of operationalization attempts culminating in Allport and Ross (3.9). In that investigation, extrinsically oriented individuals tended to report greater prejudice than did intrinsically oriented individuals, as Allport had suspected (although the import of such findings with self-report measures remains open to question; see Batson & Burris, 1994).

Unfortunately, additional conceptual clarification and empirical research concerning the religious orientation framework by Allport himself were cut short by his death in 1967. Nonetheless, research by others has mushroomed so much that the religious orientation scale and its various spin-offs included for review in this chapter are among the most frequently used measures in the psychology of religion (see Kirkpatrick & Hood, 1990, for further discussion). Allport's conceptualization has not gone unchallenged, however. Indeed, it has been suggested (e.g., Wulff, 1997) that Allport's uncanny popularity among psychologists of religion may have as much or more to do with his apostolic reputation than with the conceptual soundness of his religious orientation framework or the instruments used to assess it. Because of the heuristic value of Allport's framework and because the Allport and Ross scale has been used so frequently for empirical research, the review of the measure itself (3.9) is more detailed than what is typically found in this volume.

Among the scales reviewed in this chapter are several that are modifications of the original Allport and Ross measure. Hoge's Intrinsic Religious Motivation Scale (3.6) differs from Allport and Ross in two regards: (a) the scale is useful for measuring religious orientation in some religions outside a Christian context and (b) intrinsic and extrinsic religious motivation anchor opposite ends of one dimension instead of representing two separate dimensions, as they do in the Allport and Ross scale. The Duke Religion Index (3.4) authored by Koenig and his colleagues is a brief scale of intrinsic religiousness (along with two other dimensions: organizational and nonorganizational religiousness) where three items of Hoge's intrinsic measure were extracted. Gorsuch and Venable's Age Universal Religious Orientation Scale (3.4) is interchangeable with the Allport and Ross scale but, unlike the earlier scale, does not require a middle adolescent language ability to complete the scale. The Age Universal Scale can be used with children as young as the fifth grade. However, based on Kirkpatrick's (1989) reanalysis of data from several studies using the Allport and Ross scale showing that the extrinsic scale subdivides into a personal oriented (Ep) and social oriented (Es) extrinsicness, the Age Universal Scale itself was revised in 1989 by Gorsuch and McPherson (3.10). Also, Allen and Spilka's Committed-Consensual Measures (3.3) of religion have much overlap with the Allport and Ross scale but stress the cognitive structure of beliefs rather than belief content. Finally, King and Hunt's Religious Position Scale (3.11) operationalizes Allport's intrinsic dimension in terms of "cognitive salience," or the degree to which religion is deeply significant. The extrinsic religious orientation, also measured in the King and Hunt scale, is conceptualized along the lines of Allport.

Some scales have been developed within the religious orientation tradition as a conceptual and measurement reaction to Allport and Ross. The most noted reaction has been the study of religion as quest, where religion is understood as "an open-ended process of pursuing ultimate questions more than ultimate answers" (Batson, Naifeh, & Pate, 1978, p. 40). The champion of this position is Dan Batson. Along with colleagues, he developed the Quest Scale, the most recent version of which (1991), by Batson and Schoenrade, is reviewed in this volume (3.7). Batson's quest concept and scale are not, however, free of criticism. Arguing that their own conceptualization is more in line with Allport's thinking, Dudley and Cruise have developed an alternative measure to the Quest Scale, the Religious Maturity Scale (3.8), replacing Batson's emphasis on doubt with a tentative openmindedness, even as one seeks to find a faith worthy of sincere commitment.

Another reaction to the Allport and Ross index led to the development of the Indiscriminate Proreligiousness Scale (3.5) by Pargament and his colleagues. Allport criticized the logic of those "muddleheads" who scored high on both the intrinsic and extrinsic orientations. Pargament et al. responded that scoring high on the two orientations is not necessarily logically inconsistent in that people may both "live" (intrinsic) and "use" (extrinsic) their religion.

The other index included in this chapter measures religious orientation outside of the intrinsic-extrinsic research framework. The Christian Religious Internalization Scale (3.2) developed by Ryan, Rigby, and King assesses the degree to which Christian beliefs are internalized versus introjected.

References

Adorno, T. W., Frenkel-Brunswik, E., Levinson, D. J., & Sanford, R. N. (1950). *The authoritarian personality*. New York: Harper & Row.

Allport, G. W. (1950). *The individual and his religion*. New York: MacMillan.

Allport, G. W., & Kramer, B. M. (1946). Some roots of prejudice. *Journal of Psychology, 22*, 9–30.

Batson, C. D., Naifeh, S. J., & Pate, S. (1978). Social desirability, religious orientation, and racial prejudice. *Journal for the Scientific Study of Religion, 17*, 31–41.

Batson, C. D., & Burris, C. T. (1994). Personal religion: Depressant or stimulant of prejudice and discrimination? In M. P. Zanna & J. M. Olson (Eds.), *The seventh Ontario symposium on personality and social psychology: The psychology of prejudice* (pp. 149–169). Hillsdale, NJ: Lawrence Erlbaum.

Batson, C. D., Schoenrade, P., & Ventis, W. L. (1993). *Religion and the individual: A social-psychological perspective*. New York: Oxford.

Kirkpatrick, L. A. (1989). A psychometric analysis of the Allport-Ross and Feagin measures of intrinsic-extrinsic religious orientation. In D. O. Moberg & M. L. Lynn (Eds.), *Research in the Social Scientific Study of Religion*, Vol. 1. Greenwich, CT: JAI Press.

Kirkpatrick, L. A., & Hood, R. W., Jr. (1990). Intrinsic-extrinsic religious orientation: The boon or bane of contemporary psychology of religion? *Journal for the Scientific Study of Religion, 29*, 442–462.

Wulff, D. M. (1997). *Psychology of religion: Classic and contemporary*. New York: Wiley.

3.1
AGE UNIVERSAL RELIGIOUS ORIENTATION SCALE
(Gorsuch & Venable, 1983)

Reviewed by Peter C. Hill

Variable: The Age Universal Intrinsic-Extrinsic Religious Orientation Scale contains two separate subscales designed to measure two distinct religious orientations: an intrinsic (I) and an extrinsic (E) orientation. But, as the name suggests, this scale is useful for both adults and children. Since its publication in 1983, the scale has been revised based on further psychometric evaluation (see Gorsuch & McPherson this volume).

Description: This scale is a modified version of the Allport and Ross (1967) I-E Religious Orientation scale where each item is a rewritten version of the original. It is completely interchangeable with the Allport and Ross scale. Whereas the original scale requires language ability beyond that of the typical child or younger adolescent, this scale reliably measures religious orientation on children as young as the fifth grade as well as adults.

Nineteen of the 20 items are scored on the same 5-point Likert continuum scale, with 1 indicating strong disagreement and 5 indicating strong agreement with each statement. The other item, part of the I subscale, measures the frequency of church attendance, also on a 5-point Likert continuum where 1 indicates "a few times a year or less" and 5 indicates "more than once a week."

Like the Allport and Ross scale, the 9 intrinsic and the 11 extrinsic items should be scored separately, since they apparently reflect independent dimensions rather than two unipolar constructs (see the discussion under "Results and comments" on the I-E Religious Orientation Scale of Allport and Ross, 1967). The score of each subscale is determined by summing the scores of the 9 or 11 items, thus providing ranges of 9 to 45 for the I measure and 11 to 55 for the E measure.

Practical Considerations: This paper-and-pencil measure requires no special examiner skill to administer, score, or interpret. No instructions are provided, nor are they necessary beyond the usual guarantee of confidentiality and the emphasis on no "right" or "wrong" answers as an attempt to diffuse a socially desirable response tendency. The purpose of the test is clear: to measure I and E religious orientations in a fashion suitable for both children and adults. Face validity of the scale is high in that items are clearly related to either the I or the E orientation.

Norms/Standardization: Two primary samples were used. The first sample consisted of 101 "adult Protestant Christian volunteers" from six churches and a college dormitory. Adults were necessary to correlate the Allport and Ross items with the rewritten items of the Age Universal Scale. In some cases there were multiple rewritten items with the highest correlating item (to the corresponding Allport and Ross item) selected.

The second sample consisted of 138 fifth and 119 seventh graders of various levels of verbal comprehension, as measured by the Altus (1948) Information Inventory. The authors maintained that children at a given grade level with lower verbal abilities should respond with equal reliability as those with higher verbal abilities if the scale claims to be useful at that particular grade level. As noted later, a precaution is necessary with children below the seventh grade who score low on measures of verbal comprehension.

Reliability: With the first sample of adult Protestant volunteers, internal consistency reliability coefficients were .66 for the E subscale and .73 for the I subscale. These coefficients compare with .70 and .73 respectively with the same subjects on the Allport and Ross (1967) scale. Individual item-to-subscale correlations were not reported. The correlation between I and E subscales was $-.39$. Among the 230 fifth- and seventh-grade students (after 27 students with scores of 0 or 1 on the Information Inventory were dropped; see discussion under "validity") in the follow-up study, the alpha coefficients were .75 for E and .68 for I. The I-E correlation in the follow-up study was $-.28$.

Validity: Item-to-item correlations between the Age Universal and the Allport and Ross scales ranged from .34 to .78. The median correlation was .59. Entire subscale correlations between the Age Universal and the Allport and Ross scales were .90 for I and .79 for E. Negative correlations between I and E were virtually identical for the two scales: $-.39$ and $-.38$ respectively. On the basis of these results, the authors conclude that the Age Universal Scale is interchangeable with the Allport and Ross scale for both the I and E measures.

In the follow-up study reported in the same article, Gorsuch and Venable (1983) included a measure of verbal ability called the Information Inventory (Altus, 1948) as a check on the properties of the Age Universal Scale with fifth- and seventh-grade children of varying verbal abilities. Using multiple regression, the authors concluded that the Age Universal Scale was appropriate for all but those with the lower verbal abilities below the seventh grade. For a sample of individuals below the seventh grade, they recommended including the Information Inventory (which can be group administered in less than five minutes) and exclude those children with abilities at the two lowest levels from a range of nine levels.

Location:
Gorsuch, R. L., & Venable, G. D. (1983). Development of an "Age Universal" I-E scale. *Journal for the Scientific Study of Religion, 22,* 181–187.

Subsequent Research:

Griffin, G. A. E., Gorsuch, R. L., & Davis, A. (1987). A cross-cultural investigation of religious orientation, social norms, and prejudice. *Journal for the Scientific Study of Religion, 26*, 358–365.

Nelson, P. B. (1989). Ethnic differences in intrinsic/extrinsic religious orientation and depression in the elderly. *Archives of Psychiatric Nursing, 3*, 199–204.

References

Allport, G. W., & Ross, J. M. (1967). Personal religious orientation and prejudice. *Journal of Personality and Social Psychology, 5*, 432–443.

Altus, W. D. (1948). The validity of an abbreviated information test used in the army. *Journal of Consulting Psychology, 12*, 270–275.

Appendix

Age Universal I-E Scale

The following items are included in the Age Universal Religious Orientation Scale. Items were administered in the (random) order listed and were all scored (except the sixth item) on the same 5-point Likert continuum:

1 = I strongly disagree   4 = I tend to agree
2 = I tend to disagree   5 = strongly agree
3 = I'm not sure

1. (I) I enjoy reading about my religion.
2. (E) I go to church because it helps me to make friends.
3. (E) It doesn't much matter what I believe so long as I am good.
4. (E) Sometimes I have to ignore my religious beliefs because of what people might think of me.
5. (I) It is important to me to spend time in private thought and prayer.
6. (I) I would prefer to go to church:
      (1) a few times a year or less
      (2) once every month or two
      (3) two or three times a month
      (4) about once a week
      (5) more than once a week
7. (I) I have often had a strong sense of God's presence.
8. (E) I pray mainly to gain relief and protection.
9. (I) I try to live all my life according to my religious beliefs.
10. (E) What religion offers me most is comfort in times of trouble and sorrow.
11. (I) My religion is important because it answers many question about the meaning of life.
12. (I) I would rather join a Bible study group than a church social group.
13. (E) Prayer is for peace and happiness.
14. (E) Although I am religious, I don't let it affect my daily life.
15. (E) I go to church mostly to spend time with my friends.
16. (I) My whole approach to life is based on my religion.
17. (E) I go to church mainly because I enjoy seeing people I know there.
18. (E) I pray mainly because I have been taught to pray.
19. (I) Prayers I say when I'm alone are as important to me as those I say in church.
20. (E) Although I believe in my religion, many other things are more important in life.

Gorsuch, R. L., & Venable, G. D. (1983). Development of an "Age Universal" I-E scale. *Journal for the Scientific Study of Religion, 22,* 181–187. Coyright © 1983 Journal for the Scientific Study of Religion. Reprinted with permission.

3.2
CHRISTIAN RELIGIOUS INTERNALIZATION SCALE
(Ryan, Rigby, & King, 1993)
Reviewed by Laura Hinebaugh-Igoe

Variable: The Christian Religious Internalization Scale (CRIS) assesses the degree of internalization for Christian beliefs and practices based on self-determination theory. Internalization refers to the process through which an individual transforms an externally prescribed regulation or value into an internal one. In other words, in internalization one "takes on" the value or regulation as one's own. Theories of internalization acknowledge that there can be varied degrees of internalization. Ryan et al. (1993) identify introjection and identification as two types of religious internalization.

Introjection represents a form of internalization in which beliefs and practices are maintained through contingent self-approval, guilt, and esteem-related activities. Thus, introjected behaviors are performed because one "should" do them or because not doing so may result in anxiety, guilt, or loss of esteem. Identification, on the other hand, represents a more fully internalized regulation in that the individual experiences behavior as volitional or self-determined. Beliefs and practices associated with identification are experienced as a personal value and the individual perceives them as emanating from himself or herself to a greater extent than in introjection. Given the nature of the distinction between the two types of internalization, Ryan et al. (1993) expect divergent and largely opposing relations to adjustment and mental health, with identification associated with more positive outcomes and introjection with more negative outcomes. Thus, the intent of the CRIS is twofold: (a) to assess an individual's type of religious orientation and (b) to examine how variations in introjection and identification are associated with well-being, mental health, and other established measures of religious orientation.

Description: The CRIS is a 12-item measure designed to identify an individual's style of religious orientation. Preliminary versions of the CRIS included a 36-item pool that was administered to two large samples of Christian subjects for the purpose of factor and internal consistency analysis. These preliminary studies indicated a reliable two-factor structure and the possibility of creating a brief version consisting of the 12 items constituting the CRIS. Factor analysis with varimax rotation of the CRIS consistently yielded two factors corresponding to the two types of internalization identified as introjection (eigenvalue = 3.00, 3.49, 3.50 across three samples of Christian subjects) and identification (eigenvalue = 2.20, 2.47, 2.80 across the three samples).

In scoring the CRIS, each item receives a score of 1–4 and subjects are directed to circle the response that best describes themselves. To distinguish religious orientation from general motivation, respondents indicate the degree to which various motives would be salient to them if they were to perform a religious behavior. No items are negatively worded and two subscale scores are created for each subject representing the mean of the six items loading on each factor. No significant correlation was found between the introjection and identification subscales ($r = .07$). Likewise, gender differences in subscale scores were examined and no significant differences on either subscale were detected.

Practical Considerations: This paper-and-pencil measure requires no special skills to administer, score, or interpret. No instructions are provided, and none are necessary beyond the usual guarantee of confidentiality and the emphasis on no "right" or "wrong" answers. Face validity of the CRIS is high in that items clearly reflect one orientation or the other.

Norms/Standardization: The CRIS was sampled against four groups of Christian subjects. As indicated by Ryan et al. (1993), Christian (i.e., Catholic and varied Protestant) denominations were used because (a) they were readily available, (b) they have been the focus of past research on religious orientation with which comparisons can be drawn, and (c) pilot survey and interview studies suggested that both introjection and identification are common forms of motivation underlying Christian practices. As the title *Christian* Religious Internalization Scale suggests, generalizability remains limited to Christians until efforts are made to investigate how the CRIS functions among non-Christian religions.

The first sample consisted of 105 undergraduates (31 men and 74 women) at a secular university who identified themselves as Christian. The mean age of these participants was 20.5. The second sample consisted of 151 undergraduates (47 men and 104 women) from a Protestant college (*n* = 84) and a Catholic university (*n* = 67). The mean age of these participants was 22.5. The third sample consisted of 41 subjects drawn from an adult Sunday school class at a suburban Protestant church. The mean age of these adults was 35. The fourth sample consisted of 333 male (149) and female (184) participants in a summer evangelical project in New York City. Their mean age was 17.5. Denominationally, 47% classified themselves as Baptists, 27% claimed non-denominational status, and the remainder reported other denominational affiliation. Both evangelical (sample 4) and less behaviorally engaged Christian subjects from a secular setting (sample 1) were utilized for comparison purposes in testing for differences in introjection and identification. Subjects in all four samples participated on a volunteer basis and were assured of the confidentiality of their responses.

Reliability: With the first sample of self-identified Christian students from a secular university, factor analysis yielded two factors, representing introjection and identification, and accounted for 23.3% and 29.1%

of the explained variance, respectively. Loadings (representing the correlation between each item and the factor extracted) ranged from .73 to .52 for introjection and from .84 to .57 for identification. Internal consistency reliability estimates found that in this sample both subscales had alpha coefficients of .82, indicating adequate internal reliability.

Factor analysis results from the second sample were similar to those obtained in the first sample, with six items falling on each of the two factors representing introjection and identification. Introjection accounted for 20.5% of the explained variance and loadings ranged from .72 to .61. Identification accounted for 29.1 of the variance with loadings ranging from .84 to .57. Alpha coefficients were .82 and .69, respectively.

Insufficient sample size prevented factor analysis from being performed on the third sample of Protestant adults. However, indices of internal consistency for introjection and identification suggest adequate reliability (α = .64 and .79, respectively).

Validity: Hypothesized group differences and correlations were used to assess the construct validity of the CRIS. In a case of "known groups" validity, Ryan et al. (1993) predicted and analyses supported a significant difference in religious internalization between subjects who had volunteered to engage in evangelical work and less behaviorally involved subjects at a secular university. More specifically, analyses of variance revealed that evangelical youths scored higher on both the introjection and identification subscales of the CRIS than the comparable sample drawn from a secular environment (*p* < .001). Total score means on introjection were 11.13 (*SD* = 3.56) and 13.88 (*SD* = 2.88) for secular college Christians and their matches from the evangelical sample, respectively. Corresponding means for identification were 17.88 (*SD* = 3.96) and 22.42 (*SD* = 1.81). In demonstrating the ability of the CRIS to discriminate between groups where one might logically predict differences in degree of religious internalization, these results assist in establishing construct validity.

Convergent and discriminant construct validity were supported in a series of predicted correlations between the CRIS and other measures of religious internalization. Correlational studies in three Christian samples provide evidence that identification is closely associated with Allport and Ross's (1967) dimension of intrinsic religiosity (correlations ranged from .33 to .77) and with what Batson and Ventis (1982) called the Religion as an End orientation (correlations ranged from .22 to .78). Moderate correlations between introjection and extrinsic religiosity and Religion as a Means orientation (correlations ranged from .10 to .31 and .17 to .40, respectively) suggest that the introjection subscale of the CRIS measures something more specific than either of these constructs. Batson and Ventis's Religious as a Quest orientation was unrelated to either type of internalization. Both identification and introjection were generally associated with greater church attendance and the Doctrinal Orthodoxy Scale (Batson, 1976), though this was particularly true of identification.

Location:
Ryan, R. M., Rigby, S., & King, K. (1993). Two types of religious internalization and their relations to religious orientations and mental health. *Journal of Personality and Social Psychology, 65* (3), 586–596.

Subsequent Research: No subsequent researchy using the scale has been published.

References

Allport, G. W., & Ross, J. M. (1967). Personal religious orientation and prejudice. *Journal of Personality and Social Psychology, 5*, 432–443.

Batson, C. D. (1976). Religion as prosocial: Agent or double agent? *Journal for the Scientific Study of Religion, 15*, 29–46.

Batson, C. D., & Ventis, W. L. (1982). *The religious experience: A social-psychological perspective*. New York: Oxford University Press.

Appendix

Christian Religious Internalization Scale

The following items are included in the Christian Religious Internalization Scale. All items are scored on the same 4-point Likert continuum:

1 = not at all true
2 = usually not true
3 = usually true
4 = very true

One reason I actively share my faith with others is:
1. (Identified) Because God is important to me and I'd like other people to know about Him too.
2. (Introjected) Because I would feel bad about myself if I didn't.
3. (Introjected) Because I want other Christians to approve of me.

When I turn to God, I most often do it because:
4. (Identified) I enjoy spending time with Him.
5. (Introjected) I would feel guilty if I didn't.
6. (Identified) I find it satisfying to me.

A reason I pray by myself is:
7. (Introjected) Because if I don't, God will disapprove of me.
8. (Identified) Because I enjoy praying.
9. (Identified) Because I find prayer satisfying.

A reason I attend church is:

10.	(Introjected)	Because one is supposed to go to church.
11.	(Identified)	By going to church, I learn new things.
12.	(Introjected)	Because others would disapprove of me if I didn't.

Note: A longer version of the scale is available from Richard Ryan, Dept. of Psychology, University of Rochester, Rochester, NY 14627–0001.

Reprinted with permission of the author.

3.3
COMMITTED-CONSENSUAL MEASURES (Allen & Spilka, 1967)
Reviewed by Rodney L. Bassett

Variable: The Committed-Consensual Measures are scales designed to tap different ways of being religious across a wide range of religious traditions. The scales emphasize the cognitive structuring of religious beliefs rather than the content of specific religious beliefs. References are made to religion, God, church, and the bible; but there are no specific references to Jesus Christ or other issues that might be divisive across the broad Judeo-Christian tradition.

Originally, Allen and Spilka (1967) designed the instrument to help clarify the relationship between religiousness and prejudice. The goal was to identify two ways of cognitively structuring religious beliefs that would relate in different ways to racial prejudice. Conceptually, consensual religion was conceived of as more dogmatic and thus related to higher prejudice; committed religion was conceived of as less dogmatic and thus related to lower prejudice. In addition, it was hoped these types of religiousness would not be confounded with pathology or religious intensity.

Description: The measurement of committed and consensual religion has undergone a series of transformations. The original version of the instrument (Allen & Spilka, 1967) had an interview format. Later versions (Spilka, Read, Allen, & Dailey, 1968; Spilka & Mullin, 1977) were redesigned into a questionnaire format to facilitate administration.

The interview version of committed and consensual religion taps five cognitive components of religious belief: content, clarity, complexity, flexibility, and importance. Committed religion is anchored in abstract principles that: (a) have exact meanings, (b) involve a large number of categories or elements, (c) are open for frank and thoughtful examination, and (d) are of central importance for the individual. Consensual religion is based upon beliefs that are concrete and: (a) have vague implications, (b) have few categories or elements, (c) are closed to differing opinions, and (d) have limited impact on the overall life of the individual. These elements of religious belief are elicited through a series of questions in an interview that typically lasts one half hour to an hour. Allen and Spilka (1967) did not present the actual questions used in the interview. However, Raschke (1973) described the process as a ". . . semistructured interview using questions centering around typical belief content areas such as God, prayer, Bible, church, faith, etc." (p. 339).

The questionnaire version of committed and consensual religion utilizes a Likert-like format. There are 15 committed and 13 consensual items. Several of these items overlap with the Allport and Ross (1967) Religious Orientation Scale. The literature generally suggest that the distinction between consensual and committed religion, like that of extrinsic and intrinsic religion, taps the distinction between 'used' vs. 'lived' faith (Spilka, 1976). However, as will be discussed in more detail later, the overlap between intrinsic and committed religion seems to be greater than the overlap between extrinsic and consensual religion.

Practical Considerations: Several problems make the consensual and committed measures difficult to use.

First, in theory, consensual and committed religion represent the endpoints of a bipolar dimension. Yet, the two measures consistently show a moderate but positive correlation (Spilka, 1977). Second, although committed and intrinsic religion seem to overlap, the relationship between consensual and extrinsic religion has always been modest (Spilka, 1977). This suggests that there are at least two fairly independent versions of utilitarian religion and these differences have never been clarified. In recent years, measures of intrinsic/extrinsic faith have tended to supplant measures of committed/consensual faith. As a result, the unique aspects of consensual faith may have been lost in the literature.

It becomes apparent that many of the consensual items measure the importance of religious worship. Concern for rituals of worship could derive from a 'cultural' faith or a 'personal' faith. Religious people could recognize the significance of rituals of worship because they were raised with these rituals (cultural) or because these rituals provide an avenue of communication and worship with a personal God (personal). The second possibility might partially explain the positive relationship between consensual and intrinsic faith (Spilka, Minton, Sizemore, & Stout, 1977). Such differing motivations for worship might cloud the meaning of the consensual scale.

Norms/Standardization: The Committed-Consensual Measures have been used with a wide range of participants. However, there is no manual for the instrument, and norms for the instrument have not been published.

Reliability: In the original article by Allen and Spilka, reliability for scoring the results of the interview were reported. Scorers were given a four-hour training session and then their ability to assess participant responses in terms of the five elements of consensual and committed religion was assessed. Reliability amongst the scorers seemed to be quite high. Using an analysis of variance technique, the coefficient of reliability across the five elements was .93.

With the questionnaire version of consensual and committed, Spilka et al. (1977) reported the Kuder-Richardson 20 estimates of reliability. For committed religion, the estimate was .93. For consensual religion, the estimate was .84.

Validity: Spilka (1977) looked at the relationship between utilitarianism and consensual and committed faith. Ninety Christian college students were given several questionnaires measuring acceptance or rejection of materialism and self-aggrandizement. Committed religion was inversely related to materialism and success achievement. Consensual religion was directly related to status concern and success achievement. Similar relationships were found with the Allport and Ross (1967) and the Hoge (1972) intrinsic and extrinsic measures.

Location:
    Allen, R. O., & Spilka, B. (1967). Committed and consensual religion: A specification of religion-prejudice relationships. *Journal for the Scientific Study of Religion, 6*, 191–206.
    Spilka, B., Minton, B., Sizemore, D., & Stout, L. (1977). Death and personal faith: A psychometric investigation. *Journal for the Scientific Study of Religion, 16*, 169–178.

Subsequent Research: Little research work has been done with the consensual-committed measures. Instead, the scientific study of religion has utilized the related intrinsic-extrinsic constructs to a far greater degree.

References:

    Allport, G. W., & Ross, J. M. (1967). Personal religious orientation and prejudice. *Journal of Personality and Social Psychology, 5*, 432–433.
    Hoge, D. R. (1972). A validated intrinsic religious motivation scale. *Journal for the Scientific Study of Religion, 11*, 369–376.
    Raschke, V. (1973). Dogmatism and committed and consensual religion. *Journal for the Scientific Study of Religion, 12*, 339–344.
    Spilka, B. (1976). The complete person: Some

theoretical views and research findings for a theological-psychology of religion. *Journal of Psychology and Theology, 4,*15–24.

Spilka, B. (1977). Utilitarianism and personal faith. *Journal of Psychology and Theology, 5,* 226–223.

Spilka, B., & Mullin, M. (1977). Personal religion and psychosocial schemata: A research approach to a theological psychology of religion. *Character Potential, 8,* 57–66.

Spilka, B., Read, S., Allen, R. O., & Dailey, K. A. (1968 December). Specificity vs. generality: *The criterion problem in religious measurement.* Paper presented at the annual meeting for the American Association for the Advancement of Science, Dallas, TX.

Appendix

Commited-Consensual Measures

Indicate the extent to which you agree or disagree to each statemen below by using the following scale.

1 = Strongly Disagree	4 = Slightly Agree
2 = Moderatley Disagree	5 = Moderatley Agree
3 = Slightly Disagree	6 = Strongly Agree

1. One of the most important aspects of religion is the religious ceremonies. (Cn)

2. I try hard to carry my religion over into all my other dealings in life. (Cm)

3. My ideas about religion are one of the most important parts of my philosophy of life. (Cm)

4. Religion is most real to me during my attendance at public church or religious services. (Cn)

5. I do not think that the sequences of prayers, songs, etc., is very important in religious services. (Cn)

6. Quite often I have been keenly aware of the presence of God or the Divine Being. (Cm)

7. Every person needs to have the feeling of security given by a church. (Cn)

8. Tender concern for others is a means of finding joy in one's religion. (Cm)

9. The more a religious service is ritualized the more it has meaning for me. (Cn)

10. The purpose of prayer is to secure a happy and peaceful life. (Cn)

11. The truly religious person believes honestly and wholeheartedly in the doctrines of his church. (Cn)

12. My interest in and real commitment to religion is greater now than when I first joined the church. (Cm)

13. Religion is a subject in which I am not particularly interested. (Cm - reverse scored)

14. It is important to me to spend periods of time in private thought and meditation. (Cm)

15. The ritual of worship is a very important part of religion. (Cn)

16. My religious beliefs are what really lie behind my whole approach to life. (Cm)

17. I like to think that people all over are going through nearly the same ritual in their religious worship. (Cn)

18. I think that the placement and treatment of the various articles of worship is very important in a worship service. (Cn)

19. I often think about matters relating to religion. (Cm)

20. Believing as I do about religion is very important to being the kind of person I want to be. (Cm)

21. The precision and orderliness with which religious ceremonies are performed is important. (Cn).

22. Religion is especially important to me because it answers many questions about the meaning of life. (Cm)

23. It is important to me that religious services be standardized. (Cn)

24. If my ideas about religion were different, I believe that my way of life would be very different. (Cm)

25. The aim of missionaries should be to establish church buildings where religious services and ceremonies can be conducted. (Cn)

26. I read literature about my faith or church. (Cm)
    (a) yes (b) no

27. If I were joining a church group, I would prefer to join (1) a Bible study group or (2) a social fellowship. (Cm)
    a. I would prefer to join (1)
    b. I probably would prefer to join (1)
    c. I probably would prefer to join (2)
    d. I would prefer to join (2)

28. How much time during the week would you say you spend reading the Bible and other religious literature? (Cm)
    a. one hour or more
    b. one-half hour
    c. none

Cm—item measures Committed form of personal religion
Cn—item measures Consensual form of personal religion

Spilka, B., Minton, B., Sizemore, D., & Stout, L. (1977). Death and personal faith: A psychometric investigation. *Journal for the Scientific Study of Religion, 16,* 169–178. Copyright © 1977 Journal for the Scientific Study of Religion. Reprinted with permission.

3.4
DUKE RELIGION INDEX (Koenig, Patterson, & Meador, 1997)
Reviewed by Peter C. Hill

Variable: The Duke Religion Index (DUREL) measures three major dimensions of religiousness: organizational (OR), nonorganizational (NOR), and intrinsic religiosity (IR). The authors developed this scale as an attempt "to measure religosity in a comprehensive yet brief and non-offensive manner" (p. 885).

Description: The first and second items of this five-item scale measure OR and NOR respectively. The last three items were extracted from Hoge's (1972) intrinsic religiosity scale (items 2, 6, and 7). From a study of 458 medical patients in the Duke Hospital Study, these three items were chosen based on their intrinsic factor loading (3 of Hoge's 5 items that loaded .72 or greater), correlation with the total score of the Hoge ten-item scale (3 of Hoge's 6 items that correlated .65 or greater), and relationship with several health outcomes, including social support, functional impairment, severity of medical illness, self-related depression, major depression, and speed of recovery from depression. The five items are summed, resulting in a score range of 5 (high religiousness) to 27 (low religiousness).

Practical Considerations: This brief scale requires no special considerations and should take only a few minutes to complete.

Norms/Standardization: Though no normative data on the first two items are presented in Koenig, Patterson, and Meador (1997), the authors report that normative data on response rates in both clinical and community populations are available. These two items were adminstered to over 7,000 persons aged 18 to 90 participating in three separate studies. Descriptive statistics (e.g., means, standard deviations, etc.) were also not reported for the final three items. Again, however, such normative data is provided through the Duke Hospital Study.

Reliability: No reliability data are presented on the first two items. The three-item intrinsic religiosity subscale had a Cronbach's alpha of .75.

Validity: The 3-item intrinsic religiosity subscale strongly correlated ($r = .85$) with Hoge's full 10-item scale and only moderately correlated with OR ($r = .40$) and NOR ($r = .42$). Though the correlation between OR and NOR was not reported, correlations with physical and mental health measures suggest that these two measures of religious behavior are distinct (see also Koenig, 1997; Koenig, Hays, George, & Blazer, 1997). For example, OR is related to more social support, less depression (both self-rated and major depression), less severity of medical illness, and less functional impairment. NOR is related to more social support only, though the authors cite recent research (Koenig et al., 1997) suggesting that NOR is related to poorer physical health and has a mixed association with depression. The authors' claim that this brief instrument measures "three major dimensions of religiousness that are related in overlapping yet unique ways to social support and different health outcomes" (p. 885) appears to be valid.

Location:
   Koenig, H. G., Parkerson, G. R., & Meador, K. G. (1997). Religion index for psychiatric research: A 5-item measure for use in health outcome studies. *American Journal of Psychiatry, 154*(6), 885.

Recent Research:
   Koenig, H. G. (1997). *Is religion good for your health?* New York: Haworth Press.
   Koenig, H. G., Hays, J. C., George, L. K., & Blaxer, D. G. (1997). Modeling the cross-sectional relationships between religion, physical health, social support, and depressive symptoms. *American Journal of Geriatric Psychiatry, 5*, 131–143.

Appendix

Duke University Religion Index (DUREL)

1. How often do you attend church or other religious meetings? (OR)
   1. More than once a week
   2. Once a week
   3. A few times a month
   4. A few times a year
   5. Once a year or less
   6. Never

2. How often do you spend time in private religious activities, such as prayer, meditation, or
   Bible study? (NOR)
       1. More than once a day
       2. Daily
       3. Two or more times/week
       4. Once a week
       5. A few times a month
       6. Rarely or never

*The following section contains 3 statements about religious belief or experience. Please
mark the extent to which each statement is true or not true for you.*

3. In my life, I experience the presence of the Divine (i.e., God). (IR)
       1. Definitely true of me
       2. Tends to be true
       3. Unsure
       4. Tends *not* to be true
       5. Definitely *not* true

4. My religious beliefs are what really lies behind my whole approach to life. (IR)
       1. Definitely true of me
       2. Tends to be true
       3. Unsure
       4. Tends *not* to be true
       5. Definitely *not* true

5. I try hard to carry my religion over into all other dealings in life. (IR)
       1. Definitely true of me
       2. Tends to be true
       3. Unsure
       4. Tends *not* to be true
       5. Definitely *not* true

OR—organizational religiosity
NOR—Non-organizational religiosity
IR—intrinsic religiosity

3.5
INDISCRIMINATE PRORELIGIOUSNESS SCALE (Pargament et al., 1987)
Reviewed by Peter C. Hill

Variable: The Indiscriminate Proreligiousness Scale (IPRO) measures the tendency to be both intrinsically and extrinsically religious on personal and congregational levels. Pargament developed this scale after examining the way Allport criticized the logic of the indiscriminately proreligious individual who scored high on both the extrinsic and intrinsic subscales of the Religious Orientation Scale (Allport & Ross, 1967). Pargament suggests that intrinsic and extrinsic orientations are not necessarily logically inconsistent. Individuals who score high on both scales may, according to

Pargament, both "live" and "use" their religion.

Pargament and his colleagues operationally define indiscriminate proreligiousness as a tendency to respond positively to religious material regardless of its plausibility. For example, a person who consistently responds positively to such statements as "Members always know about all church activities" and "I always live by my religious beliefs" would be considered indiscriminately proreligious by this scale.

Description: The IPRO contains two subscales: congregational (PRO-C) and personal (PRO-P) proreligiousness. The PRO-C items focus on areas of church life, such as leadership, membership, services, activities, education, clergy, and policies. The PRO-P items deal with the devotional, consequential, ritual, and ideological facets of an individual's personal religious life.

Both the congregational and personal subscales use a true-false format to force the respondent to choose between an indiscriminate proreligious position and a more discriminating position. Each item clearly allows for a choice of a proreligious position, and, in each case, this position is not plausible. The PRO-C scale contains 16 items, 8 of which are reverse scored. The PRO-P scale has 12 items, with 5 reverse scored.

Practical Considerations: As with other measures of religious orientation, the Indiscriminate Proreligious Scale requires no special skills to administer or score. For all items, the proreligious response (some items are reverse scored) is scored 1 and the nonproreligious response is scored 0. The total score is simply the number of items answered with a proreligious response.

If a proreligious orientation is used as a categorical independent variable, it is recommended that theoretical midpoints of the scales (8 for PRO-C, 6 for PRO-P) be used rather than median splits, thereby avoiding inconsistent classification across studies due to sampling differences.

Norms/Standardization: One sample totaling 261 subjects was selected from three Michigan churches: two Lutheran (total $N = 155$) and one Presbyterian ($N = 106$). Forty-one percent of the sample was male and the median age was 43. A second sample was drawn from church-going student volunteers from a moderate-sized midwestern university. This sample of 305 subjects contained 27% males with a median age of 19 and consisted of 53% Roman Catholic, 43% Protestant, and 4% Other.

Means (and standard deviations) for the church sample were 4.51 (3.19) on the PRO-C measure and 4.01 (2.68) on the PRO-P measure. For the student sample, the respective means (and standard deviations) for PRO-C and PRO-P were 6.08 (3.75) and 4.23 (2.16).

Reliability: For the church sample, Cronbach's alpha reliability estimates of .75 for the PRO-P scale and .78 for the PRO-C scale were found. Reliability estimates with the student sample were .59 and .82 for the PRO-P and PRO-C scales respectively. The rather low PRO-P reliability estimate in the student sample was thought to be due to the low rate of endorsement of a number of items (a dichotomous item may be limited in its correlation with another variable as its proportion of endorsement increasingly differs from 50%) among the students or to a lower level of religious commitment and integration (and, hence, possibly less reliable responses). In fact, the student sample scored significantly lower than the church sample on Hoge's (1972) Intrinsic scale.

Validity: The content validity of the scale was determined by a factor analysis, using a promax rotation. All items have factor loadings of at least .20 and, with the exception of two PRO-C items, do not load on the other factor. An agreement response set is largely eliminated by the presence of negatively worded items.

Construct validity was measured in a number of ways. First, PRO-C and PRO-P correlate only moderately with the Crowne-Marlowe (1964) measure of social desirability (.52 with PRO-P and .29 with PRO-C in the church sample; .49 with PRO-P and .31 with PRO-C in the student sample). Second,

PRO-P with PRO-C correlate only moderately with each other (.40 for the church sample and of .44 for the student sample), suggesting that the two subscales assess related but distinct domains of indiscriminate proreligiousness. Third, the median correlations with measures of congregational climate and satisfaction across both church and student samples were higher with PRO-C (.43) than with PRO-P (.22) and Crowne-Marlowe (.14). Fourth, the median correlations with several religious variables (e.g., intrinsic, extrinsic, quest, God-control, orthodoxy, church attendance, frequency of prayer, and religious salience) were higher with PRO-P (.30) than with PRO-C (.10) and Crowne-Marlowe (.09). The between-sample (church and students) consistency in support of these hypotheses not only suggests high construct validity but also demonstrates evidence of generalizability. Fifth, a modest relationship was found between PRO-P and indiscriminate proreligiousness as defined through the Allport and Ross 2X2 typology on the Intrinsic-Extrinsic Religious Orientation Scale.

Location:
Pargament, K. I., Brannick, M. T., Adamakos, H., Ensing, D. S., Kelemen, M. L., Warren, R. K., Falgout, K., Cook, P., & Myers, J. (1987). Indiscriminate proreligiousness: Conceptualization and measurement. *Journal for the Scientific Study of Religion, 26,* 182–200.

Subsequent Research:
Hathaway, W. L., & Pargament, K. I. (1990). Intrinsic religiousness, religious coping, and psychosocial competence: A covariance structure analysis. *Journal for the Scientific Study of Religion, 29*(4), 423–441.

Pargament, K. I., Ensing, D. S., Falgout, K., Olsen, H., Reilly, B., Van Haitsma, K., & Warren, R. (1990). God help me (I): Religious coping efforts as predictors of the outcomes to significant life events. *American Journal of Community Psychology, 18*(6), 793–824.

Pargament, K. I., Olsen, H., Reilly, B., Falgout, K., Ensing, D. S., & Van Haitsma, K. (1992). God help me (II): The relationship of religious orientations to religious coping with negative life events. *Journal for the Scientific Study of Religion, 31*(4), 504–513.

References

Allport, G. W., & Ross, J. M. (1967). Personal religious orientation and prejudice. *Journal of Personality and Social Psychology, 5,* 432–443.

Crowne, D. P., & Marlowe, D. (1964). *The approval motive: Studies in evaluative dependence.* New York: Wiley.

Hoge, D. R. (1972). A validated intrinsic religious motivation scale. *Journal for the Scientific Study of Religion, 11,* 369–376.

Appendix

Indiscriminate Proreligiousness Scale

Please answer "true" or "false" to each of the following items.

Congregational Form (PRO-C)
1. Tensions do not exist among members of this church.
2. Differences of opinion are always welcome in this church.
3. Members of the church share all of their joys and sorrows with each other.
4. Some members complain about aspects of the church. (R)
5. Church members never gossip about one another.
6. Sometimes there is a problem about getting volunteers for activities in this church. (R)
7. Sometimes church leaders don't know members' opinions on important issues. (R)
8. Church leaders are sometimes insensitive to members' needs. (R)
9. Some church activities are boring. (R)
10. Members always know about all church activities.
11. It is sometimes hard for members to get involved in church activities. (R)

12. This church has programs to meet the needs of all the members.
13. There are no cliques in this church.
14. The ministers are sometimes unable to help solve members' problems. (R)
15. The members know all the church policies and rules.
16. Our ministers do not give their full attention to some of the members. (R)

Personal Form (PRO-P)
1. Religious services always give me new insight into my religious beliefs.
2. I am always inspired by the sermon topics.
3. Sometimes I daydream during services. (R)
4. I always try to use the message of the weekly sermon in my daily life.
5. There have been times when I doubted the existence of God. (R)
6. I always live by my religious beliefs.
7. My religious beliefs guide me in every one of my daily actions.
8. There are times when I do not feel like going to church. (R)
9. Praying always brings me inner peace.
10. Sometimes I feel that the teachings of my religion ask too much of me. (R)
11. I never disobey the teachings of my faith.
12. When things are going well for me, I sometimes forget to thank God. (R)

(R) indicates that the item is reverse scored.

Pargament, K. I., Brannick, M. T., Adamakos, H., Ensing, D. S., Kelemen, M. L., Warren, R. K., Falgout, K., Cook, P., & Myers, J. (1987). Indiscriminate proreligiousness: Conceptualization and measurement. *Journal for the Scientific Study of Religion, 26,* 182–200. Copyright © 1987 Journal for the Scientific Study of Religion. Reprinted with permission.

3.6
INTRINSIC RELIGIOUS MOTIVATION SCALE (Hoge, 1972)
Reviewed by Rodney L. Bassett

Variable: The Intrinsic Religious Motivation Scale measures different ways of being religious. Although it was developed and tested within the Christian tradition, the items are applicable to a wide range of religious groups. Only two of the ten items comprising the instrument make a specific reference to God, and no items refer specifically to Christianity. In addition, the instrument clearly avoids the potentially divisive issues of religious behaviors and beliefs. Instead, this scale measures the motivation behind religious activity. It was Hoge's (1972) hope that by limiting the instrument to the measurement of only one aspect of religiousness the instrument would produce a unidimensional scale. Hoge believed that such a scale would add conceptual clarity to the relationships between religiousness and

other factors of interest to social scientists (e.g., prejudice).

Description: The Intrinsic Religious Motivation Scale contains ten items in a Likert-like format. These items are designed to tap the dimension Hunt and King (1971) called "ultimate versus instrumental." Conceptually, this dimension is derived from the motivational aspect of Allport and Ross's (1967) Religious Orientation Scale. Unlike similar instruments (e.g., Feagin, 1964), the final items for the Hoge instrument were selected because they loaded on a single factor. On one end of the dimension are seven intrinsic items, and on the other end are three extrinsic items. Obviously, Hoge assumed that intrinsic and extrinsic faith anchor different ends of the same dimension instead of assuming that intrinsic and extrinsic faith might represent two separate dimensions. It should be noted that some of the items on Hoge's scale were taken from the Allport and Ross scale and the Feagin scale. Respondents have four response options to the scale items ranging from "strongly agree" (1) to "strongly disagree" (4). In the computation of the overall score, the extrinsic items are reversed. Thus, a low overall score indicates intrinsicness and a high score indicates extrinsicness.

Practical Considerations: The most useful source for someone using the scale is the original article by Hoge (1972). This article presents the actual items and makes a few suggestions for administering and scoring the instrument. The inclusion of intrinsic and extrinsic items may provide some protection against response bias.

Several strategies for scoring the scale appear in the literature. The strategy advocated by Hoge is to reverse score the extrinsic items, add the intrinsic and extrinsic items together, and then report an overall intrinsic score. An alternative strategy has been to separate the intrinsic and extrinsic items and report them as separate scale values (e.g., Spilka, 1977). A final variation in the literature (e.g., Sapp & Jones, 1986) is to use the Hoge instrument as a measure of intrinsicness along with some other measure of extrinsicness.

The instrument is straightforward and short, and it avoids sectarian language. It should be a particularly useful instrument for researchers that are concerned about participant fatigue effects.

Norms/Standardization: The original article by Hoge reported on two studies. In both studies, participants were nominated by local pastors because these parishioners fit a description of intrinsic or extrinsic religious orientation. Hoge reported that for the second study the average intrinsic item score was 2.00, and the average standard deviation was 1.07. For the extrinsic items, the average score was 4.11, and the average standard deviation was 1.08. When the scores for the extrinsic items were reversed and all the items were considered together,

the average item score was 1.97 and the average standard deviation was 1.08.

Reliability: Reversing the extrinsic items, Hoge reported that the reliability of the scale was .90 using the Kuder-Richardson Formula 20. The item-to-item correlations ranged from a low of .13 to a high of .72.

Reliability information was also provided by Hoge and Carroll (1978) from their survey of members of eight suburban Protestant churches. In attempting to identify determinants of commitment in suburban churches, Hoge and Carroll administered a shortened version (six items) of the Intrinsic Religious Motivation Scale. With the shortened version, Cronbach's alpha was .84.

Validity: In the original report by Hoge, participants were nominated by ministers who identified them as being either intrinsic or extrinsic in their religious orientation. Only those items that correlated with the ministers' judgments were included in the final form of the scale. The overall final version of the scale correlated .59 with these judgments. In addition, the Intrinsic Religious Motivation Scale was correlated with the Allport and Ross (1967) and the Feagin (1964) intrinsic scales. The correlations with these scales all ranged from .71 to .87. Of course, these high positive correlations can be explained in part by the common items shared by the scales.

Benson et al. (1980) researched intrapersonal factors affecting nonspontaneous helping. The participants were 69 female and 44 male students at a small midwestern liberal arts college. The data were collected through a series of questionnaires administered during a single testing session. Nonspontaneous helping involved self-reports of hours spent during the previous year in 14 different helping categories. These categories included volunteer work, visitations, leadership in youth organizations, solicitation for charities, etc. One of the intrapersonal factors was intrinsic faith (as measured by Hoge's scale). Providing construct validity for Hoge's instrument, Benson et al. found that intrinsicness was one of the best positive predictors of nonspontaneous helping.

Location:

Hoge, D. R. (1972). A validated intrinsic religious motivation scale. *Journal for the Scientific Study of Religion, 11,* 369–376.

Subsequent Research:

Hathaway, W. L., & Pargament, K. I. (1990). Intrinsic religiousness, religious coping, and psychosocial competence: A covariance structure analysis. *Journal for the Scientific Study of Religion, 29*(4), 423–441.

Pargament, K. I., Ensing, D. S., Falgout, K., Olsen, H., Reilly, B., Vanhaitsma, K., & Warren, R. (1990). God help me: 1. Religious coping efforts as predictors of the outcomes to significant negative life events. *American Journal of Community Psychology, 18,* 793–824.

References:

Allport, G. W., & Ross, J. M. (1967). Personal religious orientation and prejudice. *Journal of Personality and Social Psychology, 5,* 447–457.

Benson, P. L., Dehority, J., Garman, L., Hanson, E., Hochschwender, M., Lebold, C., Rohr, R., & Sullivan, J. (1980). Interpersonal correlates of nonspontaneous helping behavior. *Journal of Social Psychology, 110,* 87–95.

Feagin, J. R. (1964). Prejudice and religious types: A focused study of southern fundamentalists. *Journal for the Scientific Study of Religion, 4,* 3–13.

Hoge, D. R., & Carroll, J. W. (1978). Determinants of commitment and participation in suburban Protestant churches. *Journal for the Scientific Study of Religion, 17,* 107–127.

Hunt, R. A., & King, M. (1971). The intrinsic-extrinsic concept: A review and evaluation. *Journal for the Scientific Study of Religion, 10,* 339–356,

Sapp, G. L., & Jones, L. (1986). Religious orientation and moral judgment. *Journal for the Scientific Study of Religion, 25,* 208–214.

Spilka, B. (1977). Utilitarianism and personal faith. *Journal of Psychology and Theology, 5,* 226–233.

APPENDIX

Intrinsic Religious Motivation Scale

Please use the following scale to indicate your response to each statement listed below:

1 = strongly disagree   3 = moderately agree
2 = moderately disagree   4 = strongly agree

1. My faith involves all of my life. (Intrinsic)
2. One should seek God's guidance when making every important decision. (Intrinsic)
3. In my life I experience the presence of the Divine. (Intrinsic)
4. My faith sometimes restricts my actions. (Intrinsic)
5. Nothing is as important to me as serving God as best I know how. (Intrinsic)
6. I try hard to carry my religion over into all my other dealings in life. (Intrinsic)
7. My religious beliefs are what really lie behind my whole approach to life. (Intrinsic)
8. It doesn't matter so much what I believe as long as I lead a moral life. (Extrinsic)
9. Although I am a religious person, I refuse to let religious considerations influence my everyday affairs. (Extrinsic)
10. Although I believe in my religion, I feel there are many more important things in life. (Extrinsic)

3.7
QUEST SCALE (Batson & Schoenrade, 1991a, b)
Reviewed by Christopher T. Burris

Variable: Quest is a form of religious orientation, a motivational construct distinct from the extrinsic and intrinsic orientations conceptualized and measured by Allport (Allport & Ross, 1967; see also this volume). Initially proposed, in part, as the "conceptual leftovers" of the "mature religious sentiment" (Allport, 1950) that were believed to be overlooked in Allport's operationalization of the Intrinsic Scale (Batson, 1976; Batson & Ventis, 1982), quest is characterized as "the degree to which an individual's religion involves an open-ended, responsive dialogue with existential questions raised by the contradictions and tragedies of life" (Batson, Schoenrade, & Ventis, 1993, p. 169). Such dialogue appreciates the complexity of the issues involved, ascribes a positive role to doubt, and maintains a correspondingly tentative, changeable stance toward religious convictions (Batson et al., 1993).

Description: Although the conceptualization of quest has remained virtually unchanged over the course of Batson's writings related to it, numerous "Quest Scales" have appeared since the construct was initially proposed. A nine-item version used by Batson in the early seventies gave way to the six-item "Interactional" Scale (Batson, 1976), the version with which most of the substantive research related to the quest orientation has been conducted (see Batson & Ventis, 1982; Batson et al., 1993, for reviews). Prompted largely by criticisms regarding the low internal consistency associated with the 6-item scale, however, Batson and Schoenrade (1991b) constructed a 12-item Quest Scale. Reliability and other psychometric concerns also sparked three other independent scale revision/construction attempts: Altemeyer and Hunsberger (1992); Kojetin, McIntosh, Bridges, & Spilka (1987); and McFarland (1989). Only Batson and Schoenrade (1991b) will be discussed here, however.

The 12-item Quest Scale is intended to assess three distinct but interrelated aspects of the quest orientation: (a) "readiness to face existential questions without reducing their complexity," (b) "self-criticism and perceptions of religious doubts as positive," and (c) "openness to change" (Batson & Schoenrade, 1991b, p. 431). Each aspect is primarily assessed by four different items, although Batson and Schoenrade express reservations with respect to using these item clusters as subscales. Batson and colleagues typically employ a nine-point (1 = strongly disagree to 9 = strongly agree) response format; scores are reported as overall item means (range = 1–9) rather than as item totals (see "Norms/Standardization").

In addition to Quest Scale scores, Quest component scores—along with Means and End component scores—are computed based on a principal-components analysis justified by Batson's (1976) three-dimensional model of religious orientation (see "Practical Considerations"; see also *Religious Orientation Scale*, in this volume). Because the Quest component is defined almost exclusively by the Quest Scale (Batson & Schoenrade, 1991b, reported loadings of .98 and .97 in their two samples), however, the two are virtually interchangeable.

Practical Considerations: Other than a reference to deity in one item, the Quest Scale's assumptions and wording are quite nonsectarian, suggesting the scale's usefulness across a broad range of samples. The existential content and sense of time perspective present in many items may limit the scale's comprehensibility to older adolescents and beyond, although this reviewer is unaware of any data establishing a "lower limit" age range for the scale's use. Scoring of the scale itself is quite straightforward; deriving Quest component scores à la Batson's three-dimensional model requires some degree of statistical sophistication, however (see Batson, 1976, and Batson et al., 1993, for overviews of this procedure).

Norms/Standardization: In their initial presentation of the 12-item Quest Scale, Batson and Schoenrade (1991b) reported means of 5.04 and 4.95 for two groups (approximately 200 each) of Christian-background undergraduates at the University of Kansas who were at least moderately interested in religion. Burris, Jackson, Tarpley, and Smith (1996) demonstrated that Quest scores vary considerably as a function of self-identified religious preference (see "Validity"). There is also some evidence that quest is inversely related to age (from adolescence beyond), but the data are by no means unequivocal (see Batson & Schoenrade, 1991a). Moreover, all age-related data reported thus far are cross-sectional, not longitudinal, which cannot rule out possible cohort effects on the age-quest relationship.

Reliability: As noted above, Batson and Schoenrade (1991b) developed the 12-item Quest Scale in part as a response to criticisms regarding the 6-item Interactional Scale's low reliability, i.e., with the "true" Cronbach's alpha hovering "around .45 or .50" (p. 432) based on their review of several studies. The reliability of the 12-item Quest Scale, while not outstanding, is nevertheless much more adequate: Batson and Schoenrade reported Cronbach's alphas of .75 and .81 in their two samples, approximating the .71 to .78 range reported by Burris et al. (1996) across their four samples. Burris and Tarpley (in press) recently reported a two-week test-retest reliability of .79 for the 12-item scale in a sample of 61 undergraduates, again favorably comparing to the .63 for the 6-item scale in an unpublished manuscript cited by Batson and Schoenrade.

Validity: Assuming the relative interchangeability of the 6-item Interactional and the 12-item Quest scales (which seems justified given correlations ≥ .85, Batson & Schoenrade, 1991b), support for the validity of the latter scale is fairly substantial. For example, Batson has demonstrated repeatedly that the Quest Scale measures something

distinct from what the Extrinsic or the Intrinsic scales measure (see Allport & Ross, 1967; see also this volume)—although whether the quest orientation should be regarded as independent with respect to either of these orientations is open to debate (see Burris, 1994). Moreover, Burris et al. (1996) demonstrated quest to be an articulation of religion not reducible to agnosticism (Donahue, 1985), liberalism (Paloutzian, 1983; Wulff, 1997), or simple anti-orthodox sentiment (Watson, Morris, & Hood, 1989). In two university samples, Burris et al. (1996) found that individuals who declared their religious preference to be "personal religion" averaged higher on the Quest Scale than did either agnostics, liberal Protestants, or atheists. Indeed, consistent with Batson and colleagues' (1993, p. 167) suggestion that the quest-oriented individual is committed to "hammering out his or her stance on religious questions, refusing to be dominated by the religious institutions of society," Burris et al. found quest to be related to a number of variables suggestive of an individuated stance toward social participation in general (e.g., reactance, social criticism, need for uniqueness).

Two lines of evidence are consistent with Batson and colleagues' (1993, p. 166) assertion that quest centrally involves "honestly facing existential questions, while at the same time resisting clear-cut, pat answers." First, Batson and Raynor-Prince (1983) found quest (as measured by the six-item Interactional Scale) to be uniquely positively correlated with cognitive complexity specific to the religious domain. Second, Burris et al. found Quest scores to increase following confrontation with an existential dilemma (viz., reading about an infant boy who became a victim of a drive-by shooting while his grandmother prayed for his protection). Burris et al. also found quest to be uniquely positively correlated with self-reported family conflict in two undergraduate samples; moreover, cross-lag data suggested that family conflict was driving quest rather than vice-versa. Together, these two lines of evidence seem to offer quite consistent support for Batson's (1976, p. 32) assertion that quest is typified by "an endless process of probing and questioning generated by the tensions, contradictions, and tragedies in their own lives and society."

Curiously, given its origin in part as an attempt to capture aspects of so-called "mature religion" that Allport (1950) conceptualized but failed to measure (see this volume), the quest orientation seems to have taken on a life of its own. Indeed, given that it is unique among the religious orientations in its tendency to correlate negatively with a broad range of prejudice measures (Batson & Burris, 1994), and given that it also appears to correlate uniquely with victim-focused helping motivation (see Batson et al., 1993, chap. 10), quest would seem to offer the promise of many good things to the socially conscious psychologist of religion. Yet, as both critics (Hood & Morris, 1985) and defenders (Batson & Ventis, 1985) of the quest construct note, such sacralization may ultimately prove unwise. Rather, a much more fruitful approach would be to attempt to develop a general model of religious orientation that articulates not only *how* quest relates to the extrinsic and intrinsic orientations but also *why* each orientation relates to significant psychological and social variables as it does (e.g., Burris, 1997). Such integrative explanations seem all too rare.

Location:

Batson, C. D., & Schoenrade, P. (1991). Measuring religion as quest: 2. Reliability concerns. *Journal for the Scientific Study of Religion, 30*, 430–447.

Subsequent Research:

Batson, C. D., Oleson, K. C., Weeks, J. L., Healy, S. P., Reeves, P. J., Jennings, P., & Brown, T. (1989). Religious prosocial motivation: Is it altruistic or egoistic? *Journal of Personality and Social Psychology, 57*, 873–884.

Burris, C. T., Jackson, L. M., Tarpley, W. R., & Smith, G. (1996). Religion as quest: The self-directed pursuit of meaning. *Personality and Social Psychology Bulletin, 22*, 1068–1076.

McFarland, S. G., & Warren, J. C., Jr. (1992). Religious orientation and selective exposure among fundamentalist Christians. *Journal for the Scientific Study of Religion, 31*, 163–174.

References

Allport, G. W. (1950). *The individual and his religion*. New York: MacMillan.

Allport, G. W. , & Ross, J. M. (1967). Personal religious orientation and prejudice. *Journal of Personality and Social Psychology, 5*, 432–443.

Altemeyer, B. & Hunsberger, B. (1992). Authoritarianism, religious fundamentalism, quest, and prejudice. *International Journal for the Scientific Study of Religion, 2*, 113–133.

Batson, C. D. (1976). Religion as prosocial: Agent or double-agent? *Journal for the Scientific Study of Religion, 15*, 29–45.

Batson, C. D., & Burris, C. T. (1994). Personal religion: Depressant or stimulant of prejudice and discrimination? In M. P. Zanna & J. M. Olson (Eds.), *The seventh Ontario symposium on personality and social psychology: The psychology of prejudice* (pp. 149–169). Hillsdale, NJ: Lawrence Erlbaum.

Batson, C. D., & Raynor-Prince, L. (1983). Religious orientation and complexity of thought about existential concerns. *Journal for the Scientific Study of Religion, 22*, 38–50.

Batson, C. D., & Ventis, W. L. (1982). *The religious experience: A social-psychological perspective*. New York: Oxford University Press.

Batson, C. D., & Ventis, W. L. (1985). Misconception of quest: A reply to Hood and Morris. *Review of Religious Research, 26*, 398–407.

Batson, C. D., & Schoenrade, P. (1991a). Measuring religion as quest: 1. Validity concerns. *Journal for the Scientific Study of Religion, 30*, 416–429.

Batson, C. D., & Schoenrade, P. (1991b). Measuring religion as quest: 2. Reliability concerns. *Journal for the Scientific Study of Religion, 30*, 430–447.

Batson, C. D., Schoenrade, P., & Ventis, W. L. (1993). *Religion and the individual: A social-psychological perspective*. New York: Oxford University Press.

Burris, C. T. (1994). Curvilinearity and religious types: A second look at intrinsic, extrinsic, and quest relations. *International Journal for the Psychology of Religion, 4*, 245–260.

Burris, C. T. (1997, June). *Religious orientation and social identity: Towards a theoretical integration*. Paper presented at the Annual Convention of the Canadian Psychological Association, Toronto, Ontario, Canada.

Burris, C. T., Jackson, L. M., Tarpley, W. R., & Smith, G. (1996). Religion as quest: The self-directed pursuit of meaning. *Personality and Social Psychology Bulletin, 22*, 1068–1076.

Burris, C. T., & Tarpley, W. R. (1998). Religion

as being: Preliminary validation of the Immanence Scale. *Journal of Research in Personality, 32,* 55–79.

Donahue, M. J. (1985). Intrinsic and extrinsic religiousness: Review and meta-analysis. *Journal of Personality and Social Psychology, 48,* 400–419.

Hood, R. W., Jr., & Morris, R. J. (1985). Conceptualization of quest: A critical rejoinder to Batson. *Review of Religious Research, 26,* 391–397.

Kojetin, B. A., McIntosh, D. N., Bridges, R. A., & Spilka, B. (1987). Quest: Constructive search or religious conflict? *Journal for the Scientific Study of Religion, 26,* 111–115.

McFarland, S. G. (1989). Religious orientation and the targets of discrimination. *Journal for the Scientific Study of Religion, 28,* 324–336.

Paloutzian, R. F. (1983). *Invitation to the psychology of religion.* Glenview, IL: Scott, Foresman.

Watson, P. J., Morris, R. J., & Hood, R. W., Jr. (1989). Interactional factor correlations with means and end religiousness. *Journal for the Scientific Study of Religion, 28,* 337–347.

Wulff, D. M. (1997). *Psychology of religion: Classic and contemporary.* New York: Wiley.

Appendix

Quest Scale

Please indicate the extent to which you agree or disagree with each of the items by using the following scale:

1	2	3	4	5	6	7	8	9
Strongly disagree								Strongly agree

1. As I grow and change, I expect my religion also to grow and change.
2. I am constantly questioning my religious beliefs.
3. It might be said that I value my religious doubts and uncertainties.
4. I was not very interested in religion until I began to ask questions about the meaning and purpose of my life.
5. For me, doubting is an important part of what it means to be religious.
6. (-) I do not expect my religious convictions to change in the next few years.
7. (-) I find religious doubts upsetting.
8. I have been driven to ask religious questions out of a growing awareness of the tensions in my world and in my relation to my world.
9. My life experiences have led me to rethink my religious convictions.
10. There are many religious issues on which my views are still changing.
11. God wasn't very important to me until I began to ask questions about the meaning of my own life.
12. Questions are far more central to my religious experience than are answers.

Note. (-) indicates reverse-scoring. Items 4, 8, 9, and 11 tap the "existential questions" aspect. Items 3, 5, 7, and 12 tap the "doubting as positive" aspect. Items 1, 2, 6, and 10 tap the "openness to change" aspect.

3.8
RELIGIOUS MATURITY SCALE (Dudley & Cruise, 1990)
Reviewed by P. J. Watson

Variable: The Religious Maturity Scale (RMS) was developed in response to recent controversies in the psychology of religion. Widely used measures of intrinsic and committed religiousness originate in efforts to operationalize Allport's (1950) classic description of religious maturity. According to Batson and his colleagues (e.g., Batson & Ventis, 1982), these measures have failed to achieve their purpose. Allport emphasized open-mindedness as one aspect of religious maturity, whereas these instuments putatively record the orthodox fanaticism of a "true believer." Batson's Quest Scale seeks to redress this presumed problem by measuring a tolerant existential struggle for meaning. High scores on the Quest Scale are designed to reveal a more cognitively flexible religious orientation in which faith is wedded to doubt.

Like others before them, Dudley and Cruise (1990) criticize this conceptualization of Quest. They suggest that doubt is incompatible with the sincere commitment that Allport identified as another aspect of mature religion. To their way of thinking, a person who scores high on Quest "would be required to strongly agree with one set of items stressing commitment and the importance of faith while at the same time strongly agreeing with another set of items stressing religious doubts and uncertainties. To us this seems rather illogical, not to mention uncomfortable" (Dudley & Cruise, p. 100).

In their Religious Maturity Scale, Dudley and Cruise present what they hope to be a more defensible index of the personal religious search for meaning. They define religious maturity within a psychological rather than a theological framework. The focus, in other words, is on the process of being religious rather than on the content of particular theological beliefs. High scores theoretically reflect a creative tension between sincere commitment and a tentative open-mindedness, rather than doubt. As described by this scale, the religiously mature individual believes, "I want to be ready to progress in my understanding when a new piece of the 'truth' becomes clear to me. In the meantime I will live by the light I have" (Dudley & Cruise, p. 101).

Description: As a process rather than a content measure of religious commitment, this scale may be appropriate for use with all types of religious subjects, including those outside of the Judeo-Christian tradition. Items were written after a careful analysis of Allport's (1950) claim that a mature religion should be "(1) well differentiated; (2) dynamic in character in spite of its derivative nature; (3) productive of a consistent morality; (4) comprehensive; (5) integral; and (6) fundamentally heuristic" (Allport as quoted by Dudley and Cruise, p. 98). Twenty-six statements of religious maturity were combined with 28 other Intrinsic, Extrinsic, and Quest items to form a Personal Religion Inventory.

This inventory was administered to a sample of 491 mostly university students. Each statement was followed by a 5-point Likert-style agreement scale. A factor analysis of the entire inventory uncovered three orthogonal dimensions, with the third reflecting religious maturity. The 11 statements loading on this factor were combined into the Religious Maturity Scale (see appendix). Three negatively scored items articulated religious immaturity, with eight others expressing maturity. Total scores were computed by summing across all 11 items, resulting in a possible range of 11 to 55.

Practical Considerations: The Religious Maturity Scale appears to be a straightforward self-report measure. All items display an obvious face validity, and completion of the scale should be possible within ten and perhaps five minutes. Dudley and Cruise did not determine the reading level of their instrument, but comprehension of at least some items might demand a fairly high level of education. This possibility perhaps is illustrated in the following item: "I have found many religious questions to be difficult and complex so I am hesitant to be dogmatic or final in my assertions."

Norms/Standardization: Most of the 491 subjects used by Dudley and Cruise were Catholic or Seventh-day Adventist university students. Seventy older adolescents and a smaller group of adults attending various religious functions were included as well. The Religious Maturity mean and standard deviation were not reported for this sample.

Reliability: Dudley and Cruise obtained a coefficient alpha of .55. They argued that this internal reliability was not higher because the construct is a difficult one to operationalize. It is not easy, they claimed, to combine "the intelligent and informed commitment to a belief system, with the open-minded tentativeness of the searcher of truth" (Dudley & Cruise, p. 103). The authors did note, however, that a more acceptable coefficient alpha of .68 was uncovered in another investigation examining a national sample of over 400 participants.

Validity: The title of this article explicitly states that the goal of Dudley and Cruise was to present "a proposed scale." The authors consequently supplied little supportive validity evidence. They did find, however, that their instrument correlated as expected with greater Quest (.37), but not with the Intrinsic (.10) or Extrinsic (.02) religious orientations.

Location:
Dudley, R. L., & Cruise, R. J. (1990). Measuring religious maturity: A proposed scale. *Review of Religious Research, 32*, 97–109.

Recent Research:
Dudley, M. G., & Kosinski, F. A., Jr. (1990). Religiosity and marital satisfaction: A research note. *Review of Religious Research, 32*, 78–86.
Dudley, R. L., Hernandez, E. I., & Terian, S. M. K. (1992). Religiosity and public issues among Seventh-day Adventists. *Review of Religious Research, 33*, 330–348.

References

Allport, G. W. (1950). *The individual and his religion*. New York: Macmillan.
Batson, C. D., & Ventis, W. L. (1982). *The religious experience: A social-psychological perspective*. New York: Oxford University Press.

Appendix

Religious Maturity Scale

Here are some statements that show how some people feel about religion. Please indicate how much you agree or disagree with each by circling a number on a 5-point scale where 1 = strongly disagree and 5 = strongly agree.

1. My religious beliefs provide me with satisfying answers at this stage of my development, but I am prepared to alter them as new information becomes available.

2. I am happy with my present religion but wish to be open to new insights and ways of understanding the meaning of life.

3. As best as I can determine, my religion is true, but I recognize that I could be mistaken on some points.

4. Important questions about the meaning of life do not have simple or easy answers; therefore faith is a developmental process.

*5. I could not commit myself to a religion unless I was certain that it is completely true.

6. I have struggled in trying to understand the problems of evil, suffering, and death that mark this world.

*7. Churches should concentrate on proclaiming the gospel and not become involved in trying to change society through social or political action.

8. While we can never be quite sure that what we believe is absolutely true, it is worth acting on the probability that it may be.

9. I have found many religious questions to be difficult and complex so I am hesitant to be dogmatic or final in my assertions.

10. In my religion my relationships with other people are as fundamental as my relationship with God.

*11. My religious beliefs are pretty much the same today as they were five years ago.

An asterisk (*) identifies a negatively scored item for which 1 = 5, 2 = 4, 3 = 3, 4 = 2, and 5 = 1. Presented to the side of each statement is the following rating scale:

Strongly Disagree				Strongly Agree
1	2	3	4	5

Dudley, R. L., & Cruise, R. J. (1990). Measuring religious maturity: A proposed scale. *Review of Religious Research, 32,* (2), 97–109. Copyright © 1990. Review of Religious Research. Reprinted with permission.

3.9
RELIGIOUS ORIENTATION SCALE (Allport & Ross, 1967)
Reviewed by Christopher T. Burris

Variable: The Religious Orientation Scale (ROS) is based on Allport's early (1950) conceptual work where he characterized the so-called mature religious sentiment as: "1) well-differentiated [complex and critically embraced]; 2) dynamic in character in spite of its derivative nature [motivational in and of itself]; 3) productive of a consistent morality [shapes personal ethical code]; 4) comprehensive [applies to all areas of life]; 5) integral [capable of assimilating new information]; and 6) fundamentally heuristic [tentatively, though not lightly, held]" (pp. 64–65, interpretive brackets inserted). The "immature" religious sentiment, it was assumed, embodied the opposite of these characteristics. Details of the immature-mature distinction are largely absent from later discussions (Allport, 1966; Allport & Ross, 1967) of the relabeled extrinsic and intrinsic religious orientations; however, it is unclear whether this omission represented a narrowing of Allport's thinking or merely an indication that the earlier proposed differences

had become implicit assumptions. Still explicit, however, was that religious orientation (or sentiment) is a *motivational* construct: "Instrumental versus ultimate," "peripheral versus central," and "servant versus master" all capture the essence of the differential role that Allport assumed religion to occupy within the individual's life depending on whether he or she is extrinsically or intrinsically oriented, respectively. More formally, *extrinsic* religious orientation refers to a flagrantly utilitarian motivation underlying religious behaviors: The individual endorses religious beliefs and attitudes or engages in religious acts only to the extent that they might aid in achieving mundane goals, such as feeling comforted and protected or acquiring social status and approval. In contrast, *intrinsic* religious orientation refers to motivation arising from goals set forth by the religious tradition itself, and is thus assumed to have an "otherly," nonmundane, even self-denying quality: Religion is regarded as a "master motive . . . [whereas] other needs, strong as they may be, are regarded as of less ultimate significance" (Allport & Ross, 1967, p. 434, brackets inserted). Based on this distinction, many subsequent researchers have adopted the convenient, albeit simplistic, conceptual shorthand, initiated by Allport and Ross themselves, of referring to the extrinsic-intrinsic distinction as "using" versus "living" one's religion.

Description:

Subscales. Although the ROS represents Allport's capstone effort to operationalize the extrinsic and intrinsic religious orientations, there were at least two earlier efforts to tap these constructs. Specifically, Wilson (1960), with assistance from Allport, constructed a 15-item, forced-choice measure of extrinsic (but not intrinsic) "religious values." Several years later, Feagin (1964) presented 21 items from whence he derived both a 6-item Extrinsic and a 6-item Intrinsic Scale. (All but 1 of Feagin's original 21 items subsequently appeared in the ROS.) Neither of these earlier efforts has received the empirical attention that the ROS has, however.

Within the ROS itself, the Extrinsic (sub)scale assesses an individual's degree of acknowledgment of the peripheral role that religion plays in his or her life, as well as the degree to which he or she frankly admits to religious involvement in order to secure solace and/or social approval. That is, the items appear to operationalize straightforwardly the key elements of extrinsic orientation as Allport (1966; Allport & Ross, 1967) understood them.

Sampled from a variety of religious attitudes, behaviors, and intentions, Intrinsic (sub)scale items at first glance seem less conceptually focused than do Extrinsic items. To the extent that intrinsic orientation involves enshrining religion as the "master motive" of one's life as Allport and Ross (1967) suggested, however, the items make considerable sense, for they all reflect the no-nonsense fervency of commitment that such a master motive might evoke (at least as it might be articulated within a traditional

Christian context; see "Practical Considerations").

Scoring. Extrinsic and Intrinsic ROS items are best treated as composing distinct scales, owing to the absence of a straightforward inverse relationship between the two orientations (see "Validity"). Thus, given the 5-point (1 = strongly disagree to 5 = strongly agree) response format used in the original report (Allport & Ross, 1967), separate summation of the respective scale items yields score ranges of 11–55 and 9–45 for the Extrinsic and Intrinsic Scales. A 9-point response format is preferred by some researchers (e.g., Batson, 1976). Regardless of the specific response format used, it is recommended that means are scaled to the response format rather than reported as unscaled totals, for the former allows for meaningful comparisons between Extrinsic and Intrinsic scale scores within a given sample.

Another scoring issue linked to validity is whether and how individuals should be assigned religious-orientation-type labels based on their Extrinsic and Intrinsic scores (see, e.g., Burris, 1994; Hood, 1978; but also see Batson et al., 1993). This issue was initially confronted by Allport and Ross (1967) when Extrinsic and Intrinsic scores in their samples appeared to be linearly independent rather than inversely related as expected. In order to account primarily for those individuals who simultaneously tended toward agreement on both the Extrinsic and Intrinsic Scales—the so-called indiscriminately proreligious—Allport and Ross treated these respondents as a group, comparing them on pertinent dependent variables with those who tended toward agreement on only one of the two scales ("Extrinsics" or "Intrinsics"), and with those who tended toward disagreement on both scales (the "indiscriminately proreligious"). This later evolved into a median-split approach to classification, in which the four groups are created based on whether individuals score above or below the respective Extrinsic and Intrinsic medians for that sample. The chief advantage of the median-split approach is that it assures a relatively equal representation of respondents in each of the four groups regardless of sample characteristics. This is also the chief disadvantage: Extrinsic and Intrinsic score distributions—and thus, their medians—vary as a function of faith tradition (see Burris, Jackson, Tarpley, & Smith, 1996, Study 3), so labeled groups (e.g., Intrinsics) may not be comparable across samples. For this reason, the more conceptually meaningful practice of splitting the sample at the scales' theoretical mid- or neutral-point (e.g., 5 on a 1–9 scale) is preferred. Whatever the procedure, Burris (1994) has recommended that typing be employed only when adequately theoretically justified.

Spin-offs. Suggested revisions and replacements for the ROS scales have been numerous, although they have generally arisen based on one of two types of criticisms: the "pure empirical" and the "conceptual-empirical." Pure empirical criticisms focus on one or more of the ROS's perceived psychometric inadequacies, e.g., the absence of a strongly inverse Extrinsic/Intrinsic correlation (Hoge, 1972; see also this volume), low interitem correlations and/or multidimensionality of especially the Extrinsic Scale (Genia, 1993; Gorsuch & McPherson, 1989; see also this volume; Kirkpatrick 1989), or excessively abstruse item wording (Gorsuch & Venable, 1983; see also this volume). Conceptual-empirical criticisms are based more on *what* the ROS does and does not measure than on *how well* it measures. Typically, Allport's writings on immature/extrinsic and mature/intrinsic religion are compared against the content of ROS items, discrepancies are noted, and new scales are proposed to fill the presumed conceptual gaps (e.g., Dudley & Cruise, 1990). Of these, the most empirically prolific has been Batson's (1976; Batson, Schoenrade, & Ventis, 1993) means-end approach. It will thus be discussed in some detail.

According to Batson (1976), Allport's (1950) depiction of the "mature" religious sentiment actually confounds two forms of religious orientation that are conceptually and empirically distinct. The Intrinsic scale of the ROS taps only the "religion as master motive" theme that pervades Allport's discussion of the intrinsic orientation in later writings, Batson claimed: Unmeasured by either the Intrinsic or the Extrinsic Scale is the motivation to grapple with existential questions, to view religious doubts as positive, and to remain open to religious change that peppers earlier discussions of the mature sentiment. Batson and colleagues thus developed the Interactional, or Quest, Scale to tap these hitherto unmeasured themes (Batson, 1976; Batson & Schoenrade, 1991; see also this volume), and three additional scales intended to capture additional aspects of the extrinsic and intrinsic orientations that seemed implicit but unmeasured in the two constructs.

Specifically, based on his assumption that the "master motive" quality of the intrinsic orientation may be an outgrowth of needs for certainty, strength, and direction that express themselves outwardly (in part) through wholehearted endorsement of institutionally approved religious doctrines, Batson (1976) constructed the Internal and Doctrinal Orthodoxy scales. The former essentially measures an individual's "need to believe" (in religion); the latter measures an individual's degree of endorsement of a number of traditional Christian beliefs. Both scales were predicted and found to be moderately to strongly positively correlated with the Intrinsic scale. The remaining, External, scale measures the degree to which an individual's religion is affected by influential others such as peers, family members, and lay or professional religious workers. Batson (1976) initially predicted that this scale would be positively correlated with the Extrinsic scale; it has, however, almost invariantly correlated positively with the Intrinsic Scale instead, leading Batson et al. (1993, p. 169) to concede that the initial assumption has "proved wrong."

The six scales (all of which use a 9-point response format) in combination are intended to measure three dimensions of religious orientation that Batson assumes (and statistically forces) to be independent: The devout, doctrinaire End dimension (assessed by the Intrinsic, Internal, External, and Doctrinal Orthodoxy Scales), the utilitarian Means dimension (assessed primarily by the Extrinsic Scale), and the existentially toned Quest dimension (assessed primarily by the Quest Scale). The statistical procedures for deriving Means and End (as well as Quest) scores are sufficiently complex as to be beyond the scope of this volume; see Batson et al. (1993) for details.

Practical Considerations: Although Allport used the term "religion" rather generically in his theoretical works, he was undoubtedly influenced by his cultural, familial, and personal ties to a North American Protestant articulation of Christianity in his construction of the ROS (see Wulff, 1997). Hence, items including references to church and Bible study, for example, restrict the ROS's interpretability primarily to respondents with a Christian background. Modifications involving less sectarian wording, e.g., from "church" to "religious gathering," that do not alter the items' meaning substantially are therefore recommended.

Another problematic issue concerns conditional items, i.e., those containing a premise such as "although I believe in my religion. . . ." Nonreligious respondents in particular have difficulty answering such questions because they disagree with the premise. Because respondents' strategies for handling these items differ (i.e., some skip the items, some indicate strong disagreement, and some mark the scale midpoint), the reliability of particularly the Extrinsic Scale can be adversely affected. Specific instructions to assist respondents, e.g., "If you disagree with the premise on which an item is based, mark the response indicating 'strongly disagree' instead of leaving the item blank," are therefore encouraged.

Finally, as noted under "Description," the ROS has been criticized for the relatively high reading level of its items. Although this probably presents no problem in most adult samples, it is a legitimate concern when working with special adult populations or with children. An "age universal" version of the ROS has been developed for

such instances (Gorsuch & Venable, 1983; see also this volume).

Norms/Standardization: Allport and Ross's (1967) sample consisted of 309 members of six different churches/denominations (Roman Catholic, Lutheran, Nazarene, Presbyterian, Methodist, Baptist) scattered across the eastern United States, a sample that was claimed to be "in no sense representative" (p. 436). Unfortunately, Allport and Ross reported Intrinsic and Extrinsic scale means for neither each subsample nor the total sample. Donahue (1985a, p. 419) speculated that "smaller, more sect-like [religious] groups, would be expected to have higher Intrinsic and lower Extrinsic scores than larger denominations due to their more stringent membership requirements." Offering some support for this speculation, Burris et al. (1996, Study 3) found higher Intrinsic scores among conservative Protestant groups (e.g., Baptist, Pentecostal, Mormon) than among either liberal Protestants (e.g., Episcopal, Methodist, Presbyterian) or Catholics in a midwestern U.S. university sample. Conservative Protestants also averaged lower on the Extrinsic scale compared to Catholics but not compared to liberal Protestants.

Reliability: Internal consistencies reported for the ROS Intrinsic scale range from adequate to excellent, with Cronbach's alphas most typically in the mid .80s (e.g., Donahue, 1985a). Internal consistencies reported for the ROS Extrinsic scale are invariably lower, with Cronbach's alphas most typically in the low .70s (e.g., Donahue, 1985a). Burris and Tarpley (in press, footnote 3) reported two-week test-retest reliabilities of .84 and .78 for the Intrinsic and Extrinsic scales, respectively ($N = 61$). The lower reliabilities associated with the Extrinsic scale, although subject to criticism, can be attributed—at least in part—to the scale's tapping of multiple manifestations of the extrinsic orientation (e.g., Kirkpatrick, 1989). Whether the trade-off of psychometric potency for conceptual breadth is justifiable remains open to debate.

Validity: Evaluating the validity of the ROS Intrinsic and Extrinsic scales is, unfortunately, not a simple task, given the subtle shifts in emphasis in Allport's writings over time, and given the value-ladenness of the religious orientation constructs. The first issue affects evaluations of the scales' structural properties; the second raises questions as to what standards or markers should be considered relevant to validity.

Structure. As earlier noted, Allport's discussion (if not his conceptualization) of the intrinsic orientation appeared to narrow over time to a primary emphasis on the orientation's "master motive" character. Thus it could be argued that the adequacy of the Intrinsic scale as a measure of intrinsic orientation depends on whether one focuses on Allport's early or later writings. The Intrinsic scale's combination of relatively high internal consistency and breadth of item content would seem to support its validity as a measure of "religion as a master motive." Indeed, from this perspective, that intrinsic items scatter across a number of factors when factor-analyzed with other items tapping traditional religious attitudes and activities is not as problematic as Hunt and King (1971) claimed. Rather, the scattering can be interpreted as suggesting a common underlying construct, i.e., centralized religious motivation. On the other hand, the Intrinsic scale does not appear to be adequate as a comprehensive measure of "religious maturity" à la Allport (1950), as Batson (1976) has demonstrated.

In contrast, there is much less uncertainty as to whether the Extrinsic scale gets at the intended orientation. Although the scale's multidimensionality has been criticized on both conceptual and empirical grounds (e.g., Kirkpatrick, 1989) that Extrinsic items load on separable factors related to comfort-seeking, status-seeking, and the admission of religion's tangentiality conforms precisely to Allport's (1966; Allport & Ross, 1967) conceptualization. Thus, from a structural-content standpoint, the validity of the Extrinsic scale, like the validity of the Intrinsic scale, is very much a matter of perspective.

The same can be said from a structural-relational standpoint. As was earlier noted, Allport and Ross (1967) clearly expected a strong, inversely linear relationship between their Extrinsic and Intrinsic items—consistent with an hypothesized bipolar religious orientation dimension—rather than the near-zero linear correlation between the two scales that they found. In fact, the expected negative relationship has been obtained but has been restricted to theologically conservative samples (Donahue, 1985b), leading the majority of researchers (e.g., Batson, 1976) to conclude that Allport was wrong, i.e., that the extrinsic and intrinsic orientations are not opposites but are independent. Burris (1994) demonstrated, however, that the frequently observed near-zero linear relationship masks a substantial nonlinear relationship. Specifically, the Intrinsic and Extrinsic scales were shown to be inversely curvilinearly related such that, below the Intrinsic midpoint, the Intrinsic/Extrinsic correlation is positive, suggesting rejection of both forms of religious motivation, or simple irreligiosity. Above the Intrinsic midpoint, however, the Intrinsic/Extrinsic correlation is negative, suggesting that, as reported intrinsic orientation increases, reported extrinsic orientation decreases. (A similar overall relationship has been observed for the Intrinsic and Quest scales—see Burris, 1994). This pattern thus offers at least partial support of Allport and Ross's bipolarity assumption, but no support for the independence assumption.

Standards. The value-ladenness of the extrinsic/intrinsic distinction is most evident when determining what should serve as standards or markers of the ROS's validity. Allport and Ross (1967) provided no data relevant to the validity of the Extrinsic and Intrinsic scales, apparently assuming that the differential relationship observed between measures of ethnocentrism and these two scales was adequate. Their assumption was clear: As the old "mature" and "immature" labels implied, the intrinsic orientation was seen as the embodiment of "good" or "true" religion, whereas the extrinsic orientation was the embodiment of "bad" or "false" religion; "true" religion cannot, or at least should not, foster intolerance. Although perhaps quite compelling as a theological prescription, this assumption—that prejudice or its absence should ipso facto serve as a criterion for the religious orientation scales' validity—warrants clearer psychological (i.e., conceptual) justification. Much subsequent research utilizing the ROS and related measures has sidestepped issues of validity, however, by relying—as did Allport—upon an implicit "extrinsic is bad, intrinsic is good" heuristic. As a consequence, research that challenges the moral fiber and purity of motives assumed to be associated with the intrinsic orientation is often met with sharp criticism and accusations of bias. For example, consider the recurrent observation of a positive correlation between the Intrinsic scale and various measures of social desirability (e.g., Batson, Naifeh, & Pate, 1978). The straightforward interpretation of this is that higher intrinsic orientation is predictive of an increased need to "look good" to oneself and others. Defenders of the intrinsic orientation have responded by suggesting that measures of social desirability are biased against religious respondents or, alternatively, that intrinsically oriented individuals *report* being more socially desirable because they *are* more socially desirable (e.g., Watson, Morris, Foster, & Hood, 1986; Richards, 1994), although empirical support for either contention remains rather questionable (Burris, 1994; Leak & Fish, 1989). Similar denunciations (e.g., Gorsuch, 1993) have been made with respect to research linking the intrinsic orientation with subtle and not-so-subtle forms of prejudice (see Batson & Burris, 1994, for a review). In contrast, this reviewer is unaware of any comparable accusations of bias with respect to research demonstrating links between the extrinsic orientation and unsavory variables such as ethnocentrism.

To be certain, the conceptual and empirical claims and counterclaims raised regarding the extrinsic and intrinsic orientations remain sensitive and controversial. That is precisely the point: Allport's framework,

because of its implicit value assumptions, seldom elicits indifference. Moreover, researchers' personal responses to these value assumptions undoubtedly affect how questions of validity are framed. Indeed, one might suggest that, failing all else, the ROS might serve as a sort of projective test of the values and predilections of psychologists of religion! Having said this, what data (if any) might speak regarding the validity of the Extrinsic and Intrinsic scales?

If the Intrinsic scale indeed measures "religion as a master motive," it should be rather strongly positively correlated with measures tapping commitment to, or ascribed importance of, religion. This is, in fact, the case (Donahue, 1985b). Moreover, numerous studies have found a positive correlation between the Intrinsic scale and measures of one's general sense of purpose in life, also consistent with the "master motive" conceptualization (see Batson et al., 1993, chap. 8).

If the Extrinsic scale indeed taps a "hands-off" attitude toward religion, then it should *not* be positively correlated with measures of religious commitment. Once again, this is the case (Donahue, 1985b). Moreover, if the Extrinsic scale assesses one's frank admission of using religion for comfort, then it should be linked to variables suggestive of stress and maladjustment, i.e., variables that might encourage an otherwise irreligious person to "try " religion. Research is generally consistent with this suggestion: Batson et al. (1993) concluded, based on a review of findings from over 40 studies, that there is "considerable evidence that this [extrinsic, means] dimension is negatively associated with several conceptions of mental health," including "appropriate social behavior" and "freedom from worry and guilt" (p. 286, brackets inserted). Moreover, Burris, Batson, and Wagoner (1992) found that persons randomly assigned to complete an esteem-threatening writing task subsequently scored higher on the personal comfort subscale of the Extrinsic scale (Kirkpatrick, 1989) than did those who completed a neutral writing task, offering some experimental evidence for validity.

Direct evidence of this sort suggesting that the Extrinsic scale effectively taps the use of religion to bolster one's social status has yet to be produced, however.

In short, the research reviewed here—limited in scope due to the sheer breadth of the literature, and conservatively selective due the the value-ladenness of the constructs—seems generally supportive of the validity of the extrinsic and intrinsic orientations and the scales used to measure them. The research does not, however, support Allport's conceptualizations in every detail, a fact that will undoubtedly elicit sparring between apologists and critics of religious orientation for some time yet (e.g., Kirkpatrick & Hood, 1990; Masters, 1991). In this reviewer's opinion, essential to ensuring a "fair fight" is a retooling of Allport's model based upon what has been learned in the past three decades. Such a revised framework should remain true to the motive-centered spirit—if not the letter—of Allport's extrinsic-intrinsic framework, but should also be capable of incorporating religious orientations more recently identified—e.g., Batson's (1976) quest. Such a revised framework should also move beyond theological prescriptions to psychological principles as a basis for predicting and explaining relationships between religious orientation and variables of interest, e.g., prejudice, prosocial behavior, and mental health. It is a hopeful sign that attempts at such a framework are beginning to appear (e.g., Pargament, 1992; Burris, 1997). Given the fervency with which he strove to understand the vagaries of religious motivation during his own life, we can only assume that Allport would have wanted it this way.

Location: The ROS does not appear in Allport and Ross (1967), although the authors refer the reader to an address from which it can be obtained. A number of secondary sources present the ROS items, however, including Batson et al. (1993) and Wulff (1997). Batson et al. (1993) also contains the Internal, External, and Doctrinal Orthodoxy scale items.

Subsequent Research:
Batson, C. D., & Flory, J. D. (1990). Goal-relevant cognitions associated with helping by individuals high on intrinsic, end religion. *Journal for the Scientific Study of Religion*, 29, 346–360.

Burris, C. T., Batson, C. D., Altstaedten, M., & Stephens, K. (1994). "What a friend . . .": Loneliness as a motivator of intrinsic religion. *Journal for the Scientific Study of Religion*, 33, 326–334.

Hathaway, W. L., & Pargament, K. I. (1990). Intrinsic religiousness, religious coping, and psychosocial competence: A covariance structure analysis. *Journal for the Scientific Study of Religion*, 29, 423–441.

Kirkpatrick, L. A. (1993). Fundamentalism, Christian orthodoxy, and intrinsic religious orientation as predictors of discriminatory attitudes. *Journal for the Scientific Study of Religion*, 32, 256–268.

McFarland, S. G., Warren, J. C., Jr. (1992). Religious orientation and selective exposure among fundamentalist Christians. *Journal for the Scientific Study of Religion*, 31, 163–174.

References

Allport, G. W. (1950). *The individual and his religion*. New York: MacMillan.

Allport, G. W. (1966). The religious context of prejudice. *Journal for the Scientific Study of Religion*, 5, 447–457.

Allport, G. W., & Ross, J. M. (1967). Personal religious orientation and prejudice. *Journal of Personality and Social Psychology*, 5, 447–457.

Batson, C. D. (1976). Religion as prosocial: Agent or double-agent? *Journal for the Scientific Study of Religion*, 15, 29–45.

Batson, C. D., & Burris, C. T. (1994). Personal religion: Depressant or stimulant of prejudice and discrimination? In M. P. Zanna & J. M. Olson (Eds.), *The seventh Ontario symposium on personality and social psychology: The psychology of prejudice* (pp. 149–169). Hillsdale, NJ: Lawrence Erlbaum.

Batson, C. D., Naifeh, S. J., & Pate, S. (1978). Social desirability, religious orientation, and racial prejudice. *Journal for the Scientific Study of Religion*, 17, 31–41.

Batson, C. D., & Schoenrade, P. A. (1991). Measuring religion as quest: 2. Reliability concerns. *Journal for the Scientific Study of Religion*, 30, 430–447.

Batson, C. D., Schoenrade, P., & Ventis, W. L. (1993). *Religion and the individual: A social-psychological perspective*. New York: Oxford University, Press.

Burris, C. T. (1994). Curvilinearity and religious types: A second look at intrinsic, extrinsic, and quest relations. *International Journal for the Psychology of Religion, 4,* 245–260.

Burris, C. T. (1997, June). *Religious orientation and social identity: Towards a theoretical integration.* Paper presented at the Annual Convention of the Canadian Psychological Association, Toronto, Ontario, Canada.

Burris, C. T., Batson, C. D., & Wagoner, K. C. (1992, November). *Effect of esteem threat on intrinsic and extrinsic religion.* Paper presented at the Annual Convention of the Society for the Scientific Study of Religion, Washington, D. C.

Burris, C. T., Jackson, L. M., Tarpley, W. R., & Smith, G. (1996). Religion as quest: The self-directed pursuit of meaning. *Personality and Social Psychology Bulletin, 22,* 1068–1076.

Burris, C. T., & Tarpley, W. R. (1998). Religion as being: Preliminary validation of the Immanence scale. *Journal of Research in Personality, 32,* 55–79.

Donahue, M. J. (1985a). Intrinsic and extrinsic religiousness: The empirical research. *Journal for the Scientific Study of Religion, 24,* 418–423.

Donahue, M. J. (1985b). Intrinsic and extrinsic religiousness: Review and meta-analysis. *Journal of Personality and Social Psychology, 48,* 400–419.

Dudley, R. L., & Cruise, R. J. (1990). Measuring religious maturity: A proposed scale. *Review of Religious Research, 32,* 97–109.

Feagin, J. R. (1964). Prejudice and religious types: A focused study of southern fundamentalists. *Journal for the Scientific Study of Religion, 4,* 3–13.

Genia, V. (1993). A psychometric evaluation of the Allport-Ross I/E scales in a religiously heterogeneous sample. *Journal for the Scientific Study of Religion, 32,* 284–290.

Gorsuch, R. L. (1993). Religion and prejudice: Lessons not learned from the past. *International Journal for the Psychology of Religion, 3,* 29–31.

Gorsuch, R. L., & McPherson, S. E. (1989). Intrinsic/extrinsic measurement: I/E Revised and single-item scales. *Journal for the Scientific Study of Religion, 28,* 348–352.

Gorsuch, R. L., & Venable, G. D. (1983). Development of an "age-universal" I-E scale. *Journal for the Scientific Study of Religion, 22,* 181–187.

Hoge, D. R. (1972). A validated intrinsic religious motivation scale. *Journal for the Scientific Study of Religion, 11,* 369–376.

Hood, R. W., Jr. (1978). The usefulness of the indiscriminately pro and anti categories of religious orientation. *Journal for the Scientific Study of Religion, 17,* 419–431.

Hunt, R. A., & King, M. (1971). The extrinsic-intrinsic concept: A review and evaluation. *Journal for the Scientific Study of Religion, 10,* 339–356.

Kirkpatrick, L. A. (1989). A psychometric analysis of the Allport-Ross and Feagin measures of intrinsic-extrinsic religious orientation. In M. L. Lynn & D. O. Moberg (Eds.), *Research in the social scientific study of religion* (Vol. 1, pp. 1–31). Greenwich, CT: JAI Press.

Kirkpatrick, L. A., & Hood, R. W., Jr. (1990). Intrinsic-extrinsic religious orientation: The boon or bane of contemporary psychology of religion? *Journal for the Scientific Study of Religion, 29,* 442–462.

Leak, G. K., & Fish, S. (1989). Religious orientation, impression management, and self-deception: Toward a clarification of the link between religiosity and social desirability. *Journal for the Scientific Study of Religion, 28,* 355–359.

Masters, K. S. (1991). Of boons, banes, babies, and bathwater: A reply to the Kirkpatrick and Hood discussion of intrinsic-extrinsic religious orientation. *Journal for the Scientific Study of Religion, 30,* 312–317.

Pargament, K. I. (1992). Of means and ends: Religion and the search for significance. *International Journal for the Psychology of Religion, 2,* 201–229.

Richards, P. S. (1994). Religious devoutness, impression management, and personality functioning in college students. *Journal of Research in Personality, 28,* 14–26.

Watson, P. J., Morris, R. J., Foster, J. E., & Hood, R. W., Jr. (1986). Religiosity and social desirability. *Journal for the Scientific Study of Religion, 25,* 215–232.

Wilson, W. C. (1960). Extrinsic religious values and prejudice. *Journal of Abnormal and Social Psychology, 60,* 286–288.

Wulff, D. M. (1997). *Psychology of religion: Classic and contemporary.* New York: Wiley.

Appendix A

Religious Orientation Scale (ROS)

Please indicate the extent to which you agree or disagree with each item below by using the following rating scale:*

1	2	3	4	5
strongly disagree	disagree	neutral	agree	strongly agree

*Extrinsic (sub)scale**

1. Although I believe in my religion, I feel there are many more important things in my life.
2. It doesn't matter so much what I believe so long as I lead a moral life.
3. The primary purpose of prayer is to gain relief and protection.
4. The church is most important as a place to formulate good social relationships.
5. What religion offers me most is comfort when sorrows and misfortune strike.
6. I pray chiefly because I have been taught to pray.
7. Although I am a religious person I refuse to let religious considerations influence my everyday affairs.
8. A primary reason for my interest in religion is that my church is a congenial social activity.
9. Occasionally I find it necessary to compromise my religious beliefs in order to protect my social and economic well-being.
10. One reason for my being a church member is that such membership helps to establish a person in the community.
11. The purpose of prayer is to secure a happy and peaceful life.
***12. Religion helps to keep my life balanced and steady in exactly the same way as my citizenship, friendships, and other memberships do.

*Intrinsic (sub)scale**

1. It is important for me to spend periods of time in private religious thought and meditation.
2. If not prevented by unavoidable circumstances, I attend church.
3. I try hard to carry my religion over into all my other dealings in life.
4. The prayers I say when I am alone carry as much meaning and personal emotion as those said by me during services.
5. Quite often I have been keenly aware of the presence of God or the Divine Being.
6. I read literature about my faith (or church).
7. If I were to join a church group I would prefer to join a Bible study group rather than a social fellowship.
8. My religious beliefs are really what lie behind my whole approach to life.

9. Religion is especially important because it answers many questions about the meaning of life.

*Many researchers have used a 9-point response format.
**The ordering of all 20 items should be scrambled.
*** Indicates an additional Extrinsic item used by Feagin (1964) but not by Allport and Allport and Ross (1967).

Batson's Supplementary "End Dimension" Scales

Please indicate the extent to which you agree or disagree with each item below by using the following rating scale:*

1	2	3	4	5
strongly disagree	disagree	neutral	agree	strongly agree

Internal scale
1. My religious development is a natural response to our innate need for devotion to God.
2. God's will should shape my life.
3. It is necessary for me to have a religious belief.
4. When it comes to religious questions, I feel driven to know the truth.
5. (-) Religion is something I have never felt personally compelled to consider.
6. (-) Whether I turn out to be religious or not doesn't make much difference to me.
7. I have found it essential to have faith.
8. I find it impossible to conceive of myself not being religious.
9. (-) For me, religion has not been a "must."

External scale
1. The church has been very important for my religious development.
2. My minister (or youth director, camp counselor, etc.) has had a profound influence on my personal religious development.
3. A major factor in my religious development has been the importance of religion for my parents.
4. My religion serves to satisfy needs for fellowship and security.
5. Certain people have served as "models" for my religious development.
6. (-) Outside forces (other persons, church, etc.) have been relatively unimportant in my religious development.

Doctrinal Orthodoxy scale
1. I believe in the existence of a just and merciful personal God.
2. I believe God created the universe.
3. I believe God has a plan for the universe.
4. I believe Jesus Christ is the divine Son of God.
5. I believe Jesus Christ was resurrected (raised from the dead).
6. I believe Jesus Christ is the Messiah promised in the Old Testament.
7. I believe one must accept Jesus Christ as Lord and Savior to be saved from sin.
8. I believe in the "second coming" (that Jesus Christ will one day return to judge and rule the world).
9. I believe in "original sin" (we are all born sinners).
10. I believe in life after death.

11. I believe there is a transcendent realm (an "other" world, not just this world in which we live).

12, I believe the Bible is the unique authority for God's will.

Note. (-) indicates a reverse-scored item. For additional unscored buffer items, as well as details regarding scoring procedures, see Batson et al. (1993).

Batson, C. D., Schoenrade, P., & Ventis, W. L. (1993). Religion and the Individual: A social-psychological perspective, New York: Oxford University Press. Copyright © 1993 Oxford University Press. Reprinted with permission.

3.10
RELIGIOUS ORIENTATION SCALE-REVISED
(Gorsuch & McPherson, 1989)

Reviewed by Peter C. Hill

Variable: The Religious Orientation Scale-Revised, referred to by the authors as Intrinsic/Extrinsic—Revised (I/E-R), measures both the intrinsic and extrinsic religious orientation originally posited by Allport (1950). Kirkpatrick's (1989) conclusion, based on a reanalysis of several studies using Allport and Ross's (1967) original Religious Orientation Scale (see this volume), that the extrinsic scale subdivides into two categories, a personally oriented (Ep) and socially oriented (Es) extrinsicness, suggested that a revision of the I-E scales may be necessary.

Description: Gorsuch and Venable (1983) (also see this volume) had already revised the Allport and Ross (1967) scales to make the religious orientation measure more amenable to individuals at all educational levels. A confirmatory factor analysis of the Age-Universal scale found the Ep and Es distinctions proffered by Kirkpatrick (1988). Thus, this scale is a revision of Gorsuch and Venable's 20-item "Age-Universal" I-E Scale with items designed to measure the intrinsic as well as both extrinsic categories. The result is a 14-item scale measured on the same 5-point "strongly disagree" (1) to "strongly agree" (5) format used with the Age-Universal Scale. The authors report, however, that six or more intervals could be used with college students or "other relatively sophisticated respondents."

Eight items (3 reversed scored) tap the intrinsic orientation, whereas three items each measure the personal and social categories of extrinsicness. In addition, the authors attempted to identify single items to represent the constructs (arguing that there are times when single item scales are necessary or preferred). By identifying an item that correlated highly with its own factor and low correlations with the other factors, the authors identified three single items for each of the three orientations (no.12 for intrinsic, no.8 for extrinsic-personal, no.13 for extrinsic-social). The score of each scale is determined by summing its items' responses, resulting in a range of 8–40 for the I (Revised) scale and 3–15 for each E (Revised) scale.

Practical Considerations: This paper-and-pencil measure requires no special examiner skill to administer, score, or interpret.

Norms/Standardization: Participants in the original study were 771 students from secular and religious colleges in Southern California. The mean and standard deviation for I (Revised) were 37.2 and 5.8. The mean and standard deviation for E (Revised) were 25.6 and 5.7.

Reliability: The reliability estimate for I (Revised) was .83. The relability estimates for Ep (Revised), Es (Revised), and Ep/Es (Revised) were .57, .58, and .65 respectively. The reliability of the intrinsic scale is sufficient and is comparable to the reliability estimate of the original Age Universal

Scale. Though the reliabilities of the extrinsic scales are low, partly due to the fewer number of items making up each extrinsic scale, the authors are mindful that the brevity of the scales may make their use appealing for relatively large samples, thereby retaining the scales' statistical power. The authors also suggest that additional items for each extrinsic scale would help increase the reliability of these scales and thus would be highly desirable.

Validity: This scale confirms the factors found by Kirkpatrick (1988) in his reanalysis of several studies using traditional religious orientation scales. No other direct measures of validity are reported.

Location:

Gorsuch, R. L., & McPherson, S. E. (1989). Intrinsic/extrinsic measurement: I/E-revised and single-item scales. *Journal for the Scientific Study of Religion, 28*(3), 348–354.

Subsequent Research:

Giesbrecht, N. (1995). Parenting style and adolescent religious commitment. *Journal of Psychology and Christianity, 14*(3), 228–238.

Kirkpatrick, L. A. (1993). Fundamentalism, Christian orthodoxy, and intrinsic religious orientation as predictors of discriminatory attitudes. *Journal for the Scientific Study of Religion, 32*(3), 256–268.

Schaefer, C. A., & Gorsuch, R. L. (1991). Psychological adjustment and religiousness: The multivariate belief-motivation theory of religiousness. *Journal for the Scientific Study of Religion, 30*(4), 448–461.

Schaefer, C. A., & Gorsuch, R. L. (1992). Dimensionality of religion: Belief and motivation as predictors of behavior. *Journal of Psychology and Christianity, 11*(3), 244–254.

References

Allport, G. W. (1950). *The individual and his religion.* New York: MacMillan.

Allport, G. W., & Ross, J. M. (1967). Personal religious orientation and prejudice. *Journal of Personality and Social Psychology, 5,* 432–443.

Gorsuch, R. L., & Venable, G. D. (1983). Development of an "Age Universal" I-E scale. *Journal for the Scientific Study of Religion, 22,* 181–187.

Kirkpatrick, L. A. (1989). A psychometric analysis of the Allport-Ross and Feagin measures of intrinsic-extrinsic religious orientation. In D. O. Moberg and M. L. Lynn (Eds.), *Research in the Social Scientific Study of Religion* (Vol. 1.) Greenwich, CT: JAI Press.

Appendix

Intrinsic/Extrinsic-Revised (I/E-R) Scale

Following are the items included in the I/E-R scale. All items are scored as follows:

1 = I strongly disagree	4 = I tend to agree
2 = I tend to disagree	5 = I strongly agree
3 = I'm not sure	

1. (I)   I enjoy reading about my religion.
2. (Es)   I go to church because it helps me to make friends.
3. (I)** It doesn't much matter what I believe so long as I am good.
4. (I)   It is important to me to spend time in private thought and prayer.
5. (I)   I have often had a strong sense of God's presence.
6. (Ep)   I pray mainly to gain relief and protection.
7. (I)   I try hard to live all my life according to my religious beliefs.
8. (Ep)* What religion offers me most is comfort in times of trouble and sorrow.
9. (Ep)   Prayer is for peace and happiness.
10. (I)** Although I am religious, I don't let it affect my daily life.
11. (Es) I go to church mostly to spend time with my friends.
12. (I)   My whole approach to life is based on my religion.

13. (Es)*   I go to church mainly because I enjoy seeing people I know there.
14. (I)**   Although I believe in my religion, many other things are more important in life.

* Single-item measures for that factor
** Reversed-scored

3.11
RELIGIOUS POSITION SCALE (King & Hunt, 1972a; Jennings, 1972)
Reviewed by Michael J. Boivin

Variable: The Religious Position Scale consists of two portions: the dimensions of "Cognitive Salience" and "Extrinsic Religious Orientation." The Cognitive Salience portion evaluates the deeper significance of one's religion to his or her personal life. The Extrinsic Religious Orientation portion evaluates the extent to which one's religion serves a more superficially pragmatic or "means to an end" role.

Description: Using an empirical rather than theoretical approach, King and Hunt published a series of studies beginning in 1965 which sought to verify the multidimensional nature of religiosity and develop scales to describe its major dimensions (King & Hunt, 1990). Jennings (1972) used two of the scales refined by King and Hunt, and he labeled these The Religious Position Scale.

Developing a pool of 130 items taken from previous studies or developed from three exploratory surveys, King and Hunt used intercorrelational, cluster, and factor analysis to explore and describe the multidimensional nature of religiosity. Using factor and cluster analysis with a sample of 575 Methodist church members in the Dallas area, King (1967) initially proposed nine dimensions for the religious variable, one of which he characterized as an extrinsic/dogmatism factor. King and Hunt (1969) then amended these findings after using item-scale analysis on the same data. Inspired by the contributions of Allport, Glock and Lenski in the proposed theoretical dimen-

sions of religiosity, they then developed an expended item pool which they administered to four Protestant denominations in the Dallas-Fort Worth metropolitan area (King & Hunt, 1972a; King & Hunt, 1972b). The factor analysis they performed on these data resulted in ten scales which defined different dimensions of religious behavior and congregational involvement. Two of these factors were Salience/Cognition and Extrinsic Orientation (Hunt & King, 1971), which comprised the items in the Religious Position Scale used by Jennings (1972). Jennings cited King and Hunt (1970) as his source for the Religious Position Scale.

King and Hunt (1975) went on to administer their complete set of scales to a nationwide sample of main-line Presbyterians, and obtained similar findings in terms of the major factors that emerged in their item pool. An overview of the evolution of their scales and the theoretical basis for their work is presented in King and Hunt (1990).

The Religious Position Scale used by Jennings (1972) contains a total of 12 items posed in 5-point Likert format statements (strongly disagree to strongly agree). Five of the items pertain to the Cognitive Salience subscale, and the remaining seven make up the Extrinsic Religious Orientation subscale. The difference between these two subscales corresponds closely to Allport and Ross' (1967) distinction between intrinsic and extrinsic orientation.

This instrument does not assess any particular religious faith. All of the items are unidirectional, in that the more one agrees with each item, the higher the total score for that scale.

Practical Considerations: Presentation and scoring of the instrument are clear and straightforward. The instrument is brief and easily combined with other instruments for a more comprehensive set of measures. Items are phrased appropriately for a wide variety of Christian and non-Christian religious groups.

Norms/Standardization: Since King and Hunt were primarily interested in refining the major scales comprising religiosity by examining their factor structure, they do not report normative means or standard deviations for their data. The only published normative data (sample means and standard deviations) for this scale are found in Jennings (1972) survey of 364 students (61% male, 39% female) at a metropolitan junior college in Dallas, Texas. The model age range of this sample was 20–24 years. Approximately 48% of the subjects were single, while 45% were married. For the five items comprising the Cognitive Salience portion of the Religious Position Scale, the overall normative mean is 16.03 (SD = 4.01). Males had a mean of 15.74 (SD = 4.02) while the females had a mean of 16.48 (SD = 3.98). The overall mean for the seven items comprising the Extrinsic Religious Orientation portion of the Religious Position Scale was 18.29 (SD = 5.22). Normative scores for this factor were not presented by gender.

Reliability: Jennings (1972) reported both mean inter-item correlation coefficients and Spearman-Brown modifications of split-half coefficients. Both coefficient values for the Extrinsic Religious Orientation subscale were relatively low (interitem: $r = 0.15$; Spearman-Brown: $r = 0.51$). The coefficients were somewhat stronger for the Cognitive Salience subscale (r =.56, $r = 0.74$). Given the low inter-item correlation and split-half coefficient values, the internal consistency

for the Extrinsic Religious Orientation subscale should be viewed as suspect.

Validity: In terms of construct validity, Jennings (1972) found no significant differences with respect to age or gender. The Cognitive Salience subscale was moderately related to the Scriptural Literalism Scale (Hogge & Friedman, 1967; $r = 0.63$) and Religious World View Scale (McLean, 1952; $r = 0.65$). The Extrinsic Religious Orientation subscale was less strongly related to each scale respectively ($r = 0.35$; $r = 0.31$).

Location:
Jennings, F. L. (1972). A note on the reliability of several belief scales. *Journal for the Scientific Study of Religion, 11*, 157–164.
King, M. B., & Hunt, R. A. (1975). Measuring the religious variable: National replication. *Journal for the Scientific Study of Religion, 14*, 13–22.

Subsequent Research: None found.

References

Allport, G., & Ross, J. (1967). Personal religious orientation and prejudice. *Journal of Personality and Social Psychology, 5,* 432–443.

Hogge, J., & Friedman, S. T. (1967). The Scriptural Literalism Scale: A preliminary report. *Journal of Psychology, 66,* 275–279.

Hunt, R. A., & King, M. B. (1971). The intrinsic-extrinsic concept: A review and evaluation. *Journal for the Scientific Study of Religion, 10,* 339–356.

King, M. (1967). Measuring the religious variable. Nine proposed dimensions. *Journal for the Scientific Study of Religion, 6,* 173–190.

King, M. B., & Hunt, R. A. (1969). Measuring the religious variable: Amended findings. *Journal for the Scientific Study of Religion, 8,* 321–323.

King, M. & Hunt, R. A. (1970). *Religion, prejudice and cognitive style.* Unpublished paper.

King, M. B., & Hunt, R. A. (1972a). Measuring the religious variable: Replication. *Journal for the Scientific Study of Religion, 11,* 240–251.

King, M. B., & Hunt, R. A. (1972b). Measuring religious dimensions: Studies of congregational involvement. *Studies in Social Science,* no. 1. Dallas: Southern Methodist University.

King, M. B., & Hunt, R. A. (1990). Measuring the religious variable: Final comment. *Journal for the Scientific Study of Religion, 29,* 531–535.

McLean, M. (1952). Religious world views. *Motive, 12,* 22–26.

Appendix

Religious Position Scale

Please answer the following statements by *circling* the number that most accurately describes your beliefs based on the choices provided below.

1 = strongly agree   4 = moderately disagree
2 = moderately agree   5 = strongly disagree
3 = neutral

I. *Cognitive Salience*

1. I try hard to grow in understanding of what it means to live as a child of God.   1   2   3   4   5

2. I frequently feel very close to God in prayer, during public worship, or at important moments in my daily life.   1   2   3   4   5

3. I try hard to carry my religion over into all my other dealings in life.   1   2   3   4   5

4. My religious beliefs are what really lie behind my whole approach to life.   1   2   3   4   5

5. Religion is especially important to me because it answers many questions about the meaning of life.   1   2   3   4   5

II. *Extrinsic Religious Orientation Scale*

1. What religion offers me most is comfort when sorrows and misfortune strike.   1   2   3   4   5

2. The purpose of prayer is to secure a happy and peaceful life.   1   2   3   4   5

3. It is part of one's patriotic duty to worship in the church of his choice.   1   2   3   4   5

4. Religion helps to keep my life balanced and steady in exactly the same way as my citizenship, friendships, and other memberships do.   1   2   3   4   5

5. One reason for my being a church member is that such membership helps to establish a person in the community.   1   2   3   4   5

6. The church is most important as a place to formulate good social relationships.   1   2   3   4   5

7. Church membership has helped me to meet the right kind of people.   1   2   3   4   5

Jennings, F. L. (1972). A note on the reliability of several belief scales. *Journal for the Scientific Study of Religion, 11,* 157–164. Copyright © 1972 Journal for the Scientific Study of Religion. Reprinted with permission.

Chapter 4

Scales of Religious Development

Like many constructs in psychology, religious experience is not static; it changes over time. In response, psychologists of religion have established a number of indices designed to assess religious development. Many people assume that religious development occurs after adolescence. While this may be true with regard to basic religious identity (e.g., most religious "conversions" occur by adolescence), people often report religious or spiritual "growth" throughout adulthood. Such growth may include, for example, new religious experiences, new understandings of already existing religious beliefs or experiences, a greater sense of purpose or meaning in life, or a greater perceived awareness of divine involvement in everyday life.

There is a surprising dearth of scales that specifically measure faith development during the formative years, despite a rather extensive literature investigating religious development in children and adolescents. Granted, many of the scales in this volume use adolescents (or even children in a few cases) as part of the original sample to collect normative data. Oftentimes, of course, these are convenience samples of high school or college students or the studies are designed to test whether an existing measure can be used with a younger population. However, the research specifically designed to measure religious development in children and adolescents has generally shunned the use of the kind of scales reviewed in this volume, perhaps for good reason. After all, establishing valid measures of religion in a language understandable to children is not a simple task. Furthermore, children are often a more captive audience for other measurement techniques, such as informal interviews, picture drawing, or nonparticipant observation. The concept of God literature, for example, has frequently relied on picture drawing (often with subsequent explanation) to investigate the child's perception of the divine.

The eight assessment tools reviewed in this chapter provide a variety of techniques for measuring religious and faith development. Several of the scales provide a self-report inventory of religious or spiritual maturity. Five of these scales relate specifically to Christian maturity: Alter's Christian Experience Inventory (4.1), the Barnes et al. Faith Development Scale (4.3) based on James Fowler's theory of faith development, Benson and colleagues' Faith Maturity Scale (4.4), Malony's Religious Status Inventory (4.7), and Ellison's Spirituality Maturity Index (4.8). In contrast, Marthai's Religious Index of Maturing Survey (4.5) pertains to religion in general and is not specific to any particular religious tradition.

The other two measures included in this chapter are interview tools. The first tool is the Fowler's Faith Development Interview Guide (4.2), which is not restricted to Christianity. The other interview tool, Malony's Religious Status Interview (4.6), was designed specifically to assess Christian maturity.

4.1
CHRISTIAN EXPERIENCE INVENTORY (Alter, 1986, 1989)
Reviewed by John D. Scanish and Mark R. McMinn

Variable: The Christian Experience Inventory (CEI) measures believing adults' experience of their ongoing relationship with God as Person, that is, their daily "inner" experience of being in a divinely initiated, interactive relationship that affects their attitudes and values (Alter, 1986). Five subscales yield scores for one's experience of (1) growth in faith, (2) trust in God, (3) cost of faith, (4) concern for others, and (5) justification by faith.

Description: The CEI is a brief, 24-item scale based on the author's three-stage model of religious development (see Alter, 1986; Alter, 1994). Development through these three stages is believed to be facilitated by an individual's interaction with God.

This model assumes that religious development is a multifaceted phenomenon that begins with an individual's conscious choice to enter into religious commitment. It subsequently influences a person's attitudes and values about self, others, and God. It is not a natural chronological development because it requires a personal commitment to interact with God. Alter (1989) suggests that the human component of Christian experience can be observed, described, and to some extent measured.

Originally composed of 106 "faith statements," the process used to establish the CEI's reliability and to develop usable subscales led to the elimination of all but 21 items. A few years later, three "action statements" were added to the end of the inventory; no statistical procedures have been applied to these items. All 24 items are scored on a 4-point Likert scale, "very much like me" (3 points), "somewhat like me" (2 points), "not much like me" (1 point), and "definitely not like me" (0 points).

Three to six items load on each of the five subscales mentioned above. The CEI is scored by adding together a participant's points in each of these five areas. A participant is then said to have either a "modest," "medium," or "strong" level experience of God as person in that area (M. G. Alter, personal communication, September 20, 1995).

The five subscales were determined through factor analysis and identified as Experience of Growth in Faith (items 2, 5, 7, 11, 12, 22), Experience of Trust in God (items 8, 9, 13, 15, 17, 18), Experience of Cost of Faith (items 4, 10, 20, 23), Experience of Concern for Others (items 6, 16, 19, 21, 24), and Experience of Justification by Faith (items 1, 3, 14). Given the broad foundation of moral development and values orientation on which the CEI is based, it seems reasonable to conclude that these five factors would contribute to a person's experience of an ongoing relationship with God as person. It seems premature, however, to conclude that these five factors are the only, or the best, factors by which to measure such a phenomenon. The small number of items loading onto each factor likewise suggest that any analyses based on an individual participant's scores should remain tentative.

Practical Considerations: This pencil-and-paper inventory requires no special examiner skill to administer, score, or interpret. Directions for scoring are available from the author. Participants usually complete it in 10 to 15 minutes, and it can be used with individuals, groups, or entire churches. The language used is specifically and intentionally religious, "too Christian" for some and "not Christian enough" for others in mainline Protestant and Roman Catholic traditions (Alter, 1989).

Norms/Standardization: The normative sample was composed of 125 volunteer respondents from two large Presbyterian churches in California. It was a highly educated sample, with no respondents having less than three years of high school and two thirds of them having either college or graduate-level degrees.

Reliability: Test-retest reliability data were collected from 20 volunteers from an Oakland (CA) church and 17 assorted seminarians. Intervals ranged from two weeks to three months. Pearson product moment correlations ranged from .66 for the Justification by Faith scale to .91 for the Trust in God scale.

Validity: The author contacted seven religious professionals (four Catholic and three Protestant) who were interested in and involved with persons trying to grow in their faith. Each of these seven was asked to give the CEI to several people and to identify the respondents as "beginning," "intermediate," or "advanced" in their religious maturity. Response patterns were then compared to those obtained from a group of seminarians and from two church groups. Though specific comparisons are not reported, the author reports that higher scores on CEI subscales, particularly on the first, second, and fourth subscales, indicate higher levels of Christian maturity.

Location:
   Alter, M.G. (1986). A phenomenology of Christian religious maturity. *Pastoral Psychology, 34,* 151–160.
   Alter, M.G. (1989). An empirical study of Christian religious maturity: Its implications for parish ministry. *Pastoral Psychology, 37,* 153–160.
The scale itself is not published in either article.

Recent Research:
   Muse, J.S., Estadt, B.K., Greer, J.M., & Cheston, S. (1994). Are religiously integrated therapists more empathic? *The Journal of Pastoral Care, 48,* 14–23.

References

   Alter, M.G. (1986). A phenomenology of Christian religious maturity. *Pastoral Psychology, 34,* 151–160.
   Alter, M.G. (1989). An empirical study of Christian religious maturity: Its implications for parish ministry. *Pastoral Psychology, 37,* 153–160.
   Alter, M.G. (1994). *Resurrection psychology: An understanding of human personality based on the life and teachings of Jesus.* Chicago: Loyola University Press.

Appendix

Christian Experience Inventory (24)

The following items are designed to help us understand how people experience faith in their lives. The statements vary widely, and not all will apply to you and to your experience. Some may even feel offensive to you. That is expected. Simply mark them as seems correct for your experience of faith and continue on. Please answer spontaneously without pausing to ponder any one item. Most participants report that the questions took them about 10 to 15 minutes to complete.

In the blank to the left of each statement, circle 3 if the statement is very much like you and your experience; circle 2 if the statement is somewhat like you and your experience; circle 1 if the statement is not much like you and your experience; circle 0 if the statement is definitely not like you and your experience.

3—2—1—0 1. My imperfections don't bother me as much as they used to because God's acceptance of me is more important even though it's hard to accept.

3—2—1—0 2. I've found again and again that when I live in the Spirit of the Gospels problems don't overwhelm me and life is meaningful.

3—2—1—0 3. I am realizing that I have areas of "light and darkness," or good and evil, in my life, but God's transforming power is of greater importance.

3—2—1—0 4. I feel that I am doing something wrong in my prayer life when I can't feel God's closeness.

3—2—1—0 5. The goodness and mercy of God have begun to come alive for me.

3—2—1—0 6. If I take Jesus' teachings seriously, it makes good sense to feel concern for flood and disaster victims.

3—2—1—0 7. It seems that the Spirit of God pushes me into new cycles of learning and growth.

3—2—1—0 8. In my relationship with God, I sometimes feel like talking a lot and sometimes very little, but I always know God is there.

3—2—1—0 9. I sense that God has always been in my life.

3—2—1—0 10. Because of my commitment to God, I am sometimes called to say hard things in spite of my reluctance.

3—2—1—0 11. I feel I know or will know what God wants our relationship to become.

3—2—1—0 12. I am learning to trust my ongoing relationship with God.

3—2—1—0 13. Even amid confusion and turmoil I find comfortable peacefulness in God's love.

3—2—1—0 14. The Christian understanding that I will never be perfect is a relief.

3—2—1—0 15. I have no doubt that I continue to be held in God's hand.

3—2—1—0 16. My faith leads me to an active concern for people and for the whole living world.

3—2—1—0 17. In times of greatest distress, I am most deeply aware of God's faithfulness.

3—2—1—0 18. Whatever happens, I will find that the Spirit of God moves in my life.

3—2—1—0 19. To be serious about Christian values means that I take an active interest in justice for all people.

3—2—1—0 20. I feel troubled when I realize how much I participate in a sinful society.

3—2—1—0 21. My Christian faith pervades my entire life.

3—2—1—0 22. Within the past two years, I have taken a class or workshop or participated in some other activity which directly influences my faith development.

3—2—1—0 23. Within the past year I have felt it necessary to speak out on some issue because of my faith.

3—2—1—0 24. Because of my faith, I participate practically, financially, politically or prayerfully in helping people less fortunate than I am.

Reprinted with permission by author.

4.2
FAITH DEVELOPMENT INTERVIEW GUIDE (Fowler, 1981)
Reviewed by Christopher T. Burris

Variable: The Faith Development Interview Guide provides a basic outline for a semidirective interview, the purpose of which is to determine an individual's global level of faith development. In this context, the term "faith" refers to the process by which an individual constructs a personal framework for making the world coherent and meaningful. This process-oriented conceptualization thus does not focus on the framework's content per se but rather on how its various components are assembled and maintained. As such, explicitly religious frameworks are subsumed by, but not exhaustive of, the faith domain.

Description: In the tradition of structural-developmental theorists such as Piaget, Kohlberg, and Erikson, Fowler's (1981) faith development theory postulates that an individual's maturation with respect to tackling the universal human task of meaning construction is subject to identifiable stages that are "invariant, sequential, and hierarchical" in nature (Fowler, 1996, p. 169). That is, although a given individual will not necessarily progress through all the stages of faith, he or she will go through them in a specified order, never making the transition to a "higher" stage before necessary earlier stages are experienced. Throughout this process, previous stages are assimilated but not obliterated.

Fowler postulated seven stages of faith, although his assessment approach is designed to tap only six. Thus, "Primal Faith"—or what Fowler (1994) later refers to as "Undifferentiated Faith"—defined in term's of an infant sense of basic trust and immediate sensory experience, remains but an inferred starting point in his approach. In Stage 1, or Intuitive-Projective Faith, the child—aided by newly acquired language and a blossoming imagination—begins to grasp the possibilities inherent in symbols, develops a rudimentary self-awareness, and is powerfully affected by stories and experiences with caregivers. In Stage 2, or Mythic-Literal Faith, the engrossment with stories—predominantly those endorsed by one's culture—continues; although the child's capacity to distinguish between fantasy and reality improves, story learning and telling remain rather concrete, as is his or her adherence to rules (moral and otherwise). In Stage 3, or Synthetic-Conventional Faith, interpersonal awareness is sufficiently developed to ensure a central influential role of peers, significant others, and authority figures; the (adolescent or older) individual is now capable of assuming an ideology which becomes the basis for values and ethics, although the ideology is more inherited (from one's social surround) than created (through personal reflection). Stage 4, or Individuative-Reflective Faith, is typified by an emergent awareness of inconsistencies inherent in one's inherited worldview as it is subjected to critical analysis; rationality and self-sufficiency are enshrined as reference groups and their shared symbols are dethroned. The central theme of Stage 5, Conjunctive Faith (or Paradoxical-Consolidative Faith in Fowler, 1994), might be characterized as reconciliation: Instead of dealing with the tension inherent in paradox by compartmentalization as in Stage 4, boundaries—both intrapersonal and interpersonal—are dissolved as much as possible and prior, seemingly disparate, themes are allowed to intermix freely; symbols are embraced anew, with a concurrent appreciation of their validity and incompleteness. Finally, in the "Universalizing Faith" of Stage 6, the reconciliation begun in Stage 5 is perfected sufficiently that the individual's vision of the interconnectedness of self, others, and planet is translated into a contagious call for transformation of social conditions, a role roughly corresponding to the Eastern and Western concepts of "bodhisattva" and "prophet," respectively.

The Faith Development Interview Guide

presented herein (from Fowler, 1981) should be regarded as just that: a guide, sample, or starting point. It is highly unlikely that mechanical administration of the questions contained therein can yield information of sufficient quantity or quality to determine the individual's level of faith development with any confidence. Rather, a successful interview likely requires considerable clinical acumen, as well as familiarity with the theory and the cultural context (see Snarey, 1991) in order to know when and how to direct the interviewee, and attend to the underlying meanings in his or her responses.

Scoring of faith development interviews is described in detail in Moseley, Jarvis, and Fowler (1993; also see Fowler, 1981, pp. 217–268, 307–310, for an annotated example and brief overview). Only an oversimplified sketch can be offered in this volume. In general, taped interviews are transcribed and then inspected for themes, both in terms of specific contents and underlying process(es). More specifically, a stage score is assigned to an interviewee for each of seven different aspects of faith (see Fowler, 1981, pp. 244–245, for a tabular summary). *Form of logic* refers to the characteristic decision rules used in reasoning about issues of faith and meaning. *Perspective taking* involves the individual's relative capacity for seeing himself or herself from the standpoint of either an interpersonal other or a third party. *Form of moral judgment* refers to one's foundation for ethics. *Bounds of social awareness* are concerned with an individual's degree of incorporation of diverse experiences into the process of meaning construction. *Locus of authority* refers to one's primary source of guidance and/or approval. *Form of world coherence* is concerned with an individual's degree of awareness of the subjectivity and internal consistency of his/her assumptions. Finally, *symbolic functioning* focuses on the depth and malleability of meaning(s) associated with an individual's core symbols. An individual's scores on the seven aspects of faith are then averaged to yield a global faith development stage score ranging from 1 to 6, including half-stage or transitional scores, e.g., 4/5.

***Practical Considerations*:** Practical considerations associated with administration and scoring of the Faith Development Interview Guide should not be taken lightly. As noted above, a considerable degree of clinical acumen and interviewing skill, along with familiarity with faith development theory, is needed to conduct each interview. Fowler (1994) estimated that 1–3 hours of contact time are required for each interview, with the average being somewhat lower for children. Although optional, transcription of each taped interview is strongly recommended. Scoring requires thorough familiarity with the scoring manual (Moseley et al., 1993); moreover, Fowler (1981) recommends at least three reads of a given transcript before assigning scores. To ensure accuracy and provide an index of interrater reliability, a co-rater is also required. Thus, research involving the Faith Development Interview Guide should be planned with the utmost care, for it is both time and labor intensive (see also "Validity").

***Norms/Standardization*:** Fowler's (1981) original sample consisted of 359 predominantly White women and men, ages ranging from 4 to 84. Nearly half were Protestant and slightly more than one-third were Catholic, with the balance comprised of Jewish and "other" respondents. Because faith stages are assumed to correspond—albeit roughly—with chronological age, age-stage distributions are discussed under "Validity" below.

***Reliability*:** Snarey (1991) reported an interrater reliability of .88, which he claimed to be fairly typical. He also reported an internal consistency (based on the seven aspects of faith scores) of .93, which he admitted may be inflated somewhat by the raters' desire to appear self-consistent. This caution notwithstanding, interrater reliability and internal consistency taken together are impressive, given the relative complexity of the scoring procedure.

***Validity*:** Fair empirical support exists for the validity of the Faith Development Interview Guide. In Fowler's (1981) original sample, an overall positive, if weak, relationship between age and faith stage was observed. Modal stages for the age groups represented in the sample were: 1 for 0–6 years; 2 for 7–12 years; 3 for 13–20 years; 4 for 21–30 years; 3 for 31–40 years; 4 for 41–50 years; 3 for 51–60 years and 4 for 61+ years. Moreover, no Stage 5 individuals occurred below the 31–40 age group. Overall, these data are consistent with Fowler's contention that advancing age is a necessary but not sufficient condition for advanced faith stage development. At the same time, it must be remembered that the data are cross-sectional and are thus not capable of ruling out possible cohort effects. Fowler (1994) reported that a five-year longitudinal study was underway in the early 1990s; thus, it remains to be seen whether strong support for the "invariant sequence" hypothesis of faith development theory is supported.

Snarey's (1991) study made several important contributions to the validity of faith development constructs and the related assessment procedure. First, the distribution of faith stage scores in his sample of 60 predominantly atheistic current or former dwellers in an Israeli kibbutz was similar to that of a comparable theistic sample, suggesting that the faith development conceptual scheme is not biased in favor of traditional (theistic) religion. Second, faith stage scores were moderately positively correlated with both moral and ego development scores, suggesting that both of the latter are related to, but not redundant with, the former. Moreover, faith stage was positively correlated with the presence of subtle versus obvious symbols of Jewish identity in the interviewees' dwellings, consistent with Fowler's (1981) postulation that symbol systems are employed in a more flexible, abstract manner at higher levels of faith development.

Snarey (1991) also found the average faith stage of former kibbutz dwellers who moved to Israeli cities to be higher (4.2) than the average among current kibbutz dwellers (3.8); former kibbutz dwellers who moved to North American cities averaged in between these two groups (4.0) and did not significantly differ from either. Snarey in-terpreted this finding as supportive of the construct validity of the faith development assessment approach, suggesting that the heterogeneous, cosmopolitan environment of Israeli cities provided exposure to diversity—essential fodder for advanced faith development—that was less salient in the more homogeneous environment of the kibbutz. This finding, in combination with observed positive correlations between faith stage scores and variables such as level of education and social class, raises concerns about possible intellectualist and classist biases inherent in the faith development framework, however (see Leak & Randall, 1995). That faith development theory is subject to these sorts of criticisms is not unique. Indeed, this seems to be an inevitable outcome of positing an invariant series of stages culminating in an idealized endpoint (see Wulff, 1997, pp. 401–405, for a review of conceptual criticisms): Moral development theory has been similarly criticized. It remains to be seen whether faith development theory can withstand the ideological criticisms of this sort it has provoked.

Location:

Fowler, J. W. (1981). *Stages of faith: The psychology of human development and the quest for meaning*. San Francisco: Harper & Row.

Recent Research:

Barnes, M., Doyle, D., & Johnson, B. (1989). The formation of a Fowler scale: An empirical assessment among Catholics. *Review of Religious Research, 30*, 412–420.

Green, C. W., & Hoffman, C. L. (1989). Stages of faith and perceptions of similar and dissimilar others. *Review of Religious Research, 30*, 246–254.

Leak, G. K., & Randall, B. A. (1995). Clarification of the link between right-wing authoritarianism and religiousness: The role of religious maturity. *Journal for the Scientific Study of Religion, 34*, 245–252.

Snarey, J. (1991). Faith development, moral development, and nontheistic Judaism: A construct validity study. In W. M. Kurtines and J. L. Gewirtz (Eds.), *Handbok of moral behavior and development, Volume 2: Research*. Hillsdale, NJ: Lawrence Erlbaum.

Comment:
There is little question that faith development theory is an exceedingly rich, if

complex and value-laden, theoretical frame-work. One can present hardly more than a caricature of it in the space allotted herein. Ironically, its greatest strength—attention to individuals' meaning-making life journeys in narrative detail—is its greatest weakness, for the investment required has apparently re-sulted in the empirical investigation of faith development lagging far behind armchair discussion. Quickening the empirical pace is thus a vital task for future researchers.

References

Fowler, J. W. (1981). *Stages of faith: The psy-chology of human development and the quest for meaning.* San Francisco: Harper & Row.

Fowler, J. W. (1994). Moral stages and the de-velopment of faith. In W. Pupa (Ed.), *Moral Devel-opment, Volume 2: Fundamental research in moral development* (pp. 130–160). New York: Garland.

Fowler, J. W. (1996). Pluralism and oneness in religious experience: William James, faith-develop-ment theory, and clinical practice. In E. P. Shafranske (Ed.), *Religion and the clinical practice of psychology* (pp. 165–186). Washington, DC: American Psychological Association.

Moseley, R., Jarvis, D., & Fowler, J. W. (1993). *1993 Manual for faith development research.* (Rev. Karen B. DeNicola.) Atlanta, GA: Center for Re-search in Faith and Moral Development, Emory University.

Wulff, D. M. (1997). *Psychology of religion: Classic and contemporary.* New York: Wiley.

Appendix

Faith Development Interview Guide

Part I: Life Review

1. Factual Data: Date and place of birth? Number and ages of siblings? Occupation of pro-viding parent or parents? Ethnic, racial, and religious identifications? Characterization of social class—family of origin and now?

2. Divide life into chapters: (major) segments created by changes or experiences—"turning points" or general circumstances.

3. In order for me to understand the flow or movement in your life and your way of feeling and thinking about it, what other persons and experiences would be important for me to know about?

4. Thinking about yourself at present: What gives your life meaning? What makes life worth living for you?

Part II: Life-Shaping Experiences and Relationships

1. At present, what relationships seem most important for your life? (E.g., intimate, famil-ial, or work relationships.)

2. You did/did not mention your father in your mentioning of significant relationships.
   When you think of your father as he was during the time you were a child, what stands out? What was his work? What were his special interests? Was he a religious person? Explain.
   When you think of your mother...[same questions as previous]?
   Have your perceptions of your parents changed since you were a child? How?

3. Are there other persons who at earlier times or in the present have been significant in the shaping of your outlook on life?

4. Have you experienced losses, crises or suffering that have changed or "colored" your life in special ways?

5. Have you had moments of joy, ecstasy, peak experience, or breakthrough that have shaped or changed your life? (e.g., in nature, in sexual experience or in the presence of inspiring beauty or communication?)

6. What were the taboos in your early life? How have you lived with or out of those taboos? Can you indicate how the taboos in your life have changed? What are the taboos now?

7. What experiences have affirmed your sense of meaning in life? What experiences have shaken or disturbed your sense of meaning?

Part III: Present Values and Commitments

1. Can you describe the beliefs and values or attitudes that are most important in guiding your own life?

2. What is the purpose of human life?

3. Do you feel that some approaches to life are more "true" or right than others? Are there some beliefs that all or most people *ought* to hold and act on?

4. Are there symbols or images or rituals that are important to you?

5. What relationships or groups are most important as support for your values and beliefs?

6. You have described some beliefs and values that have become important to you. How important are they? In what ways do these beliefs and values find expression in your life? Can you give some specific examples of how and when they have had effect? (e.g., times of crisis, decisions, groups affiliated with, causes invested in, risks and costs of commitment.)

7. When you have an important decision to make regarding your life, how do you go about deciding? Example?

8. Is there a "plan" for human lives? Are we—individually or as a species—determined or affected in our lives by power beyond human control?

9. When life seems most discouraging and hopeless, what holds you up or renews your hope? Example?

10. When you think about the future, what makes you feel most anxious or uneasy (for yourself and those you love; for society or institutions; for the world)?

11. What does death mean to you? What becomes of us when we die?

12. Why do some persons and groups suffer more than others?

13. Some people believe that we will always have poor people among us, and that in general life rewards people according to their efforts. What are your feelings about this?

14. Do you feel that human life on this planet will go on indefinitely, or do you think it is about to end?

Part IV: Religion

1. Do you have or have you had important religious experiences?

2. What feelings do you have when you think about God?

3. Do you consider yourself a religious person?

4. If you pray, what do you feel is going on when you pray?

5. Do you feel that your religious outlook is "true"? In what sense? Are religious traditions other than your own "true"?

6. What is sin (or sins)? How have your feelings about this changed? How did you feel or think about sin as a child, an adolescent, and so on?

7. Some people believe that without religion morality breaks down. What do you feel about this?

8. Where do you feel that you are changing, growing, struggling or wrestling with doubt in your life at the present time? Where is your growing edge?

9. What is your image (or idea) of mature faith?

4.3
FAITH DEVELOPMENT SCALE (Barnes, Doyle & Johnson, 1989)
Reviewed by Randie L. Timpe

Variable: James Fowler's Faith Development Scale is based on (1981, 1991a, 1991b) his theory of faith development that parallels Erik Erikson's psycho-social, Jean Piaget's cognitive, and Lawrence Kohlberg's moral developmental theories. Fowler's faith development theory builds on the foundations set by cognitive and moral development, so that Fowler's proposition is an extension and elaboration of Piaget and Kohlberg's developmental stage theories. Fowler (1981) advanced the concept that individuals may hold the same beliefs in different ways, some in very literal ways and others in a very symbolic, abstract fashion. He proposed that the most primitive style was the *projective-intuitive faith* of a little child. In the second stage, *mythical-literal faith*, the person accepts uncritically and literally the traditional faith stories. In the third stage, *synthetic-conventional faith*, the individual aligns more explicitly with group religiosity and lives a more complex story. The fourth stage, *individuative-reflective*, employs a more abstract and individually reasoned universal form of faith. Individuals exhibiting the fifth stage, the *conjunctive* stage, recognize the symbolic nature of truth. Only a few individuals achieve *universalizing faith* in which motivation and vision so focus on justice and the needs of others that the self is decentered.

Description: Fowler (1981) developed his stages of faith through an interview methodology. He failed to develop a quick, simple, reliable, and valid measure to assess one's stage of faith development. Barnes, Doyle and Johnson (1989) sought to develop an assessment instrument for faith development like that developed by Rest (1979, 1986) for Kohlberg's (1976) moral development theory. But rather than define faith in a stage orientation, Barnes, Doyle and Johnson (1989) described faith in terms of styles. The individual's score is determined by the nine sets of paired items. Each item represents a faith "style" indicative of one of Fowler's faith stages.

Practical Considerations: The scale is an easy-to-administer paper and pencil test, but it could be given orally. The items require that the respondent has given some logical reflection to religion. The scale seems inappropriate for individuals who have given little cognitive reflection to their participation in religion; agnostics, children, and individuals who are intellectually challenged could not be anticipated as providing reliable, valid self-assessments. Individuals whose religious experience is primarily affectively oriented might challenge the test's cognitive orientation. The scale may not effectively assess a behavioral orientation to religion.

The items were originally developed for a Catholic audience, but the item content relates to adults from the mainstream Catholicism and Protestantism. Using the scale with religious extremists may result in data of questionable utility. Individuals from a rigid, right-winged fundamentalist cult or from a left-winged liberal society may react adversely to item content rather than reveal their thinking preference. The God and Christ language renders the scale inappropriate for a Hindu, Islamic, Jewish, or even non-western religious devotee. That is, some respondents might reject the theological tenets assumed in the scale's construction.

Norms/Standardization: Barnes, Doyle and Johnson (1989) tested the items on three groups of individuals who, they reasoned, should be different in their style of faith: members of a prayer group, parishioners from a Catholic congregation in Dayton, OH, and a group of college/seminary religious studies teachers and theologians. The total usable sample was 576. They suggested that this grouping should differentiate individuals along a continuum from literal faith to symbolic faith. They found that a discriminant analysis predicted membership well in the norming groups (94% correct prediction in the prayer group, 61% in the parish group, and 81% in the college/seminary faculty group).

Reliability: No findings are reported that suggest that the scale developers or those using it in subsequent research addressed the issue of reliability.

Validity: Barnes, Doyle and Johnson (1989) sought to establish concurrent validity by predicting membership in varying groups of faith style. That discriminant analysis study was described earlier. They also developed a survey of beliefs that varied along the literal-symbolic dimension. The survey of religious beliefs was comprised of twenty pairs of statements about essential church doctrine. One statement in each pair was literal, while the other was symbolic in form. Individuals identified as faith style 2 and 3 consistently preferred the more literal statement of belief, while those identified by the scale as faith style 4 and 5 consistently preferred the symbolic statements.

Goldsmith and Bayless (1991) reported a moderate correlation between the Fowler Faith Scale and Rest's Defining Issues Test, as would be anticipated by Kohlberg's and Fowler's theories. They also found that individuals with a more intrinsic orientation to religion had a more symbolic expression of faith. Those of higher faith stages were less dogmatic. Similar results were reported in a later study (Goldsmith, Bayless, & Hines, 1992).

Location:
Barnes, M., Doyle, D., & Johnson, B. (1989). The formulation of a Fowler Scale: An empirical assessment among Catholics. *Review of Religious Research*, 30(4), 412–420.

Subsequent Research:
Goldsmith, W. M., & Bayless, S. L. (1991, August). *Male and female seminarians' personality and moral reasoning: Protestants, Catholics and Jews*. Paper presented to the American Psychological Association, San Francisco, CA.

Goldsmith, W. M., Bayless, S. L., & Hynes, V. J. (1992, August). *Faith development, moral development and values*. Paper presented to the American Psychological Association, Washington, DC.

References

Barnes, M., Doyle, D., & Johnson, B. (1989). The formulation of a Fowler Scale: An empirical assessment among Catholics. *Review of Religious Research*, 30(4), 412–420.

Fowler, J. (1981). *Stages of faith: The psychology of human development and the quest for faith*. San Franciso: Harper and Row.

Fowler, J. (1991a). The vocation of faith development theory. In J. W. Fowler, K. E. Nipkow, and F. Schweitzer (Eds.), *Stages of faith and religious development: Implications for church, education, and society*. New York: Crossroad Publishing Company.

Fowler, J. (1991b). *Weaving the new creation: Stages of faith and the public church*. San Francisco: Harper & Row.

Goldsmith, W. M., & Bayless, S. L. (1991, August). *Male and female seminarians' personality and moral reasoning: Protestants, Catholics and Jews*. Paper presented to the American Psychological Association, San Francisco, CA.

    Goldsmith, W. M., Bayless, S. L., & Hynes, V. J. (1992, August). *Faith development, moral development and values*. Paper presented to the American Psychological Association, Washington, DC.

    Kohlberg, L. (1976). Moral stages and moralization: The cognitive-developmental approach. In T. Lickona (Ed.), *Moral development and behavior: Theory, research, and social issues*. New York: Holt, Rinehart & Winston.

    Rest, J. R. (1979). *The Defining Issues Test*. Minneapolis: University of Minnesota Press.

    Rest, J. R. (1986). *Manual for the Defining Issues Test: An objective test of moral development* (3rd ed.). Minneapolis, MN: University of Minnesota Press.

Appendix

Instrument

(2)* 1. A. Those who do what God wants are given special rewards.
(3)   B. God grants comfort and strength to those who are loyal and faithful.

(2) 2. A. God can do whatever God wants without any particular reason.
(4)   B. It is important to try to make sense out of how God acts and why.

(2) 3. A. A good way to relate to God is to do what God wants, so that God will help you in return.
(5)   B. It is best to think of God as utterly and freely giving.

(3) 4. A. Following Christ with loving devotion is more important than having a thorough and correct understanding of true doctrine.
(4)   B. It is important to reflect on one's beliefs to make them reasonable and logically coherent.

(3) 5. A. True followers of Christ will often find themselves rejected by the world.
(5)   B. Most people in the world are doing their best to live decent lives.

(4) 6. A. God's revealed truth is meant for all people everywhere.
(5)   B. No set of religious beliefs is the whole and final truth for everyone.

(3) 7. A. It is important to follow the leaders to whom God has entrusted his church.
(4)   B. Religious leaders must respect the need for reasonableness, consistency, and coherence in their interpretation of doctrines.

(3) 8. A. It is often hard to understand why people are disloyal to their family and religion.
(5)   B. People have to make their own best choices about religion, even if it means following new ways.

(4) 9. A. The moral teachings of the church are objectively valid for all people, even though many do not realize this.
(5)   B. Love of neighbor requires being open to new ideas and values.

    *The number in parentheses indicates the Fowler stage ("style" here) that the statement is intended to identify. The respondents were asked to express a preference for one of the two statements on each of the nine items.

4.4
FAITH MATURITY SCALE (Benson, Donahue, & Erickson, 1993)
Reviewed by Theresa C. Tisdale

Variable: The Faith Maturity Scale (FMS) is designed to measure "the degree to which a person embodies the priorities, commitments, and perspectives characteristic of vibrant and life transforming faith, as these have been understood in 'mainline' Protestant traditions" (p.3). This definition focuses intentionally on values and behavioral manifestations or indicators of faith rather than exclusively on an assent to particular religious beliefs or tenets. The scale is appropriate for use with both adolescents and adults.

Description: The Faith Maturity Scale (FMS) was developed as part of The National Study of Protestant Congregations (NSPC), which had as its goal the assessment of personal faith, denominational loyalty, and their determinants (Benson & Eklin, 1990). This study involved 11,000 adolescents and adults from six Protestant denominations: (a) Christian Church, Disciples of Christ (CC), (b) Evangelical Lutheran Church in America (ELCA), (c) Presbyterian Church, U.S.A. (PCUSA), (d) United Church of Christ (UCC); (e) United Methodist Church (UMC), and (f) Southern Baptist Convention (SBC). Working in conjunction with three advisory panels comprising seminary scholars, denominational experts, and clergy from diverse racial and ethnic backgrounds, the Search Institute of Minneapolis developed the scale utilizing a criterion-based approach. Development was guided by eight considerations: (a) faith maturity occurs along a continuum; (b) there are multiple core dimensions of faith maturity; (c) faith maturity involves both one's personal relationship with God (vertical faith), as well as one's relationship with others and behavioral manifestations of faith (horizontal faith); (d) the scale should have

heuristic value; (e) the length of the instrument and its response format should make it useful; (f) the scale should minimize economic, educational, and racial-ethnic specificity; (g) the indicators of faith maturity should not presume an institutional attachment or involvement; and (h) denominational specificity should be minimized.

Utilizing a thorough and systematic process, the investigators generated the FMS in a three-stage process which consisted of (a) naming the core dimensions, (b) defining faith-maturity indicators, and (c) developing survey items. The result of their work is a 38-item, 7-point Likert scale that yields a global faith-maturity score with a potential range of scores between 1 and 7.

Practical Considerations: This paper-and-pencil measure does not require any particular skill to administer, score, or interpret. Brief instructions are provided and the global score is derived by calculating the mean of the 38 items. Five items (13%) are reversed scored. The possibility of alternate scoring by subscale and/or according to a four-fold typology, as well as the development of two shorter versions are discussed, but further research is needed before these methods possess the same reliability and validity as the original FMS measure and scoring criteria.

Norms/Standardization: From a nationally representative sample of congregations, 150 were randomly selected from each of the six participating denominations. Samples were stratified by size of the congregation to ensure representative distribution. Within each congregation, adolescents, adults, Christian Education teachers, pastors, and Christian Education coordinators (10 from each category) were randomly selected. Norms in the form of mean scores are provided for each of these groups. Sample size ranged from 3,582 (adult) to 404 (Christian Education Coordinator), reflecting a 65% response rate for most groups. These norms are provided based on a total of five of the six groups; one denomination, Southern Baptist, was eliminated due to sample anomalies.

Reliability: Cronbach Coefficient Alpha reliabilities are reported by age, gender, denomination, and respondent category (i.e. adults, pastors, etc.). Coefficients across all categories range from .84 (females over 69 years) to .90 (males 60–69 years), demonstrating high reliability for the measure.

Validity: The authors present evidence to support face, content, and construct validity. Because the FMS is criterion-based and panels of experts were utilized to aid with construction, face validity is apparent at least for the denominations represented. Content validity is supported by the three-stage process that was utilized to develop the items. Items were derived based on indicators of the eight core dimensions postulated by the authors in conjunction with the expert panels. Construct validity of the measure was assessed utilizing the techniques of known groups, expert raters, comparison scores by age, and comparison with other measures. Results of these evaluations yielded confirmation of all predictions. Pastors received the highest scores (known group), significant correlations existed between expert raters and actual scores obtained on the FMS by individuals, faith maturity increased linearly with age, and the FMS correlated with intrinsic religiousness and was unrelated to extrinsic religiousness. Evidence supporting the validity of the FMS makes it quite suitable for research use.

Location:

Benson, P. L., Donahue, M. J., & Erickson, J. A. (1993). The Faith Maturity Scale: Conceptualization, measurement, and empirical validation. In M. L. Lynn & D. O. Moberg (Eds.), *Research in the social scientific study of religion* (Vol. 5, pp. 1–26). Greenwich: JAI Press.

Subsequent Research:

Benson, P. L. & Donahue, M. J. (1990). *Value-genesis: Report 1. A study of the influence of family, church, and school on the faith, values and commitment of Adventist youth.* Paper presented to the General Conference, North American Division, Seventh-day Adventist Church, Silver Spring, MD.

Additionally, the instrument has been used in local and regional studies of Catholic, Episcopal, American Baptist, and the Reform Church of America as well as with the Seventh-Day Adventist Church in Australia. No specific references were given in the Benson and Donahue (1990) article.

Reference

Benson, P. L. & Eklin, C. E. (1990). *Effective Christian education: A national study of Protestant congregations: A summary report on faith, loyalty, and congregation life.* Unpublished manuscript, Search Institute, Minneapolis, MN.

Appendix

FMS

Mark one answer for each. Be as honest as possible, describing how true it really is and now how true you would like it to be.

Choose from these responses:

1 = never true   5 = often true
2 = rarely true   6 = almost always true
3 = true once in a while   7 = always true
4 = sometimes true

	Never True						Always True
	1	2	3	4	5	6	7

1. I am concerned that our country is not doing . . . . enough to help the poor   1 2 3 4 5 6 7

2. I know that Jesus Christ is the Son of God who . . died on a cross and rose again   1 2 3 4 5 6 7

3. My faith shapes how I think and act each . . . . and every day   1 2 3 4 5 6 7

4. I help others with their religious questions . . . . . . and struggles   1 2 3 4 5 6 7

5. I tend to be critical of other people (R) 1 2 3 4 5 6 7

6. In my free time, I help people who . . . . have problems or needs   1 2 3 4 5 6 7

7. My faith helps me know right from wrong ˋ1 2 3 4 5 6 7

8. I do things to help protect the environment 1 2 3 4 5 6 7

9. I devote time to reading and studying the Bible . .   1 2 3 4 5 6 7

10. I have a hard time accepting myself (R) 1 2 3 4 5 6 7

11. Every day I see evidence that God is active . . . . . in the world   1 2 3 4 5 6 7

12. I take excellent care of my physical health 1 2 3 4 5 6 7

13. I am active in efforts to promote social justice . . .   1 2 3 4 5 6 7

14. I seek out opportunities to help me . . . . grow spiritually   1 2 3 4 5 6 7

15. I take time for periods of prayer or meditation . . .   1 2 3 4 5 6 7

16. I am active in efforts to promote world peace 1 2 3 4 5 6 7

17. I accept people whose religious beliefs are . . . . . . different from mine   1 2 3 4 5 6 7

18. I feel a deep sense of responsibility for reducing. . pain and suffering in the world   1 2 3 4 5 6 7

19. As I grow older, my understanding of . . . . God changes   1 2 3 4 5 6 7

20. I feel overwhelmed by all the responsibilities . . . . and obligations I have   1 2 3 4 5 6 7

21. I give significant portions of my time and . . . . money to help other people   1 2 3 4 5 6 7

22. I speak out for equality for women . . . . and minorities   1 2 3 4 5 6 7

23. I feel God's presence in my relationships . . . . with other people   1 2 3 4 5 6 7

24. My life is filled with meaning and purpose 1 2 3 4 5 6 7

25.	I do not understand how a loving God can . . . . . . allow so much pain and suffering in the world (R)	1	2	3	4	5	6	7
26.	I believe that I must obey God's rules and . . . . . . commandments in order to be saved (R)	1	2	3	4	5	6	7
27.	I am confident that I can overcome any . . . . problem or crisis no matter how serious	1	2	3	4	5	6	7
28.	I care a great deal about reducing poverty in. . . . . the United States and throughout the world	1	2	3	4	5	6	7
29.	I try to apply my faith to political and . . . . social issues	1	2	3	4	5	6	7
30	My life is committed to Jesus Christ.	1	2	3	4	5	6	7
31.	I talk with other people about my faith	1	2	3	4	5	6	7
32.	My life is filled with stress and anxiety.	1	2	3	4	5	6	7
33.	I go out of my way to show love to. . . . . people I meet	1	2	3	4	5	6	7
34.	I have a real sense that God is guiding me	1	2	3	4	5	6	7
35.	I do not want the churches of this nation. . . . . getting involved in political issues (R)	1	2	3	4	5	6	7
36.	I like to worship and pray with others.	1	2	3	4	5	6	7
37.	I think Christians must be about the business . . . . of creating international understanding and harmony	1	2	3	4	5	6	7
38.	I am spiritually moved by the beauty of God's . . . creation enough to help the poor	1	2	3	4	5	6	7

(R)—reversed scored

4.5
RELIGIOUS INDEX OF MATURING SURVEY (Marthai, 1980)
Reviewed by Michael J. Boivin

Variable: The Religious Index of Maturing Survey (RIMS) assesses religious maturity by evaluating an individual's feelings and orientation pertaining to his or her religious life. This measure pertains to religion in general and does not assess any particular religious commitment.

Marthai (1980) began with the notion that religious maturity has some basis in an individual's self concept or ego identity. He then listed the following criteria as defining his construct of religious maturity: (a) phenomenal in nature; (b) a process and not necessarily a set of objective standards; (c) reality based; (d) intrinsically motivated; (e) involving a religious identity, either with an organization or as personally defined; (f) involving a religious self concept in that one has a sense of acceptance of self in light of one's religion; (g) reflecting wholeness; (h) volitionally based; (i) involving changes in behaviors, attitudes and/or values; (j) reflecting growth towards more complete and whole behaviors; (k) associated with satisfaction; (l) somewhat related to physical and cognitive maturity; and (m) an unending growth process.

Description: Marthai constructed 79 statement items using, as a guideline, Clark's (1970) 10 questions for appraising mature religion. Other general statements were included reflecting religious concepts, theological issues, and generally accepted religious behaviors. After administering this initial version of the instrument to 250 Baptist church members in and around the Grand Rapids, Michigan area, Marthai (1980) used a factor analysis of his initial sample results to refine the instrument down to the 19 items having the highest loadings on the primary factor. This factor seemed to be "centered around the constructs of growth, satisfaction and positive behavioral change in and through one's religion" (p. 25).

The statements were formatted according to a five point Likert format ranging from "completely true" (A) to "completely false" (E). To prevent a response set, five of the items were negatively worded and six new nonscored negatively worded statements were randomly added for a total of 25 statement items.

To score the instrument, Marthai (1980) simply totaled the Likert ratings for the 19 scored items (e.g., A/Completely true = 5, E/Completely false = 1), reversing the values for the five negatively worded items. The Likert ratings were then totaled for an overall score on the RIMS.

Practical Considerations: The administration of the instrument is straightforward. Statements are clear, concise, and appropriate for a variety of religious and nonreligious contexts. This instrument is short and can be easily completed by normal adults in 15 minutes or less. The format allows the measure to be easily combined with other instruments.

Norms/Standardization: The instrument was administered to 216 adolescents (grades 8–12) at three conservative Christian schools in the south. Each school was advertised as nondenominational and conservative in doctrinal beliefs (holding to the fundamentals of the Christian faith).

All but one of the students were white, and 45% of the respondents were male. Mean grade level was 9.3 years and mean age was 15.5 years. Mean years since conversion as self-reported was 7.04 years. The denominational preference was 48% Baptist, 12% Presbyterian, 8% Methodist, 7% Independent, 3% Pentecostal and Full Gospel, 3% Lutheran, and 19% nonrespondent. The students were described as middle class by school administrators.

Reliability: Thirty-three students from one school were tested twice within a period of 10 days. The test/retest reliability coefficient was .81. The Cronbach inter-item coefficient for internal consistency was .93. The high level of internal consistency might be expected based on the selection criterion for the items to be included in the final draft of the instrument.

Validity: Since Marthai hypothesized a strong relationship between positive self-concept and religious maturity, the Tennessee Self-Concept Scale (TSCS) (Fitts, 1965) was administered along with several other instruments in addition to the RIMS. The statistically significant positive correlations with the TSCS Total-P scores ($r = 0.39$, $p < .01$) and TSCS Moral-Ethical subscale ($r = 0.54$, $p < .01$) indicated good construct validity for the RIMS.

The Spielberger State-Trait Anxiety Inventory (Spielberger, Gorsuch, & Lushene, 1970) was administered as part of the above battery to test the hypothesis that the religiously mature individual would demonstrate wholeness, in part by being less anxious. The significant negative correlations with both state ($r = -0.22$, $p < .01$) and trait anxiety ($r = 0.21$, $p < .01$) indicate good construct validity here as well.

Finally, Allport and Ross' (1967) measure of Intrinsic/Extrinsic religious orientation was included to evaluate the hypothesis that religious maturity would correspond in a positive manner to intrinsic religiosity, and negatively to extrinsic religiosity. RIMS performance was significantly correlated to intrinsic religiosity ($r = 0.79$, $p < .01$) and extrinsic religiosity ($r = -0.31$, $p < .01$). These correlations support Marthai's conceptual basis for maturity measure, and lend further validity to this measure.

Location:

Marthai, R. (1980). Construction and validation of a measure of phenomenal process and religious maturity. (Doctoral dissertation, Southern Mississippi University, Hattiesburg, MS, 1980). *Dissertation Abstracts International*, 41–05B, 1893.

Subsequent Research: None found.

References:

Allport, G., & Ross, J. (1967). Personal religious orientation and prejudice. *Journal of Personality and Social Psychology*, 5, 432–443.

Clark, W. (1970). *The psychology of religion*. New York: Macmillan.

Fitts, W. (1965). *Manual for Tennessee Self Concept Scale*. Los Angeles: Western Psychological Services.

Spielberger, C. D., Gorsuch, R. L., & Lushene, R. E. (1970). *STAI manual for the State-Trait Anxiety Inventory*. Palo Alto, CA: Consulting Psychological Press.

Appendix

RIMS: A Self-Perception Scale

Name _____   Class or Position _____

Date _____   Religious Preference _____

Years since religious conversion _____   Age_____

This is a survey that will be used to find out how people think about their religion. Please answer the following statements by circling the choice which best describe you.

        A = completely true
        B = partly true
        C = partly true and partly false
        D = partly false
        E = completely false

Please respond with your first impression about yourself and do not deliberate on any one question. Please answer for how you personally agree or disagree with the statement and *not* how other people might expect you to answer. Religion in this survey means all of your personal beliefs about God and spiritual things. There are no right or wrong answers. They are only right if they reflect your personal beliefs.

A B C D E   1. My religion is the primary factor in my life.

A B C D E   2. My religion is not fresh each day.

A B C D E   3. My religious beliefs play a vital role when I make everyday choices.

A B C D E   4. My religion does not fully satisfy me.

A B C D E   5. My religion gives me a wholeness to living.

A B C D E   6. I feel an urge to know more about my religion's deeper truth.

A B C D E   7. I am unconcerned that others find the same things I have found in my religion.

A B C D E   8. I rarely or never think of myself being part of the universe.

A B C D E   9. My religion is growing daily within me.

A B C D E   10. Many things have changed in my life since I have followed my religion.

A B C D E   11. Almost no one knows what I really believe about my religion.

A B C D E   12. I often become confused about what to believe about my religion.

A B C D E   13. I have a better understanding of myself than I have about my religion.

A B C D E   14. I see myself as part of a master plan.

A B C D E   15. In persecution for my religion, I am uncertain I would hold up.

A B C D E   16. Because of my religion, I continually experience a new joy.

A B C D E   17. I have no doubts about religious miracles.

A B C D E   18. God interacts with me.

A B C D E   19. I have a lot of hope in my religion.

A B C D E   20. My religion has helped me be more open in my relationships with other people.

A B C D E   21. My views of my religion have not changed since I have followed them.

A B C D E   22. I read the Scriptures rarely.

A B C D E   23. The criterion I use to decide whether or not to do something is to ask if it would be pleasing to God.

A B C D E   24. God actively directs my life.

A B C D E   25. My religion does not really give me a sense of reality.

Reprinted with permission of the author.

4.6
RELIGIOUS STATUS INTERVIEW
(Malony, 1985, 1988; Malony & Nelson, 1982)

Reviewed by Peter C. Hill

Editors' Note: The Religious Status Interview and The Religious Status Inventory (reviewed next) were designed by the same research team. The purpose of both instruments is to measure Christian maturity as an indicator of optimal religious functioning. The major difference is that one is an interview and the other is a paper-and-pencil inventory.

Variable: The Religious Status Interview (RSI) is a measure of Christian religious maturity. Malony (1985) defines Christian maturity in the following way:

Mature Christians are those who have identity, integrity and inspiration. They "identify" in that their self-understanding is as children of God—created by Him and destined by Him to live according to a divine plan. They have "integrity" in that their daily life is lived in the awareness that they have been saved by God's grace from the guilt of sin and that they can freely respond to God's will in the present. They have "inspiration" in that they live with the sense that God is available to sustain, comfort, encourage, and direct their lives on a daily basis. (p. 28)

Description: This one-hour interview schedule was originally intended to provide mental health professionals with an instrument that assesses religious maturity, particularly as it relates to optimal religious functioning. Malony (1985) maintains that this tool is useful for the mental health professional in three types of decisions: diagnosis, general mental status, and treatment. The interview's use, however, is not limited to the mental health professional.

The RSI assesses eight dimensions of religious experience based on Pruyser (1976): (a) Awareness of God (6 questions), (b) Acceptance of God's Grace and Steadfast Love (4 questions), (c) Being Repentant and Responsible (5 questions), (d) Knowing God's Leadership and Direction (3 questions), (e) Involvement in Organized Religion (4 questions), (f) Experiencing Fellowship (3 questions), (g) Being Ethical (4 questions), and (h) Affirming Openness in Faith (4 questions). The instrument measures overall religious maturity across all dimensions, though a more specific maturity may be evaluated on any of the dimensions as well.

Malony (1985) identifies several assumptions or characteristics of the RSI. First, "religion," as identified in the RSI, is understood as a "substantive social reality rather than a dynamic subjective motivation" (p. 26). Second, the interview is limited to Christian religion, not religion in general. Third, the interview attempts to assess how substantive beliefs function in the life of the individual being evaluated. Fourth, the interview assumes that what people say about their religion is the essence of their religious faith and, therefore, is admittedly confounded with verbal ability. Fifth, it is assumed that people should be able to talk about their faith spontaneously.

Scoring of responses is provided within the interview itself, with the highest score (5) reflecting the most mature response and the lowest score (1) reflecting the least mature response. The rating for each item is placed on the score sheet provided at the beginning of the instrument and the responses across the items for each of the eight dimensions are simply summed. The total range of scores is between 32 and 160.

Practical Considerations: Great care must be taken in adminstering any interview. The key to a good interview is to not lead the respondent toward any response and to make the interview process as standard as possible. Training for interviewers is recommended. The authors have provided a set of instructions at the beginning of the interview instrument.

The procedure usually involves writing down answers in the space provided on the interview form and then later going back and scoring the responses. It is recommended that the interview sessions also be taped. The authors estimate that scoring each interview takes approximately one hour in addition to the interview itself.

Norms/Standardization: Normative data for this hour-long interview schedule has not been collected.

Reliability: Malony (1988) reports that the RSI is a tool with "uneven" reliability. Yagel (1982, as reported in Malony, 1988) found inter-rater reliability coefficients among three raters of interview responses of .66 to .74, with an intraclass correlation coefficient of .85, when using the total maturity score over all eight categories. These results indicated acceptable inter-rater reliability. However, only one subcategory, Involvement in Organized Religion, with an intraclass correlation coefficient of .75, had acceptable inter-rater reliability. Thus, when comparing raters, only the total RSI maturity score was acceptably reliable.

Davis (1985, as reported in Malony, 1988) discovered reasonably high test-retest reliability over a two week period with female Protestant church members. The total maturity score reliability coefficient was .93. All of the subcategory reliability coefficients were above .84 except the Being Repentant and Responsible scale, which was .60. It appears that the RSI assesses a trait of religious functioning that is stable over time.

The reliability results from these two studies utilized an earlier version of the RSI. The version of the RSI included here showed overall maturity scores to be reliable both in terms of test-retest ($r = .74$, Jackson, 1987, as reported in Malony, 1988) and between raters ($r = .89$, Hadlock, 1987, as reported in Malony, 1988). Once again, with one exception (the Being Ethical scale), the individual categories were not found to be acceptably reliable.

Validity: Several studies reported in Malony (1988) indicate that the RSI is a clinical tool of "moderate" validity. Nelson (1985) found that the total RSI score could discriminate among persons judged by their pastors to be very mature, moderately mature, and immature. Tilley (1984) discovered that Christians in mental hospitals scored lower on the RSI than Christians who came to visit them. Tilley later (1985) found that Christian psychiatric inpatients scored lower on the RSI than Christian psychiatric outpatients. Atkinson (1986) discovered that the RSI had predictive validity in that women who scored high on the measure subsequently reported less distress from stressful life events, after controlling for the number and recency of such stressful events.

Location: The interview is unpublished but information may be obtained from the author through the Graduate School of Psychology, Fuller Theological Seminary, 180 N. Oakland Ave., Pasadena, CA 91101. The most thorough discussion of the measure found in the published literature is Malony (1988).

Subsequent Research: Other than a number of unpublished master's theses and doctoral dissertations at Fuller Seminary, no subsequent research using this measure was found.

References

Atkinson, B. E. (1986). *Religious maturity and psychological distress among older Christian women*. Unpublished doctoral dissertation, Graduate School of Psychology, Fuller Theological Seminary, Pasadena, CA.

Davis, S. P. (1985). *Interviewer reliability of the Religious Status Interview*. Unpublished master's thesis, Graduate School of Psychology, Fuller Theological Seminary, Pasadena, CA.

Hadlock, M. N. (1987). *Assessing religious maturity: Inter-rater reliability of the Religious Status Interview*. Unpublished master's thesis, Graduate School of Psychology, Fuller Theological Seminary, Pasadena, CA.

Jackson, C. (1987). *The test-retest reliability of the Religious Status Interview: A reconfirmation*. Unpublished master's thesis, Graduate School of Psychology, Fuller Theological Seminary, Pasadena, CA.

Malony, H. N. (1985). Assessing religious maturity. In E. M. Stern (Ed.), *Psychotherapy and the religiously committed patient* (pp. 25–34). New York: Hayworth Press.

Malony, H. N. (1988). The clinical assessment of optimal religious functioning. *Review of Religious Research, 30*(1), 3–17.

Nelson, D. O. (1985). *The construction and initial validation of the Religious Status Interview*. Unpublished doctoral dissertation, Graduate School of Psychology, Fuller Theological Seminary, Pasadena, CA.

Nelson, D. O., & Malony, H. N. (1982). *The Religious Status Interview*. Unpublished manuscript.

Pruyser, P. (1976). *The minister as diagnostician*. Philadelphia: Westminster Press.

Tilley, S. B. (1984). *The relationship between religion and mental health: An application of the Religious Status Interview*. Unpublished master's thesis, Graduate School of Psychology, Fuller Theological Seminary, Pasadena, CA.

Tilley, S. B. (1985). *Religious maturity and mental health: Verification of the Religious Status Interview*. Unpublished doctoral dissertation, Graduate School of Psychology, Fuller Theological Seminary, Pasadena, CA.

Yagel, J. C. (1982). *Initial inter-rater reliability of the Religious Status Interview*. Unpublished master's thesis, Graduate School of Psychology, Fuller Theological Seminary, Pasadena, CA.

Appendix

Religious Status Interview

Interviewer:_____ Interviewee:_____ Setting:_____ Date:_____

Directions for Interviewer:

1. Ask the interviewee the questions numbered 1 through 33 in order.
2. Take down his/her answers in the appropriate places in abbreviated form.
3. Score each subscale as you go along by glancing over the ratings from 1 to 5 (and sometimes back to 1 again), and *circling the one rating* which is best reflected in the interviewee's answer. Remember that a rating of 5 always reflects the most mature answer and a rating of 1 the least mature answer.
4. Do *not* ask additional questions which are not indicated on this interview. However, several prompting questions may on occasion be appropriate when the information received in the answer is not sufficient to render a rating. These prompting questions are limited to the following:

   "Could you tell me more about that?"
   "Could you explain that more fully?"
   "Can you give me an example of that?"
   "Can you think of another example?"

5. Place ratings in the blanks indicated below. Total scores within each subscale first, and then total these for an overall score. Norms have not yet been established, but the higher the score, the more mature the faith.

Scoring Totals:	A	B	C	D	E	F	Total
I. Awareness of God	____ +	____ +	____ +	____ +	____ +	____ =	____ *
II. Acceptance of God's Grace and Steadfast Love	____ +	____ +	____ +	____			= ____
III. Being Repentant and Responsible	____ +	____ +	____ +	____ +	____		= ____
IV. Knowing God's Leadership and Direction	____ +	____ +	____				= ____
V Involvement in Organized Religion	____ +	____ +	____ +	____			= ____
VI. Experiencing Fellowship	____ +	____ +	____				= ____

---

*The number of items added to create a total score varies. For example, six items are used to score the Awareness of God subscale but only four items to score the Acceptance of God's Grace and Steadfast Love subscale, etc.

VII. Being Ethical   ___ + ___ + ___ + ___   = ___

VIII. Affirming
       Openness in Faith
       Faith   ___ + ___ + ___ + ___   = ___

TOTAL SCORE: _____

RELIGIOUS STATUS INTERVIEW
I. Awareness of God

QUESTION: ANSWER:
  1. Who or what is God to you?

SUBSCALE: A. Attitude toward God
RATING:
  1 = This person demonstrates an indifferent or impersonal attitude towards God.
  *2 =
  3 = This person merely acknowledges that God has a role in his/her life.
  4 =
  5 = This person stands in awe before God as a creature aware of his/her Creator.

QUESTION: ANSWER:
  2. Who or what is
      Jesus Christ to you?

SUBSCALE:
RATING:
  1 = This person has an indifferent or impersonal attitude toward Christ.
  2 =
  3 = This person merely names one or two roles Christ plays in general but is unable to apply
      them personally.
  4 =
  5 = This person mentions several of the roles Christ plays in human life and is able to apply
      them personally.

QUESTION: ANSWER:
  3. In your *day to day* life, for
     which things do you depend upon
     God and for which things do you not?

SUBSCALE: B. Sense of Dependence of God
RATING:
  1 = This person is totally independent of God. They completely deny God's capacity to in-
      fluence their life.

---

*descriptions of even-numbered ratings were not provided in the original instrument.

2 =

3 = This person overemphasizes his/her *independence* from God.

4 =

5 = This person expresses awareness of his/her dependence upon the Creator, but also recognizes his/her own capabilities.

4 =

3 = This person overemphasizes his/her *dependence* on God.

2 =

1 = This person is overly dependent on God, totally denying his/her own capabilities or power to act.

QUESTION: ANSWER:

4. When problems seem out of your
   control, what do you do?

SUBSCALE: C. Sense of Creatureliness
RATING:

1 = This person shows an attitude of total resignation, giving up on life and is discounting of his/her own power.

2 =

3 = This person is troubled by his/her creaturely limitations.

4 =

5 = This person shows humility in the face of life's besetting problems and a realistic awareness of his/her own creaturely limitations but does not deny his/her own capacity for productive action.

4 =

3 = This person minimizes some of the real limitation of his/her creatureliness.

2 =

1 = This person is thoroughly self-aggrandizing, denying his/her own creaturely limitations.

QUESTION: ANSWER:

5. Why do you worship God?

SUBSCALE: D. Use of worship
RATING:

1 = This person sees worship as something he/she *should* do as a *duty* or *obligation*.

2 =

3 = This person's worship serves as a means of meeting his/her own needs.

4 =

5 = This person's worship serves primarily as an expression of reverence and love towards God.

QUESTION: ANSWER:

6. In what situations
 do you pray to God and why?

SUBSCALE: E. Use of Prayer
RATING:

1 = This person sees prayer as something he/she *should* do as a *duty* or an *obligation*.

2 =

3 = This person's prayer serves as a means of meeting his/her own needs.

4 =

5 = This person's prayer serves basically as a means of spiritual sustenance and communication with God, including honest expression of concerns.

II. Acceptance of God's Grace and Steadfast Love

QUESTION: ANSWER:

7. How does *God* seem to respond
   to you when you sin?

SUBSCALE: A. View of God's Love
RATING:

1 = This person views God as basically punitive, judgmental and distant, not loving.

2 =

3 = This person sees God's love as conditional, as dependent on his/her actions.

4 =

5 = This person views God as loving him/her unconditionally.

QUESTION: ANSWER:

8. How do *you* respond
   to God's love and forgiveness?

SUBSCALE: B. Response to God's Love
RATING:

1 = This person completely fails to use God's love and forgiveness as a motivation for responsible change or action.

2 =

3 = This person uses God's love and forgiveness as an impetus for some minimal change.

4 =

5 = This person uses God's love and forgiveness as an impetus for new living and responsible action.

QUESTION: ANSWER:

9. What feelings come up when
   you think of God's love?

SUBSCALE: C. Appreciation of God's Love
RATING:

1 = This person does not appreciate and experience God's love.

2 =

3 = This person has some appreciation or experience of God's love, but lacks a sense of joy and gratitude.

4 =

5 = This person appreciates and experiences God's love, manifested by a sense of joy and gratitude.

QUESTION: ANSWER:
10. Why do you think God allows
    personal suffering in your life?

SUBSCALE: D. Personal Meaning in Life's Problems
RATING:
1 = This person completely denies his/her problems and sorrows.
2 =
3 = This person admits he/she has problems or sorrows but sees no higher meaning to them.
4 =
5 = This person has the ability to find meaning in the suffering and difficulties of life. This
    meaning is based on trust in God and His goodness.
4 =
3 = This person struggles with why God allows suffering in his/her life.
2 =
1 = This person is totally unable to meaningfully integrate life's difficulties and sorrows
    with his/her faith.

III. Being Repentant and Responsible

QUESTION: ANSWER:
11. In general, who or what
    causes your problems?

SUBSCALE: A. Locus of Control
RATING:
1 = This person projects sole responsibility for personal difficulties or sin onto God, parents,
    friends, or situations.
2 =
3 = This person lays excessive blame on others for difficulties or sin.
4 =
5 = This person accurately perceives personal responsibility without denying other factors
    such as the environment in personal difficulties or sin.
4 =
3 = This person tends to internalize excessive personal responsibility for difficulties or sin.
2 =
1 = This person sees himself/herself as having total responsibility for personal difficulties or
    sin, completely denying any environmental factors.

QUESTION: ANSWER:
12. How do you handle
    your own angry feelings?

SUBSCALE: B. Acceptance of Feelings
RATING:
1 = This person denies his/her feelings and impulses. He/she does not see them as a part of
    being human.
2 =

3 = This person is aware of his/her negative feelings, but does not accept them as a legitimate part of being human.

4 =

5 = This person is aware of his/her negative feelings and accepts them as a legitimate part of being human.

QUESTION: ANSWER:

13. How do you *feel* when you
have wronged someone?

SUBSCALE: C. Motivation and Repentance
RATING:

1 = This person's attitude of repentance is based on guilt feelings or self-depreciation rather than concern for the offended person or solution of the problem.

2 =

3 = This person's attitude of repentance shows elements of both guilt and concern for the other.

4 =

5 = This person's attitude of repentance is based on concern to correct the situation, a feeling of constructive sorrow.

4 =

3 = This person recognizes minimal need for repentance.

2 =

1 = This person completely denies any need for repentance, showing no concern for the offended person or solution of the problem.

QUESTION: ANSWER:

14. What do you do when *you
have wronged someone?*

SUBSCALE: D. Requesting Forgiveness
RATING:

1 = This person completely denies or rationalizes any need to ask for forgiveness from another person.

2 =

3 = This person seldom asks for forgiveness.

4 =

5 = This person is able to request and accept forgiveness from others without feeling threatened or self-depreciating.

4 =

3 = This person has some difficulty accepting forgiveness from others.

2 =

1 = This person may ask for forgiveness, but is unable to really accept it. This individual feels very unworthy of receiving forgiveness.

QUESTION: ANSWER:

15. When *someone has wronged you,*
    how do you respond to him or her?

SUBSCALE: E. Granting Forgiveness
RATING:

1 = This person cannot forgive others. This individual continues to feel anger, resentment, bitterness or suspicion towards them.

2 =

3 = This person forgives superficially, but still feels resentment.

4 =

5 = This person is forgiving of others without experiencing continued resentment towards them.

IV. Knowing God's Leadership and Direction

QUESTION: ANSWER:

16. How do you make major decisions
    in your life?

SUBSCALE: A. Trust in God's Leadership
RATING:

1 = This person totally lacks trust in God's leadership, taking on complete responsibility for directing his/her life.

2 =

3 = This person minimizes the role of God's leadership in his/her decision-making process.

4 =

5 = This person expresses trust in God's leadership for his/her life yet also recognizes his/her role in that process.

4 =

3 = This person tends to overspiritualize guidance in life, minimizing his/her own power.

2 =

1 = This person demonstrates a naive trust in God, completely denying his/her own power to direct his/her life.

QUESTION: ANSWER:

17. What do you think your future
    is going to be like?

SUBSCALE: B. Sense of Hope
RATING:

1 = This person feels hopeless. He/she has an attitude of resignation in life.

2 =

3 = This person feels somewhat pessimistic.

4 =

5 = This person expresses an optimistic, but realistic hope based on trust in God, without denying present problems. This person is confident that God is in control.

4 =

3 = This person feels somewhat unrealistically optimistic.

2 =

1 = This person completely denies his/her problems, expressing a naive, unrealistic optimism.

QUESTION: ANSWER:

18. How does your faith relate to your various
    roles in your family, occupation,
    and community?

SUBSCALE: C. Role Identity
RATING:

1 = This person has a thoroughly diffuse or unclear role identity, which does not provide any meaning in relation to his/her faith.

2 =

3 = This person has a partially defined role identity, but does not relate it to his/her faith.

4 =

5 = This person has a sense of positive role identity which provides meaning in relation to his/her faith.

V. Involvement in Organized Religion

QUESTION: ANSWER:

19. How often do you attend the activities of
    your church or religious community?

SUBSCALE: A. Level of Involvement
RATING:

1 = This person attends church only on holidays.

2 = This person attends church once a month.

3 = This person attends church every other week.

4 = This person attends church one time a week.

5 = This person attends church twice a week or more.

QUESTION: ANSWER:

20. What part do you
    play in church activities?

SUBSCALE: B. Active-Passive Involvement
RATING:

1 = This person completely avoids participation in worship or other religious activities.

2 =

3 = This person participates when asked, but does not initiate involvement.

4 =

5 = This person shows active involvement and commitment in worship and other religious activities.

QUESTION: ANSWER:
21. Do you give money to the church or other
    religious organizations? What percentage of
    your income would you estimate you give?

SUBSCALE: C. Commitment of Finances
RATING:
1 = This person gives no money to the church.
2 =
3 = This person gives periodically to the church, but less than 10% of his/her income.
4 =
5 = This person regularly gives 10% or more of his/her income to the church.

QUESTION: ANSWER:
22. Why do you attend
 church?

SUBSCALE: D. Reason for Involvement
RATING:
1 = This person views involvement in a religious community as unnecessary for expression
    of his/her faith.
2 =
3 = This person is ambivalent about the importance of his/her involvement in a religious
    community.
4 =
5 = This person is involved in church or group as an expression of a desire to grow in his/her
    faith (i.e., service, study, fellowship, worship).
4 =
3 = This person is involved for both social gain and expression of his/her faith.
2 =
1 = This person is involved in a church or religious group solely for emotional or status
    needs, rather than to grow in his/her faith.

VI. Experiencing Fellowship

QUESTION: ANSWER:
23. Tell me about your friendships?
    Who are they? Where did you meet them?
    How close are you to them?

SUBSCALE: A. Intimacy with other Believers
RATING:
1 = This person is excessively dependent on other believers as a means of protecting him-
    self/herself from non-Christian influences.
2 =
3 = This person seems to overly rely on relationships with Christians, and to neglect his/her
    relationships with non-Christians.
4 =

5 = This person experiences relationships at various levels of intimacy, including inter-de-
pendent, growth-oriented, intimate relationships with at least a few believers and a few
non-believers.

4 =

3 = This person has very few intimate relationships with believers.

2 =

1 = This person totally lacks intimate relationships with either Christians or non-Christians,
perhaps feeling isolated, estranged and suspicious.

QUESTION: ANSWER:

24. What does being
part of the family
of God mean to you?

SUBSCALE: B. Identification as a Child of God
RATING:

1 = This person expresses a sense of exclusiveness in his/her identity with the family of God.
This individual may display a self-righteous, judgmental attitude or condemn others who
express their faith differently.

2 =

3 = This person's identity with the family of God includes some sense of superiority over
those seen to be outside the family of God.

4 =

5 = This person identifies positively with the family of God, including a sense of community
with the "people of God" and an attitude of humble appreciation for salvation.

QUESTION: ANSWER:

25. How do you feel about people
from different cultures or races?

SUBSCALE: C. Identification with Humanity
RATING:

1 = This person displays a parochial, ethnocentric attitude an overidentification with one
subculture, group or sect only, excluding all unlike self.

2 =

3 = This person identifies with humanity to some degree, but shows considerable favoritism
for his/her own group.

4 =

5 = This person expresses an identification with all of humanity, a sense of commonality as
God's creatures.

VII. Being Ethical

QUESTION: ANSWER:
26. How do you decide
    what is right or wrong?

SUBSCALE: A. Ethical Commitment and Flexibility
RATING:
1 = This person lacks clear commitment to meaningful ethical principles for his/her life.
2 =
3 = This person has commitment to ethical principles, but the commitment is weak or ill defined.
4 =
5 = This person follows his/her ethical principles in a flexible but committed manner.
4 =
3 = This person is committed to some ethical principles, but lacks some flexibility.
2 =
1 = This person views his/her ethical principles as absolute law, following them in a very rigid manner.

QUESTION: ANSWER:
27. How does your faith influence
    your sense of what is right and wrong?

SUBSCALE: b. Relationship between Faith and Ethics
RATING:
1 = This person's faith is completely unrelated to his/her ethics. This person's ethics may be based primarily on a social convention or a fear of punishment.
2 =
3 = This person's ethics are affected by both social convention and some less integrated aspects of his/her faith.
4 =
5 = This person's religious faith strongly underlies and guides all of his/her ethics.

QUESTION: ANSWER:
28. What personal and social ethical issues
    are you concerned about and how do you
    deal with them?

SUBSCALE: C. Emphasis on Personal and Social Ethics
RATING:
1 = This person expresses no concern about either personal or social ethics.
2 =
3 = This person neglects either personal or social ethics.
4 =
5 = This person shows concern for personal and social ethics. He/she acts from awareness of both and is concerned about individual responsibility and social justice.

QUESTION: ANSWER:

29. What satisfaction do you receive
    from your job, vocation, or what you do?

SUBSCALE: D. Serving Others in Work Situation
RATING:
1 = This person is very self-centered in his/her work or vocation, focusing only on his/her
    own status, financial, or social needs.
2 =
3 = This person focuses his/her motivations partially on his/her own needs and partially on
    the needs of others.
4 =
5 = This person has a sense that he/she is serving others in his/her work or vocation, rather
    than just focusing on his/her own needs.

VIII. Affirming Openness in Faith

QUESTION: ANSWER:

30. How does your faith affect
    different aspects of your life?

SUBSCALE: A. Centrality of Faith
RATING:
1 = This person's faith is very compartmentalized in that it does not seem to relate to any
    other aspects of life.
2 =
3 = This person's faith is only moderately related to some aspects of his/her life.
4 =
5 = This person's faith provides a directive for all aspects of his/her life.

QUESTION: ANSWER:

31. How many times during the past year
    did you do some reading about
    your faith or had some discussions
    about faith with others?

SUBSCALE: B. Growth in Faith
RATING:
1 = This person spent no time in the last year discussing or reading about his/her faith.
2 =
3 = This person spent considerable time in the last year discussing or reading about his/her
    faith, but expressed no desire to grow in faith, reflecting instead motives of duty or habit.
4 =
5 = This person spent significant time in the last year reading about his/her faith and/or dis-
    cussing it with others, as an expression of a desire to grow in faith.

QUESTION: ANSWER:
32. How do you respond to people
    who do not believe as you do?

SUBSCALE: C. Openness to Divergent Viewpoints
RATING:
1 = This person's faith is very rigid and unable to tolerate differing ideas. This individual
    may reject or distort these different ideas and practices in order to maintain his/her
    own position.
2 =
3 = This person is unable to tolerate new ideas in some areas of faith.
4 =
5 = While expressing confidence in his/her own view, this person shows a tolerance for
    others' viewpoints and a willingness to examine and try to understand other people's be-
    liefs.
4 =
3 = This person is easily influenced by others' beliefs and frequently vacillates among them.
2 =
1 = This person is unsure about his/her beliefs. His/her beliefs change completely depending
    upon whom he/she is with.

QUESTION: ANSWER:
33. Can you name some dimensions, or parts, of your faith that are important to you.

SUBSCALE: D. Differentiation of Faith
RATING:
1 = This person's faith is thoroughly undifferentiated and composed of a small number of
    categories or elements. Ideas are global and overgeneralized. (1 part)
2 =
3 = This person's faith is composed of only a few categories or elements. These ideas
    include generalizations. (3 parts)
4 =
5 = This person's faith is differentiated and is composed of a relatively large number of cat-
    egories or elements. Ideas are multiple and specific rather than overgeneralized. (5 parts)

Reprinted with permission of author.

4.7
RELIGIOUS STATUS INVENTORY
(Hadlock, 1988; Jackson, 1994; Massey, 1988)

Reviewed by Peter C. Hill

Editors' Note: The Religious Status Interview (p. 178) and The Religious Status Inventory were
designed by the same research team. The purpose of both instruments is to measure Christian
maturity as an indicator of optimal religious functioning. The major difference is that one is an
interview and the other is a paper-and-pencil inventory.

Variable: The Religious Status Inventory is a measure of Christian religious maturity. Malony (1985) defines Christian maturity in the following way:

> Mature Christians are those who have identity, integrity and inspiration. They "identify" in that their self-understanding is as children of God—created by Him and destined by Him to live according to a divine plan. They have "integrity" in that their daily life is lived in the awareness that they have been saved by God's grace from the guilt of sin and that they can freely respond to God's will in the present. They have "inspiration" in that they live with the sense that God is available to sustain, comfort, encourage, and direct their lives on a daily basis. (p. 28)

Description: The Religious Status Inventory contains 160 items measured on a 5-point scale ranging from "not true of me" (1) to "true of me" (5). Scores are simply added together. Thus, total scores may range from a low of 160 to a high of 800, with higher scores indicating greater religious maturity.

The Religious Status Inventory, like the Religious Status Interview (RSI), was originally designed to assess eight dimensions of religious experience based on Pruyser (1976): (a) Awareness of God, (b) Acceptance of God's Grace and Steadfast Love, (c) Being Repentant and Responsible, (d) Knowing God's Leadership and Direction, (e) Involvement in Organized Religion, (f) Experiencing Fellowship, (g) Being Ethical, and (h) Affirming Openness in Faith. Each dimension consists of 20 items, half of which are reversed scored, resulting in a range for each dimension of 20 (low religious maturity) to 100 (high religious maturity).

However, a factor analysis conducted by Jackson (1994) found seven rather than eight dimensions: (a) Importance of Religion in Daily Life (64 items), (b) Worship and Commitment (44 items), (c) Complexity of Faith (7 items), (d) Rejection of Simplistic Faith (7 items), (e) Involvement in Organized Religion (5 items), (f) Social

Ethics (5 items), and (g) Optimal Religious Functioning (49 items—a higher order factor consisting of items from Factors 2 and 5). A scoring key is provided at the end of instrument in this volume for both the seven- and eight-dimension analyses.

Malony (1985) identifies several assumptions or characteristics of the Religious Status Interview. Many of the same assumptions or characteristics apply to the Religious Status Inventory as well. First, "religion," is understood as a "substantive social reality rather than a dynamic subjective motivation" (p. 26). Second, the inventory is limited to Christian religion, not religion in general. Third, the inventory attempts to assess how substantive beliefs function in the life of the individual being evaluated.

Practical Considerations: No special considerations are necessary in administering or scoring this instrument.

Norms/Standardization: Normative data for the Religious Status Inventory were based on 451 Christian college and seminarian students throughout the United States. Means and standard deviations of the eight original dimensions were reported. Means (with a possible range of 20–100 on each dimension) were quite consistent across the eight dimensions, ranging from a low of 69.06 (Involvement in Organized Religion) to a high of 77.87 (Knowing God's Leadership). Standard deviations were less consistent, ranging from a low of 6.27 (Being Repentant and Responsible) to a high of 14.57 on (Involvement in Organized Religion).

Lukaszewski, Archer, Malony, Newton, and Jackson (1996) report mean scores of Jackson's (1994) seven factors based on 810 protocols. Mean scores were quite variable, ranging from a low of 2.72 (on a 1–5 range) for Involvement in Organized Religion to a high of 3.92 for Social Ethics.

Reliability: Lukaszewski et al. (1996), based on Jackson's (1994) seven factors, report alpha coefficients ranging from .54 (on the higher order factor of Optimal Religious

Functioning) to .98 (Importance of Religion in Daily Life). Test-retest reliability coefficients range from .70 (Social Ethics) to .92 (Worship and Commitment; Optimal Religious Functioning).

Validity: Porter (1995) found, as predicted, no significant differences of religious maturity as measured by the Religious Status Inventory between four modes of religious experience: verbal, affective, social-relational, and transcendental. Research in progress at the time of this writing is investigating the relationship between the Religious Status Inventory's assessment of religious maturity and measures of both happiness as well as neuroticism and psychoticism.

Location: This scale is unpublished. Information may be obtained by contacting H. Newton Malony through the Graduate School of Psychology, Fuller Theological Seminary, 180 N. Oakland Ave., Pasadena, CA 91101.

Subsequent Research: A number of unpublished master's theses and doctoral dissertations at Fuller Theological Seminary are further establishing the metric properties of the scale. No other subsequent research using this measure was found.

References

Hadlock, M. N. (1988). *Construction and initial validation of the Religious Status Inventory.* Unpublished doctoral dissertation, Graduate School of Psychology, Fuller Theological Seminary, Pasadena, CA.

Jackson, C. (1994). *A factor analysis of the Religious Status Inventory.* Unpublished doctoral dissertation, Graduate School of Psychology, Fuller Theological Seminary, Pasadena, CA.

Lukaszewski, M., Archer, P. , Malony, H. N., Newton, S., & Jackson, C. (1996). *Factorial stability of the Religious Status Inventory: Empirical and ideological implications.* Paper presented at the Society for the Scientific Study of Religion, Nashville, TN.

Massey, D. (1988). *Construction and factor analysis of the Religious Status Inventory.* Unpublished doctoral dissertation, Graduate School of Psychology, Fuller Theological Seminary, Pasadena, CA.

Malony, H. N. (1985). Assessing religious maturity. In E. M. Stern (Ed.), *Psychotherapy and the religiously committed patient* (pp. 25–34). New York: Hayworth Press.

Pruyser, P. (1976). *The minister as diagnostician.* Philadelphia: Westminster Press.

Porter, R., Jr. (1995). *Religious maturity and preferred mode of religious experience.* Unpublished doctoral dissertation, Graduate School of Psychology, Fuller Theological Seminary, Pasadena, CA.

Appendix A

Religious Status Inventory

Instructions: This inventory contains 160 items designed to study the way people think about their Christian faith and how it interacts with their lives. It may be taken by those who consider themselves Christians. Items will reflect what you believe, feel, and do in connection with your faith. There are no right or wrong answers. Just answer what is true for you.

On the answer sheet provided for you please write your name and other information that has been asked for. Then begin by reading each statement and deciding whether this is true for you or not true of you. For each item, indicate on the answer sheet a number representing the following answers:

Not true of me				True of me
1	2	3	4	5

1. I'm always happy because God takes care of all my problems.
2. I have read many books about my faith in the past year.
3. Making a decision is as simple as praying to God and waiting for an answer.
4. I regularly attend church or a religious community.
5. Religion is just one aspect of my life.
6. I pray for help in my decisions rather than ask for specific answers.
7. I have little desire to read a religious book.
8. When someone asks me to forgive them, I am able to do so.
9. Whatever problems I have I bring on myself.
10. I have been unable to find a group of Christians where I feel accepted.
11. I contribute a lot of money to social causes.
12. When I've done something wrong, I try to do something to correct the situation.
13. Both prayer and personal action are needed to deal with difficult problems. One without the other is insufficient.
14. Without my Christian faith I would be a much different person.
15. I change my religious beliefs frequently.
16. I usually find something else to do rather than go to church.
17. When God forgives me, I feel like I'm "off the hook."
18. I would be free of problems if life treated me better.
19. There are a lot of different parts of my faith that I want to explore.
20. God can use my anger in positive ways.
21. I make most of my decisions based on the idea that I should do to others what I want them to do to me.
22. I feel a desire to worship God throughout the week.
23. Jesus Christ is the Lord of my life.
24. I am trying to help change many things that are unfair in the world.
25. When I've wronged someone, it is useless to apologize to them.
26. I know that God will bring good out of all my painful situations because he loves me.
27. Being with non-Christians makes me feel uncomfortable.
28. It's important to do what other people want you to do.
29. God is more important to me than anything else in my life.
30. I feel accepted and understood when I am with other Christians.
31. I am conscious that my relationship to God affects how I relate to my family.
32. I decide if something is right or wrong by what happens to me.
33. I feel safe and secure knowing that God loves me.
34. When I sin, I have a sense that God cares less about what happens to me.
35. I consider myself very active in moral issues.
36. I consistently give a large amount of my income to a church or religious organization.
37. It is difficult for me to relate to Christians who believe differently than I do.

38. When making major decisions, I ask for help from my family, friends, and God.

39. I trust that the future is in God's hands and that I will accept whatever he has for me.

40. I need God's help in every minor decision I make.

41. One reason I go to church is to feel important in my community.

42. Denominational differences mean little to me.

43. When I am with a group of Christians, I feel at home.

44. I feel good about what I do because I know I am contributing to society.

45. I have little desire to be involved in social action.

46. Receiving God's forgiveness inspires me to worship and praise God.

47. I feel comfortable receiving God's love and forgiveness.

48. All I can do is take what comes in life.

49. When I have hurt someone, I feel so guilty that I find myself avoiding them.

50. I fail to understand why things have to happen to me.

51. It bothers me that God does so little to make my life better.

52. I try to keep my religion separate from other aspects of my life.

53. I lack direction from God in how to fulfill my roles with my work and family.

54. If someone hurts me, it makes it hard for me to trust them again.

55. I have a regular devotional time in order to grow in my faith.

56. Some problems and sins are so complex that it is difficult to put blame on any one thing.

57. I expect some hard times in the future but trust that God will help me through them.

58. I have difficulty handling someone getting angry at me.

59. I feel a common bond with other Christians.

60. God is an impersonal force.

61. I can do little to make my future better.

62. I'm uneasy around people from different cultures or races.

63. I am quick to ask for forgiveness when I have hurt someone.

64. I consistently go to church or a religious community twice a week or more.

65. My religious beliefs should be kept separate from what I do in my daily life.

66. I can know God merely by interacting with people.

67. I respect beliefs that are different than mine.

68. The causes of my problems include both myself and my surroundings.

69. Prayer helps me feel closer to God.

70. I am involved in my community as an expression of my faith.

71. I continue to wish the best for someone who has hurt me.

72. I volunteer quite often for church positions.

73. Prayer is useless in helping make major decisions.

74. I enjoy being around other people of different cultures or races.

75. I think about what God would want for my life when I make any major decision.

76. I have a great deal of problem with people who feel that our culture is better than others.

77. I see Jesus mainly as the founder of Christianity.

78. I feel forgiven by God when I sin.

79. It bothers me when religious differences keep people from becoming friends.

80. I would lose interest in my job if it paid less.

81. In the midst of prayer I sometimes stop and just listen.

82. Sometimes anger allows me to be productive in my actions.

83. I rarely go to church or a religious community.

84. I stand in awe and wonder of God my creator.

85. To make Jesus relevant to my daily life seems to be taking religion too far.

86. I continue to give money to the church during times when it is hard to pay my bills.

87. As a Christian everything is wonderful and will continue to be.

88. I have close friendships with both Christians and non-Christians.

89. God punishes sin.

90. I am careful to do what is right for fear that I will be punished by God.

91. I fail to see how my religious life relates to what I do every day.

92. Often I wonder if God really forgives me.

93. When problems are difficult, I recognize there is nothing I can do so I give it all to God.

94. My faith affects every aspect of my life.

95. My main reason for going to church is to make me feel better.

96. When I think of God's love, I get a warm and tender feeling inside.

97. I believe that God has a purpose for me in my job or what I do.

98. I seldom take time to think about my relationship with God.

99. My decisions are always founded on my faith.

100. Pain makes me question God's role in my life.

101. I have a hard time accepting God's forgiveness because I feel unworthy to receive it.

102. It is hard to be open and honest with other Christians.

103. I feel good about how God uses me in what I do.

104. When I have wronged someone my first thought is how that person might be feeling.

105. I lack close relationships with any group of Christians.

106. I rarely give money to the church.

107. I expect to have both good times and bad times in my future.

108. People from other cultures who become Christians will need to give up much of their cultural lifestyle.

109. I try to serve God through my work.

110. I have little desire to give money to the church.

111. The church lacks a feeling of being like a family to me.

112. I rarely consider what God would think about my actions.

113. I enjoy my work because it makes me feel good about myself.

114. When someone has wronged me, I give them the cold shoulder.

115. What is right or wrong is sometimes unclear.

116. I refuse to listen to someone who says things contrary to the Bible.

117. I rely solely on my own resources to make major decisions in my life.

118. People from some cultures or races are difficult to trust.

119. Suffering seems to develop and refine my faith and character.

120. I need friendships with both Christians and non-Christians to help me grow.

121. God will still love me regardless of what I do.

122. Without my faith in God I would be lacking much of my sense of what is right or wrong.

123. I live my life without need of God's assistance.

124. When I have hurt someone, I try to ask myself what I can do to make it right.

125. My faith is renewed when I attend church.

126. I seldom struggle with decisions of what is right or wrong.

127. I avoid volunteering for church positions.

128. I need to be more involved in church than just being a member.

129. If you follow the Bible, you will know what is right or wrong in all situations.

130. The main reason I worship God is that I feel I should.

131. Involvement in a religious community seems unnecessary to me.

132. I avoid churches that encourage a lot of involvement.

133. I don't get angry.

134. I try to keep a balance between what I can do for myself and what God can do for me.

135. It is important for Christians to separate themselves from non-Christians.

136. It would be hard to refrain from worshiping God.

137. Both God's guidance and my capabilities are important for dealing with difficult situations.

138. It's hard for me to understand how other people get so excited about God's love.

139. My concern for others is based on my love for God.

140. Knowing that God loves me gets me very excited.

141. I am comfortable with other people believing differently than I.

142. I go to church mainly to worship God and fellowship with other Christians.

143. If I've done something wrong, it is better to let it go than to bring it up again and apologize for it.

144. Because God loves and forgives me, it makes me want to go out of my way to help someone else.

145. I pray mainly when things are out of my control.

146. I have little need to deal with moral issues because very few affect me.

147. I like to just sit and enjoy a church service. I dislike being asked to participate in it.

148. My religious beliefs are complex.

149. I feel an absence of God's love in my life.

150. I go to church because I want to grow as a Christian.

151. I feel guilty when I fail to pray.

152. Talking to people from different cultures helps me to have a broader view of life.

153. Some people would say that my faith is too simple.

154. I am very active in church activities.

155. To know that God loves me is the only thing I need to know about my faith.

156. God is disappointed with me when I get angry.

157. I have discussed my faith with others on many occasions within the past year.

158. I live my daily life without thinking about my religious beliefs.

159. Discussing my faith with others seems unnecessary.

160. I try to keep an open mind about others' beliefs and am willing to change my beliefs if necessary.

Reprinted with permission of author.

Appendix B

Scoring the Religious Status Inventory

There are two ways to score the Religious Status Inventory (RSI). One way is by using the eight dimensions on the basis of which the RSI was originally constructed. The other way is by using the seven factors found in a factory analysis done in 1993 by Dr. Cynthia Jackson. These two alternatives are described below.

When the phrase "reverse score" is used, it means that when you add the answers to "reverse score" items to the score for that dimension or factor, you should change all 5s to 1s, all 2s to 4s, and leave all 3s as they are. This will make sense with an example.

Item 7 is "I have little desire to read a religious book" (the person taking the RSI answers along a 5-point scale where 5 equals "true of me" and 1 equals "not true of me").

Item 7 is a "reverse score" item on Dimension 7: Affirming Openness in Faith and on Factor 1: Religious Omissions. Since all scores on dimensions and on factors are additive (in the sense that you add up scores on the items to get a score for that dimension or factor), the higher the score, the more that dimension or factor characterizes them. Thus, it can be seen that if a participant checked 1 on this item, it should be weighted as a 5 in adding to the person being more Open in their Faith (Dimension 7) as well as adding to the number of things they do that should not do (Factor 1: Religious Omissions). Note that Dimension 7 is positive; higher scores contribute to greater religious maturity while Factor 1 is negative; higher scores contribute to less religious maturity.

SCORING FOR DIMENSIONS OF THE RSI

Dimension 1: Awareness of God
	Items:	13	22	23	29	69	81	84	134	136	137		
(Reverse Score)			40	60	66	77	85	93	123	130	145	151

Dimension 2: Acceptance of God's Grace and Steadfast Love
Items:	26	33	46	47	78	96	119	121	140	144
(Reverse Score)	1	17	34	50	89	92	100	101	138	149

Dimension 3: Knowing God's Leadership and Direction
Items:	6	31	38	39	57	70	75	103	107	109
(Reverse Score)	3	48	51	53	61	65	73	87	91	117

Dimension 4: Being Ethical
Items:	11	21	24	35	44	97	99	115	122	139
(Reverse Score)	28	32	45	80	90	112	113	126	129	146

Dimension 5: Being Repentant and Responsible
Items:	8	12	20	56	63	71	82	104	124	
(Reverse Score)	9	18	25	49	54	58	114	133	143	156

Dimension 6: Involvement in Organized Religion
Items:	4	36	64	72	86	125	128	142	150	154
(Reverse Score)	16	41	83	95	106	110	127	131	132	147

Dimension 7: Experiencing Fellowship
Items:	30	42	43	59	74	76	79	88	120	152
(ReverseScore)	10	27	37	62	102	105	108	111	118	135

Dimension 8: Affirming Openness in Faith
Items:	2	14	19	55	67	94	141	148	157	160
(Reverse Score)	5	7	15	52	98	116	153	155	158	159

The range for each dimension is 20 to 100. A total score can be obtained by adding up all dimensions. The range for the total score is 160 to 800.

Appendix C

Scoring for the Seven Factors (Jackson, 1993)

Factor 1: Importance of Religion in Daily Life (64 items)
Items:	25	146										
(Reverse Score)	7	10	15	16	18	27	28	32	34	37	41	
	45	48	50	51	52	53	60	61	62	65	66	73	80
	83	85	87	89	90	91	92	95	98	100	101	102	105
	106	108	110	111	112	113	114	117	118	123	127	130	131
	132	133	135	138	143	145	147	149	155	158	159	

Factor 2: Worship and Commitment (44 items)
Items:	4	13	14	22	23	26	29	30	31	33	38	39
	43	46	47	55	57	59	64	69	70	75	78	81	84
	86	94	96	97	99	103	109	119	121	122	125	128	136
	137	139	140	142	144	150						

Factor 3: Complexity of Faith (7 items)
Items:	56	68	115	120	148	152	160

Factor 4: Rejection of Simplistic Faith (7 items)
    Items: 1   3   40   93   116   129   156

Factor 5: Involvement in Organized Religion (5 items)
    Items: 2   11   36   72   154

Factor 6: Social Ethics (5 items)
    Items: 1   22   36   72   154

One Higher Order Factor: Optimal relgious Functioning (items from Factors 2 & 5; 49 total items)

4.8
SPIRITUAL MATURITY INDEX (Ellison, 1983)
Reviewed by Daryl H. Stevenson

Variable: The Spiritual Maturity Index (SMI) is a general measure of religious maturity that conceptualizes the construct as a continuous developmental process. Derived from evangelical Christian theology, the SMI is "marked by qualities that are similar to psychological maturity" (Ellison, 1984). Ellison conceives of the maturing person as exhibiting autonomy (not basing faith beliefs on the consensus of others), keen perception of reality, and creativity in everyday life. He suggests that the spiritually mature person does not rely on support from others to maintain beliefs but develops those beliefs through critical self-reflection.

Ellison sees religious practices and beliefs as an integral part of life's daily activities. Ellison believes spiritual maturity, unlike the closley related concept of spiritual well-being, implies meeting attitudinal and behavioral criteria not suggested in the concept of well-being. The spiritually mature person is self-principled and is able to enter into many full relationships with others. Hence, maturity reflects interdependence as well as a strong sense of self.

Spiritually mature persons are willing to make sacrifices for the welfare of others as well as cope with suffering and pain. Such individuals define their personal identity in relationship to closeness and communion with God. They tend to be conscientious regarding regular devotional time with God,

seeing it as essential for spiritual growth. Self-principled and autonomous, these persons actively use their gifts and talents and are committed to cultivating and expressing the classic Christian virtues and disciplines.

Description: The SMI consists of 30 self-report items, logically derived, and scaled on a 6-point Likert-style format with reverse scoring on 12 items due to negative wording. The respondent circles the letters corresponding to the phrases which most adequately describe one's attitude. These phrases are "strongly agree" (SA), "moderately agree" (MA), "agree" (A), "disagree" (D), "moderately disagree" (MD), "strongly disagree" (SD). Eighteen of the 30 items, if marked in the strongly agree direction, are said to be indicators of mature spirituality. Face validity of the scale is quite high because items are directly related to Ellison's conceptualized quality of spiritual maturity.

Practical Considerations: The instrument is easily self-administered and takes 10 minutes or less to complete. The scoring key indicates the nature of each item. They are scored from 1 to 6, with the higher number representing the more favorable direction (i.e., maturity). The total score is the sum of the scores obtained on all items, making the range of scores 30 to 180. No items are included as a check for social desirability or other response biases. The instructions indicate that there is no "right" response in an attempt to diffuse a social desirability tendency. Other than four sentences of instruction at the top of the instrument, no other special guidelines are provided.

Norms/Standardization: Several studies report group means and standard deviations without further explanation of how these are interpreted. Mack et al. (1987) report a mean of 138.1 (*SD* = 16.8), using a sample of 319 adult Sunday School attendees from the same church. Buhrow et al. (1987) reported a mean of 140.73 (*SD* = 17.78) based on 117 students from three seminaries. Bassett et al. (1991) report results from 84 Catholic and 131 Protestant college students. Their mean scores were 128.45 and 140.26, respectively (no *SD* reported). The heterogeneity of the combined samples is quite restricted, and norms have not been established to aid interpretation.

Unfortunately, there has been no significant work on standardization. No manual is currently available, so it is difficult to know how best to administer, score, or interpret the measure. Further work needs to be done for the SMI to be used with confidence for a variety of applications in religious or educational settings. The SMI may be useful for research purposes, however.

Reliability: Buhrow et al. (1987) report that "a portion" of the initial seminarian sample participated in a retest six months later, but no results were reported. The researchers reported an internal consistency coefficient of .87 (Cronbach's alpha). Bassett et al. (1991) reported the same statistic with a value of .92.

Validity: Much of the research with the SMI has yielded moderately significant correlations with Ellison's Spiritual Well-Being Scale (SWBS). Ellison (1984) initially hypothesized and found this relationship (r = .57, p = .001) based on the assertion that both were actually measuring different aspects of spiritual health. Bufford (1984) also found this relationship (r = .62), spawning several papers and dissertations exploring that relationship further (Boliou et al., 1987; Cooper, 1986; Davis et al., 1987; Mack et

al., 1987; see also Bassett et al., 1991). Some studies correlated the SMI with other religiosity measures. Several factor analytic studies consistently yielded a single dominant factor that accounted for much of the variance. For example, Bassett et al. (1991) combined items from several religiosity scales, including the SMI and the SWBS, and found confirmation of a single factor that "looked like (it) measured the extent to which personal commitment was manifested in belief" (p. 90), consistent with Gorsuch's (1984) suggestion that religious measures tend to tap a general factor of religiosity. Construct validity appears quite weak since it is not measuring a discrete dimension separate from the SWBS.

Using known groups, Buhrow et al. (1987) found only modest support for this construct. No gender differences emerged. Those who "profess Christ as Savior" versus those who only "follow Christ's teachings" were discriminated by the instrument. Further research requires greater heterogeneity in the samples and more studies on criterion-related and content validity. Perhaps further refinement of the theoretical construct itself, and its behavioral domain, would yield items that discriminate better.

Location:

Ellison, C. W. (1984). *Personality, religious orientation, and spiritual well-being.* Unpublished manuscript, Alliance Theological Seminary, Nyack, NY.

The SMI may be obtained from the author: Craig W. Ellison, Ph.D., Alliance Theological Seminary, South Highland Avenue, Nyack, New York 10960

Subsequent Research:

Bressem, M. R. (1986). The relationship between individual differences in imaginal abilities, Christian imaginal frequency, and Christian spirituality (Doctoral dissertation, Western Conservative Baptist Seminary). *Dissertation Abstracts International, 48–12,* 3714B.

Colwell, J. C. (1986). A correlational study of self-concept and spirituality in seminarians (Doctoral dissertation, Western Conservative Baptist Seminary). *Dissertation Abstracts International, 47–11,* 4645B.

McPherson, S. E. (1990). Studies in optimal religious functioning, personality traits, religious orientation, and spiritual maturity (Doctoral dissertation, Fuller Theological Seminary, School of Psychology). *Dissertation Abstracts International, 49–12,* 3757A.

Pramann, R. F., Jr. (1987). Commitment to spouse and God: The relationship among measures of marital commitment and spiritual maturity (Doctoral dissertation, Western Conservative Baptist Seminary). *Dissertation Abstracts International, 48–12,* 3717B.

References

Barker, G., DeWitt, J., Godwin, A., & Spotts, S. (1987). *A construct validity study of the SMI: A systematic replication.* Unpublished manuscript, Western Conservative Baptist Seminary, Portland, OR.

Bassett, R., Camplin, W., Humphrey, D., Dorr, C., Biggs, S., Distaffen, R., Doxtator, I., Flaherty, M., Hunsberger, P., Poage, R., & Thompson, H. (1991). Measuring Christian maturity: A comparison of several scales. *Journal of Psychology and Theology, 19*(1), 84–93.

Boliou, N. (1988). *Spiritual maturity: A review of construct and research.* Unpublished manuscript, Western Conservative Baptist Seminary, Portland, OR.

Boliou, N., Chapman, S., & Davis, K. (1987). *An empirical examination of the Spiritual Maturity Index and Spiritual Well-being Scale in an Evangelical church population.* Unpublished manuscript, Western Conservative Baptist Seminary, Portland, OR.

Bufford, R. (1984). *Empirical correlates of Spiritual Well- Being and Spiritual Maturity Scales.* Paper presented at the meeting of the Christian Association for Psychological Studies, Dallas, TX.

Buhrow, W., Calkins, P., Haws, J., & Rost, K. (1987). *The Spiritual Maturity Index: A study of reliability and validity.* Unpublished manuscript, Alliance Theological Seminary, Nyack, NY.

Cooper, R. L. (1987). An empirical examination of the construct validity of the Spiritual Maturity Index. *Dissertation Abstracts International, 47,* 4645B. (University Microfilms International, 87-04712)

Davis, W., Longfellow, D., Moody, A., & Moynihan, W. (1987). *Spiritual Maturity Index: Construct Validation.* Unpublished manuscript, Western Conservative Baptist Seminary, Portland, OR.

Ellison, C. W. (1984). *Personality, religious orientation, and spiritual well-being.* Unpublished manuscript, Alliance Theological Seminary, Nyack, NY.

Gorsuch, R. L. (1984). Measurement: The boon and bane of investigating religion. *American Psychologist, 39,* 228–236.

Mack, K., Stone, K., Renfroe, W., & Lloyd, K. (1987). *Spiritual well-being and maturity construct.* Unpublished manuscript, Western Conservative Baptist Seminary, Portland, OR.

Appendix

Spiritual Maturity Index

Instructions: Please circle the choice that best indicates the extent of your agreement or disagreement with each of the following statements. *Please note that there is no "right" response;* your response should honestly describe your personal experience. Do not choose an answer that would make you look "spiritual" if it is not true of yourself. All responses will be confidential; please do not put your name on the questionnaire.

SA = strongly agree	D = disagree
MA = moderately agree	MD = moderately disagree
A = agree	SD = strongly disagree

1. My faith doesn't primarily depend on the formal church for its vitality.

2. The way I do things from day to day is often affected by my relationship with God.

3. I seldom find myself thinking about God and spiritual matters during each day. (R)

4. Even if the people around me opposed my Christian convictions, I would still hold fast to them.

5. The encouragement and example of other Christians is essential for me to keep on living for Jesus. (R)

6. I feel like I need to be open to consider new insights and truths about my faith.

7. I am convinced that the way I believe spiritually is the right way.

8. People that don't believe the way that I do about spiritual truths are hard-hearted. (R)

9. I feel that a Christian needs to take care of his or her own needs first in order to help others. (R)

10. My faith doesn't seem to give me a definite purpose in my daily life. (R)

11. I find that following Christ's example of sacrificial love is one of my most important goals.

12. My identity (who I am) is determined more by my personal or professional situation than by my relationship with God. (R)

13. Walking closely with God is the greatest joy in my life.

14. I feel that identifying and using my spiritual gifts is not really important. (R)

15. I don't seem to be able to live in such a way that my life is characterized by the fruits of the Spirit. (R)

16. When my life is done, I feel like only those things that I've done, as part of following Christ will matter.

17. I believe that God has used the most "negative" or difficult times in my life to draw me closer to Him.

18. I feel like God has let me down in some of the things that have happened to me. (R)

19. I have chosen to forego various gains when they have detracted from my spiritual witness or violated spiritual principles.

20. Giving myself to God regardless of what happens to me is my highest calling in my life.

21. I don't regularly study the Bible in depth on my own. (R)

22. I actively look for opportunities to share my faith with non-Christians.

23. My relationships with others are guided by my desire to express the love of Christ.

24. I don't regularly have times of deep communion with God in personal (private) prayer. (R)

25. More than anything else in life I want to know God intimately and to serve Him.

26. Worship and fellowship with other believers is a significant part of my Christian life.

27. It seems like I am experiencing more of God's presence in my daily life than I have previously.

28. I feel like I am becoming more Christ-like.

29. I seem to have less consistent victories over temptation than I used to. (R)

30. On the whole, my relationship with God is alive and growing.

(R)—reversed-scored item

Reprinted with permission by author. Copyright © 1983 by Craig W. Ellison.

Chapter 5

Scales of Religious Commitment and Involvement

Rather than simply asking respondents how important religion is or how committed they are to their religion, the five scales reviewed in this chapter attempt to measure specific aspects of religious commitment or involvement. The length and detail of the scales vary from the 3-item Salience in Religious Commitment Scale (5.4) to the 17-item Religiousness Measure (5.3).

Two of the scales emphasize Christian commitment or involvement: the Religious Commitment Scale (5.1) and the Religious Emphasis Scale (5.2). However, with cautious modification, both scales could be used in other religious traditions with a Western orientation. The Sethi and Seligman Religiousness Measure (5.3) may be useful with some religious traditions beyond a Judeo-Christian perspective. The Roof and Perkins Salience in Religious Commitment Scale (5.4) is not specific to any particular religious tradition.

As the names of the scales indicate, the Pfeifer and Waelty Scale (5.1) and the Roof and Perkins Scale (5.4) emphasize religious commitment. However, these two scales differ radically in that the first scale operationalizes religious commitment primarily in terms of behavioral practices or affective experience, whereas the latter scale relies upon self-reported assessment of religious commitment. The Religiousness Measure (5.3) assesses primarily religious involvement and contains items concerning religious beliefs, religious practices, and the influence of religious beliefs on behavioral practices.

Altemeyer's Religious Emphasis Scale (5.2) is distinctly different from the other scales in that it measures the religious environment of the home. Thus it too assesses religious commitment and involvement, not it terms of current practice, but in terms of childhood background.

5.1
RELIGIOUS COMMITMENT SCALE (Pfeifer & Waelty, 1995)
Reviewed by Kevin S. Seybold

Variable: The Religious Commitment Scale (RCS) was developed to examine religious commitment in a sample of psychiatric patients and in a control group. Scores in the RCS could then be correlated with other indicators of psychopathology (diagnosis of depression, anxiety disorders, and personality disorders).

Description: The RCS is a subscale of the Questionnaire on Religious Orientation and General Coping with Life. A total of 51 items are used in the questionnaire; 20 of the items are modified from the Religious Orientation Scale of Allport and Ross (1967). The remaining 31 items are taken from two German scales developed to measure neurosis and religiosity (Hark, 1984), and depression and re-ligiosity (Doerr, 1987). The remaining four items, assigned to detect religious attitudes and behaviors specifically in a Swiss Context, were added by Pfeifer and Waelty. Of the 51 total items, 15 serve as the Religious Commitment Scale and are scattered throughout the entire questionnaire. Of these 15 items, 10 reflect broad social conventions (e.g., "Do you feel secure in your faith?" "Do you regard yourself as a religious person?") and are given one point each. The remaining five items are given two points and reflect specific aspects of religious practice (e.g., "Do you pray before eating?" "Do you regularly attend a worship service?"). The score on these 15 items (total = 20 pts.) is used to determine religious commitment. Scores of 11 and under signify low religious commitment and scores above 11 indicate high religious commitment.

Practical Considerations: This self-reported questionnaire is easy to administer and score. The respondent answers yes or no to each of the 51 items. "Yes" responses to those 15 items that make up the Religious Commitment Scale are then scored either 1 or 2 points to determine the total religious commitment score (0–20 pts.). The responses on the remaining 36 items are not used in determining religious commitment.

Norms/Standardization: The sample consisted of 44 psychiatric patients (13 males and 31 females) and 45 nonhospitalized and preserved healthy controls (17 males and 28 females). The mean age of the psychiatric patients was 34.4 years (SD = 10.14), and the mean age of the control group was 36.6 years (SD = 16.30). The psychiatric patients

were all diagnosed according to DSM-III-R criteria. Patients with organic disorders, schizophrenia, or major depression with psychotic features or melancholia were not included in the sample. The control group was recruited from choirs, Bible study groups, and university students from the same region of Switzerland. An attempt was made to match subjects according to social, economic, and educational status.

Reliability: No specific tests of reliability were reported.

Validity: Correlations between religious commitment scores and other measures of religiosity suggest some validity of the scale. A positive correlation (.88, p < .0001) with the intrinsic factor of the Religious Orientation Scale (Allport & Ross, 1967) was noted as was a negative correlation with the extrinsic factor (−.48, p < .0001). No other tests of validity were reported.

Location:
   Pfeifer, S., & Waelty, U. (1995). Psychopathology and religious commitment: A controlled study. *Psychopathology, 28,* 70–77.

Recent Research: None

References

Allport, G. W., & Ross, J. M. (1967). Personal religious orientation and prejudice. *Journal of Personality and Social Psychology, 5,* 432–443.

Doerr, A. (1987). *Religiosität und depression* [Religious commitment and depression]. Weinheim, Germany: Deutscher Studien Verlag.

Hark, H. (1984). *Religiös neurosen: Ursachen und heilung* [Religious neuroses: Causes and healing]. Stuttgart, Germany: Kreuz.

Appendix

Quenstionnaire or Religious Orientation and General Coping with Life

      Yes No
   1. ___ ___ * Do you regard yourself a religious person? (yes = 1 pt.)
   2. ___ ___ ^ I pray chiefly because I have been taught to pray.

3. __ __   Do you feel more satisfaction today than before?

4. __ __ ^ If not prevented by unavoidable circumstances, I attend my house of worship.

5. __ __ * Do you pray before eating? (yes = 2 pt.)

6. __ __ ^ What religion offers me most is comfort when sorrows and misfortune strike.

7. __ __ * Do you pray often? (yes = 1 pt.)

8. __ __ ^ Although I believe in my religion, I feel there are many more important things in life.

9. __ __ ^ Religion is especially important to me because it answers many questions about the meaning of life.

10. __ __   Could you live without Christmas (the cause for the celebration, not the bustle associated with it)? (inverse scoring: yes = 0, no = 1 pt.)

11. __ __   Is your conscience sometimes annoying to you?

12. __ __ ^ My religious beliefs are what really lie behind my whole approach to life.

13. __ __ * Do you regard it important to marry in a religious ceremony? (yes = 1 pt.)

14. __ __ ^ Although I am a religious person, I refuse to let religious considerations influence my everyday affairs.

15. __ __ * Do you feel secure in your faith? (yes = 1 pt.)

16. __ __ ^ The purpose of prayer is to secure a happy and peaceful life.

17. __ __ ^ A primary reason for my interest in religion is that my house of worship is a congenial social activity.

18. __ __   To live a religious life means in my opinion, to hope for and trust in things which exist but cannot be seen.

19. __ __   Do you think that your parents have given you a religious education?

20. __ __ * Do you regularly attend a worship service? (yes = 2 pt.)

21. __ __ * Could you do without God? (inverse scoring: yes = 0, no = 1 pt.)

22. __ __   Does sexuality cause anxiety in you?

23. __ __   As a child, did you believe: "God sees everything"?

24. __ __ *^ If I were to join a religious group, I would prefer to join a Bible study group rather than a social fellowship. (yes = 2 pt.)

25. __ __ * My faith alone will be able to give me the feeling of security in the last hours of my life. (yes = 1 pt.)

26. __ __   When you were a child, have you often felt discriminated (or put down)?

27. __ __ ^ My house of worship is most important as a place to formulate good social relations.

28. __ __   Without faith my life would be meaningless.

29. __ __ ^ Occasionally I find it necessary to compromise my religious beliefs in order to protect my social and economic well-being.

30. __ __ ^ It doesn't matter so much what I believe so long as I lead a moral life.

31. __ __ * Through faith I have often experienced the closeness of God. (yes = 1 pt.)

32. __ __ *^ I read literature about my faith (or my church). (yes = 2 pt.)

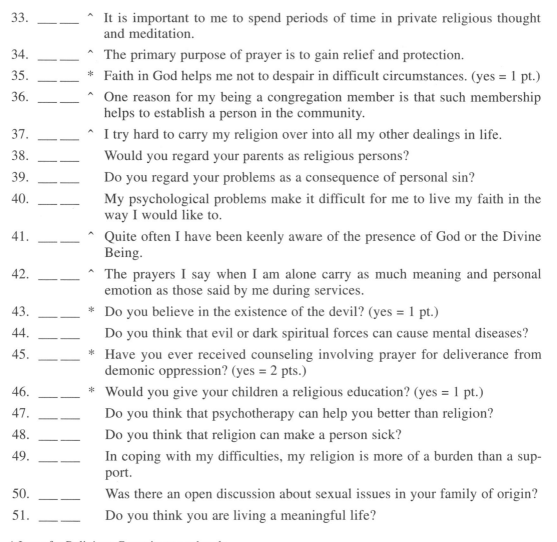

33. ___ ___ ^ It is important to me to spend periods of time in private religious thought and meditation.

34. ___ ___ ^ The primary purpose of prayer is to gain relief and protection.

35. ___ ___ * Faith in God helps me not to despair in difficult circumstances. (yes = 1 pt.)

36. ___ ___ ^ One reason for my being a congregation member is that such membership helps to establish a person in the community.

37. ___ ___ ^ I try hard to carry my religion over into all my other dealings in life.

38. ___ ___ Would you regard your parents as religious persons?

39. ___ ___ Do you regard your problems as a consequence of personal sin?

40. ___ ___ My psychological problems make it difficult for me to live my faith in the way I would like to.

41. ___ ___ ^ Quite often I have been keenly aware of the presence of God or the Divine Being.

42. ___ ___ ^ The prayers I say when I am alone carry as much meaning and personal emotion as those said by me during services.

43. ___ ___ * Do you believe in the existence of the devil? (yes = 1 pt.)

44. ___ ___ Do you think that evil or dark spiritual forces can cause mental diseases?

45. ___ ___ * Have you ever received counseling involving prayer for deliverance from demonic oppression? (yes = 2 pts.)

46. ___ ___ * Would you give your children a religious education? (yes = 1 pt.)

47. ___ ___ Do you think that psychotherapy can help you better than religion?

48. ___ ___ Do you think that religion can make a person sick?

49. ___ ___ In coping with my difficulties, my religion is more of a burden than a support.

50. ___ ___ Was there an open discussion about sexual issues in your family of origin?

51. ___ ___ Do you think you are living a meaningful life?

* Items for Religious Commitment subscale
^ Modified item from Religious Orientation Scale (Allport & Ross, 1967).

Reprinted with permission by authors.

5.2
RELIGIOUS EMPHASIS SCALE (ALTEMEYER, 1988)

Reviewed by Bruce Hunsberger

Variable: The Religious Emphasis Scale (RES) measures the extent to which one's parents emphasized the family religion as one was growing up. The scale was originally developed and reported by Altemeyer (1981) and later slightly revised (Altemeyer, 1988). The revised form is discussed here. The RES was developed in the context of Al-temeyer's (1981, 1988) work on right-wing authoritarianism and its link with religion.

Description: Respondents are asked to indicate the extent to which their parents emphasized religion while they were growing up, using a 6-point response format. Response alternatives included 0 (none at all), 1 (only a little bit), 2 (a mild amount), 3 (a moderate amount), 4 (quite a bit), and 5 (a great deal). The total scale score is determined by a summation of the 10 item scores.

Practical Considerations: This paper-and-pencil measure is relatively straightforward to use, requiring no special examiner skill to administer, score, or interpret. The test has been used both with university students and their parents in Canada. It appears to be suitable for adolescent through adult samples in similar cultures.

Norms/Standardization: Two primary samples were used in Altemeyer's (1988) work with this scale. Five hundred and thirteen introductory psychology students completed the scale as part of a course research bonus credit system. Also, 549 parents of these students responded to the scale, which was part of a questionnaire package sent and returned by regular mail. Average scores on the scale were 17.7 for the students and 25.0 for the parents; variance was 161 and 186 respectively.

Reliability: The average interitem correlation for these 10 items was .55, with a resulting Cronbach's alpha of .92, identical for both the university student sample and their parents.

Validity: Altemeyer (1988) provides documentation regarding correlations between the Religious Emphasis Scale and other measures of religion and authoritarianism. These relationships are in the expected directions. For example, correlations between Religious Emphasis and other measures developed by Altemeyer (1988), for the student and parent samples respectively, were Right-Wing Authoritarianism (.37, .30), Religious Doubts (−.30, −.23), and Religious Pressures (.59, .43). Comparable correlations for other scales included Fullerton and Hunsberger's (1982) Christian Orthodoxy Scale (.59, .49), and Allport and Ross' (1967) Intrinsic Religious Orientation (.58, .50) and Extrinsic Religious Orientation (−.20, −.15) Scales.

The correlations with a single-item measure of church attendance were .62 and .44 for the two groups respectively.

Further, in earlier work with this scale (Altemeyer, 1981), students' and parents' accounts of the emphasis placed on religion in the home correlated .70 and .73 in two studies. That is, students' accounts of the religious circumstances of their youth were corroborated by their parents. There was also a reasonably strong relationship (.48 to .53) between Religious Emphasis scores and the extent to which students still reported accepting the teachings of the home religion.

Location:
Altemeyer, B. (1988). *Enemies of Freedom: Understanding right-wing authoritarianism.* San Francisco: Jossey-Bass. (See especially pp. 205-206, 214, 218.)

Subsequent Research: Altemeyer has continued to develop this scale, and a 16-item version was recently used (Hunsberger & Altemeyer, 1995) in research on apostates, again revealing strong psychometric properties. Cronbach's alpha for the 16-item version was .95 and .96 in two samples of more than 800 university students each.

References

Allport, G. W., & Ross, J. M. (1967). Personal religious orientation and prejudice. *Journal of Personality and Social Psychology, 5,* 432–443.

Altemeyer, B. (1981). *Right-wing authoritarianism.* Winnipeg, Manitoba: University of Manitoba Press.

Altemeyer, B. (1988). *Enemies of freedom: Understanding right-wing authoritarianism.* San Francisco: Jossey-Bass.

Fullerton, J. T., & Hunsberger, B. E. (1982). A unidimensional measure of Christian orthodoxy. *Journal for the Scientific Study of Religion, 21,* 317–326.

Hunsberger, B., & Altemeyer, B. (1995, June). *Apostates from highly religious homes: Socialization anomalies.* Poster presented at the annual meetings of the Canadian Psychological Association, Charlottetown, Prince Edward Island, Canada.

Appendix

The Religious Emphasis Scale

After naming the particular religion in which they had been raised, participants are asked to respond to the following items, on a 0-5 basis, to indicate "how much their parents emphasized practicing the family religion while they were growing up" (Altemeyer, 1988, p. 205).

0 = no emphasis was placed on the behavior
1 = a slight emphasis was placed on the behavior
2 = a mild emphasis was placed on the behavior
3 = a moderate emphasis was placed on the behavior
4 = a strong emphasis was placed on the behavior
5 = a very strong emphasis was placed on the behavior

1. Going to church; attending religious services.
2. Attending "Sunday school"; getting systematic religious instruction regularly.
3. Reviewing the teachings of the religion at home.
4. Praying before meals.
5. Reading Scripture or other religious material.
6. Praying before bedtime.
7. Discussing moral "do's" and "don't's" in religious terms.
8. Observing religious holidays; celebrating events like Christmas in a religious way.
9. Being a good representative of the faith; acting the way a devout member of your religion would be expected to act.
10. Taking part in religious youth groups.

5.3
RELIGIOUSNESS MEASURE (Sethi & Seligman, 1993)
Reviewed by Kevin S. Seybold

Variable: Sethi and Seligman (1993) designed the Religiousness Measure in an attempt to correlate religiosity with attributional style and optimism. Three aspects of religiousness were included on the measure: religious influence in daily life, religious involvement, and religious hope.

Description: The Religiousness Measure consists of 17 questions. Religious hope is assessed through six questions (e.g., Do you believe that there is a heaven?, Do you believe your suffering will be rewarded?), each placed on a Likert scale ranging from 1 (strongly disagree) to 7 (strongly agree). Religious involvement is measured using three questions (e.g., How often do you

pray?) evaluated on a frequency scale. Six questions are designed to assess religious influence (e.g., How much influence do your religious beliefs have on the important decisions of your life?); these questions are also evaluated through a 7-point Likert format. In addition, the respondent is asked whether he or she believes in God and whether he or she would marry someone of another religion (to be answered yes or no).

Practical Considerations: Directions for administering the religious measure are clear. Scoring for the religious hope and religious influence items are determined by means for each subscale. Responses on the religious involvement questions are scored on a scale of 1 to 6, with the higher number indicating greater involvement. As in the other questions, a mean involvement score is then determined for each subject. The two yes/no questions are not used in quantifying religiousness.

Norms/Standardization: Members of various religious groups in the United States served as subjects (N = 623). Three broad catagories of religious affiliation were created into which these subjects were placed: fundamentalists (N = 208), moderates (N = 274), and liberals (N = 141). Orthodox Jews, Muslims, and Calvinists were placed into the fundamentalist category because these groups tend to interpret religious texts literally and because they place greater regulations upon the daily behavior of their followers. The moderate group was composed of four religions (Conservative Judaism, Catholicism, Lutheranism, and Methodism) based upon textual interpretation and less time (than fundamentalists) spent in religious activities. The liberal category consisted of Reformed Jews and Unitarians because these religions encourage a skeptical and individualistic outlook. All subjects ranged in age from 18 to 65 years and were selected from urban areas (New York, Philadelphia, Minneapolis, and Washington, D. C.). No statistically significant effects of gender, age, education, or income were found among the subjects of the three broad religious classifications.

Reliability: No formal attempt was made to establish the reliability of the measure.

Validity: Significant differences were found between the fundamentalist, moderate, and liberal classifications in religious influence in daily life, religious hope, and religious involvement. The authors interpreted these differences as confirming their original divisions of the groups into the three broad categories. No significant differences were found within the three classifications on these religious dimensions. The authors report that each of the three religious measures correlated positively with optimism as measured by the Attributional Style Questionnaire (Schulman, Castellon, & Seligman, 1989). The correlations were rather low (religious involvement, r = .08; religious influences r = 14; religious hope r = .21); however due to the large sample size, the correlations were statistically significant. No other attempt to validate the measure with established religious scales was reported.

Location:
   Sethi, S., & Seligman, M. E. P. (1993). Optimism and fundamentalism. *Psychological Science, 4,* 256–259.

Subsequent Research:
   Seith, S., & Seligman, M. E. P. (1994). The hope of fundamentalists. *Psychological Science, 5,* 58.

References

Schulman, P., Castellon, C., & Seligman, M. (1989). Assessing explanatory style: The content analysis of verbatim explanations and the Attributional Style Questionnaire. *Behavior Research and Therapy, 27,* 505–512.

Appendix

Religiousness Measure

Gender _____

Age _____

Educational Level _____

Income Level (high, middle, low) _____

Race _____

To what religious faith do you belong? _____

Please circle the response which you feel is most like you.

1. Do you believe in God?
   yes   no

2. How important would you say religion is in your life?
   1   2   3   4   5   6   7
   not at all   extremely
   important   important

3. How often do you read holy scriptures?
   a. more than once a day   d. once a week
   b. once a day   e. more than once a month
   c. more than once a week   f. less than once a month

4. How often do you pray?
   a. more than once a day   d. once a week
   b. once a day   e. more than once a month
   c. more than once a week   f. less than once a month

5. How often do you attend religious services and activities?
   a. more than once a day   d. once a week
   b. once a day   e. more than once a month
   c. more than once a week   f. less than once a month

6. How much influence do your religious beliefs have on the important decisions of your life?
   1   2   3   4   5   6   7
   none of my   some of my   all of my
   decisions   decisions   decisions

7. Would you marry someone of another religion?
   yes   no

8. How much influence do your religious beliefs have on what you wear?
   1   2   3   4   5   6   7
   not at all   somewhat   extremely
   influential   influential   influential

9. How much influence do your religious beliefs have on what you eat and drink?
   1   2   3   4   5   6   7
   not at all   somewhat   extremely
   influential   influential   influential

10. How much influence do your religious beliefs have on whom you associate with?
    1   2   3   4   5   6   7
    not at all   somewhat   extremely
    influential   influential   influential

11. How much influence do your religious beliefs have on what social activities you under-
    take?
    1   2   3   4   5   6   7
    not at all   somewhat   extremely
    influential   influential   influential

12. Do you believe that there is a heaven?
    1   2   3   4   5   6   7
    strongly   somewhat   strongly
    disagree   agree   agree

13. Do you believe it is possible for all humans to live in harmony together?
    1   2   3   4   5   6   7
    strongly   somewhat   strongly
    disagree   agree   agree

14. Do you believe there are miracles?
    1   2   3   4   5   6   7
    strongly   somewhat   strongly
    disagree   agree   agree

15. Do you believe your suffering will be rewarded?
    1   2   3   4   5   6   7
    strongly   somewhat   strongly
    disagree   agree   agree

16. Do you believe that in the future your children will be able to lead a better life than
    yourself?
    1   2   3   4   5   6   7
    strongly   somewhat   strongly
    disagree   agree   agree

17. Do you believe the future will be a better place to live?
    1   2   3   4   5   6   7
    strongly   somewhat   strongly
    disagree   agree   agree

To use items, contact Sheena Sethi-Iyengar, Ph. D., Sloan School of Management, Massachusetts Institute of Technology, Bldg. E52, Room 561, 77 Massachusetts Ave., Cambridge, MA 02139-4307.

5.4
SALIENCE IN RELIGIOUS COMMITMENT SCALE (Roof & Perkins, 1975)
Reviewed by Paul D. Young

Variable: The Salience in Religious Commitment Scale measures "the importance an individual attaches to being religious" (p. 111). The authors designed and used the scale to measure the extent to which individual adults consider their religious beliefs to be important, both in general and when making decisions. The scale was developed as part of a study to measure the relationship of religious salience with orthodoxy, church activism, political conservatism, anti-black prejudice, and racism.

Description: This is a short scale with only three items. The first two items are in a multiple-choice format, whereas the third measures degree of agreement with a general statement on a 4-point Likert-type scale. Total scores range from 3 to 11.

The authors assert that the scale attempts to measure "an orientation toward religious commitment, similar to that implied in Allport's [1966] intrinsic religiosity" (p.116). Intrinsic religiosity has effects on everyday life and decisions, and the Salience in Religious Commitment Scale attempts to measure that concept.

Practical considerations: This scale may be easily administered and may be scored in less than five minutes. Note, however, that the authors suggest that salience is not linear and that only scores of 10 or 11 (on the 11-point scale) indicate the level of religious salience that is likely to relate to other measured variables.

Norms/Standardization: Roof and Perkins used the questionnaire with 518 adult Episcopalians in North Carolina. The sample represents a rather narrow segment of American adults: predominantly Southern born, college-educated Episcopalian professionals and managers. No specialized norms were reported.

Reliability: An alpha reliability coefficient of .72, moderate at best and minimally acceptable for research purposes, is the only measure of reliability reported.

Validity: The scale relies heavily on face validity. The authors also report a correlation coefficient of .81 between this salience measure and a companion test of religious orthodoxy that focuses on doctrinal commitment. This strong relationship suggests that the salience scale is indeed measuring some characteristic of religiousness.

The usefulness of information gained from the scale may be limited by the narrow range of scores. The authors did not find that the scale enabled them to predict church activism, political conservatism, or racism with much confidence, since the highest correlation coefficient was .10. It remains to be seen, however, whether the "threshold" effect predicted by the authors (that salience has impact only on these scoring at the highest levels of the scale) is valid and heuristically useful.

Location:
  Roof, W. C., & Perkins, R.P. (1975). On conceptualizing salience in religious commitment. *Journal for the Scientific Study of Religion, 14*, 111–128.

Subsequent research. None found.

References

Allport, G. W. (1966). The religious context of prejudice. *Journal for the Scientific Study of Religion, 5*, 447–457.

Appendix

Salience in Religious Commitment Scale

Shown below are the scale items. Numbers in parentheses indicate values.

1. My religious faith is:
____ Important for my life, but no more important than certain other aspects of my life (2).

____ Only of minor importance for my life, compared to certain other aspects of my life (1).

____ Of central importance for my life, and would, if necessary come before all other aspects of my life (3).

2. Everyone must make many important life decisions, such as which occupation to pursue, what goals to strive for, whom to vote for, what to teach one's children, etc. When you have made, or do make decisions such as these, to what extent do you make the decisions on the basis of your religious faith?

____ I seldom if ever base such decisions on religious faith (1).

____ I sometimes base such decisions on my religious faith but definitely not most of the time (2).

____ I feel that most of my important decisions are based on my religious faith, but usually in a general, unconscious way (3).

____ I feel that most of my important decisions are based on my religious faith, and I usually consciously attempt to make them so (4).

3. Without my religious faith, the rest of my life would not have much meaning to it.
strongly disagree (1)   disagree (2)   agree (3)   strongly agree (4)

Note: Numbers in parentheses indicate values for scoring purposes.

Roof, W. C., & Perkins, R. P. (1975). On conceptualizing salience in religious in religious commitment Journal for the Scientific Study of Religion, 14, 111–128. Copyright © 1975 Journal for the Scientific Study of Religion. Reprinted with permission.

Chapter 6

Scales of Religious Experience

One of the distinguishing characteristics of religion is that many people find its experience to be powerful and moving. William James, viewed by many as the patriarch of American psychology of religion, insisted that any study of religion should recognize the powerful role that the element of feeling plays in religion; similarly, James argued, the intellect is subordinated in religious experience. Of course, the relationship between cognition and emotion, whether applied to religion or not, is complex. A long standing debate (that extends far beyond the purposes of this volume) about the precise nature of this relationship has only intensified during the past two decades.

With regard to religion, there has been very little research on underlying cognitive and affective mechanisms, though there has been considerable effort investigating cognitive (but less so affective) *content* of religious experience. These research efforts are reflected in the number of scales in chapter 1 measuring religious belief content versus the cognitive structure of religious belief (e.g., is there a hierarchical order to religious belief?). Perhaps because the affective domain is so difficult to study, there are few developed measures that tap the affective, experiential dimension that many people find central to religious faith. However, it appears that more measures are being developed. In addition to the three measures included here, some of the measures of spirituality and mysticism reviewed in chapter 10 and some of chapter 8's multidimensional scales contain an experiential component.

All three scales reviewed in this chapter appear to be culture bound, but only Hsieh's Word-Spirit Orientation Scale (6.3) directly measures Christian religious experience. Edwards' Religious Experience Questionnaire (6.1) would likely require some modification outside of the Christian tradition and therefore should be used with extreme caution in such a context. Edwards's scale (6.1) assesses the individual's subjective sense of God's presence, care, and forgiveness experienced through religious faith. Hsieh's scale (6.3) attempts to identify the degree to which one may emphasize in his or her own religious experience this subjective-experiential orientation by contrasting it with a more objective-rational approach to religion.

Hood's Religious Experience Episodes Measure (6.2) and, in particular, the subsequent Rosegrant version of the scale, is unique among measures in this volume. This scale assesses the degree to which religion is subjectively experienced by providing 15 first-person accounts of religious experience as reported in William James's *The Varieties of Religious Experience: A Study in Human Nature*. The respondent is then asked to indicate the degree of match between the reported religious experience with his or her own actual religious experience.

6.1
RELIGIOUS EXPERIENCE QUESTIONNAIRE (Edwards, 1976)
Reviewed by M. Elizabeth Lewis Hall

Variable: The Religious Experience Questionnaire (REQ) was designed to measure personal religious experience, which refers to the experienced reality of an affective relationship with a personal, caring God. The author differentiates between this affective, experiential dimension, and the cognitive dimension of belief in a religious system or in doctrinal statements. The construct includes a sense of being heard, cared for, and forgiven by God, as well as a sense of God's presence and of being saved. The measure is intended to assess individual, subjective experience, not group norms or values.

Description: This scale was developed in response to the observation that traditional religious measures of orthodoxy tended to have ceiling effects in religiously committed populations. It emphasized the cognitive rather than the affective aspects of religion (K. J. Edwards, personal communication, August 26, 1997). It is based on the personal religious experience factor identified by King (1967), which contained items related to experiencing the effects of God's influence on one's personal life. Edwards's scale was initially developed from items drawn from this factor and was later revised and expanded.

The original REQ consisted of eight items scored on a 4-point Likert scale ranging from "all the time" to "very seldom" for seven items, and from "constant fellowship" to "rare fellowship" for one item assessing the degree of experienced fellowship with God (Edwards, 1976). The scale was later revised and expanded to 12 items in order to include 4 reverse-scored items (K. J. Edwards, personal communication, August 17, 1997). In addition, two items were reworded in order to standardize the anchors of the Likert scales, which were expanded to 7 points ranging from "never" to "always." One item on prayer was also replaced with an item that was more relational in order to maintain the consistency of the measure's experiential emphasis.

Items 3, 5, 7, and 12 are reverse scored. The total score for the instrument is then determined by summing the responses on each item, allowing a range of 12 to 84. Alternatively, the mean of the responses may be calculated.

Practical Considerations: The REQ is a paper-and-pencil measure that does not require special examiner skill for administration or interpretation. Brief instructions are provided for the test taker that emphasize the importance of answering each item based on personal experience. The purpose and rationale of the scale are clear: to assess the subjective and experiential aspects of an individual's relationship with God. The face validity of the measure is good as all items clearly relate to the construct the scale attempts to measure.

Norms/Standardization: No normative data are reported in the available research on the REQ. Consequently, it is difficult to assess whether the instrument does, in fact, avoid the problem of a ceiling effect with religiously committed populations, as intended by the author. However, the fact that the scale correlates significantly with a number of measures in a number of religiously committed samples (e.g., college students, adults, and an inpatient clinical sample) suggests that the range is indeed wide enough to allow for research use of the instrument with religious populations.

Reliability: No specific reliability data are available.

Validity: Construct validity of an affective experience of God as close and loving is supported by significant positive correlations between REQ scores and loving, benevolent God images (Brokaw & Edwards, 1994), an intrinsic-committed religious orientation, and peer ratings of the individual's relationship to God (Wessel, 1979). Brokaw (1991) factor-analyzed the original 12 items, in addition to 16 experimental items, using a sample of 92 undergraduate students from a religiously homogeneous population. The results suggest that the original 12 items load onto a single factor with loadings ranging from .46 to .83, thus supporting the homogeneity of the construct.

In addition, the construct validity of the REQ is indirectly supported by a number of studies showing significant positive correlations between REQ scores and constructs involving inter- and intrapersonal affective and experiential dimensions: intrapersonal variables of positive self-concept (Day, 1980; Wessel, 1979), self-esteem (Edwards, 1977; Edwards, Goldberg, Hargrove, & Linamen, 1979), and self-adequacy (Tisdale et al., 1997); interpersonal variables of empathy (Edwards, 1977; Edwards et al., 1979; Wessel, 1979), an affiliative interpersonal style (Volker, 1981), dominance, autonomy, a friendly-dominant interpersonal style, expressed inclusion, expressed affection (Edwards et al., 1979), social interest, and psychosocial maturity (Wessel, 1979); and level of object relations development (Brokaw & Edwards, 1994; Tisdale et al., 1997).

Location:

Edwards, K. J. (1976). Son role behavior and religious experience. In W. J. Donaldson Jr. (Ed.), *Research in mental health and religious behavior: An introduction to research in the integration of Christianity and the behavioral sciences* (pp. 224–238). Atlanta: Psychological Studies Institute. (original version)

Information on the development of the current version has not been published. Further information on the scale can be obtained by contacting the author directly:

Keith J. Edwards, Ph.D.
Rosemead School of Psychology
Biola University
13800 Biola Ave.
La Mirada, CA 90639; (562) 903-4867

Recent Research:

Brokaw, B. F., & Edwards, K. J. (1994). The relationship of God image to level of object relations development. *Journal of Psychology and Theology, 22*(4), 352–371.

Day, N. D. (1980). *Religious orientation, God concept, religious experience, social interest, and self-concept.* Unpublished doctoral dissertation, Rosemead Graduate School of Psychology, Biola University, La Mirada, CA.

Edwards, K. J., Goldberg, G., Hargrove, J., & Linamen, C. (1979). *Religious experience as a function of self-concept and interpersonal behavior.* Unpublished manuscript, Rosemead School of Psychology, Biola University, La Mirada, CA.

Tisdale, T. C., Key, T. L., Edwards, K. J., Brokaw, B. F., Kemperman, S. R., Cloud, H., Townsend, J., & Okamoto, T. (1997). Impact of treatment on God image and personal adjustment, and correlations of God image to personal adjustment and object relations development. *Journal of Psychology and Theology, 25*(2), 227–239.

Volker, G. C. (1981). God concept as a function of interpersonal style (Doctoral dissertation, Rosemead School of Psychology, Biola University, 1981). *Dissertation Abstracts International, 42,* 1157B.

References

Brokaw, B. F. (1991). *The relationship of God image to level of object relations development.* Unpublished doctoral dissertation, Rosemead Graduate School of Psychology, Biola University, La Mirada, CA.

Brokaw, B. F., & Edwards, K. J. (1994). The relationship of God image to level of object relations development. *Journal of Psychology and Theology, 22*(4), 352–371.

Day, N. D. (1980). *Religious orientation, God concept, religious experience, social interest, and self-concept.* Unpublished doctoral dissertation, Rosemead Graduate School of Psychology, Biola University, La Mirada, CA.

Edwards, K. J. (1977). *Religious experience as a function of self-concept and interpersonal behavior.* Unpublished manuscript, Rosemead School of Psychology, Biola University, La Mirada, CA.

Edwards, K. J., Goldberg, G., Hargrove, J., & Linamen, C. (1979). *Religious experience as a function of self-concept and interpersonal behavior.* Unpublished manuscript, Rosemead School of Psychology, Biola University, La Mirada, CA.

King, M. (1967). Measuring the religion variable: Nine proposed dimensions. *Journal for the Scientific Study of Religion, 6,* 173–190.

Tisdale, T. C., Key, T. L., Edwards, K. J.,

Brokaw, B. F., Kemperman, S. R., Cloud, H., Townsend, J., & Okamoto, T. (1997). Impact of treatment on God image and personal adjustment, and correlations of God image to personal adjustment and object relations development. *Journal of Psychology and Theology, 25*(2), 227–239.

Volker, G. C. (1981). God concept as a function of interpersonal style (Doctoral dissertation, Rosemead School of Psychology, Biola University, 1981). *Dissertation Abstracts International, 42*, 1157B.

Wessel, S. J. (1979). *The relationship of psychosocial maturity to intrapersonal, interpersonal and spiritual functioning.* Unpublished doctoral dissertation, Biola University, La Mirada, CA.

Appendix

Religious Experience Questionnaire

Below are listed a number of descriptive statements concerning religious experience. We would like you to use these statements to describe *YOUR* religious experience as accurately as possible. That is, we would like you to indicate, on a scale from 1 to 7, how true of **YOUR** religious experience these various statements are. Please respond to each item using the following scale:

1	2	3	4	5	6	7
Never	Almost never	Sometimes but infrequently	Occasionally	Often	Almost all the time	Always

_____ 1. I experience an awareness of God's love.
_____ 2. I pray privately in places other than church.
_____ 3. I experience feelings of anger or resentment toward God.
_____ 4. I ask God to forgive my sins.
_____ 5. I am afraid that God is going to punish me in some way.
_____ 6. When I have decisions to make in my everyday life, I try to find out what God wants me to do.
_____ 7. I experience the feeling that God is so big and important He doesn't have time for my personal problems.
_____ 8. I feel very close to God in prayer, during public worship, or at important moments in my life.
_____ 9. I experience awareness of God's influence in my daily life.
_____ 10. When I pray to God, I feel like I'm having a conversation with a close friend.
_____ 11. My relationship to God is characterized by close fellowship.
_____ 12. I find myself doubting that God really exists.

Reprinted with permission by author.

6.2
RELIGIOUS EXPERIENCE EPISODES MEASURE (REEM)
(Hood, 1970; Rosegrant, 1976)

Reviewed by Christopher T. Burris

Variable: The REEM, as it is self-evidently labeled, is intended as "an operational measure of the degree of reported religious experience" (Hood, 1970, p. 286).

Description: Hood (1970) constructed the REEM in order to address the empirical neglect of religious experience, owing in part to what he perceived to be insufficient or unduly simplistic operationalizations of the construct at the time. In order to eliminate some of the interpretational ambiguities associated with the construct among respondents, Hood utilized a "literary exemplar" approach in constructing the REEM. Thus, the original REEM consists of 15 first-person accounts of religious experiences culled from James's (1902/1985) compilation. After reading each account, participants are asked to rate the degree to which any of their own experiences resemble the experience reported in the account, from 1 "I have had absolutely no experience like this" to 5 "I have had an experience almost identical to this." Possible scores can thus range from 15 to 75.

Rosegrant (1976) reported research using a modified version of the REEM. Three changes were implemented: (a) The archaic wording present in some of the turn-of-the-century accounts was eliminated; (b) the five most explicitly Christian-sounding accounts were deleted; and (c) The 5-point response format was dropped in favor of a 9-point format.

Practical Considerations: Both Hood's (1970) and Rosegrant's (1976) versions of the REEM require little administration time, and instructions to the respondent are clear and straightforward. Scoring is also uncomplicated. One noteworthy limitation of the REEM is that its content is rather culture bound, a point that Hood himself (Hood, Spilka, Hunsberger, & Gorsuch, 1996) noted. Because it is adapted from James's (1902/1985) compilation of religious experiences from available autobiographies, diaries, letters, etc., the content and language of the REEM bears the imprint of North American Protestantism. Indeed, Holm's (1982) respondents found the James-based accounts of religious experiences presented in a literal Swedish translation of the REEM to be rather confusing, forcing Holm to construct a culture-specific version of the REEM based, in part, upon the Nordic experiential literature. Thus, administration of either the original or the shortened REEM outside of a religiously committed North American Christian sample may be ill-advised.

Norms/Standardization: Hood (1970) reported a mean of 31.5 for the 15-item REEM among his original sample of 51 psychology undergraduates at South Dakota State University; he suggested that this average might be somewhat higher than that for the general population, owing to the rural, religious background of many of the respondents. Rosegrant's (1976) sample of 91 participants in an outdoor program in North Carolina yielded an item mean of 3.4 (9-point response format).

Some cultural variation in REEM scores is evident. For example, Hood and Hall (1977) found, using a 5-item "culture-fair" version of the REEM, that Catholics of nonacculturated Mexican-American or Native American descent reported higher average levels of religious experience than did Catholics of either European-American or acculturated Mexican-American descent.

Reliability: Hood (1970) reported a 2-week test-retest reliability coefficient of .93 for the original REEM. Internal consistency (Kuder-Richardson formula) was .84. Rosegrant (1976) reported a Cronbach's alpha of .73. Thus, both the original and shortened versions of the REEM appear sufficiently reliable for research purposes.

Validity: Both in the original and in a subsequent study, Hood (1970; 1978b) found REEM scores to be moderately positively correlated with intrinsic, and uncorrelated with extrinsic, religious orientation, as measured by the Allport and Ross (1967) scales. Holm (1982) reported that the Christian-based items of his Swedish adaptation of the REEM were related to the religious/noetic subscale of Hood's (1975) Mysticism Scale, whereas the non-Christian-based items were related to the general/phenomenological subscale. Moreover, Hood (1978a) found the REEM sufficiently sensitive to shifts in reported religious experience to function as a dependent variable in a quasi-experimental investigation of the effects of stress and expectancy on religious experience in a nature setting. Thus there appears to be reasonable evidence for the REEM scale's construct validity.

Location: Both Hood (1970) and Rosegrant (1976) give descriptions and sample items from the original and revised versions of the REEM, although neither source reproduces a scale version in its entirety. Interested readers are instead instructed to contact the respective authors for versions of the scale.

Recent Research: In addition to studies that have direct implications on the scale's validity, versions of the REEM have been used to investigate the relationship between reported religious experience and both hypnotic susceptibility (Hood, 1973) and psychological adjustment (Hood, 1974), and to differentiate among individuals whose report or denial of religious experiences is either false or genuine (Hood, 1978b). Nevertheless, the REEM scale in its various forms has been underutilized in empirical research relative to Hood's (1975) Mysticism Scale. This underuse may be attributable, in part, to Hood's (e.g., 1978a, 1978b) and others' (e.g., Holm, 1982) equating what the REEM measures with "mysticism." To the extent that this is true, then the Mysticism Scale (also in this volume) is probably the more adaptable and informative of the two measures.

References

Allport, G. W., & Ross, J. M. (1967). Personal religious orientation and prejudice. *Journal of Personality and Social Psychology, 5,* 432–443.

Holm, N. G. (1982). Mysticism and intense experiences. *Journal for the Scientific Study of Religion, 21,* 268–276.

Hood, R. W., Jr. (1970). Religious orientation and the report of religious experience. *Journal for the Scientific Study of Religion, 9,* 285–291.

Hood, R. W., Jr. (1973). Hypnotic susceptibility and reported religious experience. *Psychological Reports, 33,* 549–550.

Hood, R. W., Jr. (1974). Psychological strength and the report of intense religious experience. *Journal for the Scientific Study of Religion, 13,* 65–71.

Hood, R. W., Jr. (1975). The construction and preliminary validation of a measure of reported mystical experience. *Journal for the Scientific Study of Religion, 14,* 29–41.

Hood, R. W., Jr. (1978a). Anticipatory set and setting: Stress incongruity as elicitors of mystical experience in solitary nature situations. *Journal for the Scientific Study of Religion, 17,* 278–287.

Hood, R. W., Jr. (1978b). The usefulness of the indiscriminately pro and anti categories of religious orientation. *Journal for the Scientific Study of Religion, 17,* 419–431.

Hood, R. W., Jr., & Hall, J. R. (1977). Comparison of reported religious experience in Caucasian, American Indian, and two Mexican American samples. *Psychological Reports, 41,* 657–658.

Hood, R. W., Jr., Spilka, B., Hunsberger, B., & Gorsuch, R. (1996). *The psychology of religion: An empirical approach.* New York: Guilford.

James, W. (1985). *The varieties of religious experience: A study in human nature.* Cambridge, MA: Harvard University Press. (Original work published in 1902)

Rosegrant, J. (1976). The impact of set and setting on religious experience in nature. *Journal for the Scientific Study of Religion, 15,* 301–310.

Appendix

Religious Experience Episodes Measure: Form 2 (Rosegrant, 1976)

Instructions: People sometimes have very moving and powerful experiences. It is hard to measure this sort of thing, especially since there can be many kinds of moving experiences. What I want you to do is compare your experience with the following descriptions of significant experiences that different people have had. Most of the descriptions use religious language. What I want you to decide is not whether you like the language used, but whether you think that your experience was moving and powerful in the same way as the experience that the person was trying to describe.

Below each description are numbers running from 1 to 9. Please circle one number for each experience; the higher the number, the more similar it is to your experience.

1. Indicates that your experience was not at all like the experience described.
3. Indicates that your experience was vaguely similar to the experience described.
5. Indicates that your experience was similar to the experience described.
7. Indicates that your experience was quite similar to the experience described.
9. Indicates that your experience was almost identical to the experience described.

Once, a few weeks after I came to the woods, I thought that perhaps it was necessary to be near other people for a happy and healthy life. To be alone was somewhat unpleasant. But during a gentle rain, while I had these thoughts, I was suddenly aware of such a good society in nature, in the pattern of the drops and in every sight and sound around my house, that the fancy advantages of being near people seemed insignificant, and I haven't thought about them since. Every little pine needle expanded with sympathy and befriended me. I was so definitely aware of something akin to me that I thought no place could ever be strange to me again.

1   2   3   4   5   6   7   8   9

My mind, deeply under the influence of the thoughts and emotions called up by the reading and talk, was calm and peaceful. I was in a state of quiet, almost passive enjoyment, not actually thinking but letting thoughts and emotions flow by themselves through my mind. All at once, without any warning, I found myself wrapped in a flamecolored cloud. For an instant I thought a great fire might be in the nearby city; the next moment I knew that the fire was within myself. Directly afterward I felt a sense of exultation, of immense joy and intellectual insight impossible to describe.

1   2   3   4   5   6   7   8   9

I have several times felt that I have enjoyed a period of communion with the divine. These meetings are unexpected but clear, and consist of the disappearance of the conventionalities that fill my life. Once it happened when from the top of a high mountain I looked over a rugged landscape extending to a long curve of ocean which reached the horizon. Another time it happened when from the same point I could see nothing beneath me but an endless expanse of white cloud. Above the windblown clouds a few high peaks, including the one I was on, seemed to be plunging about as if they were dragging their anchors. On these occasions I felt a temporary loss of my identity, and I realized that life was more significant than I had thought.

1   2   3   4   5   6   7   8   9

My thoughts went back to what they had been busy with for three years—the search for God. I wondered how I had ever come by the idea of God. And with this thought a glad desire for life arose in me. Everything in me became meaningful. I realized that I did not have to look farther. To acknowledge God and to live are one and the same thing. God is what life is.

1   2   3   4   5   6   7   8   9

I would suddenly feel the mood coming when I was at church, or with people, or reading, but only when my muscles were relaxed. It would irresistibly take over my mind and will, last what seemed like forever, and disappear in a way that resembled waking up from anesthesia. One reason that I disliked this kind of trance was that I could not describe it to myself; even now I can't find the right words. It involved the disappearance of space, time, feeling, and all the things that I call my self. As ordinary consciousness disappeared, the sense of underlying or essential consciousness grew stronger. At last nothing remained but a pure, absolute, abstract self.

1   2   3   4   5   6   7   8   9

I remember the night and almost every spot on the hilltop where my soul opened out and the inner and outer worlds rushed together. My own deep struggle was being answered by the unfathomable deep without, reaching beyond the stars. I stood alone with him who had made me, and all the beauty, love, and sorrow of the world. I felt the union of my spirit with his. The ordinary sense of things around me faded, and for the moment nothing remained but an indescribable joy.

1   2   3   4   5   6   7   8   9

I felt something within me had broken on which my life had always rested, that I had nothing to hold on to, and that my life no longer had meaning. I felt forced to commit suicide. It wouldn't exactly be right to say I wished to kill myself, because the force which drew me away from life was more powerful and more general than any mere wish. It was a force like my old desire to live, but it moved me in the opposite direction. I was driven to die, and in spite of that I still hoped for something from life.

1   2   3   4   5   6   7   8   9

God is more real to me than any thought or thing or person. I feel God's presence and I feel it more as I live in closer harmony with his laws. I feel God in the sunshine or rain, and my feelings are best described as awe mixed with delirious restfulness.

1   2   3   4   5   6   7   8   9

The highest experiences I have had of the presence of God have been rare and brief—flashes of consciousness which have made me exclaim with surprise, or less intense moments of happiness and insight, only gradually passing away. I have severely questioned whether these moments were worthwhile, but I find that after every questioning, they stand out today as the most real experiences of my life.

1   2   3   4   5   6   7   8   9

I have never had such an immediate, powerful experience. I don't know what it was in that flower, what shape or secret, that made me see it in a limitless beauty. I will never enclose in a conception this power, this indescribable greatness, this uncontainable form, this ideal of a better world, which I felt but which nature has not made actual.

1   2   3   4   5   6   7   8   9

6.3
WORD-SPIRIT ORIENTATION SCALE (Hsieh, 1981)
Reviewed by Christopher T. Burris

Variable: The Word-Spirit Orientation Scale (WSOS) is intended to measure the degree to which a Christian individual tends to emphasize the objective-rational ("Word" orientation) or subjective-experiential aspects ("Spirit orientation") of his or her faith tradition.

Description: Based on a conceptual distinction introduced by Stewart (1974), with conceptual ties to the field independent/dependent cognitive style distinctions of Witkin and colleagues (e.g., Witkin, Dyk, Faterson, Goodenough, & Karp, 1962), the WSOS is comprised of 16 forced-choice items (including 3 fillers). Scoring consists of adding up a respondent's total number of Word-oriented choices. It assumes an underlying bipolar continuum from low (Spirit-oriented) to high (Word-oriented; possible score range is 0–13).

Practical Considerations: The WSOS is brief, can be administered in paper-and-pencil format, and is easy to score. Written instructions to the respondent are adequate for scale completion, although no rationale for scale completion is provided therein. The scale's content and wording (e.g., "personal testimonies," "witnessing") assumes familiarity and agreement with a number of beliefs and practices distinct to evangelical Protestant Christianity; administration and interpretation of the scale among other populations is thus probably ill-advised.

Norms/Standardization: The original sample (Hsieh, 1981) consisted of 82 psychology undergraduate students attending a theologically conservative Christian college in the midwestern United States. Classification of respondents was based on a tertiary split, with the top third being designated as "Word-oriented" and the bottom third as "Spirit-oriented." Men were overrepresented in the Word-oriented group; women were overrepresented in the Spirit-oriented group. Actual cutoff scores, as well as the total sample mean, were not reported.

Hsieh (1987), using a sample of 127 Christian college students, utilized cutoff scores of 6 and above for Word orientation and 5 and below for Spirit orientation, approximating a median split. The sample mean was 5.09 ($SD = 2.04$); sex differences were not reported.

Reliability: Using a sample of 24 evangelical Christian college undergraduates, Hsieh (1981) reported a two-week test-retest reliability of .88. No internal consistency or factor structure information was reported, however.

Validity: Information concerning the WSOS's validity is fragmentary. Hsieh (1981) alluded to a pool from which scale items were chosen, but item selection was based on face validity alone. To the extent that the WSOS is assumed to be linked conceptually to cognitive style, then Hsieh's (1981) finding that Word-oriented persons are more field-independent than Spirit-oriented persons offers some evidence for the WSOS's construct validity. Hsieh (1987) referred to two unpublished manuscripts linking Word-Spirit orientation to preferences for both religious denomination and preaching style, which may contribute to the scale's predictive validity. At least two problematic issues remain, however. First, conceptual and psychometric justification for the assumed bipolarity of Word-Spirit orientation is needed. It is unclear, for example, whether the middle-scoring WSOS respondents excluded from Hsieh's (1981) primary investigation should best be conceptualized as neither Spirit- nor Word-oriented, or as a mixture of both orientations. Second, discriminant validity of the WSOS needs to be established. It is unclear, for example, whether the apparent link between Word-Spirit orientation and gender is indicative of construct validity or is a confound.

Location:

Hsieh, T. T. Y. (1981). Cognitive styles and word versus spirit orientations among Christians. *Journal of Psychology and Theology*, 9, 175–182.

Recent Research:

Hsieh, T. T. Y. (1987). Heavenly-minded and earthly good: A study of social interest, ethical style, and word-spirit orientation among Christians. *Journal of Psychology and Theology*, 15, 141–147.

References

Hsieh, T. T. Y. (1981). Cognitive styles and word versus spirit orientations among   Christians. *Journal of Psychology and Theology*, 9, 175–182.

Hsieh, T. T. Y. (1987). Heavenly-minded and earthly good: A study of social interest, ethical style, and word-spirit orientation among Christians. *Journal of Psychology and Theology*, 15, 141–147.

Stewart, V. M. (1974). Cognitive style, North American values, and the body of Christ. *Journal of Psychology and Theology*, 2, 77–88.

Witkin, H. A., Dyk, R. B., Paterson, H. F., Goodenough, D. R., & Karp, S. A. (1962). *Psychological differentiation*. New York: Wiley.

Appendix

Word-Spirit Orientation Scale

Instructions: There are two statements in each of the following questions. Please choose the one that *you believe describes you accurately or is more true. There are no right or wrong answers.* However, it is important that each statement you choose applies to you more than the other. Try to answer each item independently when making your choice; do not be influenced by your previous choices.

1. a.   I feel regular church attendance is an integral part of the Christian faith.
   b.   I feel that one can maintain Christian growth without regular church attendance.

2. a.   When reading the Bible for the purpose of understanding and interpretation, I tend to rely more often upon my own resources to shed light upon the subject.
   *b. When reading the Bible for the purpose of understanding and interpretation, I tend to seek help from other people's writings to shed light upon the subject.

3.*a.   When I am with a group of new people, I am more often concerned with just being myself.
   b.   When I am with a group of new people, I am more often concerned with making a good impression.

4. a.   When witnessing to others, I tend to present the lovingkindness of Christ.
   *b. When witnessing to others, I tend to present claims of Christ's life, death, and resurrection.

5.*a.   I feel that a church should be more concerned with a vision for worldwide evangelization.
   b.   I feel that a church should be more concerned with the fellowship and growth of its own members.

6. a.   I feel the biblical concept of the nature of man places him in a position of being basically good.
   b.   I feel the biblical concept of the nature of man places him in a position of being basically evil.

7.*a.   I feel the scriptural teachings and doctrines are better defenses of Christian faith.
  b.   I feel personal testimonies and experiences are better defenses of Christian faith.

8. a.   I feel the main emphasis of Sunday School should be to teach children application of faith, such as acceptance of others and themselves.
  *b.   I feel the main emphasis of Sunday School should be to give children solid biblical teaching, such as the doctrine of salvation.

9. a.   When making life decisions, I tend to rely mostly upon what I feel to be God's will.
  *b.   When making life decisions, I tend to rely mostly upon my own intellectual capacities.

10. a.   If I were to hold some leadership position in my church, I would feel more comfortable allowing members to help me in the decisions and delegating responsibilities to those members.
  *b.   If I were to hold some leadership position in my church, I would feel more comfortable making decisions and being responsible for following them through myself.

11.*a.   When getting together with a few of my close friends for reasons of Christian growth, I prefer to spend time in Bible study, group discussion, and interpretation of the passages read.
  b.   When getting together with a few of my close friends for reasons of Christian growth, I prefer to spend time in sharing personal experiences we have had with God and praying together.

12.*a.   In my own personal Bible study times, I spend more time concentrating on finding the correct interpretation of Bible passages, even going to commentaries once in a while for further insight.
  b.   In my own personal Bible study times, I spend more of my time reading for inspiration and strength to meet present problems.

13. a.   I feel that it is an important part of my faith to give 10 percent or more of my income to the local church.
  b.   I feel that my spiritual growth will not suffer by giving less than 10 percent of my income to the local church.

14. a.   I feel that God wants a church to listen for a call to outreach on a day-to-day basis.
  *b.   I feel that God wants a church to have a well-structured, long-range, ongoing program of outreach.

15.*a.   Most of my reading materials are theological and doctrinal in nature.
  b.   Most of my reading materials are devotional and inspirational in nature.

16. a.   I see my ministry as a Christian as dealing with those who are lonely, suffering, and overcome by temptations (even as a layperson).
  *b.   I see my ministry as a Christian in the area of teaching, pastoring, and administration (even as a layperson).

* Indicates "Word-oriented" statements. Items 1, 6, and 13 are fillers.

Hsieh, T.T.Y. (1981). Cognitive style and word versus spirit orientations among Christians. *Journal of Psychology and Theology, 9*, 175–182. Copyright © 1981 by Rosemead School of Psychology, Biola University. Reprinted with permission.

Chapter 7

Scales of Religious/Moral Values or Personal Characteristics

People often report that their system of values is influenced by their religious faith. Most religious traditions not only prescribe a value system but also provide a set of guidelines for personal character development. For example, in his letter to the churches in the Roman province of Galatia (Galatians 5:22–23) the apostle Paul describes the "fruit of the spirit"—a wholistic lifestyle characterized by qualities such as love, joy, and peace that is expected of all Christians.

Two of the scales reviewed in this chapter are operationalizations of biblical teachings. Schmidt's 225-item Character Assessment Scale (7.1) measures moral strengths and weaknesses based on specific criteria culled from New Testament writers. Wichern's Spiritual Leadership Qualities Inventory (7.5) measures nineteen specific character qualities from two Pauline passages that are expected of Christians in leadership positions within the church.

The other four measures are value surveys. Two of these surveys evaluate the degree to which values prescribed by the Judeo-Christian tradition are supported. The Christian Moral Values Scale (7.2), authored by Francis and Greer, is a brief ten-item scale listing behaviors that either are clearly not advocated by traditional Judeo Christian teaching (e.g., drunkenness, premarital intercourse, etc.) or are debated within the Christian community (e.g., artificial birth control, divorce, etc.). The other measure, the highly specialized Missionary Kids' Value Scales (7.3), is a lengthy composite of several subscales (including some that could be reviewed in other chapters in this volume, such as a religious orthodoxy subscale). It has been tested with adolescents who have grown up in other cultures (primarily children of missionaries).

The other two surveys do not measure values as explicitly religious constructs. Both instruments, however, operationalize variables that have been and likely will continue to be of interest to psychologists of religion. The first of these is the widely used Rokeach Value Survey (7.4), which assesses the relative importance of different values as life-guiding principles. Respondents are asked to rank-order a list of eighteen "terminal values," or end-states toward which people strive, and a list of eighteen "instrumental values," or means to those end-states. The other scale is the Value Profile (7.6) of Bales and Couch, in which rated values fall into four interpersonal value dimensions: acceptance of authority, need-determined expression versus value-determined restraint, equalitarianism, and individualism.

7.1
CHARACTER ASSESSMENT SCALE (Schmidt, 1987)
Reviewed by Michael J. Boivin

Variable: The Character Assessment Scale assesses personal character traits within the framework of an evangelical Christian commitment. This instrument is designed for the helping professional as a reliable and valid instrument for assessing a person's moral strengths and weaknesses according to biblical standards. It is intended to be a resource tool within the therapeutic or counseling setting.

Description: The CAS is part of a family of similar instruments that endeavor to operationalize the moral teaching of Christ as expressed by the New Testament authors. These include the Sinful Attitudes Inventory by Backus (1969, 1976) and Schmidt, Backus, and Oates (1978), as well as the Spiritual Leadership Qualities Inventory (Wichern, 1980-see review in this volume).

In the initial development of the instrument, Schmidt composed 300 true-false items consisting of a revised list of Backus's seven deadly sins. Revisions were made to in order for the items to more fully encompass the interpersonal and behavioral dimensions of the sins. Also, some of the traits were renamed to reflect a more psychological, contemporary emphasis. Seven corresponding virtues were added (character strengths) to the seven deadly sins, and two scales to measure an additional dimension (Honesty). Pretesting with a sample of 60 individuals eventually resulted in the selection of 225 of these items for the final version of the instrument.

The test measures eight basic moral resources divided into four attitudes of the heart (those dealing with Truth, Respect, Concern, and Anger) and four attitudes of the flesh (involving the use of Money, Time and Energy, Sexuality, and Bodily Health). Each of these character traits is composed of two subscales: a character strength and a related moral weakness. The score for each of the eight moral resources is derived from subtracting the weakness score from the strength score.

Practical Considerations: The CAS manual provides detailed step-by-step instructions for scoring the answer sheet to the instrument. Scoring the various subscale measures and plotting them along the response profile is a rather involved process, although a computer program was available at one time from the author to automate scoring on computers running MS-DOS. Schmidt notes that once the scorer becomes familiar with the process, he or she can score an instrument by hand in seven to eight minutes.

Since the instrument is intended as a resource tool within the therapeutic setting, the manual provides very detailed guidelines for interpreting the results and debriefing those results with the client. Included are numerous biblical illustrations and insight suggestions that can be shared with the client for each of the subscales.

Norms/Standardization: In the CAS manual, Schmidt provides a detailed descriptive overview of the roughly 600 individuals from across America (92%) and Canada (8 %) who completed the instrument (Schmidt, 1987, appendix A). The normative sample was composed of 54% female with an average age of 38 years and an average of 17 years of education. They represented 45 American states and 7 Canadian provinces. Sixty-four percent were married; 76% identified themselves as Protestant; and the majority of respondents were middle income. In terms of occupation, 19% were pastors and pastoral counselors and another 3% were secular counselors. Fourteen percent were homemakers and 15% were students. Seventy-five percent of the normative sample were not receiving any treatment or counseling for emotional problems at the time of testing, whereas the remaining 25% were under psychological or psychiatric care. Most of the sample were regular church attenders.

Appendixes B and C of the manual describe the effects of various normative characteristics and demographic variables on CAS scale profiles. These include the relationship between CAS scale profiles and the following demographic variables: age, sex, education, geographic location, marital status, occupation, income level, psychological treatment status, church attendance, and religious denomination.

Reliability: Cronbach's alpha was computed across items for each of the eight basic subscale measures. The resulting coefficient values ranged from 0.61 to 0.83 with an average of 0.75, reflecting interitem consistency for the various subscales that are adequate but not exceptionally high. There is a strong pattern of high intercorrelations among the various subscales.

Validity: All subjects were asked before taking the test which of the eight moral resources they considered to be their strongest and weakest areas. A significantly higher percentage of respondents had test outcomes that agreed with their predictions than would be anticipated by chance ($\chi^2 = 55.4$, $p < .0001$). The same was true when counselors were asked to predict their client's strongest and weakest resources ($\chi^2 = 23.7$, $p < .001$).

A final test of validity by Schmidt (1983) involved asking 25 seminary students to take the test a second time and purposely present themselves in the most positive a manner possible. This significantly increased the Denial score in the instrument, the subscale used by the administrator to partially assess the validity of the client's response.

Location: The instrument, answer sheets, and manual can be obtained from:

Paul F. Schmidt
1209 West Main Street
Shelbyville, Kentucky, 40065

Schmidt, P. F., (1987). *Manual for use of the Character Assessment Scale* (3rd ed.). Shelbyville, Kentucky: Institute for Character Development.

Subsequent Research:

Boivin, M. J., Beuthin, T. M., & Hauger, G., (1993). Why Christian students leave Christian colleges: Evaluating the dynamics of adjustment in a Christian community. *The Journal of the Freshman Year Experience*, 5, 93–125.

Elzerman, J. H., & Boivin, M. J. (1987). The assessment of Christian maturity, personality, and psychopathology among college students. *Journal of Psychology and Theology*, 6, 50–64.

Schmidt, P. F., (1983). *Manual for use of the Character Assessment Scale* (2nd ed.). Shelbyville, Kentucky: Institute for Character Development.

Underwood, L. K., Maes, B. J., Alstadt, L. A., & Boivin, M. J. (1996). Evaluating changes in social attitudes, character traits, and liberal-arts abilities during a four-year program at a Christian college. *Research on Christian Higher Education*, 3, 115–128.

References

Backus, D. W. (1969). *The seven deadly sins: Their meaning and measurement*. Unpublished doctoral dissertation, University of Minnesota. Ann Arbor, MI: University Microfilms.

Backus, D. W. (1976). The seven deadly sins: Their meaning and measurement. In W. Donaldson (Ed.), *Research in Mental Health and Religious Behavior*, Atlanta: Psychological Studies Institute, 444–448.

Schmidt, P. F., Backus, D.W., & Oates, W.E. (1978) *The Sinful Attitudes Inventory: A manual for administration, scoring, interpretation, and follow-up counseling*. Unpublished manuscript.

Wichern, F. B. (1980) *The Spiritual Leadership Qualities Inventory: Manual for administration and instruction*. Available from the author, 300 Northview, Richardson, TX 75080. Unpublished manuscript.

Appendix

The Character Assessment Scale

This test is designed to help you understand yourself better. It is based on the belief that a healthy personality reflects a balanced respect and concern for both yourself and other people. In particular, the test measures how you tend to use and invest your respect, concern, anger, money, time, body, and sexuality.

You will receive scores on 15 traits of character, plus a scale that suggests how carefully and honestly you have described yourself on the test. Your scores will be given back to you, along with descriptions of the traits and guidelines to help you interpret you scores.

Some statements will assume that you have a mate, a job, or an income. If you don't now have one, then answer the question to describe how you think you would be if you *did* have a mate, a job, or an income.

To answer some of these questions honestly, you will have to stop and think for a moment. Do not be in a *hurry*. A good half the value of taking the test should be what you learn about yourself in responding to the items that make you stop and think.

If you simply cannot decide which answer to make, just skip the question. But answer as many questions as you possibly can because blank answers reduce the value of the test.

You are to mark your answers on the answer sheet. If statement number one is more true than false for you, then circle the T. If statement number one is more false than true, then circle the F.

Make all of your marks on the answer sheet, and do not mark on the pages of questions that follow.

1. At times I have done things which I know weren't good for my body.   T   F

2. I enjoy laughing at myself when I do stupid things.   T   F

3. When someone I know is happy, I feel almost as much joy myself in response.   T   F

4. It is best to forgive people who hurt you, even when they don't deserve it and might try the same thing again.   T   F

5. The more money you have, the more responsibility you should feel to support others in need.   T   F

6. I am deeply moved by the needs of others, and I spend most of my time working hard to help other people.   T   F

7. In looking at attractive members of the opposite sex, I always follow the rule "Admire, but don't desire."   T   F

8. I would level with *anyone* who asked how much I weigh, how much exercise I get, or what things I put into my body.   T   F

9. I do not enjoy having so much to eat that afterwards all I feel like doing is just lying around until my stomach recovers.   T   F

10. People need religion's and society's taboos against sexual freedom.   T   F

11. During the day, it is rare for me to check the time out of boredom.   T   F

12. I imagine that I could be truly happy below the middle income bracket.   T   F

13. I don't like to feel angry, so I get it out of my system as quickly and politely as possible.   T   F

14. I have no appetite for gossip.   T   F

15. I would not like to climb to a level in life where I would   T   F
be above being hurt by other people.

16. I sometimes enjoy looking down on others and feeling superior.   T   F

17. I sometimes want to have sex primarily for my own pleasure.   T   F

18. I am morally opposed to abortions and to mercy killing   T   F
(withholding treatment to let medically hopeless people die).

19. I always rejoice with people over pleasant surprises in their lives,   T   F
even when they don't seem to deserve such good luck.

20. One of the best ways to get back at enemies is being   T   F
kind to them when they don't deserve it.

21. I never splurge and buy things I don't really need just   T   F
for the fun of it.

22. I enjoy dreaming about the future and then working   T   F
hard to make my dream come true.

23. Sex outside of marriage results in a dishonest cover-up   T   F
with the spouse, and this causes more emotional problems
than any affair is worth.

24. When I'm around people who are talking about dieting   T   F
or exercising, I would never exaggerate or cover up my
behavior to impress them.

25. I would not especially enjoy having a good wine with my   T   F
evening meals every day.

26. I don't get very excited watching a fleshy love scene in a movie.   T   F

27. I seldom find myself looking forward to going to bed and   T   F
falling off to sleep.

28. It is not a top priority for me to have enough money and   T   F
assets so that I won't be poor in the future.

29. I never act rude to people unless I have been repeatedly   T   F
provoked by them.

30. I am not bothered by people who seem to have no faults.   T   F

31. When I see somebody embarrassed in public, I usually   T   F
get a kick out of it.

32. These days there just isn't much recognition or respect   T   F
for the people who deserve it most.

33. I am sometimes so tired I don't want to do things I really believe in.   T   F
34. In a group I like to let other people see what I don't   T   F
know so they can teach me things.

35. I am a sympathetic person, ready and willing to share the   T   F
sorrow of anyone who is suffering from loss.

36. When people hurt me, I usually feel sad and try to make   T   F
up or work it out before I get angry with them.

37. Learning to enjoy sharing your money is one way to   T   F
protect yourself against hard times.

38. I feel no need to pretend to anyone that I work any harder than I actually do.   T   F

39. For married people who have had sex with others beside their spouses, I do not believe that "what spouses don't know won't hurt them."   T   F

40. Keeping my body fit and healthy is very important to me.   T   F

41. Between meals I don't think about food very often.   T   F

42. Having some sexual inhibitions is necessary for mental health.   T   F

43. The fear of failure and rejection very rarely keep me from doing my best.   T   F

44. Labor unions shouldn't try so hard to get the highest possible wages for their members.   T   F

45. I would not feel any pleasure at seeing someone who had wronged me back his car into a telephone pole.   T   F

46. When I am really mad, my anger often lasts for several days.   T   F

47. When people get more recognition than they deserve, I like seeing them called down for making a mistake.   T   F

48. If other people don't appreciate me, it results from their own limitations.   T   F

49. When I am short on money, I am sometimes reluctant to give to a needy cause or person.   T   F

50. I enjoy serving others behind the scenes more than impressing them from where all can see.   T   F

51. I can be a pretty good companion and friend for a person who is feeling miserable.   T   F

52. I am a patient person.   T   F

53. I don't want anyone to notice when I give away money.   T   F

54. I generally work harder when I am alone than I do when someone is watching me.   T   F

55. Satisfying my partner's sexual needs gives me more enjoyment than having my own needs satisfied.   T   F

56. I am careful to get enough exercise and to watch what I put into my body.   T   F

57. When I am uptight, depressed, or bored, I am not tempted to drink or take pills.   T   F

58. I don't enjoy thinking of new and unusual ways to increase my pleasure in making love.   T   F

59. I seldom get to the point where I feel like giving up and have to force myself to keep at it.   T   F

60. I feel no need to "keep up with the Joneses" by having as much or more money and possessions than my friends.   T   F

61. It's hard to be generous unless you have enough money to afford it.   T   F

62. I usually let resentments grow into long-range grudges because I don't know how to express my anger constructively. T F

63. I sometimes resent it when a person I know is honored for some achievement. T F

64. I usually get irritated when someone in authority over me pulls rank and tells me what to do. T F

65. When people take advantage of me or hurt me intentionally, I don't always forgive them right away. T F

66. I care more about making others happy and glorifying God than I do about making sure my life is happy. T F

67. I am very considerate and sensitive to the feelings of others. T F

68. I am not one to appear as if I am trying to settle an argument when I am really still enjoying it. T F

69. I would not feel embarrassed if people found out how much money I contribute to people in need. T F

70. I am a very intense person—whether working or playing, I give it all I've got. T F

71. When it comes to lovemaking, I am unselfish. T F

72. Except for times of rest, it is important for me to stay as alert and energetic as I can. T F

73. Within the last week, I have not regretted anything that I have eaten. T F

74. I don't like to read dirty books. T F

75. When I get depressed, I can usually stay on top of it and keep going. T F

76. Although it's no fun being sick, I really do enjoy having such a good excuse to do nothing for awhile. T F

77. If I charge something in a store and they keep forgetting to bill me, I figure that's their problem. T F

78. Sometimes when I am mad at people, I enjoy just clamming up and watching them climb the walls. T F

79. I am sometimes envious and even bitter about the good fortune of others. T F

80. It is sad that there are so many boring, unintelligent, and uneducated people in the world. T F

81. At times I have been so preoccupied with my own needs that I didn't care very much how people around me felt. T F

82. I easily accept and support the leadership of those over me in a group. T F

83. I can't think of any situation where I would act more concerned about other people than I really feel. T F

84. Under no circumstances would I ever act like I had forgiven someone when I knew in my heart that I hadn't done it yet. T F

85. When I don't have enough money to pay for something   T   F
    I want, I learn not to want it so much.

86. I'm a "self-starter": I like to get myself going and keep   T   F
    busy at work.

87. I believe it is always best if a bride and groom can both   T   F
    go to the altar as virgins.

88. Being a success at my work depends largely on my health   T   F
    and physical attractiveness.

89. I do not eat so much food that I am overweight.   T   F

90. Talking about genitals and the sexual act in obscene   T   F
    terms is very repulsive to me.

91. The amount of passion in act of love-making is primarily   T   F
    determined by energy, physical attractiveness, and "chemistry."

92. Often I feel like there is nothing worth doing at the present time. T   F

93. One of the nice things about being rich would be not   T   F
    giving a darn what anybody else thought of me.

94. I seem to have more enemies than most other people do.   T   F

95. When I am standing near someone much more popular,   T   F
    wealthy, or intelligent than I am, it makes me feel like a
    small and worthless person by comparison.

96. We all try to avoid feeling lonely, confused, and afraid, and   T   F
    I have succeeded at this better than most.

97. Sometimes I am too proud to admit that I have made a   T   F
    mistake or to let someone else teach me something I don't know.

98. I would never try to impress someone else by acting more   T   F
    modest and humble than I feel.

99. When I hear a friend has suffered a loss, I seldom act   T   F
    more concerned and sympathetic than I really am.

100. When I am in an argument, I almost always try to settle   T   F
     it with peaceful compromise before walking away.

101. I enjoy spending my money more when I know that I have already   T   F
     given a fair share of it to those who need it more than I do.

102. I especially enjoy being with people who like to work   T   F
     hard at whatever they do.

103. I consistently try not to imagine having intercourse with   T   F
     someone other than my spouse.

104. I am an energetic and alert person because I have been   T   F
     careful about putting food, alcohol, and drugs into my body.

105. Within the past year, I have not done or said anything   T   F
     while using drugs or alcohol which I later regretted.

106. Sometimes I get so wrapped up in the pleasure of tasting   T   F
     and eating food that I am inconsiderate of those around
     me at the time.

107. People who talk about finding meaning in making love   T   F
are mostly trying to justify the natural experience of pleasure.

108. Some people think of me as spoiled.   T   F

109. Sometimes I like to daydream and wonder what it would   T   F
be like to have lots of money.

110. It really gripes me the way some people are forgiven   T   F
without being punished for their mistakes.

111. Some people seem to have it easy, and when I see them   T   F
get something else they have wanted, I usually have to
fight feeling sorry for myself.

112. I often realize that I could help other people so much   T   F
more if only they could see things my way.

113. To get a point across, sometimes I exaggerate or leave   T   F
out part of the truth.

114. When God or other people help me do something, I   T   F
usually express my appreciation honestly without
secretly giving myself more credit than I let on.

115. I really get worked up identifying with the characters in   T   F
a good movie or TV drama.

116. When I don't know how to settle an argument with a   T   F
loved one, I am usually willing to bring in another person to help us.

117. I include in my regular budget giving a certain portion of   T   F
my income to people less fortunate than I.

118. A vacation "re-creates" me, and leaves me all fresh and   T   F
ready to go back to work.

119. People who wait until their wedding night to enjoy   T   F
intercourse are smart.

120. I can experience and enjoy no more of life than my body   T   F
will let me, so I try hard to keep it in good shape.

121. I don't work hard enough to keep my appearance pleasant   T   F
and attractive.

122. When there are delicious foods around, I simply cannot   T   F
eat just a little and stop there.

123. When I see a particularly attractive member of the opposite   T   F
sex, I'll sometimes wonder what he or she would
look like undressed.

124. Although the doctor cannot explain why, I just seem to   T   F
be low on energy.

125. It gives me pleasure to count the money in my pocket,   T   F
purse, or bank account to see just how much money I have.

126. I sometimes enjoy planning elaborate ways of getting   T   F
even with people who intentionally hurt me.

127. I sometimes can't keep from spreading bad news about someone   T   F
     I know, even when I don't have anything against the person.

128. In some situations, I try to hide how much I'm looking   T   F
     down on others, and how I think of myself.

129. Sometimes I like to brag on myself a little bit.   T   F

130. Every human being can grow to be a positive, unselfish   T   F
     person, regardless of intelligence, health, or present
     moral habits.

131. When I hear of someone I know who has suffered a loss,   T   F
     my heart instantly goes out to them.

132. I am always kind and polite to strangers, even when I am   T   F
     worked up or mad about something.

133. I believe I could learn to be content no matter what kind   T   F
     of income I have.

134. Doing things for others usually turns me on, and leaves   T   F
     me feeling I have more energy than I had to start with.

135. Adultery is stealing—it's taking what belongs to somebody else.   T   F

136. Sexually, I find that at times forbidden fruit seems a little   T   F
     extra tasty to me.

137. I don't take very good care of my body.   T   F

138. Other people tell me I am now physically or emotionally   T   F
     dependent on drugs or alcohol.

139. The idea of making love with a complete stranger   T   F
     someimes appeals to me.

140. I sometimes get to the point where I feel totally worthless   T   F
     as a person.

141. Nearly all people who give away money do it mostly for   T   F
     show or for a tax break.

142. Some of my resentments have lasted for months and months.   T   F

143. I sometimes have to hide a twinge of pleasure at watching   T   F
     the embarrassment of people more popular than I.

144. Sometimes I try to act humbly interested and impressed   T   F
     with someone when I really just want that person to be
     impressed with me.

145. Sometimes I feel a little bit relieved or tickled when a   T   F
     very vain person is embarrassed.

146. When I experience the vastness and beauty of nature, my heart   T   F
     and mind humbly bow down before the God who created it.

147. When people I know are hurting, it hurts me, and I always   T   F
     try my best to help them out.

148. I hate being in an argument, and I always try to settle it   T   F
     as fairly and quickly as possible.

149. If I were a millionaire, I would give money secretly to people who really need it.   T   F

150. When I tell people I'll do something, they can always count on me to be on time and ready to go.   T   F

151. I don't seem to have a great deal of willpower.   T   F

152. When two unmarried people both want to make love just for pleasure, I believe they will usually feel satisfied afterward.   T   F

153. When I eat and talk about food, I am not very careful to be considerate of those around me who are struggling with their weight.   T   F

154. Having a little booze or drugs helps me to relax, and talk more easily with people I don't know very well.   T   F

155. At times the thought of sex gets stronger and stronger until I have satisfied myself.   T   F

156. People take me for granted—no one really appreciates the effort I make.   T   F

157. The security that comes from a good income is a top priority for my future.   T   F

158. Sometimes I secretly try to get back at people who have done me wrong.   T   F

159. I try to hide that little bit of resentment I sometimes feel when lucky people get another lucky break.   T   F

160. When I get into an argument, I usually know when I am right and the other person is wrong.   T   F

161. At times I have been so mad that I have said something hurtful that I later regretted.   T   F

162. I nearly always practice building others up by pointing out their strengths and believing in them to put those strengths to work.   T   F

163. The more I cling to my own security when others need me to act with courage, the more insecure I get.   T   F

164. I don't usually express anger too quickly because I have learned to hold my tongue.   T   F

165. When I give someone money, I don't expect anything in return, not even appreciation.   T   F

166. I am not extremely careful about wasting money.   T   F

167. I have never been described as an overly optimistic person.   T   F

168. Under certain circumstances, having a secret love affair could help a person's marriage more than it would hurt it.   T   F

169. I don't exercise as often as I need to keep my body fit and trim.   T   F

170. My use of tobacco, drugs, alcohol, or food has taken a toll on my health and probably has reduced my life expectancy by more than a year.   T   F

171. Sometimes I like to look at the pictures in pinup magazines.   T   F

172. I could accomplish a lot more in life if I could just get a few decent breaks.   T   F

173. To succeed in business, it helps to be a little bit deceptive and not always tell the entire truth.   T   F

174. Sometimes I might exaggerate or pass on a rumor about a person who has hurt my feelings.   T   F

175. I sometimes get preoccupied imagining the misery others must be feeling, but it usually makes me feel a little better about my own life.   T   F

176. I don't rely very much on things I can't predict or control.   T   F

177. At times I imagine money to be more important than it really is.   T   F

178. My life clearly reflects the belief that my most important responsibility is to love and serve God.   T   F

179. Playing it safe in life is risky business, so I usually take the risks getting involved.   T   F

180. When I feel like talking out quickly in anger, I usually restrain myself until I can think of something more constructive to say.   T   F

181. I am seldom the first one to apologize to end an argument.   T   F

182. I give to church or charities only from what I have left over from my other expenses.   T   F

183. When the going gets tough, my concentration and effort seem to drop off a bit.   T   F

184. To ensure a healthy sexual relationship in marriage, in some cases it can help if two people try making love before they get married.   T   F

185. It is not a high priority now for me to have good health in my old age because my personal habits reflect this lack of concern.   T   F

186. In the past year, while under the influence of drugs or alcohol, I have probably said or done something that hurt someone else.   T   F

187. Sometimes I am frustrated by my unfulfilled sexual needs.   T   F

188. I sometimes arrange it so that I can goof off without anybody knowing it.   T   F

189. I would be embarrassed if other people knew how much time I spend thinking about money.   T   F

190. Sometimes I enjoy the sense of power and energy I get when I express my anger.   T   F

191. I like to daydream about what my life would be like if I were more intelligent or good-looking.   T   F

192. I take pride in being able to solve most of my problems without help.   T   F

193. I occasionally put off until tomorrow things I could just as easily do today.   T   F

194. I believe that a loving God created and rules over the universe and that I must answer to God for my actions both now and after death.   T   F

195. Some people suffer more than their share of hurt and sadness,   T   F
     and I feel especially drawn to helping these people.

196. I have a lot of trouble putting myself in another's place   T   F
     and feeling what that person must feel in the situation.

197. To forgive someone who has hurt me is really hard for me.   T   F

198. Sometimes I think that if I always had enough money, I   T   F
     would always be happy.

199. When I'm in a group that's doing something, I'm generally   T   F
     not one of the hardest workers.

200. People who have intercourse with only one person in   T   F
     their lives will never know what good times they have missed.

201. Sometimes I feel a bit down because I haven't worked   T   F
     hard enough to stay healthy and trim.

202. It would bother me if my family and friends found out   T   F
     about all the times I put things into my body that
     aren't good for it.

203. If a person could make sure no one would find out, a   T   F
     one-night sexual affair wouldn't hurt his and her marriage much.

204. I sometimes try to make others think that I am more   T   F
     ambitious, concerned, or busy than I really am.

205. It really gets to me when I see how other people flaunt   T   F
     their new possessions.

206. At times I wonder how I can get even with someone   T   F
     who has done me wrong.

207. I often spend time wondering what it would be like to   T   F
     be rich and famous.

208. Sometimes life seems like a big contest, and I have become   T   F
     skilled at the art of being a winner.

209. I have sometimes gotten a little excited just thinking about sex.   T   F

210. Guilt is usually a constructive feeling for me, and so I   T   F
     react fairly well to criticism.

211. The people I respect the most are those who have become   T   F
     famous by accomplishing great things.

212. When my friends are feeling very up and very down, I seem   T   F
     to draw a blank and don't know how to respond emotionally.

213. When I am in the middle of an argument, I am seldom open-minded   T   F
     or trying to learn something from the other person involved.

214. I never give money to strangers who ask for a handout.   T   F

215. When someone comes up to me and asks, "Will you do   T   F
     me a favor?" my first reaction is negative.

216. I would rather marry an experienced lover than a virgin.   T   F

217. I am not very faithful to follow doctors' advice in keeping   T   F
     myself fit and healthy.

218. Within the past month, I have probably lied about or   T   F
     sneaked a drink, a smoke, a pill, or a fattening snack.

219. I have not been completely honest with my spouse concerning   T   F
     my sexual behavior.

220. The actions of other people have caused most of my problems.   T   F

221. I enjoy keeping in reserve a supply or stash of money   T   F
     that no one else knows about.

222. I sometimes lose control of what I say or do when I get mad.   T   F

223. I often compare myself to others in my mind.   T   F

224. Due to my questioning mind, I have trouble putting   T   F
     much pure faith in anything or anyone.

225. I don't always stop eating when I should.   T   F

7.2
CHRISTIAN MORAL VALUES SCALE (Francis & Greer, 1990, 1992)
Reviewed by Richard L. Gorsuch

Variable: The Christian Moral Values Scale measures individual differences in the evaluation of traditional values supported by the Judeo-Christian tradition. In particular these are moral issues that the authors felt to be important in analyzing the differences between active and inactive Catholics and Protestants in Northern Ireland.

The approach is a "common-sense" based selection of behaviors having high face/content validity to the investigators. There is little attention given to interfacing this behavioral list with other research for either measurement or theoretical purposes.

Francis and Greer (1992) point out that research on attitudes is more common than on ethical issues. This scale is a response to that need by dealing explictly with moral values. In Francis and Greer (1992), the emphasis on values is also provided by the possible responses to each behavior. These ranged from "always wrong" to "never wrong." Thus the responses also stress moral evaluation. This is appropriate given other research (reviewed by Gorsuch, 1986) clearly showing that the traditional attitude scale is primarily composed of affect, and

lacks the moral oughtness of ethical issues. It also shows that moral evalutions add in predicting moral behaviors over affect evaluations as measured by the usual attitude scale (Gorsuch & Ortberg, 1983). This response scale is more consistent with the expressed goal than the "strongly disagree" to "strongly agree" response scale used in Francis and Greer (1990) for rating the same behaviors.

Description: The items consist of 10 behaviors selected primarily by content (see items below) based on the authors' knowledge of the traditions. "Exploratory factor analysis" (details about the methods used are not given) resulted in a single factor from which the best 10 behaviors were selected. The behaviors in this scale are primarily single words (e.g., stealing) and thus are somewhat more simplified than others using the same intuitive approach.

The respondents rate each of the behaviors on a 5-point scale. "Aways wrong" or "strongly disagree" is given a score of 5 and "never wrong" or "strongly agree" is scored 1 so that a higher score is a higher moral judgment. Since there are no positive ethical values on the questionnaire, those with a negativistic bias will score higher.

Practical Considerations: The scale is easily administered and scored. Since the items are so short, it is easy for one teenager to glance at another's response, which may lead to students' commenting on each others' responses if the test is given in a classroom setting.

Note that two different response scales have been used, the traditional Likert and one based on how wrong a behavior is. The latter is more consistent with the expressed purpose of the scale.

Norms/Standardization: Some item response summaries and descriptive statistics are given in the research studies for students in Northern Ireland. No other normative data are provided.

Reliability: Internal consistency reliabilities are adequate for research purposes. They range from .70 (*N* = 571; Francis & Greer, 1990) to .76 (*N* = 1,177; Greer & Francis, 1990). All respondents were pupils in forms 4 to 6 in Protestant and Catholic coeducational schools in Northern Ireland.

Validity: The validity is assumed based on the item content. However, some of the behaviors are not distinctly Christian, since secularists also strongly support them.

Other behaviors have little consensus across variations in Christianity. Construct validity is supported in the research to date (although it may be more appropriate to subscore for behaviors judged wrong within particular Christian traditions; see Greer & Francis, 1990, for Protestant-Catholic differences to establish subscoring).

Location:
    Francis; L. J. & Geer, J. E. (1990). Catholic schools and adolescent religiosity in Northern Ireland: Shaping moral values. *Irish Journal of Education, 2,* 40–47.
    Francis, L. J., & Greer, J. E. (1992). Measuring Christian moral values among Catholic and Protestant adolescents in Northen Ireland. *Journal Moral Education, 21.* 59–65.

Recent Research:
    Greer, J. E., & Frances, L. J. (1990). The religious profile of pupils in Northern Ireland. *Journal of Empirical Theology, 3,* 35–50.

References

Gorsuch, R. L. (1986). Measuring attitudes, interests, sentiments, and values. In R. Johnson & R. B. Cattell (Eds), *Functional psychological testing* (pp. 316–333). New York: Brunner/Mazel.

Gorsuch, R. L. & Ortberg, J. (1983). Moral obligations and attitudes: their relations to behavioral intentions. *Journal of Personality and Social Psychology, 44,* 1025–1078.

Appendix

Christian Moral Values Scale

The authors are flexible as to format and instructions. The 10 behaviors are given separately or included with other items using the same response format. The typical directions for such questionnaires are used. For example:

Below is a set of behaviors. Please print a number from 1 to 5 on the line in front of each item to tell us how wrong that behaviors is. The "right" response is what you think about that behavior.

Here is what each of the numbers from 1 to 5 mean:

    1. = never wrong.
    2. = usually excusable.
    3. = undecided.
    4. = usually wrong.
    5. = always wrong.

Write the number in front of each behavior to tell us if you believe it is wrong or not.

_____ Gambling

_____ Drinking alcohol

_____ Drunkenness

_____ Stealing

_____ Drug taking

_____ Sexual intercourse before marriage

_____ Abortion

_____ Artificial birth control

_____ Suicide

_____ Divorce

Reprinted with permission by author.

7.3
MISSIONARY KIDS' VALUE SCALES (Sharp, 1988, 1990)
Reviewed by M. Elizabeth Lewis Hall and Beth Fletcher Brokaw

Variable: The Missionary Kids' Value Scales (MKVS) contains 18 measures of the value constructs of religiosity, worldmindedness, and commitment to justice, as well as different aspects of the cross-cultural context of individuals who have grown up overseas. The specific value constructs measured are Religiosity, Religious Orthodoxy, Religious Action, Attitudinal Worldmindedness, World Systems, Social Distance, and Justice Commitment. The contextual scales are Religious Interaction as Youth, Religious Interaction at School, Religious Interaction in the Home, Cross-Cultural Involvement as Youth, Cross-Cultural Interaction in School, Leadership, Justice Interaction as Youth, Parent-Child Relationship, Teacher-Student Relationship, School Involvement, and School Rating. The measure was created specifically for use with children of missionaries in Brazil (referred to as "missionary kids" or "MKs"), although it can easily be modified for use with MKs from other countries or other individuals who have lived cross-culturally.

The value scales make up the core of this instrument and will be reviewed briefly here. The Religiosity scale is a measure of a person's commitment to his or her religion. It is operationalized in this measure as commitment to the specific beliefs, values, and behaviors of evangelical Christianity. Religious Orthodoxy is a measure of the degree to which a person agrees with the beliefs of orthodox Protestant Christianity. Religious Action is a measure of a person's willingness to return overseas, either on a short-term basis or for an indefinite period. The Attitudinal Worldmindedness scale measures attitudes and behaviors that demonstrate acceptance and tolerance of people from other cultures and value systems. World Systems measures a person's attitudinal acceptance of differing concepts of national identity. Social Distance assesses an individual's willingness to become socially involved with different ethnic and socioeconomic groups, on a continuum ranging from minimal social contact to intermarriage. Justice Commitment is a measure of a person's reactions to the poor and needy and is operationalized as frequency of actions to help these groups in the past 12 months. Particularly noteworthy among the contextual variables is the Crosscultural Involvement as Youth scale, which is a measure of behaviors and attitudes that demonstrate involvement with the foreign culture in which the individual has lived.

Description: The measure is heterogeneous in that it is not intended to measure a related group of constructs. Rather, its intent is to survey many areas relevant to the life experience of individuals who live in other cultures during their formative years. Of the 18 scales, only 6 are explicitly religious (Religiosity, Religious Orthodoxy, Religious Action, Religious Interaction-Youth, Religious Interaction-School, Religious Interaction-Home). The remaining scales address behaviors and attitudes related to living in a different culture. The Religiosity and World-mindedness scales can be combined to measure the construct of World Christianity. This construct is not widely used in the social sciences but has commonly been used in evangelical missiology in recent years. Individuals who demonstrate an expanded view of the world (in contrast to ethnocentrism) and a commitment to the values of historic Christianity are considered World Christians.

The religiously oriented scales were constructed on the basis of items developed by King and Hunt (1972, 1975), Fichter (1954), Glock and Stark (1965), Bibby and Brinkerhoff (1973, 1983), and Brinkerhoff and Mackie (1985). The Worldmindedness items were drawn from a scale developed by Sampson and Smith (1957). Several contextual variables were drawn from the International Mobile Student Questionnaire developed by the Institute of International Studies at Michigan State University. For several of the scales within the overall measure, particularly the religiously oriented ones, similar scales exist that have been much more extensively validated. The present measure does, however, make a unique contribution. Its primary value lies in the comprehensiveness of the constructs surveyed, providing in one measure an array of constructs relevant to international populations. Researchers in this area can make use of individual scales as well as the complete measure.

Most items are forced choice and utilize a variety of types of 4- and 5-point Likert scales, including "strongly disagree" to "strongly agree," "never" to "very often," and "yes, definitely" to "no." A smaller number of items require rank ordering and yes/no answers. Each of the subscales is scored separately. No special instructions are provided for scoring.

Practical Considerations: The MKVS is a paper-and-pencil measure that does not require special examiner skill for administration or interpretation. No instructions are provided for the subject, as each item is self-explanatory. The face validity of the measure is high, as each scale clearly relates to the construct it attempts to measure. Given the heterogeneity of the measure, one disadvantage is that the relationship of the different scales to each other is not clearly articulated. However, use of the entire instrument is not necessary. An additional disadvantage is that many of the subscales have a variety of answer formats, which is awkward both for the respondent and for measurement purposes.

Norms/Standardization: The measure was normed on 533 adult children of Brazil missionaries, representing a 60.8% response rate. The population was 49.9% male and 50.1% female with a mean age of 26.3 (range 17–43) years. Fifty-four percent were married. Ninety-nine percent stated that they were raised as evangelicals, and 97.3% considered themselves to be "born again." They had lived in Brazil for an average of 12.4 years. Professionally, they represented a range of occupations, with a large number in the religious and management categories. Educationally, 56.9% had completed college degrees and 33.6% were still students. The population with which the complete measure can be used is limited, as it is aimed at adults who have lived cross-culturally and have attended Christian schools. The following descriptive statistics were reported for this sample: for Religiosity, a mean of 52.0, with a standard deviation of 8.87; for Religious Orthodoxy, a mean of 23.41, with a standard deviation of 1.62; for Religious Action, a mean of 5.97, with a standard deviation of 1.77; for Attitudinal Worldmindedness, a mean of 17.38, with a standard deviation of 1.88; for World Systems, a mean of 4.42, with a standard deviation of 1.41; for Social Distance, a mean of 21.26, with a standard deviation of 4.33; for Justice Commitment, a mean of 7.80, with a standard deviation of 2.21. Descriptive statistics for the remainder of the scales are available in the source reference.

Reliability: The internal consistency of the scales was estimated using Cronbach's coefficient alpha. The values for the scales were as follows: Religiosity, .93; Religious Orthodoxy, .86; Religious Action, .81; Attitudinal Worldmindedness, .64; World Systems, .59; Social Distance, .93; and Justice Commitment, .66. The Religiosity, Religious Orthodoxy, Religious Action, and Social Distance scale alphas indicate good lower-bound estimates of scale reliability for research purposes. The remaining scales have marginal internal consistency. These figures do not support the use of this instrument for the testing of individuals, with the exception of the Religiosity and Social Distance scales, which have high reliabilities. No test-retest reliability data are reported for this measure.

Validity: Each scale was submitted to an exploratory factor analysis using principal factoring with iterations. An eigenvalue of 1.0 or higher was used as a cutoff, although "Religious Interaction in the Home" had an eigenvalue of .75 but was retained as an exploratory variable. Loadings of the individual items varied from .38 to .89. All items that did not load on the first factor of each scale were dropped, reducing the total number of items from 171 to 88. The first factor explained 100 percent of the variance for each scale, except Religiosity in which it accounted for 92.7 percent. All scales demonstrated internal consistency coefficients of .60 or higher except "Religious Interaction in the Home" (.45). The factor analysis of the scales provides moderate support for the construct validity of the individual scales. The relationships among the different scales, in the form of correlations, are avail-

able in the source reference. Convergent and divergent validity data are not reported for this measure.

One validity issue that is not addressed by the author is the uneven weighting of items in scales that have several response formats. For example, the Religious Interaction-Home subscale has three items, two of which have 4-point Likert scales, whereas the remaining item is in a yes/no format. Summing the responses to arrive at a total score gives greater weight to the 4-point Likert items. While the MKVS is a helpful tool for measuring multiple variables of interest to those in missiology, the variety of constructs and ways of measuring them do present some measurement difficulties. Further reliability and validity testing seems in order as researchers use this instrument in the future.

Location:

Sharp, L. W. (1990). How missionary children become world Christians: The role of the MK school and the local culture. *Journal of Psychology and Theology, 18*(1), 66–74.

Sharp, L. W. (1988). Patterns of religiosity, worldmindedness, and commitment to justice issues for Brazil-experienced missionary children (Doctoral dissertation, University of Calgary, 1987). *Dissertation Abstracts International, 49*(2).

Subsequent Research:

No further research has been done utilizing this measure.

References

Bibby, R. W., & Brinkerhoff, M. B. (1973). The circulation of the saints: A study of people who join conservative churches. *Journal for the Scientific Study of Religion, 12*, 273–283.

Bibby, R. W., & Brinkerhoff, M. B. (1983). Circulation of the saints revisited: A longitudinal look at conservative church growth. *Journal for the Scientific Study of Religion, 22*(3), 253–262.

Brinkerhoff, M. B., & Mackie, M. (1985). Religion and gender: A comparison of Canadian and American student attitudes. *Journal of Marriage and the Family,* 415–429.

Fichter, J. H. (1954). *Social relations in the urban parish.* Chicago: University of Chicago Press.

Glock, C. Y., & Stark, R. (1965). *Religion and society in tension.* Chicago: Rand McNally.

King, M., & Hunt, R. (1972). Measuring the religious variable: Replication. *Journal for the Scientific Study of Religion*, *11*, 240–251.

King, M., & Hunt, R. (1975). Measuring the religious variable: National replication. *Journal for the Scientific Study of Religion*, *14*, 13–22.

Sampson, D.L., & Smith, H. P. (1957). A scale to measure world-minded attitudes. *The Journal of Social Psychology, 45,* 99–106.

Appendix

Missionary Kids' Value Scales

Religiosity

1. In general, how religious minded would you say you are (not necessarily related to formal or institutionalized religion)?
   1. Very religious-minded   2. More than average   3. Average
   4. Less than average   5. Not at all

2. Last year, approximately what percentage of your money was contributed to a church or to religious endeavors?
   1. 1 % or less   2. Between 1 % and 10 %   3. 10 %
   4. Between 10 % and 20 %   5. More than 20 %

3. Normally, how often do you attend religious services?
   1. 2–3 times per week or more   2. 1 time per week   3. 1–2 times per month
   4. Monthly   5. A few times per year   6. Rarely or almost never
   7. Never

How often do you . . .	Never	Occasionally	Quite often	Very often
4. pray before meals?	1	2	3	4
5. pray and meditate privately in places other than church?	1	2	3	4
6. read the Bible?	1	2	3	4
7. personally try to share your faith in God with unbelievers?	1	2	3	4
8. in the last year shared with others the problems and joys of trying to live a life of faith in God?	1	2	3	4
9. ask God to forgive your sins?	1	2	3	4
10. feel God has answered your prayers?	1	2	3	4
11. read literature about your faith, church, or missions?	1	2	3	4
12. attend a weekday Bible study?	1	2	3	4

	Strongly disagree	Disagree	Agree	Strongly agree
13. Without my faith the rest of my life would *not* have much meaning to it.	1	2	3	4
14. It is important to me that my children be taught my Christian beliefs.	1	2	3	4
15. I try hard to carry my faith into all my other dealings in life.	1	2	3	4
16. I consistently seek the "will of God" for my life.	1	2	3	4

Religious Orthodoxy	Strongly disagree	Disagree	Agree	Strongly agree
1. The Bible is the literal inspired word of God.	1	2	3	4
2. There is *no* eternal life.	1	2	3	4

Religious Orthodoxy	Strongly disagree	Disagree	Agree	Strongly agree
3. Jesus Christ is the divine Son of God and I have no doubts about him.	1	2	3	4
4. Salvation is attained through personal faith in Christ.	1	2	3	4
5. I believe biblical miracles are stories that never really happened.	1	2	3	4
6. Christ was crucified, died, was buried, and on the third day rose from the dead.	1	2	3	4

Religious Action

1. Suppose your church or a familiar mission organization asked you to return to Brazil for 6–12 months on a special assignment for which you are qualified. Would you go?
   1. Yes, definitely   2. Probably   3. Maybe, unsure
   4. No

2. Suppose your church or a familiar mission organization asked you to return to Brazil for an indefinite period as a missionary. Would you likely go?
   1. Yes, definitely   2. Probably
   3. Maybe, unsure   4. No

Religious Interaction-Youth

1. How frequently did your parents talk with you about Christian values and your faith?
   1. Consistently, many times   2. Quite often
   3. Occasionally as it came up   4. Rarely

How often did you	Never	Occasionally	Quite often	Very often
2. lead a church activity?	1	2	3	4
3. participate in religious-oriented youth activities?	1	2	3	4

Religious Interaction in School

1. Did your school have required Bible or religion lessons?   ___ Yes   ___ No
2. Did your school have required regular chapel time?   ___ Yes   ___ No
3. Rate your school spiritual guidance (bible instruction, prayer groups, spiritual emphasis weeks, sharing times):
   1. Poor   2. Fair   3. Good   4. Very good

Religious Interaction-Home

1. How frequently did your parents talk with you about Christian values and your faith?
   1. Consistently, many times   2. Quite often
   3. Occasionally as it came up   4. Rarely

2. My parents lived up to the truths they professed.
    1. Strongly disagree   2. Disagree   3. Agree   4. Strongly agree
3. Our family had regular devotional time in the home.   ___ Yes   ___ No

Attitudinal Worldmindedness

	Strongly disagree	Disagree	Agree	Strongly agree
1. The school curriculum should include courses on world history and culture and not only the history of the home country.	1	2	3	4
2. I would accept my friends marrying someone of another race or nationality.	1	2	3	4
3. I am just as comfortable with foreigners as I am with my fellow countrymen.	1	2	3	4
4. My cross-cultural heritage is important to me.	1	2	3	4
5. I can say I learned to really love Brazilians.	1	2	3	4

Crosscultural Involvement as Youth
1. Rate your ability to speak Portuguese:
    1. Excellent   2. Good   3. Fair   4. Minimal   5. Not at all
2. Which of the following would you say provided the most meaningful experience for you in your *teen* years? Rank order using numbers 1 to 4, with a (1) for most meaningful and a (4) for least.
    The school community   ____
    The church   ____
    My home life   ____
    The Brazilian community   ____

How often did you . . .	Never	Occasionally	Quite often	Very often
3. lead Brazilian community activities?	1	2	3	4
4. date a Brazilian or other Third World national?	1	2	3	4
5. voluntarily attend a Brazilian culture or music festival?	1	2	3	4
6. attend professional soccer games?	1	2	3	4
7. help a Brazilian in poverty?	1	2	3	4
8. have interaction with local Brazilian citizens?	1	2	3	4

World Systems

	Strongly disagree	Disagree	Agree	Strongly agree
1. It would be better to be a citizen of the world than of a particular country.	1	2	3	4
2. My country is probably no better than many others.	1	2	3	4

Social Distance
Listed below are the names of various groups of people. Also listed (across the top) are various kinds of social contacts people have with one another. Thinking of the typical members

of each group, please circle as many of the *types of contact you would be willing to have with each group.* (Circle as many as applicable).

	Marry into group	Welcome as fellow members of club or church	Speak to as an acquaintance	Avoid contact
1. Upper-class Brazilians	1	2	3	4
2. Middle-class Brazilians	1	2	3	4
3. Brazilian Indians	1	2	3	4
4. African refugees	1	2	3	4
5. Poor Brazilians	1	2	3	4
6. Orientals	1	2	3	4
7. Jews	1	2	3	4

Cross-Cultural Interaction in School
1. Did your school have studies in Brazilian culture, history, or religion/philosophy?   ___ Yes   ___ No
2. Did your school have required Portuguese language study?   ___ Yes   ___ No

Leadership

How often did you . . .	Never	Occasionally	Quite often	Very often
1. coach or teach younger children?	1	2	3	4
2. lead Brazilian community activities?	1	2	3	4
3. lead a church activity (e.g. Sunday school class, singing, etc.)?	1	2	3	4

Justice Commitment
Below are some categories of *reactions to the poor and needy* of this world. Within the past 12 months, how often have you done any of the following? (Circle the appropriate number.)

	Never	Occasionally	Quite often	Very often
1. helped with a community program	1	2	3	4
2. prayed for the poor or suffering	1	2	3	4
3. contributed money to the poor in the community	1	2	3	4
4. campaigned for social justice	1	2	3	4

Justice Interaction as Youth
1. As you think of your father's work and social contacts in Brazil, to what extent was he *practically involved* in issues related to the poor, needy and suffering?
   1. Not at all   2. Occasionally as the need was apparent
   3. Quite a bit   4. Continuously
2. How often did you help a Brazilian in poverty?
   1. Never   2. Occasionally   3. Quite often   4. Very often
3. How often did you help sick, suffering, or uneducated people?
   1. Never   2. Occasionally   3. Quite often   4. Very often

Parent-child Relationship
1. In general, how happy would you say your home life as a child was?
   1. Very happy   2. Happy   3. Not very happy   4. Unhappy   5. Very unhappy

2. How would you describe the amount of time your parents spent with you as you were growing up?
   1. Adequate, about right   2. Not enough, but satisfactory
   3. Inadequate   4. Other (specify) _____
3. I could always count on my parents to accept me.
   1. Strongly disagree   2. Disagree   3. Agree   4. Strongly agree
4. I had trouble getting along with my parents as a teenager.
   1. Strongly disagree   2. Disagree   3. Agree   4. Strongly agree
5. Which of the following would you say provided the most 'meaningful' experience for you in your *teen* years? Rank order using numbers 1 to 4, with a (1) for most meaningful and a (4) for least meaningful.
   ____ The school community
   ____ My home life
   ____ The church
   ____ The Brazilian community

Teacher-Student Relationship
1. I discussed my personal problems with one or more teachers in my high school in Brazil.
   1. Strongly disagree   2. Disagree   3. Agree   4. Strongly agree
2. A teacher had a powerful influence on my direction in life.
   1. Strongly disagree   2. Disagree   3. Agree   4. Strongly agree
3. In reflecting on your experience in the Brazilian high school that you attended, how would you rate the teacher/teacher relationships (evidence of harmony and teamwork among faculty and administration)?
   1. Poor   2. Fair   3. Good   4. Very good
4. How would you rate the teacher/student relationships (accessibility and friendliness of teacher to student)?
   1. Poor   2. Fair   3. Good   4. Very good

School Involvement
Below is a list of activities in which overseas teenage students sometimes participate. Circle the appropriate number depending on how often you participated in the following activities:

	Never	Occasionally	Quite often	Very Often
1. Participated in student government	1	2	3	4
2. Sang in a school choir or choral group	1	2	3	4
3. Participated in school drama activities	1	2	3	4
4. Worked on a school literary project (e.g., yearbook, newspaper, etc.)	1	2	3	4

School Rating
In reflecting on your experience in the Brazilian high school that you attended, how would you rate the following?

	Poor	Fair	Good	Very good
1. Academic preparation: my classes prepared me for college	1	2	3	4
2. Spiritual guidance: Bible instruction, prayer groups, spiritual emphasis weeks, sharing, etc.	1	2	3	4

3. Career instruction: availability of information to help decide on possible career options	1	2	3	4
4. College guidance: materials to help make a choice about college and prepare for entrance	1	2	3	4
5. Teacher/teacher relationships: evidence of harmony and teamwork among faculty and administration	1	2	3	4
6. Teacher/student relationships: accessibility and friendliness of teacher to student	1	2	3	4
7. Preparation for return to country of parents: instruction for probable adjustment experiences	1	2	3	4
8. Teacher attitudes as positive toward Brazilian culture: seemed to understand and accept Brazil's culture, values, etc.	1	2	3	4

Sharp, L.W. (1990). How missionary children become world Christians: The role of the MK school and the local culture. *Journal of Psychology and Theology, 18,* 66–74. Copyright © 1990 by Rosemead School of Psychology, Biola University. Reprinted with permission.

7.4
ROKEACH VALUE SURVEY (RVS) (Rokeach, 1973)
Reviewed by Ronald Burwell

Variable: The Rokeach Value Survey (RVS) measures general human values that include both religious and nonreligious values. The values contained in the survey are sufficiently diverse that they could be used in a variety of cultural settings. Thirty-six values are contained in the survey divided into two categories: terminal values and instrumental values.

According to Rokeach (1973), a value is a prescriptive or proscriptive belief that a specific mode of behavior or end-state of existence is preferred to an opposite mode of behavior or end-state. This definition reflects Rokeach's view that values can be sorted into two basic categories: terminal values and instrumental values. Terminal values are "end-states of existence," whereas instrumental values are "modes of conduct." These two categories represent a distinction between means and ends.

Rokeach estimates that there are fewer terminal values, approximately 18 to 24, and more instrumental values, 60 to 72, that are held by the average person. The total possible universe of human values is larger than this, but each individual, as well as different culture, narrows the possible collection of values to a relatively small number.

Description: The Rokeach Value Survey (RVS) uses a total of 18 terminal values and 18 instrumental values. These values were obtained from a variety of sources, including an extensive review of the literature on human values. In addition, various groups of people were surveyed and asked to produce lists of values. Following this inductive process, Rokeach and his associates were able to reduce the values to the final group after considering the following criteria:

Eliminating synonymous or near synonymous values.
Using values that were maximally different.
Using values that represented the most important values in American society.
Retaining those values that might pertain to all cultures.
Using values that one could accept or admit to without appearing immodest or boastful.

Perhaps the most important consideration was methodological: how many values can a person be reasonably expected to rank order? Eighteen values were judged to be the maximum bits of information that a person could manipulate and reorder.

The actual survey is quite simple. The subject is presented first with the list of terminal values (e.g., a comfortable life, salvation, wisdom, etc.) and asked to rank them from high to low according to "their importance to you as guiding principles in your life." The same procedure is then repeated with a list of the 18 instrumental values (e.g., independent, obedient, self-controlled, etc.).

Rokeach has used several forms of the RVS but has found that two forms (Forms D and E) are the most reliable forms. Form E presents the list and asks the subject to place a number between 1 and 18 in front of the appropriate value. Form D uses removable stickers with the values printed on them, which the subject can remove and paste in the appropriate order on a separate sheet of paper. Form D has some advantages over Form E in terms of reliability (see below). Rokeach reports that the vast majority of people are able to complete the survey in ten to twenty minutes.

Practical Considerations: The Rokeach Value Survey is easy to administer and does not require significant training to score and interpret. The RVS has high face validity. Rokeach's book covering the RVS (1973) gives a great deal of information about the survey and provides data for comparison to those using the survey.

For some people, creating and using a sticker version of the survey (Form D) might present some obstacles (e.g., printing the labels on stickers). One alternative that has been used is to provide the values on small slips of paper or card stock that the subject could sort into order. Otherwise, researchers could simply use Form E, which is a more standard paper and pencil version of the survey.

In reporting the results, Rokeach (1973) uses medians and composite rank orders together with frequency distributions. The median was considered the most appropriate

measure of central tendency. He also notes that other measures have been used, including t-tests, Anovas, and the Kruskal-Wallis test, and that there is a high level of consistency among the tests. It would seem possible to use means as well as medians, particularly if the size of the group to be compared is relatively large.

One other methodological note is that since the survey asks for a rank ordering of the values, each rank is dependent on the others so that individual items are interrelated. In other words, if the subject changes the rank of one value the corresponding ranks of all the other values also shift.

The most appropriate use of this survey would be to develop comparative group data or to study changes in values. This survey is less useful in individual assessment or evaluation.

Norms/Standardization: Rokeach (1973) presents data on a national sample that was obtained in 1968 through the National Opinion Research Center (NORC) on a sample of adult Americans over twenty one years of age ($n = 1409$). In addition, Rokeach (1973) reports results for age groups from 11 to 90 years old. Since the publication of the RVS, there have been several hundred reported studies using this survey. In these studies a wide range of samples are used, including cross-cultural comparisons (e.g., Feather, 1973). Most comparisons involve how different groups rank the two sets of values. In his manual Rokeach provides data on his original sample broken down by social class, race, age, religious values, and political values.

Reliability: There has been extensive research on the reliability of the RVS. For Form D, median test-retest reliabilities of college students run from .78 – .80 (terminal values) to .70 – .72 (instrumental values). The time intervals between test and retest vary from 3 to 7 weeks. For a longer time between test and retest the reliabilities drop about .03 – .05 (a 2 to 4 month interval).

The reliability for Form E is slightly lower than for Form D (.74 for terminal values and .65 for instrumental values). Rokeach suggests this difference is due to the fact that in Form E (the paper/pencil version) the subject can only change an answer by crossing out the initial response. In contrast, Form D allows the respondent to continue to re-sort the values until he or she is satisfied with the final ranking. For this reason, Rokeach recommends Form D if it is possible to use it. In all cases, terminal value reliabilities are consistently higher than instrumental value reliabilities.

Validity: The RVS represents a different approach to measuring values and is not easily compared with other value measures. It has face validity. Although Rokeach does not address the issue of the validity of the RVS, he does offer some comparative data. In comparing the RVS results with variations of needs as measured by the TAT, correlations were found between certain needs and the values. These results suggest that there is a similarity between the measure of values and the measure of needs, although they are not the same thing.

Other research connected the RVS with Osgood's evaluative factor in a semantic differential analysis (Homant, 1969). The results indicate that the RVS measures the same kind of meaning as Osgood's evaluative factor.

Location: The test and extensive documentation can be found in Rokeach (1973). The test can also be ordered from: Consulting Psychologists Press, Inc., 3803 E. Bayshore Road., P.O. Box 10096, Palo Alto, CA 94303

Recent Research:

This is a widely used instrument. An extensive review of the literature can be found in several editions of the *Buros Mental Measurement Yearbook* (e.g., Conoley & Impara, 1995).

Allen, M.W. (1994). Reliability and accuracy of cultural-level judgments of personal values. *Perceptual and Motor Skills, 79,* 16–18.

Diessner, R., Mayton, D., & Dolen, M.A. (1993). Values heirarchies and moral reasoning. *The Journal of Social Psychology, 133,* 869–871.

Faase, T. P. (1982). International differences in value ranking and religious style among Jesuits. *Review of Religious Research, 24,* 3–18.

Feather, N.T. (1988). Moral judgements and human values. *British Journal of Social Psychology, 27,* 239–246.

Gibbons, K., & Walker, I. (1993). Multiple interpretations of the Rokeach Value Survey. *The Journal of Social Psychology, 133,* 797–805.

Thompson, B., Leviton, J. E., & Mieden, P. A. (1982) Validity of the Rokeach Value Survey. *Educational and Psychological Measurement, 42,* 899–905.

References

Conoley, J. C., & Impara, J. C. (1995). *The twelfth mental measurements yearbook*. Lincoln University of Nebraska Press.

Feather, N. T. (1973). Value change among university students. *Australian Journal of Psychology, 25,* 57–70.

Homant, R. (1969). Semantic differential ratings and rank-ordering of values. *Educational and Psychological Measurement, 29,* 885–889.

Rokeach, M. (1973). *The nature of human values*. New York: Free Press.

Permission was not granted to reproduce the Rokeach Value Survey. You may obtain a copy of the survey through: Consulting Psychologists Press, Inc., 3803 East Bayshore Rd., P.O. Box 10096, Palo Alto, CA 94303.

7.5
SPIRITUAL LEADERSHIP QUALITIES INVENTORY (Wichern, 1980)

Reviewed by Daryl H. Stevenson

Variable: The Spiritual Leadership Qualities Inventory (SLQI) was designed to reflect "the characteristics and qualities of spiritual maturity described by Paul in I Timothy 3:1–7 and Titus 1:5–9" (Townsend & Wichern, 1984, p. 306). The authors assert that in these passages the apostle Paul sets forth an outline of the spiritual character qualifications for elders (leaders) of the church. Their exegesis identifies, a total of 22 distinct traits or qualities. Of these, the SLQI measures 19 qualities.

The instrument's theory base assumes that the beliefs and behaviors of leaders in Christian evangelical churches are on a spiritual level measurably higher than those of the population at large. Although other instruments are available and are used for measuring attitudes and interests of religiously oriented people, broad spiritual maturity levels, or leadership abilities, those instruments deal with a wide range of thoughts, feelings, and values. They tend to be normed primarily for ministers or seminarians, or they have no explicit biblical basis for determining levels of spiritual maturity. Thus this inventory of spiritual leadership qualities was developed to be applicable not only for clergy but also for laity. A hallmark is the explicit and specific biblical content as the basis for both trait and item development. This assumption is that an individual who has a marked degree of these "biblically-derived" qualities of spiritual maturity could be considered for spiritual leadership. This instrument's purpose, then, is to "help an individual recognize areas of spiritual and psychological growth," rather than to "be a diagnostic instrument of overall spiritual maturity" (Townsend and Wichern, 1984, p. 306). This distinction, however, is not entirely clear.

Description: The SLQI contains 222 items identifying 19 traits of spiritual maturity. A thorough exegetical study of the Timothy and Titus passages resulted in the following traits: being upright, having a good reputation, being above reproach, being respectable, having a desire to be overseer, being holy, having an ability to teach, being temperate, being prudent, being able to manage family, being the husband of one wife, being gentle, not being quick-tempered, being self-controlled, not being addicted to wine, not being greedy, being a lover of good, not being self-willed, and being hospitable. Specific scriptural passages, Greek words, and principles of exegesis are detailed in Appendix A of the Instruction Manual (Wichern, 1980).

The spiritual traits were logically derived to confirm or disconfirm the presence of those traits in a person's daily behavior. Means and standard deviations of pastors, elders, seminary students, and non-Christians are reported in Wichern's (1980) Manual, providing a general frame of reference for interpretation.

Practical Considerations: The SLQI provides a 22-page Instruction Manual, which explains the instrument's purpose and historical development, contains directions for administration, and offers interpretation guidelines. The Manual has two sample case studies to clarify the use of the SLQI in interpretation. Appendix D provides helpful and simple action plans for developing each of the leadership qualities measured by this instrument. The inventory may be completed in about 50 minutes.

The scoring key is a single transparent overlay with seven columns, one for each page. Scoring is straightforward for anyone familiar with hand-scoring procedures. The two-sided SLQI Scoring Record explains the four-step procedure. Raw scores from one side of the Scoring Record are plotted on the Analysis Profile on the reverse side.

Norms/Standardization: The Analysis Profile is a graph of an individual's scores. Shaded portions of the profile indicate "new believer," "normal Christian," and "spiritually mature." The distinctions are based on the mean score for all populations.

The Manual reminds the user that the usefulness of test results is directly related to the skillfulness of the administrator. Scores can be analyzed in one of three ways: as individual traits, as general trends, or as reflections of certain social attitudes and behaviors. No explanation is offered for using these levels of analysis. At several points in the Manual, users are reminded that the SLQI is not to be used as the sole basis for any administrative decision as to one's qualification for leadership. The instrument may be combined with an educational and small group process, thereby providing informal feedback for the spiritual strengths and weaknesses of potential leaders.

Reliability: Support of the SLQI's reliability is reported both in the Manual and in the follow-up study by Townsend and Wichern (1984). Test-retest correlations are reported from 100 Christians randomly selected to take the SLQI twice. The interval between administrations was eight weeks. The coefficient values for the 19 traits ranged from .30 to .63, with an overall reliability of .94. All correlations were significant at the .05 level.

Validity: The SLQI Manual asserts that "numerous personal interviews and surveys have confirmed that the SLQI accurately assesses the traits it measures. In addition, several studies have shown that the SLQI discriminates between church leader and non-church leader populations" (Wichern, 1980, p. 6). Aside from these assertions, no other citations provide actual empirical data to evaluate the instrument's validity for its intended purpose. However, Townsend and Wichern (1984) cite several studies that demonstrate acceptable convergent and divergent validity for each scale (Ewing, Parker, & Quinn, 1983). Campbell, Carr, and Parker (1983) performed a factor analysis of the SLQI, resulting in a five-factor solution accounting for 70% of the variance. Parker (1984), and later Carr (1987), explored construct validity again using a principle components factor analysis and produced a feasible five-factor explanation and a two-to-six factor solution, respectively. Unfortunately, a large percentage of the total variance was attributed to one factor, further questioning the theoretical analysis and item pool of Wichern's original study.

Townsend and Wichern (1984) attempted a comparison validation study of the original data, using 71 adults from the Dallas, Texas, area. Their sample included 22 elders, 22 deacons, and 27 non-Christians, ranging in age from 18–65. Comparisons among these known groups were analyzed using *t*-tests. On none of the 19 traits was the non-Christian group higher than the church-leader group in total scores. Several significant differences were found on individual traits, including "gentle" and "not self-willed" (the elders were higher than deacons in both groups). In general, the SLQI did not effectively distinguish between these two leadership groups, although they distinguished the leadership groups from the non-Christian group.

The correlational results are mixed. There were high intercorrelations among the 19 trait variables, indicating high internal consistency. These results also evidence significant overlap in these scales, demonstrating lack of discrimination of these character qualities. Rockwood (1986) reported a significant relationship between the spiritual development traits of the SLQI and the psychological maturity scores yielded on the Personal Authority in the Family System Questionnaire, an instrument based on family of origin theory. Rockwood found a significant difference between age-group scores on both instruments, lending some credence to the SLQI's ability to distinguish leadership qualities in younger versus older participants.

Based on these findings and on the shortage of current validity studies for this instrument, most researchers suggest further development focusing on reexamining the exegesis of the passages and the items drawn from them. The instrument as a whole seems to have promise, but individual scales may not make the sensitive discriminations the author expected. The available findings suggest the viability of discriminating spiritual leadership qualities from nonleadership qualities, but the length of the SLQI might be discouraging for researchers when briefer instruments measure similar constructs (Bassett et al., 1991). Thus, caution is warranted in using this as a pure clinical instrument for determining roles within a fellowship, but it might be used effectively as an educational and discussion tool for developing spiritual leadership qualities, assuming that any feedback given is tentative.

Location:

Wichern, F. B. (1980). *Spiritual Leadership Qualities Inventory Instruction Manual.* Richardson, TX: Believer Renewal Resources.

The author of the SLQI allows purchasers of the administration packet to make up to 100 copies of the test booklet and profile sheets without further charge. The Manual may also be reproduced as needed, but the scoring template may not be reproduced (Wichern, personal communication, September 18, 1995).

For purchasing information, write to: Frank B. Wichern, Ph.D., 600 West Campbell Road, Suite 5, Richardson, TX 75080

Subsequent Research:

Campbell, C., Carr, S., & Parker, T. (1983). *Factor analysis of the Spiritual Leadership Qualities Inventory.* Unpublished manuscript, Western Conservative Baptist Seminary, Portland, OR.

Carr, S. A. (1987). A theoretical and empirical examination of the construct validity of the Spiritual Leadership Qualities Inventory (Doctoral dissertation, Western Conservative Baptist Seminary, 1987). *Dissertation Abstracts International, 48,* 3714B.

Ewing, B., Parker, T., & Quinn, J. (1983). *Correlates of the Spiritual Leadership Qualities Inventory, the Religious Orientation Scale, and the Spiritual Well-Being Scale.* Unpublished manuscript, Western Conservative Baptist Seminary, Portland, OR.

Parker, T. G. (1984). An empirical examination of the construct validity of the Spiritual Leadership Qualities Inventory (Doctoral dissertation, Western Conservative Baptist Seminary, 1984). *Dissertation Abstracts International, 48,* 3724B.

Rockwood, J. T. (1986). The relationship of spiritual development to psychological development based on family of origin theory (Doctoral dissertation, Texas Womens' University, 1986). *Dissertation Abstracts International, 47–10,* 4132B.

References

Bassett, R. L., Camplin, W., Humphrey, D., Door, C., Biggs, S., Distaffen, R., Doxtator, I., Flaherty, M., Hunsberger, P., Poage, R., & Thompson, H. (1991). Measuring Christian maturity: A comparison of several scales. *Journal of Psychology and Theology, 19*(1), 84–93.

Greene, M. P. (1987). The relationship between faculty-led small groups and character development of seminarians in an evangelical seminary (Doctoral dissertation, University of North Texas, 1987). *Dissertation Abstracts International, 48–04,* 0890A.

Townsend, J. S., & Wichern, F. B. (1984). The development of the Spiritual Leadership Qualities Inventory. *Journal of Psychology and Theology, 12*(4), 305–313.

Wichern, F. B. (1980). *Spiritual Leadership Qualities Inventory Instruction Manual.* Richardson, TX: Believer Renewal Resources.

Appendix

Spiritual Leadership Qualities Inventory

This survey is one way of describing human beings in terms of their beliefs, attitudes, and values. The survey consists of numbered statements. Read each statement and decide whether it is *true as applied to you or false as applied to you.*

You are to mark your answers directly on the survey sheet. If a statement is *true* or *mostly true,* as applied to you, blacken in the circle in the column headed 'T'. If a statement is *false* or *not usually true,* as applied to you, blacken in the circle in the column headed *F.*

Remember to give *your own* opinion of yourself. *Do not leave any blank spaces if you can avoid it.* Be sure to let your responses reflect how you feel at the present time.

1. If others fail to recognize how good I am, it is because of their own limitations.
2. I rarely find myself so overcome by emotion that I cannot meet the people I work with.
3. At times I am afraid that things I have done in the past will catch up with me.
4. I have little trouble because of a guilty conscience.
5. At my work area or desk, I frequently create such a mess that I can't get anything done.
6. My will power is strong when it comes to passing up food.
7. It makes me angry when others refuse to accept my good ideas.
8. If you don't look out for yourself, nobody else will.
9. There are a few people who know things about me which if told, could cause me great embarrassment.
10. I am sometimes depressed because of things that I did in my past.
11. I admire someone who will point out an error even though it may cost them.
12. I am often bothered by feelings of guilt.
13. I believe each person has complete freedom to eat, drink, or act however he wants.
14. I don't mind being asked to do a humbling job which no one else will take.
15. At times I feel like swearing.
16. My conscience often bothers me with the feeling that I am not doing what I ought to be doing.
17. I often laugh at a dirty joke or story just so my friends or coworkers don't think I'm stuck-up.
18. If I took a test and the grader missed a mistake I made, I wouldn't tell him.
19. I believe that there is a code which demands that all men act fairly toward one another.
20. If I could get into a movie without paying and be sure I was not seen, I would probably do it.
21. I usually feel irritated when I have to take orders from others.
22. People in my community would say that I am a person with high moral values.
23. At times I feel like swearing.
24. I frequently laugh at dirty jokes.
25. What others think of me does not bother me.
26. I secretly enjoy someone who is good at fooling others even if it sometimes embarrasses them.
27. Most people are too soft and if they were more critical they wouldn't get taken advantage of.
28. I think nearly anyone would tell a lie to keep out of trouble.
29. I frequently find myself going out of my way to make sure the other guy has an equal chance.
30. I really enjoy a good hot argument.

31. I don't enjoy conversations in which the faults or misdeeds of others are being discussed.

32. I secretly feel good when I learn that someone I dislike has gotten into trouble.

33. Sometimes when others speak too highly of an acquaintance, I try to point out his defects.

34. If I am given the wrong change by a clerk, I usually try to return the incorrect amount.

35. If I had to choose, I would rather be spiritually close to God than be physically and emotionally close to people.

36. People who invest their time in studying the Bible are not aware of the real problems facing man.

37. I have often thought that I would like to be a leader in a local church.

38. The main purpose of man is to know God and worship Him.

39. Frankly, there are so many religions and cults that I doubt if any of them are right.

40. I sometimes find myself continuing a discussion just because I don't want to be wrong.

41. I am not impressed by the men who lead the church I attend.

42. Being able to teach a subject well is as important as knowing that subject.

43. I don't have any desire to be a church leader.

44. I would rather read a good novel or a true life adventure than to read the Bible.

45. I wouldn't mind being an elder or deacon if I was chosen.

46. While I may not consistently study truths about God, I do make it a priority to seek Him.

47. A regular program of Bible study should be a priority for most people.

48. I would like to be an elder or deacon if chosen.

49. I believe that by meditating on the Bible and praying one may know God better.

50. I enjoy being able to get up in front of a group and sharing new ideas I have had.

51. Elders or deacons are sincere people who should be praised for their work.

52. The life of Jesus shows that all men can know God if they just look in themselves.

53. Some of the greatest moments of my life have come through seeking to know God.

54. Theologians have so confused people about religion that I would rather watch TV than read a religious book.

55. Elders or deacons are just like anyone else, only they try to look good.

56. Serving in activities at my church is more important than having time just for myself.

57. I have made the study of the Bible and seeking God my highest priority.

58. I would rather help a person grow spiritually than develop my own interests.

59. I would feel good about working regularly on projects for my church.

60. Christians overemphasize the abstract knowledge of God and forget to see the good in human beings.

61. I am a doer, not a planner.

62. Planning ahead makes things turn out better.

63. I don't easily become impatient with people.

64. Talking in front of a group of people makes me very anxious.

65. The main purpose of man is to know God and worship Him.

66. I am not easily swayed by others' opinions.

67. I have periods of days, weeks, or months when I can't take care of things because I can't "get going."

68. I am called on by my friends in times of trouble.

69. I feel I am well suited to be a leader.

70. I usually have to stop and think before I act even in trifling matters.

71. I have been asked to lead groups where a difficult decision had to be made.

72. I do many things which I regret afterward (regret things more or more often than others seem to).

73. I sometimes feel a good goal for myself would be to never have to rely on anyone for anything.

74. I don't easily become impatient with people.

75. I have met problems so full of possibilities that I have been almost unable to make up my mind about them.

76. There is no respect these days for people who really know what is going on.

77. When I get into a conversation, I am uncomfortable unless I get people to talk about subjects I know a great deal about.

78. If other people fail to recognize how good I am, it is because of their limitations.

79. I have had periods in which I carried on activities without knowing later what I had been doing.

80. The human mind has so much potential that it will be able to bring world peace, end pollution, and bring in a "new age."

81. I feel resentment when others fail to notice and praise me for my achievements.

82. People who say that man is innately bad are just too pessimistic and are overlooking the human potential for justness.

83. One of my greatest desires is to be a truly wise man.

84. I rarely experience times when I am so confused I can't decide what to do.

85. I have good success in settling disputes between people.

86. In order to be really successful, I must be willing to take big risks.

87. I find it hard to set aside a task that I have undertaken, even for a short time.

88. I am a doer, not a planner.

89. At times I feel like smashing things.

90. I frequently feel like swearing.

91. I feel better about my life than I ever have.

92. At times my thoughts have raced ahead faster than I could speak them.

93. I get mad easily and then get over it soon.

94. I frequently find myself worrying about something.

95. When you do something wrong, there is very little you can do to make it right.

96. Wishing can make good things happen.

97. Planning ahead makes things turn out better.

98. I sometimes feel a good goal for myself would be to never have to rely on anyone for anything.

99. I find it hard to set aside a task that I have undertaken, even for a short time.

100. Society has surrounded man's sex drive with too many prohibitions.

101. I have very few quarrels with members of my family.

102. I want my wife/husband to feel that she/he is the most important person in my life.

103. Teenagers have too many problems and should be ignored.

104. When I have problems with my family life, I usually try to work harder at my job.

105. I think that any religion which teaches that God made man with a sex drive and then sets up restrictions is unreasonable.

106. I spend time thinking about new and unusual ways to enjoy sex.

107. Because mothers spend more time with their children they are better able to make decisions about privileges and discipline.

108. The main part of man's life is his work, and a woman should take care of the home.

109. An occasional visit to an adult bookstore never hurt anyone.

110. If my children talked back to me, I'd spank them.

111. Sexual enjoyment is God's greatest gift to mankind.

112. My wife/husband and I rarely agree on any decision.

113. My interest in sex is about average, but I sometimes find myself having long periods of erotic fantasy.

114. I find I can talk more openly and honestly to friends at work than I can my family (or wife).

115. If I have a choice, I will go see a sexy movie in preference to others.

116. If I had teen-age children, I wouldn't be particularly embarrassed if they were arrested for alcohol or drug use.

117. At times when I am around an attractive person of the opposite sex, I am preoccupied with thoughts of touching, embracing, and going to bed with that person.

118. It is probably better not to tell your children about sex, since they probably learn more about it at school.

119. In the final analysis, pleasure is not the most important thing in life.

120. I agree with the concept that "kids will be kids" and should be allowed to sow their "wild oats."

121. I think I could give up about anything except sexual feelings, thoughts, and pleasures.

122. Children should make up their own minds on religion without their parent's prejudices.

123. I would rather read a magazine about current events than a magazine which contains sex-related articles.

124. Most of the time parents listen to what their children have to say.

125. It is useless to try to get my way at home.

126. No one can tell me when and how and with whom I can make love.

127. I have little to say about what I eat at home.

128. I don't especially enjoy watching movies depicting intimate love scenes.

129. I have little to say about what my family does.

130. Sexual enjoyment is God's greatest gift to mankind.

131. I want my wife/husband to feel that she/he is the most important person in my life.

132. I have resentments which I have stored up and harbored for long periods.

133. Although I am usually aware of my immediate response to a situation, I have little difficulty with impulsiveness.

134. At times I enjoy a good argument.

135. Most people are uninformed and need someone to tell them what to do.

136. I will go out of my way to avoid causing a fight.

137. When someone insults or hurts me, I think for hours about things I should have said or done to get even.

138. I do not let interruptions in my schedule disorganize me so that I cannot finish my jobs.

139. In meetings I feel I should have something to say about every issue.

140. Frequently I feel frustrated because I cannot think of a way to get even with someone who deserves it.

141. I have frequently found myself so overwhelmed by anger that I have thrown something or cursed.

142. I enjoy seeing a shrewd lawyer change a jury's mind.

143. When I think how many stupid people are allowed to drive, I get angry.

144. Doing things on the spur of the moment is just not characteristic of me.

145. If I propose an idea or belief, I usually will push it until the majority of people accept it.

146. If I were in the military, I would have some problems in accepting the discipline.

147. I am not surprised when someone goes out of his way to please me or to help me.

148. It makes me angry when others refuse to accept my good ideas.

149. I am known to my friends as a man who exhibits self- discipline.

150. It is impossible to expect that any group of thinking men could agree consistently.

151. The best defense is a strong offense.

152. I believe that I can stop myself from catching a cold.

153. I really enjoy a good hot argument.

154. I hate to talk to people who I know have talked badly about me in the past.

155. I believe that if somebody studies hard enough, he or she can pass any subject.

156. I admire the concept, "an eye for an eye and a tooth for a tooth."

157. God made the world but He expects men to work out their own problems.

158. Some people make me so angry I'd like to shout at them or slap their face.

159. It makes me impatient to have people ask my advice or interrupt me when I am working on something important.

160. I frequently find myself daydreaming about ways to get back at people who have hurt me.

161. I think most people mislead their friends just to gain sympathy and help.

162. I can't think of anyone I really hate.

163. I have sometimes opposed people who were trying to do something not because of what they were doing but just to oppose them.

164. If I am angry, I think it's best to keep it to myself for several days.

165. It takes a lot of argument to convince most people of the truth.

166. If a credit card company doesn't bill me, I simply figure that it's their problem.

167. I have used alcohol excessively.

168. When I lose money, I get so uncomfortable I can hardly think about anything else.

169. It's too bad so many people who haven't worked for it have money and position.

170. In the final analysis, pleasure is the main thing in life.

171. I would prefer an easy comfortable life where I need to exert myself as little as possible to a life full of challenges and demands.

172. I couldn't care less what people think of me as long as I have plenty of money.

173. One of the things I would like to do is keep a well-stocked liquor collection.

174. If I am given the wrong change by a clerk, I usually try to return the incorrect amount.

175. I feel I sometimes misuse medicines I have been given.

176. I secretly dream of finding an envelope of money on the street.

177. I prefer the company of people who drink very little or not at all.

178. One of my major goals in life is to acquire enough money so I can be sure of a secure future.

179. I frequently find I am jealous when I hear about friends who have made fantastic savings on expensive items such as cars.

180. I believe there is some truth in the old saying that you can "drown your sorrows" with alcohol.

181. I enjoy telling my friends about tricking a salesman into making a good deal.

182. At times I have so enjoyed the cleverness of a crook that I wished he would get away with it.

183. I frequently use medication.

184. I enjoy movies or stories about men who "beat the system" either by taking valuables or escaping the authorities.

185. My will-power is strong when it comes to passing up food or drink.

186. I would rather have a savings account of over $5,000 than to have close relationships with my friends.

187. I worry over money and business.

188. I find it difficult to share food or drink with others.

189. My health is not good, and I frequently use medicines to keep going.

190. I don't enjoy conversations in which the faults or misdeeds of others are being discussed.

191. The philosophy of looking out for yourself appeals to me.

192. People who get all the breaks need to experience a few more troubles.

193. I sometimes enjoy conversations in which the faults or misdeeds of others are being discussed.

194. It would give me pleasure to be at a party where someone more popular than I am suffered embarrassment.

195. I enjoy having friends come over for supper or an evening.

196. God's plan for mankind is still the best plan.

197. I secretly feel good when I learn that someone I dislike has gotten into trouble.

198. I support missionaries because I believe they are doing a necessary job.

199. Sometimes when others speak too highly of an acquaintance, I try to point out his defects.

200. My friends feel that I am optimistic about life.

201 My meals are more enjoyable when I can feel free to eat as fast as I wish without worrying about others at the table.

202. The world is full of too many idealistic Pollyannas; life is hard.

203. Frequently I find that I have eaten so much I just don't feel like doing anything but lying around.

204. When I get into a conversation, I am uncomfortable unless I get people to talk about subjects I know a great deal about.

205. I wish I could get rid of the feeling of inferiority and resentment which the good fortunes of others frequently arouse in me.

206. Providing overnight lodging for my friends or even strangers does not bother me.

207. I often think, "I wish I were a child again."

208. I don't have problems saying no to my own desires over spending time with my family.

209. People who seek their own self-interests before the needs of others probably have inferiority feelings.

210. I think most people exaggerate their misfortunes in order to gain the sympathy and help of others.

211. Most people will use somewhat unfair means to gain profit or advantage rather than to lose it.

212. Some people are just born lucky.

213. I am against giving money to beggars.

214. People often disappoint me.

215. I have a good luck piece.

216. I find it hard to make talk when I meet new people.

217. I basically am a selfish person.

218. My motto is "when the going gets tough, the tough get going."

219. I don't believe in letting the "grass grow under my feet."

220. I believe that things will turn out as the Bible says.

221. I feel good when I learn that someone I dislike has gotten into trouble.

222. Mankind has never really understood God's redemptive plan through Jesus Christ.

7.6
VALUE PROFILE (Bales & Couch, 1969)
Reviewed by P. J. Watson

Variable: The Value Profile comprehensively records the values that guide interpersonal relations. From diverse sources, Bales and Couch collected a large array of relevant normative statements, which they submitted to methodical interpretrative and factor analytic procedures. Four interpersonal value dimensions were identified.

Acceptance of Authority measured values that social scientists typically attribute to the authoritarian personality. Loading most strongly on this factor was the belief that "obedience and respect for authority are the most important virtues children should learn." High scores on the Need-Determined Expression versus Value-Determined Restraint factor were indicative of an active pursuit of pleasure. This value was most evident in the assertion that "since there are no values that can be eternal, the only real values are those that meet the needs of the given moment." Equalitarianism was defined most strongly by the claim that "everyone should have an equal chance and an equal say." A final Individualism factor was most obvious in the statement that "to be superior a man must stand alone."

Description: In attempting to create an exhaustive list of interpersonal values, Bales and Couch consulted well-known social scientific treatments of values, had access to a several unpublished dissertations, and developed a number of new items. They collected 872 normative statements. A conceptual framework based on previous research was utilized to organize these items into 16 meaningful categories. Within each category, duplicate articulations of a value were eliminated. Others were combined in a single sentence.

The remaining 252 items were included in a self-report questionnaire. Reactions to each value occurred along a 6-point agreement scale with no mid-point. Scores on the response format ranged from 1 to 7; "4" was reserved for instances in which no response was made. This scale was administered to a sample of 552 individuals consisting of undergraduates from Harvard University, Radcliffe University, and Bennington College; a few faculty members and graduate students from Harvard; and officer candidates from an Air Force base. Based on preliminary analyses, two types of statements were eliminated: those that displayed little response variability and those that in correlational data proved to be empirically redundant. The remaining 143 items were factor analyzed.

The final Value Profile included only those articulations of a value that loaded exclusively on a single factor. In other words, the goal was to create independent measures of the four broad value domains. Ten items were used to define each factor, and except for three statements from the Need-Determined Expression Scale, all were positively worded.

In a previous review of this instrument, Robinson and Shaver (1973) concluded that "this scale is useful because it is extremely comprehensive, seemingly representing a very large domain of value positions on which people differ" (p. 529). Subsequent research has confirmed that the Value Profile can be useful (e.g., Watson & Morris, 1994).

Practical Considerations: The Value Profile is a fairly standard self-report questionnaire. Four- and five- rather than six-point response options have been used successfully in at least some studies (e.g., Tyson, Doctor, & Mentis, 1988; Watson & Morris, 1994).

Robinson and Shaver (1973) estimated that the profile could be completed within 25 to 40 minutes. The reading level does not appear to be especially challenging.

Norms/Standardization: Bales and Couch did not supply norms, nor would such data have been particularly useful. As these researchers stressed in evaluating their subjects, "This sample, though decently large, is not so diverse as one would like for general theoretical purposes, since values differ so markedly cross-culturally" (pp. 5-6).

Reliability: Internal and temporal consistency data were not reported. Factor loadings ranged from .56 to .76 for Acceptance of Authority, .20 to .62 for Need-Determined Expression, .36 to .57 for Equalitarianism, and .28 to .49 for Individualism. Based on these loadings, Robinson and Shaver (1973) estimated that the average interitem correlation for Acceptance of Authority was in the .40s whereas these figures were were presumed to be in the high teens for the other three measures.

Validity: In the Bales and Couch study, authoritarianism as measured by the F Scale loaded strongly on the Acceptance of Authority factor. The implications of this finding remain unclear given subsequent controversies over the meaning of the F Scale (e.g., Ray, 1976). Bales and Couch supplied no additional data that could testify to the validity of their instrument. Again, however, at least some supportive evidence has been presented elsewhere (e.g., Watson & Morris, 1994).

Location:
Bales, R. F., & Couch, A. S. (1969). The Value Profile: A factor analytic study of value statements. *Sociological Inquiry*, *39*, 3–17

Subsequent Research: The Value Profile has been employed in recent investigations in the psychology of religion. With religious subjects, some of the subscales have covaried directly, and Equalitarianism has included factors that produce contrasting patterns of correlations. These observations suggest that the Value Profile failed in its goal to measure four fully independent value domains and that Bales and Crouch were justified in being concerned about the insufficient diversity of their sample. Still, the Value Profile has helped clarify the value commitments of religious individuals and should continue to do so in the future.

Watson, P. J., Morris, R. J., & Hood, R. W., Jr. (1989). Sin and self-functioning, Part 5: Antireligious humanistic values, individualism, and the community. *Journal of Psychology and Theology*, *17*, 157–172.

Watson, P. J., Folbrecht, J., Morris, R. J., & Morris, R. W., Jr. (1990). Values, "irrationality," and religiosity. *Journal of Psychology and Theology*, *18*, 348–362.

References
Ray, J. J. (1976). Do authoritarians hold authoritarian attitudes? *Human Relations*, *29*, 307–325.

Robinson, J. P., & Shaver, P. R. (1973). *Measures of Social Psychological Attitudes (Revised ed)*. Ann Arbor, MI: Institute for Social Research.

Tyson, G., Doctor, E. A., & Mentis, M. (1988). A psycholinguistic perspective on bilinguals' discrepant questionnaire responses. *Journal of Cross-Cultural Psychology*, *19*, 413–426.

Watson, P. J., & Morris, R. J. (1994). Communal orientation and individualism: Factors and correlations with values, social adjustment, and self-esteem. *Journal of Psychology*, *128*, 289–297.

Appendix

Value Profile[1]

This questionnaire is designed to measure the extent to which you hold each of several general attitudes or values common in our society. On the following pages you will find a series of general statements expressing opinions of the kind you may have heard from other persons around you. After each statement, there is a set of possible responses as follows:

strongly disagree, disagree, slightly disagree, slightly agree, agree, strongly agree

You are asked to read each of the statements and then to *circle* the response which best *represents* your immediate reaction to the opinion expressed. Respond to each opinion as a whole. If you have reservations about some part of a statement, circle the response which most clearly approximates your *general feeling*.

Acceptance of Authority

1. Obedience and respect for authority are the most important virtues children should learn.

2. There is hardly anything lower than a person who does not feel a great love, gratitude, and respect for his parents.

3. What youth need most is strict discipline, rugged determination, and the will to work and fight for family and country.

4. You have to respect authority and when you stop respecting authority, your situation isn't worth much.

5. Patriotism and loyalty are the first and the most important requirements for a good citizen.

6. Young people sometimes get rebellious ideas, but as they grow up they ought to get over them and settle down.

7. A child should not be allowed to talk back to his parents, or else he will lose respect for them.

8. The facts on crime and sexual immorality show that we will have to crack down harder on young people if we are going to save our moral standards.

9. Disobeying an order is one thing you can't excuse—if one can get away with disobedience, why can't everybody?

10. A well-raised child is one who doesn't have to be told twice to do something.

Need-Determined Expression vs. Value-Determined Restraint

1. Since there are no values which can be eternal, the only real values are those which meet the needs of the given moment.

2. Nothing is static, nothing is everlasting; at any moment one must be ready to meet the change in environment by a necessary change in one's moral views.

3. Let us eat, drink, and be merry, for tomorrow we die.

4. The solution to almost any human problem should be based on the situation at the time, not on some general moral rule.

---

[1] The instructions preceding this questionnaire were taken from Robinson and Shaver (1973). For positively worded statements, the six-response options presented in the instructions are scored 1, 2, 3, 5, 6, and 7 respectively. An asterisk (*) identifies a negatively scored item in which this sequence of numbers is reversed. Missing responses are assigned a score of 4.

5. Life is something to be enjoyed to the full, sensuously enjoyed with relish and enthusiasm.

6. Life is more a festival than a workshop or a school for moral discipline.

7. The past is no more, the future may never be, the present is all that we can be certain of.

*8. Not to attain happiness but to be worthy of it is the purpose of our existence.

*9. No time is better spent than that devoted to thinking about the ultimate purposes of life.

*10. Tenderness is more important than passion in love.

Equalitarianism
1. Everyone should have an equal chance and an equal say.

2. There should be equality for everyone because we are all human beings.

3. A group of equals will work a lot better than a group with a rigid hierarchy.

4. Each one should get what he needs—the things we have belong to all of us.

5. No matter what the circumstances, one should never arbitrarily tell people what they have to do.

6. It is the duty of every good citizen to correct antiminority remarks made in his presence.

7. Poverty could be almost entirely done away with if we made certain basic changes in our social and economic system.

8. There has been too much talk and not enough real action in doing away with racial discrimination.

9. In any group it is more important to keep a friendly atmosphere than to be efficient.

10. In a small group there should be no real leaders—everyone should have an equal say.

Individualism
1. To be superior, a man must stand alone.

2. In life an individual should for the most part "go it alone," assuring himself of privacy, having much time to himself, attempting to control his own life.

3. It is the man who stands alone who excites our admiration.

4. The rich internal world of ideals, of sensitive feelings, of reverie, of self-knowledge, is man's true home.

5. One must avoid dependence upon persons or things; the center of life should be found within oneself.

6. The most rewarding object of study any man can find is his own inner life.

7. Whoever would be a man, must be a nonconformist.

8. Contemplation is the highest form of human activity.

9. The individualist is the man who is most likely to discover the best road to a new future.

10. A man can learn better by striking out boldly on his own than he can by following the advice of others.

Chapter 8

Multidimensional Scales of Religiousness

Any construct as complex as religion is likely to be multidimensional in nature. For example, as Marty and Appleby note in the introduction to the first of their five edited volumes on religious fundamentalism, religion deals with people's ultimate concerns and provides both personal and social identity within the context of a cosmic or metaphysical background. They also point out that religion usually stipulates behavior patterns and encourages adherents to practice certain forms of religious expression. Researchers have tried to capture the multidimensional nature of religious experience in a number of ways, and such attempts have often resulted in the development of measurement scales, many of which are reviewed in this chapter. Measures included in the other chapters in this volume usually assess some limited dimension of religiousness. The use of a single dimension instrument is fine as long as it adequately taps the desired component of the religious experience. If it is necessary, however, to broadly measure the whole of religious experience (as difficult as that may be), the use of a multidimensional measure is recommended.

The fifteen multidimensional scales reviewed in this chapter vary widely, and it is neither possible nor desirable to describe the intricacies of each measure in this brief introduction. The number of dimensions also vary substantially, ranging from two to twelve dimensions, though the majority of scales have between four and six dimensions. The instruments also differ in terms of their range of applicability. Some are restricted to Christianity, whereas others may be cautiously applied to other Western religions.

Many of the measures maintain some variation of cognitive, affective, and behavioral dimensions, most with an individual or personal religious orientation, although some also include an institutional component. One of the better-known taxonomies, Glock and Stark's Dimensions of Religious Commitment Scale (8.3), will be discussed as a prototype for most of the scales included in this chapter. Glock and Stark developed their measure around five dimensions of religiosity: belief, ritual (behavioral), experience, knowledge, and consequences. While the belief and knowledge dimensions may overlap, empirical research on the other dimensions suggest they are independent of each other. Many of the other scales in this chapter include some or all of Glock and Stark's dimensions: the Cross-Cultural Dimensions of Religiosity (8.1), the Dimensions of Religiosity Scale (8.2), the Five-Dimension Scale of Religiosity (8.5), the Rohrbaugh and Jessor Religiosity Measure (8.8), the Religious Involvement Inventory (8.12), Lenski's Religious Orientation and Involvement Scale (8.13), and the Ten Religious Variable Scales of King and Hunt (8.14). This is *not* to say that all of these scales are interchangeable. Many of these scales incorporate a number of other important dimensions not included in the Glock and Stark scale. Also, some scales (e.g., Hilty & Morgan's Religious Involvement Inventory, 8.12) were developed as either a conceptual or methodological reaction to other scales (e.g., King & Hunt's scale, 8.14). However, most of these instruments assess the multidimensional nature of religion, at least in part, in categories similar to those proposed by Glock and Stark.

The other scales reviewed in this chapter assess the multidimensional nature of religion in different terms. For example, though Putney and Middleton (8.4) include a measure of belief in their Dimensions of Religious Ideology Scale, they also assess religious importance, fanaticism, and ambivalence. Funk's Religion and Philosophy of Life Scale (8.7) measures a belief component, but also includes such dimensions as religious conflict, philosophy of life, hostility toward the church, religious tranquillity, religious solace, and change in religious attitudes. Similarly, while Maranell (8.10) assesses behavior ("ritualism") and belief ("theism"), he conceived six other dimensions of religiosity: church orientation, altruism, fundamentalism, idealism, superstition, and mysticism.

Four other scales reflect a unique multidimensional conception of religiousness: the love vs. guilt orientations of Christian belief (8.6), the nearness to God and fundamentalism-humanitarianism dimensions of Broen's Religious Attitude Inventory (8.9), the intellectual versus affective expressions of religious faith found in Boan's Religious Expression Scale (8.11), and Hoge's extensive twelve-dimensional Theological Index (8.15).

8.1
CROSS-CULTURAL DIMENSIONS OF RELIGIOSITY
(DeJong, Faulkner, & Warland, 1976)
Reviewed by Ronald Burwell

Variable: The Cross-Cultural Dimensions of Religiosity Scale measures the following: belief, experience, religious practices, religious knowledge, individual moral consequences, and social consequences. These scales are related to the dimensions of religiosity identified by Glock and Stark (1966) and are part of the ongoing debate about the unidimensionality or multidimensionality of religion. In this regard, Hilty, Morgan and Burns (1984) as well as Hilty and Morgan (1985), present more recent discussion of some of the same issues. The Hilty et al. conclusion, based on a different set of items and different analytic techniques, supports a multidimensional view. Their seven dimensions of religiosity, however, are only partially similar to DeJong's six dimensions of religiosity.

Description: DeJong, Faulkner, and Warland (1976) have revised and modified a set of religious measures that had originally been developed using Guttman scaling techniques (Faulkner & DeJong, 1966). These

measures assume a multidimensional model of religiosity like that advocated by Glock and Stark (1966). However, DeJong and colleagues' version used a variety of factor analytic techniques to refine a pool of 54 items. The items were of varying formats, including Likert-type questions, open-ended questions, forced-choice questions, factual questions, matching questions, and so on. An initial factor analysis (oblique method) reduced the pool of items to the final set of 38 items. The scales and the number of associated items are described as follows:

Belief Dimension (8 items): Belief about God, immortality, prayer, and scripture

Experience Dimension (4 items): Experiencing the presence of God, forgiveness, peace

Religious Practice Dimension (5 items): Church attendance, financial support, bible reading, church activity

Individual Moral Consequences Dimension (6 items): Agreement or disagreement with ethical issues such as dishonesty, sexuality, violence

Religious Knowledge Dimension (10 items): Ability to identify biblical characters, persons in church history

Social Consequences Dimension (5 items): Concern about selected social issues such as poverty, housing, unemployment

Practical Considerations: The scales produced by DeJong et al. (1976) are straightforward and easy to use. The entire set of 38 items takes about 20 minutes to administer. Although DeJong et al. give no directions for scoring the scales, simple addition of the answers produces composite scores. In many cases the higher the number of the answer, the higher the level of religiosity for that item. However, to guard against a response set, DeJong et al. reversed the answers in some scales, especially those for experience, religious practice, and social consequences. Therefore, some items must be reverse scored.

Norms/Standardization: These scales were tested using a cross-cultural sample. The sample was composed of students at Pennsylvania State University and the University of Bielefeld, Germany. In the fall of 1970, a total of 536 usable schedules for the American students and a total of 390 usable schedules from the German respondents (total *n* = 926) was obtained. In both universities, the sample was a purposive nonrandom aggregate sample.

De Jong et al. (1976) report that the American and German students displayed a "strikingly similar dimensional pattern" of religiosity (p. 879). Although they answered the questions in rather different ways, the underlying pattern of religiosity was the same. This gives support to the idea that the six dimensions presented may transcend American religious settings and represent, at least, a more general Judeo-Christian pattern. The specific differences observed between the American and German students were that the German students were less likely to attend church, less likely to endorse traditional Judeo-Christian beliefs

about God and death, less likely to report they have experienced repentance, more likely to be knowledgeable about biblical and theological personalities, and more concerned about issues of social justice.

More recently Hilty and Stockman (1986) conducted a replication of the DeJong et al. (1976) research with two samples of Americans. One sample was composed of 503 adults in American Lutheran churches in Ohio, whereas the second sample was drawn from undergraduate students at Ohio State University (*n* = 385). Using the 38 items created by DeJong and his colleagues, Hilty and Stockman found corroboration for five out of the six dimensions of religiosity. Essentially their work duplicated the findings of DeJong et al., with the exception that the religious practice dimension did not emerge in the factor analysis. They also dropped one of the items from the Social Consequences Dimension (the item on capital punishment). The resulting pool of 32 items and five factors seems to fit the data better and give higher degrees of fitness using goodness of fit statistics.

In addition, Hilty and Stockman sought to corroborate DeJong's second order factor analysis. In this case, however, they found greater differences between the two studies. Instead of finding three second order factors as did DeJong, Hilty and Stockman found only two second order factors for their first sample and only one factor for the second sample. Their conclusion is that although the multidimensionality of religion is supported by some studies (including data from their Lutheran study), the possibility remains that a single dimension of religiosity focusing on the area of ideology or religious belief may capture much of what is included under the notion of religiosity. In general, the replication by Hilty and Stockman reveals that the DeJong et al. (1976) measures fare quite well in their estimation.

Reliability: No reliability data were reported.

Validity: The only validity checks were alternative statistical analyses. DeJong et al. (1976) report that analyses based on techniques of image analysis and a derived solution based on a varimax rotation (factor analysis) produced no significant differences in the factor structure.

Location:

DeJong, G. F., Faulkner, J. E., & Warland, R. H. (1976). Dimensions of religiosity reconsidered: Evidence from a cross-cultural study. *Social Forces*, *54* (4), 866–889.

Subsequent Research:

Hilty, D. M., & Stockman, S. J. (1986). A covariance structure analysis of the DeJong, Faulkner and Warland Religious Involvement Model. *Journal for the Scientific Study of Religion, 25(4)*, 483–493.

Thompson, E. H. (1991). Beneath the status characteristic: Gender variations in religiousness. *Journal for the Scientific Study of Religion, 30*(4), 381–394.

References

Clayton, R. R. (1971). 5-D or 1? *Journal for the Scientific Study of Religion*, *10*, 37–40.

Clayton, R. R. (1974). The five dimensions of religiosity: Toward demythologizing a sacred artifact. *Journal for the Scientific Study of Religion*, *13*, 135–143.

DeJong, G., Faulkner, J., & Warland, R. (1976). Dimensions of religiosity reconsidered: Evidence from a cross-cultural study. *Social Forces*, *54*, 866–889.

Faulkner, J. E., & DeJong, G. (1966). Religiosity in 5-D: An empirical analysis. *Social Forces*, *45*, 246–254.

Glock, C., & Stark, R. (1966). *Christian beliefs and anti-semitism*. New York: Harper & Row.

Hilty, D. M., Morgan, R., & Burns, J. (1984). King and Hunt revisited: Dimensions of religious involvement. *Journal for the Scientific Study of Religion*, *23*(3), 252–266.

Hilty, D. M., & Morgan, R. (1985) Construct validation for the Religious Involvement Inventory: Replication. *Journal for the Scientific Study of Religion*, *24*(1), 75–85.

Hilty, D. M., & Stockman, S. J. (1986). A covariance structure analysis of the DeJong, Faulkner and Warland Religious Involvement Model. *Journal for the Scientific Study of Religion*, *25*(4), 483–493.

Roof, W. C. (1979). Concepts and indicators of religious commitment: A critical review. In R. Wuthnow (Ed.), *The religious dimension: New directions in quantitative research*. New York: Academic Press.

Weigert, A. J., & Thomas, D. L. (1969). Religiosity in 5-D: A critical note. *Social Forces*, *48*, 260–262.

Appendix

Dimensions of Religiosity

Belief Dimension

1. What do you believe about immortality?

    1. I do not believe in immortality in any sense.

    2. I believe in reincarnation.

    3. I believe immortality is the continued influence of a person's life on family or society.

    4. While its meaning is somewhat imprecise, I believe in the continued existence of the personality as a part of a universal spiritual principle.

    5. I believe in the resurrection of one's being and life after death.

2. What do you feel will probably happen to you after death?
    1. Simply stop existing.

    2. Reincarnation.

    3. I have no idea.

    4. Uncertain.

    5. My "spirit" will have some continuation in the universe.

    6. Depending on the will of God, I will go to heaven or hell.

3. What do you believe about God?
    1. I don't believe in God.

    2. I don't know whether there is a God and there probably is not a way to find out.

    3. God is a "spirit" within us.

    4. I don't believe in a personal God, but I do believe in a higher power of some kind.

    5. I feel that I do believe in God even though I am not able to explain fully who or what God is.

    6. I know God really exists and I have no doubts about it.

4. What do you believe about Jesus?
    1. Frankly, I am not sure the historical Jesus existed.

    2. I think Jesus was only a man.

    3. I think Jesus was only a man, although an extraordinary one.

    4. I feel that Jesus was a great religious prophet, but I don't feel He was the Son of God any more than all of us are the children of God.

    5. Jesus is best understood as a symbol of goodness; whether he existed or not is unimportant.

    6. I feel basically that Jesus is Divine, but I have some problems understanding the concept of His Divinity.

    7. Jesus is the Divine Son of God and I have no doubts about it.

5. What do you believe about the idea that God has and continues to act in the history of man?
    1. There is no evidence of any intervention of "God" in human history.

    2. People who have believed in God have influenced history.

    3. I believe the unfolding history of man has been within a natural order established by a higher power.

    4. While I am unable to explain fully who or what God is, I believe he has an influence in the history of man.

    5. I believe God has and continues to intervene directly and indirectly in the history of man.

6. Which of the following comes closest to expressing your conception of prayer?
    1. "Prayer" is not a meaningful term to me.

    2. Prayer is self-evaluation and working out one's problems.

    3. Prayer is meditation in which thought is directed toward beauty, goodness, comfort, etc.

    4. Prayer is directing one's thoughts toward a higher power.

    5. Prayer is speaking to God.

7. Which of the following statements comes closest to expressing your conception of sin?
   1. I do not believe in "sin."

   2. I believe people err but do not "sin."

   3. Sin is behavior which goes against my own personal principles.

   4. Sin is behavior which harms others.

   5. Sin is behavior which goes against accepted social and ethical principles.

   6. Sin is failure to live up to the highest spiritual ideals I know.

   7. Sin is the individual's rejection of God's will for his life.

8. What is your view of the Bible?
   1. The Bible is a collection of myths and fantasies.

   2. The Bible is a collection of literary and historical writings.

   3. The Bible contains some of man's significant moral and ethical thinking.

   4. The Bible was written by inspired men and contains valuable spiritual teachings.

   5. The Bible is God's Word.

Experience Dimension

1. Have you ever had an experience which, at the time, you thought of as a religious experience? If so, which of the following comes closest to expressing the dominant characteristics of your experience?
   1. I have never had what I would call a religious experience.

   2. I can't recall that I have had what I would call a religious experience.

   3. I have had moments of unusual appreciation of truth, beauty, goodness, etc.

   4. At some time I have had an awareness of the divine.

   5. I have had an experience (or experiences) when I felt a mutual encounter between myself and God.

For questions 2-4, answer according to the following:
   1. Strongly agree
   2. Agree
   3. Uncertain
   4. Disagree
   5. Strongly disagree

*2. There are particular moments in my life when I feel "close" to the Divine.

*3. I know what it feels like to repent and experience forgiveness of sin.

*4. I have experienced the joy and peace which comes from recognizing that one is a forgiven sinner.

Religious Practice Dimension

*1. How often do you attend Sabbath worship services?
   1. Every week.
   2. About twice a month.
   3. About once a month.
   4. A few times a year.
   5. Never.

*2. Do you presently belong to a church (or synagogue)?
   1. Yes.
   2. No.

3. Do you contribute funds to the church?
   1. Never.
   2. Pays church tax (German students).
   3. Sometimes.
   4. Regularly.

*4. How would you describe your use of the Bible?
   1. I read the Bible regularly for devotional purposes.
   2. I read the Bible, somewhat irregularly, primarily for devotional purposes.
   3. I read the Bible occasionally for its ethical and moral teachings.
   4. I read the Bible occasionally for literary or historical purposes.
   5. I read the Bible for diverse purposes.
   6. I seldom, if ever, read the Bible.
   7. I never read the Bible.

5. In how many religiously affiliated organizations, groups, or activities (such as choir, youth groups, committees, and boards, etc.) do you participate?
   0. None
   1. One
   2. Two
   3. Three
   4. Four
   5. Five or more

Individual Moral Consequences Dimension

For each of the following statements, answer according to the following.
   1. Strongly agree
   2. Agree
   3. Uncertain
   4. Disagree
   5. Strongly disagree

1. Misrepresenting your age to be served alcoholic beverages is acceptable behavior.
2. It would not bother my conscience to use marijuana.
3. Premarital sexual relations between a boy and a girl who are "in love" is not immoral.
4. Stealing hubcaps or shoplifting minor items is not immoral.
5. Violence can be a justifiable form of civic protest.
6. A woman should be able to obtain an abortion for any reason.

Religious Knowledge Dimension

Are the following persons mentioned in the (1) Old Testament, (2) New Testament, or not mentioned in Bible? Check the appropriate column.

	Old Testament	New Testament	Not in Bible
Aquinas			
Moses			
Joshua			
Wesley			
David			
Paul			
Isaiah			
Luther			
Timothy			
Augustine			

Social Consequences Dimension

For the following statements, answer according to the following.
   1. Strongly agree
   2. Agree
   3. Uncertain
   4. Disagree
   5. Strongly disagree

*1. I am for better housing for disadvantaged groups in society.

*2. I stand for the eradication of poverty among groups of this society.

*3. I support full employment opportunities for all.

*4. I support programs which guarantee economic security for old age.

*5. I think capital punishment should be abolished.

*Item is reversed scored

Reprinted with permission from *Social Forces* (Vol. 54, No. 4, 1976). Dimensions of religiosity reconsidered: Evidence from a cross-cultural study by G. DeJong, J. Faulkner, and R. Warland. Copyright © 1976 The University of North Carolina Press.

8.2
DIMENSIONS OF RELIGIOSITY SCALE
(Cornwall, Albrecht, Cunningham, & Pitcher, 1986)
Reviewed by Keith J. Edwards

Variable: The Dimensions of Religiosity (DOR) Scale is based on a model of spirituality that makes a distinction among three components of religiosity: knowing (cognition), feeling (affect), and doing (behavior). For each of these components, the authors identify two modes of religious involvement: the personal mode and the institutional mode. The cross-classification of these two components identifies six dimensions of religiosity: traditional and particularistic orthodoxy (cognitive), spiritual and church commitment (affective), and religious behavior and participation (behavioral).

Description: The scale was developed to operationalize the conceptual model just described. Sets of items were formulated for each of the six hypothesized dimensions. Subsequent psychometric analyses resulted in the identification of seven subscales. The seventh subscale appears to measure familial religious behavior, an area of interest to the Mormon church because of its explicit teachings and expectations regarding family life and religion. The subscales are as follows: Traditional Orthodoxy (5 items), Particularistic Orthodoxy (4 items), Spiritual Commitment (5 items), Church Commitment (5 items), Religious Behavior (4 items), Christian Behavior (4 items), and Home Religious Observances (4 items). There are a total of 31 items. The items in the first 6 categories are rated on five-point Likert scales. The participation items request quantitative reports of the extent of involvement (e.g., frequency of prayer.)

While the instrument was developed to test a general model of religiousness, some of the item content is very specific to the Mormon Church (e.g., one item measures the authority of *The Book of Mormon*). All of the Particularistic Orthodoxy subscale and four of the five Church Commitment subscale items are directly related to Mormon doctrine. The specific nature of this content will limit the general utility of the scale.

The Traditional Orthodoxy scale consists of five items that state central doctrines of Christian theology. The Spiritual Commitment, Religious Behavior, and Christian Behavior scales measure the person's religious experience and relationship to God as well as a range of behaviors and attitudes consistent with religious belief. Some items on these three scales are similar to items on the Intrinsic/Extrinsic religious orientation scale by Allport and Ross (1967).

Practical Considerations: This paper and pencil measure can be completed in less than 15 minutes. There are no special instructions or scoring procedures. The subscales are scored by calculating the mean of the scale item responses. The measure has limited usefulness outside the Mormon Church. If one were to want to use this scale with non-Mormon groups, some of the items which are only applicable to Mormon subjects would need to be rewritten. On the other hand, if one were specifically interested in a religious measure appropriate for use with Mormons, this may be the measure of choice.

Norms/Standardization: There are no reported norms or standardization samples given in the original study.

Reliability: Internal consistency estimates of reliability were calculated using a sample of over 1400 active and inactive members of the Mormon Church. The coefficient alphas for each of the final scales were: Traditional Orthodoxy (.76) Particularistic Orthodoxy (.92) Spiritual Commitment (.88) Church Commitment (.80) Religious Behavior (.83) Christian Behavior (.75) Home Religious Observance (.87).

Validity: A principle components factor analysis with varimax rotation of the factors yielded five factors with eigenvalues greater than one. The five factors were: a belief factor, two commitment factors, and two behavior factors. Subsets of items were also subjected to factor analyses. On the basis of the results of all the factor analyses, seven scales were created using the thirty-one religiosity items. No other validity data were available.

Location
Cornwall, M., Albrecht, S.L., Cunningham, P.H., & Pitcher, B.L. (1986). The dimensions of religiosity: A conceptual model with an empirical test. *Review of Religious Research, 27,* 226–244

Subsequent Research:
Cornwall, M. (1989). The determinants of religious behavior: A theoretical model and empirical test. *Social Forces, 68,* 572–592.

References

Allport, G. W. & Ross, J. M. (1967). Personal religious orientation and prejudice. *Journal of Personality and Social Psychology, 5,* 432–433.

Appendix

Dimensions of Religiosity

The following are the final 31 items included in the Dimensions of Religiosity Scale. Items are scored on one of three scales. The scales were as follows:

   A. 1 = not at all 2 = slightly 3 = somewhat 4 = moderately 5 = exactly
   B. 1 = strongly disagree 2 = disagree 3 = not sure 4 = agree 5 = strongly agree
   C. 1 = never 2 = a few times a year 3 = monthly 4 = a few times a month 5 = weekly
      6 = a few times a week 7 = daily

The letters next to the items indicate which response scale was used for that item.

(Traditional Orthodoxy)
1. I believe in the divinity of Christ. (A)
2. I have no doubts that God lives and is real. (A)
3. There is life after death. (B)
4. The Bible is the word of God. (B)
5. Satan actually exists. (B)

(Particularistic Orthodoxy)
6. The president of the LDS Church is a prophet of God. (B)
7. The Book of Mormon is the word of God. (B)
8. The Church of Jesus Christ of Latter-day Saints is the only church on earth. (B)
9. Joseph Smith actually saw God the Father and Jesus Christ. (B)

(Spiritual Commitment)
10. My relationship with the Lord is an important part of my life. (A)
11. The Holy Ghost is an important influence in my life. (A)
12. I love God with all my heart. (A)
13. Without religious faith the rest of my life would not have much meaning. (A)
14. I am willing to do whatever the Lord wants me to do. (A)

(Church Commitment)
15. Some doctrines of the LDS Church are hard for me to accept. (A) (reverse scored)
16. I don't really care about the LDS Church. (A) (reverse scored)

17. I do not accept some of the standards of the LDS Church. (A) (reverse scored)
18. The LDS Church puts too many restrictions on its members. (A) (reverse scored)
19. Church programs and activities are an important part of my life. (A)

(Religious Behavior)
20. I encourage others to believe in Christ. (A)
21. I seek God's guidance when making important decisions in my life. (A)
22. I admit my sins to God and pray for forgiveness. (A)
23. How often do you pray? (C)

(Christian Behavior)
24. I try to carry my religion over in to all my other dealings in life. (A)
25. I live a Christian life. (A)
26. I share what I have with the poor. (A)
27. I forgive others. (A)

(Home Religious Observances)
28. How often do you have family prayer? (C)
29. How often do you have family religious discussions? (C)
30. How often do you read the Bible or other scripture? (C)
31. How often do you have family discussions about right or wrong? (C)

Cornwall, M., Albrecht, S. L., Cunningham, P. H., & Pitcher, B. L. (1986). The dimensions of religiosity: A conceptual model with an empirical test. *Review of Religious Research, 27,* 226–244. Copyright © 1986 Review of Religious Research. Reprinted with permission.

8.3
DIMENSIONS OF RELIGIOUS COMMITMENT (Glock & Stark, 1966)
Reviewed by Ronald Burwell

Variable: The Dimensions of Religious Commitment Scale is an extensive set of religious measures designed to cover five dimensions of religiosity: belief, ritual, experience, knowledge, and consequences. The latter dimension (consequences) is omitted because it is not strictly a measure of religiosity itself. The remaining four dimensions are covered by a set of 48 different items, many with multiple subsections.

Glock and Stark made an important contribution to the study of religiosity by attempting to develop a comprehensive way of measuring religiosity. Prior to their work most studies picked up on only one or two dimensions of religiosity. Subsequent to Glock and Stark's work it appears no longer satisfactory to measure religiosity in this way.

Weigert and Thomas (1969) raised criticisms about the Glock and Stark approach. They pointed to a significant overlap between the belief dimension and knowledge dimension, arguing that both are really part of the ideological domain. Nevertheless, apart from the possibility of an overlap between these categories, the independence of the other dimensions is not questioned. However, a more critical analysis of Glock and Stark's work by Clayton (1971) and Clayton and Gladden (1974) suggested that all of the dimensions, with the possible exception of a consequential scale, might really be measuring aspects of religious belief.

In contrast, the extensive research program conducted by King and Hunt (1975) has offered strong corroboration for the multidimensionality claimed by Glock and

Stark. Using an inductive approach via the technique of factor analysis, King and Hunt found six basic scales that were very close to Glock's belief, experiential, and ritual dimensions. More recently, Hilty (1988) reported results from an ongoing religious measures project that also support a multidimensional approach.

Description: Glock and Stark's dimensions of religious commitment measures are an important element in the evolution of sociologically oriented attempts to measure religion. They represent the growing realization in the 1960s that religion was a complex phenomenon that demanded a multidimensional approach to its measurement. Influenced by earlier work of Gerhard Lenski, Glock and Stark approached the issue of creating religious measures by identifying the important components or dimensions of religion. For each of these dimensions they created a set of survey questions that could be combined into indices. The following dimensions of religiosity produced these indices:

Belief Orthodoxy Index (central religious beliefs—7 items)

Particularism Index (beliefs about what leads to salvation—3 items)

Ethicalism Index (beliefs about relationships with others—2 items)

Practice Ritual Involvement Index (involvement in organized public worship—6 items)

Devotionalism Index (private devotional practices— 3 items)

Experience Religious Experience Index (extent to which one reports personal contact with the supernatural—5 items)

Knowledge Religious Knowledge Index (degree of knowledge of biblical content—10 items)

Glock and Stark's dimensions of religious commitment measures can be viewed as a pool of survey items that could be used by researchers studying religion. As Glock and Stark themselves demonstrated, one might not need to use all the possible items that are available. Furthermore, if only certain aspects of religiosity are deemed important to the research, then one or more of the indices could be used independently. Care should be taken not to claim that religion is being measured comprehensively. Others have followed essentially the same basic framework but have created different specific items (Faulkner & DeJong, 1966; King & Hunt, 1969). One could compare the Glock and Stark items with alternatives and create a composite set of measures that suits exactly the needs of a particular study.

Practical Considerations: A major consideration with the use of a multidimensional set of religious measures is whether or not the precision gained in such an approach is necessary for the purposes of the study. Generally, including all of the Glock and Stark measures as part of a larger instrument would necessitate a fair amount of time for the subject to complete all the items. Researchers would have to allow up to 30 minutes for these items to be completed. In some cases fewer items could be used with an accompanying loss of precision.

The scoring procedure for the items is straightforward. The indices are simply constructed by assigning numbers to the possible answers and summing the totals. Answers deemed as indicating religiosity are assigned higher values and answers indicating a lack of religiosity are not given any value. Thus the higher the total score, the more religious the respondent is on that particular dimension.

In a number of cases Glock and Stark did not use all of the possible items created for a given dimension. In some cases, items were omitted because they were relevant only to a specific religious subgroup. In other cases, Glock and Stark found through index validation analysis that a smaller group of items served as well as a larger set of questions.

Norms/Standardization: The 1966 publication by Glock and Stark reports the results for two samples. The first was a 1963 study of over 3,000 church members drawn from

118 Protestant and Roman Catholic congregations in four counties in northern California. The second sample was a national study (N = 1,976) that was part of a National Opinion Research Center (NORC) survey of the nation in 1964. The first sample completed self-administered mail surveys and the second sample involved in-person interviews.

A major concern was to discover if the results of the regional study (California) would be similar to the national sample. Glock and Stark reported that the national data confirmed empirically the findings of the regional study.

Since publication of Glock and Stark's study other researchers have adopted some of the same measures. But there have been no systematically replicated studies of the exact same instrument. Nevertheless, Glock and Stark (1966) provides useful normative data to anyone using these measures.

Reliability: No reliability data were reported.

Validity: Extensive item intercorrelations were conducted to see if the various measures were logically connected. Individual items did, in fact, correlate well with the indices that were created. In some cases Glock and Stark present product moment correlations for these correlations (range: .404 to .766); in other cases, they do cross tabulations between items and indices. Beyond item analysis, Glock and Stark do not offer any external validity checks. They report data that can be intuitively confirmed such as differences between various denominations on religious orthodoxy, participation, etc. For example, more theologically conservative Protestant groups such as Baptists demonstrate higher levels on the measures of religious orthodoxy.

Location:
Glock, C., & Stark, R. (1966). *Christian beliefs and anti-Semitism.* New York: Harper & Row.

Note: Most of the religiosity items are found on pages 1–7 of the questionnaire (items 1–43). Information on index construction is also found in their book.

Subsequent Research:
Clayton, R. R. (1971). 5-D or 1? *Journal for the Scientific Study of Religion, 10*(1), 37–40.

Clayton, R. R., & Gladden, J. (1974). The five dimensions of religiosity: Toward demythologizing a social artifact. *Journal for the Scientific Study of Religion, 13*(2), 135–143.

Hilty, D. M. (1988). Religious belief, participation and consequences: An exploratory and confirmatory analysis. *Journal for the Scientific Study of Religion, 27*(2), 243–259.

Roof, W. C. (1979). Concepts and indicators of religious commitment: A critical review. In R. Wuthnow (Ed.), *The religious dimension: New directions in quantitative research* (Chap. 1). New York: Academic Press.

References

DeJong, G., Faulkner, J., & Warland, R. (1976). Dimensions of religiosity reconsidered: Evidence from a cross-cultural study. *Social Forces, 54*, 866–889.

Faulkner, J. E., & DeJong, G. F. (1966). Religiosity in 5-D: An empirical analysis. *Social Forces 45*, 246–254.

Glock, C., & Stark, R. (1966). *Christian beliefs and anti-Semitism.* New York: Harper & Row.

King, M., & Hunt, R. (1969). Measuring the religious variable: Amended findings. *Journal for the Scientific Study of Religion 8*, 321–323.

King, M., & Hunt, R. (1975). Measuring the religious variable: National replication. *Journal for the Scientific Study of Religion, 14*, 13–22.

Weigert, A., & Thomas, D. (1969). Religiosity in 5-D: A critical note. *Social Forces, 48*, 260–263.

Appendix

Dimensions of Religious Commitment

To begin with, we would like to ask about your present church going habits and about your activities more generally.

1. What is the name and denomination of the church to which you presently belong?

2. How long have you been a member of your present congregation or parish?
   a. I have always been a member
   b. Less than one year
   c. One to two years
   d. Three to five years
   e. Six to ten years
   f. More than ten years

3. Have you ever been a member of a denomination other than your present one?
   Yes   No

   If yes, what denomination was that? (If more than one, list them in order from the most recent to the earliest.)

4. How often do you attend Sunday worship services?
   a. Every week
   b. Nearly every week
   c. About three times a month
   d. About twice a month
   e. About once a month
   f. About every six weeks
   g. About every three months
   h. About once or twice a year
   i. Less than once a year
   j. Never

5. Have you received Holy Communion in the last year?
   Yes   No

6. Have you been baptized?
   a. Yes, in my present denomination
   b. Yes, in another denomination
   c. No

7. Have you been confirmed?
   a. Yes, in my present denomination
   b. Yes, in another denomination
   c. No

8. In an average week, how many evenings do you spend in church, including church meetings such as study groups that may not actually meet in the church building?

9. IF YOU HAVE CHILDREN, PLEASE ANSWER THE FOLLOWING QUESTIONS. IF NOT, SKIP TO QUESTION 10.
   What kind of school do your children attend?
   a. A parochial or church-affiliated school
   b. A public school
   c. A private school not affiliated with any church
   d. They do not attend school

   How frequently, if at all, do your children attend Sunday school or religious instruction classes that are not part of their regular school day?
   a. They do not attend
   b. They attend regularly
   c. They attend often
   d. They attend sometimes

10. All in all, how important would you say your church membership is to you?
    a. Extremely important
    b. Quite important
    c. Fairly important
    d. Not too important
    e. Fairly unimportant

11. In *Column A*, please list all of the church organizations, groups, or activities in which you participate, such as choir, church committees and boards, men's clubs, women's clubs, etc.
    In *Column B*, please indicate how many of the last five meetings of each of these organizations you have attended.
    In *Column C*, please indicate whether or not you have ever held an office in each organization you list.

    Column A   *Column B*   *Column C*

12. IF YOU ARE NOW OR EVER HAVE BEEN MARRIED, PLEASE ANSWER THE FOLLOWING QUESTIONS. If you have been married more than once, answer for your most recent spouse.
    a. To what denomination does (or did) your spouse belong?
    b. In what denomination was your spouse raised?
    c. Would you say you are (or were) more or less interested in religion than your spouse?
       a. More   b. Less   c. About the same
    d. About how often does (or did) your spouse attend Sunday worship services?
       a. Every week
       b. Nearly every week
       c. About three times a month
       d. About twice a month
       e. About once a month
       f. About every six weeks
       g. About every three months
       h. About once or twice a year
       i. Less than once a year
       j. Never

13. All in all, how well do you think you fit in with the group of people who make up your church congregation (or parish)?
    a. I really don't fit in too well with this group of people
    b. I fit in, but not too well
    c. I fit in quite well
    d. I fit in very well

14. Generally speaking, would you say most of the people you associate with in activities aside from church affairs are or are not members of your congregation (or parish)?
    a. Most are members of my congregation (or parish)
    b. About half are and half aren't
    c. Most are not members of my congregation

15. Of your five closest friends, how many are members of your congregation (or parish)?

16. Turning now to other religious activities besides attending church, how often, if at all, are table prayers or grace said before or after meals in your home?
    a. We say grace at all meals
    b. We say grace at least once a day
    c. We say grace at least once a week
    d. We say grace but only on special occasions
    e. We never, or hardly ever, say grace

17. How often do you read the Bible at home?
    a. To be frank, I never read the Bible or I read it so rarely that it probably shouldn't even count
    b. I read it regularly once a day or more
    c. I read it regularly several times a week
    d. I read it regularly once a week
    e. I read it quite often, but not at regular intervals
    f. I read it once in a while
    g. I read it only on very special occasions

18. Thinking now of your daily life and the decisions that you have to make constantly about how to spend your time, how to act with other people, how to bring up your children, presuming you have them, and so on, to what extent does what you read in the Bible help you in making everyday decisions in your life?
    a. To be frank, I hardly ever think of the Bible and what it has to say as I go about my daily life
    b. While I can't think of specific examples, nevertheless I feel sure that the Bible is still of help in my daily life
    c. I can think of specific examples when it has helped me in a very direct way in making decisions in life
    d. Other (please specify)

19. If you were asked, do you think you could recite the Ten Commandments?
    a. Yes, but not the exact words
    b. Yes, the exact words
    c. I'm not sure that I would remember all ten

20. Which of the following were Old Testament prophets?
    a. Elijah
    b. Deuteronomy
    c. Jeremiah
    d. Paul
    e. Leviticus
    f. Ezekiel
    g. None of these

21. Which one of Christ's disciples denied Him three times?
    a. James
    b. Paul
    c. Judas
    d. Mark
    e. Peter
    f. Jacob

22. Would you say that the book of Acts was an eyewitness account of Jesus' ministry?
    a. Yes
    b. No
    c. Don't know

23. Would you please read each of the following statements and do *two* things: *first*, decide whether this statement is from the Bible or not; and *second*, please indicate whether or not you agree with the statement, even if you think the statement is not from the Bible.

    For it is easier for a camel to go through a needle's eye than for a rich man to enter the kingdom of God.

From the Bible?	a. Yes	b. No
Do you agree?	a. Yes	b. No

    Blessed are the strong, for they shall be the sword of God.

From the Bible?	a. Yes	b. No
Do you agree?	a. Yes	b. No

    Thou shalt not suffer a witch to live.

From the Bible?	a. Yes	b. No
Do you agree?	a. Yes	b. No

    Blessed are the meek, for they shall inherit the earth.

From the Bible?	a. Yes	b. No
Do you agree?	a. Yes	b. No

    Let your women keep silence in the churches, for it is not permitted unto them to speak.

From the Bible?	a. Yes	b. No
Do you agree?	a. Yes	b. No

    For I the Lord thy God am a jealous God, visiting the iniquity of the fathers upon the children unto the third and fourth generation of them that hate me.

From the Bible?	a. Yes	b. No
Do you agree?	a. Yes	b. No

We'd like to shift now from asking about the Bible to asking about prayer. Prayer is a very private thing and we frankly are not sure whether we should ask people about their prayers. We hope that you will find the questions not too delicate to answer, but if you do, please tell us by writing in the margins.

24. How often do you pray privately?
    a. I never pray, or only do so at church services
    b. I pray only on very special occasions
    c. I pray once in a while, but not at regular intervals
    d. I pray quite often, but not at regular times
    e. I pray regularly once a day or more
    f. I pray regularly several times a week
    g. I pray regularly once a week

IF YOU EVER PRAY, OTHER THAN IN CHURCH, PLEASE ANSWER THE FOLLOWING QUESTIONS.

1. When you pray, why do you pray? (Answer as many as apply)
    a. As a Christian duty
    b. To find comfort when I am feeling low
    c. To strengthen my faith
    d. To try to learn God's will
    e. To ask God's guidance in making decisions
    f. Because it gives me a feeling of being closer to God
    g. To ask forgiveness for something I have done
    h. To ask God to bring someone else to Christian faith and belief
    i. To give thanks to God
    j. To be worshipful of God

Now look back at the list above, and please circle the answer that you feel is the *most* important reason that you pray.

2. Have you ever prayed during your adult years for the following purposes? (Answer as many as apply)
    a. To ask for some material thing, for example, a new car or a new house
    b. To ask God to keep some misfortune from happening to me
    c. To ask God to restore my health
    d. To ask God to restore someone else's health
    e. None of these

3. Do you feel your prayers are answered?
    a. Yes, I have no doubt that they are
    b. I feel that they are, but I'm not entirely sure
    c. I don't really know
    d. I feel that they aren't, but I'm not entirely sure
    e. I guess I don't feel that they really are
    f. Other (please specify)

4. How important is prayer in your life?
    a. Extremely important
    b. Fairly important

c. Not too important
d. Not important at all

25. How important is the idea of sin in your life?
    a. I am rather concerned with trying to live as sinless a life as possible
    b. I accept the idea of sin, but do not really think about it very often
    c. The idea of sin means very little to me
    d. None of the above represents my feelings; what I do feel is that _____

26. How often do you ask for forgiveness for your sins?
    a. Very often
    b. Quite often
    c. Occasionally
    d. Rarely
    e. Never

27. How certain are you that your sins are forgiven?
    a. I am absolutely certain they are
    b. I am fairly certain
    c. I feel they are forgiven sometimes, but not always
    d. I am never quite sure whether my sins are forgiven or not
    e. I usually feel that my sins are not forgiven
    f. I don't think of sin in this way

28. Have you personally tried to convert someone to your religious faith?
    a. Yes, often
    b. Yes, a few times
    c. Yes, once or twice
    d. No, never

29. There has always been a good deal of discussion among Christians about how people ought to act in their daily lives. It is not always clear what characteristics ought to be admired and which ones we should disapprove of. Below you will find a series of descriptions of ways in which people act.
    1. Drinks moderately
    2. Is very ambitious
    3. Thinks he is better than others
    4. Dresses in a flashy way
    5. Prefers to be with people like himself
    6. Is very patriotic
    7. Feels that Christian holidays should not be celebrated in the public schools
    8. Is very rich
    9. Is very anxious to be thought of as an intellectual
    10. Is satisfied with his lot in life

For each one, decide how much you would admire or disapprove of a person who acted in this way. Complete the following sentence with one of the choices:
    If a person were like this, I would:
    a. Admire him for it
    b. Think it was all right
    c. Be mildly disapproving of him
    d. Be highly disapproving of him

30. We would like you to imagine, for a moment, that for some reason you could no longer continue to attend a church of your present denomination. Below is a list of other denominations that it would be possible for you to attend. We would like you to consider each and decide for yourself how comfortable and "at home" you think you would feel in each. The choices for answering are:
    a. Very comfortable
    b. Comfortable
    c. A little uncomfortable
    d. Uncomfortable
    e. Don't know enough about this denomination to say

    The denominations are:
    a. Baptist
    b. Jehovah's Witnesses
    c. Jewish
    d. Lutheran
    e. Presbyterian
    f. Roman Catholic
    g. Unitarian
    h. Mormon

We now turn to another part of religious life—religious belief. We are concerned to learn not only what people believe but also how important their beliefs are to them. We hope you will find that the questions allow you to express your own beliefs. If not, please write a comment next to any question that you would consider to be inappropriate.

31. Which of the following statements comes closest to expressing what you believe about God?
    a. I know God exists and I have no doubts about it
    b. While I have doubts, I feel that I do believe in God
    c. I find myself believing in God some of the time, but not at other times
    d. I don't believe in a personal God, but I do believe in a higher power of some kind
    e. I don't know whether there is a God and I don't believe there is any way to find out
    f. I don't believe in God
    g. None of the above represents what I believe. What I believe about God is_____

32. Which of the following statements comes closest to expressing what you believe about Jesus?
    a. Jesus is the Divine Son of God and I have no doubts about it
    b. While I have some doubts, I feel basically that Jesus is Divine
    c. I feel that Jesus was a great man and very holy, but I don't feel Him to be the Son of God any more than all of us are children of God
    d. I think Jesus was only a man, although an extraordinary one
    e. Frankly, I'm not entirely sure there really was such a person as Jesus
    f. None of the above represents what I believe. What I believe about Jesus is _____

33. The Bible tells of many miracles, some credited to Christ and some to other prophets and apostles. Generally speaking, which of the following statements comes closest to what you believe about biblical miracles.
    a. I am not sure whether these miracles really happened or not
    b. I believe miracles are stories and never really happened

c. I believe the miracles happened, but can be explained by natural causes

d. I believe the miracles actually happened just as the Bible says they did

34. Please think about each of the religious beliefs listed below and indicate how certain you are that it is true according to these choices: Completely true, probably true, probably not true, definitely not true

a. There is life beyond death

b. Jesus was born of a virgin

c. The devil actually exists

d. Jesus was opposed to all drinking of alcohol

e. What we do in this life will determine our fate in the hereafter

f. Jesus walked on water

g. Man cannot help doing evil

h. The pope is infallible in matters of faith and morals

i. Jesus was born a Jew

j. Only those who believe in Jesus Christ can go to heaven

k. A child is born into the world already guilty of sin

35. When you think of salvation, do you think primarily of being granted eternal life beyond the grave or do you think primarily of being released from sin and protected from evil in this life?

a. I think primarily of being granted eternal life beyond death

b. I think primarily of being released from sin and protected from evil in this life

c. Other

36. Please read each of the items listed below and decide whether you think it is:

1. Absolutely necessary for salvation

2. Probably would help in gaining salvation

    or

3. Probably has no influence on salvation

    a. Belief in Jesus Christ as Savior

    b. Holy Baptism

    c. Membership in a Christian church

    d. Regular participation in Christian sacraments, for example, Holy Communion

    e. Holding the Bible to be God's truth

    f. Prayer

    g. Doing good for others

    h. Tithing

    i. Being a member of your particular religious faith

    j. Loving thy neighbor

37. Now looking at the following items, please indicate for each whether you think it will:

1. Definitely prevent salvation

2. May possibly prevent salvation

    or

3. Probably has no influence on salvation

    a. Drinking liquor

    b. Breaking the Sabbath

    c. Being completely ignorant of Jesus, as might be the case for people living in other countries

    d. Taking the name of the Lord in vain

    e. Being of the Jewish religion
    f. Practicing artificial birth control
    g. Being of the Hindu religion
    h. Marrying a non-Christian
    i. Discriminating against other races
    j. Being anti-Semitic

38. Do you believe Jesus will actually return to the earth some day?
    a. Definitely
    b. Probably
    c. Possibly
    d. Probably not
    e. Definitely not

IF YOU THINK JESUS WILL DEFINITELY OR PROBABLY RETURN, PLEASE AN-
SWER THE FOLLOWING QUESTION:
    How soon do you expect Jesus' return to happen?
    a. In the next 10 years
    b. In the next 25 years
    c. In the next 50 years
    d. In the next 100 years
    e. 200 to 500 years from now
    f. 1,000 to 10,000 years from now
    g. 50,000 or more years from now
    h. Other _____

39. What do you feel will probably happen to you after death? I feel that I will:
    a. Go to purgatory
    b. Go to hell
    c. Simply stop existing
    d. Go to heaven

40. How certain do you feel about the answer you have just given?
    a. Very certain
    b. Fairly certain
    c. Not very certain
    d. Not at all certain

41. How sure are you that you have found the answers to the meaning and the purpose of
    life?
    a. I am quite certain and I pretty much grew up knowing these things
    b. I am quite certain, although at one time I was pretty uncertain
    c. I am uncertain whether or not I have found them
    d. I am quite sure I have not found them
    e. I don't really believe there are answers to these questions

So far, we have asked about your religious activities, your religious knowledge, and your religious beliefs. The next series of questions has to do with your religious experiences, that is,
with what feelings you may have had which you would think of as religious.

42. To begin, would you describe briefly any experience which you have had in your life which at the time you thought of as a distinctly religious experience.

43. Listed below are a number of experiences of a religious nature which people have reported having. Since you have been an adult, have you ever had any of these experiences, and how sure are you that you had it? Answer either: Yes, I'm sure I have; Yes, I think I have; or No

    a. A feeling that you were somehow in the presence of God
    b. A sense of being saved in Christ
    c. A feeling of being afraid of God
    d. A feeling of being punished by God for something you had done
    e. A feeling of being tempted by the devil

    IF YOU HAVE ANSWERED NO TO ALL OF THE ABOVE, do you feel that it is possible for people to have religious experiences?
    a. Yes   b. No   c. I'm not sure

The following questions give attention to still another topic—the history of Christianity. Here we are interested to learn how church people view the events of early Christianity and the Reformation period.

44. The Old Testament tells that God picked a certain group to be his "Chosen People." Can you tell us who God picked as his "Chosen People"?
    a. The Romans
    b. The Greeks
    c. The Jews
    d. The Christians
    e. None of these

45. Who do you think are God's "Chosen People" today?
    a. The Americans
    b. The Roman Catholics
    c. The Jews
    d. The Christians
    e. The Protestants
    f. None
    g. Other _____

46. Do you think of Moses, David, and Solomon as:
    a. Romans
    b. Greeks
    c. Jews
    d. Christians
    e. None of these

47. When you think of Peter and Paul and the other apostles, do you think of them as:
    a. Romans
    b. Greeks
    c. Jews
    d. Christians
    e. None of the above

48. When you think of Judas, who betrayed Christ, do you think of him as:
    a. A Roman
    b. A Greek
    c. A Jew
    d. A Christian
    e. None of these

8.4
DIMENSIONS OF RELIGIOUS IDEOLOGY (Putney & Middleton, 1961)
Reviewed by Rodney L. Bassett

Variable: This scale measures four dimensions of Christian ideology: (a) orthodoxy (the belief in some traditional Christian doctrines), (b) fanaticism (the desire to share Christianity with others), (c) importance (the personal significance of religion), and (d) ambivalence (the self-awareness of having contradictory attitudes toward religion).

The instrument clearly assesses religious identity and ways of being religious within that identity, but it is not as clear that the items necessarily tap Christian identity. For example, the orthodoxy items refer to the church, a divine plan, and devil and hell, but there is no specific reference to God or Jesus Christ. The other dimensions simply refer to "religion." Christians would understand and probably agree with most of these items, but the questionnaire doesn't seem to allow Christians to affirm many beliefs that are distinctly Christian. Interestingly, although the instrument seems to have been used largely with Christian populations, researchers have generally referred to the instrument as a "religious" measure (e.g., Benson et al., 1980), instead of using the more narrow concept of "Christian."

Description: The Orthodoxy, Fanaticism, and Importance Scales were constructed using the Likert method, which emphasizes internal consistency and discriminatory power. Each of these scales has six items with most of the items positively worded (some of the items are negatively worded).

The ambivalence scale contains only one item: "Although one is stronger than the other, there is part of me that believes in religion and part of me that does not." Participants respond to all 19 items using a 7-point scale with the end points of "strong agreement" and "strong disagreement."

Practical Considerations: Putney and Middleton presented the actual items in their article, but they did not specify the instructions given participants. When the instrument is scored, a participant's score is computed separately for each scale by reversing any negatively worded items and then summing the responses for that scale. When using the scale, Putney and Middleton used the strategy of splitting participants into high and low categories using the theoretical midpoints for each scale (e.g., on the Orthodoxy Scale, where scores can range from 6 to 42, the cutoff for "highs" and "lows" was 24).

An interesting question is whether the scales are independent. Putney and Middleton administered the instrument to 1,200 college and university students in the northeastern and southeastern parts of the United States. When Jewish and other non-Christian students were excluded from the analyses, 1,126 students remained. Using a nonparametric measure of association (Yule's Q), the authors found that the Orthodoxy, Fanaticism, and Importance scales were positively related. The ambivalence scale was negatively related to the other three scales. Further, the positive relationships were stronger than the negative relationships.

Norms/Standardization: The only published normative data has been reported by Cygnar, Jacobson, and Noel (1977) with Catholic high school students. However, this information is hard to interpret and apply to new samples because some of the items may have been dropped from the scales and the means and standard deviations that are reported appear to be based on factor scores.

Reliability: Cygnar, Jacobson, and Noel (1977) also reported data on the reliability of the Orthodoxy, Fanaticism, and Importance Scales. To make sure the scales were unidimensional, Cygnar et al. factor-analyzed the items for each scale, dropping the items that did not load on each first factor and computing factor scores for the remaining items. Using these factor scores, the reliability coefficients for the scales were (a) orthodoxy = .50, (b) fanaticism = .49, and (c) importance = .60.

Seyfarth et al. (1984) administered the Fanaticism Scale to 124 introductory psychology students. The mean age for these students was 20.7, and 55% of the sample was male. The researchers used the Spearman-Brown prophecy formula for computing split-half reliability and the resulting coefficient was .77.

Validity: In the Seyfarth et al. (1984) study, the fanaticism scale was used to provide construct validity for a measure of evangelism that the authors developed. This Attitude Toward Evangelism Scale included items like: (a) "I like to listen to a religious evangelist," (b) "Religious soliciting is an infringement on my right to privacy" (reverse scored), and (c) "There is a strong need for more people to openly attempt to convert others." When this scale was correlated with the fanaticism scale, the resulting validity coefficient was .76.

Cygnar et al. (1977) administered modified versions of the ritual, ideology, knowledge, experience, and consequence scales from Faulkner and DeJong (1966) along with the Orthodoxy, Fanaticism, and Importance Scales. The responses of Catholic high school students were factor analyzed and factor scores were computed for each student (dropping items that did not load on the factors). When the results for all of the scales were compared, the scales from Dimensions of Religious Ideologies correlated positively with all of the Faulkner and DeJong scales (the correlations ranged from .32 to .52). The only exception to this pattern was the Consequence Scale. This scale measures the extent to which religion is integrated into everyday life. The correlations between the Consequence Scale and the Dimensions of Religious Ideologies scales were lower (ranging from .04 to .16).

Location:
    Putney, S., & Middleton, R. (1961). Dimensions and correlates of religious ideologies. *Social Forces, 39,* 285–290.

References

Benson, P. L., Dehority, J., Garman, L, Hanson, E., Hochschwender, M., Lebold, C., Rohr, R., & Sullivan, J. (1980). Intrapersonal correlates of non-spontaneous helping behavior. *Journal of Social Psychology, 110,* 87–95.

Cygnar, T. E., Jacobson, C. K., & Noel, D. L. (1977). Religiosity and prejudice: An interdimensional analysis. *Journal for the Scientific Study of Religion, 16,* 183–191.

Faulkner, J. E., & DeJong, G. (1966). Religiosity in 5-D: An empirical analysis. *Social Forces, 45,* 246–254.

Pargament, K. I., Ensing, D. S., Falgout, K., Olsen, H., Reilly, B., Van Haitsma, K., & Warren, R. (1990). God help me: (I): Religious coping efforts as predictors of the outcomes to significant negative life events. *American Journal of Community Psychology, 18,* 793–824.

Seyfarth, L. H., Larsen, K. S., Lamont, K., Haasch, C., Hale, T., & Haskin, D. (1984). Attitude toward evangelism: Scale development and validity. *Journal of Social Psychology, 123,* 55–61.

Appendix

Dimensions of Religious Ideology

Please read the following statements carefully, and then indicate agreement according to the following scale:

    7 = strongly agree   3 = slightly disagree
    6 = moderately agree   2 = moderately disagree
    5 = slightly agree   1 = strongly disagree
    4 = no response

Orthodoxy Scale

1. I believe that there is a physical hell where men are punished after death for the sins of their lives.
2. I believe there is a supernatural being, the devil, who continually tries to lead men into sin.
3. To me the most important work of the church is the saving of souls.
4. I believe that there is a life after death.
5. I believe there is a divine plan and purpose for every living person and thing.
6. The only benefit one receives from prayer is psychological. (reverse scored)

Fanaticism Scale

1. I have a duty to help those who are confused about religion.
2. Even though it may create some unpleasant situations, it is important to help people become enlightened about religion.
3. There is no point in arguing about religion because there is little chance of changing other people's minds. (reverse scored)
4. It doesn't really matter what an individual believes about religion as long as he is happy with it. (reverse scored)
5. I believe the world would really be a better place if more people held the views about religion which I hold.
6. I believe the world's problems are seriously aggravated by the fact that so many people are misguided about religion.

Importance Scale

1. My ideas about religion are one of the most important parts of my philosophy of life.
2. I find that my ideas on religion have a considerable influence on my views in other areas.
3. Believing as I do about religion is very important to being the kind of person I want to be.
4. If my ideas about religion were different, I believe that my way of life would be very different.
5. Religion is a subject in which I am not particularly interested. (reverse scored)
6. I very often think about matters relating to religion.

Ambivalence Scale

1. Although one is stronger than the other, there is part of me which believes in religion and part of me which does not.
   Items should be placed in random order.

Putney, S., & Middleton, R. (1961). Dimensions and correlates of religious ideologies. *Social Forces, 39,* 285–290. Copyright © 1961 University of North Carolina Press. Reprinted with permission.

8.5
FIVE-DIMENSION SCALE OF RELIGIOSITY (Faulkner & DeJong, 1966)
Reviewed by Daryl H. Stevenson

Variable: The Five-Dimension Scale of Religiosity (FDSR) measures the major dimensions of religiosity first described by Glock (1962). They include the ideological (belief), intellectual(knowledge), ritualistic (religious behavior), experiential (feeling and emotion), and consequential (effect of religion in everyday life) dimensions. Five Guttman-type scales were constructed, one for each aspect. Faulkner and DeJong assume that his typology represents separate and distinct components of religiosity.

Description: Faulkner and DeJong base their measure on the assumption that these dimensions are crucial. Unfortunately, there has not been a consensus about the nature of this multidimensional construct in more than a decade of research.

The authors propose a Guttman scaling procedure that results in five individual scores rather than a single summary score on Glock's dimensions. The items for each scale are arranged sequentially from stronger to weaker statements of attitude, and it is presumed that respondents who agree with stronger statements also agree with all weaker items.

The five scales are composed either of four or five items, each containing from two to six options. Scoring involves counting the positive responses indicated by the asterisk on the scales provided in the appendix. For example, if a person has a score of three on the ideological scale, we know she is not as high as a score-four person but is higher than a score-two person. Further, this indicates that she "affirmed the keyed re-sponse on questions three through five, but to no others." This allows the researcher, theoretically, to know an individual's pattern of response for an entire scale.

Practical Considerations: This instrument's 23 items require less than 10 minutes to complete. Beyond providing the actual scales in the initial article, no special instructions are provided for administering or scoring. Presumably the scales are presented in the order given, but without the labels. Some scoring confusion may result from referring at times to the whole instrument as a scale, the five scales, individual items on each scale, and each option in every item. Lettering the options and sequentially numbering all 23 items might reduce confusion.

Since these scales were developed for research purposes, the authors assume more knowledge of the Guttman scaling procedure than many users will have. For further detail regarding Guttman scaling and scoring, see Ford (1950). Basically, one's score on a scale is the total number of items indicating a traditional religious response. For a five-item scale, the scores range from 0 through 5. Grouped data are then translated into percentage of positive responses.

Norms/Standardization: The five scales have not been standardized. Since these scales are used exclusively for research purposes, no manual is provided to assist in administration, scoring, or interpretation.

Reliability: Test-retest or other reliability coefficients were not reported, but the coefficient of reproducibility indicates the unidimensionality strength of a Guttman-type scale. The accepted minimum level is .90. All five scales met this minimum standard when initially tested at Pennsylvania State University in 1966 on a sample of 362 undergraduates. In 1968, Clayton reported statistics on 873 undergraduate respondents from a Southern Protestant private university. Clayton's sample yielded five coefficients of reproducibility equal to or higher than the Penn State sample. It appears that these scales have demonstrated an acceptable level of reliability.

Validity: Faulkner and DeJong (1966), Clayton (1968), Clayton and Gladden (1974), and DeJong, Faulkner, and Warland (1976) provide evidence that all five scales more than adequately met the minimum criteria of unidimensionality. However, the fact that all five scales in all data sets are unidimensional says nothing about their *independence* from one another. Intercorrelation of these scales on widely diverse samples, as well as many factor analyses (both varimax and oblique rotation), yield empirical results that are vehemently argued in one of two directions. Either the five-dimensional scales measure five real and separate dimensions of religiosity or the five-dimensional scales measure different aspects of ideological commitment manifested in several directions.

Researchers agree on the dominance of the ideological factor over all other dimensions. In a factor analytic study, Clayton and Gladden (1974) report that the ideological commitment factor accounts for 78 percent of the common variance for their 1967 sample and 83 percent of the variance for the 1970 sample. Other minor factors were extracted, but a second-order factor analysis yielded one general factor. Clayton and Gladden conclude that "religiosity is essentially a single-dimension phenomenon composed primarily of ideological commitment with experience and practice being evidence of the strength of that initial and core commitment at the belief level" (p. 141).

In the initial study, the between-scale correlation coefficients ranged between .58 (between ideological and intellectual) and .36 (between experience and consequential) (Faulkner & DeJong, 1966). These are typical moderate correlations as reported from several studies. They argued that the moderate correlations supported the obvious multidimensionality of such a complex phenomenon as religiosity. By 1976, they make a small concession that "the time may have come to consider social consequences as primarily a dependent variable rather than an integral part of religiosity" (DeJong, Faulkner & Warland, 1976, p. 883). They concede that the consequential dimension may only be a result of the other dimensions operating. Nevertheless, they hold fast to multidimensional theory, arguing that their instrument has validly tapped the construct.

The problem seems to be one of specificity versus generality in measuring the religious variable. DeJong, Faulkner, and Warland (1976) argue that generalized and specific definitions of religiosity are compatible. While they believe their findings support multidimensionality, it is their judgment that "the one-not-five or the three-not-eleven debates over the number of dimensions of religiosity are primarily a function of level of abstraction and the subdivision of dimensions" (p. 884).

Another criticism by Weigert and Thomas (1969) is the wording of items used to measure Glock's dimensions. They criticize the validity of this instrument on the grounds that the same semantic categories of stimuli (i.e., use of the words "view," "opinion," and "believe" in items found on the ideological as well as the intellectual dimensions) are used. There are further examples: the knowledge dimension contains three "belief" items; the ritualistic dimension has two items that use the words "feel" and "believe." While this is not exhaustive, the point is made that Weigert and Thomas believe the authors do not faithfully construct items that validly measure the original dimensions proposed by Glock. Faulkner and DeJong (1969) wrote a rejoinder to Weigert and Thomas that effectively blunted much of their critique.

The question of construct validity, then, is still open, and it amounts to a debate over the interpretation of the findings of diverse data sets. The scales are designed for research only and are not recommended for clinical assessment of religiosity.

Location:

Faulkner, J. E., & DeJong, G. (1966). Religiosity in 5-D: An empirical analysis. *Social Forces, 45,* 246–254.

Subsequent Research:

Cole, G. E. (1982). Relationships among measures of mental health, stress, and religiosity (Doctoral dissertation, Southern Illinois University at Carbondale, 1982). *Dissertation Abstracts International, 43–05,* 1433A.

Courtenay, B. C., Poon, L., Martin, P., & Clayton, G. (1992). Religiosity and adaptation in the oldest-old. *International Journal of Aging & Human Development, 34*(1), 47–56.

Domino, G., & Miller, K. (1992). Religiosity and attitudes toward suicide. *Omega-Journal of Death & Dying, 25*(4), 271–282.

Lenes, M. S., & Hart, E. J. (1975). The influence of pornography and violence on attitudes and guilt. *Journal of School Health, 45*(8), 447–451.

Ruppel, H. J. (1970). Religiosity and premarital sexual permissiveness: A response to the Reiss-Heltsley and Broderick debate. *Journal of Marriage & the Family, 32*(4), 647–655.

References

Clayton, R. R. (1968). Religiosity in 5-D: A southern test. *Social Forces, 47,* 80–83.

Clayton, R. R., & Gladden J. W. (1974). The five dimensions of religiosity: Toward de-mythologizing a sacred artifact. *Journal for the Scientific Study of Religion, 13,* 135–144.

DeJong, G., Faulkner, J. E., & Warland, R. (1976). Dimensions of religiosity reconsidered: Evidence from a cross-cultural study. *Social Forces, 54*(4), 866–889.

Ford, R. N. (1950). A rapid scoring procedure for scaling attitude questions. *Public Opinion Quarterly, 14,* 507–532.

Faulkner, J. E., & DeJong, G. (1966). Religiosity in 5-D: An empirical analysis. *Social Forces, 45,* 246–254.

Faulkner, J. E., & DeJong, G. (1969). On measuring the religious Variable: Rejoinder to Weigert and Thomas. *Social Forces, 48*(2), 263–267.

Glock, D. (1962). On the study of religious commitment. *Religious Education: Research Supplement, 42,* 98–110.

Weigert, A. J., & Thomas, D. L. (1969). Religiosity in 5-D: A critical note. *Social Forces, 48*(2), 260–263.

Appendix

Five-Dimension Scale of Religiosity

The exact wording of items included in the religiosity scales is shown below, with an asterisk (*) marking the response defined as indicating a traditional religious response.

Ideological Scale
1. Do you believe that the world will come to an end according to the will of God?
   *1. Yes, I believe this.
    2. I am uncertain about this.
    3. No, I do not believe this.

2. Which of the following statements most clearly describes your idea about the Deity?
   *1. I believe in a Divine God, creator of the Universe, who knows my innermost thoughts and feelings, and to whom one day I shall be accountable.
    2. I believe in a power greater than myself, which some people call God and some people call Nature.
    3. I believe in the worth of humanity but not in a God or a Supreme Being.
    4. The so-called universal mysteries are ultimately knowable according to the scientific method based on natural laws.

    5. I am not quite sure what I believe.
    6. I am an atheist.

3. Do you believe that it is necessary for a person to repent before God will forgive his sins?
   *1. Yes, God's forgiveness comes only after repentance.
    2. No, God does not demand repentance.
    3. I am not in need of repentance.

4. Which one of the following best expresses your opinion of God acting in history?
   *1. God has and continues to act in the history of mankind.
    2. God acted in previous periods but is not active at the present time.
    3. God does not act in human history.

5. Which of the following best expresses your view of the Bible?
   *1. The Bible is God's Word and all it says is true.
   *2. The Bible was written by men inspired by God, and its basic moral and religious teachings are true, but because writers were men, it contains some human errors.
    3. The Bible is a valuable book because it was written by wise and good men, but God had nothing to do with it.
    4. The Bible was written by men who lived so long ago that it is of little value today.

Intellectual Scale
1. How do you personally view the story of creation as recorded in Genesis?
   *1. Literally true history.
    2. A symbolic account which is no better or worse than any other account of the beginning.
    3. Not a valid account of creation.

2. Which of the following best expresses your opinion concerning miracles?
   *1. I believe the report of the miracles in the Bible; that is, they occurred through a setting aside of natural laws by a higher power.
    2. I do not believe in the so-called miracles of the Bible. Either such events did not occur at all, or, if they did, the report is inaccurate, and they could be explained upon scientific grounds if we had the actual facts.
    3. I neither believe nor disbelieve the so-called miracles of the Bible. No evidence which I have considered seems to prove conclusively that they did or did not happen as recorded.

3. What is your view of the following statement: Religious truth is higher than any other form of truth.
   *1. Strongly agree
   *2. Agree
    3. Disagree
    4. Strongly disagree

4. Would you write the names of the four Gospels?
   What are the first five books of the Old Testament?
   (The second question was used for Jewish respondents.)
   *Three or more books correctly identified.

Ritualistic Scale
1. Do you feel it is possible for an individual to develop a well-rounded religious life apart from the institutional church?
   *1. No
    2. Uncertain
    3. Yes

2. How much time during a week would you say you spend reading the Bible and other religious literature?
   *1. One hour or more
   *2. One-half hour
   3. None

3. How many of the past four Sabbath worship services have you attended?
   *1. Three or more
   *2. Two
   3. One
   4. None

4. Which of the following best describes your participation in the act of prayer?
   *1. Prayer is a regular part of my behavior.
   *2. I pray primarily in times of stress and/or need, but not much otherwise.
   3. Prayer is restricted pretty much to formal worship services.
   4. Prayer is only incidental to my life.
   5. I never pray.

5. Do you believe that for your marriage the ceremony should be performed by:
   *1. A religious official.
   2. Either a religious official or a civil authority.
   3. A civil authority.

Experiential Scale
1. Would you say that one's religious commitment gives life a certain purpose which it could not otherwise have?
   *1. Strongly agree
   2. Agree
   3. Disagree

2. All religions stress that belief normally includes some experience of "union" with the Divine. Are there particular moments when you feel "close" to the Divine?
   *1. Frequently
   *2. Occasionally
   3. Rarely
   4. Never

3. Would you say that religion offers a sense of security in the face of death which is not otherwise possible?
   *1. Agree
   2. Uncertain
   3. Disagree

4. How would you respond to the statement: "Religion provides the individual with an interpretation of his existence which could not be discovered by reason alone."
   *1. Strongly agree
   *2. Agree
   3. Disagree

5. Faith, meaning putting full confidence in the things we hope for and being certain of things we cannot see, is essential to one's religious life.
   *1. Agree
   2. Uncertain
   3. Disagree

Consequential Scale

1. What is your feeling about the operation of nonessential businesses on the Sabbath?
   *1. They should not be open.
   2. I am uncertain about this.
   3. They have a legitimate right to be open.

2. A boy and a girl, both of whom attend church frequently, regularly date one another and have entered into sexual relations with each other. Do you feel that people who give at least partial support to the church by attending its worship services should behave in this manner? Which of the following statements expresses your opinion concerning this matter?
   *1. People who identify themselves with the church to the extent that they participate in its worship services should uphold its moral teachings as well.
   2. Sexual intercourse prior to marriage is a matter of individual responsibility.

3. Two candidates are seeking the same political office. One is a member and a strong participant in a church. The other candidate is indifferent, but not hostile, to religious organizations. Other factors being equal, do you think the candidate identified with the church would be a better public servant than the one who has no interest in religion?
   *1. He definitely would.
   *2. He probably would.
   3. Uncertain.
   4. He probably would not.
   5. He definitely would not.

4. Suppose you are living next door to a person who confides in you that each year he puts down on his income tax a $50.00 contribution to the church in "loose change," even though he knows that while he does contribute *some* money to the church in "loose change" each year, the total sum is far below that amount. Do you feel that a person's religious orientation should be reflected in all phases of his life so that such behavior is morally wrong—that it is a form of lying?
   *1. Yes
   2. Uncertain
   3. No

Faulkner, J. E., & DeJong, G. (1966). Religiosity in 5-D: An empirical analysis. *Social Forces, 45,* 246–254. Copyrigth © 1966 University of North Carolina Press. Reprinted with permission.

8.6
LOVE AND GUILT-ORIENTED DIMENSIONS OF CHRISTIAN BELIEF
(McConahay & Hough, 1973)

Reviewed by Leslie J. Francis

Variable: The Love and Guilt-Oriented Dimensions Scale attempts "to distinguish types of religious belief based upon the theological content of belief." The resulting instrument distinguishes between love-oriented and guilt-oriented interpretations of atonement in Christianity. To these dimensions is added an index of culture-oriented or conventional religiosity.

Description: Centering their typology around the meaning of atonement in Christianity, involving notions of love, guilt, and forgiveness, the authors hypothesized four types of religious belief. The *guilt-oriented extrapunitive* dimension characterizes individuals who emphasize punishment for evildoers, vengeance, triumph of the righteous, and their own certain identification with the forces of good. The *guilt-oriented intropunitive* dimension characterizes individuals who emphasize punishment for evildoers and vengeance, and their own identification with unworthiness, badness, and guilt. The *love-oriented self-centered* dimension characterizes individuals who emphasize the benevolence of God and the complete forgiveness of their own sins. The *love-oriented other-centered* dimension characterizes individuals who emphasize the common humanity of all persons as creatures of God and God's loving redemption of the whole world. To these four understandings of atonement, the authors added a fifth dimension, which they styled *culture-oriented, the conventional.* The conventionally religious were hypothesized to hold values that are more culturally than theologically oriented. Such individuals would argue that their children should attend church to prepare them to be good citizens.

A pool of 48 items was generated from an unspecified number of conversations with members of Southern Baptist and United Church of Christ congregations and from "previous experience." There were 10 items for each of the guilt-love scales and 8 items for the culture-oriented scale. These items were then assessed on a 5-point Likert scale by 160 white seminary students in Southern California. Item rest of test correlations were computed for the items selected to represent each of the five hypothesized dimensions.

The sets of items constructed to assess the *love-oriented self-centered, love-oriented other-centered*, and *culture-oriented, the conventional* dimensions all produced satisfactory item rest of test correlations. The best five items were selected in each case. The *guilt-oriented extrapunitive* and *guilt-oriented intropunitive* sets of items functioned less satisfactorily. The two sets of items were therefore collapsed and the best five selected to produce a *guilt-oriented* scale.

In its present form the instrument contains 20 items, 5 items for each of four scales styled as: *guilt-oriented, love-oriented self-centered, love-oriented other-centered*, and *conventional religiosity.* Each item is assessed on a 5-point scale anchored as follows: definitely agree, tend to agree, neither agree nor disagree, tend to disagree, and definitely disagree. Scale scores are computed as a product of the respective items. This means that scores on the four scales range between 5 and 25. In each case a high score indicates agreement with the dimension being assessed and a low score means disagreement with the dimension being assessed.

Practical Considerations: This paper-and-pencil measure requires no special examiner skill to administer or score. Minimal instructions are provided or necessary. Although the theoretical debate underlying the development of this instrument remains highly relevant, the operational form may be heavily constrained by the generation and location of its development. Some contemporary groups may feel alienated by the noninclusive use of language.

Norms/standardisation: Using the original sample of 160 seminarians, the authors published the following mean scores: guilt-oriented scale, 14.80 (*SD*, 4.85); love-oriented self-centered scale, 14.62 (*SD*, 3.36); love-oriented other-centered scale, 18.22 (*SD*, 3.51); conventional religiosity scale, 12.85 (*SD*, 3.52).

Reliability: The authors reported the following alpha coefficients: guilt-oriented scale, .807; love-oriented self-centered scale, .561; love-oriented other-centered scale, .533; conventional religiosity scale, .660. For the guilt-oriented scale, item rest of test correlations ranged between .52 and .62. For the love-oriented self-centered scale, item rest of test correlations ranged between .22 and .43. For the love-oriented other-centered scale, item rest of test correlations ranged between .27 and .40. For the conventional religiosity scale, item rest of test correlations ranged between .29 and .48.

Validity: No factor analysis was undertaken to assess the independence of the hypothesized dimensions. Intercorrelations show that the guilt-oriented scale correlates +.48 with the love-oriented self-centered scale, +.47 with the conventional religiosity scale, and −.46 with the love-oriented other-centered scale. The love-oriented self-centered scale correlated +.34 with the conventional religiosity scale and −.06 with the love-oriented other-centered scale.

Construct validity was examined by correlation with a measure of attitude toward church involvement in social action. As hypothesized, there was a positive correlation between this measure and the love-oriented other-centered scale (+.53), but negative correlations between this measure and the love-oriented self-centered scale (−.31), the guilt-oriented scale (−.52) and the conventional religiosity scale (−.27).

In a subsequent analysis, McConahay and Hough (1976) demonstrated positive correlations between symbolic racism and the conventional religiosity scale (+.41), the guilt- oriented scale (+.32) and the love-oriented self-centered scale (+.22), but a negative correlation between symbolic racism and the love-oriented other-centered scale (−.24).

Location:

McConahay, J. B., & Hough, J. C., Jr. (1973). Love and guilt-oriented dimensions of Christian belief. *Journal for the Scientific Study of Religion, 12,* 53–64.

Subsequent Research:

McConahay, J. B., & Hough, J. C., Jr. (1976). Symbolic racism. *Journal of Social Issues, 32*(2), 23–45.

Watson, P. J., Hood, R. W., Foster, S. J., & Morris, R. J. (1988). Sin, depression and narcissism. *Review of Religious Research, 29,* 295–305.

Watson, P. J., Hood, R. W., & Morris, J. R. (1985). Religiosity, sin and self-esteem. *Journal of Psychology and Theology, 13,* 116–128.

Watson, P. J., Morris, R. J., & Hood, R.W. (1987). Antireligious humanistic values, guilt and self-esteem. *Journal for the Scientific Study of Religion, 26,* 535–546.

Watson, P. J., Morris, R. J., & Hood, R. W. (1988). Sin and self-functioning, part 1: grace, guilt and self-consciousness. *Journal of Psychology and Theology, 16,* 245–269.

Watson, P. J., Morris, R. J., & Hood, R. W. (1989). Intrinsicness, religious self-love, and narcissism. *Journal of Psychology and Christianity, 8* (1), 31–37.

Watson, P. J., Morris, R. J., & Hood, R. W. (1990). Extrinsic scale factors: correlations and construction of religious orientation types. *Journal of Psychology and Christianity, 9* (3), 35–46.

Appendix

Love and Guilt-Oriented Dimensions of Christian Belief

Please use the following scale to indicate the extent to which you agree with each item below.

    1 = definitely disagree   4 = tend to agree
    2 = tend to disagree   5 = definitely agree
    3 = neither agree nor disagree

Guilt-Oriented Scale

1. The fires of Hell are the right place for adulterers, murderers, drunkards, and other persons who violate God's laws.
2. The thought of God's anger should strike terror in the hearts of wild livers.
3. Whatever God's punishment for me, I have no doubt that I deserve it.
4. At the final judgment, we can be sure that those who sin in this life will be exposed.
5. Nobody in the world is really good, least of all am I.

Love-Oriented Self-Centered Scale

6. The way the world can be changed is for each man to know that God loves him.

7. The important thing in religion to me is the knowledge that God loves me like a father loves his children.
8. When I have trouble, all I have to do is pray to God, who loves me, and he will help.
9. Heaven is my home, and so I do not worry about this world.
10. The main thing that Jesus taught was that God loves individual human beings just as they are.

Love-Oriented Other-Centered Scale

11. The greatest sin is man's sin against his fellow man.
12. There is a goodness in man, even in the worst of us which is put there by God and which cannot be destroyed.
13. If a man wants to serve God, let him serve mankind.
14. We are all part of each other, because God's love for us is bound up in his love for others.
15. It is love and not wrath that is the essence of the nature of God.

Conventional Religiosity Scale

16. Americans who are really good Americans are interested in the church.
17. I want my children to have the experience of church attendance to prepare them to be good citizens.
18. A religious man should be thrifty and honest, clean and hard working.
19. A great advantage of churches is the friendly atmosphere they provide for one's associations with the right kind of people.
20. One of the marks of a good family is that they attend church somewhere, especially at Christmas and Easter.

McConahay, J. B., & Hough, J. C. (1973). Love and guilt-oriented dimensions of Christian belief. *Journal for the Scientific Study of Religion, 12,* 53–64. Copyright © 1973. Journal for the Scientific Study of Religion. Reprinted with permission.

8.7
RELIGION AND PHILOSOPHY OF LIFE ATTITUDES SCALE
(Funk, 1955, 1958)

Reviewed by Bernard Spilka and Kevin L. Ladd

Variable: The Attitudes Toward Religion and Philosophy of Life Survey is a set of seven scales designed to assess relationships between various aspects of individual religion among college students. These are measures of Religious Conflict, Philosophy of Life, Hostility toward the Church, Religious Tranquility, Religious Solace, and Change of Religious Attitudes. It also contains a modified version of the Myers (1952) Orthodoxy Scale.

Description: The scales are defined as follows:

1. *Religious Conflict.* (22 items). This is defined as "simultaneous tendencies to react in opposing and incompatible ways to the same religious attitude object" (Funk, 1958, p. 240).
2. *Religious Orthodoxy.* (9 items). Five of Meyers (1952) originally developed items were supplemented by four new statements. Orthodoxy is conceptualized as "the tendency to accept the teachings of religious authorities, and conform to prescribed religious practices" (Funk, 1958, p. 240).
3. *Philosophy of Life.* (5 items). This is defined as "an integrated system of

meanings and purposes which relates the individuals goals to the goals of humanity and the wider structure of the universe" (Funk, 1958, p. 241). This may or may not involve religion.

4. *Hostility toward the Church.* (6 items). This is denoted as "aggression or withdrawal toward religious attitude objects" (Funk, 1958, p. 242).

5. *Religious Tranquility.* (6 items). Religious tranquility is said to "characterize the attitude of those who see religion, not as a compensation, but an aid to happiness and favorable socio-psychological adjustment" (Funk, 1958, p. 242).

6. *Religious Solace.* (7 items). This measure assesses the "use of religion as a means of compensating for the unhappiness and disappointments of life" (Funk, 1958, p. 242).

7. *Change of Religious Attitudes.* (10 items). This measure was designed to assess the "stability or instability of religious beliefs since college entrance" (Funk, 1958, p. 243).

Practical Considerations. Administering a 65-item instrument might be regarded as rather demanding and time-consuming. One may however select among the scales and employ those that are appropriate to one's theoretical stance. Taking the items out of context, placing them in a different order, and considering that this overall measure was primarily utilized about 40 years ago, researchers should recompute reliabilities and also reexamine issues of validity. Scoring is quite simple (true and false), and no special training is required.

Norms/Standardization: The scales were administered to 255 Purdue University undergraduates and were developed on this sample. Essentially no further data are available on the use of this instrument. The items for all scales were randomly mixed in the final survey.

Reliability: Only test-retest reliabilities for a three-week period are available. Generally, these look good, but there is need to

examine internal consistency. The coefficients for the scales are as follows: Religious Conflict (.84), Religious Orthodoxy (.95), Philosophy of Life (.81), Hostility toward the Church (.88), Religious Tranquility (.84), Religious Solace (.87), and Change of Religious Attitudes (.90).

Validity: The individual scales are likely to correlate highly, and therefore, the face validity of the various instruments must be doubted. In all likelihood, they would reduce to a smaller set of item composites if treated factor-analytically.

Construct and content validity for the Religious Conflict Scale is supported by a highly significant .43 correlation with the Taylor Manifest Anxiety Scale (Taylor, 1953). It also correlates significantly and negatively with orthodoxy. Shaw and Wright (1967) question the distinctiveness of the Religious Solace and Religious Tranquility scales from each other. In addition, the Hostility toward the Church scale comes across more as a general hostility toward religion. The meaning of the change of attitude scores is in considerable doubt since the original stance of the respondents is not known. Overall, lack of use of these instruments severely limits our knowledge of their validity.

Location:

Funk, R. A. (1955). *A survey of religious attitudes and manifest anxiety in a college population.* Unpubl. Doctoral Dissertation, Purdue University.

Funk, R. A. (1958). Experimental scales used in a study of religious attitudes as related to manifest anxiety. *Psychological Newsletter, 9,* 238–244.

References

Myers, M. S. (1952). The latent role of religious orientation. *Studies in Higher Education, Purdue University,* No. 78.

Shaw, M. E., & Wright, J. M. (1967). *Scales for the measurement of attitudes.* New York: McGraw-Hill.

Taylor, J. A. (1953). A personality scale of manifest anxiety. *Journal of Abnormal and Social Psychology, 48,* 285–290.

Appendix

A Survey of Attitudes toward Religion and Philosophy of Life

Instructions: This inventory consists of numbered statements. Read each statement and decide whether it is *true as applied to you or false as applied to you*. If the question is multiple choice, blacken in the space corresponding to your choice.

You are to make your answers on the answer sheet you have. If a statement is *true or mostly true*, as applied to you, blacken between the lines in the column headed T. If a statement is *false or not usually true* as applied to you, blacken between the lines in the column headed F.

Religious Conflict Scale

1. I cannot decide what to believe about religion.
10. I sometimes wonder just what life is all about and why we are here.
12. I am actively trying to decide by reading or other means what the truth is about religion.
14. At times I have felt guilty because of my religious upbringing.
20. I sometimes feel disloyal to my parents because I cannot entirely accept their religious beliefs.
24. I wish I was perfectly sure of my belief in God.
26. I am not as strict in my religious practices as I feel I should be.
28. My church is too strict.
38. There are too many things about religion that I don't understand.
42. I am in danger of losing my faith.
44. Sometimes I feel guilty because of my lack of faith.
46. Education has led me to question some teachings of my church.
50. Sometimes I believe in Hell and sometimes I don't.
56. I wish I could be sure my religious beliefs are correct.
60. Contradictory religious ideas make one wonder which ones to accept.
64. I feel that I shouldn't question my religion, but I sometimes do, anyway.
66. I feel that I should be more religious than I am.
68. I might be happier if I did not believe in my religion.
72. I wish I did not believe in Hell, but I do
76. I sometimes wonder why God lets terrible things happen to people.
84. It is hard to reconcile science with religion.
86. Although basically I believe in my religion, my faith often wavers.

The Orthodoxy Scale

1.(a) I believe in the basic teachings of my church and attend regularly.
4. I believe firmly in the teachings of my church.
6. I never doubt the teachings of the church.
90. I believe that religious faith is better than logic for solving life's important problems.
92. I believe our fate in the hereafter depends on how we behave on earth.
94. I believe God knows our every thought and movement.
96. I believe God controls everything that happens everywhere.
98. I think my prayers are answered.
    a. Always (2)   b. Sometimes (1)
100. I attend church
    a. Once a week or more (2)   b. Once a month or more (1)

Each true response = 1; Note on 98 and 100, scores of 2 and 1.

Philosophy of Life Scale

1.(d) I do not believe in any particular religion; instead I have a philosophy of life. (If checked, score as 2.)
8. Although at one time I believed in a religion, I now believe in a code of ethics.
62. If you are a strong person, you do not need religion.
82. Promoting a better world is more important to me than religion is.
88. We make our own heaven or hell here on earth.

The Religious Tranquility Scale

30. Religion has brought me peace of mind.
32. Religion's chief purpose is to make people happy.
40. Religion makes me feel safe and secure.
70. Religion helps me to be a better person.
74. I feel secure in the knowledge that God is always with me.
80. I believe in a merciful God, not a punishing one.

Religious Solace Scale

16. Religion helps me when I feel blue.
18. Some unhappy experiences have made me turn to God for help.
22. Sometimes religion is the only thing we can rely on.
34. If I were to lose my belief in God, there would be little comfort left.
36. I feel a strong need to believe in God.
52. You can always turn to God when you are in trouble.
78. At times only my belief in God has prevented me from feeling hopeless.

Hostility to the Church Scale

1.(e) I believe that religion is of little use in present-day society. (If answered true, score as 2.)
2. I am indifferent to the subject of religion.
48. I have little use for religion.
54. Religion has not kept pace with the times.
58. Religion has too often been used to promote prejudice.
82. Promoting a better world is more important to me than religion is.

Item 82 also contributes to the Philosophy of Life Scale score.

Religious Attitude Change Scale

(Here are a number of beliefs. Please indicate, by checking the appropriate column, whether your attitude toward each is the same (S), partly different (P), or very different (D) from what it was when you entered college).

Item no. Item	S	P	D
104. The church	———	———	———
105. A personal God	———	———	———
106. The immortality of the soul	———	———	———
107. Hell	———	———	———
108. Heaven	———	———	———
109. Adam and Eve	———	———	———
110. Angels	———	———	———
111. The divine inspiration of the Bible	———	———	———

112. The power of prayer   ___   ___   ___

113. The divine authority of the church   ___   ___   ___

Item D is checked, score as 2; P is scored as 1; $S = 0$.

Note: Items for all scales were randomly mixed in the final survey, and a true-false response mode was employed. A separate standard IBM true-false answer sheet was used. The original item numbers are presented above as a guide to mixing the items.

Funk, R. A. (1958). Experimental scales used in a study of religious attitudes as related to manifest anxiety. *Psychological Newsletter, 9,* 238–244. Copyright © 1958 Psychological Newsletter. Reprinted with permission.

8.8
RELIGIOSITY MEASURE (Rohrbaugh & Jessor, 1975)
Reviewed by Michael J. Boivin

Variable: The Religiosity Measure was developed in an attempt to evaluate the impact of religion on the respondent's daily, secular life as well as to determine the extent of individual participation in ritual practices. The emphasis is on one's cognitive orientation concerning a transcendent reality. The measure is intended to be applicable to religiosity in general. No particular religious affiliation or denominational creed is assumed.

Description: Glock's (1959) four dimensions of religiosity (ritual, consequential, ideological, and experiential) were operationalized in two-item subscales, yielding an eight-item multiple-choice instrument. Each item is scored from 0 (option indicating least religiosity) to 4 (option indicating greatest religiosity) with the exception of the "attendance at religious services" question. This item was categorized according to four meaningful breaks in the response distribution. The maximum score for each of the four subscales is 8 with a total possible score of 32 for the subscales combined.

Some of the items are reverse worded and can be randomly ordered to minimize any kind of obvious systematic structure. Items of an ideological nature contain the verb "believe," whereas experiential items are oriented towards "feelings." Items pertaining to ritual participation are behavioral in nature.

Practical Considerations: The instrument is easy to administer and is relatively short. The level of reading competency needed to take the instrument is a high school range reading competency.

Norms/Standardization: In their original study, Rohrbaugh and Jessor initially contacted a random sample of 2,220 students stratified by sex and grade level at several junior and senior high schools in a small city located in the Rocky Mountain region. Of those, 949 provided individual and parental consent and were included in the study. The college sample was drawn from a random selection of 497 freshman students on a freshman registration list from the College of Arts and Sciences at a large university in the Rocky Mountain region. Of the designated sample, 276 participated in their freshman year and formed the cohort sample that was monitored longitudinally throughout their college experience. High school females (mean = 17.2) and high school males (mean = 15.2) scored significantly higher than their same-sex counterparts in college (college female mean = 12.7; college male mean = 12.5). Rohrbaugh and Jessor also present mean religiosity scores for their sample partitioned on the basis of such descriptors as gender, high school versus college, length of involvement with marijuana, length of sexual involvement, and social activism status.

Reliability: Cronbach coefficient alphas were over .90, indicating high internal consistency for the instrument. The measure was unidimensional and homogeneous, as indicated by an average of .55 for Homogeneity Ratios (Scott, 1960).

Validity: In terms of construct validity, females were consistently more religious than males and high school-age students were more religious than college age, indicating good construct validity with other consistent findings in the field. In their survey, Rohrbaugh and Jessor (1975) also asked subjects to note their overall religiosity on a 10-point linear rating scale. The overall religiosity score from the present instrument correlated well with this self-rating (college males $r = 0.78$, college females $r = 0.81$, high school males $r = 0.83$, high school females $r = 0.84$). Strong internal validity was indicated by the four subscales for the four student groups having an overall average correlation matrix coefficient value of 0.69. Finally, a discriminant validity analysis indicated that this instrument assessed the personal religious orientation of the individual, and was not primarily the result of his/her identification with an external religious network or social structure.

Location:
Rohrbaugh, J., & Jessor, R. (1975). Religiosity in youth: A personal control against deviant behavior. *Journal of Personality, 43,* 136–155.

Subsequent Research:
Demaria, T., & Kassinove, H. (1988). Predicting guilt from irrational beliefs, religious affiliation and religiosity. *Journal of Rational-Emotive and Cognitive-Behavior Therapy.* 6(4), 259–272.

Friedberg, B. A., & Friedberg, R. D. (1985). Locus of control and religiosity in college students. *Psychological Reports, 56,* 757–758.

Heintzelman, H. E. (1976). Relationship between religious orthodoxy and three personality variables. *Psychological Reports, 38, 756–758.*

References:

Glock, C. (1959). The religious revival in America? In J. Zahn (Ed.) *Religion and the face of America.* Berkeley: University of California Press.

Scott, W. A. (1960). Measures of test homogeneity. *Educational and Psychological Measurements, 20, 751–757.*

Appendix

Religiosity Measures Questionnaire

Instructions: The following questionnaire consists of seven multiple-choice items with one fill-in-the-blank item. Please answer the following questions by *circling* the appropriate letter for the multiple-choice items and providing the most accurate number for the fill-in-the-blank question.

Ritual Religiosity

1. How many times have you attended religious services during the past year? _____ times.

2. Which of the following best describes your practice of prayer or religious meditation?

    a. Prayer is a regular part of my daily life.
    b. I usually pray in times of stress or need but rarely at any other time.
    c. I pray only during formal ceremonies.
    d. I never pray.

Consequential Religiosity

3. When you have a serious personal problem, how often do you take religious advice or teaching into consideration?

   a. Almost always
   b. Usually
   c. Sometimes
   d. Never

4. How much influence would you say that religion has on the way that you choose to act and the way that you choose to spend your time each day?

   a. No influence
   b. A small influence
   c. Some influence
   d. A fair amount of influence
   e. A large influence

Theological Religiosity

5. Which of the following statements comes closest to your belief about God?

   a. I am sure that God really exists and that He is active in my life.
   b. Although I sometimes question His existence, I do believe in God and believe He knows of me as a person.
   c. I don't know if there is a personal God, but I do believe in a higher power of some kind.
   d. I don't know if there is a personal God or a higher power of some kind, and I don't know if I ever will.
   e. I don't believe in a personal God or in a higher power.

6. Which one of the following statements comes closest to your belief about life after death (immortality)?

   a. I believe in a personal life after death, a soul existing as a specific individual spirit.
   b. I believe in a soul existing after death as a part of a universal spirit.
   c. I believe in a life after death of some kind, but I really don't know what it would be like.
   d. I don't know whether there is any kind of life after death, and I don't know if I will ever know.
   e. I don't believe in any kind of life after death.

Experiential Religiosity

7. During the past year, how often have you experienced a feeling of religious reverence or devotion?

   a. Almost daily
   b. Frequently
   c. Sometimes
   d. Rarely
   e. Never

8. Do you agree with the following statement? "Religion gives me a great amount of comfort and security in life."

a. Strongly disagree
b. Disagree
c. Uncertain
d. Agree
e. Strongly Agree

Rohrbaugh, J., & Jessor, R. (1975). Religiosity in youth: A personal control against deviant behavior. *Journal of Personality, 43,* 136–155. Copyright © 1975 by Blackwell Publishers, Malden, MA. Reprinted with permission.

8.9
RELIGIOUS ATTITUDE INVENTORY (BROEN, 1957)

Reviewed by Kevin L. Ladd & Bernard Spilka

Variable: The Religious Attitude Inventory (RAI) is an early attempt to study religion as a multidimensional construct. Broen (1957a, 1957b) sought to identify how an individual's religious attitude might be composed of several relatively independent, differentially weighted aspects.

Description: No particular theory was cited as a driving force behind the development of the RAI. The scale is most noted as an attempt to distinguish between two broad types of religiosity: a "nearness of God" perspective (where high scores emphasize the Deity's loving presence and guidance) and a "fundamentalism-humanitarianism" view (where high scores emphasize humanity's sinfulness and the need for a punishing God). Gorsuch and Smith (1983) provided a revised edition of each dimension (see 11.6 and 12.2 in this volume), retaining only those items that appear to transcend the cultural and theological shifts during that twenty-five year interval.

Practical Considerations: The 58 item scale is easily administered. This paper and pencil instrument requires approximately 10–15 minutes to complete. However, reliability and validity apparently remain untested beyond the original study (see *Reliability* and *Validity*). Additionally, the user must be aware of the fact that responses in 1957 to items such as "Dancing is a sin" or "All public places of amusement should be closed on Sunday" may well be different half a century later.

Norms/Standardization: Broen first hypothesized the existence of five fairly discrete religious types: (a) those who stress sin, (b) individuals who need religion to fill a void, (c) emphasizers of moral aspects of religion, (d) highlighters of God's love and glory, and (e) "spirit-filled" practitioners of glossolalia. Through a variety of selection techniques, a total of 133 statements regarding God's nature and human relationships with God were identified as representing these categories.

Five groups of four people each were chosen to represent the above noted types; four other individuals, deemed "moderate" Catholics and Lutherans, composed a sixth group. These 20 participants Q-sorted the 133 items into nine groups along a continuum of agree—disagree. A normal distribution was forced; each of the nine groups had a predetermined limit on the number of items it could contain (i.e., 2–7–15–26–33–26–15–7–2). The sort vectors were then correlated between subjects to provide a matrix that was used to perform an inverse (Q) factor analysis.[1]

---

[1]For a thorough explanation of this technique, see a text such as Guertin and Bailey (1970).

Two primary factors emerged initially (r = .32); four were carried into rotation to increase the stability of the final loadings of subjects on the two main factors. Subjects were then divided into two sets for each factor, depending on whether they loaded high or low on the two main factors of interest. Average Q-sort placements for each of the 133 statements were next calculated for each of the four sets of subjects. Those items having the greatest mean differences and least overlap between high and low loading below (see appendix). An examination of these statements resulted in general factor descriptions: (a) nearness to God and (b) fundamentalism-humanitarianism. The RAI thus derived is presented as a dichotic choice instrument: agree or disagree. With the item numbers from the instrument (see appendix), the factors were constructed as follows:

FACTOR 1 (Nearness of God)
Agree statements
1 5 9 13 17 21 25 29 33 37 40 43 46 48 50
Disagree statements
3 7 11 15 19 23 27 31 35
FACTOR 2 (Fundamentalism-Humanitarianism)
Agree statements
2 6 10 14 18 22 26 30 34 38 41 44 47 49 51
Disagree statements
4 8 12 16 20 24 28 32 36 39 42 45
Reported As Belonging to Both Factors
52 54 55 (Disagree = Factor 1; Agree = Factor 2)
58 (Agree = Factor 1; Disagree = Factor 2)
53 (Agree = Factors 1 & 2)
56 57 (Disagree = Factors 1 & 2)

T tests were introduced as evidence for the utility of (a) a summation of all "agree" responses as a measure of general religiosity which discriminated between groups and (b) a measure of religious emphasis obtained as a difference score between mean "agree" responses on the two factors.

Reliability: Several issues address the reliability Broen's factors. First, the loadings do not inspire great confidence. Though Factor 2 reports adequate reliability loadings, 8 of 14 loadings on Factor 1 are .42 or less. This pattern begs further exploration with additional samples.

Second, the exact parameters used to reduce the initial 133 statements to arrive at the final 58 are not clear. A refactoring of the original 133 items could serve the purpose of verifying the accuracy of these final choices.

It is also not made clear why, when both positive and negative aspects of the two factors are represented in the 58 statements, only "agree" responses are used in determining general religiosity or religious emphases. Since the dichotic choice already severely limits potential variance, it would seem advantageous to reverse score the appropriate endorsements of "disagree" items.

Validity: Cross-validation was attempted using 113 participants from 4 religious orientations. Summations of "agree" responses were made for each factor's constituent items. On this basis, eight t tests were presented as indications that groups of people respond differentially to the two factors. (These remain significant after applying a Bonferroni correction to the alpha level.)

Such a procedure does not help to better understand the actual structure of the two factors. Further investigation may help to clarify the factor composition.

This "cross-validation" procedure also shifts from an idiographic to a topological level of analysis. Strictly speaking, the comparison is not one of equals; it is not fully apparent how the differences between groups address the issue of an individual's unique pattern. In fact, the intentional selection of individuals to compose the different groups probably overestimates the discriminative properties of the RAI.

While such aspects of Broen's methodology raise questions, the overall approach is intriguing. Much research in the psychology of religion focuses on nomothetic descriptions or generalized individual differences.

Broen's research paradigm is predominately one of idiographic depictions. His approach illustrates how different facets of religiosity may combine to form a single individual's predilections. This focus is one that is very beneficial and is to be encouraged if we wish to describe real people instead of a mythical average.

Location:

Broen, W. E., Jr. (1957a). A factor-analytic study of religious attitudes. *Journal of Abnormal and Social Psychology, 54,* (2), 176–179.

Subsequent Research:

Gorsuch, R. L., & Smith, C. S. (1983). Attributions of responsibility to God: An interaction of religious beliefs and outcomes. *Journal for the Scientific Study of Religion, 22,* 340–352.

References

Broen, W. E., Jr. (1957a). A factor-analytic study of religious attitudes. *Journal of Abnormal and Social Psychology, 54,* (2), 176–179.

Broen, W. E., Jr. (1957b). Factor I key: Religious attitude inventory. American Documentation Institute, Auxiliary Publications Project, Photoduplication Service, Library of Congress, Washington, D. C., Document 5066.

Gorsuch, R. L., & Smith, C. S. (1983). Attributions of responsibility to God: An interaction of religious beliefs and outcomes. *Journal for the Scientific Study of Religion, 22,* 340–352.

Guertin, W. H., & Bailey, J. P., Jr. (1970). *Introduction to modern factor analysis.* Ann Arbor, MI: Edwards Brothers.

Stevens, J. (1992). *Applied multivariate statistics for the social sciences.* Hillsdale, N. J.: Lawrence Earlbaum.

Appendix

Religious Attitude Inventory

Instructions: Circle the *A* if you agree with a statement; circle the *D* if you disagree with the statement. Make a choice for each statement. Do not spend too much time on any one statement. A person who does not believe in the existence of a God may have difficulty in answering a statement such as "God watches over us." (Disagree might be interpreted as meaning "There *is* a God who does not watch over us.") If you do not believe in the existence of a God, show your disagreement with the *concept* by circling the disagree when you come to such a statement.

A D   1. God is constantly with us.

A D   2. Christ died for sinners.

A D   3. The Ten Commandments were good for people of olden times but are really not applicable to modern life.

A D   4. There is really no such place as Hell.

A D   5. Miracles are performed by the power of God even today.

A D   6. It is through the righteousness of Jesus Christ and not because of our own works that we are made righteous before God.

A D   7. Dancing is a sin.

A D   8. Christ's simple message of concern for your fellow man has been twisted by the superstitious mysticism of such men as Paul.

A D   9. God can be approached directly by all believers.

A D   10. The death of Christ on the cross was necessary to blot out man's sin and make him acceptable in the eyes of God.

A D   11. It was too bad that Christ died so young or He could have been a greater power for good.

A D 12. "God" is an abstract concept roughly equivalent to the concept "nature."

A D 13. God exists in all of us.

A D 14. Man is born in sin.

A D 15. The wearing of fashionable dress and worldly adornment should be discontinued because it tends to gratify and encourage pride.

A D 16. Man's essential nature is good.

A D 17. I am sometimes very conscious of the presence of God.

A D 18. Man is by nature sinful and unclean.

A D 19. All public places of amusement should be closed on Sunday.

A D 20. The stories of miracles in the Bible are like the parables in that they have some deeper meaning or moral but are not to be taken literally.

A D 21. God is very real to me.

A D 22. The Bible is the word of God and must be believed in its entirety.

A D 23. I believe in God but I am not sure what I believe about Him.

A D 24. Man has a spark of the divine in him which must be made to blossom more fully.

A D 25. When in doubt it's best to stop and ask God what to do.

A D 26. Sin brings forth the wrath of God.

A D 27. A person should follow his own conscience in deciding right and wrong.

A D 28. The most important idea in religion is the golden rule.

A D 29. God should be asked about all important matters.

A D 30. The wrath of God is a terrible thing.

A D 31. It is more important to love your neighbor than to keep the Ten Commandments.

A D 32. The Scriptures should be interpreted with the constant exercise of reason.

A D 33. Because of His presence we can *know* that God exists.

A D 34. Everyone will be called before God at the judgment day to answer for his sins.

A D 35. Man's idea of God is quite vague.

A D 36. Reason is not depraved and untrustworthy for then the natural foundations of religion which rest upon it, would fall.

A D 37. Miracles are sometimes performed by persons in close communion with God.

A D 38. Everyone has sinned and deserves punishment for his sins.

A D 39. The church is important because it is an effective agency for organizing the social life of a community.

A D 40. My faith in God is complete, for "though He slay me yet will I trust Him."

A D 41. No one should question the authority of the Bible.

A D 42. The content of various doctrines is unimportant. What really matters is that they help those who believe in them to lead better lives.

A D 43. When the Scriptures are interpreted with reason, they will be found to be consistent with themselves and with nature.

A D 44. Because of his terrible sinfulness, man has been eternally damned unless he accepts Christ as his savior.

A D 45. Religion is a search for understanding, truth, love and beauty in human life.

A D 46. True love of God is shown in obedience to His moral laws.

A D 47. Every person born into this world deserves God's wrath and damnation.

A D 48. If we live as pure lives as we can, God will forgive our sins.

A D 49. The world is full of condemned sinners.

A D 50. Persons who are in close contact with the Holy Spirit can and do at times speak in unknown tongues.

A D 51. The Devil can enter a man's body and take control.

A D 52. The people of the world must repent before it is too late and they find themselves in Hell.

A D 53. No one who has experienced God like I have could doubt His existence.

A D 54. The Christian must lead a strict life, away from worldly amusements.

A D 55. In his natural state of sin, man is too evil to communicate with God.

A D 56. Christ was not divine but his teachings and the example set by his life are invaluable.

A D 57. The question of Christ's divinity is unimportant; it is his teachings that matter.

A D 58. God is the final judge of our behavior, but I do not believe that he is as punishing as some seem to say He is.

8.10
RELIGIOUS ATTITUDES SCALES (Maranell, 1974)
Reviewed by David M. Wulff

Variables: The Religious Attitudes Scales were designed to measure what are conceived of as eight dimensions of religiosity or religious attitudes: church orientation, ritualism, altruism, fundamentalism, theism, idealism, superstition, and mysticism. (1) *Church orientation* refers to positive attitudes toward and active involvement in the church, conceived mainly as a local institution. (2) *Ritualism* gives primacy to formal worship services that are carried out with precision and orderliness. (3) *Altruism* consists of concern for and helpfulness toward others and a corresponding valorization of the church's teachings against selfishness and individualism. (4) *Fundamentalism* is defined here primarily as biblical literalism and the conviction that the Bible is an infallible personal guide for living. (5) *Theism* designates an affirmation of the existence of God as a personal, omniscient, and omnipotent caretaker and guide. (6) *Idealism* is de-

fined as an uncompromising dedication to ideals and principles apart from any theistic assumptions. (7) *Superstition* refers to belief in ordinary superstitions, in astrology and psychic phenomena, and in ultimately mysterious spiritual forces. (8) *Mysticism* entails an affirmation of the possibility of ineffable knowledge of and union with God or some ultimate reality, which are thought to be attainable by means of silent waiting, meditation, or prayer.

Description: Each of the eight dimensions is represented by a 12-item scale. Four of the statements on the Church Orientation Scale as well as four on the Altruism Scale were taken from Thurstone and Chave's (1929) Attitude Toward the Church Scale. Similarly, four items on the Superstition Scale were borrowed from the Fascism (F) Scale developed by Adorno, Frenkel-Brunswik, Levinson, and Sanford (1950), and four on the Idealism scale were taken from still other sources. The scales may be individually administered or the 96 items may be randomly mixed, as the author himself chose to arrange them. Subjects respond to each item on a 5-point Likert scale that ranges from "strongly disagree" to "strongly agree," with the midpoint designated "undecided." Numerical equivalents to the five categories range from 0 to 4. Twenty-three of the items are reversed in their wording; scoring of these items is thus likewise reversed. Scores on each scale range from 0 to 48. A total religiosity score can also be derived, by averaging the individual's eight scale scores. Maranell used this mean scale score only for an initial ordering of the eleven denominational groups he studied.

Practical Considerations: There is no fixed format required for the administration of this instrument. On some occasions, the 5-point response scale was printed after each of the 96 statements. At other times, a test booklet with the randomly arranged statements was accompanied by a standardized answer sheet that could then be easily scored with a set of eight templates.

Maranell recommends that, in randomizing the questionnaire items, researchers should be careful not to begin the questionnaire with negative statements that might damage rapport with certain subjects. Maranell gives no indication of the order he himself employed. Users will have to format their own versions of the questionnaire and design their own scoring templates.

Norms/Standardization: Because this instrument was designed primarily for correlational and experimental research, no effort was made to develop formal norms for these scales. Yet Maranell (1974) does provide mean scores for various subject groupings, which were formed according to occupation, dwelling area, house type, educational level, and region of the country. Thus he does offer some basis for interpreting individual scores.

Reliability: Test-retest reliabilities were twice calculated for the eight scales, the first time with a one-week interval between administrations and the second time, using a different but likewise unspecified group of subjects, with an interval of one and a half weeks. In both cases the mean reliability coefficient—the coefficient of stability—was .87, with individual scales ranging in reliability from .68 to .99. Under both conditions, seven out of eight scales had reliabilities in the .80s or .90s.

Validity: To ensure the highest possible level of reliability and validity, Maranell constructed his scales using an item-analysis technique developed by Allen Edwards. For each scale, Maranell selected for his two criterion groups those students who fell either in the top or in the bottom 25% of the distribution of total scores. He then compared the item means for these two groups by using the statistic t, which measures the extent to which the two groups score differently on the item. Edwards proposed a minimum t of 1.75 for including an item on a scale; all of Maranell's 96 items meet this minimum requirement and t values typically range much higher. Following Maranell, scale items are listed at the end of this review in descending order of t values, which are listed to the right of each item.

Maranell asserts that the scale statements say what one would expect them to and thus that the scales have "face validity." Useful though this quality is for enlisting a subject's cooperation, it does not assure us that the instrument genuinely measures the variables after which its scales are named. Far more significant for assessing the scales' construct validity is the accumulation of research evidence that Maranell lays out in the chapters of his book. He features in particular the pattern of denominational differences that he found in a stratified random sample of clergy. On the total religiosity score, Catholic priests had a strikingly higher mean than the clergy in the other ten groups, and the Unitarian-Universalist ministers had a notably lower one; the clergy of the remaining nine denominations were only slightly distinguished from each other. On the individual scales, a diversity of patterns appeared. In some cases—the Ritualism Scale, for example, on which the Catholic and Episcopal clergy stood out from the rest—the pattern seems to confirm that the scale measures more or less what it is supposed to. In other cases, however, the trends raise questions about the scale's precise meaning.

On the Altruism Scale, to illustrate, the Catholic, Seventh Day Adventist, and Church of Christ clergy scored highest and the Lutheran, Episcopal, Presbyterian, and Unitarian-Universalist clergy scored lowest. While there may be some truth in Maranell's claim that these results reflect genuine differences in altruism resulting from exclusivistic tendencies or social class, an examination of the items on the Altruism Scale suggests that a high score does not reflect "unselfish concern for others" per se, but the conviction that the church is vital for overcoming human selfishness and that the respondent is interested in the church mainly "because of its work for moral and social reform." It is telling that, for all of the subject groups, the Altruism Scale tends to correlate more highly with the Fundamentalism Scale than with any of the others, including the Idealism Scale. Moreover, the Altruism Scale shows the same tendency to correlate positively with superpatriotic, authoritarian, and anticivil-liberty attitudes that appear for all of the other scales except Idealism. Only on anti-Black, anti-Semitic, and antiforeign attitudes does it consistently diverge from the others and join with the Idealism scale in opposition to these attitudes. And whereas the Idealism Scale correlates −.78 with a measure of general maladjustment, the Altruism Scale correlates a significant .37. This scale is obviously something more than a simple measure of altruism.

The Ritualism Scale, which shows an even stronger positive relation with politically conservative attitudes than the Fundamentalism Scale does, tends like some of the other scales to correlate positively with suggestibility, perceptual rigidity, anxiety, general maladjustment, dependency, and fanaticism, and negatively with scholastic aptitude, ego strength, and social desirability. Instead of representing a thoughtful appreciation for ritualization, as we find in the work of Erik Erikson (1977), the Ritualism Scale's emphasis on precision and orderliness tips the scale in the direction of what Erikson himself called ritualism, defined as a pathological distortion of playful ritualization. Thus any would-be user of Maranell's scales should carefully take into account the scale items themselves and the patterns of Maranell's findings instead of simply relying on the names of the scales.

Location:

Maranell, G. M. (1974). *Responses to religion: Studies in the social psychology of religious belief.* Lawrence: University Press of Kansas.

Subsequent Research: Maranell's (1974) book-length work sums up a series of research undertakings that were earlier reported in the journal literature. The scales have apparently not been used subsequently.

References

Adorno, T. W., Frenkel-Brunswik, E., Levinson, D. J., & Sanford, R. N. (1950). *The authoritarian personality.* New York: Harper & Brothers.

Christie, R., & Geis, F. A. (1970). *Studies in Machiavellianism.* New York: Academic.

Erikson, E. H. (1977). *Toys and reasons: Stages in ritualization of experience.* New York: W. W. Norton.

Thurstone, L. L., & Chave, E. J. (1929). *The measurement of attitude: A psychophysical method and some experiments with a scale for measuring attitude toward the church.* Chicago: University of Chicago Press.

Appendix

Maranell's Religiosity Scales

Please use the following scale to indicate the extent to which you agree with each statement:

0 = strongly disagree   1 = somewhat disagree   2 = undecided
3 = somewhat agree   4 = strongly agree

Note: Scoring for the items followed by (R) should be reversed.

Church Orientation Scale   *t value*

*1. I don't believe churchgoing will do anyone any harm.	6.65
*2. I believe in the church and its teachings because I have been accustomed to them since I was a child.	5.41
3. The church is important as it helps in deciding one's role in the community.	5.03
*4. I believe that membership in a good church increases one's self-respect.	4.88
5. The history of the church qualifies it as a lasting institution of which one would want to be a part.	4.88
*6. I believe that membership in a good church increases one's usefulness to society.	4.88
7. The church affords an atmosphere favorable to the furthering of the ideals of the good life.	4.83
8. Church members are especially good people to associate with.	4.72
9. Church attendance helps me to rid myself of any guilt feelings for not living up to the proposed ideals of the church.	4.00
10. Church is a good place for one to win social approval.	2.73
11. When one fails to live up to certain ideals of the good life, he finds a way to make restitution for these failures through the church.	2.54
12. Few important members of our society maintain any degree of religious affiliation. (R)	2.17

*From Thurstone and Chave (1929).

Ritualism Scale   *t value*

1. The ritual of worship is a very important part of religion.	9.17
2. One of the most important aspects of religion is the religious service itself.	7.71
3. The precision and orderliness with which religious ceremonies are performed is important to me.	7.51
4. The more a religious service is ritualized the more it has meaning for me.	7.23
5. Religion is most real to me during my attendance at public church or religious services.	7.07
6. I think that the placement and treatment of the various articles of worship is very important in a worship service.	7.00
7. When I recall my experiences with religion I most readily remember the impressive formal rites and rituals.	6.74
8. I like to think that people all over are going through nearly the same ritual in their religious worship.	6.67

9. A religious service must be beautiful to be really meaningful to me.   6.02
10. It is important to me that a religious service be standardized.   4.96
11. I do not think that the sequence of prayers, songs, etc., is very important
    in religious services. (R)   4.76
12. Prayers in religious services are better if they are formalized—as litanies,
    that is, with responses.   4.73

Altruism Scale   *t* value

 *1. The paternal and benevolent attitude of the church is quite distasteful
     to me. (R)   9.76
  2. The church is helping me to develop the social attitudes of understanding,
     sympathy, and cooperation.   8.28
 *3. I believe the church is absolutely needed to overcome the tendency to
     individualism and selfishness, for it seeks to practice the golden rule.   8.14
  4. We should be concerned with our own private welfare and stop trying to help
     others by butting into their private lives. (R)   6.44
 *5. I am interested in the church because of its work for moral and social reform
     in which I desire to share.   5.96
  6. Unselfish love is the prerequisite for any real knowledge of religion.   5.23
  7. Tender concern for others is a means of finding joy in one's religion.   5.06
  8. Religion causes one to love his enemies.   3.72
  9. Brotherly love was the heart of the teaching of Jesus.   3.72
 10. "Do-gooders" usually do much more harm than good. (R)   3.29
*11. I believe that the church is attempting to correlate science and religion for the
     good of humanity.   2.45
 12. Our world is in need of a more positive emphasis on life.   1.93

* From Thurstone and Chave (1929).

Fundamentalism Scale   *t* value

  1. The Bible is completely and everlastingly true.   12.15
  2. The Bible is the Word of God.   12.00
  3. The Bible is His message to me as His son or daughter.   11.44
  4. The Bible is the book upon which I should try to base my living.   9 53
  5. The Bible is too illogical. (R)   8.50
  6. The Bible is an instrument which brings me closer to God.   6.79
  7. The Bible is only a group of myths. (R)   5.89
  8. The Bible is one of the best history books ever written.   5.76
  9. The Bible should not be taken seriously. (R)   5.50
 10. The Bible contains the teaching given by God to His disciples and
     other peoples.   5.12
 11. Any scholar can see that the Bible just isn't true. (R)   3.12
 12. The Bible is a book in which the moral values of the world in general
     can be found.   2.84

Theism Scale   *t* value

  1. God is always watching over us.   10.62
  2. I do not feel that a belief in God is necessary. (R)   10.19
  3. God is my Father.   9.74

4.	God is a divine spirit guiding my life.	9.67
5.	There is no proof for the existence of God. (R)	9.57
6.	God is not a certainty. (R)	7.87
7.	God is hard to visualize as really existing. (R)	6.92
8.	God is all-powerful and all-knowing.	6.87
9.	God is an all-pervading spirit.	6.79
10.	God's voice keeps me on the straight and narrow path.	6.00
11.	I personally feel that the notion of God is inappropriate in this world of science. (R)	5.78
12.	God is nothing. (R)	4.63

Idealism Scale t value

*1.	In the end justice will prevail.	5.43
2.	Great causes must be supported.	4.53
3.	Brotherhood, freedom, and equality are workable concepts for man.	4.46
**4.	The best way to handle people is to tell them what they want to hear. (R)	4.23
5.	Men will never learn to live peacefully with one another. (R)	4.06
6.	If individuals would act in accord with their consciences, the world would be a lot better off.	3.94
7.	An individual without principles is an individual without honor.	3.90
8.	We must behave as if men were completely honest.	3.56
9.	Identification with a "cause" is an important part of life.	3 35
**10.	It is better to compromise with existing evils than to go out on limb in attacking them. (R)	3.10
**11.	When you come right down to it, it's human nature never to do anything without an eye to one's own advantage. (R)	2.90
12.	The people who get ahead in the world are individuals who are willing to compromise with their principles. (R)	2.77

*From Goldman-Eisler (1953)
**From Christie and Geis (1970)

Superstition Scale t value

1.	One should never step on or walk across a grave.	8.56
2.	To be perfectly honest, I am bothered by a black cat crossing my path.	5.15
3.	It is silly to believe that people are born under certain stars or planets which influence their futures. (R)	5 05
4.	Failure to live up to the laws of God will result in hard times for an individual.	4.29
5.	One should never treat a Bible disrespectfully or tear it.	4.00
6.	Every person should have a deep faith in some supernatural force higher than himself.	3.50
7.	It is conceivable that there are spirits and spiritual beings in our world today.	3.00
8.	Only fools and extremely gullible individuals believe in extrasensory perception, that is, such things as telepathy and clairvoyance. (R)	2.77
9.	Sickness is a result of present or past sins on the part of an individual or some of his relatives.	2.75
*10.	It is entirely possible that this series of wars and conflicts will be ended once and for all by a world-destroying earthquake, flood, or other catastrophe.	2.69

*11. Although many people may scoff, it may yet be shown that astrology
can explain a lot of things.   2.42
*12. Sciences like chemistry, physics, and medicine have carried men very far,
but there are many important things that can never possibly be understood
by the human mind.   1.83

*From Adorno, Frenkel-Brunswik, Levinson, & Sanford (1950).

Mysticism Scale   *t* value

1. The true seeker will eventually reach his goal of union with God.   8.54
2. The final authority in religion is the inner light or the testimony of the
   Holy Spirit.   6.36
3. True religious experience occurs in periods of profound silence.   5.81
4. Communion with God is a result of the complete loss of one's will
   (or the subjection of it), giving way to a superior power.   5.30
5. The visible manifestations of life are a partial manifestation of the spiritual. 5.27
6. Real worship involves a perfect union between man and God.   5.12
7. Religion finds its working expression in intellectual speculation and
   not in prayer. (R)   3.94
8. Man must endeavor with the human mind to grasp the divine essence or the
   ultimate reality of things, and to enjoy the blessedness of actual communion
   with the highest.   3.62
9. The mind has a higher state of existence beyond reason and in this
   superconscious state, knowledge beyond reasoning comes.   3.33
10. Meditation is the most important phase of one's religious experience.   2.42
11. Purely intellectual life does not have a mystical state.   2.41
12. Our verbal language isn't adequate to express or communicate real religious
    experience.   2.01

Maranell, G. M. (1974). *Response to religion studies in the social psychology of religious belief.*
Lawrence: Univ. of Kansas Press. Copyright © 1974 by the University of Kansas Press. Reprinted with permission.

8.11
RELIGIOUS EXPRESSION SCALE (Boan, 1978)
Reviewed by Michael J. Boivin

Variable: The Religious Expression Scale is a multidimensional assessment of religious expression within the context of evangelical Christian faith. Boan's scale measures a predominantly intellectual versus predominantly affective expression of religious faith.

In developing this instrument, Boan built upon James's (1902) distinction between intuitive/experiential and doctrinal/intellectual expressions of religious faith. More recently, theorists have speculated that these two tendencies might somehow be anchored in the distinctive functions of the right and left cortical hemispheres of the brain (see Ash, Crist, Salisbury, Dewell, & Boivin, 1996 for a concise review of this literature). Boan developed a questionnaire that he hoped would allow for an evaluation of the extent to which the respondent favored doctrinal/intellectual modes of religious expression (left brain) versus tendencies more consistent with an affective/intuitive approach (right brain).

Description: The first part of the instrument consists of 59 statements which the respondent evaluates on a Likert scale (1 = disagree strongly to 6 = agree strongly). The second part of the questionnaire consists of 24 questions that are either descriptive (e.g., age, sex, educational level) or pertain to present religious practices and recent life experiences (e.g., "Have you ever spoken in tongues?" "What is the number of times you attend church each month?" "Have you moved in the last five years?").

A factor analysis of the data provided from Boan's sample of several hundred participants from a variety of church backgrounds revealed nine factors:

1. General religious commitment (general religiosity).
2. Intellectual emphasis (intellectuality of religious expression)
3. Affective emphasis (emotionality of religious expression)
4. Philosophical orientation (religious philosophical and existential concerns)
5. Intense affective experience (concern with intense emotional experiences)
6. Social/emotionally-dependent style (emphasis on an emotional faith that relies on the support of others)
7. Bible teaching orientation (emphasis on the teaching and study of the scriptures)
8. Social affective style (emphasis on witnessing, outreach, and sharing one's emotional experience with others)
9. Miscellaneous religiosity items (statements that did not load significantly with any of the previous eight factors).

Practical Considerations: The instrument is self-explanatory and easy to administer. However, there is no standard procedure for scoring the instrument. In one study (Ash et al., 1996) the results of the factor analysis in Boan's dissertation were used to develop subscale scores for the factors in the instrument. This was done by multiplying item responses by the factor loading for that item, and summing these products for a total score for that factor.

Norms/Standardization: Three groups of subjects were selected for Boan's dissertation study, with the expectation that they would differ in the extent to which they represented a more "intellectual" as opposed to "affective" orientation in their Christian faith. The first group consisted of 46 students from Talbot Theological Seminary (intellectual emphasis) in La Mirada, California. The second group consisted of 61 students at Melodyland School of Theology (charismatic/affective) in Anaheim, California. The third group consisted of 176 subjects were from various churches and organizations in the Southern California area (fundamentalist, evangelical, and charismatic groups participated). However, no group means or standard deviations are reported by Boan.

Reliability: Spearman-Brown correlation coefficients were calculated for each factor to evaluate the internal consistency for the items within each factor, with coefficient values above 0.80 for all of the factors. Test-retest coefficients are not available.

Validity: Validation of this instrument was divided into four steps: The first step consisted of an evaluation of the sensitivity of the instrument by examining the form of the frequency distribution for the entire groups of respondents for each Likert-scale item. These distributions were examined for any obvious ceiling or basement effects. The second step involved the factorial analysis of the total sample to evaluate the extent to which a clear factor structure emerged in terms of intellectual versus emotional/intuitive modes of religious expression. The factors emerging from this analysis are listed above in the description of the instrument. The third step, in order to determine criterion-related validity, was to measure the extent to which each factor could allow for a reasonable prediction of whether each seminarian respondent was from Talbot or Melodyland. It was anticipated by Boan that the Talbot seminarians would display more of a verbal/intellectual cognitive orientation (i.e., left brain), while the Melodyland seminarians would exhibit a more perceptual/affective orientation (i.e., right brain). The discriminant analysis predicted seminary membership with 72.9% accuracy, indicating reasonable predictive validity. Step four, which pertained to construct validity, was assessed by the relationship between the factors (part 1) and actual religious practices (part 2) of the subjects. Generally, the distinctive types of religious practices noted in part 2 of the questionnaire tended to correspond with the favored mode of religious expression as apparent in part 1 for the respondents.

Location:

Boan, D. M. (1978). The development and validation of a measure of religious expression (Doctoral dissertation, Rosemead Graduate School of Professional Psychology, Biola University, La Mi-rada, CA, 1977). *Dissertation Abstracts International*, 40–04B, 1864.

Subsequent Research:

Ash, C., Crist, C., Salisbury, D., Dewell, M., & Boivin, M. J. (1996). Unilateral and bilateral brain hemispheric advantage on visual matching tasks and their relationship to styles of religiosity. *Journal of Psychology and Theology*, 24, 133–154.

References

Ash, C., Crist, C., Salisbury, D., Dewell, M., & Boivin, M. J. (1996). Unilateral and bilateral brain hemispheric advantage on visual matching tasks and their relationship to styles of religiosity. *Journal of Psychology and Theology*, 24, 133–154.

James, W. (1902). *The varieties of religious experience*. New York: Random House.

Appendix

Religious Expression Survey (Boan, 1978)

The following is a survey designed to determine the manner in which a person expresses his/her religious faith. It consists of a list of statements about religion and religious experiences, followed by a series of more general questions.

I would like you to rate each item as to whether or not you agree with it as a description of your own religious faith or behavior. This rating will be done according to the following scales:

1 - disagree strongly   4 - agree slightly
2 - disagree mildly   5 - agree mildly
3 - disagree slightly   6 - agree strongly

In making your answer, just circle the appropriate number after each item. All information is strictly confidential, so please do not put your name anywhere on this test.

Thank you for your help with this study.

I.   *Statements concerning religious expression.*

1. For myself, reading the Bible is most important for understanding the truths of God's revelation.   1   2   3   4   5   6

2. In relating to non-Christians, I would feel most comfortable speaking about the philosophical soundness of my experience.   1   2   3   4   5   6

3. I would say that I express my faith primarily through the intellectual areas of my life.   1   2   3   4   5   6

4. For myself, the Bible is interpreted   1   2   3   4   5   6
   through the direct and immediate guidance
   of the Holy Spirit.

5. To me, the beauty of Christianity lies in   1   2   3   4   5   6
   the way it helps me through the joys and
   trials of each day.

6. I would say that I "think" my religion.   1   2   3   4   5   6

7. I need other people to help me through the 1   2   3   4   5   6
   emotional aspects of my life.

8. I tend to express my faith through the
   emotional aspects of my life.   1   2   3   4   5   6

9. In speaking to non-Christians I would   1   2   3   4   5   6
   probably emphasize the emotional security
   I experience with my faith.

10. Religion should not be "intellectual."   1   2   3   4   5   6

11. For myself, the Bible is best interpreted so that 1   2   3   4   5   6
    it will be consistent with history and science.

12. In emphasizing the "rational" aspects of faith 1   2   3   4   5   6
    there is a danger in losing the applicability
    of that faith.

13. I experience the Holy Spirit working actively 1   2   3   4   5   6
    in my life.

14. I prefer to witness about the love I   1   2   3   4   5   6
    experience in Christ.

15. During a church service I may become   1   2   3   4   5   6
    emotionally overwhelmed by the Spirit of God.

16. The Holy Spirit works primarily through   1   2   3   4   5   6
    such means as culture and history.

17. I find the Body of Christ to be a place where 1   2   3   4   5   6
    His Word is emphasized.

18. To evangelize means to work within groups, 1   2   3   4   5   6
    developing relationships.

19. I prefer to witness to the truth found in Christ. 1   2   3   4   5   6

20. I spend time reflecting on the wonder of God. 1   2   3   4   5   6

21. To evangelize means to witness to individuals. 1   2   3   4   5   6

22. Society will change when institutions are changed. 1   2   3   4   5   6

23. I would say that I "feel" my religion.   1   2   3   4   5   6

24. I tend to be concerned about the political 1   2   3   4   5   6
    and social implications of the gospel.

25. I prefer to listen to a minister who is a   1   2   3   4   5   6
    good Biblical scholar.

26. I seek God's guidance through prayer and   1   2   3   4   5   6
    meditation.

27. When troubled I prefer to talk to a person
    who will show me compassion.   1   2   3   4   5   6

28. I prefer a church group which emphasizes
    personal sharing.   1   2   3   4   5   6

29. I seek God's guidance through the study
    of scripture.   1   2   3   4   5   6

30. I rely on the Bible to help me understand
    what a conversion experience is.   1   2   3   4   5   6

31. I am willing to accept another's con-
    version experience as real even if it is
    quite different from my own.   1   2   3   4   5   6

32. I am an unemotional person.   1   2   3   4   5   6

33. For myself, becoming a believer was the
    result of much study of Scripture.   1   2   3   4   5   6

34. Christianity may be seen as a logical
    system of beliefs.   1   2   3   4   5   6

35. The content of a person's testimony is more
    important than the feelings surrounding it.   1   2   3   4   5   6

36. I have never actually felt God's presence.   1   2   3   4   5   6

37. As Christians, we are living in the Church
    Age; therefore, we should not expect God
    to intervene by supernatural means.   1   2   3   4   5   6

38. For me, worship services are most meaning-
    ful where we do not have to follow a set program.   1   2   3   4   5   6

39. I dislike it when a minister speaks with a lot of
    emotion and tries to create certain feelings.   1   2   3   4   5   6

40. Midweek services at my church emphasize
    sharing needs rather than studying Scripture.   1   2   3   4   5   6

41. What a person thinks is more important
    than how he feels.   1   2   3   4   5   6

42. In church I expect to be taught the Word of God.   1   2   3   4   5   6

43. Worship is when you reflect on God rather
    than His "filling" you.   1   2   3   4   5   6

44. I may lose control of myself during prayer or worship. 1 2   3   4   5   6

45. Miracles and supernatural events are a
    regular part of a "spirit-filled" Christian's life. 1   2   3   4   5   6

46. I am more emotional about my faith than
    other people.   1   2   3   4   5   6

47. I don't need other people to help me
    grow in my faith.   1   2   3   4   5   6

48. I have had an emotional conversion experience.   1   2   3   4   5   6

49. I feel more comfortable doing things in
    groups than alone.   1   2   3   4   5   6

50. I tend to be more individualistic than other people.	1	2	3	4	5	6
51. I would say that I have an analytic mind.	1	2	3	4	5	6
52. I am not as concerned about the details of the Bible as other people are.	1	2	3	4	5	6
53. I can say for certain that I have felt God's presence.	1	2	3	4	5	6
54. My beliefs are well organized and thought out.	1	2	3	4	5	6
55. I am more intellectual about my beliefs than other people.	1	2	3	4	5	6
56. I would describe myself as a very rational person.	1	2	3	4	5	6
57. I am a very sociable person.	1	2	3	4	5	6
58. My religion is very important to me and touches all of my life.	1	2	3	4	5	6
59. I would describe myself as a very emotional person.	1	2	3	4	5	6

II. *General Survey*. Please answer all of the following briefly. Remember that all information will be kept in strict confidence. Feel free not to answer any questions you object to.

Age _____ Sex _____ Education _____

Annual Income_____ Occupation_____

Marital Status_____ Denomination _____

Denomination of Parents (if different) _____

Number of times you attend church each month? _____

Number of times you study your Bible each week? _____

Number of people you witness to each month? _____

Have you ever spoken in tongues?_____ How often?_____

Do you consider yourself saved? _____

Do you believe you can lose your salvation? _____

Have you had more than one conversion experience? _____

Have you had an experience of being in the presence of God? _____

Is your church a place of fellowship for you? _____

Do you worry about whether or not you are saved? _____

Do you now or have you in the past had doubts about your faith? _____

How often have you moved in the past five years? _____

How often have you changed jobs in the last five years? _____

Is there a problem (stress) situation in your home? _____

Check where appropriate:

_____ Physical Illness	_____ Financial
_____ Marital	_____ Alcoholism
_____ Drugs	_____ Emotional Illness
_____ Death	_____ Other

8.12
RELIGIOUS INVOLVEMENT INVENTORY
(Hilty & Morgan, 1985; Hilty, Morgan, & Burns, 1984)

Reviewed by Randall Lehmann Sorenson and Todd W. Hall

Variable: The Religious Involvement Inventory (RII) measures seven dimensions of religiosity: (1) Personal Faith; (2) Intolerance of Ambiguity: Revised, (3) Orthodoxy, (4) Social Conscience, (5) Knowledge of Religious History, (6) Life Purpose, and (7) Church Involvement.

Description: The Religious Involvement Inventory (RII) arose out of the author's critiques of the earlier scales by King and Hunt (1968, 1969, 1972, 1975). The authors hailed King and Hunt's 11-factor, multivariate approach as an improvement over earlier, merely conceptual typologies. But they questioned King and Hunt's reliance on (a) factors that were forced to be uncorrelated, (b) items that loaded on multiple factors, and (c) extraempirical criteria for item rejection from various factors.

By subjecting King and Hunt's questionnaire to an oblique rotation, using only empirical criteria for scale construction with repeated and various religious populations, the authors found seven factors to best account for the data. A 4-point rating system (e.g., "strongly agree" to "strongly disagree," and "regularly" to "seldom or never") generated raw data for the following factors: (1) *Personal Faith*, which reflects the degree of an active religious faith and an intrinsic orientation with regard to the importance of religion; (2) *Intolerance of Ambiguity: Revised*, which measures rigid, categorical thinking; (3) *Orthodoxy*, which reflects the degree to which an individual acknowledges acceptance of traditional beliefs in church doctrines; (4) *Social Conscience*, which measures belief about the church's and one's personal role in society; (5) *Knowledge of Religious History*, which measures an individual's knowledge of religion; (6) *Life Purpose*, which merges the two King and Hunt Purpose in Life scales into one, represents a general life purpose factor; and (7) *Church Involvement*, which indicates the extent of financial and social involvement within the church context and reflects an extrinsic orientation toward public religious practice.

Practical Considerations: This is a paper-and-pencil measure requiring no special skill to administer and score. No instructions are provided and no norms have been developed to allow use of the inventory with individuals.

Norms/Standardization: Seven hundred fifty-eight members of the Mennonite Church Conference (53% females, 47% males, 16 to 90 years old) were the participants in the first study (Hilty et al., 1984). A second study (Hilty & Morgan, 1985) replicated Hilty et al. 1984 outcomes, this time using three groups: the first was 367 females and 221 males affiliated with the West Ohio Conference of the United Methodist denomination; the second and third groups were subjects reported in the King and Hunt 1972 and 1975 studies.

Reliability: Coefficient alphas for the seven scales are as follows: Personal Faith (.87), Intolerance of Ambiguity: Revised (.83), Orthodoxy (.85), Social Conscience (.79), Knowledge of Religious History (.80), Life Purpose (.84), and Church Involvement

(.81). These coefficients indicate good lower-bound estimates of scale reliability.

Validity: In two of the three samples from the Hilty and Morgan (1985) replication the authors found the same seven oblique factors (consisting of a total of 82 items), with essentially the same items loading on each factor as in the 1984 study by Hilty et al. Coefficients of congruence between factors across samples ranged from .84 to .98. In sample three, however. a five-factor solution was a better fit with those data, which was a different outcome than the seven-factor model suggested from samples one and two. From these results, the authors concluded that the Hilty et al. (1984) multidimensional model based on their seven (or fewer) factor structure was more parsimonious than the 11 King and Hunt scales.

In both studies (Hilty et. al., 1984; Hilty and Morgan, 1985) the authors seem to have taken a LISREL confirmatory factor model—derived from the just completed exploratory factor analyses—and then tested this confirmatory model, in part, on the same datasets from which the exploratory factor structures were extracted. When they did use data from other samples, the chi-square tests for the authors' proposed factor structures indicated the models were not acceptable statistically, although they were an improvement compared to the null model. Various goodness-of-fit indices for the three samples were only .712, .734, and .819, leading Hilty and Morgan (1985) to conclude that the results offered, at best, "substantial inroads" into understanding the true factor structure of the data.

Location:

Hilty, D. M., & Morgan, R. L. (1985). Construct validation for the Religious Involvement Inventory: Replication. *Journal for the Scientific Study of Religion, 24*(1), 75–86.

Subsequent Research: The RII has been used in subsequent research to assess reli-giosity among African Americans (Jacobson, 1992; Johnson, Matre & Armbrecht, 1991) and political activists (Guth & Green, 1990), as well as a variety of other considerations within social psychology (Abbott, Berry & Merideth, 1990; Bernt, 1989; Ellison, Gay & Glass, 1989; Watson, Howard, Hood & Morris, 1988).

References

Abbott, D., Berry, M., & Merideth, W. (1990). Religious belief and practice: A potential asset in helping families. *Family Relations, 39,* 443–448.

Bernt, F. (1989). Being religious and being altruistic: A study of college service volunteers. *Personality and Individual Differences, 10,* 663–669.

Ellison, C., Gay, D., & Glass, T. (1989). Does religious commitment contribute to individual life satisfactory? *Social Forces, 68,* 100–123.

Guth, J., & Green, J. (1990). Religiosity and participation among political activists. *Western Political Quarterly, 43,* 153–179.

Hilty, D. M., Morgan, R. L., & Burns, J. E. (1984). King and Hunt revisited: Dimensions of religious involvement. *Journal for the Scientific Study of Religion, 22,* 252–266.

Jacobson, C. (1992). Religiosity in a black community: An examination of secularization and political values. *Review of Religious Research, 33,* 215–228.

Johnson, G., Matre, M., & Armbrecht, G. (1991). Race and religiosity: An empirical evaluation of a causal model. *Review of Religious Research, 32,* 252 266.

King, M., & Hunt, R. (1968). 1968 Questionnaire. Unpublished test.

King, M., & Hunt, R. (1969). Measuring the religious variable: Amended findings. *Journal for the Scientific Study of Religion, 8,* 321–323.

King, M., & Hunt, R. (1972). Measuring the religious variable: Replication. *Journal for the Scientific Study of Religion, 11,* 240–251.

King, M., & Hunt, R. (1975). Measuring the religious variable: National replication. *Journal for the Scientific Study of Religion, 14,* 13–22.

Watson, P., Howard, R., Hood, R., & Morris, R. (1988). Age and religious orientation. *Review of Religious Research, 29,* 271–280.

Appendix

The Religious Involvement Inventory

Most items are answered on a 4-point scale from "strongly agree" to "strongly disagree." The "how often" items have four alternatives: "regularly," "fairly frequently," "occasionally," and "seldom or never." The Knowledge of Religious History items have six choices that are listed in parentheses next to the items.

Personal Faith
1. The amount of time I spend trying to grow in understanding of my faith is:
2. How often do you read literature about your faith (or church)?
3. How often in the last year have you shared with another church member the problems and joys of trying to live a life of faith in God?
4. When faced by decisions regarding social problems, how often do you seek guidance from statements and publications provided by the church?
5. How often do you read the Bible?
6. How often do you pray privately in places other than at church?
7. How often do you talk about religion with your friends, neighbors, or fellow workers?
8. When you have decisions to make in your everyday life, how often do you try to find out what God wants you to do?
9. During the last year, how often have you visited someone in need, besides your own relatives?
10. In talking with members of your family, how often do you yourself mention religion or religious activities?
11. How often have you personally tried to convert someone to faith in God?
12. I must admit that I don't do very much to increase my knowledge of God.
13. I have had some unusual religious experiences.
14. It is important to me to spend periods of time in private religious thought and meditation.

Intolerance of Ambiguity: Revised
15. There is only one right way to do anything.
16. It is part of one's patriotic duty to worship in the church of his choice.
17. A person either knows the answer to a question or he doesn't.
18. Church leaders should pay attention to recent scientific studies which prove that the white race is best.
19. What religion offers me most is comfort when sorrows and misfortune strikes.
20. There are two kinds of people in the world: the weak and the strong.
21. A person is either a 100% American or he isn't.
22. The purpose of prayer is to secure a happy and peaceful life.
23. There are two kinds of women: the pure and the bad.
24. You can classify almost all people as either honest or crooked.
25. It doesn't take very long to find out if you can trust a person.

Orthodoxy
26. Estimate the extent to which you feel religion is important in your life today.
27. To what extent has God influenced your life?
28. How often do you ask God to forgive your sins?
29. How often do you pray privately in places other than at church?
30. I know that God answers my prayers.

31. I believe in eternal life.
32. Private prayer is one of the most important and satisfying aspects of my religious experience.
33. Property (house, automobile, money, investments, etc.) belongs to God; we only hold it in trust for him.
34. I believe that God revealed Himself to man in Jesus Christ.
35. Religion is especially important to me because it answers many questions about the meaning of life.
36. The church is important to me as a place where I get strength and courage for dealing with the trials and problems of life.
37. I believe that the Bible provides the basic moral principles to guide every decision of my daily life: with family and neighbors, in business and financial transactions, and as a citizen of the nation and world.
38. I believe in salvation as release from sin and freedom for new life with God.
39. I believe that the word of God is revealed in the Scriptures.
40. I believe in God as Heavenly Father who watches over me and to whom I am accountable.
41. I believe that Christ is a living reality.
42. I know how it feels to repent and experience forgiveness of sin.
43. I have about given up trying to understand "worship" or get much out of it.
44. I frequently feel very close to God in prayer, during public worship, or at important moments in my daily life.
45. I know that I need God's continual love and care.

Social Conscience
46. I believe that my local congregation should sponsor projects to improve the economic well-being of blacks and other minority groups.
47. The church should take the lead in ending injustice toward blacks and other minority groups.
48. I am proud that my denomination has taken a stand in favor of equal rights for blacks and other minority groups.
49. Churches should support the struggle of black people to achieve equal rights.
50. I believe that my local congregation should sponsor projects to protect the rights of blacks and other minority groups.
51. I believe that my local congregation should accept as members persons of all races.

Knowledge of Religious History
52. Which of the following were among the twelve disciples? (Daniel; John; Judas; Paul; Peter; Samuel)
53. Which of the following books are in the Old Testament? (Acts; Amos; Galatians; Hebrews; Hosea; Psalms)
54. Which of the following denominations in the U.S. have bishops? (Disciples; Episcopal; Lutheran; Methodist; Presbyterian; Roman Catholic)
55. Which of the following books are included in the four Gospels? (James; John; Mark; Matthew; Peter; Thomas)
56. Which of the following were Old Testament prophets? (Deuteronomy; Ecclesiastes; Elijah; Isaiah; Jeremiah; Leviticus)
57. Which of the following men were leaders of the Protestant Reformation? (Aquinas; Augustine; Calvin; Cranmer; Hegel; Luther)
58. Which of the following acts were performed by Jesus Christ during his earthly ministry? (Resisting the temptations of Satan; healing ten lepers; leading his people against the

priests of Baal; parting the waters to cross the Red Sea; overcoming Goliath; turning water into wine)

59. Which of the following principles are supported by most Protestant denominations? (Bible as the word of God; separation of church and state; power of clergy to forgive sins; final authority of the church; justification by faith; justification by good works)

Life Purpose

60. If I should die today, I would feel that my life has been worthwhile.
61. I am satisfied that most of the time I live in right relationship to God and to men.
62. Most of the time my life seems to be out of my control.
63. I usually find life new and exciting.
64. My life is full of joy and satisfaction.
65. I have discovered satisfying goals and a clear purpose in life.
66. My personal existence often seems meaningless and without purpose.
67. My life is often empty, filled with despair.
68. Facing my daily tasks is usually a source of pleasure and satisfaction to me.

Church Involvement

69. Of all your closest friends, how many are also members of your local congregation?
70. How would you rate your activity in this congregation?
71. Last year, approximately what percentage of your income was contributed to the church?
72. In proportion to your income, what do you consider that your contributions to the church are?
73. During the last year, what was the average monthly contribution of your family to your local congregation?
74. During the last year, how often have your made contributions to the church in addition to the general budget and Sunday School?
75. If not prevented by unavoidable circumstances, I attend church.
76. I make financial contributions to the church.
77. How often do you get together with members of your congregation in addition to church-sponsored meetings?
78. How often have you taken Holy Communion (the Lord's Supper; the Eucharist) during the last year?
79. How often do you spend evenings at church meetings or in church work?
80. Church activities (meetings, committee work, etc.) are a major source of satisfaction in my life.
81. I keep pretty well informed about my congregation and have some influence on its decisions.
82. I enjoy working in the activities of the church.

Hilty, D. M. & Morgan, R. L. (1985). Construct validation for the Religious Involvement Inventory: Replication. *Journal for the Scientific Study of Religion, 24*(1), 75–86. Copyright © 1985 Journal for the Scientific Study of Religion. Reprinted with permission.

8.13
RELIGIOUS ORIENTATION AND INVOLVEMENT (LENSKI, 1961)

Reviewed by Ronald Burwell

Variable: The Religious Orientation and Involvement Inventory identifies four dimensions of religiosity: doctrinal orthodoxy, devotionalism, associational involvement, and communal involvement. The first two dimensions are considered measures of religious orientation, whereas the latter two dimensions are measures of religious involvement.

Description: This study is based on data gathered in 1958 from residents of Detroit, Michigan. Historically, it is important because it was one of the early attempts to specify a multidimensional approach to religiosity. Lenski created his measures in light of a definition of religion that involved religious beliefs (orthodoxy), religious practices (devotionalism) and involvement in socioreligious groups (associational and communal involvement). He defined the four dimensions as follows:

Doctrinal orthodoxy: The degree to which a person accepts the presented doctrines of his or her church; an intellectual assent; a passive, intellectual dimension.
Devotionalism: That orientation that emphasizes the importance of private or personal communion with God; pietism; frequency of prayer and seeking God's will. An active, behavioral, dimension.
Associational involvement: The degree of involvement in the formal, corporate religious structures of one's faith; measured by frequency of attendance at worship services and other formal activities.
Communal involvement: The degree to which one's primary social relationships are limited to persons of one's own religious group; indicated by religious endogamy and friends or relatives who share common religious identity.

The purposes of Lenski's research were directed toward intergroup comparisons among Protestants, Catholics, and Jews in Detroit. Lenski believed that the multidimensional measures he created were suited to a variety of religious groups. Hence, the dimensions of religiosity were adapted to fit all three groups (e.g., word changes in some questions from church to synagogue, etc.). Significant components of this research were designed to test contemporary applications of Max Weber's theories about the connections between religion and economics. In addition, Lenski examined how the "religious factor" as measured

by these four dimensions related to politics, education, family life, and science. In a subsequent study, Lenski examined some of the differences among clergy drawn from the three major religious groups.

Practical Considerations: This collection of measures is a multidimensional approach to measuring religiosity. Lenski uses a total of 14 different questions to cover the four dimensions. Since each question takes less than a minute to answer, the whole group of questions can be administered in approximately 10 minutes. This makes these measures attractive for use in longer interviews or questionnaires. However, later approaches to a multidimensional measure of religiosity are more elaborate and offer greater precision. The decision one would have to make, therefore, is whether Lenski's more limited approach is adequate for the researcher's purposes.

Norms/Standardization: The original study by Lenski is based upon 656 completed interviews (87% of the initial sample of 750). Lenski appeared successful in gathering a representative sample of the population of Detroit. Someone using his measures could find comparative data presented in study. However, the date of that study (late 1950s) may make such comparative data less useful for contemporary researchers.

Lenski (1961, appendix 1) estimated that sampling errors range from four percentage points to about eight percentage points for the bulk of the study. Statistical data from smaller subgroups (e.g., Jews) are more likely to have somewhat higher sampling error levels.

Reliability: No information on reliability was given.

Validity: Lenski did not conduct any rigorous procedures to check the validity of these measures. The scale has high face validity. In addition, Lenski reported other comparable studies that have discovered similar patterns. For example, he noted that, in the area of religion and economics, his data are consistent with that of Mack, Murphy, and Yellin (1956).

The research on which these measures are based is part of a larger cluster of research studies called the Detroit Area Study (Freedman, 1953). These studies were begun in the 1950s in conjunction with the Department of Sociology of the University of Michigan. Lenski's study was a part of this work and he reports many comparisons between his findings and other studies in this series.

Location:

Lenski, G. (1961). *The religious factor*. Garden City, NY: Doubleday.

Recent Research: Although subsequent studies used many of the same measures created by Lenski, they tend to be revised and modified (in some cases, entirely new scales were developed).

DeJong, G., Faulkner, J., & Warland, R. (1976). Dimensions of religiosity reconsidered: Evidence from a cross-cultural study. *Social Forces, 54*, 866–889.

Glock, C., & Stark, R. (1966). *Christian beliefs and anti-semitism*. New York: Harper & Row.

King, M., & Hunt, R. (1969). Measuring the religious variable: Replication. *Journal for the Scientific Study of Religion, 11*, 240–251.

Winter, G. (1962). Methodological reflection on "the religious factor." *Journal for the Scientific Study of Religion, 2*, 53–63.

References

Freedman, R. (1953). The Detroit area study: A training and research laboratory in the community. *American Journal of Sociology, 59*, 30–33.

Mack, R., Murphy, R., & Yellin, S. (1956). The Protestant ethic, level of aspiration, and social mobility. *American Sociological Review, 21*, 295–300.

Appendix

Religious Orientation and Involvement

I. Types of Involvement

A. *Associational*

1. About how often, if ever, have you attended religious services in the last year?
   a) Once a week or more
   b) Two or three times a month
   c) Once a month
   d) A few times a year or less
   e) Never
2. Do you take part in any of the activities or organizations of your church (synagogue, temple) other than attending services? _____ Yes _____ No
   (if yes)
   How often have you done these things in the last year? (Use same response categories as for 1 above.)

Scoring: Lenski labeled "actively involved" all those who attended worship services every week, plus those who attended services two or three times a month and also some church related group at least once a month. All the others he called "marginal members."

B. *Communal*

1. What is (was) your husband's (wife's) religious preference?_____
2. Of those relatives you really feel close to, what proportion are (*same religion as respondent*)?
   a) All of them
   b) Nearly all of them
   c) More than half of them

d) Less than half of them
e) None of them
3. Thinking of your closest friends, what proportion are *(same religion as respondent)*? (Use same response categories as for previous question.)

Scoring: High communal involvement was inferred for all those who were married to someone of the same socioreligious group, and who also reported that all or nearly all of their close friends were of the same group. Low communal involvement was attributed to all the others.

II. Types of Religious Orientation

A. *Doctrinal Orthodoxy*

1. Do you believe there is a God, or not? _____ Yes _____ No
2. Do you think God is like a Heavenly Father who watches over you, or do you have some other belief?_____ Yes _____ Some other belief
3. Do you believe that God answers people's prayers, or not? _____ Yes _____ No
4. Do you believe in a life after death, or not? _____ Yes _____ No
   If so, do you also believe that in the next life some people will be punished and others rewarded by God, or not? _____ Yes _____ No
5. Do you believe that, when they are able, God expects people to worship Him in their churches and synagogues *every week*, or not? _____ Yes _____ No
6. Do you believe that Jesus was God's only son sent into the world by God to save sinful men, or do you believe that he was simply a very good man and teacher, or do you have some other belief? _____ Yes _____ No

Scoring: (It should be noted that Jews were not classified according to this scale.) Christians were classified as unorthodox unless they held all six beliefs.

B. *Devotionalism*

1. How often do you pray?_____
2. When you have decisions to make in your everyday life, do you ask yourself what God would want you to do? (Often, sometimes, or never)

Scoring: Respondents were ranked high in devotionalism if (a) they reported praying more than once a day, plus asking what God would have them do either *often* or *sometimes*; or if (b) they reported praying once a day, but *often* asked what God would have them do.

Lenski, G. (1961). *The religious factor.* Garden City, N.Y.: Doubleday. Copyright © 1961 by Doubleday. Reprinted with permission by Doubleday, a division of Bantom Doubleday Dell Publishing Group, Inc.

8.14
RELIGIOUS VARIABLES: TEN SCALES (King & Hunt, 1972)
Reviewed by Ronald Burwell

Variable: King and Hunt offer a set of 10 scales covering a variety of religious dimensions. Their scales are clustered under six headings: creedal assent, devotionalism, congregational involvement, religious knowledge, orientation to religion, and salience of religious beliefs.

Description: The scales are derived from earlier work by King (1967) and King and Hunt (1969). They created a pool of items that represented some of the emerging consensus about the multidimensionality of religiosity. Their original formulations assumed a total of 11 hypothetical dimensions, including some developed by Allport and Ross (1967), Glock (1962), and Lenski (1961). Analysis of data gathered in 1965 and 1968 led King and Hunt to amend their findings (King & Hunt, 1969). They found that eight of their original hypothetical scales were confirmed through new computer-assisted statistical analysis. Furthermore, some two or three new dimensions were discovered.

On the basis of their earlier studies, King and Hunt repeated their general approach on a larger and more diverse population of subjects using a somewhat modified universe of items. Their research produced the following ten scales, which reflect some degree of homogeneity and internal consistency. Note that the first six scales are similar to dimensions discussed by Glock (1962) and Lenski (1961):

> 1. Creedal Assent (7 items): similar to Glock's ideological dimension and Lenski's doctrinal orthodoxy; seeks to find agreement with set of beliefs common to a broad spectrum of believing Christians.
> 2. Devotionalism (5 items): related to Lenski's devotionalism; items deal with personal prayer, closeness to and communication with God.
> 3–5. Congregational Involvement: three subscales related to Glock's ritualistic dimension and Lenski's associational dimension.
> Church Attendance (3 items): church worship attendance; attendance at Communion.
> Organizational Activity (6 items): self-reported rating of activity; the number of evenings spent on church work; church offices held.
> Financial Support (5 items): part of income given to church; estimated contributions; giving to more than just general budget.
> 6. Religious Knowledge (8 items): similar to Glock's (1962) intellectual dimen-

sion; covers biblical knowledge; knowledge of church history; denominational and church polity.

> 7–8. Orientation to Religion: Two subscales in how a person sees religion functioning in daily life.
> Growth and Striving (6 items): the extent to which a person is either satisfied or dissatisfied with his or her present religious state.
> Extrinsic (7 items): derived from Allport and Feagin items (Feagin, 1964; Allport & Ross, 1967); assumes an instrumental, selfish attitude toward religion.
> 9–10. Salience: two subscales measuring the relevance and importance of religion.
> Behavior (7 items): the importance of religious activities outside of the formal structure of the church, such as witnessing, reading the Bible, talking about religion, and visitation.
> Cognition (5 items): somewhat related to the intrinsic dimension outlined by Feagin (1964) and Allport and Ross (1967); the importance of religion for one's thoughts, feelings, beliefs; how important religious beliefs are to the rest of life.

Most items are measured on a 4-point ("strongly disagree" to "strongly agree") scale. Religious knowledge items have six choices or possible answers. Items that deal with the frequency of activities have alternatives of regularly, fairly regularly, occasionally, and seldom or never as alternatives.

The final scale consisted of 59 items. Thirty-two items were rejected as being redundant or statistically unrelated to the 10 dimensions.

Practical Considerations: These scales are straightforward and simple to use. The items are additive and unweighted, making analysis relatively easy. Like any set of multidimensional measures of religiosity, potential users must decide if the use of an extensive set of items like these is warranted given the purposes of their research. If it is important to measure the religious dimension with a high level of precision and complexity, these scales are an excellent choice. They have the advantages of being a refinement of several earlier versions and researchers may have some confidence that the items do form internally consistent scales. Thirty minutes should be allowed for test administration.

Norms/Standardization: In earlier studies, King (1967) and King and Hunt (1969) used data from a sample of 575 Methodists located in Dallas, Texas and its suburbs. In this study they used subjects from Protestant denominations in the Dallas-Fort Worth metropolitan area. A systematic sample of all members 16 years old and older was drawn. Questionnaires were distributed by mail and resulted in 1,356 usable returns (a response rate of 44%). The four denominations represented were Disciples ($n = 314$), Missouri-Synod Lutheran ($n = 344$), Presbyterian ($n = 346$), and United Methodists ($n = 339$). Generally, this sample reflected white, mainline Protestants in urban north Texas. The authors later (King & Hunt, 1975) conducted a replication with a more geographically diverse sample of 872 individuals from the United Presbyterian denomination.

King and Hunt do note some limitations of their work. First, they note that these scales have been largely developed from data gathered from mainline Protestant denominations. Therefore, use of these scales with Roman Catholics and Protestant Pentecostals (1972, p. 248) should be approached with caution. However, in principle it would seem that these scales have a wider application than either mainline Protestantism or even just Christianity in general. With some modification they might be used with Jewish or Muslim subjects.

Reliability: Test-retest reliabilities are not presented. However, King and Hunt do offer internal consistency reliability coefficients. Their final selection of scale items was based upon two criteria: (a) a Cronbach's alpha of .75 for a coefficient of homogeneity and (b) some demonstration of analytical power when correlated with other variables. The scales are listed with their alpha coefficients (see scales). They range from .734 (Financial Support; Extrinsic) to .852 (Devotionalism).

In addition, King and Hunt report item to scale correlations for each of the 59 items. These generally range from .39 to .70. In each scale the items are listed from high to low in order of item to scale correlation coefficients.

Validity: King and Hunt argue that the validity of their scales may be judged in terms of utility or explanatory power. Intercorrelations among the 10 religiosity scales are presented in this volume with the scale. In addition, intercorrelations between the religious dimensions and 5 other cognitive style scales is presented. One low but statistically significant positive correlation was between certain ethnic attitudes and church attendance, organizational activities, religious knowledge, growth and striving, and salience (1972, p. 244). In other words, there was a positive correlation between racial tolerance (i.e., less prejudice) and congregational activity, knowledge about the faith, dissatisfaction with religious attainment, and importance of religion. This is similar to some of the findings of Allport and Ross (1967).

Location:
King, M. B., & Hunt, R. A. (1972). Measuring the religious variable: Replication. *Journal for the Scientific Study of Religion, 11,* 240–251.

Subsequent Research:
Hilty, D. M., Morgan, R. L., & Burns, J. E. (1984). King and Hunt revisited: Dimensions of religious involvement. *Journal for the Scientific Study of Religion, 23,* 252–266.

Hilty, D. M., & Morgan, R. L. (1985). Construct validation for the religious involvement inventory: Replication. *Journal for the Scientific Study of Religion, 24,* 75–86.

References

Allport, G. W., & Ross, J. M. (1967). Personal religious orientation and prejudice. *Journal of Personality and Social Psychology, 5,* 432–433.

De Jong, G., Faulkner, J., & Warland, R. (1976). Dimensions of religiosity reconsidered: Evidence from a cross-cultural study. *Social Forces, 54,* 866–889.

Feagin, J. R. (1964). Prejudice and religious types: A focus study of southern fundamentalists. *Journal for the Scientific Study of Religion, 4,* 3–13.

Glock, C. Y. (1962). On the study of religious commitment: Review of recent research bearing on religious and character formation. A research supplement to *Religious Education*, July-August, S98–S110.

Glock, C. Y., & Stark, R. (1966). *Christian beliefs and anti-Semitism*. New York: Harper & Row.

King, M. (1967). Measuring the religious variable. *Journal for the Scientific Study of Religion, 6*, 173–190.

King, M., & Hunt, R. (1969). Measuring the religious variable: Amended findings. *Journal for the Scientific Study of Religion, 8*, 321–323.

King, M., & Hunt, R. (1972). Measuring the religious variable: Replication. *Journal for the Scientific Study of Religion, 11*, 240–251.

King, M., & Hunt, R. (1975). Measuring the religious variable: National replication. *Journal for the Scientific Study of Religion, 14*, 13–22.

Lenski, G. (1961). *The religious factor*. New York: Doubleday, 1961.

Appendix

Items for Ten Religious Scales[1]

The various scales are simple, additive, and unweighted. See endnotes for more information. Generally, each item has four possible answers (e.g., strongly agree = 4, agree = 3, disagree = 2, and strongly disagree = 1), which are added together to produce a combined score. Some items are used on more than one scale.

I. Creedal Assent (.834)[2]

1. (.70)[3] I believe that the word of God is revealed in the Scriptures.[4]
2. (.65) I believe in God as a Heavenly Father who watches over me and to whom I am accountable.
3. (.58) I believe that God revealed Himself to man in Jesus Christ.
4. (.58) I believe that Christ is a living entity.
5. (.58) I believe in eternal life.
6. (.54) I believe in salvation as release from sin and freedom for new life with God.
7. (.53) I believe honestly and wholeheartedly in the doctrines and teaching of the church.

II. Devotionalism (.852)

1. (.74) How often do you pray privately in places other than at church?
2. (.73) How often do you ask God to forgive your sin?
3. (.65) Private prayer is one of the most important and satisfying aspects of my religious experience.
4. (.63) When you have decisions to make in your everyday life, how often do you try to find out what God wants you to do?
5. (.59) I frequently feel very close to God in prayer, during public worship, or at important moments in my daily life.

III. Congregational Involvement

A. Church Attendance (.821)

1. (.71) How often have you taken Holy Communion (the Lord's Supper, the Eucharist) during the past year?
2. (.69) During the last year, how many Sundays per month on the average have you gone to a worship service: (None—Three or more).

3. (.64) If not prevented by unavoidable circumstances, I attend Church: (more than once a week—less than once a month).

B. Organizational Activity (.831)

1. (.69) How would you rate your activity in this congregation (very active—inactive)?

2. (.63) How often do you spend evenings at church meetings or in church work?

3. (.59) I enjoy working in the activities of the church.

4. (.59) Church activities (meetings, committee work, etc.) are a major source of satisfaction in my life.

5. (.57) I keep pretty well informed about my congregation and have some influence on its decisions.

6. (.55) List the church offices, committees, or jobs of any kind in which you have served during the past 12 months.

C. Financial Support (.734)

1. (.56) Last year, approximately what percentage of your income was contributed to the church? (Answer in terms of your individual income *or* that of your family, whichever is appropriate.) (1% or less—10% or more).

2. (.53) I make financial contributions to church: (in regular, planned amounts—seldom or never).

3. (.51) During the last year, what was the average *monthly* contribution of your family to your local congregation? (Under $5—$50 and up)

4. (.48) In proportion to your income, do you consider that your contributions to the Church are: (generous—small)?

5. (.40) During the last year, how often have you made contributions to the church *in addition to* the general budget and Sunday school? (regularly—never)

IV. Religious Knowledge (.769)

1. (.56) Which of the following were Old Testament prophets? (Deuteronomy, Ecclesiastes, Elijah, Isaiah, Jeremiah, Leviticus)

2. (.54) Which of the following books are included in the four Gospels? (James, John, Mark, Matthew, Peter, Thomas)

3. (.53) Which of the following were among the twelve disciples of Christ? (Daniel, John, Judas, Paul, Peter, Samuel)

4. (.50) Which of the following acts were performed by Jesus Christ during his earthly ministry? (resisting the temptations of Satan; healing ten lepers; leading his people against the priests of Baal; parting the waters of the Red Sea; overcoming Goliath; turning water into wine)

5. (.48) Which of the following men were leaders of the Protestant Reformation? (Aquinas; Augustine; Calvin; Cranmer; Hegel; Luther)

6. (.44) Which of the following principles are supported by most Protestant denominations? (Bible as the word of God; separation of church and state; power of clergy to forgive sins; final authority of the church; justification by faith; justification by good works)

7. (.43) Which of the following books are in the Old Testament? (Acts; Amos; Galatians; Hebrews; Hosea; Psalms)

8. (.41) Which of the following denominations in the United States have bishops? (Disciples; Episcopal; Lutheran; Methodist; Presbyterian; Roman Catholic)

V. Orientation to Religion

A. Growth and Striving (.806)

1. (.61) How often do you read literature about your faith (or church)? (Frequently—Never)
2. (.60) How often do you read the Bible?
3. (.59) I try hard to grow in understanding of what it means to live as a child of God.
4. (.57) When you have decisions to make in your everyday life, how often do you try to find out what God wants you to do?
5. (.54) The amount of time I spend trying to grow in understanding of my faith is: (Very much—Little or none)
6. (.52) I try hard to carry my religion over into all my other dealings in life.

B. Extrinsic (.734)

1. (.52) It is part of one's patriotic duty to worship in the church of his choice.
2. (.49) The church is the most important place to form good social relationships.
3. (.46) The purpose of prayer is to secure a happy and peaceful life.
4. (.45) Church membership has helped me to meet the right kind of people.
5. (.42) What religion offers me most is comfort when sorrows and misfortune strike.
6. (.39) One reason for my being a church member is that such membership helps to establish a person in the community.
7. (.39) Religion helps to keep my life balanced and steady in exactly the same way as my citizenship, friendships, and other memberships do.

VI. Salience

A. Behavior (.825)

1. (.68) How often in the last year have you shared with another church member the problems and joys of trying to live a life of faith in God?
2. (.60) How often have you personally tried to convert someone to faith in God?
3. (.59) How often do you talk about religion with your friends, neighbors, or fellow workers?
4. (.57) When faced by decisions regarding social problems, how often do you seek guidance from statements and publications provided by the Church?
5. (.54) How often do you read the Bible?
6. (.53) How often do you talk with the pastor (or some other official) about some part of the worship service: for example, the sermon, scripture, choice of hymns, etc.?
7. (.49) During the last year, how often have you visited someone in need, besides your own relatives?

B. Cognition (.808)

1. (.64) My religious beliefs are what really lie behind my whole approach to life.
2. (.64) I try hard to grow in understanding of what it means to live as a child of God.
3. (.59) Religion is especially important to me because it answers many questions about the meaning of life.
4. (.56) I try hard to carry my religion over into all my other dealings in life.
5. (.54) I frequently feel very close to God in prayer, during public worship, or at important moments in my daily life.

1. The items on each scale are ranked by their item-scale correlation coefficients, from highest to lowest.
2. A coefficient of homogeneity (Cronbach's alpha).
3. The item-scale correlation, with that item dropped from the scale.
4. Items have four alternative answers, except the knowledge items (IV), which have six. Most items are answered on a 4-point scale from "strongly agree" to "strongly disagree." Sixteen "how often" items have "regularly," "fairly frequently," "occasionally," and "seldom or never" as alternatives. The alternatives to other items are indicated in parentheses.

King, M. B., & Hunt, R. A. (1972). Measuring the religious variable: Replication. *Journal for the Scientific Study of Religion, 11,* 240–251. Copyright © 1972 Journal for the Scientific Study of Religion. Reprinted with permission.

8.15
THEOLOGICAL INDEX (Hoge, 1976)

Reviewed by Duane Kauffmann

Variable: The Theological Index was developed to identify areas of disagreement among members of the Protestant community of faith. The index, which is comprised of numerous subscales, was one of many measures used in a series of research studies using Presbyterian samples.

Description: The Theological Index consists of 53 questions. These items arc intended to measure 12 components of theological position: spiritual-secular dualism (6 items), freewill behavior (6 items), otherworldliness (3 items), scriptural authority (1 item), social optimism (3 items), ethicalism (4 items), religious nationalism (3 items), creedal assent (6 items), religious despair (5 items), orientation to growth and striving (5 items), devotionalism (4 items), and salience: behavior (6 items).

The items for subscales creedal assent, religious despair, orientation to growth and striving, devotionalism, and salience: behavior, were taken from King and Hunt (1972). Only the devotionalism scale was identical to that of King and Hunt, with the other theological index subscales omitting one or two of the King and Hunt items. For an analysis of the King and Hunt scales, the reader is referred to page 334 (Religious Variables: Ten Scales review) in this volume.

Respondents are asked to indicate their position by a circle around one of 4 responses: Strongly Agree, Agree, Disagree, Strongly Disagree. Appropriate changes in response catagories are made for a few questionnaire items which deal with behavior frequency. Some items must be reverse scored. Subscale scores require summation of numerical scores for items appropriate to that concept.

Practical Considerations: Administration of the questionnaire is straightforward, with very minimal need for instructions.

Wording of questionnaire items reflects traditional use of theological concepts and pronouns. Many persons using the index today would wish to edit scale items to reflect more inclusive language.

Norms/Standardization: For the scales constructed by Hoge, 10 to 15 items were written for each of the constructs to be measured. Two pretests were conducted, one with 48 Presbyterian laypersons and ministers and the other with 53 laypersons and ministers. Final items for the subscales were selected based on reliability coefficients and face validity.

Reliability: The sample for which Cronbach's alpha coefficients are reported for each subscale from a sample of 872 Presbyterian laity and 667 Presbyterian clergy. Reliabilities for the scales prepared by Hoge are spiritual-secular dualism, .65 for ministers and .56 for laypersons, freewill behavior, .68 for ministers and .50 for laypersons, otherworldliness, .75 for ministers and .71 for laypersons, social optimism, .63 for ministers and .44 for laypersons, and ethicalism, .68 for laypersons.

Validity: No validity coefficients are provided in Hoge (1976) or in the Technical Supplement. The Technical Supplement indicates that items were chosen for their face validity.

Location:

Hoge, D. (1976). *Division in the protestant house*. Philadelphia: Westminster.

References

King, M., & Hunt, R. (1972). Measuring the religious variable: Replication. *Journal for the Scientific Study of Religion, 11,* 240–251.

Appendix

Theological Index

Unless instructed otherwise, please indicate the extent to which you agree or disagree with each item by using the following scale

1 = strongly disagree	3 = agree
2 = disagree	4 = strongly agree

Spiritual-Secular Dualism Index

1. The true Christian's loyalties must be to the spiritual part of man, not the bodily part.

2. Spiritual, and not worldly, affairs in human life should be the concern of the Christian.

3. Christians should look at man as a total unity and not concern themselves with only a "spiritual" part. (R)

4. The true Christian should avoid much involvement in the secular structures of society; his loyalties should first of all be to spiritual things.

5. Christianity is clear about separating spiritual and secular realms and putting emphasis on spiritual values.

6. The Christian should identify himself with secular social forces working for justice and humanization in society. (R)

Freewill Behavior Index

1. Most human behavior is a result of social pressures and conditions. (R)

2. Any person's behavior is largely determined by the influences of society upon him. (R)

3. The individual, and not his society, determines his personal fate in life.

4. Converting men to Christ must be the first step in creating a better society.

5. To bring peace in the world, we must first of all cleanse men's hearts of sin.

6. Freedom in Christ has little meaning for persons living amid oppressive social conditions. (R)

Otherworldliness Index
1. The primary purpose of man in this life is preparation for the next life.
2. I believe in a divine judgment after death where some shall be rewarded and others punished.
3. It is not as important to worry about life after death as about what one can do in this life. (R)

Scriptural Authority Item
1. Scripture is the inspired and inerrant Word of God, not only in matters of faith but also in historical, geographical, and other secular matters.

Social Optimism Index
1. The world is so full of human sin that we can expect little improvement in the human condition in history. (R)
2. All human undertakings are corrupted by sin and therefore will eventually fail. (R)
3. Human action can create a substantially better world than we now have.

Ethicalism Index
1. For the Christian, the man-to-man relationship should be at least as important as the man-to-God relationship.
2. A good Christian should be as concerned about personal and social ethics as about his own spiritual growth.
3. A correct relationship to God is far more important than proper ethical behavior toward other people. (R)
4. It is the correct relationship to God and not good works in society which should be the foremost concern of the Christian. (R)

Religious Nationalism Index
1. A good Christian should never criticize an American president while he is in office.
2. America is a nation chosen by God to lead in the regeneration of the world.
3. In the church Christianity should be distinguished as much as possible from patriotism. (R)

Creedal Assent Index
1. I believe in eternal life.
2. I believe that God revealed himself to man in Jesus Christ.
3. I believe in salvation as release from sin and freedom for new life with God.
4. I believe that the Word of God is revealed in the Scriptures.
5. I believe in God as a Heavenly Father who watches over me and to whom I am accountable.
6. I believe that Christ is a living reality.

Religious Despair Index
1. The Communion Service (Lord's Supper, Eucharist) often has little meaning to me.
2. I find myself believing in God some of the time, but not at other times.
3. My personal existence often seems meaningless and without purpose.

4. My life is often empty, filled with despair.
5. I have about given up trying to understand "worship" or get much out of it.

Orientation to Growth and Striving Index
1. I try hard to grow in understanding of what it means to live as a child of God.
2. I try hard to carry my religion over into all my other dealings in life.
3. How often to you read literature about your faith (or church)?
   _____ infrequently _____ fairly infrequently _____ fairly frequently _____ frequently
4. How often do you read the Bible?
   _____ infrequently _____ fairly infrequently _____ fairly frequently _____ frequently
5. The amount of time I spend trying to grow in understanding of my faith is:
   _____ very little _____ somewhat little _____ somewhat much _____ very much

Devotionalism Index
1. Private prayer is one of the most important and satisfying aspects of my religious experience.
2. I frequently feel very close to God in prayer, during public worship, or at important moments in my daily life.
3. How often do you ask God to forgive your sin?
   _____ infrequently _____ fairly infrequently _____ fairly frequently _____ frequently
4. How often do you pray privately in places other than at church?
   _____ infrequently _____ fairly infrequently _____ fairly frequently _____ frequently
5. When you have decisions to make in your everyday life, how often do you try to find out what God wants you to do?
   _____ infrequently _____ fairly infrequently _____ fairly frequently _____ frequently

Salience: Behavior Index
1. How often do you talk with the pastor (or other official) about some part of the worship service, for example, the sermon, Scripture, choice of hymns, etc.?
   _____ infrequently _____ fairly infrequently _____ fairly frequently _____ frequently
2. How often in the past year have you shared with another church member the problems and joys of trying to live a life of faith in God?
   _____ infrequently _____ fairly infrequently _____ fairly frequently _____ frequently
3. When faced with decisions regarding social problems, how often do you seek guidance from statements and publications provided by the church?
   _____ infrequently _____ fairly infrequently _____ fairly frequently _____ frequently
4. How often do you talk about religion with your friends, neighbors, or fellow workers?
   _____ infrequently _____ fairly infrequently _____ fairly frequently _____ frequently
5. During the last year, how often have you visited someone in need, besides relatives?
   _____ infrequently _____ fairly infrequently _____ fairly frequently _____ frequently
6. How often have you personally tried to convert someone to faith in God?
   _____ infrequently _____ fairly infrequently _____ fairly frequently _____ frequently

(R) indicates item to be reverse scored

Chapter 9

Scales of Religious Coping and Problem-Solving

How people handle life's problems and how to help people through difficult periods is a topic of obvious interest for psychologists. Until recently, however, psychologists have overlooked the important role that religious faith often plays in the coping process. Those who have explored religion and coping tend to view religion as a process (versus personality) variable, investigating when and how religion becomes involved as problems arise.

Religion often presents itself forcefully during life's difficult times. This is not to say that religious faith is appealed to only during times of crises. In fact, a leading researcher in this field suggests that people bring an already established "reservoir of religious resources with them when they face stressful times. For many, the depth and nature of this reservoir is unknown. . . . However, when people are stressed, the religious reservoir is often tapped and revealed for whatever it does (or does not) hold" (Pargament, 1997, p. 5). Thus religious faith itself is often an important source of strength for the individual facing a crisis.

The foremost systematic effort in exploring the religion and coping connection is the work of Pargament and colleagues at Bowling Green State University. Their multidimensional Religious Coping Activities Scale (9.1) identifies and measures six types of religious coping: spiritually based coping, good deeds coping, coping by expressing discontent, coping through interpersonal religious support, coping by pleading, and religious avoidance coping. Pargament's research team also developed the Religious Problem-Solving Scale (9.2). In measuring the degrees of responsibility assigned to God or self in solving problems, this scale measures three general approaches: self-directing, collaborative, or deferring (to God).

The other instrument included in this chapter is the Royal Free Interview for Religious and Spiritual Beliefs (9.3). As the scale's name indicates, this is an interview developed at the Royal Free Hospital in London that determines the extent to which spiritual, religious, and philosophical beliefs can influence the outcome of acute physical illness.

The first of these three measures is clearly a measure of Christian religious coping. The second measure is less restricted. The authors' intent with the third measure was to make the intake interview as religiously inclusive as possible.

Reference

Pargament, K. I. (1997). *The psychology of religion and coping: Theory, research, practice.* New York: Guilford.

9.1
RELIGIOUS COPING ACTIVITIES SCALE
(Pargament, Ensing, Falgout, Olsen, Reilly, Van Haitsma, & Warren, 1990)
Reviewed by P. J. Watson

Variable: The Religious Coping Activities Scale measures the extent to which people turn to religion to cope with stressful life circumstances. Research prior to the development of this instrument was based on fairly crude assessments of religious commitment (e.g., church attendance, frequency of prayer, etc.) and progress in clarifying the issue seemed to require a more sophisticated index of religiously based coping responses. Pargament et al. (1990) sought to supply such an instrument.

The Religious Coping Activities Scale monitors six types of religious coping. The Spiritually Based Activities subscale records an individual's reliance on a loving relationship with God. With the Good Deeds subscale, high scores reveal attempts to cope by behaving more in conformity with religious commitments. The Discontent subscale records an angry and alienated reaction to God and to the church. Interpersonal Religious Support operationalizes tendencies to lean on the support of clergy and church members. The Plead subscale reveals tendencies to question and bargain with God in hopes of obtaining a miraculous solution to personal problems. Religious Avoidance measures a religiously based attempt to divert attention away from stressful circumstances.

Description: Pargament et al. constructed a list of religiously based coping activities by consulting previous research, analyzing written accounts of people who used their faith to meet personal challenges, and asking clergy and religious individuals to indicate how religion had played a role in their attempts to cope. A list of 31 religious coping activities was created. These items were combined into a questionnaire that was administered to 528 churchgoers. All of these subjects had used religion to confront stressful experiences within the past year. Respondents noted how strongly they relied on each activity by using

a 4-point Likert scale ranging from "not at all" to "a great deal."

Five of the six Religious Coping Activities subscales emerged when these data were submitted to a factor analysis. These five factors explained close to 100% of the variance. Three items that did not load on a common factor were combined into a sixth subscale because they seemed to define a theoretically meaningful construct. In the factor analysis, the Spiritually Based Activities subscale was defined by 12 items, with 6 for Good Deeds, 3 each for Discontent and Plead, and 2 for Interpersonal Religious Support. Religious Avoidance was the subscale created out of three items that did not load on a common factor.

Practical Consideration: This instrument presents a straightforward list of religiously based coping activities and should be easy for subjects to read and understand. Most respondents should be able to complete the scale within 15 minutes.

Norms/Standardization: Pargament et al. supplied useful normative data. Their sample consisted of adults belonging to 10 different Roman Catholic, Lutheran, Presbyterian, Episcopalian, American Baptist, and nondenominational congregations in the midwestern United States. Of the stressful events recently experienced by these subjects, the illness or injury of family or friends was most common (25%), followed by the death of a friend or family member (18%), interpersonal problems (14%), employment difficulties (8%), and personal injuries or illness (8%). Anyone with a MMPI Lie score greater than two was eliminated.

Care was taken to ensure that samples from each congregation were as representative as possible. The final group of 586 participants was 66% female, 96% white, 38% college educated, and 64% married. Average age was 46. With regard to socioeconomic status, 30% had average family incomes of less than $25,000, with 38% between $25,000 and $49,999 and 32% at or above $50,000. Given the nature of these congregations, males and infrequent church attenders were slightly underrepresented. As Pargament et al. made clear, however, this is a common problem in psychology of religion research.

Ratings of all activities within a subscale were averaged, and means ranged from 2.64 (SD = 0.70) on the four-point scale for Spiritually Based Activities to 1.37 (SD = 0.60) for Discontent. Normative data also were supplied for the other subscales: Good Deeds, M = 2.22, SD = 0.72; Interpersonal Religious Support, M = 2.02, SD = 1.01; Plead, M = 1.75, SD = 0.74; and Religious Avoidance, M = 2.01, SD = 0.99.

Reliability: Internal reliabilities for all six subscales were adequate for research purposes. Cronbach's alphas were described as ranging from low to moderately high: Religious Avoidance, alpha = .61; Plead, alpha = .61; Discontent, alpha = .68; Interpersonal Religious Support, alpha = .78; Good Deeds, alpha = .82; and Spiritually Based Activities, alpha = .92.

Validity: Pargament et al. used their scale to predict three outcome measures of coping: a mental health questionnaire, five items estimating general nonreligious effects of the stressful event (e.g., how much had been learned, success in controlling emotions, whether individuals were strengthened or made better, etc.), and three other items operationalizing religious outcomes (changes in closeness to God, sense of belonging to church, and spiritual growth).

The Spiritually Based Activities subscale proved to be an especially strong predictor of successful coping according to all three outcome measures. The Good Deeds, Religious Support, and Religious Avoidance subscales also displayed consistently positive effects. Mixed consequences were evident for Plead, as this subscale was associated with poorer mental health but positive religious outcomes. Discontent was consistently negative in its apparent influences.

Use of multiple regression procedures demonstrated that the six Religious Coping Activities contributed to the predictability of all three outcomes over and above the variance explained by a wide array of other frequently employed religious measures. The six subscales also exhibited significant correlations with measures of nonreligious coping activities, and the Religious Coping Activities Scale once again produced an increment in the predictability of outcomes even when entered into the prediction equation after these nonreligious coping activities.

These data clearly documented the validity of the Religious Coping Activities Scale. Particularly impressive were the multiple regression findings in which the six subscales accounted for unique variance not explained by other religious variables or by nonreligious responses to stress. Without doubt, the Religious Coping Activities Scale should be an invaluable research tool for investigators interested in the influence of religion on reactions to stress.

Location:
Pargament, K. I., Ensing, D. S., Falgout, K., Olsen, H., Reilly, B., Van Haitsma, K., & Warren, R. (1990). God help me: (I): Religious coping efforts as predictors of the outcomes to significant negative life events. *American Journal of Community Psychology, 18*, 793–824.

Recent Research:
Pargament, K. I., Ishler, K., Dubow, E. F., Stanik, P., Rouiller, R., Crowe, P., Cullman, E. P., Albert, M., & Royster, B. J. (1994). Methods of religious coping with the Gulf War: Cross-sectional and longitudinal analyses. *Journal for the Scientific Study of Religion, 33*, 347–361.

Pargament, K. I., Olsen, H., Reilly, B., Falgout, K., Ensing, D. S., & Van Haitsma, K. (1992). God help me (II): The relationship of religious orientations to religious coping with negative life events. *Journal for the Scientific Study of Religion, 31*, 504–513.

Park, C. L., & Cohen, L. H. (1993). Religious and nonreligious coping with the death of a friend. *Cognitive Therapy and Research, 17*, 561–577.

Shortz, J. L., & Worthington, E. L., Jr. (1994). Young adults' recall of religiosity, attributions, and coping in parental divorce. *Journal for the Scientific Study of Religion, 33*, 172–179.

Appendix

Religious Coping Activities Scales

Please read the statements listed below and for each statement please indicate to what extent each of the following was involved in your coping with the event. Please use the following scale to record your answers:

1 = not at all
2 = somewhat
3 = quite a bit
4 = a great deal

Spiritually Based Coping

1. Trusted that God would not let anything terrible happen to me.
2. Experienced God's love and care.
3. Realized that God was trying to strengthen me.
4. In dealing with the problem, I was guided by God.
5. Realized that I didn't have to suffer since Jesus suffered for me.
6. Used Christ as an example of how I should live.
7. Took control over what I could and gave the rest to God.
8. My faith showed me different ways to handle the problem.
9. Accepted the situation was not in my hands but in the hands of God.
10. Found the lesson from God in the event.
11. God showed me how to deal with the situation.
12. Used my faith to help me decide how to cope with the situation.

Good Deeds

13. Tried to be less sinful.
14. Confessed my sins.
15. Led a more loving life.
16. Attended religious services or participated in religious rituals.
17. Participated in church groups (support groups, prayer groups, Bible studies).
18. Provided help to other church members.

Discontent

19. Felt angry with or distant from God.
20. Felt angry with or distant from the members of the church.
21. Questioned my religious beliefs and faith.

Interpersonal Religious Support

22. Received support from the clergy.
23. Received support from other members of the church.

Plead

24. Asked for a miracle.
25. Bargained with God to make things better.
26. Asked God why it happened.

Religious Avoidance

27. Focused on the world-to-come rather than the problems of this world.
28. I let God solve my problems for me.
29. Prayed or read the Bible to keep my mind off my problems.

9.2
RELIGIOUS PROBLEM-SOLVING SCALE
(Pargament, Kennell, Hathaway, Grevengoed, Newman, & Jones, 1988)
Reviewed by Nancy Stiehler Thurston

Variable: The Religious Problem-Solving Scale (RPS) explores the significant role that religion plays in the problem-solving process. It measures several religiously-based problem-solving styles or orientations. This scale was developed, in part, to test the hypothesis that one's religious problem-solving style is significantly associated with one's mental health.

Description: The Religious Problem-Solving Scale is actually comprised of three separate subscales. They were designed to distinguish different degrees of responsibility assigned to self or God in solving problems, as well as the level of initiative taken in problem solving. The Self-Directing, Collaborative, and Deferring subscales were based on the hypothesis that responsibility and initiative in problem solving is associated with greater mental health. The Self-Directing scale was based on Fromm's (1960) notion of a humanistic religion which places the responsibility for problem solving on people rather than God. The Collaborative scale was based on a notion of persons acting as co-partners with God, working together to solve life's problems (Abelson, 1969; Hart, 1984). The Deferring scale was derived from Fromm's concept of an authoritarian religion which stresses the passive submission of persons to an omnipotent God when faced with problems.

The RPS was also based conceptually on the literature which has outlined several phases to the problem-solving process: definition of the problem; generation of solutions; selection and implementation of the solution; and re-definition of the problem once it has been solved. Each of these phases was used in drafting items for the RPS.

The full form of the RPS consists of 36 items (12 for each sub-scale) scored on the same five point continuum from "Never" to "Always." Items from the three subscales are presented in random order. The short form of the RPS and its subscales are half the length of the full scales. A separate score is obtained for each of the three subscales by summing the points assigned to each item. The range of possible scores for each of the three scales is 5–60.

Practical Considerations: This paper-and-pencil measure takes approximately twenty minutes to complete in its long form (half as long in the short form). The instructions ask respondents to state how often each of the statements apply to them. No special examiner skills are needed to score or interpret this self-administered measure. The items in the scale are easy to comprehend.

Norms/Standardization: Normative data were collected from a sample of 197 members drawn from one Presbyterian church and one Missouri Synod Lutheran Church in the Midwest. The means and standard deviations obtained for each of the three scales were: Collaborative (mean = 36.02, standard deviation = 10.67); Self-Directing (mean = 29.70; standard deviation = 10.71); and Deferring (mean = 25.81; standard deviation = 9.19). Members were sampled through a procedure designed to control the effects of the degree of involvement in one's church. The sample was 57% female, 69% married, and varied in educational background. The lack of racial diversity in the sample raises questions as to the generalizability of the norms among a racially diverse population.

Reliability: Both internal consistency and test-retest reliability were found to be high. Cronbach's alpha coefficients obtained for Self-Directing, Collaborative, and Deferring problem solving were .91, .93, and .89, respectively. A test-retest reliability analysis of the scales over a one week period among a sample of 97 college students yielded the following reliability estimates: .93 (Collaborative), .94 (Self-Directing), and .87 (Deferring).

The short form of this measure also evidenced high reliability. Cronbach's alpha coefficients demonstrated high internal consistency (Collaborative = .93; Self-Directing = .91; Deferring = .89). The short form correlated highly with the full form: Collaborative (r = .97), Self-Directing (r = .98), and Deferring (r = .97).

Validity: As the authors predicted, the three problem-solving styles were found to be differentially associated with measures of religiousness as well as psychosocial competence. As expected, the Deferring orientation was associated with a religious style characterized by high religious involvement and reliance on external rules. The Collaborative style was linked to an internalized form of religiousness based on an intimate, interactive, and highly involved relationship with God. The Self-Directing style was not associated with traditional religious interest and practices, favoring instead a quest orientation to religion.

Also consistent with the authors' predictions, the Deferring style of problem solving was negatively associated with such aspects of competence as personal control, self-es-

teem, and tolerance of ambiguity. In contrast, the Self-Directing style was positively associated with personal control and self-esteem. When the effects of the Deferring and Self-Directing styles were statistically removed, the Collaborative style was also found to be positively associated with personal control and self-esteem.

A factor analysis of the 36 items of the RPS resulted in a three-factor solution which conformed well to the three scales of the RPS. This three factor solution lends strong support to the hypothesis that people use either a Self-Directing, Collaborative, or Deferring problem-solving style in their relationship with God. This finding, along with the data linking the Deferring style with poor psychosocial competence, and the data linking the Self-Directing/Collaborative styles with higher psychosocial competence, combine to support the validity of this measure.

Location:

Pargament, K. I., Kennell, J., Hathaway, W., Grevengoed, N., Newman, J., & Jones, W. (1988). Religion and the problem-solving process: Three styles of coping. *Journal for the Scientific Study of Religion, 27*, 90–104.

Subsequent Research:

Friedel, L. A., & Pargament, K. I. (1995). *Religion and coping with crises in the work environment.* Paper presented at the 103rd annual convention of the American Psychological Association, New York, NY.

Hathaway, W. & Pargament, K. I. (1990). Intrinsic religiousness, religious coping, and psychosocial competence: A covariance structure analysis. *Journal for the Scientific Study of Religion, 29*, 448–461.

Schaefer, C. A., & Gorsuch, R. L. (1991). Psychological adjustment and religiousness: The multivariate belief-motivation theory of religiousness. *Journal for the Scientific Study of Religion, 30*, 136–147.

Schaefer, C. A., & Gorsuch, R. L. (1993). Situational and personal variations in religious coping. *Journal for the Scientific Study of Religion, 32*, 136–147.

Stiehler, N. (1991). *Attitude and personality characteristics of conservative and mainline/liberal church congregations.* Unpublished doctoral dissertation, Central Michigan University, Mount Pleasant, MI.

References

Abelson, J. (1969). *The immanence of God in rabbinical literature*. New York: Hermon Press.

Fromm, E. (1960). *Psychoanalysis and religion*. New York: Holt, Rinehart, & Winston.

Hart, A. D. (1984). *Coping with depression in the ministry and other helping professions*. Waco: Word Books.

Appendix

Religious Problem-solving Scale

Following are the items included in the Religious Problem-Solving Scale. Items from the three subscales (Collaborative, Self-Directive, and Deferring) were mixed together to form a single questionnaire. All items were scored on the same 5-point Likert continuum ranging from "never" to "always." The short form of this measure consists of the first 18 of the 36 items listed below.

1. [C]   When I have a problem, I talk to God about it and together we decide what it means.

2. [D]   Rather than trying to come up with the right solution to a problem myself, I let God decide how to deal with it.

3. [S]   When faced with trouble, I deal with my feelings without God's help.

4. [D]   When a situation makes me anxious, I wait for God to take those feelings away.

5. [C]   Together, God and I put my plans into action.

6. [C]   When it comes to deciding how to solve a problem, God and I work together as partners.

7. [S]   I act to solve my problems without God's help.

8. [S]   When I have difficulty, I decide what it means by myself without help from God.

9. [D]   I don't spend much time thinking about troubles I've had; God makes sense of them for me.

10. [C]   When considering a difficult situation, God and I work together to think of possible solutions.

11. [D]   When a troublesome issue arises, I leave it up to God to decide what it means for me.

12. [S]   When thinking about a difficulty, I try to come up with possible solutions without God's help.

13. [C]   After solving a problem, I work with God to make sense of it.

14. [S]   When deciding on a solution, I make a choice independent of God's input.

15. [D]   In carrying out the solutions to my problems, I wait for God to take control and know somehow He'll work it out.

16. [D]   I do not think about different solutions to my problems because God provides them for me.

17. [S]   After I've gone through a rough time, I try to make sense of it without relying on God.

18. [C] When I feel nervous or anxious about a problem, I work together with God to find a way to relieve my worries.

19. [C] When I'm upset, I try to soothe myself, and also share the unpleasantness with God so He can comfort me.

20. [S] When faced with a decision, I make the best choice I can without God's involvement.

21. [D] God solves problems for me without my doing anything.

22. [D] When I have a problem, I try not to think about it and wait for God to tell me what it means.

23. [C] In carrying out solutions, I work hard at them knowing God is working right along with me.

24. [S] When a difficult period is over, I make sense of what happened on my own without involvement from God.

25. [C] When faced with a question, I work together with God to figure it out.

26. [S] When I feel nervous or anxious, I calm myself without relying on God.

27. [S] God doesn't put solutions to my problems into action; I carry them out myself.

28. [D] I don't worry too much about learning from difficult situations, since God will make me grow in the right direction.

29. [S] When I am trying to come up with different solutions to troubles I am facing, I do not get them from God but think of them myself.

30. [C] When a hard time has passed, God works with me to help me learn from it.

31. [C] God and I talk together and decide upon the best answer to my question.

32. [D] When faced with a decision, I wait for God to make the best choice for me.

33. [D] I do not become upset or nervous because God solves my problems for me.

34. [D] When I run into trouble, I simply trust in God knowing that He will show me the possible solutions.

35. [S] When I run into a difficult situation, I make sense out of it on my own without divine assistance.

36. [C] The Lord works with me to help me see a number of different ways that a problem can be solved.

[C]   Collaborative
[S]   Self-Directing
[D]   Deferring

Pargament, K. I., Kennell, J., Hathaway, W., Grevengoed, N., Newman, J., & Jones, W. (1988). Religion and the problem-solving process: Three styles of coping. *Journal for the Scientific Study of Religion, 27,* 90–104. Copyright © 1988 Journal for the Scientific Study of Religion. Reprinted with permission.

9.3
THE ROYAL FREE INTERVIEW FOR RELIGIOUS AND
SPIRITUAL BELIEFS (King, Speck, & Thomas, 1995)
Reviewed by Kevin S. Seybold

Variable: The Royal Free Interview for Religious and Spiritual Beliefs attempts to establish whether spiritual, religious, or philosophical beliefs can be empirically measured in patients admitted into the hospital with an acute physical illness and, ultimately, to determine if those beliefs have any influence on the outcome of the illness. The interview is meant to assess beliefs that are based not just upon North American Christianity (a serious limitation of most published religious measures according to the authors), but upon a broader understanding of the religious, spiritual, and philosophical. As such, religion in the survey refers to the practice of and/or the framework for a system of beliefs, codes, rituals, and values. Spiritual is taken in its broad sense to mean an individual's belief in a power extraneous to him or herself. A search for meaning in life without reference to an external power is referred to as philosophical belief in the survey.

Description: An early version of the interview was used in a study of 300 patients admitted into the Royal Free Hospital of London (King, Speck, & Thomas, 1994). The results of that study led to the refinement of the instrument into its present form as reported in King et al. (1995). The scale consists of a section (Section A) for demographic data and a second section (Section B) for a physician's assessment of the patient's condition. After a paragraph of instructions, the third section (Section C) contains the main body of the religious survey. This third section follows a branching format and has questions about the nature of the subject's spiritual beliefs and religious and philosophical understanding. (Questions in Section C could be used in settings other than hospitals or where the subjects are ill.) Depending on the answers given by the subject, the interviewer will take various branches through the survey. Some of the questions require the subject to respond quantitatively by indicating on an 11 point scale (0–10) how strongly he or she holds a particular belief.

Following these questions, there are six questions that deal specifically with the subject's understanding about any association between his or her illness and religious beliefs. Two scales are derived from the survey: (a) a scale measuring spiritual belief (sum of answers to questions 3,9,10,11, and 12), and (b) a philosophical scale (sum of answers to questions 3,15,16, and 17).

Practical Considerations: The survey is easy to administer and score, requiring only the summation of scores given on the quantitative scales for interpretation. An exception to this is the scoring of Question 2, which requires the test administrator to determine, based on an open response question, whether the subject has expressed a religious understanding, a spiritual understanding without religious observance, or a philosophical understanding without any religious or spiritual understanding. Directions for administration are provided within the questionnaire as are definitions of religion, spiritual, and philosophy to be used by the subject as he or she takes the survey.

Norms/Standardization: Three reference populations were used to standardize the interview. In each of the three populations, only those individuals who could read and speak English were included. The populations used and the number of subjects included from each were the following: (a) a convenience sample of staff working in various departments at the Royal Free Hospital (n =153), (b) a consecutive series of non-acutely ill patients at a general practice in London (n =123), and (c) individuals strongly associated with a religious faith (e.g., chaplains, ministers, nuns, daily observant Muslim staff at the Royal Free Hospital, administrative staff associated with religious organizations) selected from among personal contacts in order to validate the spiritual section of the survey (*n* = 29).

Subjects from the staff at the Royal Free Hospital (RFH) differed from the general practice (GP) subjects in that they came from a higher social class (Mantel-Haenszel test for linear association = 33.16, df = 1, *p* < .0001) and were older (Mann-Whitney *U* = 7507.5, *p* = .0039). Religious faith was reported by 45% of the RFH staff and 47% of the GP subjects and was equally likely among men and women. The Christian faith was reported in 75% of the total subjects. Of those reporting religious faith, 67% of the RFH group and 45% of the GP group practiced their faith on a daily basis (prayer, reading, etc.); 21% and 25% weekly; and 10% and 31% monthly or less. Again, there were no differences in frequency of religious practice among males and females.

Of the RFH staff, 71% reported having a spiritual belief, compared to 75% of the GP subjects. The GP patients reported a higher mean score on the spiritual scale, questions 3+9+10+11+12 (30.2 vs 25.3), but there was no difference between the two groups on the philosophical scale, questions 3+15+16+17 (22.1 vs 22.0). Finally, there were no significant associations between age or social class and spiritual or philosophical scale scores. Mean scores on the spiritual scale were higher for men (30.0), however, than for women (26.6), *t*(199) = 1.81, *p* = .07.

Although the stated purpose of the interview was to assess religious, spiritual, and philosophical beliefs in populations not limited to a particular religious creed or philosophy, a limitation of the standardization procedure, as pointed out by the authors, was that the number of non-Christian people interviewed was insignificant. Standardization in people of other ethnic, religious, and cultural groups remains to be performed.

Reliability: Internal reliability was computed for the spiritual and philosophical scales. The alpha coefficient for the spiritual scale was 0.81 and 0.60 for the philosophical scale. Test-retest reliability was measured by assessing 103 of the hospital staff subjects a second time one week later. Correlation coefficients for the questions scored using the 11 point scale were high and ranged from 0.76 to 0.93 (Five correlations were above .90, four were above .85, and four were below .85.). Kappa coefficients for the categorical questions (4,5,8,13,14) were also high ranging from 0.67 to 1.0. Test-retest reliability coefficients for the spiritual and philosophical scales were 0.95 and 0.91 respectively.

Validity: Comparisons with other measures of religious or spiritual belief were not made, so concurrent validity is unknown. Criterion validity was assessed in two ways: (a) measuring the strength of the association between spiritual belief (spiritual scale score) and religious observance, and (b) comparing the spiritual scale score of the third reference group (the individuals strongly associated with a religious faith) with the spiritual scores of the other two reference groups. The hypothesis was that the scores for the third group would be higher than for the other two populations.

The Pearson correlation for the association between the spiritual scores and religious observance was 0.41 (p < .0005); a linear relationship between frequency of religious observance and strength of belief was seen. The mean spiritual scale score of the third reference group (37.1) was significantly higher than the combined scores of the RFH and GP groups (27.6), *t*(228) = 4.06, *p* < .0005.

Location:
King, M., Speck, P., & Thomas, A. (1995). The Royal Free Interview for Religious and Spiritual Beliefs: Development and standardization. *Psychological Medicine*, 25, 1125–1134.

Recent Research: None.

Reference

King, M., Speck, P., & Thomas, A. (1994). Spiritual and religious beliefs in acute illness: Is this a feasible area for study? *Social Science and Medicine*, 38, 631–636.

Appendix

The Royal Free Interview for Religious and Spiritual Beliefs

PATIENT INTERVIEW   Research ID Number: . . . .

Section A

Demographic Data   Address:

Hospital Record Number:
Name:
Age: Sex: Telephone:
Marital Status: Employed/Unemployed:
Job Description: Spouse's Job:
Job Status (e.g. manager):
Ethnic Origin: Country of Birth:
Who is at home with you at present?
(record detail of other residents/ family members)

Section B

Clinician's Assessment of Patient's Condition at Time of Admission

Nonacute   [ ]
Moderate   [ ]
Serious   [ ] i.e., potentially life threatening
Very serious   [ ] i.e., life threatening now

Section C

Introduction by interviewer:
Thank you for agreeing to be interviewed. We are trying to understand whether a person's beliefs affect what happens to them. I am going to ask you some questions about your beliefs. In using the word *"religion,"* we are meaning the actual practice of a faith, e.g., going to church or synagogue. Some people don't follow a specific religion but do have *spiritual* beliefs (for example, they believe that there is some other power or force outside themselves which might influence their life). Some people make sense of what happens to them in life without a belief in a God or any outside power. This could be called their philosophy of life. (Interviewer may need to amplify this statement to make sure the patient understands.)

1. In the way I've just described, would you say you have a *religious* or *spiritual* or some other *philosophical* understanding of your life?
   YES/NO *If NO, go to Question 3*

2. *If Yes*, can you explain briefly what form this has taken?

3. In respect to belief or non-belief where would you place yourself, at present, on this scale?

(*Interviewer show scale*)

Interviewer:

      If the subject expresses (in Q2) a religious understanding, continue with *Question 4.*

      If the subject expresses a spiritual understanding without religious observance, go to *Question 9.*

      If the subject expresses a philosophical understanding in the absence of any religious or spiritual understanding, continue with *Question 14.*

      If subject expresses no belief at all, go to *Question 19.*

Religious Understanding

  4. What religion do you observe?

  5. If Christian, which denomination?
     If other, orthodox or liberal?

  6. How important to you is the actual practice of your faith?

(*Interviewer show scale*)

  7. What form does this take:

      private prayer
      worship attendance
      reading about my faith
      sharing with others
      one to one contact with religious leader
      observing religious rituals (e.g. diet)
      other (specify)

  8. How often do you practice your faith, in any form?
     At least daily/monthly/yearly or less

Now continue with question 9

Spiritual Belief

  9. You said that you believe in a power or force outside of yourself. How much does this influence what happens to you in your life? (i.e., can this affect your day-to-day life, e.g., chance meetings, accidents, illness or unexpected opportunities?).

(*Interviewer show scale*)

10. How much can this power affect how you respond to things that happen to you? (i.e., how much does it help you to cope when you are affected personally by change or other events in your life?)
    (Interviewer to make sure patients understand the focus is on the personal nature of life events)

(*Interviewer show scale*)

11. How much does this power help you to understand why things happen in the world, outside of your day-to-day activities? (e.g., political events, wars, accidents?)

(Interviewer show scale)

12. What about natural disasters, like earthquakes, floods?

(Interviewer show scale)

13. Do you communicate in any way with this power?
        Yes/No/Unsure
     If yes, describe form of communication (e.g., prayer, contact through a medium)

Now go to *Question 18*

Philosophical Understanding

14. Can you tell me about your philosophical approach to life? Does it have a specific name?
     (Interviewer may add: existentialism (man is free and responsible for his own acts),
     atheism (belief that there is no God), humanism (belief in human effort rather than reli-
     gion), free thinkers (skeptic who forms his own opinions).)

15. How much does this philosophy influence how you respond to day-to-day events? (i.e.,
     How much does it help you to cope with things that happen to you?)
     (Interviewer to make sure patients understand the focus is on the personal nature of life
     events)

(Interviewer show scale)

16. How much does this philosophy help you to understand why things happen in the world,
     outside of your day-to-day activities? (e.g., political events, wars, accidents?)

(Interviewer show scale)

17. What about natural disasters, like earthquakes, floods?

(Interviewer show scale)

----

18. How much have your beliefs helped you during this illness?

(Interviewer show scale)

ALL SUBJECTS TO ANSWER THE REMAINDER

19. I should now like to ask you what you think about views people sometimes express
     about illness.
     a. Do you feel illness is a punishment for wrong doing?

(Interviewer show scale)

     b. Do you feel illness is predetermined/due to fate?

(Interviewer show scale)

     c. Do you feel illness is sent to test/try us?

(Interviewer show scale)

     d. Do you feel that illness is a consequence of lifestyle (e.g., smoking, drinking, sex)?

(*Interviewer show scale*)

20. With these thoughts in mind, would you think there is any link/association between *your* illness and *your* religious/spiritual/philosophical approach to life?

(*Interviewer show scale*)

This Section to be given to Interviewee

FOR EACH QUESTION CIRCLE THE NUMBER ON THE LINE WHICH IS CLOSEST TO YOUR VIEW

Question 3 Totally disbelieve	0 1 2 3 4 5 6 7 8 9 10	Very strongly believe
Question 6 Not necessary	0 1 2 3 4 5 6 7 8 9 10	Essential
Question 9 No influence	0 1 2 3 4 5 6 7 8 9 10	Very strong influence
Question 10 No influence	0 1 2 3 4 5 6 7 8 9 10	Very strong influence
Question 11 No help at all in my understanding	0 1 2 3 4 5 6 7 8 9 10	Greatly helps my understanding
Question 12 No help at all in my understanding	0 1 2 3 4 5 6 7 8 9 10	Greatly helps my understanding
Question 15 No influence	0 1 2 3 4 5 6 7 8 9 10	Very strong influence
Question 16 No help at all in my understanding	0 1 2 3 4 5 6 7 8 9 10	Greatly helps my understanding
Question 17 No help at all in my understanding	0 1 2 3 4 5 6 7 8 9 10	Greatly helps my understanding

Question 18													
No help at all	0	1	2	3	4	5	6	7	8	9	10		Greatly helped

Question 19a													
Strongly disagree	0	1	2	3	4	5	6	7	8	9	10		Strongly agree

Question 19b													
Strongly disagree	0	1	2	3	4	5	6	7	8	9	10		Strongly agree

Question 19c													
Strongly disagree	0	1	2	3	4	5	6	7	8	9	10		Strongly agree

Question 19d													
Strongly disagree	0	1	2	3	4	5	6	7	8	9	10		Strongly agree

Question 20													
Convinced there is NO link	0	1	2	3	4	5	6	7	8	9	10		Convinced there IS a link

King, M., Speck, P., & Thomas, A. (1995). The Royal Free Interview for Religious and Spiritual Beliefs: Development and standardization, *Psychological Medicine 25*, 1125–1134. Copyright © 1995 Cambridge University Press. Reprinted with permission of Cambridge University Press.

Chapter 10

Scales of Spirituality and Mysticism

Spirituality has captured the attention of researchers in the psychology of religion just as it has become a topic of interest in the culture at large now for the past few decades. In fact, during the 1980s and particularly the 1990s, we continue to witness an explosion of research on the topic, with many measures of spirituality now being reported in the literature. Although this volume is expressly a handbook of *religious* measures, we also recognize that religion and spirituality are closely connected. In fact, the word "spirituality" is taken from the Latin root *spiritus* meaning breath or life, with the Latin *spiritulis* designating simply a person "of the spirit." Spirituality is frequently mentioned in both the Hebrew Old Testament (*ruach*) and the Greek New Testament (*pneuma*), and the term has historically been referenced only in the context of religion. For many, spirituality is experienced and expressed through conventional religious understanding, and the contemporary conception of spirituality as separate from religion has a surprisingly short history. Indeed, it was with the rise of secularism in this century and a growing disillusionment with religious institutions, particularly in Western society since the 1960s, that spirituality began to acquire distinct meanings and connotations separate from religion.

There are six measures reviewed in this chapter, including one scale on mystical experience, a phenomenon central to spirituality. This is but a small sample of the large number of spirituality scales that have recently been published and a subsequent volume to review many of these measures is now planned. Other than the Saur and Saur Spiritual Themes and Religious Responses Test (10.4), which is a projective measure, and Hood's Mysticism Scale (10.2), all of the scales reviewed here use the term "God," though the Index of Core Spiritual Experiences (10.1) qualifies its use of the term and encourages respondents to use their own definition of God when responding to the questions. It is precisely these three scales (10.1, 10.2, and 10.4) that are probably the least culture bound measures reviewed in this chapter, though their applicability to non-Western religion has not been established.

In contrast, Moberg's Spiritual Well-Being Questionnaire (10.5) makes specific references to the Bible, church, religious television programs, etc., and is thus limited to a Christian population. Hall and Edwards's Spiritual Assessment Inventory (10.3) mentions the Bible in one item only and contains expressions that may be unique to Judeo-Christian or at least Western religion. Among the most widely used instruments in this entire volume, the Spiritual Well-Being Scale (10.6), authored by Paloutzian and Ellison, is clearly useful beyond the Judeo-Christian tradition, but it too appears limited to Western thought.

10.1
INDEX OF CORE SPIRITUAL EXPERIENCES (Kass, Friedman, Lesserman, Zuttermeister & Benson, 1991)

Reviewed by Laura Hinebaugh-Igoe

Variable: The Index of Core Spiritual Experiences (INSPIRIT) was developed to identify experiences that are described in more intense or concrete terms than an amorphous "belief in God." The characteristic elements of core spiritual experiences are (a) a distinct event and a cognitive appraisal of that event resulting in a personal conviction of God's existence and (b) the perception of a highly internalized relationship between God and the person (i.e., God dwells within and a corresponding feeling of unity or closeness to God).

The intent of the INSPIRIT is twofold to (a) identify core spiritual experiences that satisfy the aforementioned criteria and (b) investigate any relationships between this scale and health outcomes.

Description: The INSPIRIT contains 7 items. Items 5, 6, and 7 were newly developed for this index. Items 1, 2, and 4 are modifications of items originally developed by the National Opinion Research Center (NORC) (Davis & Smith, 1985). Item 3 was developed by NORC, in conjunction with Greeley (1974). Scale items were devised or chosen to operationalize the two key characteristics that distinguish core spiritual experiences.

The original item pool contained 11 questions. These included 4 additional items developed by NORC in conjunction with Greeley. Principal components analysis with orthogonal varimax rotation of the 11 items yielded three factors. However, there was a dramatic gap in loadings separating the first factor, containing items 1–7 (eigenvalue = 4.58), from the latter two (items 9–10; eigenvalue = 1.96 and items 8, 11; eigenvalue = 1.29). Because questions 8–11 did not form a unified factor, and because items 1–7 contained the two key aspects of core spiritual experiences, the final version of the INSPIRIT consists of items 1–7, which Kass et al. (1991) identified as assessing the

two fundamental aspects of Core Spiritual Experiences. Items 3, 5, and 7 identify experiences leading to a conviction of God's existence, whereas items 1, 2, 4, and 6 measure behaviors and attitudes that would be present among those experiencing a closeness to God.

In scoring the INSPIRIT, each item receives a score of 1–4, and subjects are directed to circle the response that best describes themselves. The subject's total INSPIRIT score is the mean of all items weighted equally. Scores range from 1.75 to 4.0. Scores ranging from 3.5 to 4.0 were considered a strong indication of the occurrence of at least one core spiritual experience.

Scoring the checklist format of item 7 has produced recent controversy. The author utilizes the highest score recorded for any of the 12 subtypes as the score for the whole question (Kass et al., 1991). VandeCreek, Ayres, and Bassham (1995) suggest including all responses on the 12-part checklist. VandeCreek et al. (1995) claim that the Kass method of scoring excludes significant data of potential clinical importance. Utilizing the VandeCreek method of scoring, approximately 80% acknowledged at least one experience that strengthened their belief in God (coding at least one item as "3" or "4"), whereas the Kass method reported between 5% and 30%.

Practical Considerations: The administration of this paper-and-pencil measure requires no special skills. In an attempt to diffuse social desirability, instructions emphasize that there are no "right" or "wrong" answers, and respondents are encouraged to employ their personal definition of what they call "God" when responding to the items.

Norms/Standardization: The INSPIRIT was sampled against a group of 83 adult outpatients participating in a hospital-based behavioral medicine program for various medical diagnoses, including hypertension, cancer, musculoskeletal disorders, and chronic pain. This rather unique standardization group was necessary in order to measure the hypothesized relationship between core spiritual experiences and health improvements. The sample consisted of predominantly white (94%), female (66%) outpatients of divergent religious backgrounds; Catholic (37%), Protestant (23%), and Jewish (40%). The educational background was significantly above average, with a mean indicating most participants had received some degree of postsecondary schooling (M = 16.1 years, SD = 2.5). There is both an overrepresentation of whites and an underrepresentation of the less educated, which limits the generalizability of the INSPIRIT beyond this selective sample.

In response to this limitation, a second study by VandeCreek et al. (1995) tested the INSPIRIT in a more generalized health-care setting with a larger group of respondents. Data were collected from 247 outpatients at a cancer hospital and 124 family members in a surgical waiting room. The majority of respondents were married (72%), white (91%), and male (60%). The mean age was 50 years (range = 17 to 78) and the level of education was almost equally distributed: 38% had completed high school, 30% had taken some college courses, and 32% had graduated from college. Differences between the two samples had little effect, with mean scores and standard deviations produced in the VandeCreek et al. study (M = 2.97, SD = .74) similar to those reported by Kass; (M = 2.80, SD = .83). While the normative data are based on a wide variety of respondents, generalizability is still limited until efforts are made to investigate how the INSPIRIT functions among minority groups.

Reliability: A principal components analysis of the INSPIRIT retained all seven items in a single component (eigenvalue = 4.42), accounting for 63% of the explained variance and loadings (representing the correlation between each item and the single component extracted) ranging from .69 to .85. Utilizing Cronbach's coefficient alpha, an internal-consistency reliability estimate, the INSPIRIT yielded a .90 correlation, indicating an impressive degree of internal reliability.

Reliability estimates are also available for the VandeCreek method of scoring. When the number of factors was limited to two, factor analysis of the six items and the 12 parts of the checklist resulted in one factor accounting for 34% of the variance and a second factor accounting for 8.4% of the variance. Loadings ranged from .52 to .68 for the first factor, and from .65 to .79 for the second factor. Cronbach's coefficient alpha was .88.

Validity: Hypothesized group differences and correlations were used to assess the construct validity of the INSPIRIT. Based on several studies that concluded that meditation is significantly related to the occurrence of spiritual experiences (Davidson, 1976; Kornfield, 1979; Walsh, 1978), Kass et al. (1991) hypothesized a relationship between INSPIRIT scores and meditative experience. At the onset of treatment, subjects in the sample were divided into two groups: those with less than one month of meditative experience and those with more than one month of meditative experience. As predicted, a significant difference (p < .04) in means was found between the less experienced (M = 2.70) and the more experienced (M = 3.15). In demonstrating the ability of the INSPIRIT to discriminate between groups where one might logically predict differences in degree of core spiritual experiences, these results assist in establishing construct validity.

Convergent and discriminant construct validity were supported in a series of predicted correlations between the INSPIRIT and other measures of religious or spiritual experiences. More specifically, Kass et al. (1991) hypothesized, and analysis supported, a positive correlation between the INSPIRIT and the Intrinsic scale of the Religious Orientation Inventory (ROI) (Allport

& Ross, 1967) and a weak negative correlation with the Extrinsic Scale of the ROI ($r = .69$, $p < .0001$ and $r = -.26$, $p < .06$; respectively).

Additional assessments of construct validity were reported in the VandeCreek et al. study (1995). Correlations between the INSPIRIT and the Intrinsic Religious Motivation Scale (IRMS) (Hoge, 1972) were substantial, further suggesting that the INSPIRIT scale reflects intrinsic religiosity. VandeCreek then compared INSPIRIT correlations with the IRMS using the Kass method for scoring item 7 ($r = .61$) and the VandeCreek method for scoring item 7 ($r = .54$). VandeCreek explains this discrepancy by suggesting that the spiritual experiences reported in the seventh item may not be reflective of intrinsic religiosity. Alternatively, because the Kass scoring method places less emphasis on the quantity of spiritual experiences and more emphasis on the cognitive impact of spiritual experiences (irrespective of their number), it is possible that this scoring method is more reflective of intrinsic religiosity.

Further investigation of both scoring methods are required for clarification of these issues.

Location:

Kass, J. D., Friedman, R., Lesserman, J., Zuttermeister, P., & Benson, H. (1991). Health outcomes and a new index of spiritual experience. *Journal for the Scientific Study of Religion, 30*(2), 203–211.

Subsequent Research:

VandeCreek, L., Ayres, S., & Bassham, M. (1995). Using the INSPIRIT to conduct spiritual assessments. *Journal of Pastoral Care, 49*(1), 83–89.

References

Allport, G. W., & Ross, J. M. (1967). Personal religious orientation and prejudice. *Journal of Personality and Social Psychology, 5*(4), 434–443.

Davidson, J. (1976). The physiology of meditation and mystical states of consciousness. *Perspectives in Biology and Medicine, 19*, 345–379.

Davis, J. A., & Smith, T. W. (1985). *General social surveys: 1972–1985.* Chicago: National Opinion Research Center.

Greeley, A. (1974). *Ecstasy: A way of knowing.* Englewood Cliffs, New Jersey: Prentice Hall.

Hoge, D. (1972). A validated intrinsic religious motivation scale. *Journal for the Scientific Study of Religion, 11*(4), 369–376.

Kornfield, J. (1979). Intensive insight meditation: A phenomonological study. *The Journal of Transpersonal Psychology, 2*(1), 41–58.

Walsh, R. (1978). Initial meditative experiences. *Journal of Transpersonal Psychology, 10*(1), 1–28.

Appendix

Index of Core Spiritual Experiences

Instructions: The following questions concern your spiritual or religious beliefs and experiences. There are no right or wrong answers. For each question, circle the number of the answer that is most true for you.

1. How strongly religious (or spiritually oriented) do you consider yourself to be? (strong; somewhat strong; not very strong; not at all; can't answer)

2. About how often do you spend time on religious or spiritual practices? (several times per day-several times per week; once per week-several times per month; once per month-several times per year; once a year or less)

3. How often have you felt as though you were very close to a powerful spiritual force that seemed to lift you outside yourself? (never; once or twice; several times; often; can't answer)

    People have many different definitions of the "Higher Power" that we often call "God." Please use your definition of God when answering the following questions.

4. How close do you feel to God? (extremely close; somewhat close; not very close; I don't believe in God; can't answer)

5. Have you ever had an experience that has convinced you that God exists? (yes; no; can't answer)

6. Indicate whether you agree or disagree with this statement: "God dwells within you." (definitely disagree; tend to disagree; tend to agree; definitely agree)

7. The following list describes spiritual experiences that some people have had. Please indicate if you have had any of these experiences and the extent to which each of them has affected your belief in God.

   The response choices are:

   I had this experience and it:

   4) Convinced me of God's existence

   3) Strengthened belief in God; or

   2) Did not strengthen belief in God.

   1) I have never had this experience.

A. An experience of God's energy or presence

B. An experience of a great spiritual figure (e.g., Jesus, Mary, Elijah, Buddha)

C. An experience of angels or guiding spirits

D. An experience of communication with someone who has died

E. Meeting or listening to a spiritual teacher or master

F. An overwhelming experience of love

G. An experience of profound inner peace

H. An experience of complete joy and ecstasy

I. A miraculous (or not normally occurring) event

J. A healing of your body or mind (or witnessed such a healing)

K. A feeling of unity with the earth and all living beings

L. An experience with near death or life after death

M. Other

Kass, J. D., Friedman, R., Lesserman, J., Zuttermeister, P., & Benson, H. (1941). Health outcomes and a new index of spiritual experience. *Journal for the Scientific Study of Religion, 30 (2)*, 203–211. Copyright © 1991 Journal for the Scientific Study of Religion. Reprinted with permission.

10.2
THE MYSTICISM SCALE: RESEARCH FORM D (M SCALE) (Hood, 1975)
Reviewed by Christopher T. Burris

Variable: The M scale is a self-report instrument intended to assess an individual's intense experiences, characterized by a sense of unity with the outside world and/or with "nothingness," which may or may not be religiously interpreted.

Description: The M scale consists of 32 items—drawn from an original pool of 108 on the basis of face validity and ability to differentiate between high- and low-scale scorers—explicitly intended to operationalize eight of Stace's (1960) nine phenomenological criteria for mystical experience. Specifically, four items each are devoted to the following: (a) Ego Quality (loss of self—nos. 3, 4, 6, and 24); (b) Unifying Quality (perceptions of oneness—nos. 12, 19, 28, and 30); (c) Inner Subjective Quality (perception of all objects as animate—nos. 8, 10, 29, and 31); (d) Temporal/ Spatial Quality (distortion of time and space—nos. 1, 11, 15, and 27); (e) Noetic Quality (perceptions of special knowledge or insight—nos. 13, 16, 17, and 26); (f) Ineffability (difficulty with articulation—nos. 2, 21, 23, and 32); (g) Positive Affect (experience of peace or bliss—nos. 5, 7, 18, and 25); and (h) Religious Quality (perceptions of sacredness or wonder—nos. 9, 14, 20, and 22). Half of the items are reverse worded.

A −2 (definitely not true) to +2 (probably true) Likert-type response format is used. There is no midpoint per se, although respondents are instructed to write a question mark (equivalent to 0) when they cannot decide on an answer. Scoring is accomplished by first reverse scoring all negatively worded items, adding three to each item's value (including "?s"), and finally summing item scores. M scale scores can thus range from a low of 32 to a high of 160.

The M scale's basis in Stace's (1960) eight mysticism criteria notwithstanding, Hood and other researchers have made little use of the eight subscales, instead analyzing reported mystical experience at a more molar level. Specifically, the M subscales of choice have until recently been based on the two-component structure reported by Hood (1975)—the first component corresponding to intense experience of unity, the second to affectively charged, religiously interpreted insight. At least two notable alternative structures have been proposed, however. Caird (1988; N = 115) suggested a three-factor solution, retaining the general or unity factor and splitting the interpretation factor into religious- and knowledge-based subscales. Hood, Morris, and Watson (1993) reported a different three-factor solution based on a much larger sample (N = 740)—the first component corresponding to "extrovertive" mysticism (experienced unity

with the external world), the second to religious interpretation, and the third to "introvertive" mysticism (experienced unity with "nothingness"). Hood, Spilka, Hunsberger, and Gorsuch (1996) have recently recommended that subscales based on this three-factor solution be used in subsequent research in order to tap the potentially important conceptual distinction between introvertive and extrovertive unitive experience. For a more detailed presentation of conceptual issues and research relating to the M scale, see Hood et al. (1996).

Practical Considerations: Administration is typically paper-and-pencil, although oral administration using a yes/no response format has also been done (Hood, Morris, & Watson, 1990). Instructions to the respondent are clear and straightforward, as is scoring. The M scale in general appears nonsectarian and nonsexist in wording and content, and can therefore be administered without modification across a broad range of samples.

Norms/Standardization: Hood's (1975) initial validation sample consisted of 300 predominantly Protestant undergraduates. M scale means were 109.3 for males and 119.4 for females; no significance test was reported for the apparent sex difference (see also Smurthwaite & McDonald, 1987; Swartz & Seginer, 1981). Hood also reported M scale means for an additional four samples: two groups of undergraduates, sizes 65 and 52, at a fundamentalist Christian college in the southern United States (Ms = 132.2 and 114.9, respectively), and two groups, sizes 83 and 29, at the University of Tennessee at Chattanooga (Ms = 110.2 and 104.9, respectively). As Hood noted, the anomalously high mean of the first Christian college sample may have been attributable, at least in part, to a situational demand for responses attesting to one's personal religiosity.

Reliability: Total M scale reliability appears adequate: Hood (1975) reported corrected item-total correlations ranging from .29 (#2) to .55 (#28) in his original size-300 sample.

Hood et al. (1993) reported reasonable relia-bilities for subscales based on their 3-factor solution as well: Alpha coefficients were .76, .69, and .76 for the Extrovertive, Intro-vertive, and Religious Interpretation Scales, respectively.

Validity: The validity of the M scale is rather well documented. Supportive of its convergent validity, the M scale has been found to be related to measures of openness to experience, religious experience broadly construed, and traditional religious motiva-tion (Hood, 1975). It is also related to ab-sorption and hypnotizability, but unrelated to social desirability (Spanos & Moretti, 1988). Supportive of its discriminant valid-ity, relationships between the M scale and various indices of psychopathology have been generally unremarkable. Caird (1987), for example, found no relationship between M scale scores and either neuroticism or psychoticism as measured by the Eysenck Personality Questionnaire, for example. Moreover, although Stifler, Greer, Sneck, and Dovenmuehle (1993) found that reli-giously delusional psychotic individuals and members of contemplative groups reported similar levels of mystical experience as compared to "normals" (i.e., a group of hos-pital employees), contemplatives were more similar to the "normal" versus the psychotic group in terms of reported (relatively low) levels of psychopathology. Indeed, Hood, Hall, Watson, and Biderman (1979) found self-reported mysticism to be related to a number of positive personality characteris-tics such as creativity and tolerance (see also Cowling, 1985; Hood, 1975; Spanos & Moretti, 1988).

Location:
Hood, R. W., Jr. (1975). The construction and preliminary validation of a measure of reported mystical experience. *Journal for the Scientific Study of Religion, 14*, 29–41.

Subsequent Research:
Hood, R. W., Jr. (1977). Eliciting mystical states of consciousness with semistructured nature experi-ences. *Journal for the Scientific Study of Religion, 16,* 155–163.
Hood, R. W., Jr., Morris, R. J., & Watson, P. J.

(1990). Quasi-experimental elicitation of the differ-ential report of religious experiences among intrin-sic and indiscriminately pro-religious types. *Jour-nal for the Scientific Study of Religion, 29,* 164–172.
Propst, L. R. (1979). Effects of personality and loss of anonymity on aggression: A reevaluation of deindividuation. *Journal of Personality, 47,* 531–545.
Smurthwaite, T. J., & McDonald, R. D. (1987). Examining ecological concern among persons re-porting mystical experiences. *Psychological Re-ports, 60,* 591–596.

References

Caird, D. (1987). Religiosity and personality: Are mystics introverted, neurotic, or psychotic? *British Journal of Social Psychology, 26*, 345–346.
Caird, D. (1988). The structure of Hood's mysti-cism scale: A factor-analytic study. *Journal for the Scientific Study of Religion, 27*, 122–127.
Cowling, W. R. (1985). Relationship of mystical experience, differentiation, and creativity. *Percep-tual and Motor Skills, 61*, 451–456.
Hood, R. W., Jr. (1975). The construction and preliminary validation of a measure of reported mystical experience. *Journal for the Scientific Study of Religion, 14*, 29–41.
Hood, R. W., Jr., Hall, J. R., Watson, P. J., & Bi-derman, M. (1979). Personality correlates of the re-port of mystical experience. *Psychological Reports, 44*, 804–806.
Hood, R. W., Jr., Morris, R. J., & Watson, P. J. (1993). Further factor analysis of Hood's Mysti-cism Scale. *Psychological Reports, 73*, 1176–1178.
Hood, R. W., Jr., Spilka, B., Hunsberger, B., & Gorsuch, R. (1996). *The psychology of religion: An empirical approach.* New York: Guilford.
Stace, W. T. (1960). *Mysticism and philosophy.* Philadelphia: J. B. Lippincott.
Swartz, P., & Seginer, L. (1981). Response to body rotation and tendency to mystical experience. *Perceptual and Motor Skills, 53*, 683–688.
Spanos, N. P., & Moretti, P. (1988). Correlates of mystical and diabolical experiences in a sample of female university students. *Journal for the Sci-entific Study of Religion, 27*, 105–116.
Stifler, K. R., Greer, J., Sneck, W., & Doven-muehle, R. (1993). An empirical investigation of the discriminability of reported mystical experi-ences among religious contemplatives, psychotic inpatients, and normal adults. *Journal for the Sci-entific Study of Religion, 32*, 366–372.

Appendix

Mysticism Scale—Research Form D

Instructions: The attached booklet contains brief descriptions of a number of experiences. Some descriptions refer to phenomena that you may not have experienced. In each case note the description carefully and then place a mark in the left margin according to how much the description applies to your own experience. Write +1, +2, or –1, –2, or ? depending on how you feel in each case.

+1: This description is probably true of my own experience or experiences.
–1: This description is probably not true of my own experience or experiences.
+2: This description is definitely true of my own experience or experiences.
–2: This description is definitely not true of my own experience or experiences.
?:   I cannot decide.

Please mark each item trying to avoid if at all possible marking any item with a ?. In responding to each item, please understand that the items may be considered as applying to one experience or as applying to several different experiences. After completing the booklet, please be sure that all items have been marked—leave no items unanswered.

1.   I have had an experience which was both timeless and spaceless.
*2. I have never had an experience which was incapable of being expressed in words.
3.   I have had an experience in which something greater than myself seemed to absorb me.
4.   I have had an experience in which everything seemed to disappear from my mind until I was conscious only of a void.
5.   I have experienced profound joy.
*6. I have never had an experience in which I felt myself to be absorbed as one with all things.
*7. I have never experienced a perfectly peaceful state.
*8. I have never had an experience in which I felt as if all things were alive.
*9. I have never had an experience which seemed holy to me.
*10. I have never had an experience in which all things seemed to be aware.
11. I have had an experience in which I had no sense of time or space.
12. I have had an experience in which I realized the oneness of myself with all things.
13. I have had an experience in which a new view of reality was revealed to me.
*14. I have never experienced anything to be divine.
*15. I have never had an expcrience in which time and space were nonexistent.
*16. I have never experienced anything that I could call ultimate reality.
17. I have had an experience in which ultimate reality was revealed to me.
18. I have had an experience in which I felt that all was perfection at that time.
19. I have had an experience in which I felt everything in the world to be part of the same whole.
20. I have had an experience which I knew to be sacred.
*21. I have never had an experience which I was unable to express adequately through language.
22. I have had an experience which left me with a feeling of awe.
23. I have had an experience that is impossible to communicate.
*24. I have never had an experience in which my own self seemed to merge into something greater.

*25. I have never had an experience which left me with a feeling of wonder.

*26. I have never had an experience in which deeper aspects of reality were revealed to me.

*27. I have never had an experience in which time, place, and distance were meaningless.

*28. I have never had an experience in which I became aware of the unity of all things.

29. I have had an experience in which all things seemed to be conscious.

*30. I have never had an experience in which all things seemed to be unified into a single whole.

31. I have had an experience in which I felt nothing is ever really dead.

32. I have had an experience that cannot be expressed in words.

*Item is reverse scored.

Note. Items corresponding to the 2-component solution are: nos. 1–2, 4, 6, 8, 10–12, 15, 18–19, 21, 23, 24, 27–32 (intense experience of unity); and nos. 3, 5, 7, 9 ,13, 14, 16–17, 20, 22, 25, 26 (affectively charged religious revelation). Items corresponding to the three-component solution are: nos. 6, 8, 10, 12, 15, 19, 24, 27–31 (extrovertive mysticism); nos. 5, 7, 9, 13–14, 16–18, 20, 22, 25, 26 (religious interpretation); and nos. 1–4, 11, 21, 23, 32 (introvertive mysticism).

Hood, R. W., Jr. (1975). The construction and preliminary validation of a measure of reported mystical experience. *Journal for the Scientific Study of Religion, 14,* 29–41. Copyright © 1975 Journal for the Scientific Study of Religion. Reprinted with permission.

10.3
SPIRITUAL ASSESSMENT INVENTORY (Hall & Edwards, 1996)
Reviewed by Theresa C. Tisdale

Variable: The Spiritual Assessment Inventory (SAI) measures an individual's spiritual development or spiritual maturity from both an object relations and a contemplative spirituality perspective. It is constructed on the premise that spiritual maturity is composed of two primary dimensions: (a) the equality of an individual's relationship with God and (b) the degree of an individual's awareness of God in his or her life. Five factors underlie the total score: Awareness, Instability, Defensiveness/Disappointment, Grandiosity, and Realistic Acceptance. The instrument is designed for use with adults.

Description: The development of the (SAI) was informed by both the object relations and contemplative spirituality literature. Theoretical and empirical works supporting a relationship between an individual's level of object relations development and the nature of one's relationship with God (Brokaw & Edwards, 1994; Carter & Barnhurst, 1986; Hall & Brokaw, 1995; Jones, 1991; Pingleton, 1984; Shackelford, 1978; Tis-

dale, Brokaw, Edwards, & Key, 1993) informed the conceptualization of the first dimension of the instrument; that is, the quality of a person's relationship with God.

The spiritual direction literature (Barry & Connolly, 1982; Conn, 1989; Edwards, 1986) was utilized as a source when constructing items related to the second dimension of the instrument: the degree of an individual's awareness of God in his or her life. This awareness is theorized to be only moderately related to an individual's level of object relations development because a person will be relating to God in a way influenced by early life relationships, but may or may not be aware of God's presence in his or her life.

The instrument consists of 43 items and is self-administered. The items are presented in a 5-point Likert format, with 1 indicating nonendorsement and 5 indicating endorsement. Some items consist of two parts in order to explore the respondent's reaction to negative experiences with God. Five subscale scores (Awareness, Instability, Defensiveness/Disappointment, Grandiosity, and Realistic Acceptance) are generated by totaling the items pertaining to each.

Practical Considerations: This paper-and-pencil measure requires no special examiner skills and takes approximately 15 minutes to complete. Instructions to respondents are provided at the top of the first page of the instrument, and scoring instructions and an interpretive guide are available from the authors. Face validity appears high in that items can be readily identified as assessing quality of relationship with God and/or awareness of God's presence.

Norms/Standardization: To date, norms have been generated utilizing a nonclinical sample of college students from two universities in southern California. The initial factor analysis was computed based on results from 193 subjects, and the revision was based on results from 449 subjects. Specific normative data such as subscale means are not reported.

Reliability: Results from the second factor analysis of the SAI (449 subjects) suggest a five-factor solution; eigenvalues ranged from 11.14 to 1.56 and account for 50.5% of the total variance. Reliability of the five factors was estimated using Cronbach's coefficient alpha measure of internal consistency. The values reported were Instability, .88; Defensiveness, .91; Awareness, .90; Realistic Acceptance, .76; and Grandiosity, .52.

Test-retest coefficients were computed for a subsample of 17 subjects; the length of time between administrations was two weeks. Reliability coefficients were Instability, .94; Defensiveness, .93; Awareness, .83; Realistic Acceptance, .59; and Grandiosity, .56. All estimates provided to date render the SAI a promising research tool, but further refinement of the psychometric properties is warranted before widescale use of the measure could be endorsed.

Validity: Construct validity of the SAI is promising, based on the results of the factor analysis, with the possible exception of the Grandiosity factor (Cronbach's alpha = .52), which the authors admit requires further investigation to assess what this factor is re-

ally measuring. Correlation of the scores on the SAI with scores on the Bell Object Relations Inventory (BORI; Bell, 1991) were also computed as an additional measure of construct validity, since both have a similar theoretical basis. The pattern of correlations between the SAI and the BORI was consistent with theoretical expectations with the exception of the Grandiosity factor, which echoes the low Cronbach's alpha reliability estimate reported for this factor.

At this point, the SAI appears to be a reasonably reliable and valid measure for use with religious college students. Wider use will need to be determined through additional investigations assessing different sample groups combined with additional psychometric refinement.

Location:
Hall, T. W., & Edwards, K. J. (1996). The initial development and factor analysis of the Spiritual Assessment Inventory. *Journal of Psychology and Theology, 24*(3), 233–246.

Subsequent Research: Due to the relatively recent development of this scale, no subsequent research has been reported.

References

Barry, W. A., & Connolly, W. J. (1982). *The practice of spiritual direction.* San Francisco: HarperCollins.

Bell, M. (1991). *An introduction to the Bell Object Relations and Reality Testing Inventory.* Los Angeles: Western Psychological Services.

Brokaw, B. F., & Edwards, K. J. (1994). The relationship of God image to level of object relations development. *Journal of Psychology and Theology, 22,* 352–371.

Carter, J. D., & Barnhurst, L. F. (1986). Maturity, intimacy and spirituality. Paper presented at Midwest CAPS Convention, August 8–10.

Conn, J. W. (1989). *Spirituality and personal maturity.* New York: Paulist Press.

Edwards, J. (1986). Spiritual direction: A delicate weaving of life and religious experience. *Studies in Formative Spirituality, 7,* 177–191.

Hall, T. W., & Brokaw, B. F. (1995). The relationship of spiritual maturity to level of object relations development and God image. *Pastoral Psychology, 43,* 373–0391.

Jones, J. W. (1991). *Contemporary psycho-*

analysis and religion. New Haven: Yale University Press.

Pingleton, J. P. (1984). *An integrative analysis of psychological and Christian concepts of relational maturity*. Unpublished doctoral dissertation, Rosemead School of Psychology Biola University, La Mirada, CA.

Shackelford, J. F. (1978). *A comparison of psychological and theological concepts of dependency*. Unpublished doctoral dissertation, Rosemead School of Psychology, Biola University, La Mirada, CA.

Tisdale, T., Brokaw, B., Edwards, K., & Key, T. (1993, August). Impact of Psychotherapy Treatment on Level of Object Relations Development, God Image, and Self-Esteem. In J. W. Jones (Chair), *Varieties of psychoanalytic research on religion*. Symposium conducted at the annual convention of the American Psychological Association, Toronto, Canada.

Appendix

SAI

Instructions:

1. Please respond to each statement by circling the number that best represents your experience: Circle:

    1 if the statement is not true of you at all;
    2 if the statement is slightly true of you;
    3 if the statement is moderately true of you;
    4 if the statement is substantially true of you; and
    5 if the statement is very true of you.

2. It is best to answer according to what *really reflects* your experience rather than what you think your experience should be.
3. Give the answer that comes to mind first. Don't spend too much time thinking about an item.
4. Give the best possible response to each statement even if it does not provide all the information you would like.
5. Try your best to respond to all statements. Your answers will be completely confidential.

Factor		Not true of me			True of me	
		1	2	3	4	5
A	1. I have a good sense of how God is working in my life	1	2	3	4	5
A	2. I regularly sense God speaking to me through other people.	1	2	3	4	5
D	3. (a). There are time when I feel disappointed with God	1	2	3	4	5
	(b). When this happens, I still want our relationship to continue	1	2	3	4	5
RA	4. Listening to God is an essential part of my life	1	2	3	4	5
A	5. I am frequently aware of God prompting me to do something.	1	2	3	4	5

Factor		Not true of me				True of me
		1	2	3	4	5
D	6. (a). There are times when God frustrates me	1	2	3	4	5
RA	(b). When I feel this way, I still desire to put effort into our relationship	1	2	3	4	5
A	7. My experiences of God's responses to me impact me greatly	1	2	3	4	5
I	8. I frequently bargain with God	1	2	3	4	5
A	9. I am regularly aware of God's presence in my interactions with other people	1	2	3	4	5
I	10. I am very afraid that God will give up on me	1	2	3	4	5
I	11. My emotional connection with God is very unstable . . .	1	2	3	4	5
A	12. I am very sensitive to what God is teaching me in my relationships with other people	1	2	3	4	5
I	13. I almost always feel completely cut off from God	1	2	3	4	5
D	14. (a) There are times when I feel irritated at God	1	2	3	4	5
RA	(b) When I feel this way, I am able to come to some sense of resolution in our relationship	1	2	3	4	5
A	15. I am aware of God responding to me in a variety of ways	1	2	3	4	5
I	16. I frequently feel that God is angry at me and punishing me	1	2	3	4	5
A	17. I am aware of God attending to me in times of need . . .	1	2	3	4	5
G	18. God seems to understand that my needs are more important than most people's	1	2	3	4	5
D	19. (a). There are times when I feel angry at God	1	2	3	4	5
RA	(b). When this happens, I still have the sense that God will always be with me	1	2	3	4	5
G	20. My relationship with God is an extraordinary one that most people would not understand	1	2	3	4	5
A	21. I have a good sense of the direction in which God is guiding me	1	2	3	4	5
D	22. There are times when I feel like God doesn't come through for me	1	2	3	4	5
G	23. God's way of dealing with other people does not apply to me	1	2	3	4	5
D	24. (a). There are times when I feel betrayed by God	1	2	3	4	5
RA	(b). When I feel this way, I put effort into restoring our relationship	1	2	3	4	5
I	25. My emotional connection with God is very unstable . . .	1	2	3	4	5

Factor		Not true of me			True of me	
		1	2	3	4	5
I	26. No matter how hard I try to avoid them, I still experience many difficulties in my relationship with God.	1	2	3	4	5
RA	27. When I sin, I still have a sense that God cares about what happens to me.	1	2	3	4	5
I	28. I often worry that I will be left out of God's plans	1	2	3	4	5
A	29. When I consult God about decisions in my life, I am aware of His direction and help.	1	2	3	4	5
D	30. (a). There are times when I feel frustrated by God for not responding to my prayers	1	2	3	4	5
RA	(b). When I feel this way, I am able to talk it through with God	1	2	3	4	5
I	31. I often feel I have to please God or he might reject me .	1	2	3	4	5
D	32. (a). There are times when I feel like God has let me down	1	2	3	4	5
RA	(b). When this happens, my trust in God is not completely broken	1	2	3	4	5
I	33. I often completely withdraw from God	1	2	3	4	5
G	34. God recognizes that I am more spiritual than most people	1	2	3	4	5
I	35. God does not seem to exist when I am not praying or reading/hearing the Bible	1	2	3	4	5
G	36. Manipulating God seems to be the best way to get what I want.	1	2	3	4	5

Factors: I = Instability; D = Defensive/Disappointment; A – Awareness; RA = Realistic Acceptance; G = Grandiosity

Note: This scale is undergoing further revision. Therefore, researchers are encouraged to contact the autors at the Rosemead School of Psychology, Biola University, La Mirada, CA before using this scale.

Hall, T. W., & Edwards, K. J. (1996). The initial development and factor analysis of the Spiritual Assessment Inventory *Journal of Psychology and Theology, 24*(3), 233–246. Copyright © 1996 Rosemead School of Psychology, Biola University. Reprinted with permission.

10.4
SPIRITUAL THEMES AND RELIGIOUS RESPONSES TEST
(Saur & Saur, 1993)

Reviewed by Beth Fletcher Brokaw

Variable: The Spiritual Themes and Religious Responses Test (STARR) is a projective instrument designed to generate data of a general spiritual and religious nature. Modeled after the Thematic Apperception Test (TAT), it attempts to tap conscious and unconscious material from the individual being tested. Depending on the instructions given, the instrument may elicit information on a number of specific dimensions of religious experience, including representation of God, relationship with God, religious institutions, nature of the world, life themes, religious symbols, prayer, and dependency. In addition, self and object representations are often reflected in the test material.

Description: The test consists of 11 stimulus cards that are black and white photographs of people in postures that may be construed as prayerful. The photographs tend to elicit not only prayer content but also universal themes such as solitude, grief, joy, awe, celebration of life, family relatedness, and death. A broad range of ages, religious practices, and races is represented. In a number of cards, gender is ambiguous, which seems to increase the extent to which subjects of both sexes project onto the cards. Likewise, the photographs are ambiguous regarding affect and outcome, encouraging projection of the subject's own thoughts, emotions, concerns, and conflicts in response to the cards.

Similar to the TAT, the test is based on the assumption that individuals may project their own conscious and unconscious strivings, dispositions, and conflicts onto unstructured or ambiguous stimuli. The STARR photographs were chosen to elicit religious themes beyond those of personality and world view typically generated by the TAT. The authors of the STARR were particularly interested in assessing unconscious aspects of God representation and religious development, which have been increasingly addressed in contemporary psychoanalytic literature (Jones, 1991; McDargh, 1983; Meissner, 1984; Rizzuto, 1979), yet have seldom been adequately tested.

The authors suggest that at least 8 of the 11 stimulus cards be administered to each subject to ensure adequate repetition of themes. A number of instructional sets may be used, depending on which religious variables are of interest to the interviewer. The Saurs describe two primary instructional sets. In Instructional Set I, the test administrator states that he or she is interested in studying prayer, thus offering a broad religious backdrop to the testing process. Then the subject is presented with each card and is asked to tell a story describing what is happening in each situation, what leads up to it, and how it ends. In addition, the subject is asked what the main character is thinking and feeling. The data elicited by this process may be interpreted in a number of ways, though the authors suggest seven categories into which much of the data can be organized. These categories are religious institutions, representation of God, nature of the world, life themes, religious symbols, prayer, and dependency. In Instructional Set II, the test administrator states that "these are photographs of people in prayer. Your task is to make up or describe the prayer." A helpful prompt may be added: "Please talk about the prayer in the photograph." Data gathered in this manner may be more specific to the person's relationship to God. The authors suggest that this material be organized into the categories of prayer descriptions, self representations, object representations, and relationship to God.

The authors also note that alternative instructional sets may be used to elicit other types of religious material. Information about stages of faith may be prompted by asking the subjects, "What does the person in the photograph believe about God?" Another alternative instructional method provides a story along with a picture and then asks for the outcome. This seems to elicit expectations that the person has of God and the assumptions made about the action of God in the person's life. Spear (1993) added to Instructional Set I a prompt about what God was thinking and feeling, which helped elicit further information regarding God representation.

The authors suggest that interpretations of the data may be based on various thematic categories or specific research questions at hand, although they note that material gathered in testing may also be organized by offering a basic descriptive and thematic summary of the responses of each subject. Although the authors have primarily used qualitative approaches to interpret the test material, they do note that less subjective quantitative methods of scoring are possible. Thusfar, three other researchers have used quantitative techniques for scoring the STARR. Spear (1993) scored the STARR by rating responses according to the factors in Gorsuch's Adjective Ratings of God. Ozorak and Kosiewicz (1994) coded responses for themes of separation and connectedness, themes of power and love, nature of prayers, focus of prayers, and whether the prayers were answered or not. Misner (1995/1994), in an attempt to create an objective, reliable means of scoring responses to the STARR, developed a scale that assesses 12 dimensions of spirituality, including psychological mindedness, identification with others, capacity for mature relatedness, affect prior to prayer, affect following prayer, world view, degree of resolution experienced following prayer, attachment style, coping style, type of prayer, type of need expressed, and theological theme expressed.

Practical Considerations: This test must be administered and interpreted by someone trained in the use of projective testing, with specific approval of the author, Marilyn Saur. It takes approximately 45 minutes to administer, depending on the instructional set and number of cards used. While the authors offer suggestions regarding interpretation of the data, professional training and skills in assessing projective material are required to adequately interpret the data. Use of quantitative scoring systems for the STARR likewise requires rater training. The specific purpose of the test may vary, depending on the questions of concern to the interviewer and the instructional sets chosen. Given the variety of instructional sets suggested by the author, researchers or clinicians may find the test particularly adaptable for use in testing conscious and unconscious aspects of a number of different religious variables. Although the test has been used only in research to date, Marilyn Saur is currently developing administration, interpretation, and training guidelines for use of the STARR in psychotherapy and spiritual direction as well.

Norms/Standardization: Normative data for the STARR is quite limited, given the projective nature of the test and limited use of the test in quantitative research. The instrument was first pilot tested on five male and five female adults between the ages of 40 and 48. A later study by the authors included 15 adults between the ages of 35 and 50, a third of whom were active participants in a conservative Jewish congregation, a third of whom were active in the Episcopal Church, and third of whom were not currently active in any religious tradition. Subsequent studies have gathered data from 39 students attending a Christian college and 29 students attending a private liberal arts college in California (Spear, 1993), 72 college students attending a liberal arts college in Pennsylvania (Ozorak & Kosiewicz, 1994), and 42 adults between the ages of 28 and 51 recruited from Lutheran, Methodist, and Presbyterian churches in the Midwest (Misner, 1994/1995). The last three studies used quantitative scoring systems for the STARR, although means for religious variables tested by the STARR were reported only in the Ozorak and Kosiewicz study.

Reliability: Reliability data on the STARR is also quite limited. Interscorer reliability for the scoring system developed by Misner (1994/1995), following thorough rater training, was reported to range from .46 for the subscale of type of need expressed to .88 for the subscales of psychological mindedness and identification with others. Internal consistency reliability is not reasonable to determine, since different cards were chosen to tap varying aspects of religious experience, and responses in projective testing tend to vary over the course of testing administration. No other types of reliability have been determined for the STARR at this time.

Validity: Validity is also difficult to determine for this projective test and has been addressed only in a limited way. The authors have addressed the question of whether the STARR offers access to unconscious qualities of one's relationship with God by evaluating data gathered in their initial studies. They found that many subjects' responses reflected a range of religious affective content that had been out of their conscious awareness prior to the testing process (Saur & Saur, 1993b). One purpose of Misner's (1994/1995) study was to test the concurrent validity of the STARR, scored according to the Misner Spiritual Development Scale. Misner correlated STARR scores with scores on other measures of religious and psychological functioning, including the Age Universal Intrinsic-Extrinsic Scale, Quest Scale, MMPI-2, Measures of Psychosocial Development, and Rorschach Egocentricity Index. Most notable were a number of significant correlations, ranging from .36 to .58, between the Intrinsic Scale and seven of the subscales of Misner's scoring system for the STARR, including psychological mindedness, identification with others, capacity for mature relatedness, and attachment style. These and other findings reported in Misner's work suggest that the STARR is useful for measuring one's capacity for and style of religious relating, to God and others, as well as a number of other religious and psychological variables.

Location:
Saur, M. S., & Saur, W. G. (1993a). *Spiritual Themes and Religious Responses Test (STARR): Preliminary Manual*. Chapel Hill, NC: Author.

Saur, M. S., & Saur, W. G. (1993b). Transitional phenomena as evidenced in prayer. *Journal of Religion and Health, 32*, 55-65.

Permission to use this test must be obtained from Marilyn Saur, 907 Cedar Fork Trail, Chapel Hill, NC 27514-1706.

Subsequent Research:
Misner, C. (1995). The construction and preliminary validation of a spiritual development scale for coding a projective technique of spirituality and prayer (Doctoral dissertation, Central Michigan University, 1994). *Dissertation Abstracts International, 56,* 6006B.

Ozorak, E. W., & Kosiewicz, J. D. (1994, November). *The relationship of self-schema to religious schemas and behaviors.* Paper presented at the annual meeting of the Society for the Scientific Study of Religion, Albuquerque, NM.

Spear, K. (1993). *Conscious and pre-conscious God-concepts: An object relations perspective.* Unpublished doctoral dissertation, Graduate School of Psychology, Fuller Theological Seminary, Pasadena, CA.

References

Jones, J. W. (1991). *Contemporary psychoanalysis and religion.* New Haven: Yale University Press.

McDargh, J. (1983). *Psychoanalytic object relations theory and the study of religion.* Lanham, MD: University Press of America.

Meissner, W. W. (1984). *Psychoanalysis and religious experience.* New Haven: Yale University Press.

Rizzuto, A. (1979). *The birth of the living God.* Chicago: University of Chicago Press.

Appendix

Spiritual Themes and Religious Responses Test

Given that the STARR is a projective test consisting of eleven photographs, the instrument cannot be reprinted in this book. A copy of the 21-page instruction manual may be obtained from Marilyn Saur, 907 Cedar Fork Trail, Chapel Hill, NC 27514-1706.

10.5
SPIRITUAL WELL-BEING QUESTIONNAIRE (Moberg, 1984)
Reviewed by Michael J. Boivin,

Variable: The Spiritual Well-Being Questionnaire (SWB) is a multidimensional assessment tool useful for evaluating religiosity in terms of spiritual growth and maturity from a wholistic perspective. The conceptual basis of the SWB consists of one's relationship with God, self, community, and environment.

Description: The instrument is comprehensive because it includes individual items pertaining to social attitudes, self-perceptions, theological orientation, religious beliefs, opinions, experiences, preferences, affiliations, and various charitable endeavors. In developing this instrument, Moberg attempted to address the following requirements for a useful measure of spiritual well-being. These consist of:

1. A need for an instrument in evaluation research to plan activities and monitor progress in religious groups and organizations (Moberg, 1980)
2. A concern for the measuring the vital signs of a healthy church (Wagner, 1976)
3. A concern for addressing issues related to church growth and decline (Kelley, 1977; Hoge & Roozen, 1979)
4. An interest in evaluating the intensity of faith (Wagner & Johnson, 1977)

Initially, Moberg instituted a survey study to gather data used for constructing the SWB Questionnaire. From the data gathered, an 82-item instrument was constructed consisting of 6-point Likert scale statements, matrix questions, multiple choice questions, and self-identifying information through four major parts of the questionnaire. Through personal correspondance, the author states that all four parts of the questionnaire are "indicators, reflectors, or aspects of 'spiritual well-being' but not necessarily 'measures' of it (Moberg, personal communication, January 5, 1995). Items pertain to social attitudes, self-perceptions, theological orientation, and activ-

ities serving others in charitable, political, and religious contexts. Also included are religious beliefs, Christian doctrine, opinions, experiences, preferences, and affiliations. Scoring is somewhat complex and is explained in this volune at the end of the instrument.

Moberg (1984) identifies 13 different scales and indices.

1. Existential Well-Being Scale (from Ellison & Paloutzian, 1982)
   Part I: 5, 6, 12, 15, 17, 25, 27, 29, 32, 34
2. Religious Well-Being Scale (from Ellison & Paloutzian, 1982)
   Part I: 4, 6, 8, 14, 16, 18, 26, 28, 31, 33
3. Internal Well-Being Scale (from Farmham, 1979)
   Part III: 1, 2, 3, 4, 5, 6, 7, 8
4. Christian Faith Index
   Part I: 19, 20, 21, 24, 35, 47, 49
   Part IV: 15
5. Self Satisfaction Index
   Part I: 1, 3, 13, 22, 46
6. Personal Piety Index
   Part IV: 9, 10, 11, 13, 14
7. Subjective Spiritual Well-Being Index
   Part I: 36, 37, 38, 39
8. Optimism Index
   Part I: 2, 9, 23, 40
9. Religious Cynicism Index
   Part I: 41, 42, 44
10. Elitism Index
    Part I: 30, 43
11. Political Involvement Index
    Part II: 51, 54, 55, 56, 57
12. Religious Involvement Index
    Part II: 52, 58, 59, 60, 61
13. Charitable Involvement Index
    Part II: 53, 62, 63, 65, 66

The four strongest indexes or spiritual well-being are the Christian Faith Index, the Self-Satisfaction Index, the Personal Piety Index, and the Subjective Spiritual Well-Being Index. One measure of spiritual well-being could, therefore, just include the items involved in these indices. The indexes of Optimism, Religious Cynicism, and Elitism are the weakest statistically and the author, through personal correspondence, recommends that these items be dropped.

Practical Considerations: The directions for administering, scoring, and interpreting this instrument are specifically addressed in Moberg's (1984) article. This questionnaire can easily be administered to respondents in a private or group setting (i.e., classes, clubs, senior citizen forums, or church-related gatherings).

The instrument is comprehensive and requires approximately 30 to 60 minutes to complete. Because of its length, it may not be useful for subjects who tire easily or grow impatient with a lengthy questionnaire.

Norms/Standardization: The original sample consisted of 761 respondents in 17 group settings in three regions of the United States, and 320 respondents in 15 groups from all major regions of Sweden. It was selected in such a manner as to insure a diverse representation. However, means and standard deviations were not reported for these data.

Reliability: No measures of reliability were reported in Moberg (1984).

Validity: Paloutzian and Ellison (1982) administered their Spiritual Well-Being measure (consisting of Existential Well-Being and Religious Well-Being) along with Moberg's instrument. These two measures corresponded very well with each other. The Existential Well-Being portion of Paloutzian and Ellison's measure had a correlation coefficient of 0.73 with Moberg's Self-Satisfaction index. Likewise, Paloutzian and Ellison's Religious Well-Being Scale had a coefficient value of 0.86 with Moberg's Christian Faith index, 0.70 with Moberg's Personal Piety index, 0.63 with the Subjective Social Well-Being index, and 0.63 with the Religious Involvement index.

Location:
    Moberg, D. O. (1984). Subjective measures of spiritual well-being. *Review of Religious Research*, *25*, 351–359.

Subsequent Research :
    Koenig, H. G., Moberg, D. O., & Kvale, J. N. (1988). Religious activities and attitudes of older adults in a geriatric assessment clinic. *Journal of the American Geriatrics Society*, *36*, 362–374.
    Mickley, J. R., Soeken, K., & Belcher, A. (1992). Spiritual well-being, religiousness and hope among women with breast cancer. *Journal of Nursing Scholarship*, *24*, 267–272.
    Reed, P. G. (1986). Religiousness among terminally ill and healthy adults. *Research in Nursing & Health*, *9*, 35–41.
    Reed, P. G. (1992). An emerging paradigm for the investigation of spirituality in nursing. *Research in Nursing & Health*, *15*, 349–357.
    Walton, C. G., Shultz, C. M., Beck, C. M., & Walls, R. C. (1991). Psychological correlates of loneliness in the older adult. *Archives of Psychiatric Nursing*, *5*, 165–170.

Note: A further resource of more recent research using Moberg's scale as well as other assessments of spiritual well-being in the health care setting, can be found in the

Proceedings of the Spiritual Well-Being
    Conference
Program for Continuing Education in
    Nursing
Marquette University
510 N. 16th St.
Milwaukee, WI 53233

References

Hoge, D. R., & Roozen, D. A. (1979). *Understanding church growth and decline*: New York: Pilgrim Press.
    Kelley, D. M. (1977). *Why conservative churches are growing*. New York: Harper & Row.
    Moberg, D. O. (1980). Social indicators of spiritual well-being. In J. A. Thorsen & T. C. Cook, Jr. (Eds.). *Spiritual well-being of the elderly* (pp. 20–37). Springfield, IL: Charles C. Thomas.
    Paloutzian, R. F., & Ellison, C. W. (1982). Spiritual well-being and quality of life. In L. A. Peplau & D. Perlman (Eds.), *Loneliness: A sourcebook of current theory, research, and therapy*. New York: Wiley Interscience.
    Wagner, P. C. (1976). *Your church can grow: Seven vital signs of a healthy church*. Los Angeles: Regal Books.
    Wagner, P. C., & Johnson, A. (1977). Intensity of belief: A pragmatic concern for church growth. *Christianity Today*, *21*, 372–382.

Appendix

Well-Being Questionnaire

I. BELIEFS AND ATTITUDES Circle the answer for each item that is closest to your own personal opinion or belief. (If you wish, you may add comments to explain your answers.)

SA = I strongly agree.   TD = I tend to disagree.
 A = I agree.   D = I disagree.
TA = I tend to agree.   SD = I strongly disagree.

1. I have inner peace.	SA	A	TA	TD	D	SD
2. The world owes me a living.	SA	A	TA	TD	D	SD
3. Right now my life is happy.	SA	A	TA	TD	D	SD
4. I don't find much satisfaction in private prayer with God.*	SA	A	TA	TD	D	SD
5. I don't know who I am, where I came from or where I'm going.*	SA	A	TA	TD	D	SD
6. I believe that God loves me and cares about me.	SA	A	TA	TD	D	SD
7. I feel that life is a positive experience.	SA	A	TA	TD	D	SD
8. I believe that God is impersonal and not interested in my daily situations.*	SA	A	TA	TD	D	SD
9. I believe in the goodness of all people.	SA	A	TA	TD	D	SD
10. Heaven is a reward for people who earn it by living a good life.	SA	A	TA	TD	D	SD
11. The only home for Heaven is through personal faith in Jesus Christ.	SA	A	TA	TD	D	SD
12. I feel unsettled about my future.*	SA	A	TA	TD	D	SD
13. I love myself.	SA	A	TA	TD	D	SD
14. I have a personally meaningful relationship with God.	SA	A	TA	TD	D	SD
15. I feel very fulfilled and satisfied with life.	SA	A	TA	TD	D	SD
16. I don't get much personal strength and support from God.*	SA	A	TA	TD	D	SD
17. I feel a sense of well-being about the direction my life is headed in.	SA	A	TA	TD	D	SD
18. I believe that God is concerned about my problems.	SA	A	TA	TD	D	SD
19. I know that God has forgiven my sins.	SA	A	TA	TD	D	SD
20. My religious faith gives meaning to my life.	SA	A	TA	TD	D	SD
21. My faith helps me to make decisions.	SA	A	TA	TD	D	SD
22. Most people are friendly to me.	SA	A	TA	TD	D	SD
23. All that I am and ever hope to be I owe to others.	SA	A	TA	TD	D	SD

24. All people are sinners.   SA   A   TA   TD   D   SD

25. I don't enjoy much about life.*   SA   A   TA   TD   D   SD

26. I don't have a personally satisfying   SA   A   TA   TD   D   SD
    relationship with God.*

27. I feel good about my future.   SA   A   TA   TD   D   SD

28. My relationship with God helps me not   SA   A   TA   TD   D   SD
    to feel lonely.

29. My life is full of conflict and unhappiness.*   SA   A   TA   TD   D   SD

30. I am annoyed when people ask me to   SA   A   TA   TD   D   SD
    help them out of a jam.

31. I feel most fulfilled when I'm in close   SA   A   TA   TD   D   SD
    communion with God.

32. Life doesn't have much meaning.*   SA   A   TA   TD   D   SD

33. My relation with God contributes to my   SA   A   TA   TD   D   SD
    sense of well-being.

34. I believe there is some real purpose for   SA   A   TA   TD   D   SD
    my life.

35. The Holy Spirit lives in me.   SA   A   TA   TD   D   SD

36. If my ideas about religion were   SA   A   TA   TD   D   SD
    different, my lifestyle would be different.

37. I personally do have spiritual well-being.   SA   A   TA   TD   D   SD

38. My friends believe that I have spiritual   SA   A   TA   TD   D   SD
    well-being.

39. My family members or relatives believe   SA   A   TA   TD   D   SD
    that I have spiritual well-being.

40. Most people have spiritual well-being.   SA   A   TA   TD   D   SD

41. I try hard to keep religion separate   SA   A   TA   TD   D   SD
    from the rest of my life.

42. Efforts to deal with difficult problems   SA   A   TA   TD   D   SD
    of humanity by religious means are a
    waste of time and resources.

43. I do not want a group resident or half-   SA   A   TA   TD   D   SD
    way house for ex-convicts, alcoholics,
    drug addicts, or mentally ill people near
    my home.

44. Organized religion (church, synagogue,   SA   A   TA   TD   D   SD
    etc.) has harmed my own spiritual well-
    being more than it has helped.

45. Religious rituals or sacraments improve   SA   A   TA   TD   D   SD
    my well-being.

46. I once had spiritual well-being but have lost it.*   SA   A   TA   TD   D   SD

47. Jesus Christ died for my sins.   SA   A   TA   TD   D   SD

48. Jesus was a great religious teacher,   SA   A   TA   TD   D   SD
    but He was not the Son of God.

49. I have the peace of God.   SA   A   TA   TD   D   SD

50. The Bible is the Word of God and is   SA   A   TA   TD   D   SD
without mistakes in its statements and teachings.

II.   SOCIAL ACTIVITIES   Please check each of the following that you have done *during the past 12 months.*

51. _____ Contributed money to a political cause or campaign.

52. _____ Contributed money to a church or other religious organization.

53. _____ Contributed money to a charity.

54. _____ Signed a petition to a government office or for a politician.

55. _____ Voted in an election.

56. _____ Tried to influence the way others vote.

57. _____ Supported human rights or other causes by attending a rally marching, distributing leaflets, organizing, wearing a button, putting a bumper sticker on your car or other actions.

58. _____ Encouraged someone to accept your religious beliefs.

59. _____ Taught in a church school, synagogue, Sunday school or vacation Bible school.

60. _____ Held office or served on a committee in a church, synagogue, or other religious organization.

61. _____ Prayed for other people or for problems in the world.

62. _____ Donated food, clothing, or other things to a community project to help needy people.

63. _____ Donated your services to the Scouts, a service club, or some other community program to help people.

64. _____ Helped a family member or close relative when he or she was in trouble.

65. _____ Visited a sick or shut-in person who is not a family member.

66. _____ Helped a disabled or elderly person who is not a family member.

III. FEELINGS   (Use these pairs of words to describe how you feel about your life at the present time.)

     If your life now is *very closely related* to one of the words, check the space next to it under the 1 or 7.

     If your life is *quite closely related*, check the space under 2 or 6.

     If your life is *only slightly related*, check the space under 3 or 5.

     If your life seems either *unrelated* or *equally related* to both words, check the middle space under the 4.

     It is important to *check only one* space on each line.

		1	2	3	4	5	6	7	
1.	Boring	___ :	___ :	___ :	___ :	___ :	___ :	___	Interesting[*]
2.	Rewarding	___ :	___ :	___ :	___ :	___ :	___ :	___	Disappointing
3.	Hopeless	___ :	___ :	___ :	___ :	___ :	___ :	___	Hopeful[*]
4.	Many friends	___ :	___ :	___ :	___ :	___ :	___ :	___	Lonely

5. Filled with guilt   ___ : ___ : ___ : ___ : ___ : ___ : ___   Free from guilt*

6. Filled with worry   ___ : ___ : ___ : ___ : ___ : ___ : ___   Free from worry*

7. Useless   ___ : ___ : ___ : ___ : ___ : ___ : ___   Meaningful*

8. Brings out the best in me   ___ : ___ : ___ : ___ : ___ : ___ : ___   Brings out the worst in me

IV. RELIGIOUS ACTIVITIES AND IDENTITY Check the answer to each item that best indicates your own characteristics.

9. How often do you usually attend religious services in a church or synagogue? Twice or more each week ___ ; Once a week ___ ; Once or more each month ___ ; Several times a year ___ ; Once a year or less ___ ; Never ___ .

10. How often do you attend or take part in other religious activities, such as Bible studies, prayer groups, religious discussions, etc.? Twice or more each week ___ ; Once a week ___ ; Once or more each month ___ ; Several times a year ___ ; Once a year or less ___ ; Never ___ .

11. How often do you read the Bible or other devotional literature? Every day ___ ; Several times each week ___ ; At least once a week ___ ; Occasionally ___ ; Rarely ___ ; Never ___ .

12. How often do you tune in to religious programs on radio or television? Every day ___; Several times each week ___ ; At least once a week ___ ; Occasionally ___ ; Rarely ___ ; Never ___ .

13. How often do you pray privately? Several times each day ___ ; Daily ___ ; Several times each week ___ ; Occasionally ___ ; Only when I have a crisis or emergency ___ ; Never ___ .

14. How often do you meditate? Several times each day ___ ; Daily ___ ; Several times each week ___ ; Occasionally ___ ; Only when I have a crisis or emergency ___ ; Never ___ .

15. How important to you are your religious beliefs? Extremely important ___ ; Very important ___ ; Fairly important ___ ; Somewhat unimportant ___ ; Fairly unimportant ___ ; Not at all important ___ .

16. Compared to ten years ago, is your spiritual well-being now: Very much better ___ ; Much better ___ ; Somewhat better ___ ; About the same ___ ; Somewhat worse ___ ; Much worse ___ ; Very much worse ___ .

17. Have you been "born again" or had a "born again" experience—that is, a turning point in your life when you committed yourself to Jesus Christ? Yes ___ ; No ___ . If yes, is it still important to you? Yes ___ ; No ___ .

18. Are you now, or have ever been, a member of a church or synagogue? Yes, I am an *active* member now ___ ; Yes, but I am an *inactive* member now ___ ; No, but I was a member ___ ; No, and I never was a member ___ .

19. Is your church membership identity the same as that of your parents? Same as both ___ ; Same as mother's but not father's ___ ; Same as father's but not mother's ___ ; Different from both ___ .

20. What is your religious preference? Protestant ___ ; Catholic ___ ; Jewish ___ ; Eastern Orthodox ___ ; None ___ ; Other (what?) _____ .

21. If Protestant, what denomination do you prefer? Baptist ___ ; Episcopal ___ ; Lutheran ___ ; Methodist ___ ; Pentecostal or Holiness ___ ; Presbyterian or Reformed ___ ; United Church of Christ ___ ; Other (what?)_____ .

22. Which theological position is closest to your own? Atheist ___ ; Agnostic or skeptic ___ ; Jewish ___ ; Charismatic Christian ___ ; Evangelical Christian ___ ; Fundamentalist Christian ___ ; Liberal Christian ___; Neo-Orthodox Christian ___ ; Other (what?) _____ .

V. PERSONAL CHARACTERISTICS

23. Is your health: Excellent ___ ; Good ___ ; Fair ___ ; Poor ___ ?

24. What is the highest level of education you have completed? 8 grades or less ___ ; Some high school ___ ; High school graduate ___ ; 1 to 3 years of college ___ ; College graduate ___ ; Master's degree ___ ; Doctoral degree ___ ; Other (what?)_____ .

25. What is your primary occupation? (Check only one) Student ___ ; Homemaker___ ; Service worker ___ ; Skilled crafts ___ ; Laborer ___ ; Secretarial, clerical, or sales ___ ; Professional or managerial ___ ; Retired ___ ; Other (what?)_____ .

26. What is your race? Black ___ ; White ___ ; Hispanic ___ ; East Asian ___ ; Native American ___ ; Other (what?) _____ .

27. Are you: Female ___ ; or Male ___ ?

28. What is your age? 18 or less ___ ; 19–24 ___ ; 25–34 ___ ; 35–44 ___ ; 45–54 ___ ; 55–64 ___ ; 65–74 ___ ; 75 or over ___ .

* Reverse Scored.

Scoring Instructions

Part I: SA = 1   A = 2   TA = 3   TD = 4   D = 5   SD = 6
(except items 4, 5, 8, 12, 16, 25, 26, 29, 32, 46 which are reverse scored).

Part II: Items left blank are coded "1."
Items checked are coded "0."

Part III: Code by the sequential numbers by the blanks
(except items 1, 3, 5, 6, 7 which are reverse scored).

Part IV: Items 9–16: Each blank is represented sequentially in order by 1, 2, . . . 6, and for item 22 a 7.

Item 17: Yes and Yes (still important) = 1
Yes and No (not important) = 2
No (on 1st part) = 3
No and Yes = 4

Items 18–28 Codes are sequentially number in order of the response categories.

10.6
SPIRITUAL WELL-BEING SCALE (Paloutzian & Ellison, 1982; Ellison, 1983)
Reviewed by Michael J. Boivin, Allison L. Kirby,
Laura K. Underwood, and Heather Silva

Variable: The Spiritual Well-Being (SWB) Scale was developed as a general measure of the subjective quality of life. It serves as a global psychological measure of one's perception of spiritual well-being. SWB is understood to be wholistic. The scale is intended to measure people's overall SWB as it is perceived by them in both a religious well-being (RWB) sense and an existential well-being (EWB) sense.

Two points are highlighted in the conceptualization of SWB. First, it is not the same as spiritual health or spiritual maturity, since these might be prescribed by different religions or denominations. Second, SWB involves transcendence by focusing on well-being in relation to that which lies beyond oneself, understood in two senses: religious and existential. Thus, the SWB scale is intended to measure psychological dimensions, not theological ones.

Description: By design, the construction of the SWB scale includes both a religious and a social psychological dimension. The religious, "vertical" dimension (RWB) focuses on how one perceives the well-being of his or her spiritual life as this is expressed in relation to God. The social psychological, "horizontal" dimension (EWB) concerns how well the person is adjusted to self, community, and surroundings. This component involves the existential notions of life purpose, life satisfaction, and positive or negative life experiences.

Based on these concepts, the SWB scale is a 20-item self-assessment instrument constructed of two subscales, one that represents the vertical RWB dimension and one that represents the horizontal EWB dimension. Each subscale contains 10 items. All of the RWB items contain the word "God." The EWB items contain no specifically religious language, instead asking about such things as life purpose, satisfaction, and relations with the people and situations around

us. In order to control for response set bias, approximately half of the items are worded in a reverse direction so that disagreement with the item represents higher well-being.

Each item is rated on a 6-point Likert Scale with answer options ranging from "strongly agree" to "strongly disagree," with no midpoint. The items are scored from 1 to 6, with a higher number representing more well-being. These scores are summed in order to yield three scale scores: one score for RWB, one score for EWB, and one score for total SWB. RWB and EWB scores can range from 10 to 60. SWB total scores can range from 20 to 120.

Practical Considerations: The scale is easily understood, requires 10-15 minutes to complete, and has clear scoring guidelines. It is nonsectarian and can be used in a variety of religious, health, and research contexts.

Norms/Standardization: The original sample consisted of 206 students from Biola College, Westmont College, Pepperdine University, and the University of Idaho. Various initial studies employed over 500 subjects, including men and women (married and single), college and high school students, senior citizens, religious and non-religious people, and people from large cities, small towns, and rural areas. Subsequent research has included a wide variety of samples including people with AIDS, terminal cancer patients, nurses, sociopathic convicts, medical outpatients, outpatient counselees, people with eating disorders, sexually abused outpatients, and people in several Christian denominations.

Some normative data have been published that permit interpretation of scores in comparison to some identified populations (Bufford, Paloutzian, & Ellison, 1991; Paloutzian & Ellison, 1991). Means and standard deviations for RWB, EWB, and SWB are typically reported separately. Although RWB and EWB are moderately correlated with each other (r = .32), scores for the two subscales can behave differently. Mean scores for several different religious (mostly Christian) groups ranged from 34 to 56 for RWB, 46 to 53 for EWB, and 82 to 109 for total SWB. Similarly, for various other groups the mean scores for RWB, EWB, and SWB, respectively were: 51, 48, and 99 for medical outpatients; 35, 40, and 76 for nonreligious sociopathic convicts; and 44, 38, and 83 for combined sexually abused, eating disorder, and outpatient counselees.

Reliability: Test-retest reliability coefficients for four different samples with 1, 4, 6, and 10 weeks between testings ranged from .88 to .99 for RWB, .73 to .98 for EWB, and .82 to .99 for SWB. The internal consistency reliability coefficients, based on data from over 900 subjects across seven studies, ranged from .82 to .94 for RWB, .78 to .86 for EWB, and .89 to .94 for SWB. These data indicate high internal consistency and reliability.

Validity: The SWB Scale appears to measure what is intended. Face validity is evident by examination of the content of the items. Also, the authors report a factor analysis of the items, whose results yield factors that correspond to the two subscales. The RWB items cluster strongly together on one factor. The EWB items tend to cluster together on two subfactors that connote life direction and satisfaction. These results are generally consistent with the conceptual structure guiding the development of the scale. Some subsequent research may suggest a more complex factor structure (Ledbetter et al., 1991).

Validity is also indicated by correlations between the SWB scale and other measures with which it ought to be associated on theoretical grounds. For example, people who tended to score high on SWB scored lower on loneliness, higher on self-confidence, and higher on intrinsic religious orientation. The SWB, RWB, and EWB scores were all positively correlated with a sense of purpose in life (Paloutzian & Ellison, 1982).

Subsequent research shows that RWB, EWB, and SWB are associated with a variety of psychological, religious, health, and relational variables (Ellison & Smith, 1991).

The authors report that a ceiling effect can occur in RWB and SWB scores in some religious samples, making it harder to distinguish among subjects high in well-being in those groups. On the other hand, the scale is particularly sensitive at the low end. It may be a useful tool to point our attention to those experiencing spiritual distress or lack of well-being, and may assist as an instrument to assess global indications of distress in personal functions.

Location:

Ellison, C. W. (1983). Spiritual well-being: conceptualization and measurement. *Journal of Psychology and Theology, 11*, 330–340.

Ellison, C. W., & Smith, J. (1991). Toward an integrative measure of health and well-being. *Journal of Psychology and Theology, 19*, 35–48.

Paloutzian, R. F., & Ellison, C. W. (1982). Loneliness, spiritual well-being and quality of life. In L. A. Peplau & D. Perlman (Eds.), *Loneliness: A sourcebook of current theory, research and therapy*. New York: Wiley Interscience, pp. 224–237.

Paloutzian, R. F., & Ellison, C. W. (1991). *Manual for the Spiritual Well-being Scale*. Nyack, NY: Life Advance, Inc.

Subsequent Research:

Bassett, R. L., Camplin, W., Humphrey, D., Dorr, C., Biggs, S., Distaffen, R., Doxtator, I., Flaherty, M., Hunsberger, P. J., Poage, R., & Thompson, H. (1991). Measuring Christian maturity: A comparison of several scales. *Journal of Psychology and Theology, 19*, 84–93.

Carson, V. B., & Green, H. (1992). Spiritual well-being: A predictor of hardiness in patients with acquired immunodeficiency syndrome. *Journal of Professional Nursing, 8*, 209–220.

Genia, V. (1996). I, E, Quest, and Fundamentalism as predictors of psychological and spiritual well-being. *Journal for the Scientific Study of Religion, 35*, 56–64.

Kaczorowski, J. M. (1989). Spiritual well-being and anxiety in adults diagnosed with cancer. *The Hospice Journal, 5*, 105–115.

Note: This is one of the most widely used scales for research and clinical purposes. In their 1991 manual, the authors report they

have received over 300 requests to use the
scale.

References

Bufford, R. K., Paloutzian, R. F., & Ellison, C.
W. (1991). Norms for the spiritual well-being scale.
Journal of Psychology and Theology, 19, 35–48.

Ledbetter, M. F., Smith, L. A., Fischer, J. D.,
Vosler-Hunter, W. L., & Chew, G. P. (1991). An
evaluation of the construct validity of the spiritual
well-being scale: A confirmatory factor analytic approach. *Journal of Psychology and Theology, 19*,
94–102.

Appendix

SWB Scale

For each of the following statements, circle the choice that best indicates the extent of your
agreement or disagreement as it describes your personal experience:

SA = Strongly Agree		D = Disagree	
MA = Moderately Agree		MD = Moderately Disagree	
A = Agree		SD = Strongly Disagree	

1. I don't find much satisfaction in private prayer
   with God.   SA   MA   A   D   MD   SD
2. I don't know who I am, where I came from,
   or where I'm going.   SA   MA   A   D   MD   SD
3. I believe that God loves me and cares about me.   SA   MA   A   D   MD   SD
4. I feel that life is a positive experience.   SA   MA   A   D   MD   SD
5. I believe that God is impersonal and not interested
   in my daily situations.   SA   MA   A   D   MD   SD
6. I feel unsettled about my future.   SA   MA   A   D   MD   SD
7. I have a personally meaningful relationship with God. SA   MA   A   D   MD   SD
8. I feel very fulfilled and satisfied with life.   SA   MA   A   D   MD   SD
9. I don't get much personal strength and support
   from my God.   SA   MA   A   D   MD   SD
10. I feel a sense of well-being about the direction
    my life is headed in.   SA   MA   A   D   MD   SD
11. I believe that God is concerned about my problems.   SA   MA   A   D   MD   SD
12. I don't enjoy much about life.   SA   MA   A   D   MD   SD
13. I don't have a personally satisfying relationship
    with God.   SA   MA   A   D   MD   SD
14. I feel good about my future.   SA   MA   A   D   MD   SD
15. My relationship with God helps me not to
    feel lonely.   SA   MA   A   D   MD   SD
16. I feel that life is full of conflict and unhappiness. SA   MA   A   D   MD   SD
17. I feel most fulfilled when I'm in close communion
    with God.   SA   MA   A   D   MD   SD

18. Life doesn't have much meaning.	SA	MA	A	D	MD	SD
19. My relation with God contributes to my sense of well-being.	SA	MA	A	D	MD	SD
20. I believe there is some real purpose for my life.	SA	MA	A	D	MD	SD

Note: Items are scored from 1 to 6, with the higher number representing more well-being. Negatively worded items (#1, 2, 5, 6, 9, 12, 13, 16, 18) are reversed scored. Odd number items assess religious well-being; even numbered items assess existential well-being.

Chapter 11

God Concept Scales

One's vision of the divine undoubtedly influences religious experience. The scales reviewed in this chapter monitor various images of God, sometimes through a particular theoretical perspective. For many, a psychological analysis of the God concept begins with Freud's view of God as the exalted father. Rooted in the entanglements of the Oedipus Complex and the resulting feelings of fear and guilt, Freud maintains that we longingly search for and willingly submit obedience to an omnipotent father whom we project as God. Though not direct tests of Freud's theory, two of the instruments reviewed in this chapter are rooted in psychoanalytic concepts. Vergote and colleagues' Concepts of God and Parental Images (11.2) scale measures God image in light of both maternal and paternal characteristics. Rizzuto's God/Family Questionnaires (11.3) are two separate open-ended instruments: one on the topic of God and one on the topic of family. These two questionnaires are part of an overall protocol designed to reveal internalized images of God as well as self and others from psychoanalytic and object relations perspectives.

The other scales are less wedded to a particular theoretical perspective. The multidimensional nature of one's image of God is clearly captured, though in different dimensions, in three scales. The 91-item Adjective Ratings of God scale (11.1) by Gorsuch assesses five factors: traditional Christian, deistic, wrathful, "omni-ness" (i.e, omnipotence, omnipresence, omniscience, and an infinite nature), and irrelevance. Lawrence's 156-item God Image Inventory (11.4) identifies six dimensions of God image: influence, providence, presence, challenge, acceptance, and benevolence. The 10-item Loving and Controlling God Scales (11.5) provides separate scores on these two dimensions of the God concept.

One of the other two scales included for review (11.6) assesses, primarily within the context of a Christian perspective, how much one feels God is near and accessible. The last measure reviewed, Bassett and colleagues' Nonverbal Measure of God Concept (11.7), is different from the other measures in that it relies on printed drawings to test developmental differences in God image. By virtue of the very nature of this topic, these measures reflect a Western conception of the divine. With caution, some of these measures may be useful outside of a Judeo-Christian context.

11.1
ADJECTIVE RATINGS OF GOD (Gorsuch, 1968)
Reviewed by Kevin L. Ladd and Bernard Spilka

Variable: The purpose of the Adjective Ratings of God Scale is to push beyond the vague (but often asked) survey question, "Do you believe in God?" In particular, the scale measures specific concepts regarding the type of God (e.g., kindly, wrathful, etc.) in whom belief is placed.

Description: Two primary theories were explored as potential bases for these perceptions. One (Spilka, Armatas, & Nussbaum, 1964) focused on the usefulness of anthropomorphic characterizations of God. Researchers used 63 adjectives to derive five factors descriptive of a religious individual's God perceptions (stern father, impersonal, kindly father, "omni-ness," and supreme ruler).

The other (Osgood, Suci, & Tannenbaum, 1957) stressed linguistic characteristics of frequently used adjectives (e.g., good vs. bad). Working under the Semantic Differential rubric, 28 adjectives were reduced to three factors associated with the linguistic properties of adjectives (evaluation: good vs. bad; potency: strong vs. weak; and activity: active vs. passive).

To these 91 words, Gorsuch added nine marker items (eight random variables and one denoting sex); the nine additional items are not a part of the final scale. Words were rated: (a) "the word does not describe 'God,'" (b) "the word describes 'God,'" and (c) "the word describes 'God' particularly well."

Ultimately, eight first-order, two second-order, and one third-order potentially correlated factors were determined. From among the general items composing each dimension, Gorsuch isolated items on 5 of the 11 factors to construct reliable subscales. These five subscales compose the overall scale and consist of the following; Traditional Christian (Items 1, 3, 5, 7, 8, 9, 10, 11, 19, 20, 21, 22, 23, 26, 29, 30, 32, 33, 34, 35, 37, 38, 40, 42, 44, 45, 46, 48, 50, 51, 53, 54, 56, 57, 58, 59, 62, 63, 65, 66, 68, 74, 75, 76, 78, 79, 82, 85, 86, 88); Deisticness (Items 18, 39, 41, 55, 60); Wrathfulness (Items 4, 6, 12, 13, 14, 36, 43, 64, 70, 71, 76, 81, 90); Omni-ness (Items 42, 56, 57, 58); and Irrelevancy (Items 24, 28, 87, 89).

Practical Considerations: Completion time for this paper-and-pencil instrument is approximately 5–10 minutes. The five final

scales are easily extractable and are readily related to other constructs (e.g., intrinsic-extrinsic, etc.).

Norms/Standardization: Responses were initially obtained from 585 undergraduate students (234 females, 351 males). The sample was moderately religious (29% attended services at least once per week) and primarily Christian Protestant (77%).

Reliability: The five final subscales evidenced high to moderately high reliabilities:

Traditional Christian	.94
Deisticness	.71
Wrathfulness	.83
Omni-ness	.89
Irrelevancy	.49[1]

Eighty-five males randomly selected from the original sample and set aside as a cross-validation sample displayed similar results.

Two unpublished studies that have recently utilized the adjective checklist items (Fairchild et al., 1993, Sundin, Ladd, & Spilka, 1995) offer further support. Reliabilities for the scales in college student samples of 116 (Fairchild et al., 1993) and 149 (Sundin et al., 1995) respondents, respectively, were as follows:

	A	B
Traditional Christian	.83	.94
Deisticness	.65	.71
Wrathfulness	.89	.79
Omni-ness	.69	.86
Kindliness[2]	.94	.95

These two studies with only moderate sample sizes did not attempt confirmatory factoring of the scales, nor did they treat "traditional Christian" as a higher order factor. Although the basic scales extracted ap-

---

[1] A lack of variance on responses to items in this scale severely attenuated reliability estimates.

[2] The scale "kindliness" was not one of Gorsuch's suggested scales, although it was present as a first order factor; it was used for heuristic purposes, even as "irrelevancy" was not used since that scale did not pertain to the research in question.

pear solid, a full replication has not been conducted.

Validity: Overall, support was lacking for a purely semantic differential explanation of God concepts. The five factor finding of Spilka et al. (1964) was, however, essentially replicated, albeit in complex relation to Osgood et al. (1957). This replication suggests that the factors in question appear consistently. What remains is to compare directly the Gorsuch scales with others that purport to measure similar constructs.

Location:

Gorsuch, R. L. (1968). The conceptualization of God as seen in adjective ratings. *Journal for the Scientific Study of Religion, 7,* 56–64.

Subsequent Research:

Schaefer, C. A., & Gorsuch, R. L. (1992). Dimensionality of religion: Belief and motivation as predictors of behavior. *Journal of Psychology and Christianity, 11,* 244–254.

References

Fairchild, D., Roth, H., Milmoe, S., Gotthard, C., Fehrmann, L., Richards, S., Kim, B. H., Sedlmayr, J., Carely, B., Pan, P., & Spilka, B. (1993). *God images and prayer behavior: Consonance in the psychology of religion.* Paper presented at the joint convention of the Rocky Mountain and Western Psychological Associations, Phoenix, AZ.

Gorsuch, R. L. (1968). The conceptualization of God as seen in adjectiveratings. *Journal for the Scientific Study of Religion, 7,* 56–64.

Osgood, C. E., Suci, G. J., & Tannenbaum, P. H. (1957). *Measurement of meaning.* Urbana: Urbana University of Illinois Press.

Spilka, B., Armatas, P. & Nussbaum, J. (1964). The concept of God: A factor analytic approach. *Review of Religious Research, 6,* 28–36.

Sundin, H., Ladd, K. L., & Spilka, B. (1995). *The relation between God images and perceptions of God's control.* Paper presented at the annual convention of the Rocky Mountain Psychological Association, Boulder, CO.

Appendix

Religious Concept Survey

The following is a survey to determine what descriptive words apply to God. Please print a "1," "2," or "3" on the line before each word according to how well you think it describes what the term "God" means to you. There are no right or wrong answers; we are interested in what this concept means to each person. Use the following scale:

1. The word does not describe "God."
2. The word describes "God."
3. The word describes "God" particularly well.

1____ Absolute	12____ Critical	23____ Faithful	34____ Gracious
2____ Active	13____ Cruel	24____ False	35____ Guiding
3____ All-wise	14____ Damning	25____ Fast	36____ Hard
4____ Avenging	15____ Dangerous	26____ Fatherly	37____ Helpful
5____ Blessed	16____ Demanding	27____ Fearful	38____ Holy
6____ Blunt	17____ Democratic	28____ Feeble	39____ Impersonal
7____ Charitable	18____ Distant	29____ Firm	40____ Important
8____ Comforting	19____ Divine	30____ Forgiving	41____ Inaccessible
9____ Considerate	20____ Eternal	31____ Formal	42____ Infinite
10____ Controlling	21____ Everlasting	32____ Gentle	43____ Jealous
11____ Creative	22____ Fair	33____ Glorious	44____ Just

45___ Kind	57___ Omnipresent	69___ Safe	81___ Tough
46___ Kingly	58___ Omniscient	70___ Severe	82___ True
47___ Lenient	59___ Patient	71___ Sharp	83___ Unchanging
48___ Loving	60___ Passive	72___ Slow	84___ Unyielding
49___ Majestic	61___ Permissive	73___ Soft	85___ Valuable
50___ Matchless	62___ Powerful	74___ Sovereign	86___ Vigorous
51___ Meaningful	63___ Protective	75___ Steadfast	87___ Weak
52___ Meek	64___ Punishing	76___ Stern	88___ Warm
53___ Merciful	65___ Real	77___ Still	89___ Worthless
54___ Moving	66___ Redeeming	78___ Strong	90___ Wrathful
55___ Mythical	67___ Restrictive	79___ Supporting	91___ Yielding
56___ Omnipotent	68___ Righteous	80___ Timely	

11.2
CONCEPTS OF GOD AND PARENTAL IMAGES
(Vergote, Tamayo, Pasquali, Bonami, Pattyn, & Custers, 1969)

Reviewed by Caro E. Courtenay and Lee A. Kirkpatrick (see p. 785)

Variable: The Concepts of God and Parental Images Scale, developed at the Catholic University of Louvain in Belgium, is designed to measure the relationship between individuals' symbolic images of Mother, Father, and God with respect to maternal and paternal characteristics.

Description: This scale has been referred to as the *God-Parent-Score* or *Score-Dieu-Parent* (Tamayo & Desjardins, 1976), and as the *Semantic Differential Parental Scale* (*SDPS*; Vannesse & De Neuter, 1981). Originally constructed in Dutch, it has been translated into French, English, Spanish, and Italian. Like earlier research on God and parental images (e.g., Nelson & Jones, 1957; Strunk, 1959), it is theoretically grounded in psychoanalytic concepts and methodologically grounded in the *Semantic Differential* technique (Osgood, Suci, & Tannenbaum, 1957).

The Vergote et al. (1969) approach differs importantly from previous work in that subjects are asked to rate, on both maternal and paternal qualities, their ideals of each parent at a "symbolic" level, not in terms of actual experience. Vergote et al. (1969) showed, as expected, that the God image involves a mixture of both maternal and paternal qualities, although the particular patterns observed varied across a variety of samples.

The scale itself contains 36 items, 18 of which are descriptions of maternal qualities and 18 of which are considered paternal qualities. Mother, Father, and God images are each rated on all 36 qualities, which are distributed randomly within the measure. Each item consists of a word or phrase to be rated in a Likert-style format denoting the degree to which the quality described in the item applies to the target image. All items are worded in a positive direction (i.e., higher ratings mean more maternal or more paternal, respectively).

In contrast to the more usual psychometric approach in contemporary work, items are not summed to create total or subscale scores. Instead, specialized statistical techniques are used to assess the distance or similarity between entire profiles of scores (cf. Osgood et al., 1957).

A revised 72-item version of the measure (*SDPS II*) is presented in Pasquali (1981), but to our knowledge no research has been conducted with this version other than that reported by Pasquali.

Practical considerations: The scale is easy to administer. Because no items are reverse scored and because items are not summed to create aggregate scores, no further scoring is required. However, statistical analysis of the similarities/distances between images requires knowledge of specialized statistics.

To use the scale as intended, care must be taken to instruct respondents to evaluate the Mother and Father images at a "symbolic" rather than a "memory image" level, that is, "not as they really are, but as they should be" (Vergote et al., 1969, p. 80). None of the sources reviewed provided more specific detail about the appropriate wording for these instructions; however, Vergote and Tamayo (1981) provide a detailed explanation of the intended theoretical distinction.

Norms/Standardization: Vergote et al. (1969) derived their original items from "more than a hundred psychological, philosophical, religious, and literary works" (Vergote et al., 1969, p. 80), which are listed in an appendix to Vergote and Tamayo (1981). From these sources they compiled a list of 226 maternal and paternal qualities, which were then rated by graduate students from various fields to determine those items that most clearly differentiated maternal from paternal images. The scale was further developed through a series of interview and paper-and-pencil studies, employing high school students, college students, and college faculty, to determine the selection and final wording of the 36 items and to ensure equivalence of the various translations. (See Vannesse & de Neuter, 1981, and Vergote et al., 1969, for reviews of scale development procedures.)

Vergote et al. (1969) reported results on an American sample of 180 Roman Catholic students, half male and half female, including equal numbers of high school students, college liberal arts majors, and college science majors. Mean ratings on each of the 36 images were presented with respect to Mother, Father, and God, as well as various measures designed to assess the degree of correspondence among these images. Further breakdowns by sex, age, and field of study were also presented, and informal comparisons were made between these results and those from previous research with two Belgian samples.

Reliability: Because items are not summed to create a composite index, internal consistency reliability (e.g., Cronbach's alpha) is not applicable. No test-retest data were reported in the sources reviewed.

Validity: In a mixed sample of 62 American high school and college students (Vergote et al., 1969), a sample of 200 French-speaking Canadian students (Tamayo & Dugas, 1977), and a larger sample of 300 American university students (Vannesse & De Neuter, 1981), all 36 items were shown to discriminate significantly between the Mother and Father figures. In the latter study it was also shown that different results are obtained when the "symbolic image" instructions are given as compared to the "memory image" instructions.

Location:
Vergote, A., Tamayo, A., Pasquali, L., Bonami, M., Pattyn, M., & Custers, A. (1969). A concept of God and parental images. *Journal for the Scientific Study of Religion, 8*, 79–83. [Note: one maternal item is missing, presumably due to a misprint, from the item list in this article; the complete scale is reproduced in Vannesse & de Neuter, 1981.]

Subsequent research: This scale seems to have been used by few if any researchers outside of the Belgian research group that developed it. A book-length collection of research reports translated into English is available (Vergote & Tamayo, 1981), which includes studies employing the *SDPS* in a variety of cross-cultural comparisons (e.g., samples from Belgium, Italy, Zaire, Colombia, Indonesia, the Philippines, and the United States) and in various special populations (the elderly, juvenile delinquents, and schizophrenics). Other English-language publications reporting research utilizing the scale include:

Tamayo, A., & Dugas, A. (1977). Conceptual representation of mother, father, and God according to sex and field of study. *Journal of Psychology*, 97, 79–84.

Tamayo, A., & Desjardins, L. (1976). Belief systems and conceptual images of parents and God. *The Journal of Psychology*, 92, 131–140.

References

Osgood, C. E., Suci, E. J., & Tannenbaum, P. H. (1957). *The measurement of meaning*. Urbana: University of Illinois Press.

Nelson, M., & Jones, E. (1957). An application of the Q Technique to the study of religious concepts. *Psychological Reports*, 3, 293–297.

Pasquali, L. (1981). The representation of God and parental figures among North American students. In A. Vergote & A. Tamayo, *The parental figures and the representation of God: A psychological and cross-cultural study.* (pp. 169–184). The Hague: Mouton.

Strunk, O., Jr. (1959). Perceived relationships between parental and deity concepts. *Psychological Newsletter*, 10, 222–226.

Vannesse, A., & de Neuter, P. (1981). The semantic differential parental scale. In A. Vergote & Tamayo, *The parental figures and the representation of God: A psychological and cross-cultural study.* (1981), pp. 25–41. The Hague: Mouton.

Vergote, A., & Tamayo, A. (Eds.) (1981). *The parental figures and the representation of God: A psychological and cross-cultural study*. The Hague: Mouton.

[1]Preparation of this review was facilitated by a Charles Center Research Fellowship to Caro Courtenay, and a Summer Research Grant to Lee Kirkpatrick, from the College of William and Mary.

Appendix

Semantic Differential Parental Scale

Please rate the degree to which each of the following characteristics are associated with your mother/father/God using the following scale.

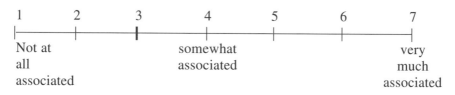

1   2   3   4   5   6   7

Not at all associated   somewhat associated   very much associated

Maternal Items:

_____ The one who is most patient
_____ Warmth
_____ A warm-hearted refuge
_____ Who takes loving care of me
_____ Who will sympathize with the child's sorrows
_____ Tenderness
_____ Who is intimate
_____ Who gives comfort
_____ Who brings out that which is delicate and refined
_____ Close to whom one feels at home
_____ Self-giving love
_____ Sensitive
_____ Who welcomes me with open arms

_____ Who is always waiting for me
_____ Intuition
_____ Who is all-embracing
_____ Charming
_____ Who is always ready with open arms

Paternal Items:
_____ Strength
_____ Power
_____ Who gives the directions
_____ Systematic mind
_____ Who is the principle, the rule
_____ Who takes the initiative
_____ The one who has the knowledge
_____ The authority
_____ The one who acts
_____ Who makes the decisions
_____ Firmness
_____ The judge
_____ Dynamic
_____ The one who maintains order
_____ Who gives the law
_____ Stern
_____ Who examines things
_____ Protection against danger

Note: Subjects rate all 36 items (which are randomly arranged) for their mother/father, then all 36 items for their other parent, then 36 items for God.

Vergote, A., Tamayo, A., Pasquali, L., Bonami, M., Pattyn, M., & Custers, A. (1969). A concept of God and parental images. *Journal for the Scientific Study of Religion, 8,* 79–83. Copyright © 1969 Journal for the Scientific Study of Religion. Reprinted with permission.

11.3
GOD/FAMILY QUESTIONNAIRES (Rizzuto, 1979)

Reviewed by Theresa C. Tisdale

Variable: The God and Family Questionnaires were developed by Rizzuto (1979) as part of a clinical study exploring the formation of an individual's God representation. Rather than consisting of a static image or a purely cognitive understanding, this representation is conceptualized as a complex mental process that evolves across the life span and is impacted and influenced by past, present, and anticipated experiences with others. Furthermore, it is mitigated by actual interactions, memories, wishes, needs, fears, and defenses.

That early interactions with significant others (primarily parents) form the basis for what one believes about God has been well documented in the literature (Beit-Hallahmi & Argyle, 1975; Godin & Hallez, 1965; Justice & Lambert, 1986; Nelson, 1971; Strunk, 1959; Tamayo & Disjardins, 1976; Tamayo & Dugas, 1977; Vergote & Aubert, 1972; Vergote et al., 1969). However, Rizzuto departs from Freud's classic (1907/1959) psychodynamic position that God is merely an exalted father by contending that in addition to both parents and other significant persons contributing to a child's God representation, the wished-for parents and the feared parents that exist in a child's imagination also contribute to the process.

Rizzuto contends that the God representation is formed in what Winnicott (1971) termed the transitional space between reality and fantasy, which is significant developmentally as the child begins to develop a sense of the continuing nature of people and relationships. This space is also occupied by objects such as teddy bears and blankets, which the child lays aside as development progresses. Unlike these objects, one's God representation is never completely put aside, but persists throughout life in an individual's internal world.

Description: The God and Family Questionnaires are based on psychoanalytic, object relations, and self psychological theories of development and are designed to reveal the nature of an individual's internalized images of (and beliefs about) self, others, and God. The questionnaires are presented in a parallel format consisting of sentence stems, one with questions about God and the other with questions about family. The respondent completes the sentence stems according to his or her own beliefs and God representation.

Practical Considerations: Administration of the God and Family Questionnaires is straightforward and fairly easy; the respondent merely completes the sentence stems. The questionnaires are not scored per se but are interpreted in light of developmental and psychodynamic theory. The details of this criteria were not reported in Rizzuto's (1979) original study.

Norms/Standardization: Because the purpose of Rizzuto's (1979) original study was an in-depth investigation into the roots of the formation of God representation and because much of the data was clinical in nature, no norms were developed. However, when the clinical sample on which the published results are based was compared with a pilot project sample of 20 nonclinical subjects, Rizzuto found no clinically significant

differences in the way these two groups related to God.

Reliability: No statistical reliabilities are reported for the God and Family Questionnaires. Development and interpretation of the questionnaires were done according to psychoanalytic, object relations, and self psychological theory, which suggests some measure of internal reliability of the items.

Validity: The face validity of the questionnaires is high; the items clearly relate to one's experience of God and family. The data obtained from the questionnaires were corroborated by information obtained from the patient's families, medical and psychiatric records, a psychodynamic evaluation, and a formulation of the patient's religious development.

Location:
Rizzuto, A. M. (1979). *The birth of living God: A psychoanalytic study.* Chicago: University of Chicago Press.

Subsequent Research:
Fay, M. A. (1983). An object relations analysis at the conscious symbolic and memory content levels of the maternal and paternal components of the representation of God in five Christian women. *Dissertation Abstracts International, 43,*(12-B), 4125.

Lawrence, R. T. (1991). The God Image Inventory: The development, validation and standardization of a psychometric instrument for research, pastoral and clinical use in measuring the image of God (Rizzuto, Ana-Maria). *Dissertation Abstracts International, 52,*(o3A), 0952.

Stephens, L. D. (1991). A path analysis of a God image model among hospital psychiatric patients. *Dissertation Abstracts International, 52,*(10A), 3534.

Stevens, B. A. (1987). Religious responses to the Rorschach test: An application of the Urist (1977) "Mutuality of Autonomy in Portrayed Relationships" scale. *Dissertation Abstracts International, 48*(05B), 1547.

References

Beit-Hallahmi, B., & Argyle, M. (1975). God as father projection: The theory and evidence. *British Journal of Medical Psychology, 48,*71–75.

Freud, S. (1959). Obsessive actions and religious practices. In J. Strachey (Ed. and Trans.), *The standard edition of the complete psychological works of Sigmund Freud* (Vol. 9, pp. 115–127). London: Hogarth Press (Original work published 1907).

Godin, A., & Hallez, M. (1965). Parental images and divine paternity. In A. Godin (Ed.), *From religious experience to a religious attitude* (pp. 65–96). Chicago: Loyloa University Press.

Justice, W. G., & Lambert, W. (1986). A comparative study of the language people use to describe the personalities of God and their earthly parents. *Journal of Pastoral Care, 40,* 166–172.

Nelson, M. O. (1971). The concept of God and feelings toward parents. *Journal of Individual Psychology, 27,* 46–49.

Strunk, O. (1959). Perceived relationships between parental and deity concepts. *Psychology Newsletter, 10,* 222–226.

Tamayo, A., & Desjardins, L. (1976). Belief systems and conceptual images of parents and God. *Journal of Psychology, 92,* 131–140.

Tamayo, A., & Dugas, A. (1977). Conceptual representation of mother, father, and God according to sex and field of study. *Journal of Psychology, 97,* 9–84.

Vergote, A., & Aubert, C. (1972). Parental images and representations of God. *Social Compass, 19,* 431–444.

Vergote, A., Tamayo, A., Pasquali, L., Bonami, M., Pattyn, M., & Custers, A. (1969). Concept of God and parental images. *Journal for the Scientific Study of Religion, 8,* 79–87.

Winnicott, D. W. (1971). *Playing and reality.* London: Tavistock.

Appendix

God Questionnaire

I

1. I feel/do not feel close to God because
2. The time of my life when I felt the closest to God was when   and I was   years old because
3. I think that in general, as a person I have pleased/dissatisfied God because
4. I think that God wants/does not want me to be good because
5. I believe/do not believe in a personal God because

II

6. The time in my life when I felt the most distant from God was when I was because
7. My most important duties toward God are

III

8. For me, the love of God towards me is/is not important because
9. For me, my love for God is/is not important because
10. The feeling I get/used to get from my relationship with God is one of because

IV

11. I feel that the fear of God is/is not important because
12. What I like the most about God is because
13. What I resent the most about God is because
14. What I dislike the most about religion is because

V

15. Emotionally, I would like to have the   that God has
    because

VI

16. Among all the religious characters I know, I would like to be like
    because

VII

17. My favorite saint or Bible character is
    because

VIII

18. I believe/do not believe in the devil because
19. I think that he wants to
    because
20. Sometimes I have/have not felt that I hated God because

IX

21. I feel that what God expects from me is
    because
22. I feel that to obey the Commandments is/is not important because
23. I pray/do not pray because I feel God will

X

24. I feel that God punishes/does not punish you if you
    because
25. I think that God considers my sins as
    because
26. I think that the way God has to punish people is
    because
27. I believe that the way God rewards people is
    because

XI

28. I think that God provides/does not provide for my needs because
29. The most important thing I expect from God is
    because

XII

30. In my way of feeling, for me to fully please God I would have to
    because
31. If I could change my past, I would like to change my
    because
32. If I can change myself now, I would like to be
    because
    If I can change myself now, I would like to change my
    because

If I can change myself now, I would like to improve my
because
If I can change myself now, I would like to increase my
because

XIII

33. If I am in distress, I resort/do not resort to God because
34. If I am happy, I thank/do not thank God because
35. Religion has/has not helped me to live because
36. If I receive an absolute proof that God does not exist, I will
    because
37. Prayer is/is not important to me because
38. I wish/don't wish to be with God after death because

XIV

39. I think that God is closest to those who
    because

XV

40. I consider God as my
    because
41. I think that God sees me as
    because

XVI

42. If I have to describe God according to my experiences with him, I would say that he is
    because

XVII

43. The day I changed my way of thinking about God was
    because

XVIII

44. Religion was always/never/at one time important to me (during the years from _____ to
    _____) because
45. For me, the world has/has not an explanation without God because

Appendix B

Family Questionnaire

Please read carefully the following questions and answer them, giving as long an explanation as you need for us to understand your real feelings.

If the answer does not need an explanation, just write the proper answer.

1. The member of my family whom I felt the closest to was my
   because

2. The member of my family whom I felt the most distant from was my
   because

3. The member of the family whom I loved the most was my
   I loved her/him this much because

4. The member of my family whom I disliked the most was my
   because she/he

5. Physically I resemble my   because

6. Emotionally I resemble my   because

7. The favorite member of my family was my
   because

8. The member of my family whom I admired the most is my
   because

9. Please write down the names of the members of your family in order of preference according to how much you like them.
   1.   6.
   2.   7.
   3.   8.
   4.   9.
   5.   10.

10. The member of my family whom I despised the most is
    because

11. The boss in my family was my   because

12. The disciplinarian in my family was my   because

13. The provider in my family was my   because

14. If I could change myself, I would like to be like my
    because

15. In my family we were close/very close/not close at all because

16. My father was closest to me/to my   because

17. My mother was closest to me/to my   because

18. The most important person in my family was   because

19. In my family the children were considered as

20. My family was/was not divided into groups
    The groups were my   and my
                       my   and my
                       my   and my   etc.

21. If I described myself as I feel I actually am, I would say I am

22. When I drew the picture of the family I felt and drew myself as being   years old
    because

23. When I drew the picture of my family, I thought the family was living in   and the
    year was   .

11.4
GOD IMAGE INVENTORY (Lawrence, 1991)
Reviewed by Todd W. Hall, and Randall Lehamann Sorenson

Variable: The God Image Inventory (GII) contains six subscales measuring different aspects of God image: Influence, Providence, Presence, Challenge, Acceptance, and Benevolence. In addition, the God Image Scales contain shortened versions of each of the six subscales for use in research.

Description: The GII contains a total of 156 items. Each of the six main scales consists of 22 items, while the two control scales (Faith and Salience) each contain 12 items. The instrument is scored on a four-point likert scale with 1 indicating strong agreement and 4 indicating strong disagreement with each statement. Many negatively worded items must be reverse scored. Each subscale should be scored separately by simply summing the items contained in it. Scores range from 22 to 88 for the six main subscales, and from 12 to 48 for the two control scales. A higher score represents a greater degree of the particular trait identified by the scale name.

Lawrence (1991) distinguishes between a person's God *concept* and his or her God *image*. The God concept is an intellectualized definition of God that is largely an artifact of cultural and religious education. God image, by contrast, is one's intuitive sense of God—what Lawrence describes as "a set of remembered and interpreted associations and experiences" (Lawrence, 1991, p. 134). Thus instead of focusing on beliefs about God, it focuses on a more affectively laden experience of God.

In light of this theory, Lawrence created the God Image Inventory to assess individuals' felt sense of who God is for them. Lawrence (1991) constructed six principal scales (Influence, Providence, Presence, Challenge, Acceptance, and Benevolence) and two control scales (Faith and Salience). Based on Rizzuto's (1979) suggestion that the God image is created, altered, and used primarily for the purpose of preserving a tolerable tension between affectively laden experiences of self and others, Lawrence concluded that God image and self image are highly related to one another, and he sought to measure the relationship between the two. Lawrence used three basic themes for the self image as a framework for the six subscales: feelings of control, belonging, and fundamental goodness.

The theme of control was divided into two basic questions, one being more primitive and focused more on the self (How much can I control God?), the other being more focused on God (How much does God control me?). The first subdivision was labeled Influence, and the second, Providence.

The theme of belonging was likewise divided into two basic considerations, the first of which, drawn from the work of Winnicott (1953), suggests that "belonging" for the infant relates to the issue of presence and is experienced as the question "Is mother there for me?" Thus the first and most primitive belonging issue was labeled "Presence," which is reflected by the question Is God there for me? The second aspect of belonging relates to the work of Kirkpatrick (1986), who, following Bowby (1969), outlined two roles for attachment figures. The first, which corresponds well to the issue of presence, is labeled "Safe Haven" and refers to a person to whom the child may retreat and find present. The second consideration, called "Secure Base," relates to the same person's availability as he or she provides empowerment for the child to move out and explore the world. Thus the second belonging issue was labeled "Challenge," which can be represented by the question "Does God want me to grow?"

The theme of Goodness was again divided into two components. The first component, with more primitive emphasis on self image, can be characterized by the question "Am I good enough for God to love?" This dimension was labeled "Acceptance." The second component, more reflexive and oriented toward God image, can be summarized by the question "Is God the sort of Being who would want to love me?" This dimension was labeled "Benevolence." Since these six dimensions are hypothesized to be fundamental questions about God image, self image, and the relationship between the two throughout life, these are viewed as being relatively independent of developmental stages or theories. Lawrence (1991) points out that although this does not mean that these basic questions remain static throughout life, they are nonetheless measurable throughout life.

In addition to these six main scales, Lawrence (1991) added two shorter control scales for the convenience of the interpreter. The first one, Faith, attempts to measure the degree to which the subject believes in God as an existing being. The second, Salience, purports to measure the degree to which people find their relationships with God important to their personal lives.

Practical Considerations: The test is self-administered and requires no special examiner skill to administer or score. The instructions explain the meaning of each choice (i.e., strongly disagree, disagree, agree, strongly agree) and emphasize that there are no "right" or "wrong" answers. It is designed for research as well as pastoral and clinical use.

Norms/Standardization: Lawrence (1991) standardized the GII on a national sample of 1,580 respondents. These standards were demonstrated to be adequate for the interpretation of scores of adult American Christians across sex, age, education, and marital status. The means for the eight subscales ranged from 36.1 (Salience) to 73.3 (Benevolence). Standard deviations ranged from 7.0 (Faith) to 12.5 (Presence).

Reliability: Lawrence (1991) found internal consistency reliability coefficients ranging from .86 (Challenge) to .94 (Presence) for the main scales and the control scales. In a later phase of the study, Lawrence (1991) rechecked the internal consistency of the eight scales on a new sample, since the previous reliability data was based on recomputations from the original 490-item survey. The results indicated essentially identical internal consistency reliability coefficients ranging from .85 (Challenge) to .94 (Presence).

Lawrence (1991) computed interscale correlations on two occasions and found the average difference between the two sets of interscale correlations to be .03. The correlations ranged from .84 (Presence with Influence) to .44 (Providence with Benevolence). Thus Lawrence concluded that the GII scales demonstrate a stable pattern of intercorrelations, which indicates good temporal stability.

Validity: Contrary to the eight theoretical factors Lawrence hypothesized, a factor analysis with oblique rotation yielded 10 factors. Seven factors contained items from at least two different scales.

In order to establish convergent and discriminate validity, Lawrence (1991) correlated the GII scales with seven other measures (Extrinsic, Intrinsic, Achievement, Self-Esteem, Altruism, Locus of Control, and God Control) with which GII scales were predicted to relate in particular ways. The extrinsic scale, as predicted, was found to correlate negatively with all the GII scales. However, not all the correlations were small, as predicted. Lawrence predicted that overall intrinsic religiosity would correlate most highly with Salience, since it measures the relational importance of the God image to the subject. Lawrence further hypothesized that subjects with a greater sense of God's availability for them (Presence) would report a more satisfactory relationship with God, and thus would be more religious overall. Lawrence also predicted that intrinsicness would correlate second best with the Presence scale. As hypothesized, the Presence scale correlated the highest with the Salience scale (.76) and second highest with the Presence scale (.69), thus supporting the validity of these two scales.

The Achievement Scale did not perform as Lawrence had hypothesized, namely, that it would correlate positively with the Challenge

Scale. However, it related negatively with all the GII scales and reached significance only with the Providence Scale. Since it did not correlate significantly with Challenge, it neither confirmed nor falsified the validity of the Challenge Scale. Confirming Lawrence's hypothesis, the Self-Esteem Scale correlated positively with the GII Acceptance Scale (.54). Although Lawrence expected the Altruism Scale to relate significantly better with the GII Benevolence Scale than with the other GII scales, and second best with the GII Acceptance Scale, it actually failed to discriminate the two GII scales, and demonstrated a very narrow range of correlations with all the GII scales (.22 to .26).

Lawrence hypothesized that Internal Locus of Control would correlate positively and most highly with the GII Influence Scale. However, it produced the second weakest correlation (–.42; the negative sign is due the way the Locus Control Scale is scored), thus not confirming the validity of the Influence Scale. Finally, consistent with Lawrence's expentations, the GII Providence Scale, which measures how much God controls the subject, related most highly to the God Control Scale (.63). The God Control Scale also correlated second highest with the GII Influence Scale (.50), the other control scale. This supports the construct validity of the Providence scale.

Location:

Lawrence, R. T. (1991). *The God Image Inventory: The development, validation, and standard-*ization of a psychometric instrument for research, pastoral and clinical use in measuring the image of God. Unpublished doctoral dissertation, The Catholic University of America, Washington D. C.

Subsequent Research:

Key, T. L. (1995). Impact of inpatient psychiatric treatment on object relations maturity, self-esteem and God image (Doctoral dissertation, Rosemead Graduate School of Psychology, Biola University, 1995). *Dissertation Abstracts International, 55, B5568.*

Knapp, C. L. (1993). *Personality transformation and belief in God: An object relations understanding of the spiritual awakening program of alcoholics anonymous.* Unpublished doctoral dissertation, Andover Newton Theological School, Newton Center, MA.

References

Lawrence, R. T. (1991). *The God Image Inventory: The development, validation, and standardization of a psychometric instrument for research, pastoral and clinical use in measuring the image of God.* Unpublished doctoral dissertation, The Catholic University of America, Washington D. C.

Bowlby, J. (1969). *Attachment and loss: Vol. 1: Attachment.* New York: Basic Books.

Kirkpatrick, L. A. (1986). *Developmental psychology and religion: Potential application of attachment theory for the psychology of religion.* Paper presented at the annual meeting of the Society for the Scientific Study of Religion, Washington D. C.

Rizzuto, A. (1979). *The birth of the living God.* Chicago: University of Chicago Press.

Winnicott, D. W. (1953). Transitional objects and transitional phenomena. *International Journal of Psychoanalysis, 34,* 91.

Appendix:

God Image Inventory

Please respond to each statement by circling the response that comes closest to describing your feelings:

SA, for Strongly Agree, if the statement is a particularly good way of describing how you feel about God.
A, for agree, if the statement just adequately describes your feelings about God.
D, for Disagree, if the statement does not adequately describe your feelings about God.
SD, for Strongly Disagree, if the statement is a particularly bad way of describing your feelings about God.

1. God does not notice me. (P)*

2. I would live the same way whether I believed in God or not. (S)*

3. I sometimes think of God while drifting off to sleep. (P)

4. When I do wrong, God's back is turned on me. (A)*

5. When I obey God's rules, God makes good things happen for me. (I)

6. God lifts me up. (P)

7. God keeps calling me to develop myself. (C)

8. I think human achievements are a threat to God. (C)

9. The world would make no sense to me without God. (F)

10. I imagine God to be rather formal, almost standoffish. (B)*

11. I can see the direct hand of God in many things. (Pr)

12. God guides me like a good parent. (Pr)

13. God wants me to avoid the world as much as possible. (C)*

14. My growth in maturity is pleasing to God. (C)

15. I am sometimes anxious about whether God still loves me. (A)*

16. My belief in God is as solid as a rock. (F)

17. Asking God for help rarely does me any good. (I)*

18. I am confident of God's love for me. (A)

19. I am never sure that God is really listening to me. (P)*

20. I know I'm not perfect, but God loves me anyway. (A)

21. God does not seem to notice when I cry. (P)*

22. I have sometimes felt that I have committed the unforgivable sin. (A)*

23. The voice of God tells me what to do. (Pr)

24. My belief in God has made a big difference in my life. (S)

25. Even when I mess things up, I know God will straighten them out. (Pr)

26. I am not very sure what God is really like. (F)*

27. God never challenges me. (C)*

28. Thinking too much could endanger my faith. (C)*

29. I think of God as more compassionate than demanding. (B)

30. One source of my own self-respect is God's love for me. (A)

31. I get what I pray for. (I)

32. I try to be good because I know how much God love's me. (A)

33. I can feel God deep inside of me. (P)

34. God's love for me has no strings attached. (A)

35. God doesn't feel very personal to me. (P)*

36. No matter how hard I pray, it doesn't do any good. (I)*

37. Even when I do bad things, I know God still loves me. (A)

38. My belief in God is central to my life. (S)

39. I can talk to God on an intimate basis. (P)

40. God is always there for me. (P)

41. I have often changed my beliefs about God. (F)*

42. God nurtures me. (P)

43. God always has time for me. (P)

44. I get no feeling of closeness to God, even in prayer. (P)*

45. God is very patient. (B)

46. God loves me only when I perform perfectly. (A)*

47. I am not sure that my prayers matter to God. (I)*

48. What happens in my life is largely a result of decisions I make. (Pr)*

49. My faith in God helps me make decisions for myself. (C)

50. I think God even loves atheists. (B)

51. God loves me regardless. (A)

52. God takes pleasure in my achievements. (C)

53. I can't imagine anyone God couldn't love. (B)

54. God wants me to help transform the world. (C)

55. Sometimes I feel that God doesn't love me anymore. (A)*

56. I get no help from God even if I pray for it. (I)*

57. I look on challenges in life as gifts from God. (C)*

58. Prayer for me feels like talking to God almost face to face. (P)

59. God can easily be provoked by disobedience. (B)*

60. I am sure there has to be a God. (F)

61. God is not terribly relevant to my life. (S)*

62. God knows me better than to push me very hard. (C)*

63. I often worry about whether God can love me. (A)*

64. God is more of an observer of my life than a participant. (Pr)*

65. God is in control of my life. (Pr)

66. God wants me to achieve all I can in life. (C)

67. I am a very powerful person because of God's help. (I)

68. Prayer changes things. (I)

69. God will always provide for me. (Pr)*

70. Not even God can change how things will come out. (Pr)*

71. God has always seemed approachable to me. (B)

72. God helps me when I ask for help. (I)

73. My belief in God makes a major difference in the way I live. (S)

74. I doubt that God interferes very much in human affairs. (Pr)*

75. I would pray more if I thought it made a difference, but I don't think it does. (I)*

76. I think God mostly leaves people free. (Pr)*

77. Everyday things are more important to me than trying to be close to God. (S)*

78. If God listens to prayers, you couldn't prove it by me. (I)*

79. God helps me to keep going, no matter how hard things are. (C)

80. God is looking for a chance to get even with me. (B)*

81. God's mercy is for everyone. (B)*

82. God has to forgive my sins, but probably doesn't really want to. (B)*

83. I doubt that I will be rewarded for following God's rules. (I)*

84. God's love for me is unconditional. (A)

85. When I think of God, I feel at peace. (A)

86. My faith gives me some control over what happens to me. (I)

87. I trust in God to take care of me. (Pr)*

88. I know what to do to get God to listen to me. (I)

89. I ask God to help me grow from my troubles. (C)

90. God loves a lot of other people better than me. (A)*

91. I have confidence when I pray. (I)

92. God walks beside me and shows me where to go. (Pr)

93. Learning too much about the world could endanger my faith in God. (C)*

94. God asks me to keep growing as a person. (C)

95. I think God only loves certain people. (B)*

96. I sometimes don't know where to look for God. (P)*

97. God almost always answers my prayers. (I)

98. My faith in God is very strong. (F)

99. God doesn't want me to ask too many questions. (C)*

100. I have often doubted the existence of God. (F)*

101. I do not think about God very often. (S)*

102. I get a great deal out of the time I spend in prayer. (S)

103. God makes few demands on me. (C)*

104. God does not do much to determine the outcome of my life. (Pr)*

105. I am not very firm in my beliefs about God. (F)*

106. God lets the world run by its laws. (Pr)*

107. Sometimes I feel that God is persecuting me. (B)*

108. I would say that I am a God-centered person. (S)

109. Even if my beliefs about God were wrong God would still love me. (B)

110. I am not good enough for God to love. (A)*

111. I think it is best not to get too involved with God. (S)*

112. I have confidence in my beliefs about God. (F)

113. If I became convinced that God did not exist, nothing much in my life would change. (S)*

114. God's compassion knows no religious boundaries. (B)

115. I sometimes feel cradled in God's arms. (P)

116. God has never asked me to do hard things. (C)*

117. In making major decisions, I almost always think about my relationship with God. (S)

118. Running the world is more important to God than caring about people. (B)*

119. I often feel that I am in the hands of God. (Pr)*

120. I don't think my faith gives me any special influence with God. (I)*

121. I am sure that God really exists. (F)

122. Mostly, I have to provide for myself. (Pr)*

123. I feel that God knows me by name. (P)

124. I am particularly drawn to the image of God as a shepherd. (Pr)

125. God does not answer when I call. (P)*

126. I most often feel that I must face my problems alone. (Pr)*

127. God feels distant to me. (P)*

128. I often feel abandoned by God. (P)*

129. I think human achievements are a delight to God. (C)

130. I feel that God has a very specific plan for my life. (Pr)

131. It doesn't matter if I pray or not. (I)*

132. I rarely feel that God is with me. (P)*

133. I cannot imagine anyone more compassionate than God. (B)*

134. God for me is like a faithful friend. (A)

135. I feel warm inside when I pray. (P)

136. God loves me because God wants to. (B)*

137. I have a hard time believing in God's mercy. (B)*

138. God's love is a constant source of comfort to me. (A)

139. I am pretty much responsible for my own life. (Pr)*

140. God has very little influence over my life. (Pr)*

141. I often have nightmares about going to hell. (A)*

142. My ideas about God are pretty vague. (F)*

143. God rarely if ever seems to give me what I ask for. (I)*

144. I think God must enjoy getting even with us when we deserve it. (B)*

145. God encourages me to go forward on the journey of life. (C)

146. God sometimes intervenes at my request. (I)

147. I think God loves us all equally. (B)*

148. I have sometimes wondered whether God really exists. (F)*

149. I am more likely to succeed at something if I ask God for help. (I)

150. God never reached out to me. (P)*

151. God doesn't mind if I don't grow very much. (C)*

152. No matter how hard I try to please God, it doesn't seem to do me any good. (I)*

153. Sometimes I think that not even God could love me. (A)*

154. Sometimes I have nightmares about God. (B)*

155. God's mercy is only for the chosen few. (B)*

156. I would have to be a lot better person to be sure of God's love. (A)*

Notations:
  P - Presence subscale items
  C - Challenge subscale items
  A - Acceptance subscale items
  B - Benevolence subscale items
  I - Influence subscale items
  Pr - Providence subscale items
  F - Faith subscale items
  S - Salience subscale items

*Denotes negatively worded item (reverse-scored)

Note: The author has subsequently published a 72-item God Image Scale. Lawrence, R. T. (1997). Measuring the image of God: The God Image Inventory and the God Image Scales, *Journal of Psychology and Theology, 25*(2), 214–226.

Reprinted with permission of author.

11.5
LOVING AND CONTROLLING GOD SCALES (Benson & Spilka, 1973)

Reviewed by Todd W. Hall and Randall Lehmann Sorenson

Variable: The Loving and Controlling God scales measure two primary dimensions of God image: a loving God image and a controlling God image.

Description: Five parts of adjectives were used for the Loving God index: rejecting-accepting, loving-hating, damning-saving, unforgiving-forgiving, and approving-disapproving. Likewise, five pairs of adjectives were used for the Controlling God index: demanding-not demanding, freeing-restricting, controlling-uncontrolling, strict-lenient, and permissive-rigid. Each of the 10 items is scored on a semantic differential scale from 0 to 6; thus, scores for each scale range from 0 to 30.

Practical Considerations: This is self-administered paper-and-pencil measure that requires no special examiner skill to administer, score, or interpret. No instructions are

provided. The items for each scale clearly relate to their respective God image scales.

Norms/Standardization: The sample consisted of 128 male Catholic high school subjects. In order to obtain a homogeneous religious sample, these subjects were drawn from an original sample of 205 male subjects on the basis of criteria such as having been a member of a local Catholic parish for at least the past ten years. The final sample consisted of the following educational distribution: 44 freshmen, 31 sophomores, 19 juniors, and 34 seniors. The mean age for the sample was 15.4 years.

Reliability: Benson and Spilka (1973) examined scale homogeneity on a sample of 50 Lutheran subjects and found the coeficients to be .72 for the Loving God scale and .60 for the Controlling God scale.

Validity: Benson and Splilka (1973) found self-esteem to be, as predicted, positively related to the Loving God scale. In addition, they found locus of control to be unrelated to the Controlling God scale. Brokaw and Edwards (1994) found the Loving God scale to be positively correlated with and the Controlling God scale to be negatively correlated with level of object relations development as measured by the Ego Function Assessment Questionnaire Revised (EFAQ-R).

Location:

Benson, P., & Spilka, B. (1973). God image as a function of self-esteem and locus control. *Journal for the Scientific Study of Religion, 12*, 297–310.

Subsequent Research: The Loving and Controlling God Scales have been a consistently fertile source for subsequent theoretical and empirical investigation since the scale was first published in 1973. The following is only a representative list of research studies that have employed this measure.

Bowman, E. S., Coons, P. M., Jones, R. S., & Oldstrom, M. (1987). Religious psychodynamics in multiple personalities: Suggestions for treatment. *American Journal of Psychotherapy, 41*, 542–554.

Brokaw, B. F., & Edwards, K. J. (1994). The relationship of God image to level of object relations development. *Journal of Psychology and Theology, 22*, 352–371.

Gabbard, C. E., Howard, G. S., & Tageson, C. W. (1986). Assessing locus of control with religious populations. *Journal of Research in Personality, 20*, 292–308.

Hall, T. W., Tisdale, T. C., & Brokaw, B. F. (1994). Assessment of religious dimensions in Christian clients: A review of selected instruments for research and clinical use. *Journal of Psychology and Theology, 22*, 395–421.

Hertel, B. R., & Donahue, M. J. (1995). Parental influences on God images among children: Testing Durkheim metaphoric parallelism. *Journal for the Scientific Study of Religion, 34*, 186–199.

Jolley, J. C., & Taulbee, S. J. (1986). Assessing perceptions of self and God: Comparison of prisoners and normals. *Psychological Reports, 59*, 1139–1146.

Kirkpatrick, L. A., & Shaver, P. R. (1992). An attachment-theoretical approach to romantic love and religious belief. *Personality and Social Psychology Bulletin, 18*, 266–275.

Park, C. L., & Cohen, L. H. (1993). Religious and nonreligious coping with the death of a friend. *Cognitive Therapy and Research, 17*, 561–577.

Appendix

Loving and Controlling God Scales

1. Damning	0	1	2	3	4	5	6	Saving (L)
2. Rejecting	0	1	2	3	4	5	6	Accepting (L)
3. Demanding	0	1	2	3	4	5	6	Not Demanding (C)*
4. Loving	0	1	2	3	4	5	6	Hating (L)*
5. Freeing	0	1	2	3	4	5	6	Restricting (C)
6. Unforgiving	0	1	2	3	4	5	6	Forgiving (L)
7. Controlling	0	1	2	3	4	5	6	Uncontrolling (C)*
8. Approving	0	1	2	3	4	5	6	Disapproving (L)*
9. Strict	0	1	2	3	4	5	6	Lenient (C)*
10. Permissive	0	1	2	3	4	5	6	Rigid (C)

(L) = Loving God item
(C) = Controlling God item
 * = reverse-scored

11.6
NEARNESS TO GOD SCALE (Gorsuch & Smith, 1983)
Reviewed by Michael J. Boivin

Variable: The Nearness to God Scale was derived from the Religious Attitude Inventory developed by William E. Broen (1957a; reviewed in this volume). Items pertaining to the Nearness to God Scale assess the extent to which one feels God is real, constantly near, and accessible. Individuals scoring high on this scale are characterized as feeling that they "walk" and "talk" with God, communicating with God regularly. One's nearness to God is evaluated from within the context of the Christian faith.

Description: Broen's (1957a,b) scale originally contained 31 items designed to measure nearness to God (see 8.9 in this volume for a review of Broen's instrument). Gorsuch and Smith (1983) retained those items that they felt had the greatest contruct validity given the cultural and theological shifts in American society since the original development of Broen's instrument. Items 1, 9, 13, 17, 21, and 23 from Broen's instrument (Broen, 1957b, Factor 1) were retained for the Nearness to God scale.

Practical Considerations: The instrument is relatively straightforward and easily administered within a variety of settings. The scale is useful for both religious and nonreligious groups, although the instrument generally assumes a Christian orientation. Respondents simply note whether they agree or disagree with the item statements. Scoring is simple, since Gorsuch and Smith just added up the number of items with which the respondent agreed.

Norms/Standardization: Gorsuch and Smith (1983) administered their revised version of Broen's original instrument to 164 undergraduate students who were taking social science, nursing, and religion courses at a small Christian college. The Nearness to God mean was 5.24 (*SD* = 0.88).

Reliability: Reliability coefficients are unavailable for Gorsuch's six-item Nearness to God Scale. In an unpublished study, Gorsuch administered the Broen's Religious Attitude Inventory to 50 students (32 males, 18 females) at Texas Christian University. The interitem consistency coefficient for all 30 items in Broen's instrument that pertained to the nearness to God dimension was 0.60 (K-Richardson formula). This would give some indication of what might be expected with the Gorsuch and Smith scale.

Validity: No validity measures are available for the Nearness to God scale beyond what was already completed with Broen's original instrument. In terms of construct validity, Gorsuch and Smith (1983) do note that individuals with a higher "nearness to God" score are significantly more likely to attribute the responsibility to God for the outcome of life events and experiences.

The following might give some indication of the construct validity of this measure. In an unpublished study, Lawrence Wrightsman and a student administered Broen's Religious Attitude Inventory to college students attending Belmont College, Wheaton College (Wheaton, IL), and Central Michigan University. They then correlated both the "Nearness to God" and "Fundamentalism" scores with scores from the Dimensions of the Philosophies of Human Nature Scale developed by Lawrence Wrightsman. For male students at Central Michigan University, scores on the Nearness to God Scale were significantly correlated with how negatively one viewed human nature ($r = 0.27$), with the extent to which one viewed persons as being less than trustworthy ($r = 0.33$), with the extent to which one viewed persons as being less than altruistic ($r = 0.24$), and with the extent to which one viewed persons as being less than independent agents ($r = 0.31$). The findings were similar for the female students.

Location:

Gorsuch, R. L., & Smith, C. S. (1983). Attributions of responsibility to God: An interaction of religious beliefs and outcomes. *Journal for the Scientific Study of Religion, 22,* 340–352.

Subsequent Research:

Lupfer, M. B., Brock, K. F., & DePaola, S. J. (1992). The use of secular and religious attributions to explain everyday behavior. *Journal for the Scientific Study of Religion, 31,* 486–503.

References:

Broen, W. E. (1957a). A factor analytic study of religious attitudes. *Journal of Abnormal and Social Psychology, 54,* 176–179.

Broen, W. E. (1957b). Religious Attitude Inventory: The original correlation matrix, the unrotated factor matrix, and the Religious Attitude Inventory with keys for scoring (Document No. 5066). American Documentation Institute: Auxiliary Publications Project, Photoduplication Service. Washington, D.C.: Library of Congress.

Appendix

Nearness to God Scale

Directions: Circle *A* if you agree with the statement. Circle *D* if you disagree with the statement. Do not spend too much time on any one statement. We realize the difficulty a person who does not believe that God exists might have in answering a statement. If you do not believe in the existence of a God, show your disagreement with the *concept* by circling the *D* when you come to such a statement.

A   D   1. God is constantly with us.

A   D   2. God can be approached directly by all believers.

A   D   3. God exists in all of us.

A   D   4. I am sometimes very conscious of the presence of God.

A   D   5. God is very real to me.

A   D   6. Because of His presence we can *know* that God exists.

Reprinted with permission of authors.

11.7
NONVERBAL MEASURE OF GOD-CONCEPT
(Bassett, Miller, Anstey, Crafts, Harmon, Lee, Parks, Robinson, Smid, Sterner, Stevens, Wheeler, & Stevenson, 1990)
(Bassett, Perry, Repass, Silver, & Welch, 1994)

Reviewed by Beverly J. McCallister

Variable: In the tradition of Piagetian inspired religious educational researcher, Ronald Goldman, and God concept drawings interpreter, Ernest Harms, The Nonverbal Measure of God-Concept attempts to identify cognitive developmental differences in conceptions of God. Cognitive development is understood in terms of Jean Piaget's stages of cognitive development: preoperational, concrete operational, and formal operational (Piaget & Inhelder, 1969).

Description: Twenty-one black and white ink drawings printed on 5 by 7 cards constitute the 1990 version of this measure. The ink drawings are either realistic (e.g., a man with a beard, Jesus with children) or symbolic (e.g., cross, flame, and dove). These drawings were selected because they reminded subjects from different cognitive stages (pre-operational, concrete operational, or formal operational) of their God concept. In the 1990 version, 3 drawings were selected by subjects of the age usually associated with preoperational thinking (4–6 years), 4 pictures by subjects of the age usually associated with concrete thinking (8–10 years), and 14 pictures by subjects of the age usually associated with formal operational thinking (12-adult). In the 1994 version, there are 15 drawings. Five drawings each were most frequently selected by subjects determined to be in a preoperational, concrete, or formal operational stage by standard cognitive tests. The cognitive tests used to distinguish preoperational from concrete subjects were for conservation of volume, mass, and number. The cognitive tests used to distinguish concrete from formal operational thinkers were paper-and-pencil tests (Lunzer, 1965) for class inclusion (e.g., leather is to soft, shoe or hide as hard, clay or house is to brick) and for completion of sequence (e.g., 27, 18, 12, ?, 5⅓). Among the 15 available pictures selected, two pictures "seemed to differentiate the preoperational thinkers from others" (Bassett et al., 1994, p. 47) and five pictures "seemed to differentiate the formal operational thinkers from others" (Bassett et al., 1994, p. 47).

The three stages of cognitive development in which this measure is "loosely anchored" (Bassett et al., 1990, p. 20) can be identified as follows. Preoperational thought is thinking in only one dimension at a time (e.g., height or width), relying on perceptual information (e.g., authority is determined by size) and confusing causes with their effects. This stage usually characterizes children 4 to 7 years old. Concrete operational thought is being able to realize that physical dimensions (i.e., number of items, volume, and mass) remain the same despite new appearances (conservation), and being able to recognize subclasses of objects. It is typical of children between the ages of 7 and 11. Formal operational thought is being able to make inferences about unobserved entities and to think about such hypothetical constructs as ideas or thinking. It is associated with children 12 years old and above.

The authors offer this measure as a starting point in nonverbal research, and rightly so: there are reasons to be concerned about how well these drawings can differentiate between Piaget's stages of cognitive development. Utmost caution needs to be exercised when considering how graphic representations may reflect cognitive ones (Kosslyn, Heldmeyer, & Locklear, 1977). But as these drawings were developed, Piaget's stages of drawing development (i.e., synthetic incapacity, intellectual realism, visual realism) were not taken into account (Piaget & Inhelder, 1969). The forms that graphic representations take can change and may provide information about mental representations that goes beyond the development of drawing ability. For when a young child's limited ability to draw is controlled (e.g., using cutout parts), how the child forms her or his graphic representations corresponds with the undifferentiated representation seen in her or his own drawings (Bassett, 1977).

When preoperational 4-year-olds draw, they juxtapose simple shapes (i.e., circles and lines) into discontinuous patterns. Humans are often graphically represented with one large circle for a head, dots and lines for a face and some lines for legs. When 6-year-olds make the transition to the concrete operational stage, they tend to draw all features intellectually related to an object, often taking in several visual perspectives simultaneously. Two ears and eyes are included in a human profile. It is not until ages 8 through 12 that the child's mental representations begin to approach visual realism (Krampen, 1991). Most of the drawings in this measure are visually realistic. They are inconsistent with how most preoperational and concrete operational children draw. The younger children may not be reminded of their mental concept of God in this measure's disproportionately large number of realistic drawings. The large proportion of drawings associated with the formal operational stage in both versions may attest to a formal bias inherent in these realistic drawings. Moreover, since the subjects selected rather than created their own God concept, not only might their own undifferentiating tendencies be underestimated but their selection may reflect what the subject has been taught to recognize instead of what reflects their actual internal God concept.

Practical Considerations: No special skills or instructions are needed to present the drawings, one at a time, before each subject, instruct the subject to point to as many (or none) of those drawings that "most remind them of God" and then to count the number of times a drawing was selected in a predetermined group. If the comparison of interest is to determine how well these pictures differentiate between stages, then an independent measure of cognitive development is required. To analyze the data, familiarity with performing a one-way within subject analysis of variance, Kruskal-Wallis, and a post hoc Newman Keuls test is needed.

The purpose of this measure, to develop a standardized set of drawings that would nonverbally "indicate developmental changes in perceptions of God," is clearly stated. Also stated is their rationale for developing a nonverbal measure. Namely, since significant portions of religious activity are not verbal, measures that investigate such nonverbal religious expressions are needed. In addition, a nonverbal measure would be of use to researchers where language use is an issue, such as when working with young children, or persons who are speech impaired, or when working across cultures.

Norms/Standardization: To develop the first version of 21 drawings (Bassett et al., 1990), pictures of God were created by 198 members of conservative Protestant Sunday school classes with ages ranging from 2 to 75. Then these pictures were analyzed for religious themes and divided into three age-groups. On the basis on these religious themes, 35 new ink drawings were created. These 35 pictures were shown to six male and six female Protestant 6-year-olds, 7 male and 3 female Protestant 3rd graders, and 28 male and 18 female Protestants between the ages of 12 and 21. Nineteen drawings were eliminated on the basis of selections. This left 1 drawing that was regularly preferred only by 6-year-olds, 8 drawings regularly preferred by only 3rd graders, and 10 drawings regularly preferred only by adults. After adding 10 new drawings that might appeal to younger children, these 35 drawings were shown to 31 4–6 year-olds, 22 8–10 year-olds, and 38 adults. Based on the preference of these subjects' first measures, 21 drawings were identified.

In the second version of this measure (Bassett et al., 1994), the 21 drawings from the first measure plus 33 drawings with new religious themes inspired by pictures of God as drawn by 17 Catholics, 23 Methodists and 1 Orthodox Jew made up a new pool of 54 drawings. These drawings were shown to groups of females from the three different cognitive stages as determined by cognitive tests. There were 33 preoperational, 35 concrete operational, and 36 formal operational subjects. Within each cognitive group, both Protestants (conservative and mainline) and Catholics were represented. Consequently, the conservative Protestant bias of the samples used in the first study was absent in the second sample, while the size of the samples of each cognitive group was adequate (30+). Based on the preference of these subjects, the second measure's 15 drawings were identified, five from each cognitive group.

Reliability: No specific procedures were used to assess reliability, but three pictures used in the 1990 study were again in the 1994 version. Among those, two pictures—one of a bearded man and another of a cross, flames, and a dove—were preferred by subjects within the same stage as before, the preoperational and formal operational stages, respectively. The third drawing used in both studies, Jesus with children, was selected by the largest percentage among concrete operational thinkers in the first study but failed to be preferred by any group in the second study.

Validity: Using chronological age as an indicator of cognitive development, as was done for the first version, is, at best, only an indirect indicator of cognitive development, and it does not ensure the presence of certain cognitive processes. Critics of Piaget's stage theory have shown how one stage's cognitive processing can be demonstrated at earlier ages (Rosenthal & Zimmerman, 1972).

The authors' procedure of assigning consecutive numbers to the age-groups and then using these numbers as the data for an analysis of variance is not a justifiable test, as the authors acknowledge, and so does not support the idea that these drawings differentiate among age-groups. Their application of a second less powerful test, the distribution free Kruskal-Wallis, does support the idea that there is an overall difference in the frequency with which certain drawings were selected by a particular group. However, as an examination of the residuals of the chi-square analysis would have demonstrated (Lehman, 1995, p. 298), this overall difference between groups primarily reflects the formal age-group's acceptance or rejection of drawings, not the equal identifications with drawings across all groups. Even when the selection of drawings was influenced by subjects identified by a standard test for cognitive ability, most of the pictures that differentiated among cognitive groups differentiated the formal operational subjects. No drawings differentiated the concrete operational stage from the other two stages in the second version. To further this instrument's effectiveness, other representations of subformal processing, drawings or cutouts, need to be added.

But even with a more representative set of drawings, using the frequency with which a drawing is selected as a measure of cognitive differences does not necessarily mean that the religious content of the drawings reflects the content of the subject's cognitive perceptions. For it is equally possible that formal-aged subjects rejected certain drawings not because of the drawing's religious theme but because that drawing looked like what a younger child would draw (formal-aged subjects rejected the geometrically shaped man wearing a crown). If preferences for religious themes are to be investigated, then the form of a graphic representation needs to be standardized. Eventually, the relationship be-

tween the processes mediating the images and the processing mediating the words used to those images (Pavio, 1990) should be part of the discussion of religious perceptions.

Also, the meaningfulness of material derived from new versions of this measure will depend on how well the many challenges to Piaget's theory of cognitive development are addressed. The authors point out that other cognitive approaches might also be explored. Despite the limitations of the current measures, in the psychology of religion, where words are only part of entire religious experiences, the development of nonverbal measures is needed.

Location:

Copies of the pictures can obtained from Rodney L. Bassett, Ph.D., Roberts Wesleyan College, 2301 Westside Drive, Rochester, New York 14624.

Subsequent Research: none

References

Bassett, E. (1977). Production strategies in the child's drawing of the human figure: Towards an argument for a model of syncretic perception. In G. Butterworth (Ed)., *The child's representation of the world.* NY: Plenum Press.

Bassett, R. L., Miller, S., Anstey, K., Crafts, K., Harmon, J., Lee, Y., Parks, J., Robinson, M., Smid, H., Sterner, W., Stevens, C. Wheeler, B., & Stevenson, D. H. (1990). Picturing God: A nonverbal measure of God concept for conservative Protestants. *Journal of Psychology and Christianity, 9*, 73–81.

Bassett, R. L., Perry, K., Repass, R., Silver, E., & Welch, T. (1994). Perceptions of God among persons with mental retardation: A research note. *Journal of Psychology and Theology, 22*, 45–49.

Harms, E. (1944). The development of religious experience in children. *American Journal of Sociology, 50*, 112–122.

Kosslyn, S. M., Heldmeyer, K. H., & Locklear, E. D. (1977). Children's drawings as data about internal representations. *Journal of Experimental Child Psychology, 23*, 191–211.

Krampen, M. (1991). *Children's drawings: Iconic coding of the environment.* New York: Plenum Press.

Lehman, R. (1995). *Statistics in the behavioral sciences: A conceptual approach.* Pacific Grove, CA: Brooks/Cole Co.

Lunzer, E. (1965). Problems of formal reasoning

Figure 1 Man with beard.

Figure 2 Man wearing crown.

Figure 3 Jesus with children.

Figure 4 Man walking out of Bible.

Figure 5 Person in clouds.

Figure 6 Tropical nature scene.

Figure 7 Cross, flame and dove.

Figure 8 Three connected circles.

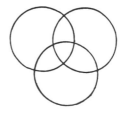

in test situations. In P. Mussen (Ed.), *European research in cognitive development: Monographs of the Society for Research in Child Development, 30,* 19–46.

Pavio, A. (1990). *Mental representations: A dual coding approach.* New York: Oxford University press.

Piaget, J., & Inhelder, B. (1969). *The psychology of the child.* (Trans. H. Weaver.) London: Routledge & Kegan Paul.

Rosenthal, T. L., & Zimmerman, B.J. (1972). Modeling by exemplification and instruction in training conservation. *Developmental Psychology, 6,* 392–401.

Appendix

Perceptions of God Pictures (Descriptions)

1990 version (name of the drawing, letters indicate which age-group reportedly preferred this drawing: P = preoperational age, C = concrete operational age, F = formal operational age)

1. Detailed sketch of a bearded man in a robe from the waist up with his left arm raised and his index finger pointing to the sky. (Man with beard, P) (see Figure 1)

2. Incomplete (no feet or hands) geometric outline with limited perspective of a panted full figure; dots for eyes and a curve for a mouth make up the face. The crown on its head sits atop long, line-drawn hair. Extending at a 90-degree angle from figure's left sleeve is a wand with a star; on its right is a rod with a ball on the top. (Man wearing crown, P) (see Figure 2).

3. An outline with limited perspective of the full figure of a robed, bearded man with a line extending downward from the fingers on his left hand. Dots for pupils encased in two curved lines for the lids and a circle for mouth with a moustache make up the face. (Man holding cane, P)

4. Impressionistic sketch of the top three quarters of a full figure with robes billowing on both sides and sleeves lifted up. Eyes, eyebrows, nostrils, mouth, and hair indicated with dots and lines. A circle sits on the hair. (Man with flowing robes, P)

5. Impressionistic sketch of a three-quarter-length profile of a robed and bearded man holding a line-drawn staff. The figure is emerging from the open pages of a book with lines on the pages. Background lines suggest movement. (Man walking out of Bible, C) (see Figure 4).

6. Impressionistic sketch of a three-quarter profile of a seated, bearded man in flowing robes holding a short-haired smaller human figure with his right arm in his lap. His left arm extends toward the profile of a standing smaller human figure facing him. The upper half of a third child appears to the right of this group. (Jesus with children, C) (see Figure 3).

7. A black geometrically shaped blot, like the skyline of a some tall buildings, one of which is a tower. This blot rests on the outline of connected curves that resemble clouds. Above and to the right of this plot is a circle with ten disconnected lines emanating from it. (Castle with clouds , C)

8. An impressionistic set of two ink-blot type curved forms, shaped like robed and hooded kneeling figures, with one larger white oval where a face would be with a smaller white circle near what would be the base of the neck, on each figure. Between these blots is the outline of a raised imperfect rectangle on crossed line with a circle on top with seven disconnected lines emanating from it. (Manger scene, F)

9. A sketch of a large mountain with a rounded top that fills most of the card. Dark wavy streaks lie above the mountain. A set of sharply angled lines extend from the upper left of the card to a point on the side of the mountain. (Mountain with lightning, F)

10. A sketch of two full human figures in non-Western dress standing to the left of the card. One figure extends a right arm into the air while the other holds a cane. The degraded outline

of many sheep stand around a bare tree down and to the right. (Shepherds looking up, F)

11. An impressionistic sketch of a robed bearded figure placed diagonally across the card. Two arms extend to the upper right side and hold two tombstone shaped objects placed at an angle to each other with scribbles in lines across them. (Man with stone tablets, F)

12. An impressionistic outdoor sketch with a black palm tree in front of a hill on the far right, a quarter moon in the upper center above foliage of various heights, hill-like shapes to the left and a broad flat river broadens out from the back to both lower corners of the card. (Tropical nature scene, F) (see Figure 6).

13. A schematic drawing of three white circles of different sizes. The large circle in the center has black areas that outline continent shaped white areas. A circle, one tenth the size of the one in the center is in the upper right corner with a quotation-mark like black curve on its left side. An even smaller circle white ring with a bulge sits in the lower left hand corner. (Outer space, F).

14. A schematic drawing of curves making clouds run along the top; and two arms extend downward from two of these clouds. (Hands in clouds, F)

15. A schematic drawing of a white hill on the left with one large and two smaller crosses on top against a black background. Shadows of the crosses extend down the hill. A white angular streak of white comes down from the upper right corner to the top of the large center cross. (Crosses with lightning, F)

16. An impressionistic drawing of the full figure of a bearded man in a robe at some distance and suspended in the foreground with the outline of three larger clouds in the background. The man holds up his right arm bent at his elbow. His other arm rests against his chest. (Person in clouds, F) (see Figure 5).

17. Three equally overlapping open circles of equal size. (Three connecting circles, F) (see Figure 8).

18. Schematic sketch of a cross left of center that extends from the top of the card to the bottom with disconnected lines emanating out around its top third. The outline of a bird with outstretched wings and a leaved twig in its mouth sits in the lower right. Three misshaped conical shapes with vertical lines appear to the left of the cross and two sit off to its right. (Cross, flame, and dove, F) (see Figure 7).

19. Impressionistic sketch of ten small bunches of flowers fill the bottom half of the card. Dense overlapping scrolling across the middle extends upward in shapes like a cypress tree. In the background to the right is the outline of a mountain. (Alpine nature scene, F)

20. (Blank card, F)

Bassett, R. L., et al. (1990). Picturing God: A noverbal measure of God-concept for conservative Protestants. *Journal of Psychology and Christianity, 8*, 73–81. Copyright © 1990 Christian Association for Psychological Studies. Reprinted with permission by author and publisher.

Chapter 12

Scales of Religious Fundamentalism

Religious fundamentalism is not easily characterized or defined. For many, it is a catch-all term that describes a rigid, dogmatic, and reactionary style of religious belief. Some mistakenly use the term "fundamentalism" interchangeably with orthodoxy or evangelicalism. Ammerman (1991) defines five central tenets of Protestant Christian fundamentalism: (a) *inerrancy of scripture*, (b) *evangelism* (of the "lost" world), (c) *premillenialism* (a particular prophetic view of the end times that strongly implies the imminent second coming of Christ), (d) *biblical literalism* (even on matters not directly related to central doctrinal issues), and (e) *separatism* (from nonbelievers). Of course, there are forms of fundamentalism in other religions as well.

A rather thorough definition of religious fundamentalism is provided by Altemeyer and Hunsberger (1992) and is included in the first paragraph of the review of their scale (12.3). Probably not everyone agrees with their definition. Our purpose is not to defend this or any other definition but to point out the complexity of the phenomenon. Investigators are encouraged to be careful in their use of the term and in their selection of fundamentalism research measures.

Only the Altemeyer and Hunsberger Religious Fundamentalism Scale (12.3) is potentially useful outside of the Christian tradition. However, this 20-item scale may require modification of some terms to be a useful measure with other religions. Each of the other four measures explicitly monitor Christian fundamentalism. Only the Fundamentalism Scale-Revised by Gorsuch and Smith (12.2) and the Wiggins Religious Fundamentalism Scale (12.5) can be considered multidimensional. The other two scales, the Gibson and Francis Christian Fundamentalist Belief Scale (12.1) and the Martin and Westie Religious Fundamentalism Scale (12.4), use religious belief as the primary criterion for defining fundamentalism.

References

Altemeyer, B., & Hunsberger, B. (1992). Authoritarianism, religious fundamentalism, quest, and prejudice. *The International Journal for the Psychology of Religion, 2*, 113-133.

Ammerman, N. T. (1991). North American Protestant fundamentalism. In M. E. Marty & R. S. Appleby (Eds.), *Fundamentalisms observed*. Chicago: University of Chicago Press.

12.1
CHRISTIAN FUNDAMENTALIST BELIEF SCALE (Gibson & Francis, 1996)

Reviewed by Ralph W. Hood Jr.

Variable: The Christian Fundamentalist Belief Scale (CFBS) was designed to provide a unidimensional scale to measure a single construct—fundamentalism. Fundamentalism is defined within the Protestant tradition and focuses primarily on the authority and inerrancy of the Bible.

Description: The CFBS is a twelve-item scale. Respondents are asked to rate each item on a 5-point Likert-type scale, ranging from disagree strongly to agree strongly.

Practical Considerations: The scale requires no special expertise to administer, score, or interpret. It is appropriate for use with adolescents and adult Protestant samples.

Norms/Standardization: The scale was administered to 395 male and 471 female adolescents attending two nondenominational, state-maintained schools in Scotland. Means and standard deviations are reported for males and females separately for grade years 7 and 8 and 9 and 10. For years 7 and 8 the mean for males (N = 224) was 33.2

(SD = 9.7) and for females (N = 262) was 35.8 (SD = 8.0). For years 9 and 10 the mean for males (N = 171) was 29.4 (SD = 10.5) and for females (N = 209) was 34.1 (SD = 10.0). No normative data has been established among samples in the United States.

Reliability: Based on the total sample of 866 students, Cronbach's alpha was 0.92.

Validity: Construct validity was explored by correlating the CFBS with three indices of Christian practice for the total sample. Significant correlations were found in all cases for frequency of chruch attendance (r = .44), prayer (r = .50), and personal Bible reading (r = .47).

Location:
Gibson, H. M., & Francis, L. J. (1996). Measuring Christian fundamentalist belief among 11–15 year old adolescents in Scotland. In L. J. Francis & W. S. Campbell (Eds.), *Research in religious education* (pp. 249–255). Leominister, UK: Fowler Wright.

Subsequent Research: None

Appendix

Instrument

Please Indicate your response to each item using the folowing scale:

1	2	3	4	5
disagree strongly	disagree	neutral	agree	agree strongly

_____ I believe that God made the world in six days and rested on the seventh.

_____ I believe that the Bible is the word of God.

_____ I believe that Jesus was born of a virgin.

_____ I believe that Jesus will return to earth some day.

_____ I believe in hell.

_____ I believe that God judges what I do and say.

_____ I believe that Jesus died to save me.

_____ I believe that Jesus changed real water into real wine.

_____ I believe that Jesus walked on water.

_____ I believe that Jesus Christ is the Son of God.

_____ I believe that God is controlling every bit of our lives.

_____ I believe that Jesus really rose from the dead.

Gibson, H. M., & Francis, L. J. (1996). Measuring Christian fundamentalist belief among 11–15 year old adolescents in Scotland. In L. J. Francis & W. S. Campbell (Eds.), *Research in religious education* (pp. 249–255). Leominster, UK: Fowler Wright. Copyright © 1996, Fowler Wright.

12.2
FUNDAMENTALISM SCALE-REVISED, (Gorsuch & Smith, 1983; Broen, 1957)
Reviewed by Michael J. Boivin

Variable: The Fundamentalism Scale was revised from the Religious Attitude Inventory developed by William E. Broen (1957a; (also reviewed in this volume). Items pertaining to this measure assess the extent to which one subscribes to the orthodox tenets of the Christian faith with an emphasis on a literal interpretation of the Bible as the word of God, the essential sinfulness of man, and the need for and rightful fear of a punishing God. Individuals scoring low on this scale would tend to adopt a more liberal view of the Scriptures and a humanistic view of the human condition, with persons having the ability to realize their innate potential through their own efforts apart from God.

Description: Gorsuch and three of his graduate students reviewed all of the fundamentalism/nonfundamentalism items in Broen's (1957a) original scale (see *8.9* in this volume for a review of Broen's instrument). They retained only those items that they could unanimously agree on as retaining face validity or relevance with regard to the religious trait of fundamentalism (33 items in all from Broen's original 58). Respondents simply note whether they agree or disagree with a series of statements.

Practical Considerations: The instrument is relatively straightforward and easily administered in a variety of settings. The scale is useful for both religious and nonreligious groups, although the instrument generally assumes a Christian orientation. In terms of scoring, Gorsuch simply added up the number of fundamentalism items with which the respondent agreed. For those fundmamentalism items that are reverse worded (denoted by an asterisk in the scale), *disagreeing* with that statement increments the total score by one.

Norms/Standardization: In an unpublished study, Gorsuch administered his selected portion of Broen's fundamentalism items in the Religious Attitude Questionnaire to 50 students (32 males, 18 females) at Texas Christian University. The mean score on the Fundamentalism Scale was 15.34 (*SD* = 5.12). Gorsuch and Smith (1983) administered their revised version of Broen's original instrument to 164 undergraduate students who were taking social science, nursing, and religion courses at a small Christian college. The Fundamentalism Scale mean was 23.94 (*SD* = 5.29).

Reliability: Reliability coefficients are unavailable for Gorsuch and Smith's (1983) 33-item Fundamentalism Scale. However, in an unpublished study, Gorsuch administered Broen's Religious Attitude Inventory to 50 students (32 males, 18 females) at Texas Christian University. The interitem consistency coefficient for all of the fundamentalism items in Broen's instrument was 0.76 (K-Richardson formula), which would give some indication of what might be expected with Gorsuch and Smith's version.

Validity: No validity measures are available for Gorsuch and Smith's (1983) version of the Fundamentalism Scale. The following might give some indication of the construct validity of this measure. In an unpublished study, Lawrence Wrightman and a student administered Broen's Religious Attitude Inventory to college students attending Belmont College, Wheaton College (Wheaton, IL), and Central Michigan University. They then correlated both the "Nearness to God" and "Fundamentalism" scores with scores from the Dimensions of the Philosophies of Human Nature Scale developed by Larry Wrightman. For male students at Central Michigan University, scores on the Fundamentalism Scale were significantly correlated with how negatively one viewed human nature ($r = 0.32$), with the extent to which one viewed persons as being less than altruistic ($r = 0.31$), and with the extent to which one viewed persons as being less than independent agents ($r = 0.36$). Students at Wheaton College had a significant correlation between fundamentalism and independence (lack of) domain of their views on human nature ($r = 0.29$). The findings were similar for the female students.

Location:
Gorsuch, R. L., & Smith, C. S. (1983). Attributions of responsibility to God: An interaction of religious beliefs and outcomes. *Journal for the Scientific Study of Religion, 22,* 340–352.

Subsequent Research: None located.

References:

Broen, W. E. (1957a). A factor analytic study of religious attitudes. *Journal of Abnormal and Social Psychology, 54,* 176–179.

Broen, W. E. (1957b). Religious Attitude Inventory: The original correlation matrix, the unrotated factor matrix, and the Religious Attitude Inventory with keys for scoring (Document No. 5066). American Documentation Institute: Auxiliary Publications Project, Photoduplication Service. Washington, D.C.: Library of Congress.

Lee, R. R. (1965). Theological belief as a dimension of personality (Doctoral dissertation, Northwestern University, 1965). *Dissertation Abstracts International, 26–06,* 3510.

Smith, C. S. (1983). Sanctioning and causal attributions to God: A function of theological position and actors' characteristics (Doctoral dissertation, Fuller Theological Seminary, Professional School of Psychology, 1983). *Dissertation Abstracts International, 44–06B,* 2016.

Appendix

Instrument

Directions: Circle the *A* if you agree with a statement, and circle the *D* if you disagree with the statement. Make a choice for each statement. Do not spend too much time on any one statement. We realize the difficulty a person who does not believe in the existence of a God might have in answering a statement such as "God watches over us." (Disagree might be interpreted as meaning that "there *is* a God who does not watch over us.") If you do not believe in the existence of a God, show your disagreement with the *concept* by circling the disagree when you come to such a statement.

A   D   1. Christ died for sinners.

A   D   2. There is really no such a place as Hell.[*]

A   D   3. It is through the righteousness of Jesus Christ and not because of our own works that we are made righteous before God.

A   D   4. Christ's simple message of concern for your fellow man has been twisted by the superstitious mysticism of such men as Paul.[*]

A   D   5. The death of Christ on the cross was necessary to blot out man's sin and make him acceptable in the eyes of God.

A   D   6. "God" is an abstract concept roughly equivalent to the concept "Nature."*

A   D   7. Man is born in sin.

A   D   8. Man's essential nature is good.*

A   D   9. Man is by nature sinful and unclean.

A   D   10. The stories of miracles in the Bible are like the parables in that they have some deeper meaning or moral but are not to be taken literally.*

A   D   11. The Bible is the word of God and must be believed in its entirety.

A   D   12. Man has a spark of the divine in him which must be made to blossom more fully.*

A   D   13. Sin brings forth the wrath of God.

A   D   14. A person should follow his own conscience in deciding right and wrong.*

A   D   15. The most important idea on religion is the Golden Rule.*

A   D   16. The wrath of God is a terrible thing.

A   D   17. The Scriptures should be interpreted with the constant exercise of reason.*

A   D   18. Everyone will be called before God at the judgment day to answer for his sins.

A   D   19. Everyone has sinned and deserves punishment for his sins.

A   D   20. The church is important because it is an effective agency for organizing the social life of a community.*

A   D   21. No one should question the authority of the Bible.

A   D   22. The content of various doctrines is unimportant. What really matters is that they help those who believe in them to lead better lives.*

A   D   23. Because of his terrible sinfulness, man has been eternally damned unless he accepts Christ as his savior.

A   D   24. Religion is a search for understanding, truth, love, and beauty in human life.*

A   D   25. Every person born into this world deserves God's wrath and damnation.

A   D   26. The world is full of condemned sinners.

A   D   27. The Devil can enter a man's body and take control.

A   D   28. The people of the world must repent before it is too late and they find themselves in Hell.

A   D   29. The Christian must lead a strict life, away from worldly amusements.

A   D   30. In his natural state of sin, man is too evil to communicate with God.

A   D   31. Christ was not divine, but his teachings and the example set by his life are invaluable.*

A   D   32. The question of Christ's divinity is unimportant; it is his teachings that matter.*

A   D   33. God is the final judge of our behavior, but I do not believe that He is as punishing as some seem to say He is.*

*Denotes reverse-scored items.

Reprinted with permission of authors.

12.3
RELIGIOUS FUNDAMENTALISM SCALE (Altemeyer & Hunsberger, 1992)

Reviewed by Raymond F. Paloutzian

Variable: This scale is designed to measure a "fundamentalist" way of holding and expressing one's religious beliefs. It is best to let the authors say, in their own words, what "fundamentalism" is intended to mean: "The belief that there is one set of religious teachings that clearly contains the fundamental, basic, intrinsic, essential, inerrant truth about humanity and deity; that this essential truth is fundamentally opposed by forces of evil which must be vigorously fought; that this truth must be followed today according to the fundamental, unchangeable practices of the past; and that those who believe and follow these fundamental teachings have a special relationship with the deity" (Altemeyer & Hunsberger, 1992, p. 118).

Description: The important feature of the Religious Fundamentalism (RF) Scale is that its items are free of doctrinal content. Past scales designed to measure fundamentalism included lists of doctrinal statements with which the adherent could express greater or lesser degrees of belief. Such measures confounded the content of one's beliefs with the mental process by which those beliefs are held. The RF Scale allows us to get beyond this problem because its items contain statements that can apply to many religions. Thus the RF Scale can measure the degree to which someone is religious in a fundamentalistic sense, whether the person is a Christian, Muslim, Jew, or other. The measure opens the door for a whole new line of research.

The measure is theoretically and empirically related to other constructs in ways that make sense. It is associated with overall right-wing authoritarianism and with each of its three components—conventionalism, submission to authority, and authoritarian aggression—and with Altemeyer's (1996) Dogmatism Scale. The measure is also correlated with degree of Christian orthodoxy, which suggests that some people who hold specific and traditional beliefs also hold

them in a rigid way. It is clear, however, that there are also exceptions to these trends and the RF Scale taps an important, separate dimension (Altemeyer & Hunsberger, 1992).

The RF Scale comprises 20 items. Half of the items are worded in the con-trait direction in order to control for a response-set bias. Each item is scored on a 9-point Likert scale for which the answer options range from "−4" to "+4" for the "very strongly disagree" and the "very strongly agree" answers, respectively. A neutral answer option of "0" is allowed. In order to eliminate negative numbers and obtain the final score, which is the sum of the scores for the 20 items, the scores are reversed for the contrait items and a constant of five is then added to the raw scores. Total scores may range from a low of 20 to a high of 180, with a theoretical midpoint of 100.

Practical Considerations: The RF Scale takes approximately 10 minutes to complete. No special training is required to administer the scale, and the scores are readily interpretable. Because the scale is nonsectarian, it is neutral with respect to specific doctrinal orientations and may be used within a variety of religious and academic contexts.

Norms/Standardization: The initial samples on which test item selection and assessment of the scale's statistical properties were based included 463 students from Wilfred Laurier University in Ontario, Canada, and 235 students from the University of Manitoba. Nearly all participants had been raised in Christian faiths. Additional data came from the parents (247 mothers and 244 fathers) of introductory psychology students at Manitoba. For the parent study, the overall mean RF score was 84.6, with a standard deviation of 33.0.

Altemeyer and Hunsberger (1992) published means and standard deviations of RF scores for the following groups of parents (sample sizes range from 20 to 158): those whose religion is "none" (M = 54.2, SD = 21.1), Catholic (M = 92.1, SD = 25.6), Anglican (M = 73.0, SD = 22.8), fundamentalist Protestant (M = 130.6, SD = 22.0), Lutheran (M = 89.1, SD = 23.7), Mennonite (M = 121.7, SD = 34.6), United Church (M = 69.8, SD = 19.6), Christian (M = 89.1, SD = 40.6), and a small sample (6) of Jews (M = 70.3, SD = 23.1). Although the parents of university students do not exactly represent the population at large, the initial data were well based on a heterogeneous sample of religious groups in Canada, no doubt with similarities to those in the rest of North America. Additional data have been published for samples of 23 Hindus (M = 84.5, SD = 31.5), 21 Muslims (M = 112.3, SD = 40.3), and 32 Jews (M = 48.3, SD = 21.1) living in Toronto (Hunsberger, 1996).

Reliability: The interitem correlations from the student samples ranged from .41 to .48; the indices of internal consistency reliability ranged from .93 to .95. For the parent sample, the mean interitem correlation was .37, and the index of internal consistency was .92. Comparable statistics were obtained from the Toronto samples of Hindus, Muslims, and Jews (Hunsberger, 1996). These statistics indicate that the RF Scale has high internal consistency reliability across various religious samples.

Validity: Examination of the content of the items suggests that the questions on the scale represent the aspects of belief that are imbedded in the authors' conceptual definition of fundamentalism. Moreover, the RF Scale has been found to correlate with other measures in ways that would be expected based on the construct that it is intended to measure. For example, in various samples RF has correlated between .66 and .75 with the Right-Wing Authoritarianism Scale (Altemeyer, 1988). It has also been found to correlate from .60 to .75 with the Christian Orthodoxy Scale (Fullerton & Hunsberger, 1982), .57 to .60 with the Dogmatism Scale, .30 with a measure of prejudice, .41 with an antihomosexuality scale, and −.79 with a balanced measure of religion as a quest. Furthermore, a group of 20 fundamentalist Protestants had a

mean score of 130.6, significantly higher than several other religious groups (Altemeyer & Hunsberger, 1992). Exploring the robustness of the RF Scale by testing it with non-Christian religious people, Hunsberger (1996) reports correlations of .42 to .65 between RF and antihomosexual attitudes for Hindus, Muslims, Jews, and Christians. Overall, although the scale is fairly new and the database is still being assembled, the available data point strongly to the scale's validity.

Location:
Altemeyer, B., & Hunsberger, B. (1992). Authoritarianism, religious fundamentalism, quest, and prejudice. *The International Journal for the Psychology of Religion, 2,* 113–133.

Subsequent Research:
Genia, V. (1996). I, E, quest, and fundamentalism as predictors of psychological and spiritual well-being. *Journal for the Scientific Study of Religion, 35,* 56–64.

Hunsberger, B. (1996). Religious fundamentalism, right-wing authoritarianism and hostility toward homosexuals in non-Christian religious groups. *The International Journal for the Psychology of Religion, 6,* 39–49

Hunsberger, B., Pancer, M. S., Pratt, M., & Alisat, S. (1996). The transition to university: Is religion related to adjustment? In M. Lynn & D. Moberg (Eds.), *Research in the Social Scientific Study of Religion* (Vol. 7, pp. 181–199). Greenwich, CT: JAI Press.

Hunsberger, B., Pratt, M., & Pancer, S. M. (1994). Religious fundamentalism and integrative complexity of thought: A relationship for existential content only? *Journal for the Scientific Study of Religion, 33,* 335–346.

Pancer, S. M., Jackson, L. M., Hunsberger, B., Pratt, M. W., & Lea, J. (1995). Religious orthodoxy and the complexity of thought about religious and nonreligious issues. *Journal of Personality, 63,* 213–232.

References
Altemeyer, B. (1988). *Enemies of freedom: Understanding right-wing authoritarianism.* San Francisco: Jossey-Bass.

Altemeyer, B. (1996). *The authoritarian specter.* Cambridge, MA: Harvard University Press.

Fullerton, J. T., & Hunsberger, B. (1982). A unidimensional measure of Christian orthodoxy. *Journal for the Scientific Study of Religion, 21,* 317–326.

Appendix

Religious Fundamentalism Scale

This survey includes a number of statements about general religious opinions. You will probably find that you *agree* with some of the statements and *disagree* with others, to varying extents. Please indicate your reaction to each of the statements by marking your opinion to the left of each statement, according to the following scale:

Mark a   – 4 if you *very strongly disagree* with the statement.
            – 3 if you *strongly disagree* with the statement.
            – 2 if you *moderately disagree* with the statement.
            – 1 if you *slightly disagree* with the statement.

Mark a   + 1 if you *slightly agree* with the statement.
            + 2 if you *moderately agree* with the statement.
            + 3 if you *strongly agree* with the statement.
            + 4 if you *very strongly agree* with the statement.

If you feel exactly and precisely *neutral* about a statement, mark a "0" next to it.

1. God has given mankind a complete, unfailing guide to happiness and salvation, which must be totally followed.

2. *All* of the religions in the world have flaws and wrong teachings.*

3. Of all the people on this earth, one group has a special relationship with God because it believes the most in his revealed truths and tries the hardest to follow his laws.

4. The long-established traditions in religion show the best way to honour and serve God, and should never be compromised.

5. Religion must admit all its past failings and adapt to modern life if it is to benefit humanity.*

6. When you get right down to it, there are only two kinds of people in the world: the Righteous, who will be rewarded by God and the rest, who will not.

7. Different religions and philosophies have different versions of the truth and may be equally right in their own way.*

8. The basic cause of evil in this world is Satan, who is still constantly and ferociously fighting against God.

9. It is more important to be a good person than to believe in God and the right religion.*

10. No one religion is especially close to God, nor does God favor any particular group of believers.*

11. God will punish most severely those who abandon his true religion.

12. No single book of religious writings contains all the important truths about life.*

13. It is silly to think people can be divided into "the Good" and "the Evil." Everyone does some good, and some bad, things.*

14. God's true followers must remember that he requires them to *constantly* fight Satan and Satan's allies on this earth.

15. Parents should encourage their children to study all religions without bias, then make up their own minds about what to believe.*

16. There *is* a religion on this earth that teaches, without error, God's truth.

17. "Satan" is just the name people give to their own bad impulses. There really is *no such thing* as a diabolical "Prince of Darkness" who tempts us.*

18. Whenever science and sacred scripture conflict, science must be wrong.

19. There is *no* body of teachings, or set of scriptures, which is completely without error.*

20. To lead the best, most meaningful life, one must belong to the one, true religion.

Note: The higher the score, the more fundamentalist the response. * = con-trait item, for which the –4 to +4 scoring key is reversed.

(emphasis in original)

Altemeyer, B., & Hunsberger, B. (1992). Authoritarianism, religious fundamentalism, quest, and prejudice. *International Journal for the Psychology of Religion, 2*(2), 113–133. Copyright © 1992, Lawrence Erlbaum Associates, Inc. Reprinted with permission.

12.4
RELIGIOUS FUNDAMENTALISM SCALE (Martin & Westie, 1959)

Reviewed by Paul D. Young

Variable: Although titled *"Religious Fundamentalism Scale* (RFS)," this instrument actually measures beliefs shared by both fundamentalists and nonfundamentalists. Martin and Westie (1959) concluded that the scale assesses "the fundamentalistic, doctrinaire, and conservative outlook" and state that it "is essentially a religious conservatism scale, stressing dogma and supernaturalism" (p. 525).

Robinson and Shaver (1973) and Hill (1995), however, suggest that the scale measures "orthodoxy." Since six of the nine scale items are derived from the Apostle's Creed, the label of fundamentalism may not be appropriate. Further, eight of the nine items ask about beliefs, and only one measures an attitude. The scale clearly does not assess behaviors, experiences, orientations, or any of the broader social factors that researchers have attempted to associate with fundamentalism, such as social concern, tolerance, or optimism.

Therefore, while people who identify themselves as Christian fundamentalists would certainly score highly on this scale, so might people who insist that they are not fundamentalists (e.g. other evangelicals, members of mainline denominations, and Roman Catholic and Eastern Orthodox believers.)

Description: Martin and Westie (1959) hypothesized that religious fundamentalism and six other personal and social characteristics would be related to the personality variable of tolerance, which they assessed using Westie's (1953) Summated Differences Scales. To test their hypotheses, the authors constructed a number of scales "by the technique of internal consistency" (p. 523). No explicit theoretical construct is presented, but the authors admit to being particularly influenced by research reported in *The Authoritarian Personality* (Adorno, Frenkel-Brunswik, Levinson, & Sanford, 1950).

The scale consists of nine statements. Respondents circle letters on a 5-point Likert scale to indicate how strongly they agree or disagree with each statement. Scoring is reversed for items 2, 3, 5 and 7.

Practical considerations: A straightforward paper-and-pencil instrument, this scale is easy to administer and may be completed in less than five minutes. It may be administered either individually or in a group. Researchers using this scale should consider adding some simple instructions as none are provided with the scale.

The authors suggest using +2 for "strongly agree," +1 for "agree," and so on, through –2 for "strongly disagree." This scoring format yields positive scores for people high in fundamentalism and negative scores for people low in fundamentalism.

Norms/Standardization: Normative data is provided for two samples, from all-Caucasian city blocks in Indianapolis in the late 1950s. The samples included 41 people who were classified as "tolerant" by the Summated Differences Scales, and 59 who were judged to be "prejudiced." The sample is small and unrepresentative.

Reliability: No reliability assessment was reported. Therefore, prior to employing this scale, researchers should determine its reliability for the current population.

Validity: The authors did not attempt to validate the scale. In their study, they found it discriminated between tolerant and prejudiced respondents at the .001 level. However, a reanalysis of their reported data (homogeneity of variance test) shows that the two groups differed in the distribution of the scores to such a degree that the validity of the reported difference is questionable. For example, 6 (14.6%) of the 41 tolerant people scored as high on the fundamentalism index as the highest of the prejudiced respondents. In addition, the distribution of fundamentalism scores for the tolerant subjects was so negatively skewed that the lower mean for the group was due to the extremely low scores of fewer than 10 individuals. The remaining 31 tolerant participants had scores that matched the prejudiced people almost perfectly.

For the tolerant group, the fundamentalism score did correlate significantly (at the .05 level) with authoritarianism (.56), child rearing attitudes (.48), nationalism (.41), intolerance of ambiguity (.32), and superstition-pseudoscience (.31). However, no variables correlated significantly with fundamentalism for the prejudiced group.

The scale may be a useful measure of Christian orthodox belief, although it would be improved by the removal of its single attitude item (number 8). As it stands, the scale has limited value for research in the scientific study of religion. If used, it must be carefully interpreted. However, it has strong historical value, and may be an appropriate base on which to construct a good measure of orthodox Christian belief.

Location:
Robinson, J. P., & Shaver, P. R. (1973). *Measures of social psychological attitudes.* Ann Arbor, MI: Institute for Social Research.

Subsequent Research:
Brown, L. B. (1981). Another test of Yinger's measure of nondoctrinal religion. *Journal of Psychology, 107,* 3–5.

Leitner, L. M., & Cado, S. (1982). Personal constructs and homosexual stress. *Journal of Personality and Social Psychology, 43,* 869–872.

References

Adorno, T. W., Frenkel-Brunswik, E., Levinson, D., & Sanford, N. (1950). *The authoritarian personality.* New York: Harper.

Ammerman, N. T. (1982). Operationalizing evangelicalism: An amendment. *Sociological Analysis, 43,* 170–172.

Hill, P. C. (1995). Fundamentalism and Christianity: A psychological perspective. Paper presented in the symposium *Psychology of Religious Fundamentalism* at the 103rd meeting of the American Psychological Association, New York City.

Martin, J. G., & Westie, F. R. (1959). The tolerant personality. *American Sociological Review, 24,* 521–528.

Robinson, J. P., & Shaver, P. R. (1973). *Measures of social psychological attitudes.* Ann Arbor, MI: Institute for Social Research.

Sethi, S., & Seligman, M. E. P. (1993). Optimism and fundamentalism. *Psychological Science, 4,* 256–259.

Westie, F. R. (1953). A technique for the measurement of race attitudes. *American Sociological Review, 18,* 73–78.

Appendix

Fundamentalism Scale

1. SA A U D SD   The Bible is the inspired word of God.

2. SA A U D SD   The religious idea of heaven is not much more than superstition.

3. SA A U D SD   Christ was a mortal, historical person, but not a supernatural or divine being.

4. SA A U D SD   Christ is a divine being, the Son of God.

5. SA A U D SD   The stories in the Bible about Christ healing sick and lame persons by His touch are fictitious and mythical.

6. SA A U D SD   Someday Christ will return.

7. SA A U D SD   The idea of life after death is simply a myth.

8. SA A U D SD   If more of the people in this country would turn to Christ we would have a lot less crime and corruption.

9. SA A U D SD   Since Christ brought the dead to life, He gave eternal life to all who have faith.

Note: Items 1, 4, 6, 8, and 9 are "positive" for scoring purposes, whereas 2, 3, 5, and 7 are "negative" items. Suggested scoring procedure: +2, +1, 0, –1, –2.

12.5
RELIGIOUS FUNDAMENTALISM SCALE OF THE MMPI (Wiggins, 1966)

Reviewed by W. Brad Johnson & Roger Olson

Variable: The Religious Fundamentalism Scale (REL) is one of 13 Minnesota Multiphasic Personality Inventory (MMPI) content scales developed by Wiggins (Wiggins, 1966). The term "fundamentalism" was not intended to refer to any specific group or formal religious body. Item content is most reflective of strong religious beliefs and religiously motivated behavior. Those with high scores on the REL see themselves as religious, churchgoing people who subscribe to a number of fundamental religious beliefs regarding interpretation of the Bible, the second coming of Christ, and the existence of hell and the devil (Wiggins, 1966). They tend to view their faith as the only true one. In addition to firm religious belief, high REL scores may be indicative of more global rigidity, dogmatism, and intolerance of those whose beliefs are different (Caldwell, 1988; Graham, 1987). Among psychiatric populations, elevated REL scores are associated with lower rates of substance abuse, impulsive behaviors, and family conflict, but higher rates of disorganization and delusional thinking (Graham, 1987; Lachar & Alexander, 1978). Low REL scores suggest nonfundamentalist religious beliefs and may indicate greater tolerance of divergent beliefs and practices (Graham, 1987). The REL does not effectively distinguish between those with rigid versus flexible religious beliefs. Therefore, researchers and clinicians must interpret the REL with caution and perhaps only in the context of an additional indicator of dogmatism/rigidity.

Description: The REL content scale was derived from the MMPI (Hathaway & McKinley, 1951), the most widely researched and utilized personality inventory in the world. In contrast to the empirical criterion keying procedures used in development of the standard MMPI scales, Wiggins (1966) developed the content scales to reflect the manifest or "overt" content of the person's self-report. He therefore applied both intuitive face validity judgments and psychometric principles to collapse the original 26 MMPI item categories (including one labeled "Religious Attitudes") into mutually exclusive content scales that represent "the major substantive clusters of the MMPI" (p. 12). Empirical criteria for inclusion of an item within a content scale were a correlation of the item with its total scale of .30 or greater and the requirement that the correlation of the item with its scale exceed its correlation with all other scales. This process resulted in adoption of 13 content scales (including the REL) with maximal homogeneity and no item overlap. The scales are internally consistent and moderately independent (Wiggins, 1969; Wiggins, Goldberg, & Applebaum, 1971).

The REL is composed of 12 items that tap fundamental religious beliefs. Half of the items are either explicitly Christian or broadly Judeo-Christian. The remaining items are clearly religious but not specifically Judeo-Christian. The 12 items are spread throughout the MMPI. Each is scored 1 if true, with the exception of the last item (491), which is scored 1 if false. Norms are available for raw scores that range from 0 to 12 (higher scores indicate greater religious fundamentalism). REL scores may also be converted to T scores for clinical evaluation. In this case, a T score of 70 is considered high, whereas 40 is low.

Practical Considerations: Unfortunately, available normative data is based on standard administrations of the full MMPI. While no norms are available for separate administration of the REL items, research indicates minimal effect on results when single MMPI scales are administered separately (Perkins & Goldberg, 1964). The MMPI contains 566 items that cover a range of subject matter from physical condition to the subject's moral and social attitudes. Time for administration varies but rarely exceeds 90 minutes. Subjects must have a sixth-grade reading level and are instructed to respond true or false to every item. The

MMPI is easily self-adminstered and requires no extra instruction or supervision. REL scale scores may be obtained by either hand scoring the 12 items or utilizing a computer scoring program. In contrast to the standard MMPI scales, no K-correction or other internal adjustment procedure is available to correct for self-favorableness versus self-criticalness on the REL scale. The Religious Fundamentalism Scale was eliminated from the MMPI-2 (Kohutek, 1992). Only one of the REL on the MMPI-2, making calculation of the REL impossible from MMPI-2 data.

Norms/Standardization: Wiggins (1966) normed the MMPI content scales using 16 small but distinct samples composed of military personnel, college students, and psychiatric patients. Mean REL scores ranged from 7.33 among psychiatric patients with "symptom reactions" to 5.11 for patients diagnosed with sociopathic personality disturbance. For a sample of 261 Air Force men, the mean was 7.16, whereas for 96 college students the mean was 5.91. Using the revised Minnesota norms (Hathaway & Briggs, 1957), REL means were 6.32 for men ($N = 225$) and 7.17 for women ($N = 315$). Subsequent state university norms (Illinois, Oregon, and Minnesota) (Wiggins et al., 1971) offered REL means of 5.75 for men ($N = 291$) and 6.32 for women ($N = 316$). Finally, Colligan and Offord (1988) recently offered updated content scale norms utilizing contemporary census-matched adult samples. Mean REL scores were 6.7 for men ($N = 646$) and 7.8 for women ($N = 762$). Across each of these normative studies, the range of REL raw scores is typically 0 to 12.

Reliability: In spite of their relative brevity, each of the Wiggins content scales demonstrates consistent reliability across divergent samples (Taylor, Ptacek, Carithers, Griffin, & Coyne, 1972). Of the 13 scales, the REL offers the highest internal consistency coefficients. Coefficient alpha reliability was .67 for Air Force men and ranged from .82 to .89 (men) and .76 to .86 (women) in three samples of university students (Wiggins,

1966). Additionally, the REL was found to have test-retest reliability of .95 (men) and .93 (women) after a six-week interval in a sample of 203 college students.

Validity: In his original monograph, Wiggins (1966) utilized the MMPI content scales in discriminant analyses on several distinct psychiatric groups. The contribution of the REL to discriminating between diagnostic groups was negligible. An evaluation of the factor analytic convergence of the content scales with the Differential Personality Inventory scales among a large psychiatric sample found the REL to load highly on a factor titled "impulse expression versus religiosity." Here REL was negatively correlated with rebelliousness, impulsivity and deviant attitudes (Hoffman & Jackson, 1976). The REL also tends to show slight positive correlations with age and small negative correlations with education (Colligan & Offord, 1988).

The REL tends to measure a highly specific dimension not represented on standard personality inventories. For example, the REL shows small and inconsistent correlations with the Adjective Checklist, California Personality Inventory, and the Edwards Personal Preference Schedule (Wiggins et al., 1971). The REL also correlates minimally and in the expected direction with the MMPI standard scales. For example, correlations with scales tapping distress and impulsivity were as follows in the Wiggins et al. (1971) study: F (distress) = −.26; Scale 2 (depression) = −.17; Scale 4 (psychopathic-deviate) = −.14; and Scale 9 (hypomania) = −.15.

Finally, convergent validity for the REL was reported by Taylor et al. (1972), who found substantial correlations between the REL and the Omnibus Personality Inventory-Religious Orientations Scale (r = .83). These authors also utilized two example anchored scale questions (e.g.,. "How religious are you, in a fundamentalist sense?") with polar anchors being "strongly religious vs. not very religious in a fundamentalist sense" (p. 546). Correlations between the two anchored scales and the REL were .759 and .774.

A subsequently developed MMPI content scale, the Religious Identification Scale (RI: Panton, 1979) measures much the same construct and includes 10 of the 12 REL items. The RI, however, currently lacks sufficient demonstration of its psychometric properties. The REL must be recommended as the best established MMPI scale of religious belief and behavior.

Location:
Hathaway, S. R., & McKinley, J. C. (1951). *The Minnesota Multiphasic Personality Inventory manual-revised.* New York: The Psychological Corporation.

Wiggins, J. S. (1966). Substantive dimensions of self-report in the MMPI item pool. *Psychological Monographs: General and Applied, 80,* (22, whole no. 630).

Subsequent Research:
Caldwell, A. B. (1988). *MMPI supplemental scale manual.* Los Angeles: The Caldwell Report.

Colligan, R. C., & Offord, K. P. (1988). Contemporary norms for the Wiggins content scales: A 45-year update. *Journal of Clinical Psychology, 44,* 23–32.

Graham, J. R. (1987). *The MMPI: A practical guide* (2nd ed.). New York: Oxford University Press.

Hathaway, S. R., & Briggs, P. F. (1957). Some normative data on new MMPI scales. *Journal of Clinical Psychology, 13,* 364–368.

Hoffman, H., & Jackson, D. N. (1976). Substantive dimensions of psychopathology derived from MMPI content scales and the Differential Personality Inventory. *Journal of Consulting and Clinical Psychology, 44,* 862.

Horton, A. M., & Timmons, M. (1982). Separation of brain-damaged from psychiatric patients: Value of the Wiggins MMPI content scales. *Perceptual and Motor Skills, 55,* 755–758.

Jarnecke, R. W., & Chambers, E. D. (1977). MMPI content scales: Dimensional structure, construct validity and interpretive norms in a psychiatric population. *Journal of Consulting and Clinical Psychology, 45,* 1126–1131.

Kohutek, K. J. (1992). Wiggins content scales and the MMPI–2. *Journal of Clinical Psychology, 48,* 215–218.

Lachar, D., & Alexander, R. S. (1978). Veridicality of self-report: Replicated correlates of the Wiggins MMPI content scales. *Journal of Consulting and Clinical Psychology, 46,* 1349–1356.

Panton, J. H. (1979). An MMPI item content

scale to measure religious identification within a state prison population. *Journal of Clinical Psychology, 35,* 588–591.

Perkins, S. R., & Goldberg, L. R. (1964). Contextual effects on the MMPI. *Journal of Consulting Psychology, 28,* 133–140.

Taylor, J. B., Ptacek, M., Carithers, M., Griffin, C., & Coyne, L. (1972). Rating scales as measures of clinical judgment, III: Judgments of the self on personality inventory scales and direct ratings. *Educational and Psychological Measurement, 32,* 543–557.

Waller, N. G., Kojetin, B. A., Bouchard, T. J., Lykken, D. T., & Tellegen, A. (1990). Genetic and environmental influences on religious interests, attitudes, and values: A study of twins reared apart and together. *Psychological Science, 1,* 138–142.

Weaver, A. J., Berry, J. W., & Pittel, S. M. (1994). Ego development in fundamentalist and nonfundamentalist Protestants. *Journal of Psychology and Theology, 22,* 215–225.

Wiggins, J. S. (1969). Content dimensions in the MMPI. In J. N. Butcher (Ed.), *MMPI: Research developments and clinical applications* (pp. 127–180). New York: McGraw-Hill.

Wiggins, J. S., Goldberg, L. R., & Applebaum, M. (1971). MMPI content scales: Interpretive norms and correlations with other scales. *Journal of Consulting and Clinical Psychology, 37,* 403–410.

Appendix

Religious Fundamentalism Scale of the MMPI

Please indicate whether you think each item below is true or false.

MMPI Item Number	Keyed Response	Item
58	True	Everything is turning out just like the prophets of the Bible said it would.
95	True	I go to church almost every week.
98	True	I believe in the second coming of Christ.
115	True	I believe in a life hereafter.
206	True	I am very religious (more than most people).
249	True	I believe there is a Devil and a Hell in the afterlife.
258	True	I believe there is a God.
373	True	I feel sure that there is only one true religion.
483	True	Christ performed miracles such as changing water into wine.
488	True	I pray several times every week.
490	True	I read the Bible several times a week.
491	False	I have no patience with people who believe there is only one true religion.

Chapter 13

Scales of Death/Afterlife, Views of

To an outside observer, religion appears preoccupied with death. For many people, concern about death and the afterlife is a major motivation for religion. Researchers have long noted that religion is a source of comfort and provides both meaning as well as a sense of personal control—benefits that are at no time greater than when confronting the unknown of death. In fact, some people may see their earthly life as only a temporary existence in the greater scheme of things as stated well in a familiar gospel tune: "This world is not my home, I'm just a passin' through."

Four of the five scales reviewed in this chapter focus in one form or another on the topic of death. Ray and Najman's Death Acceptance Scale (13.2) explores people's views on the inevitability of death. Instead of focusing on death anxiety, this instrument measures two approaches to thinking about death: denial (where death anxiety may be experienced but is not acknowledged) and acceptance (where concern about death is acknowledged but positive elements are also identified). In contrast, Templer's Death Anxiety Scale (13.3) is a composite of a number of anxiety-producing concerns about death. Templer's scale does not identify what appears to be multiple factors that influence death anxiety. Though considerably longer than Templer's scale, the Death Perspective Scales (13.4) developed by Spilka and colleagues go beyond the usual focus of fear and identify a number of emotional reactions, some negative and some positive, that people experience when thinking about death. Their measure identifies eight subscales: Death as Pain and Loneliness, Death as an Afterlife of Reward, Indifference toward Death, Death as Unknown, Death as Forsaking Dependents, Death as Courage, Death as Failure, and Death as Natural End. Hood and Morris's Death Transcendence Scale (13.5) is a measure of how people want to be remembered after they die as an attempt to seek immortality.

The only other scale included here assesses belief in afterlife (13.1). The authors, Osarchuk and Tatz, have attempted to keep the wording of this scale as broad as possible so that the scale may be useful in almost any religious tradition.

13.1
BELIEF IN AFTERLIFE SCALE (Osarchuk & Tatz, 1973)
Reviewed by James Casebolt

Variable: The Belief in Afterlife (BA) Scale is intended to measure the degree to which an individual believes that life continues, in some form, after the physical death of the body. It is not, however, intended to measure belief in any particular form of afterlife; the wording of items on the test could be equally agreed with by someone who believes in reincarnation as one with a more, for example, Orthodox Christian view of the hereafter.

431

Description: Osarchuk and Tatz (1973) proposed two forms (Form A and Form B) of the BA scale. Each consists of 10 statements reflecting acceptance or rejection of the idea of an afterlife. Form A contains seven reverse-scored items and Form B has six such items. The scale uses Likert scaling, with subjects responding on a 0 (total disagreement) to 10 (total agreement) scale. A score is derived by summing the responses after reversing those for items rejecting belief in an afterlife; therefore, a higher score indicates greater acceptance of the idea that life continues, in some form, after death.

Practical Considerations: The first, practical consideration is selecting a form of the scale to use. Two forms were developed to serve as pretest and posttest in Osarchuk and Tatz's (1973) original experiment. Of the available published sources using this scale, only one (Berman & Hays, 1973) specifically mentions that Form A was used; the other articles to be reviewed here did not specify which form of the scale was used. Two (Littlefield & Fleming, 1984; Schoenrade, 1989) were pretest-posttest experiments and presumably used both forms.

One possible variation from Osarchuk and Tatz's (1973) original instructions for the use of the scale is in the Likert scale to be used by subjects. For example, Smith, Range, and Ulmer (1992) had their subjects respond on a 1–5 scale instead of the 0–10 scale used by Osarchuk and Tatz (1973).

A potential difficulty in using the scale relates to the required reading level of the items (see appendix). Many of the items would be difficult to understand for someone without a fairly extensive vocabulary. The language used renders the scale not at all appropriate for use with children.

Norms/Standardization: Osarchuk and Tatz (1973) had 169 male and female students at C. W. Post Center (Long Island University) respond to 50 statements of belief or nonbelief in an afterlife. The two forms were constructed by randomly assigning to each form 10 of the 20 items that best distinguished the upper and lower 20% of subjects on the total score for all 50 items.

Osarchuk and Tatz (1973) used this scale in an experiment examining how inducing fear of death would affect belief in the afterlife. They did not present official norms for the scale, but their pretest scores are informative concerning both forms' psychometric characteristics. Across forms, the average score for the 311 male and female introductory psychology students who completed the experiment was 52 (Form A, $M = 53$, $SD = 24.41$; Form B, $M = 51$, $SD = 25.57$). Male and female subjects scored similarly (averaging 52.3 and 51.4, respectively). Catholic and Protestant subjects (with means of 61.4 and 62.5, respectively) scored higher than agnostics/atheists or Jews (averaging 48.9 and 42.4, respectively), though these groups were not statistically compared. Berman and Hays (1973), however, found significantly higher BA score for females than males in their study of "300 college-age subjects," though they do not report any statistical tests or means.

Schoenrade (1989), using a different scoring procedure (though not explicitly stated, apparently averaging responses on a 1–11 scale rather than summing responses on a 0–10 scale), found an average of 8.01 for the 80 University of Kansas general psychology students (all of whom were Christian and at least moderately interested in religion) who completed the BA scale as a pretest in her experiment. Similarly, Smith, Range, and Ulmer (1992) found an average score of 4.3 (determined by averaging responses on a 1–5 scale) for their 121 subjects who had experienced the death of a loved one in the last 7 years.

Reliability: Of the published sources, none report any internal consistency ratings or other statistics of reliability for the scale. Osarchuk and Tatz (1973) reported the Form A and Form B pretest scores provided above for 156 and 155 subjects, respectively, but did not perform any statistical tests to compare the scales. In one unpublished source, Casebolt (1992) used Form A of the BA scale as an experimental pretest for his 60 introductory psychology subjects and found it to have a Cronbach's alpha of .89.

Validity: In their original research, Osarchuk and Tatz selected from their initial pool of subjects a low BA and high BA group. One third of each group was presented with images and statistics relating to the chance of death for people in their age group (death threat condition); one third was told that they would be given a series of electrical shocks of varying intensity (shock threat condition); the remaining subjects, the control group, played with a child's toy for the period of time taken by the shock and death threat manipulations. Examination of pretest-posttest change scores showed that only the high BA-death threat group showed a significant change in BA score (an average increase of 9.5 points). Osarchuk and Tatz also found that the BA scale scores were significantly correlated with subjects' estimates of their own belief in an afterlife, measured on a 1–100 scale with 5-point intervals (r (309) = .428, u < .001). Similarly, Berman and Hays (1973) found a significant relationship (r = .24, p < .01) between the BA scale Form Λ and the Lester (1967) fear of death scale with their 300 college student subjects.

Kurlychek (1976) had 40 subjects 60 years of age or older complete the BA scale and the Collett and Lester (1969) fear of death scale. A significant relationship between BA and the Fear of Death of Others subscale was found (r = .44, p < .01), but not for the Fear of Death of Self, Fear of Dying of Self, or Fear of Dying of Others subscales. According to Kurlychek, the Fear of Death of Others subscale represents "the most concrete manifestation of death," as one's own death cannot be experienced but the death of another can serve a "death-threat" to one's own life.

Littlefield and Fleming (1984) used the BA scale in a pretest-posttest experiment. Their 87 introductory psychology subjects completed the BA and several death-related scales. Three weeks later the same subjects participated in an experiment in which one third faced a death threat (watched a film about death by fire), one third watched an anxiety-provoking film unrelated to death, and one third watched an innocuous film. All subjects then completed posttest BA and death scales. Change scores for the BA scale showed a decrease for the death-threat group and a slight increase for the other two groups.

Schoenrade (1989) completed a similar experiment with 100 general psychology students, all of whom were Christian in background and at least moderately interested in religion. All subjects had been asked previously to rate how strongly they believed in an afterlife on a 1–9 scale. Eighty of these subjects had also completed the Osarchuk and Tatz BA scale. They manipulated confrontation with one's own death by having subjects complete the Spilka, Stout, Minton, and Sizemore (1977) Death Perspectives scales and the other form (not specified) of the Osarchuk and Tatz BA scale either before or after listening to a tape describing the events of their own immediate and unexpected death. Subjects classified as high in belief in afterlife according to the self-report item scored higher on positive and negative death perspectives when confronted with their own deaths than did those subjects who were high in BA but not confronted with their own death first. However, there was no parallel increase in BA scale scores for those subjects who completed the Osarchuk and Tatz scales.

Location:
Osarchuk, M., & Tatz, S. J. (1973). Effect of induced fear of death on belief in afterlife. *Journal of Personality and Social Psychology, 27* (2), 256–260.

Subsequent Research:
Berman, A. L., & Hays, J. E. (1973). Relation between death anxiety, belief in afterlife, and locus of control. *Journal of Consulting and Clinical Psychology, 41*(2), 318.

Casebolt, J. (1992). [The effect of terror management and the threatening or bolstering of afterlife beliefs on attributional derogation of AIDS victims.] Unpublished raw data.

Kurlychek, R. T. (1976). Level of belief in afterlife and four categories of fear of death in a sample of 60+-year-olds. *Psychological Reports, 38*, 228.

Littlefield, C., & Fleming, S. (1984). Measuring fear of death: A multidimensional approach. *Omega, 15* (2), 131–138.

Schoenrade, P. A. (1989). When I die. . . : Belief in afterlife as a response to mortality. *Personality and Social Psychology Bulletin, 15*(1), 91–100.

Smith, P. G., Range, L. M., & Ulmer, A. (1992). Belief in afterlife as a buffer in suicidal and other bereavement. *Omega, 24*(3), 217–225.

References

Collett, L. J., & Lester, D. (1969). The fear of death and the fear of dying. *Journal of Psychology, 72*, 179–181.

Lester, D. (1967). Fear of death of suicidal persons. *Psychological Reports, 20*, 1077–1078.

Spilka, B., Stout, L., Minton, B., & Sizemore, D. Death and personal faith: A psychometric investigation. *Journal for the Scientific Study of Religion, 16*, 169–178.

Appendix

Belief in Afterlife (BA) Scale

Form A
1. Earthly existence is the only existence we have.*
2. In the premature death of someone close, some comfort can be found in knowing that in some way the deceased is still existing.
3. Humans die in the sense of "ceasing to exist."*
4. The idea of there existing somewhere some sort of afterlife is beyond my comprehension.*
5. We will never be united with those deceased whom we knew and loved.*
6. There must be an afterlife of some sort.
7. Some existentialists claim that when man dies he ceases to exist: I agree.*
8. The following statement is true: "There is no such thing as a life after death."*
9. Millions of people believe in a life after death: they are correct in so believing.
10. Enjoy yourself on earth, for death signals the end of all existence.

Form B
1. A belief in an afterlife may be useful for some, but I don't believe in it at all.*
2. The life we lead now is but a pebble cast upon the sands of our future lives.
3. Religiously associated or not, belief in an afterlife will never be shown to be true, for afterlives are nonexistent.*
4. The following statement is true: "Man must enter into some sort of existence after death, for the end of our earthly lives cannot wipe us from existence into nothingness."
5. When a human dies, that something called "life" dies with him.*
6. The millions killed by Hitler passed from existence into nothingness.*
7. Many scientists believe in a life after death: they are right, there is one.
8. There is supportive evidence for the existence of an afterlife.
9. Death ends all forms of life forever.*
10. The existence of an afterlife can never be scientifically demonstrated, for it is impossible to prove a "figment of someone's imagination."*

* Indicates reverse-scored items

Osarchuk, M., & Tatz, S. J. (1973). Effect of induced fear of death on belief in afterlife. *Journal of Personality and Social Psychology, 27* (2), 256–260. Copyright © 1973 by the American Psychological Association. Reprinted with permission.

13.2
DEATH ACCEPTANCE SCALE (Ray & Najman, 1974)
Reviewed by James Casebolt

Variable: The Death Acceptance Scale is based on the theoretical idea that the opposite of death anxiety (the construct that has received so much attention in death research) could be either denial—rejecting and refusing to deal with death—or acceptance—coming to terms with death through thought and effort. Ray and Najman (1974) suggest that subjects scoring lowest on a measure of death anxiety may actually have the most anxiety, and are very successful death deniers "in the Freudian sense—people who do feel anxiety but cannot acknowledge it" (p. 312). A person who has come to terms with death, on the other hand, may willingly acknowledge some remnant of lingering anxiety.

The variable that this scale is intended to measure is death acceptance. Ray and Najman (1974) see a death-acceptant person as someone who "will not deny that [death] does concern them but will also be able to be positive about death" (p. 312).

Description: The original scale is a 7-item Likert scale. All the items are written in the positive direction; agreement indicates a higher level of death acceptance. Ray and Najman (1974) do not include specific instructions regarding what Likert scale should be used. Several items on the scale (see appendix) are suggestive of reverse-scored death anxiety items, and at least one item (item 5), because of its gender-exclusive wording, could be potentially difficult for female subjects to respond to.

Practical Considerations: The scale is short and standardized instructions used with typical Likert-type items would work. Scoring is simple and straightforward. The items lend themselves to being nested within a longer instrument.

Norms/Standardization: The original research using the Death Acceptance Scale (Ray & Najman, 1974) was a survey of 206 Australian first-year sociology students. The Death Acceptance Scale was part of a longer instrument including measures of death anxiety, achievement orientation, and authoritarianism. No average scores or any other sort of normative information were reported.

Reliability: Ray and Najman (1974) report a high level of item-total correlation, as well as a Cronbach's alpha of .58. Alphas of .70 were found by both Durlak and Kass (1981) with their sample of 350 college psychology students, and by Warren (1982) with his mixed sample of 76 subjects.

Validity: Ray and Najman (1974) report correlations in the −.20s between the Death Acceptance Scale and two death anxiety measures (Templer, 1970; Sarnoff & Corwin, 1959). They also found that religious nonbelievers scored significantly higher on death acceptance than religious believers. They did not explain how this distinction was made. Thus difference was not found for either of the death anxiety scales, and thus was interpreted as supporting the idea that death acceptance is an independent construct from death anxiety.

Durlak and Kass (1981) included the Death Acceptance Scale, along with 15 other death-related scales, in a factor-analytic study of data from 350 college students, approximately equal in gender and averaging 21 years of age. The Death Acceptance Scale loaded moderately and negatively on two of their five factors: Negative Evaluation of Personal Death and Negative Reaction to Pain. No independent acceptance factor emerged.

Warren (1982) studied a sample consisting of death involved subjects (e.g., funeral directors, etc.), at-risk subjects (sport parachutists and hang gliders), and control subjects selected to match the age and education of the first two groups. They found that the Death Acceptance Scale was significantly and negatively correlated with measures of death fear, anxiety, and concern (r's −.23 to −.36). Subjects who identified themselves as accepting of death had higher Death Acceptance Scale scores than those who did not.

Two other pieces of research suggest modifications to or revisions of the Death Acceptance Scale. Klug and Sinha (1987) propose a two-factor conceptualization of death acceptance, confrontation of death (having accepted the idea of death, not dying, through conscious deliberation), and integration of death (a positive, emotional reaction to the idea of death). They used the Death Acceptance Scale as a basis to develop new scales for each of these constucts (the Klug Death Aceptance Scale is included as an appendix to the 1987 article). Both new scales were found to correlate in the .20s with the Death Acceptance Scale in a sample of 207 nursing students. Confrontation correlated −.19 and integration .23 with the DAS in a sample of 30 psychiatric patients. These two groups did not have significantly different scores on the DAS.

Ray and Najman (1987) propose a new balanced Death Attitude Scale, consisting of items from the Death Acceptance Scale, the Templer (1970) Death Anxiety Scale, and several new items. This new scale, scored in the direction of a more negative attitude toward death, was correlated −.35 with a measure of social desirability, .45 with a modified version of the Taylor (1953) Manifest Anxiety Scale, and .20 with the Rosenberg (1965) Self-esteem Scale. Subjects in this study were 95 volunteers who returned a survey sent to a sample of 500 registered Australian voters.

Location:

Ray, J. J., & Najman, J. (1974). Death anxiety and death acceptance: A preliminary approach. *Omega, 5*(4), 311–315.

Subsequent Research:

Durlak, J. A., & Kass, R. A. (1981). Clarifying the measurement of death attitudes: A factor analytic evaluation of fifteen self-report death scales. *Omega, 12*(2), 129–141.

Klug, L., & Sinha, A. (1987). Death acceptance: A two-component formulation and scale. *Omega, 18*(3), 229–235.

Ray, J. J., & Najman, J. M. (1987). Neoconservatism, mental health and attitude to death. *Personality and Individual Differences, 8*(2), 277–279.

Warren, W. G. (1982). Death threat, concern, anxiety, fear and acceptance in death-involved and "at-risk" groups. *Omega, 12*(4), 359–372.

References

Rosenberg, M. (1965). *Society and the adolescent self-image.* Princeton University Press: Princeton, NJ.

Sarnoff, I., & Corwin, S. (1959). Castration anxiety and the fear of death. *Journal of Personality, 27*, 375–385.

Taylor, J. A. (1953). a personality scale of manifest anxiety. *Journal of Abnormal and Social Psychology, 48*, 285–290.

Templer, D. (1970). The construction and validation of a death anxiety scale. *Journal of General Psychology, 82*, 165–177.

Appendix

Death Acceptance Scale

Please indicate the extent to which you agree with each of the following statements.

1	2	3	4	5	6	7

totally disagree — totally agree

1. Since you only do it once, death should at least be interesting.
2. I know that I have nothing to fear when I die.
3. Death is not something terrible.

4. Death is a friend.
5. Death is a good thing because it leaves the way clear for younger men to have their chance.
6. To fear pain makes sense, but death is merely a relief from pain.
7. People who worry about death must have nothing better to do.

13.3
DEATH ANXIETY SCALE (TEMPLER, 1970)
Reviewed by John D. Scanish and Mark R. McMinn

Variable: The Death Anxiety Scale (DAS) measures an individual's attitudes toward death-related topics. Unlike some similar measures, Templer's DAS (1970) takes into account a wide range of experiences related to death.

Many theorists have contributed to a growing literature on death anxiety, with the following four factors emerging as common components:

1. Concern about intellectual and personal emotional reactions to death
2. Concern about physical change
3. Awareness of and concern about the passage of time
4. Concern about the pain and stress that can accompany illness and dying (Lonetto & Templer, 1986, p. 111)

Death anxiety, by providing a vital link between our perceptions of crises and how well we cope, may be an "integral part of the flow of life itself" (1986, p. 112). While the focus may be fourfold, Templer chose to construct an instrument with one score, expecting that refined perspectives on the fear of death could be developed after gross parameters were established.

Description: The DAS is a 15-item, true/false scale that yields a single composite score. Six items are keyed false, nine true.

Although the DAS appears to have multiple factors contributing to its overall score, what these factors are and how these factors load onto the overall score is not well understood. Consequently, it is still unclear how the overall score should be interpreted.

Practical Considerations: The DAS requires no special examiner skill to administer or score. Face validity of the measure is high. The DAS has been translated into Arabic, German, Spanish, Hindi, Chinese, Korean, Afrikaans, and Japanese.

Norms/Standardizations: Comprehensive representative norms have not been established. A number of means and standard deviations relative to specific populations have, however, been published (e.g., Templer & Ruff, 1971; Lonetto & Templer, 1986). Scores for these participants range from 4.5 to 7.0, with a standard deviation of slightly more than 3.0, and with females consistently scoring higher than males.

One cross-sectional study of 226 predominantly middle class, Caucasian, well-educated individuals located throughout the United States will serve as an example (see White & Handal, 1991). The overall mean in this study was 6.16 (6.76 for males, 8.04 for females), with a standard deviation of 3.21 (2.82 for males, 3.27 for females). Some evidence suggests that DAS scores tend to decrease with age (Lonetto & Templer, 1986).

Reliability: Three weeks after the first administration, 31 community college participants completed the DAS a second time. The DAS evidenced a test-retest reliability correlation coefficient of .83. Reasonable internal consistency was demonstrated with a Kuder-Richardson reliability coefficient of .76.

Validity: Considerable validity data has been gathered on the DAS. Face validity was established by subjecting an original set of 40 items to the judgment of a clinical psychologist, two clinical psychology graduate students, and four chaplains in a state hospital. Nine items failed to evidence sufficient face validity and were therefore dropped from the scale.

Internal consistency was established by determining item-total score point biserial correlation coefficients for the 31 remaining items. Sixteen items failed to consistently reach statistical significance, leaving the 15 items that are found on the final version of the DAS.

Construct validity was addressed in two separate projects (Templer, 1970). In the first, DAS scores of 21 presumably high-death-anxiety psychiatric patients were compared to those of a matched (diagnosis, sex, approximate age) set of control patients. The high-death-anxiety patients had a DAS mean of 11.62, while the control group had a mean of 6.77 ($t = 5.78$, $p < .01$), thereby offering supporting evidence of construct validity.

In the second project, the DAS, along with Boyar's Fear of Death Scale (FODS; Boyar, 1964) and the MMPI, was administered to 77 undergraduates. Correlation with the FODS was .74, providing mutual evidence for the validity of both scales.

The MMPI was chosen because it contains three well-known anxiety scales, namely, the Manifest Anxiety Scale, the Welsh Anxiety Scale, and the Welsh Anxiety Index. If the DAS failed to correlate as highly with these scales as they do with one another, then it could be argued that the DAS is not measuring anxiety in general, but perhaps death anxiety specifically. Correlations with these scales were measured at .39, .36, and .18 respectively. Although it is clear that some correlation is present between death anxiety and anxiety in general, the DAS's correlation with the FODS was much higher than with these general measures of anxiety, providing support for the contention that Templer's DAS does possess discriminant validity, and it is not just another measure of anxiety in general.

Location:

Templer, D. I. (1970). The construction and validation of a death anxiety scale. *Journal of General Psychology*, 82, 165–177.

Recent Research: None

References

Boyar, J. I. (1964). *The construction and partial validation of a scale for the measurement of the fear of death.* Unpublished doctoral dissertation, University of Rochester, Rochester, New York.

Lester, D., & Templer, D. I. (1993). Death anxiety scales: A dialogue. *Omega*, 26, 239–253.

Lonetto, R., & Templer, D. I. (1986). *Death anxiety*. New York: Hemisphere Publishing Corporation.

McMordie, W. R. (1979). Improving measurement of death anxiety. *Psychological Reports*, 44, 975–980.

Templer, D. I. (1970). The construction and validation of a death anxiety scale. *Journal of General Psychology*, 82, 165–177.

Templer, D. I., & Ruff, C. F. (1971). Death anxiety scale means, standard deviations, and embedding. *Psychological Reports*, 29, 174–175.

White, W., & Handal, P. J. (1991). The relationship between death anxiety and mental health/distress. *Omega*, 22, 13–24.

Appendix

Templer's Death Anxiety Scale (DAS)

Key	Content
T	I am very much afraid to die.
F	The thought of death seldom enters my mind.

F	It doesn't make me nervous when people talk about death.
T	I dread to think about having to have an operation.
F	I am not at all afraid to die.
F	I am not particularly afraid of getting cancer.
F	The thought of death never bothers me.
T	I am often distressed by the way time flies so very rapidly.
T	I fear dying a painful death.
T	The subject of life after death troubles me greatly.
T	I am really scared of having a heart attack.
T	I often think about how short life really is.
T	I shudder when I hear people talking about a World War III.
T	The sight of a dead body is horrifying to me.
F	I feel that the future holds nothing for me to fear.

13.4
DEATH PERSPECTIVE SCALES (Spilka, Stout, Minton, & Sizemore, 1977)
Reviewed by James Casebolt

Variable: The Death Perspective Scales developed by Spilka et al. (1977) are intended to measure the true multidimensional nature of people's feelings about death, as opposed to the usual focus on anxiety and fear. Eight subscales are proposed to measure different aspects of people's reactions to death: Death as Pain and Loneliness, Death as an Afterlife of Reward, Indifference toward Death, Death as Unknown, Death as Forsaking Dependents, Death as Courage, Death as Failure, and Death as a Natural End. An examination of the items included in these scales suggests that what they are primarily measuring is different emotional reactions to the idea of death, especially one's own. These scales are based on the general theoretical idea that both religion and death are multidimensional domains and that different aspects of religion are related to different aspects of death.

Description: The death perspective scales presented in Spilka et al. (1977) are a development of earlier scales (Hooper & Spilka, 1970; Minton & Spilka, 1976) that had demonstrated construct validity but had possessed poor psychometric properties and were difficult to administer. There are eight scales, varying from four to six items in length, measuring each of the constructs listed above. Each item completes the phrase "Death as . . . ", to which subjects are to respond on a 6-point Likert scale.

A search of articles listed in *Social Science Citation Index* as referencing the Spilka et al. (1977) article showed that it is widely cited for its theory and findings but the scales developed have not been widely used in the published literature.

Practical Considerations: No elaborate instructions are required for the use of these scales. There are a total of 43 items, meaning that subjects should be able to complete the scales in a relatively brief period of time and that it is possible to incorporate these items into a longer instrument. The language used in the scales should be comprehensible to the average college student, but some of the wording might confuse poorly educated or younger people with less extensive vocabularies.

Norms/Standardization: Based on 180 items from Hooper and Spilka (1970),

Spilka et al. (1977) developed a pool of 60 items, 6 each to measure 10 theoretical death perspectives: natural end, pain, loneliness, unknown, punishment, forsaking dependents, failure, afterlife of reward, courage, and indifference. A total of 328 subjects completed these items. All participants were Christian; most were college students, but 74 were members of a Methodist church in Boise, Idaho. Based on the results of principal components factor analysis, an eight-factor structure was identified. Items to measure each factor were selected on the basis of the factor loadings. Items intended to measure death as punishment did not form a separate factor, and items intended to measure death as pain and death as loneliness loaded on one common factor

Reliability: After establishing scales on the basis of the results of their factor analysis, Spilka et al. (1977) computed internal consistency ratings for each scale: Death as Pain and Loneliness, K-R 20 = .79; Death as Afterlife of Reward, K-R 20 = .92; Indifference toward Death, K-R 20 = .71; Death as Unknown, K-R 20 = .87; Death as Forsaking Dependents Plus Guilt, K-R 20 = .78; Death as Courage, K-R 20 = .72; Death as Failure, K-R 20 = .77; Death as a Natural End, K-R 20 = .71.

Validity: Spilka et al. (1977) found varying levels of independence in the death perspectives scales. Of their 28 intercorrelations, 13 fell below .2 and 7 fell above .4.

In addition to the death perspectives scales, Spilka et al. had subjects who were personally involved in religion (who had regular church attendance and said that religion was important in their lives) complete the Allport and Ross (1967) Intrinsic-Extrinsic Scales and the Consensual-Committed Scales (Allen & Spilka, 1967). The Intrinsic and Committed Scales correlated positively with "the more favorable" (Spilka et al., 1977, 175) death perspectives, such as afterlife of reward and courage, whereas the negative perspectives (e.g., indifference, loneliness and pain, failure) were associated with the Extrinsic and Consensual Scales.

Along similar lines, Schoenrade (1989) used the death perspectives scales in an experiment investigating how afterlife beliefs are affected by being confronted with one's own mortality. Subjects, categorized as high or low in belief in an afterlife, completed the scales either before or after being confronted with an audiotape describing the events of the subject's own untimely death. Schoenrade submitted the scale scores to a principal axes factor analysis, which resulted in a three-factor structure: negative (pain and loneliness, unknown, forsaking dependents, failure), positive (reward, courage), and neutral (natural end). The indifference scale did not load highly on any of these factors. Regression factor scores were computed for each factor. Positive death perspective scores were highest for high belief in afterlife subjects who had previously been confronted with their own mortality; negative death perspective scores were highest for low belief in afterlife subjects who had not been so confronted. These differences would seem to be theoretically consistent with the above findings of Spilka et al. (1977) relating to religious orientation. Neutral scores did not differ across groups.

Spilka, Spangler, Rea, and Nelson (1981) had 273 clergy from 11 different Christian denominations complete the Pain and Loneliness, Forsaking Dependents, Unknown, and Afterlife as Reward Scales as part of a study of the clergy's perspectives on and experiences with terminally ill patients and their families. While their reporting of the results for these scales was customized to be appropriate for the journal in which the research appeared and therefore lacks the detail a researcher might wish, they did report that of these scales their clergy sample tended to emphasize the view of death as afterlife of reward, although "even this orientation was not held very strongly" (p. 304).

Location:

Spilka, B., Stout, L., Minton, B., & Sizemore, D. (1977). Death and personal faith: A psychometric investigation. *Journal for the Scientific Study of Religion, 16*, 169–178.

Subsequent Research:

Schoenrade, P. A. (1989). When I die . . . : Belief in afterlife as a response to mortality. *Personality and Social Psychology Bulletin, 15*(1), 91–100.

Spilka, B., Spangler, J. D., Rea, M. P., & Nelson, C. (1981). Religion and death: The clerical perspective. *Journal of Religion and Health, 20*(4), 299–306.

References

Allen, R. O., & Spilka, B. (1967). Committed and consensual religions: A specification of religion-prejudice relationships. *Journal for the Scientific Study of Religion, 6*, 191–206.

Allport, G. W., & Ross, J. M. (1967). Personal religious orientation and prejudice. *Journal of Personality and Social Psychology, 5*, 432–443.

Hooper, T., & Spilka, B. (1970). Some meanings and correlations of future time and death among college students. *Omega, 1*, 49–56.

Minton, B., & Spilka, B. (1976). Perspectives on death in relation to powerlessness and form of personal religion. *Omega, 7*, 261–268.

Appendix

Death Perspectives Scales

Responses should be made on a 6-point Likert scale (1 = strongly disagree, 6 = strongly agree).

Scale 1: Death as Pain and Loneliness
Death as . . .
1. a last agonizing moment
2. the conclusion to a time of isolation
3. the final misery
4. the fate of falling by the wayside
5. the ultimate anguish and torment
6. a lonely experience at the time of dying

Scale 2: Death as an Afterlife of Reward
Death as . . .
1. entrance to a place of ultimate satisfaction
2. leading to a cleansing and rebirth of oneself
3. leading to one's resurrection and reward
4. union with God and eternal bliss
5. opportunity to give up this life in favor of a better one
6. the doorway to heaven and ultimate happiness

Scale 3: Indifference toward Death
Death as . . .
1. unimportant in the scheme of things
2. of little consequence
3. something to be shrugged off and forgotten
4. neither feared nor welcomed
5. making no difference one way or the other

Scale 4: Death as Unknown
Death as . . .
1. the biggest uncertainty of all
2. the greatest mystery
3. the end of the known and the beginning of the unknown

4. something about which one must say "I don't know"
5. a question mark
6. the most ambiguous of life's complexities

Scale 5: Death as Forsaking Dependents Plus Guilt
Death as . . .
1. leaving one's dependents vulnerable to life's trials
2. a forsaking of loved others when one dies
3. reason to feel guilty that one may not be adequately providing for future family necessities
4. a reason for feeling guilty
5. leaving the family to fend for itself

Scale 6: Death as Courage
Death as . . .
1. a chance to show that one has stood for something during life
2. an occasion to show how one can meet this last test of life
3. a great moment of truth for oneself
4. an opportunity for great accomplishment
5. a time to refuse humiliation or defeat
6. a test of commitment to one's life values

Scale 7: Death as Failure
Death as . . .
1. an event that prevents the realization of one's potential
2. the end to one's hopes
3. the final failure of one's search for the meaning of life
4. the destruction of any chance to realize oneself to the fullest
5. defeat in the struggle to succeed and achieve

Scale 8: Death as a Natural End
Death as . . .
1. an experience which comes to each of us because of the normal passage of time
2. the final act in harmony with existence
3. a natural aspect of life
4. part of the cycle of life

13.5
THE DEATH TRANSCENDENCE SCALE (Hood & Morris, 1983)
Reviewed by Larry VandeCreek

Variable: The Death Transcendence Scale operationalizes the African proverb which states that a person is not truly dead unless he is forgotten. James (1961) observes that religion for many people means "immortality and nothing else." Lifton (1979) elaborates this sentiment by asserting that persons try to transcend death and seek immortality by several means, including mystical, religious, nature, biosocial, or creative modes.

The items in this scale seek to identify

how individuals implicitly wish to be re- membered after they die. The theoretical foundation for the scale, therefore, is strong and the items measure a cognitive orienta- tion toward death, except for the experi- ence-based mystical items.

Description: As developed, the scale con- tains 23 items with a 4-point response for- mat. The three items of the biosocial mode, and the five items for each of the other modes, create five subscales. The mysticism items are from the first factor of Hood's Mysticism Scale (1975); items for the other modes are new. The score is the sum of the responses on the Likert scale, the total of each subscale indicating the level of invest- ment in that particular mode.

In subsequent testing of the scale, Van- derCreek and Nye (1993) add three addi- tional biosocial items. They report the strength of all six. The strongest of these can now be included in the scale.

Practical Considerations: This instrument requires no special skill to administer, score, or interpret. No instructions are necessary beyond the usual guarantee of confidential- ity and the emphasis on no "right" or "wrong" answers.

Norms/Standardization: In their first study, Hood and Morris (1983) report results from three separate samples of undergraduate psychology majors. The samples consist of 587, 342, and 105 students respectively. In the same report, they describe interview re- sults from 30 female and 9 male older adults. They code these interview results in relation to four of the death transcendence modes (the mysticism items are excluded because earlier reports [Hood, 1975] indi- cated that older persons experience diffi- culty in responding to these items).

VandeCreek and Nye (1993, 1994) report results from two samples, 166 community persons and 273 general-hospital-related in- dividuals (132 patients and 141 family members waiting during surgery). Hospital patients complete the instrument alone in their rooms; family members complete it in a hospital family waiting room.

VandeCreek and Nye (1993) report one concern about the mysticism items. Some respondents found them difficult to under- stand, particularly the ones that were worded negatively.

They recommend that some items be re- worded (this problem may be an extension of that reported earlier by Hood [1975]).

Reliability: The average alpha for the Hood and Morris (1983) study is .62, ranging from .53 for the nature mode and .75 for the religious mode. Alphas from the first study of VandeCreek and Nye (1993) are .79, ranging from .84 for the mystical subscale and .55 for the nature items. In their second sample, the alpha is .74, ranging from .79 (religious mode) to .51 (nature mode).

Validity: Hood and Morris (1983) reported a principle components factor analysis fol- lowed by a quartimax rotation. It identified 23 items clearly related to Lifton's five modes, which they use in their scale.

They administered the scale to 342 un- dergraduate psychology students along with Spilka's Fear of Death Scale (1977), which contains five subscales: Fear of the Dying Process, Lack of Fear of Death, and Fear of Loss of Experience and Control in Death. The major finding was that all modes except religion were significantly correlated with the Sensitivity toward Death subscale.

In the third sample with 105 students they demonstrated that Spilka's Death Pre- spective Scale relates meaningfully to re- sults from both the Death Transcendence Scale and intrinsic/extrinsic religiosity as measured by the scale developed by Allport and Ross (1967). These results suggest that perspectives concerning death transcen- dence relate to other consciously held per- spectives on death. Additionally, intrinsic religiosity significantly correlated with all modes: positively with the religious, mysti- cism and biosocial modes and negatively with the creative and nature modes. Extrin- sic religiosity correlated positively with the creative, biosocial, and nature modes.

VandeCreek and Nye (1993) report re- sults from two factor analyses, including the three new items. The results of the second analysis using the hospital-related data are more similar to those of Hood and Morris. However, in both analyses the nature items seem to be the weakest. Larger samples are needed for more definitive results.

Location:
VandeCreek, L., & Nye, C. (1993). Testing the Death Transcendence Scale. *Journal for the Scientific Study of Religion, 32*, 279–283.

Subsequent Research:
VandeCreek, L., & Nye, C. (1993). Testing the Death Transcendence Scale. *Journal for the Scientific Study of Religion, 32*, 279–283.

VandeCreek, L., & Nye, C. (1994). Trying to live forever: Correlates to the belief in life after death. *The Journal of Pastoral Care, 48*(3), 273–280.

References
Allport, G. W., & Ross, J. M. (1967). Personal religious orientation and prejudice. *Journal of Personality and Social Psychology, 5*, 432–443.

James, W. (1961). *The Varieties of Religious Experience.* New York: Collier.

Hood, R. W., Jr. (1975). The construction and preliminary validation of a measure of reported mystical experience. *Journal for the Scientific Study of Religion, 17*, 179–188.

Hood, R. W., Jr., & Morris, R. J. (1983). Toward a theory of death transcendence. *Journal for the Scientific Study of Religion, 22*(4), 353–365.

Lifton, R. J. (1979). *The Broken Connection.* New York: Simon & Schuster.

Spilka, B., Stout, L., Minton, B., Sizemore, D, (1977). Death and personal faith: a psychometric investigation. *Journal for the Scientific Study of Religion, 16*, 169–178.

Appendix

The Death Transcendence Scale

Please respond to each of the statements below using the following rating scale.
1 = stongly disagree   3 = agree
2 = disagree   4 = strongly agree

1. I have had an experience in which I felt everything in the world to be part of the same whole.
2. I have had an experience in which I realized the oneness of myself with all things.
3. I have never had an experience in which all things seemed to be unified into a single whole. (R)
4. I have never had an experience in which I became aware of the unity of all things. (R)
5. I have never had an experience in which I felt myself to be absorbed as one with all things. (R)
6. My death does not end my personal existence.
7. Death is a transition to something even greater than this life.
8. I believe in life after death.
9. Death is never just an ending, but is part of a process.
10. There is a Force or Power that controls and gives meaning to both life and death.
11. Only nature is forever.
12. Death is as natural as anything else in nature.
13. I may die, but the streams and mountains remain.
14. No matter what, all of us are part of nature.
15. Streams, trees, and people are all one in nature.

16. Meaningless work makes for a meaningless life.

17. It is important for me to do something in life for which I will be remembered after I die.

18. If I never do anything significant, my life will have been wasted.

19. If others I love do not remember me after I die, my life will have been wasted.

20. To be creative is to live forever.

21. After death much of myself lives on through my children.

22. Without children, much of what is most precious in life would be wasted.

23. Without children, life is incomplete.

*24. My life may end, but that which is important will live on through my family.

*25. Solid relationships with family and friends is a lasting value.

*26. Relationships with family and friends are among the most lasting values.

(R) indicates reverse-scored item.

The last three items are added by VandeCreek and Nye. All items should be placed in random order.

> Mysticism Subscale = Items 1–5
> Religious Subscale = Items 6–10
> Nature Subscale = Items 11–15
> Creative Subscale = Items 16–20
> Biosocial Subscale = Items 21–26

VandeCreek, L., & Nye, C. (1993). Testing the Death Transcendence Scale. *Journal for the Scientific Study of Religion, 32*(3), 279–283. Copyright © 1993, Journal for the Scientific Study of Religion. Reprinted with permission.

Chapter 14

Scales of Divine
Intervention/Religious Attribution

Religious experience for some people functions primarily as an explanatory system that helps them understand why things happen the way they do. Religion may set the stage for the ultimate causal explanation: God's will. In many religious traditions, a sacred human responsibility is to seek (and find) God's will. Depending on one's religious outlook, questioning God's will ranges from a human responsibility (even privilege) to a blasphemous activity.

"Attribution" is the term that psychologists use to describe this search for causal explanation. Researchers have identified a number of motivational bases for attributions; among the most clearly identified are the needs for meaning, control, and self-esteem. Research indicates that people will utilize a naturalistic explanatory system to the extent that it meets the needs of meaning, control, and self-esteem. However, if their naturalistic attribution mechanism fails to meet such needs, people may shift to religious attributions. One task facing psychologists of religion is to identify factors involved in this shift. The scales reviewed in this chapter are useful in such research.

Gorsuch and Smith's Attributions of Responsibility to God Scale (14.1) uses four vignettes to measure employment of God attributions (along with attributions to personal responsibility, luck, and personal effort) by varying the degree of probability (likely vs. unlikely) and extremity (extreme vs. mild) of good outcomes. Both Degelman and Lynn's Belief in Divine Intervention Scale (14.2) and Ritzema and Young's God as a Causal Agent Scale (14.3) are more traditional scales that measure tendencies to attribute events to God rather than naturalistic causes.

The God as a Causal Agent Scale (14.3) is the only scale of these three that is clearly restricted to the Christian tradition. Beyond some possible cultural limitations embedded within the vignettes of the Attribution of Responsibility to God Scale (14.1), the other scales may be useful in Western religion other than the Judeo-Christian tradition.

14.1
ATTRIBUTIONS OF RESPONSIBILITY TO GOD SCALE
(Gorsuch & Smith, 1983)

Reviewed by Michael J. Boivin

Variable: This instrument assesses the extent to which individuals attribute certain life event outcomes to God. It does so by presenting four vignettes or stories that are varied along two dimensions: outcome probability (high vs. low) and outcome extremity (extreme vs. mild). Then it asks respondents to evaluate the extent to which personal responsibility, luck, personal efforts, or divine intervention are involved in determining the outcome of each story.

General attribution theory has been proposed as a useful theoretical perspective for an understanding of religious experience. This is because it provides a cohesive and well-developed model for understanding the major dimensions and causes of one's beliefs and interpretations about life experiences and events (Glock & Piazza, 1981; Proudfoot & Shaver, 1975). In testing this model for the evaluation of religious attributions, Lowe and Medway (1976) described some of the important situational features that would make it more likely for an individual to attribute an experience to God. In extending these findings, Gorsuch and Smith (1983) developed their instrument to evaluate how such features might interact with the religious traits of the individual in determining his or her "attribution to God" tendency for a given life situation.

Description: In the Attributions of Responsibility to God measure, all four vignettes provide events with positive outcomes. However, the outcomes can be varied along two dimensions: level of outcome probability (likely vs. unlikely) and outcome extremity (extremely good vs. mildly good). The vignettes are also constructed so that causes for the events described are ambiguous. The vignettes involve experiences and feelings with which most respondents can readily identify and empathize.

After reading each vignette, respondents are asked a series of questions that evaluate the likelihood of a given outcome on a Likert scale of 0 ("highly likely") to 11 ("highly unlikely"). Individuals are also asked to indicate whether they might find themselves in a similar situation. The response outcomes are counterbalanced in terms of likelihood of the outcome and the severity of the outcome.

The resulting measures that can be scored from this scale are:

1. To what extent is person X responsible for the outcome? (responsibility)
2. How lucky was person X to obtain the outcome? (luck)
3. How hard did person X try to obtain the outcome? (effort)
4. To what extent is God responsible for the outcome? (attribution to God) (Gorsuch & Smith, 1983, p. 343)

Practical Considerations: The test is self-administered and is relatively easy to complete. Although the required reading level has not been formally established, original data collected by Gorsuch and Smith were from college students. No other special instructions or administrator skills are mentioned.

Norms/Standardization: The original sample on which the instrument findings are based consisted of 164 undergraduate students taking social science, nursing, and religion courses at a small evangelical Christian college. Prior to being administered the four vignettes, subjects were presented with portions of the Religious Attitude Inventory (Broen, 1957), which focuses on Christian fundamentalism of belief and one's "nearness of God" (see review of Broen's instrument in this volume; also see the review of Gorsuch and Smith's Nearness to God Scale and Fundamentalism Scale).

Because of the size and selective nature of the sample, no comprehensive norms are available for the instrument. Gorsuch and Smith (1983) did provide some preliminary group averages on the extent to which individuals attributed responsibility to God for the story outcomes. For the Likert scale rating averaged across the various vignettes, individuals with higher "fundamentalism" scores ($n = 145$) had a mean of 8.5; those with lower "fundamentalism" scores ($n = 16$) had a mean of 5.8; those with higher "nearness to God" scores ($n = 145$) a mean of 8.2; and those with lower "nearness to God" scores ($n = 8$) a mean of 5.1.

Reliability: Reliability coefficients are not available from Gorsuch and Smith (1983).

Validity: This instrument has reasonable construct validity in that individuals higher on the "fundamentalist" and on the "nearness to God" dimensions of religiosity attributed more responsibility to God for extreme life event outcomes. Other studies using different measures of religiosity have noted similar findings (Ritzema, 1979; see review in this volume). Other assessments of validity with this measure have not been found.

Location:

Gorsuch, R. L., & Smith, C. S. (1983). Attributions of responsibility to God: An interaction of religious beliefs and outcomes. *Journal for the Scientific Study of Religion, 22,* 340–352.

Subsequent Research: None located.

References

Broen, W. E. (1957). A factor analytic study of religious attitudes. *Journal of Abnormal and Social Psychology, 54,* 176–179.

Glock, C. Y., & Piazza, T. (1981). Exploring reality structures. In T. Robbins & D. Anthony (Eds.). *In Gods we trust: New patterns of religious pluralism in America* (pp. 67–83). New Brunswick: Transaction.

Lowe, C. A., & Medway, F. J. (1976). Effects of valence, severity, and relevance on responsibility and dispositional attribution. *Journal of Personality, 44,* 518–538.

Proudfoot, W., & Shaver, P. (1975). Attribution theory and the psychology of religion. *Journal for the Scientific Study of Religion, 14,* 317–380.

Ritzema, R. J. (1979). Attribution to supernatural causation: An important component of religious commitment? *Journal of Psychology and Theology, 7,* 286–293.

Appendix

Attributions of Responsibility to God: Four Vignettes

Note: Due to space constraints, experimental manipulations are included without repetition of other elements of the vignettes. The parentheses, underlinings, and labels (A, B, C, and D) do not appear in the original experimental booklet.

   A: low probability manipulation
   B: high probability manipulation
   C: mild outcome manipulation
   D: extreme outcome manipulation

1. M. was in counseling because of depression with the way things were going. M. had been feeling this way for (A: *several months*/ B: *just a couple of weeks*) and thought, "I might not snap out of it so I'd better see a counselor." Although M. didn't know it, this counselor (A: *had only limited*/ B: *often had*) success in treating depressed clients.

Outcome: After a number of sessions with the counselor, M. (C: *was still a little depressed but was feeling somewhat better than at the beginning of counseling*/ D: *felt extremely better and felt no more need for further counseling*). M. said, "I feel like a changed person. I feel better than I have in years."

2.   J. was moving to a new community. In the past, J. had (A: *always*/ B: *never*) found it difficult to get settled and feel comfortable in new places. Although J. was not aware of it before the move, new people in the town (to which J. was moving) had always found it (A: *very hard*/ B: *easy*) to feel comfortable and (A: *difficult*/ B: *easy*) to fit into the life of the community during the first few months.

Outcome: Three months after moving to the new community, J. was (C: *somewhat content with*/ D: *extremely happy and even excited about*) the way things were going.

3.   D. was in the hospital because of a car accident. The doctor said that recovery would depend in part upon D's ability to maintain a positive attitude and a good emotional outlook. At first, D. was told to expect a (A: *75%/* B: *25%*) chance of permanent disability remaining after discharge from the hospital.

Outcome: D. was out of the hospital (C: *in the expected length of time/* D: *much sooner than expected*). There was (C: *some relatively minor physical disability remaining after discharge. The doctor said that there was a good chance that this disability would not be permanent/* D: *no permanent disability remaining after discharge*). D. said, "I'm just glad to be alive!"

4.   B. helped C. by offering C. a ride to a nearby town. They had met only a few days earlier. Although B. was not aware of it, C. was considered (A: *hard/* B: *easy*) to get along with by most people, had very (A: *few/* B: *many*) friends, and often expressed (A: *little/* B: *great*) appreciation for personal favors.

Outcome: (C: *C. saw the offer of the ride as a friendly act and expressed appreciation to B./* D: *After their trip, a deep and lasting friendship developed. C. later told B. how much their relationship meant to C. It was obvious that C's life had change in a positive way.*)

Gorsuch, R. L., & Smith, C. S. (1983). Attributions of responsibility to God: An interaction of religious beliefs and outcomes. *Journal for the Scientific Study of Religion, 22,* 340–352. Copyright ©, 1983, Journal for the Scientific Study of Religion. Reprinted with permission of publisher and authors.

14.2
BELIEF IN DIVINE INTERVENTION SCALE (Degelman & Lynn, 1995)

Reviewed by Cay M. Anderson-Hanley and Michael E. McCullough

Variable: The Belief in Divine Intervention Scale (BDIS) is intended to be a general measure of belief in divine intervention for use with a variety of populations and situations. The scale is reported to be unidimensional.

Description: The six items of the BDIS were selected from an initial 10-item pool. The original ten items were created to tap various categories of divine intervention (e.g., physical healing and direct communication with humans). No theoretical basis for the categories was noted by the authors. Those items with corrected item-total correlations above .6 were retained. Of the six items retained, two dealt with divine healing; two others measured divine communication; one item focused on divine intervention in nature; and a final item dealt with a global statement of belief in divine intervention. A 6-point rating scale is used to assess level of agreement or disagreement with each item; scale options range from "strongly disagree" to "strongly agree" with anchors for every point. Two of the six items are reverse scored.

Practical Considerations: The paper-and-pencil scale is easy to administer, score, and interpret. It requires no special examiner skill or training. Minimal directions are necessary for administration and scoring. The six items would take only a few minutes to complete by simply selecting a rating on the 6-point scale. Scoring likewise requires little time and is obtained by converting the scale to a 1–6 point scale and then summing the scores of the six items (after reversing items 3 and 5). The purpose of the test is clear: to measure an individual's self-reported belief in divine intervention.

Norms/Standardization: Normative data has yet to be reported. However, two subsamples used in developing the measure can provide benchmarks for puliminary reference. Participants were students from a community college (*n* = 145) and a liberal arts college (associated with the Assemblies of God; *n* = 59) who were enrolled in introductory psychology courses. Fifty-two percent of the community college subsample were European Americans, 11% were Asian

Americans, with the rest of the subsample composed of smaller percentages of students with other ethnic heritages. In the Christian college subsample, 70% were European Americans, 10% were Mexican Americans, and the rest of the subsample was composed of smaller percentages of students with other ethnic heritages. Both subsamples were reported to be predominantly middle and upper-middle class. The community college group mean was 20.38 (SD = 10.49), whereas the Christian college group mean was 32.92 (SD = 3.64). The difference in mean BDIS scores between the community college (M = 20.38, SD = 10.49) and the Christian college (M = 32.82, SD = 3.64) were significant (p < .001). No significant differences in BDIS scores were found between men and women.

A ceiling effect was observed with the Christian college group; most of the students in this sample scored near the maximum possible score. Thus it was noted that the "BDIS is not and will not be effective in discriminating among individuals within a homogeneous and extreme group" (Degelman & Lynn, 1995, p. 43). Whether or not the items would differentiate among members of different Christian traditions remains to be investigated.

Reliability: Degelman and Lynn (1995) estimated the internal consistency of the BDIS for both sub-samples as well as the combined sample. The community college sample produced a Cronbach's alpha of .898, the Christian college sample yielded .924, and Cronbach's alpha for the total sample was .910. It was noted by the authors that the low reliability found for the Christian college subsample was likely due to the restricted range of scores produced by the ceiling effect. No estimates of test-retest reliability are yet available.

Validity: The items appear clearly related to the target construct of belief in divine intervention. Preliminary support for the validity of the BDIS is found in Degelman and Lynn (1995). The authors conducted a principal components analysis using the combined sample of community and Christian college

students (N = 209). They found that all six items had high loadings on the primary component (loadings ranged from .811 to .845). This finding supported their hypothesis that the BDIS was in fact measuring a unitary construct. Similar findings were reported for a principal components analysis using only the community college subsample; no analysis was reported for the Christian college subsample.

No other data were provided to confirm the construct validity of the scale. A comparison of scores on the BDIS with the two closely related measures cited by the authors (i.e., God as Causal Agent scale [Ritzema, 1979; Ritzema & Young, 1983] and the Divine Influence scale [DeVellis et al., 1985]) might be helpful. Given the high face validity of the scale, an exploration of the role of social desirability may also be necessary.

Some supportive evidence for the concurrent validity of the BDIS can be distilled by examining the results of the authors' analyses involving three additional variables. The authors hypothesized that scores on the BDIS would be significantly and positively related to self-rated importance of religion (Gorsuch & McFarland, 1972), external locus of control (Levenson, 1981), and a belief in a just world (O'Neill et al., 1988). BDIS scores were found to be significantly related to self-reported importance of religion (r = .78, p < .001). BDIS scores were not found to be significantly related to either external locus of control or a belief in a just world (p > .10).

Location:
Degelman, D., & Lynn, D. (1995). The development and preliminary validation of the Belief in Divine Intervention Scale. *Journal of Psychology and Theology*, 23, 37–44.

Subsequent Research: Given the recent development and publication of this measure, no subsequent research has yet been published.

References
Degelman, D., & Lynn, D. (1995). The development and preliminary validation of the Belief in Divine Intervention Scale. *Journal of Psychology and Theology*, 23, 37–44.

DeVellis, R. F., DeVellis, B. M., Revicki, D. A., Lurie, S. J., Runyan, D. K., & Bristol, M. (1985). Development and validation of the Child Improvement Locus of Control (CILC) scales. *Journal of Social and Clinical Psychology*, *3*, 307–324.

Gorsuch, R. L., & McFarland, S. G. (1972). Single vs. multiple-item scales for measuring religious values. *Journal for the Scientific Study of Religion*, *11*, 53–64.

Levenson, H. (1981). Differentiating among internality, powerful others, and chance. In H. M. Lefcourt (Ed.), *Research with the locus of control construct* (Vol. 1, pp. 15–63). New York: Academic Press.

O'Neill, P., Duffy, C., Enman, M., Blackmer, E., Goodwin, J., & Campbell, E. (1988). Cognition and citizen participation in social action. *Journal of Applied Social Psychology*, *18*, 1067–1083.

Ritzema, R. J. (1979). Attribution to supernatural causation: An important component of religious commitment. *Journal of Psychology and Theology*, *7*, 286–293.

Ritzema, R. J., & Young, C. (1983). Causal schemata and the attribution of supernatural causality. *Journal of Psychology and Theology*, *11*, 36–43.

Appendix

Belief in Divine Intervention Scale

Directions: Please respond to each statement by circling the number that best reflects the extent to which you agree or disagree with each statement.

1 God sometimes directly intervenes to heal individuals of diseases like cancer.

−3	−2	−1	+1	+2	+3
strongly disagree	somewhat disagree	slightly disagree	slightly agree	somewhat agree	strongly agree

2. God sometimes communicates directly with individuals.

−3	−2	−1	+1	+2	+3
strongly disagree	somewhat disagree	slightly disagree	slightly agree	somewhat agree	strongly agree

3. God does not intervene directly in our lives. (R)

−3	−2	−1	+1	+2	+3
strongly disagree	somewhat disagree	slightly disagree	slightly agree	somewhat agree	strongly agree

4. God sometimes directly intervenes to change the course of damaging weather conditions like hurricanes.

−3	−2	−1	+1	+2	+3
strongly disagree	somewhat disagree	slightly disagree	slightly agree	somewhat agree	strongly agree

5. Real miracles of healing from God do not occur today. (R)

−3	−2	−1	+1	+2	+3
strongly disagree	somewhat disagree	slightly disagree	slightly agree	somewhat agree	strongly agree

6. God sometimes uses dreams to communicate with us.

−3	−2	−1	+1	+2	+3
strongly disagree	somewhat disagree	slightly disagree	slightly agree	somewhat agree	strongly agree

(R) indicates reverse-scored item.

14.3
GOD AS A CAUSAL AGENT SCALE (Ritzema & Young, 1983)
Reviewed by Gary L. Welton

Variable: The God as a Casual Agent (GCA) Scale is drawn from attribution theory which states that one's explanations for external events and internal states have an important effect on human behavior. This scale attempts to measure one's general predisposition to attribute events to God and divine intervention rather than naturalistic causes.

The authors argue that this scale may be a reasonable alternative for measuring religiosity. Instead of measuring religious behavior, or belief, this scale attempts to measure the extent to which one believes that God is involved in a supernatural way with the human experience. Although this belief in the supernatural intervention of God as a causal agent is only one component of religiosity, it is a very important component and thus may be an excellent way to study religious behavior.

Description: An original pool of 30 items was developed to assess one's belief in the effectiveness of prayer, the reality of miracles, and the experience of having received divine guidance. This pool was shortened to 14 items after pilot testing, based on item-whole correlations.

Of the 14 items, 8 specifically concern the respondent's beliefs about God's divine intervention. The other 6 items ask the respondent to consider and react to other people's beliefs and experiences. The reasoning behind the inclusion of this latter type of item, presumably, is that they are worded so as to indirectly assess the respondent's beliefs in light of their assessment of other people. The distinctions between these two types of items have led to criticism by Degelman and Lynn (1995). They argue that it is difficult to know what is being measured because of the confused factor structure. Item 7 seems to be a particular problem because it asks only a factual question about what other people believe.

Respondents indicate their agreement or disagreement with these items using a 5-point Likert scale, with high scores indicating agreement. Seven of the items are worded in a negative direction, and hence must be reverse scored. The result, after summation, is a range of scores from 14 to 70, indicating the extent to which the respondent is predisposed to attribute events in a supernatural manner.

Practical Considerations: The scale is a short paper-and-pencil instrument. Half of the items are worded in the positive direction, and half, in the negative direction. Item 4 may seem to be double barreled to some respondents, who may be confused as to whether they should base their answer on the statement about God's creating the world by his commands or on the particular number of days involved. (Should I disagree because it was done in six days rather than seven? or Should I disagree because I am not sure they were 24 hour days?)

Norms/Standardization: Subjects were 128 college upperclass students at a midwestern church-related college. (The homogeneity of this group would tend to deflate estimates of the reliability and validity of this instrument.) The overall mean was 52.1, the median was 52.7, the standard deviation was 6.8, and the range was 20 to 66.

Reliability: The authors obtained a coefficient alpha of .74. For 13 of the items, the item-whole correlations were between .46 and .62. The one weak item, number 7 (discussed above), had an item-whole correlation of only .09. This suggests that the deletion of this item would increase the coefficient alpha considerably. With the exception of this item, the reliability numbers are strong.

Validity: The authors developed scenarios describing hypothetical situations in which the actors received a plausible but unexpectedly favorable outcome. Subjects were asked to indicate, on a 9-point scale, the extent to which they believed these events were caused by natural or supernatural forces. These ratings were compared to the scores on the GCA scale. The analysis of variance design demonstrated that subjects who scored high on the GCA scale attributed significantly more causality to supernatural intervention than did those who scored low on the GCA. Unfortunately, the authors did not report the correlation between GCA scores and the rating of supernatural intervention. They did, however, provide enough information to enable a calculation of the correlation between the GCA and the categorization of supernatural intervention into high and low groups. This point biserial $r = .37$. The Pearson r using the data in its original form might be somewhat higher.

Research by Jackson and Coursey (1988) provides some additional evidence. They found that GCA scores were correlated with internality ($r = .26$) using Rotter's (1966) Internal vs. External Control scale. This is consistent with the discussion by Pargament, Sullivan, Tyler, and Steele (1982) that God control, though external in nature, may operate in a manner more similar to an internal LOC approach. Jackson and Coursey (1988) also found a correlation of .32 with Hoge's (1972) Intrinsic Religious Motivation Scale.

Location:

Ritzema, R. J., & Young, C. (1983). Causal schemata and the attribution of supernatural causal-ity. *Journal of Psychology and Theology, 11,* 36–43.

Subsequent Research:

Jackson, L. E., & Coursey, R. D. (1988). The relationship of God control and internal locus of control to intrinsic religious motivation, coping, and purpose in life. *Journal for the Scientific Study of Religion, 27,* 399–410.

Watson, P. J., Morris, R. J., & Hood, R. W. Jr. (1990). Extrinsic Scale factors: Correlations and construction of religious orientation types. *Journal of Psychology and Christianity, 9,* 35–46.

References

Degelman, D., & Lynn, D. (1995). The development and preliminary validation of the Belief in Divine Intervention Scale. *Journal of Psychology and Theology, 23,* 37–44.

Hoge, D. R. (1972). A validated intrinsic religious motivation scale. *Journal for the Scientific Study of Religion, 11,* 369–376.

Ritzema, R. J., & Young, C. (1983). Causal schemata and the attribution of supernatural causal-ity. *Journal of Psychology and Theology, 11,* 36–43.

Jackson, L. E., & Coursey, R. D. (1988). The relationship of God control and internal locus of control to intrinsic religious motivation, coping, and purpose in life. *Journal for the Scientific Study of Religion, 27,* 399–410.

Pargament, K. I., Sullivan, M., Tyler, F., & Steele, R. (1982). Patterns of attribution of control and individual psychosocial competence. *Psychological Reports, 51,* 1243–1252.

Rotter, J. B. (1966). Generalized expectancies for internal versus external control of reinforcement. *Psychological Monographs, 80,* Whole No. 609.

Appendix

God as a Causal Agent Scale

Following are the items included in the God as a Causal Agent Scale. Response options include (5) strongly agree; (4) agree; (3) undecided; (2) disagree; and (1) strongly disagree. Items 5, 6, 7, 9, 11,12, & 13 are to be reverse scored.

1. Every new life is a direct miracle of God.

2. A close call in a situation where an accident is likely, is probably God intervening to protect.

3. More than once I have felt that God responded specifically to a prayer that I made.

4. God created the world in 7 days by giving the commands.

5. Events happen or don't happen quite by chance in this world.

6. Many people who have claimed to feel the presence of God were probably just experiencing their own emotions.

7. Just as in the past when primitive people thought that storms, volcanoes, and other natural events were due to divine action, many people nowadays consider God or the devil responsible for things that really have completely physical causes.

8. Miracles happen much more frequently than most people suspect.

9. I'm usually skeptical when someone tells me that they're convinced that God did something to change their attitudes or beliefs.

10. God does miraculously heal diseases.

11. One problem with many Christians is that they try to give supernatural explanations for events that probably were caused by natural phenomena.

12. I have never been completely sure that anything that has happened in my life has come as an answer to prayer.

13. One thing I don't like is the tendency that some people have to call everything they don't understand a miracle.

14. There have been a number of times in my life when I was convinced that some particular event was caused by direct action of God.

Chapter 15

Scales of Forgiveness

Psychologists and others in the helping professions have demonstrated an appetite for the study of forgiveness. Forgiveness has not been operationalized in the literature as a religious construct. However, given that forgiveness is a central theme in at least Christian theology (e.g., God's forgiveness of sin), it is not surprising that it is often studied in the context of religion. Models of forgiveness now abound in the literature and are based within a number of theoretical frameworks: psychodynamic, existential, object relations, and cognitive theories, among others.

Included in this chapter are reviews of two multidimensional measures of forgiveness. The Enright Forgiveness Inventory (15.1) is a 65-item scale designed to measure six dimensions of forgiveness: the absence of negative affect, negative judgment, and negative behavior, as well as the presence of positive affect, positive judgment, and positive behavior. These specific factors, in combination, make up the definition of forgiveness used by the authors of the scale. Wade's 83-item Forgiveness Scale (15.2) identifies nine forgiveness dimensions: revenge, freedom from obsession, affirmation, victimization, positive (vs. negative) feelings, avoidance, conciliation, holding a grudge, and toward God.

15.1
ENRIGHT FORGIVENESS INVENTORY—U. S. VERSION
(Subkoviak, Enright, Wu, Gassin, Freedman, Olson, & Sarinopoulos, 1995)
Reviewed by Michael E. McCullough

Variable: The Enright Forgiveness Inventory-U. S. Version (EFI-US) was developed to measure the degree to which the respondent has forgiven a particular target person (e.g., a particular friend, family member) who has hurt or offended the respondent. Forgiveness is conceptualized as a multidimensional construct involving cognitive, affective, and behavioral components.

Subkoviak et al. (1995) define forgiveness as the overcoming of negative affect, judgment, and behavior toward an offender and the presence of positive affect, judgment, and behavior toward an offender. These changes occur in the face of consid-

erable interpersonal hurt. On this basis, Subkoviak et al. measure forgiveness with six subscales designed to measure the specific dimensions included in their definition of forgiveness: (1–3) Absence of Negative Affect, Negative Judgment, and Negative Behavior; and (4–6) Presence of Positive Affect, Positive Judgment, and Positive Behavior toward an Offender.

Subkoviak et al. (1995) see forgiveness as a universal construct that should apply to persons from all cultures and religious backgrounds. They have collected data in Brazil, Israel, Korea, Saudi Arabia, Taiwan, and the United States. The following review examines the scale and the norms that have been developed based on their U. S. sample.

Description: A panel of psychologists and graduate students who were studying forgiveness generated 25 items to measure each of the six dimensions of forgiveness that appear in their definition of forgiveness: the absence of negative affect, cognition, and behavior (NA. NC, and NB) and the presence of positive affect, cognition, and behavior (PA, PC, and PB) for the offender. In the final product, ten items are used to measure each of the six dimensions of forgiveness. Subkoviak et al. (1995) based their subscales on a priori theorizing about the important dimensions of forgiveness.

Items are scored on a 6-point Likert-type scale (1 = strongly disagree, 2 = disagree, 3 = slightly disagree, 4 = slightly agree, 5 = agree, and 6 = strongly agree). Items on the absence of affect, cognition, and behavior scales are reversed scored so that higher scores on all subscales indicate greater forgiveness. Items can be summed in two ways. First, items on each subscale can be summed to derive a set of six subscale scores, with scores ranging from 10 to 60. Second, all 60 items can be summed (after the negative items have been reverse scored) to derive a total score, with scores ranging from 60 to 360.

Practical Considerations: This paper-and-pencil measure requires no special qualifications to administer. Respondents are simply directed to think of a person who has seriously offended or hurt them, and then to indicate their agreement with items that indicate the degree to which they have experienced certain feelings, thoughts, or behavioral intentions regarding the offender.

Norms/Standardization: A sample of 204 female and 190 male college students and their same-sex parents constituted the standardization sample. The average age of the college student was 22 and the average age of the parent was 49. Based on the sample of 394 persons, the means and standard deviations for each respective subscale were:

Subscale	M	SD	Reliability (alpha)
Positive affect	36.73	14.14	.96
Negative affect	39.60	13.97	.95
Positive behavior	43.89	12.76	.96
Negative behavior	43.12	11.71	.93
Positive cognition	45.18	12.16	.96
Negative cognition	48.02	11.76	.95
EFI Total Score	256.55	69.43	.98

Reliability: Reliability was established by estimating internal consistency with Cronbach's alpha. *Alphas* were consistently high for all six subscales and the total score (.93 to .98). McCullough (1995) also found internal consistency estimates ranging from .93 to .98 for the EFI subscales and total scale.

To estimate the test-retest reliability of the EFI-US, students completed the EFI-US at one time point and were re-tested 4 weeks later. Test-retest reliabilities ranged from .67 (negative behavior) to .86 (total scale score).

Validity: Data to investigate the validity of the EFI-US were gathered in several days. First, the subscales were correlated with each other. The subscales were highly intercorrelated, with correlation coefficients ranging from .80 to .87.

Second, the subscales were correlated with a single-item measure of the degree to which respondents had forgiven the person that they rated as they completed the instrument. ("To what extent have you forgiven the person that you rated?") The EFI-US subscales were moderately correlated with this single item, (Pearson *r*'s from .60 to .68). Subdoviak et al. (1992) indicate that coefficients of this size are impressive, given that one of the variables was a single-item measure with limited reliability. Third, the EFI-US scales were correlated with the Crowne-Marlowe (1960) social desirability scale.

Fourth, Subkoviak et al. (1995) hypothesize that forgiveness should lead to reduced anxiety in relationships that are particularly intimate or developmentally significant. On this basis, they reason that an instrument that purports to measure forgiveness should be correlated with indices of mental health. Subkoviak et al. correlated the EFI-US with measures of anxiety and depression, hypothesizing that forgiveness should lead to improvements in these psychological symptoms. They found that the EFI total score had a small and negative correlation with anxiety for their total sample ($r = -.15$). For respondents in their sample who reported that the interpersonal offense that they encountered had initially caused a great deal of hurt, forgiveness had a larger negative correlation with anxiety ($r = .25$). For married respondents who rated their spouses, forgiveness was moderately and negatively correlated with trait anxiety ($r = .53$) and state anxiety ($r = -.44$). Correlations of anxiety with other particular subsets of their sample were also conducted, yielding some support for their hypothesis that forgiveness should be conductive to mental health.

Subkoviak et al. (1995) found no significant relationship between the EFI and the Beck Depression Inventory for the total sample. However, they did find that among the adult sample, the negative affect subscale of the EFI was negatively correlated with depression among those respondents who had reported that they had received a great deal of hurt from a family member.

Additional support for the instrument's validity comes from McCullough (1995), who found that the participants in a weekend seminar designed to encourage forgiveness had significantly higher EFI total scores following the intervention than did participants in a waiting-list control group. These findings suggest that the EFI might be valuable for investigating the efficacy of interventions that are designed to promote interpersonal forgiveness.

Location:

Contact Robert D. Enright, Ph. D., Department of Educational Psychology, University of Wisconsin, Madison, WI 53706-1796.

Subsequent Research:

McCullough, M. E. (1995). *Forgiveness as altruism: Toward a social-psychological theory of forgiveness and tests of its validity*. Unpublished doctoral dissertation, Virginia Commonwealth University, Richmond, VA.

References

Beck, A. T., & Steer, R. A. (1987). *Beck Depression Inventory*. San Antonio: Psychological Corporation.

Crown, D. P., & Marlowe, D. (1960). A new scale of social desirability independent of psychopathology. *Journal of Consulting Psychology, 24*, 349–354.

McCullough, M. E. (1995). *Forgiveness as altruism: Toward a social-psychological theory of forgiveness and tests of its validity*. Unpublished doctoral dissertation, Virginia Commonwealth University, Richmond, VA.

Subkoviak et al. (1995). Measuring interpersonal forgiveness in late adolescence and middle adulthood. *Journal of Adolescence, 18*, 641–655.

Appendix

Enright Forgiveness Inventory

The following six items are sample items, one for each subscale. Items are answered on a 6-point Likert Scale ranging from zero ("strongly disagree") to five ("strongly agree"). The entire scale is available through Robert D. Enright, Ph. D., Dept. of Educational Psychology, University of Wisconsin, Madison, WI 53706-1796.

Negative Affect
I feel hostile toward him/her.

Positive Affect
I feel warm toward him/her.

Negative Cognition
Regarding the person, I disapprove of him/her.

Positive Cognition
Regarding the person, I wish him/her well.

Negative Behavior
Regarding the person, I do or would put him/her down.

Positive Behavior
Regarding the person, I do or would be considerate.

15.2
FORGIVENESS SCALE (Wade, 1989)
Reviewed by Michael E. McCullough

Variable: Wade's Forgiveness Scale was developed to measure the degree to which respondent's have forgiven a specific person who has hurt them (offender). The Forgiveness Scale measures cognitions, affects, and behaviors regarding the offender. Forgiveness is conceptualized as a multidimensional construct and is measured with several different subscales.

Description: Wade (1989) criticized previous attempts to measure forgiveness because (a) they did not measure important aspects of forgiveness, (b) their items were often ambiguous, and (c) they were rarely based on clear definitions of forgiveness. Wade developed her scale to remedy some of these deficiencies. Based on a content analysis of her interviews with 20 pastors, professors, and psychologists, Wade developed fourteen dimensions of forgiveness and nine dimensions of unforgiveness. Based on these 23 dimensions, Wade generated a pool of 600 items to measure forgiveness and unforgiveness.

From this item pool, Wade (1989) produced an 83-item scale with nine intercorrelated subscales. The subscales are: Revenge, Freedom from Obsession, Affirmation, Victimization, Positive (vs. Negative) Feelings, Avoidance, Toward God, Conciliation, and Holding a Grudge. The items are responded to on a 5-point scale (1 = strongly disagree, 2 = disagree, 3 = neutral, 4 = agree, and 5 = strongly agree). Items for each subscale can be summed to derive nine distinct measures of forgiveness. Scores range from as low as 4 to 20 for the Freedom from Obsession and Holding a Grudge Scales (which both contain four items) and as high as 26 to 104 for the Feelings subscale (26 items). Higher scores on the Revenge, Victimization, Avoidance, Freedom from Obsession, Affirmation, Positive (vs. Negative) Feelings, Toward God, and Conciliation subscales indicate greater forgiveness. Subscales are designed to measure specific components of how people respond following serious interpersonal hurts (e.g., desire for revenge, avoidance, feelings, conciliation, etc.) and would be of interest to researchers interested in these components.

Practical Considerations: This paper-and-pencil measures requires no special skill to administer. The measure is scored by summing the items for each respective subscale to derive nine subscale scores. The one exception, the Feelings subscale, requires that items measuring negative feelings (e.g., betrayed, anger, and hatred) be reversed (a score of 1 is reversed to 5, a score of 2 is reversed to 4, and so on) before they are summed with the items measuring positive feelings.

Norms/Standardization: Normative data on Wade's scale has yet to be collected. The scale was developed using a sample of 282 college students, half of whom endorsed the items with a person whom they had not forgiven in mind. Means and standard deviations for their samples of church members, college students who desired to participate in a workshop to help them learn to forgive, and spouses, respectively. These might serve as tentative norms for their respective samples.

Reliability: Wade (1989), McCullough and Worthington (1995), and Woodman (1991) have estimated the internal consistency reliability of Wade's scales with Cronbach's coefficient alpha. (See table 1). All of the items correlated with their parent subscale at a minimum of $r = .50$ (Wade, 1989). No studies to date have investigated the stability of scores over time.

Table 1.
Estimates of Internal Consistency
(Coefficient Alpha) form Three Studies

Scale	Wade (1989) (N = 282)	Mc & W (1995) (N = 83)	Woodman (1991) (N = 84)
Revenge	.91	.91	.72
Freedom from Obsession	.83	.68	.65
Affirmation	.88	.87	.79
Victimization	.79	.75	.83
Feelings	.95	.92	.95
Avoidance	.91	.92	.91
Toward God	.89	.91	.90
Conciliation	.89	.85	.81
Holding a Grudge	.87	.76	.79

Note: Mc & W = McCullough & Worthington. N = number of subjects in the study.

Validity: A form of the "known groups" method was used to establish concurrent validity in Wade's (1989) study. The items were completed by 282 college students.

Half of these students were instructed to complete the instrument with an offender that they had forgiven in mind, and half were instructed to complete the instrument with an offender that they had not forgiven in mind. Wade found 11 correlated factors that appeared to measure forgiveness. Nine of these factors were retained as subscales; two were abandoned because they failed to differentiate between the group of participants that reported having forgiven their offenders and those who reported not having forgiven.

All of the subscales except for the Toward God subscale show moderate correlations with the four subscales of Spanier's (1976) Dyadic Adjustment Scale in a sample of married persons (Woodman, 1989). The subscales are modestly correlated with Christian religious maturity as measured by Massey's (1989) Religious Status Inventory (Dreelin, 1992), and narcissistic traits, as measured by the Narcissistic Personality Inventory (Davidson & Jurkovic, 1992).

Additional support for the instrument's validity comes from data suggesting that Wade's scales may be useful in measuring the efficacy of interventions designed to promote forgiveness. McCullough and Worthington (1995) used by Wade's scales to measure the effectiveness of two different one-hour psychoeducational workshops at encouraging college students to forgive persons who had offended them. They found that participation in the two workshops produced changes in the direction of forgiveness on the Revenge, Affirmation, Feelings, and Conciliation subscales of Wade's instrument.

Location:
Wade, S. H. (1989). *The development of a scale to measure forgiveness*. Unpublished doctoral dissertation, Fuller Graduate School of Psychology, Pasadena, CA.

Subsequent Research:
McCullough, M. E., & Worthington, E. L., Jr. (1995). Promoting forgiveness: A comparison of two brief psychoeducational interventions with a waiting-list control. *Counseling and Values, 40,* 55–68.

Woodman, T. (1991). *The role of forgiveness in marital adjustment.* Unpublished doctoral dissertation, Fuller Graduate School of Psychology, Pasadena, CA.

References

Massey, D. E. (1989). *The construction and initial factor analysis of the Religious Status Inventory.* Unpublished doctoral dissertation, Fuller Graduate School of Psychology, Pasadena, CA.

Spanier, G. B. (1976). Measuring dyadic adjustment: New scales for assessing the quality of marriage and similar dyads. *Journal of Marriage and Family, 38,* 15–28.

Appendix

Wade's Forgiveness Scale

Please answer the items below by using the following scale:

1	2	3	4	5
Strongly disagree	Disagree	Neutral	Agree	Strongly agree

1. Our relationship is more important than this offense. (AFF1)
2. I like them. (AFF2)
3. I'll make them pay. (REV1)
4. I wish that something bad would happen to them. (REV2)
5. There's something wrong with them. (REV3)
6. It (the offense) no longer has a hold on me. (FRE1)
7. I was victimized. (VIC1)
8. I don't replay the offense in my mind, dwelling on it. (FRE2)
9. I love them. (AFF3)
10. I blame them. (VIC2)
11. I recognize it was very painful for the offender. (AFF4)
12. They wronged me. (VIC3)
13. I have a responsibility for this relationship too. (AFF5)
14. I have stopped blaming. (FRE3)
15. I want them to get what they deserve. (REV4)
16. I have a clearer ability to see their good points. (AFF6)
17. They're guilty. (VIC4)
18. I'm going to get even. (REV5)
19. It's not fair. (VIC5)
20. I can understand where they're coming from. (AFF7)
21. I think about the good they've done. (AFF8)
22. I'm glad to be around them. (AFF9)
23. They can't do anything right. (REV6)
24. I think about them without anger. (FRE4)
25. They're scum. (REV7)
26. I want to see them hurt and miserable. (REV8)
27. I continue to think about how much I hate them. (REV9)
28. They're bad. (REV10)
29. betrayed (FEE1-R)
30. wronged (FEE2-R)
31. peace (FEE3)

32. joy (FEE4)
33. hate is dropped (FEE5)
34. anger (FEE6-R)
35. hurt rushes away, is accepted or assuaged (FEE7)
36. hurt/pain (FEE8-R)
37. victimized (FEE9-R)
38. holding a grudge (FEE10-R)
39. hatred (FEE11-R)
40. rage (FEE12-R)
41. release (FEE13)
42. respect (FEE14)
43. care (FEE15)
44. violated (FEE16-R)
45. good feeling (FEE17)
46. resentment (FEE18-R)
47. vengeance is dropped, no pleasure in it (FEE19)
48. cooperation (FEE20)
49. anger is released, gone (FEE21)
50. compassion (FEE22)
51. resentment is gone, or less (FEE23)
52. relief (FEE24)
53. acceptance (FEE25)
54. comfortable with them (FEE26)
55. I'm not letting go of the offense. (GRU1)
56. I told God I forgave them. (TOW1)
57. I asked God for forgiveness for them. (TOW2)
58. I wished them well. (CON1)
59. I keep as much distance between us as possible. (AVO1)
60. I'm holding on to the hurt and anger. (GRU2)
61. I looked for the source of the problem and tried to correct it. (CON2)
62. I took steps toward reconciliation: Wrote them, called them, expressed love, showed concern, etc. (CON3)
63. I gave my feelings to God. (TOW3)
64. I gave them back a new start, a renewed relationship. (CON4)
65. I asked God to help me forgive them, to love them. (TOW4)
66. I accept my part of the situation. (CON5)
67. I see no good in them. (AVO2)
68. I live as if they don't exist, aren't around. (AVO3)
69. I prayed for them, asking God to bless them. (TOW5)
70. I don't trust them. (AVO4)
71. I find it difficult to act warmly toward them. (AOV5)
72. I avoid them. (AVO6)
73. I accept their humanness, flaws, failures. (CON6)
74. I cut off the relationship with them. (AVO7)
75. I'm suspicious of them. (GRU3)
76. I accept them. (CON7)
77. I made an effort to be more friendly and concerned. (CON8)
78. I did my best to put aside the mistrust. (CON9)
79. I was willing to forget the past and concentrate on the present. (CON10)
80. I tried to make amends. (CON11)
81. I harbor a grudge against them. (GRU4)

82. I don't blame them. (CON12)
83. I withdraw from them. (AVO8)

REV = Revenge
FRE = Freedom from obsession
AFF = Affirmation
VIC = Victimization
FEE = Feelings
AVO = Avoidance
TOW = Toward God
CON = Conciliation
GRU = Holding a grudge
R   = Item must be reverse scored

Note: Do not include codes in parentheses in administration of this scale.

Reprinted with permission of author.

Chapter 16

Scales of Institutional Religion

The five measures reviewed in this chapter deal with the church. Church attendance is frequently operationalized as a measure of religion. Of course, such a restricted unidimensional measure of a complex construct is inadequate. If for any reason only a few questions (or even just a single question) can be asked, church attendance may *not* be the best choice. Nevertheless, the institutional nature of religion is an important part of the construct, and several measures have been developed to assess particularly the role of the church in religious experience.

The first three measures reviewed here measure attitudes toward the church. Dynes's Attitude toward Church and Religious Practices Scale (16.1) is a unidimensional scale that assesses the degree of preference for either church or sect religiousness. Church-sect typology identifies the church, or today what is commonly called a denomination, as a group that accommodates the host culture by integrating religious beliefs and practices with cultural concepts. Sects, in contrast, reject the host culture and often demand strong commitments from members.

Thurstone and Chave's Attitude toward the Church Scale (16.2), at one time a frequently used scale, is seldom used today for research purposes, though many of the items, and perhaps the entire scale itself, are relevant in measuring contemporary attitudes toward the church. The most widely used of four religious attitude scales developed by Thurstone, this instrument is probably most appreciated as a sophisticated early attempt by a respected methodologist to measure religious experience; undoubtedly, it is among a small group of early scales that helped introduce an era of measurement in psychology of religion. The third measure is Hardy's highly specialized multidimensional scale of Attitudes toward the LDS Church (16.3).

The final two scales were developed by a research team at Bowling Green State University. The five-dimensional Congregation Climate Scales (16.4) measure the "psychologically meaningful representations of the church/synagogue." The following dimensions consist of ten items each: openness to change, activity, stability, organization and clarity, and sense of community. The Congregation Satisfaction Questionnaire (16.5) assesses member satisfaction along seven dimensions: religious services, church members, church leaders, special programs and activities, religious education for children, religious education for adults, and church facilities.

16.1
ATTITUDE TOWARD CHURCH AND RELIGIOUS PRACTICES SCALE
(Dynes, 1955)

Reviewed by Duane Kauffmann

Variable: The purpose of the Attitude toward Church and Religious Pracitces Scale was to quantify church and sect so that these theoretical concepts might be incorporated into appropriate empirical studies. "Church" signifies a religious organization that is rooted securely in the prevailing social order and integrates prevailing cultural concepts into its beliefs and practices. "Sect" identifies a religious group that disdains cultural conformity and creates a separate subculture with rigid belief and practice boundaries.

Description: The original scale items were written to measure a respondent's preference for a church or a sect orientation. The scale consists of 24 items. The respondent provides a numerical response from 1 ("strongly agree") to 5 ("strongly disagree") for each question. The summed item scores may range from 24 to 120, with lower scores indicating preference for a sect religiosity and higher scores indicating preference for a church religiosity.

Practical Considerations: The scale is easy to administer, requiring only simple instructions concerning the response continuum. An individual's score is derived by adding together responses to the 24 items (with items 2, 6, 7, 10 reversed scored).

Norms/Standardization: An initial pool of 35 items was written to reflect church or sect orientation. These original questions were pretested on a sample of 55 respondents selected from a Protestant church in Columbus, Ohio. An internal consistency analysis led to the rejection of 11 items that lacked discriminatory power. Four church and 20 sect items constitute the 24 items selected for the scale.

Reliability: The split-half reliability for the pretest sample (N = 55) was .86 (corrected by the Spearman-Brown formula to .92). A subsample of 100 persons, randomly selected from the 360 residents of Columbus who constituted the final study sample, gave a split-half reliability of .70 (corrected to .82).

Validity: The theoretical background for this scale assumes a measured difference between members of groups defined by "church" and members of groups defined by "sect." As expected, a sample of church members (Episcopalian, Presbyterian) had a mean of 76.1, which was significantly different from the sect members' (Holiness, Pentecostal, Church of God, Nazarene, Baptist) mean of 58.1. Also, ten sociologists recruited from several denominations demonstrated 98% agreement in classification of items as church or sect.

Location:
Dynes, R. R. (1955). Church-sect typology and socio-economic status. *American Sociological Review*, *20*, 555–560.

Subsequent Research:
Garrison, K. C. (1962). The relationship of certain variables to church-sect typology among college students. *Journal of Social Psychology*, *56*, 29–32.

Appendix

Attitude toward Church and Religious Practices

Directions: Put a 1 before those statements with which you strongly agree, a 2 before those statements with which you mildly agree, a 3 before those statements toward which you are neutral, a 4 before those with which you mildly disagree, and a 5 before those with which you strongly disagree.

1. I think a minister should preach without expecting to get paid for it.
*2. I think it is more important to live a good life now than to be bothered about life after death.
3. I think a person who is not willing to follow *all* the rules of the church should not be allowed to belong.
4. Testifying about one's religious experience should be a part of a regular church service.
5. I feel that a congregation should encourage the minister during his sermon by saying *amen*.
*6. I think that we should emphasize education in religion and not conversion.
*7. I think that there is practically no difference between what the different Protestant churches believe.
8. I think a person should make a testimony about his religion before he joins a church.
9. In church, I would rather sing the hymns myself than hear the choir sing.
*10. I think being a success in one's job is one mark of a good Christian.
11. A minister who is "called" is better than one who is "trained."
12. I like the "old-time" religion.
13. I think churches should have more revivals.
14. I think it would be wrong for a church member to have a job as a bartender.
15. I think a person should feel his religion before he joins a church.
16. I like to sing the old gospel songs rather than the new hymns.
17. I don't believe churches do enough about saving souls.
18. Heaven and Hell are very real to me.
19. All the miracles in the Bible are true.
20. Children should not become members of the church until they are old enough to understand it.
21. I think it is more important to go to church than to be active in politics.
22. I wish ministers would preach more on the Bible and less on politics.
23. I think it is more serious to break God's law than to break man's law.
24. I think every family should have family prayers or say grace before meals.

* indicates reversed scoring

Reprinted with permission of author.

16.2
ATTITUDE TOWARD THE CHURCH SCALE
(Thurstone & Chave, 1929; Chave, 1939)

Reviewed by David M. Wulff

Variable: The Attitude toward the Church Scale was designed to measure a range of favorable and unfavorable attitudes. The scale's items represent "the church" as alternately a generalized institution or agency and a specific locus of religious services and social relations. The authors emphasize that the scale is intended as an unbiased measure without any implied judgment about persons with high or low scores. That favorable attitudes happen to be represented by low scores is the result of an arbitrary decision to assign 0 to the extremely favorable end of the scale.

Description: A Scale for Measuring Attitude toward the Church is the best known and most widely used of the several religiosity scales developed by L. L. Thurstone and his collaborators early in the twentieth century. Other scales formally published by the University of Chicago Press between 1929 and

1933 include five forms of the scale of Attitude toward God, which together assess the sensed reality of God (Forms A and B), the influence of belief in God on conduct (Forms C and D), and definitions of God (Form E, which is the only one of the five that is not quantitatively scorable); two forms of the scale of Attitude toward the Bible (Forms A and B), on which scores range from unqualified affirmation and respect to rejection and disparagement; and two forms of the scale of Attitude toward Sunday Observance, on which scores ranges from support of strict Sunday observance to total opposition to it. Several dozen related scales, checklists, and qualitative questionnaires, likewise intended for use by religious educators but less thoroughly developed than the ones listed above, were eventually published by Chave (1939). The development of the published scales was prompted by Thurstone's short-lived interest in exploring the usefulness of psychophysical methods for measuring a variety of social attitudes. The specific religious content of these scales was provided by collaborators Ernest Chave and C. K. A. Wang.

The 45 randomly ordered items of the Attitude toward the Church Scale were selected from an original list of 130 items on the basis of their content, degree of favorableness ratings, internal consistency, and median rankings. Four items were selected to represent each of 11 class-intervals of the scale; one additional item fell in an extreme, twelfth interval. Scoring is carried out by either of two methods, which reportedly yield substantially the same statistical results. One may calculate the mean scale-value (median ranking, as reported by Thurstone and Chave) of all the items that the subject has endorsed. Alternatively, after ranking the 45 statements according to their reported scale-values, one may calculate the mean rank order of the items endorsed by the individual.

Practical Considerations: The scale, which takes about 15 minutes to complete, can be used with individuals or groups. It may also be given to subjects to take at home. No time limit should be imposed. Subjects are to be told that altered statements will be ignored in the scoring process; each statement must either be endorsed as it stands or be left unchecked. There should also be no discussion of the statements before the questionnaire is completed. The authors recommend offering the respondents the opportunity to remain anonymous if local circumstances make them reluctant to be identified with their own responses.

Norms/Standardization: Instructions accompanying the Attitude toward the Church Scale provide a transformed scale-score for each statement—derived by multiplying the median ranking by 2.5 and rounding to the nearest whole number—and a table of six categories for interpreting the mean scale-scores. These categories range from "strongly favorable to the church" to "strongly antagonistic." The quasi-normative data provided in Thurstone and Chave (1929), in contrast, are based on the original median rankings. The questionnaire was administered to both undergraduate and graduate students at the University of Chicago, to divinity students, and to persons attending the Chicago Forum, a public-interest lecture series sponsored by the Illinois League of Women Voters. The number of respondents ranged from 103 (the divinity students) to 548 (the freshmen). Frequency distributions of scores for each of the groups are presented in both tabular and graphic forms; standard deviations are also provided. The four undergraduate classes and the graduate students showed no striking differences or trends, though there is among them a slight tendency toward biomodality. That tendency was clearer for the respondents at the Chicago Forum, who on the average were less favorable to the church than the other groups but also more variable. The group of divinity students was by far the most favorable as well as the least variable of the seven groups. Similar data are provided according to religious affiliation (Roman Catholics were most favorable, Jews least, and the Protestants fell in between) and sex (women were slightly more favorable than men, a tendency that also appears in the later literature).

Reliability: The exceptionally high reliability of the Attitude toward the Church Scale was calculated by means of the split-half method. To create parallel forms, the researchers first ranked the 45 statements in order of their scale values, from low to high, and then split the successive pairs of statements, alternating the form to which the higher-rank item in each pair was assigned. The extremely unfavorable statement left at the end was included in both forms. The two sets of partial scores were then correlated for two groups of respondents. An initial sample of 100 subjects yielded a correlation of .89, which, corrected by means of the Spearman-Brown formula, produced an estimated reliability of .94 for the full scale. A second group, consisting of 200 university freshmen, yielded comparable reliability coefficients of .85 and .92.

Validity: Reasonably strong evidence for validity is suggested by several findings of Thurstone and Chave. Persons who said that they attended church frequently showed strikingly higher scores than those who did not report frequent attendance. Similarly, persons claiming active church membership scored notably higher than those not reporting it. Furthermore, scale scores correlated .67 with self-ratings on a simple Likert-type scale ranging from "strongly favorable to the church" to "strongly against the church." Describing this moderately high correlation as "fairly satisfactory," Thurstone and Chave note that subjects tended to rate themselves as slightly more favorable to the church on the single rating scale than they proved to be on the more elaborate scale. This tendency, which Thurstone and Chave suspected was the result of social pressure, was particularly notable among those with negative attitudes toward the church. Subsequent research, especially correlations with other religiosity measures (e.g., Wicker, 1971), has added to the evidence for validity.

Location: All of the measures mentioned in this review with the exception of the *Sunday Observance* scale can be found in

Chave, E. J. (1939). *Measure religion: Fifty-two*

experimental forms. Chicago: The University of Chicago Bookstore.

The *Sunday Observance* scale was first published in

Thurstone, L. L. (Ed.) (1931). *The measurement of social attitudes*. Chicago: University of Chicago Press. [a collection of separately printed questionnaires and instructions]

The *Sunday Observance* scale also appears in

Shaw, M. E., & Wright, J. M. (1967). *Scales for the measurement of attitudes* (pp. 97–99). New York: McGraw-Hill.

The chief source on the development and application of the Church scale is:

Thurstone, L. L., & Chave, E. J. (1929). *The measurement of attitude: A psychophysical method and some experiments with a scale for measuring attitude toward the church*. Chicago: University of Chicago Press.

Subsequent Research: More than 30 studies have been carried out using the *Attitude toward the Church* scale, most of them looking for personality and attitudinal correlates, tracing out changes over time, or comparing various subject groups. Whereas few if any significant personality correlates have been found, several researchers have reported a tendency for those with favorable attitudes toward the church to be more conservative, authoritarian, or prejudiced. Jones (1970), in one of the most recent studies to use this scale, found that attitudes toward the church among college students had declined over a 37-year period. The Thurstone scales are seldom used today.

Heber, S. (1996). *Dimensionen der religiosität: Skalen, messomodelle und ergebnisse einer empirisch orientiernten religionspsychlolgie*. Freiburg (Switzerland): Universitätsverlag.

Jones, V. (1970). Attitudes of college students and their changes: A 37-year study. *Genetic Psychology Monographs, 81,* 3–80.

Meredith, G. M. (1968). Personality correlates to religious belief systems. *Psychological Reports, 23,* 1039–1042.

Siegman, A. W. (1962). A cross-cultural investigation of the relationship between religiosity, ethnic prejudice and authoritarianism. *Psychological Reports, 11,* 419–424.

Struening, E., & Spilka, B. (1952). A study of certain social and religious attitudes of university faculty members. *Psychological Newsletter, 43*, 1–17.

Wicker, A. W. (1971). An examination of the "other variables" explanation of attitude-behavior inconsistency. *Journal of Personality and Social Psychology, 19*, 18–30.

Appendix

Attitude toward the Church

Respondents are asked to check every statement with which they fully agree.

1. I think the church is a divine institution, and it commands my highest loyalty and respect.
2. I am neither for nor against the church, but I do not believe that churchgoing will do anyone any harm.
3. I feel the good done by the church is not worth the money and energy spent on it.
4. I regard the church as a monument to human ignorance.
5. I believe that the church is losing ground as education advances.
6. I feel the church is trying to adjust itself to a scientific world and deserves support.
7. The teaching of the church is altogether too superficial to be of interest to me.
8. I feel the church is the greatest agency for the uplift of the world.
9. I think the church has a most important influence in the development of moral habits and attitudes.
10. I believe that the church is necessary, but, like all other human institutions, it has its faults.
11. I regard the church as a harmful institution, breeding narrow-mindedness, fanaticism, and intolerance.
12. The church is too conservative for me, and so I stay away.
13. I believe in the ideals of my church, but I am tired of its denominationalism.
14. I believe that the church furnishes the stimulus for the best leadership of our country.
15. I'm not much against the church, but when I cannot agree with its leaders I stay away.
16. I regard the church as hopelessly allied with reactionary forces.
17. I believe that the church practices the Golden Rule fairly well and has a consequent good influence.
18. I am interested only to the extent of attending church occasionally.
19. I feel the church is ridiculous, for it cannot give examples of what it preaches.
20. Sometimes I feel the church is worthwhile, and sometimes I doubt it.
21. My church is the primary guiding influence in my life.
22. I like the spiritual uplift I get from the church, but I do not agree with its theology.
23. My attitude toward the church is one of neglect due to lack of interest.
24. I believe the church is bound hand and foot with monied interests and does not practice its ideals.
25. I am sympathetic toward the church, but I am not active in its work.

26. I regard the church as a parasite on society.

27. I know too little about any church to express an opinion.

28. I regard the church as the most important institution in the world outside of the home.

29. I am slightly prejudiced against the church and attend only on special occasions.

30. I do not think a man can be honest in his thinking and indorse [sic] what the church teaches.

31. There is much wrong in my church, but I feel it is so important that it is my duty to help improve it.

32. I feel that the church promotes a fine brotherly relationship between people and nations.

33. I think the church is unreservedly stupid and futile.

34. I feel that church attendance is a good index of the nation's morality.

35. I feel the church is petty, easily disturbed by matters of little importance.

36. In the church I find my best companions and express my best self.

37. I believe the church is nonscientific, depending for its influence on fear of God and hell.

38. I am loyal to the church, but I believe its influence is on the decline.

39. It seems absurd to me for a thinking man to be interested in the church.

40. My attitude toward the church is best described as indifference.

41. I believe that anyone who will work in a modern church will appreciate its indispensable value.

42. The church deals in platitudes and is afraid to follow the logic of truth.

43. My attitude toward the church is passive, with a slight tendency to disfavor it.

44. I have a casual interest in the church.

45. I have nothing but contempt for the church.

Thurstone, L. L., & Chave, E. J. (1929). *The measurement of attitude: A psychophysical method and some experiments with a scale for measuring attitude toward the church.* Chicago: University of Chicago Press. Copyright © 1929 University of Chicago Press. Reprinted with permission.

16.3
ATTITUDES TOWARD THE LDS CHURCH SCALE (Hardy, 1949)
Reviewed by Susan Sheffer

Variable: The Attitudes toward the LDS Church Scale was designed to measure the attitudes of members of the Church of Jesus Christ of Latter-Day Saints (hereafter referred to as the LDS Church) toward their church and its religious philosophy. Scale items can be categorized into several subsets. Seven items concern beliefs about religion in general. These items are not specific to the LDS Church. They address issues common to all Christian faiths, such as belief in God, belief in immortality, the divinity of Jesus Christ, and the efficacy of prayer. Other items are tied specifically to the beliefs (12 items) and practices (21 items) of the LDS Church. Other statements in the scale address more general attitudes about the LDS Church (e.g., the influence the church has on personality development, and the role of the church in community life).

Description: This scale consists of two parts. The first part contains 25 items. The five statements within each item have scale values that range from 1 (which reflects a highly favorable attitude) to 11 (which reflects a highly unfavorable attitude). The statements are randomly distributed within each item so that statements do not appear in a consistent order for every item (i.e., the most favorable statements are *not* always listed first followed by the next most favorable with the most unfavorable items always listed last). For each item, respondents are asked to choose the statement that best reflects their attitude. In the second part of the scale, 50 single-statement items are included. Respondents are instructed to place a check mark next to the statements that reflect their attitudes. Each item has a scale value associated with it, ranging potentially from 1 to 11 with "1" representing a highly favorable attitude and "11," a highly unfavorable attitude. Scoring is accomplished by taking the mean of the scale values for the statements chosen. Low scores represent more favorable attitudes and higher scores reflect unfavorable attitudes.

Hardy (1949) suggests the following interpretation of score values:

1–2.5:	Completely orthodox church member
2.5–4.0:	Orthodox member with some reservations
4.0 –6.0:	Rather unorthodox, but with favorable leanings
6.0 or above:	Unorthodox, member in name only

Practical Considerations: This scale is a paper-and-pencil measure that can be administered to a large number of people in a group setting or individually. No special skills are required for scoring or for interpreting the scores. The entire scale should take approximately 15–30 minutes to complete. Many of the items are only applicable to LDS Church members. However, many of the items could potentially be applicable to members of other faiths. Hardy (1949)

cautions that this scale is not appropriate for use with people under 15 years of age.

Norms/Standardization: In order to select the statements to be included in this scale, 80 judges were asked to rate the favorability/unfavorability of 307 statements on a scale of "1" (the statement reflects a highly favorable attitude toward the church) to "11" (the statement reflects a highly unfavorable attitude toward the church). The judges were all members of the LDS Church. Most of them (60%) were volunteers from psychology classes. The rest of the judges were volunteers from the LDS Institute of Religion. Each statement was typed on a separate piece of paper, and each judge was asked to place each statement in one of 11 piles representing the degree of favorableness reflected in the statement. Statements on which there was a high degree of agreement among the judges were retained for the final scale.

The normative sample used to validate this scale consisted of 162 adult members of the LDS Church. Door-to-door solicitation was used to obtain these individuals for participation. The individuals who distributed the scale to the respondents used a rehearsed script to solicit participation. Of the 339 surveys distributed, 162 surveys were returned from 101 different households. Although this appears to reflect a 48% response rate, the actual refusal rate was much higher because many individuals refused to accept a survey. Of the respondents, 63% were female and 37% were male. In general, this sample held extremely favorable attitudes toward the church. More than half of the sample had mean scale scores of 2.5 or less. The highest scale score of any of the respondents was 8.0, with only six individuals having scores at or above the midpoint (6.0). These very positive attitudes of the normative sample should be kept in mind when evaluating this scale.

Reliability: Data from the original normative sample, was used to calculate a split-half reliability correlation coefficient. The correlation coefficient (corrected with the Spearman-Brown formula), reported at .95, is sufficient to indicate high reliability.

Validity: A validity study (Hardy, 1949) was conducted using the normative sample of 162 LDS Church members described above. Each person completed the Attitudes toward the LDS Church Scale as well as a 26-item questionnaire. The questionnaire addressed seven issues that Hardy believed should correlate highly with attitudes toward the church, including: (a) church attendance, (b) church leadership, (c) tithing, (d) avoiding tobacco, (e) avoiding alcohol, (f) avoiding tea and coffee, and (g) frequency of prayer. A composite criterion score on the seven factors was calculated for each participant. A correlation coefficient of .79 was found for the relationship between participants' composite criterion scores and their scores on the attitude scale. This relationship was found to be nonlinear. Hardy (1949) reports that each of the criterion factors individually provides some evidence for the validity of the scale, and overall this study indicates that the scale is measuring what it is intended to measure.

Location:
Hardy, K. R. (1949). *Construction and validation of a scale measuring attitudes toward the LDS church.* Unpublished master's thesis, University of Utah, Salt Lake City.

Shaw, M. E., & Wright, J. M. (1967). *Scales for the measurement of attitudes.* New York: McGraw-Hill.

Recent Research: No subsequent studies which used the Attitudes toward the LDS Church Scale have been located in the published literature.

Appendix

Attitudes and Beliefs of LDS Church Members toward Their Church And Religion

This questionnaire has been prepared for studying the attitudes and beliefs of LDS Church members toward their church and religion. Since we are interested only in your attitude as a member of a group, we prefer that you remain anonymous; so please do not sign your name. Remember that the results of this study will be valuable only insofar as you report your true attitudes. This questionnaire is composed of two sections: one consisting of multiple-choice items, the other made up of single statements.

Section I: Read carefully each of the five statements in the item, then check (x) the statements which best expresses *your own* attitude. Then go on to the next item. If none of the statements in an item expresses your attitude fairly well, you may leave the item blank, but choose one statement whenever possible.

1. I believe that God hears prayers and may at times act upon them. (2.7)
   Prayer is a demonstration of one's ignorance and helplessness. (10.7)
   I'm not sure that God answers prayers but praying does a person good. (6.4)
   I know that God hears and responds to prayers. (1.1)
   Prayer is probably just a waste of effort and time. (10.2)

2. I feel that the Church provides only little opportunity for unselfish activity. (8.4)
   I feel that the Church provides many excellent opportunities for unselfish activity.(2.2)
   I feel that the Church provides some fine opportunities for unselfish activity. (2.6)
   I feel that the Church provides a few good opportunities for unselfish activity. (5.6)
   I feel that the Church provides no opportunities for unselfish activity. (9.7)

3. I believe the MIA program is good in general but there are some weak areas. (5.1)
    I believe the MIA program is failing to influence and appeal in many respects. (8.0)
    I believe the MIA program is a complete waste of time and energy. (10.4)
    I believe the MIA program is "on the rocks" and needs a complete revision. (9.1)
    I believe the MIA program is excellent at all age levels. (1.7)

4. I believe strongly in personal immortality: the continued existence of the individual as a separate, distinct being. (1.4)
    I have grave doubts about the possibility of personal immortality. (9.4)
    I am frequently beset with doubts about personal immortality. (7.8)
    I am at times beset with doubt about personal immortality. (7.0)
    I do not believe in immortality. (10.7)

5. I believe that missionary work is primarily an opportunity to develop the missionary. (5.6)
    I believe that missionary work affords a good opportunity to engage in unselfish activity. (2.5)
    I believe that missionary work is largely a waste of time.(10.0)
    I believe that missionary work is not much more than an opportunity to travel and meet people. (9.7)
    I believe that missionary work is a choice opportunity to serve God and help others. (1.3)

6. I believe that LDS Church members are much poorer neighbors because of the Church's influence. (10.1)
    I believe that LDS Church members are poorer neighbors because of the Church's influence. (9.9)
    I believe that LDS Church members are much better neighbors because of the Church's influence. (2.3)
    I believe that LDS Church members are somewhat better neighbors because of the Church's influence. (3.7)
    I believe that LDS Church members are no better neighbors because of the Church's influence. (7.8)

7. When other people criticize the Church, I generally strongly defend it. (2.3)
    When other people criticize the Church, I generally remain silent. (6.7)
    When other people criticize the Church, I generally passively agree. (8.0)
    When other people criticize the Church, I generally join with them in criticism.(9.7)
    When other people criticize the Church, I generally mildly defend it. (5.3)

8. The good done by the Church is not worth the money and energy spent on it. (9.8)
    There is much energy and money wasted in the Church, but the good done probably compensates for it. (5.9)
    Time and money spent in the Church are a nearly complete waste. (10.1)
    Time and money are nowhere better spent than in the Church. (1.4)
    The time and money invested in the Church are probably well spent. (3.7)

9. I feel that the Relief Society is probably a good thing but I am not impressed with it. (6.1)
    I feel that the Relief Society is a splendid organization. (2.0)
    I feel that the Relief Society is one organization which has little usefulness. (9.3)

I feel that the Relief Society is one of the better auxiliary organizations. (3.2)
I feel that the Relief Society is just a scheme to keep the women from getting dissatisfied with the Church. (9.9)

10. The Word of Wisdom is of little if any practical value. (9.6)
Some of the parts of the Word of Wisdom are good advice, but it certainly is not to be considered a commandment. (6.5)
I believe the Church is absolutely correct in its teachings about the Word of Wisdom. (1.2)
The Word of Wisdom is probably a good thing, but many other things are more important. (5.9)
I believe in the Word of Wisdom, but I think the Church leaders stress it too much. (5.3)

11. I think that the MIA is probably a good thing to have to keep the young people off the streets. (4.4)
I think that the MIA is a Church auxiliary and therefore all those eligible should attend its meetings. (2.6)
I think that the MIA is a fine auxiliary program for those interested in attending. (3.9)
I think that the MIA is something to be disregarded. (9.7)
I think that the MIA is not much better than nothing at all. (9.7)

12. I believe that a few of our present leaders are occasionally inspired by God. (5.4)
I believe that our leaders today are generally good men who are directing the affairs of the Church without supernatural aid. (6.5)
I believe that Church leaders were inspired in Joseph Smith's day but are not any more because of unworthiness. (9.6)
I believe that the Church remains under inspired leadership today. (1.2)
I believe that the Church has never been under inspired leadership. (10.8)

13. In cases where the findings of science seem to conflict with the teachings of the Church, I generally tend to:
favor the Church over scientific findings. (3.8)
defend strongly the findings of science. (9.8)
defend strongly the Church's position. (2.4)
favor neither the Church nor science to any extent. (6.1)
favor the scientific findings over the Church's position. (8.8)

14. I feel that I only rarely benefit when I attend Church meetings. (8.1)
I feel that I usually benefit when I attend Church meetings. (3.5)
I feel that I benefit occasionally when I attend Church meetings.(5.2)
I feel that I never benefit when I attend Church meetings. (9.8)
I feel that I benefit greatly whenever I attend Church meetings. (2.0)

15. I believe that the Church's method of selecting leaders is excellent. (1.5)
I believe that the Church's method of selecting leaders is good but could be improved. (5.4)
I believe that the Church's method of selecting leaders should be entirely revised and a good system substituted for it. (9.7)
I believe that the Church's method of selecting leaders is unscientific and unfair. (9.8)
I believe that the Church's method of selecting leaders is fair but could be greatly improved. (6.1)

16. I believe that the teachings of the Church have neither helped nor hindered me to any extent in enjoying life. (6.3)
I believe that the teachings of the Church have hindered me to an appreciable extent from enjoying life. (9.7)
I believe that the teachings of the Church have greatly hindered me from enjoying life. (10.0)
I believe that the teachings of the Church have helped me to an appreciable extent in enjoying life. (2.7)
I believe that the teachings of the Church have helped me tremendously in enjoying life. (1.7)

17. On the whole, I believe the missionary program is a stupid waste of time and money. (10.7)
On the whole, I believe the missionary program is excellently conceived and carried out. (1.9)
On the whole, I believe the missionary program is falling down in spots but is generally progressing well. (5.4)
On the whole, I believe the missionary program is not doing nearly as well as it should. (8.1)
On the whole, I believe the missionary program is largely wasted effort. (9.9)

18. My attitude toward the Church is passive, with some tendency to disfavor it. (8.1)
I have little but contempt for the Church. (10.9)
The Church is probably a good thing, but I'm not able to get interested in it. (6.4)
I believe that the Church is the most important organization in the world. (1.1)
I believe that the Church is one of our most important organizations. (2.9)

19. I continually receive inspiration from our Church leaders to lead a better daily life. (1.8)
I often am inspired to improve my daily behavior by the messages of our Church leaders. (2.3)
I feel that the leaders of the Church do not deal with the practical problems of life. (8.4)
I feel that the Church authorities deal too infrequently with life's practical problems. (8.0)
I feel that the Church leaders should spend a greater part of their time dealing with life's practical problems. (6.4)

20. I believe that the Church wastes much of its money. (9.2)
I believe that the Church makes only fair use of its money. (6.7)
I believe that the Church makes excellent use of its money. (2.1)
I believe that the Church generally makes good use of its money. (3.7)
I believe that the Church wastes most of its money. (10.0)

21. I feel that the Church has an excellent program for satisfying the needs of its members. (1.9)
I feel that the Church has only a fair program for satisfying the needs of its members. (6.6)
I feel that the Church in general satisfies well the needs of its members. (3.0)
I feel that the Church has a very poor program for satisfying the needs of its members. (9.8)
I feel that the Church has a fairly good program for satisfying the needs of its members. (4.2)

22. When other people argue favorably for the Church, I usually strongly disagree. (10.4)
    When other people argue favorably for the Church, I usually passively agree with them. (5.4)
    When other people argue favorably for the Church, I usually remain silent. (6.3)
    When other people argue favorably for the Church, I usually join actively with them. (3.3)
    When other people argue favorably for the Church, I usually mildly disagree. (8.2)

23. I feel that the tolerance and love fostered by the Church probably balances the intolerance fostered. (6.0)
    I feel that the Church greatly fosters intolerance and bigotry on the part of the members. (10.4)
    I feel that the Church greatly fosters an attitude of love and good will toward nonmembers. (2.2)
    I feel that the tolerance and love fostered by the Church is outweighed by the intolerance and bigotry fostered. (8.8)
    I feel that the Church on the whole fosters tolerance and love, but at times fosters intolerance and bigotry. (6.5)

24. I have strong doubts about the reality of the preexistence. (9.7)
    The reality of the preexistence seems impossible. (10.1)
    I believe strongly in the reality of the preexistence but occasionally have doubts. (4.5)
    The reality of the preexistence seems highly improbable to me. (9.8)
    I believe wholeheartedly in the reality of the preexistence. (1.2)

25. I feel that the Church is greatly declining in influence upon its membership. (8.6)
    I feel that the Church is gaining greatly in influence upon its membership. (2.4)
    I feel that the Church is measurably declining in influence upon its membership. (8.6)
    I feel that the Church is not measurably gaining or declining in influence on its membership. (6.2)
    I feel that the Church is gaining in influence on its membership to a certain degree. (4.2)

Section II: In this section, check (x) *each statement* that expresses your attitude or position fairly well.

1. I believe that Joseph Smith was an inspired prophet of God. (1.1)
2. I believe that the Church is probably justified in denying the Priesthood to the Negroes. (3.4)
3. I believe most of the Church's teachings, but I have doubts about some. (5.7)
4. I believe that the Church has hindered me to some extent from developing my personality. (8.9)
5. I would prefer that my child marry outside the Church. (10.6)
6. I believe that temple work is a fairly important work in the Church. (5.4)
7. I doubt very seriously the existence of God. (10.6)
8. I believe that a couple should generally marry in the temple from the start, but in many cases should marry in the temple later on after trying out civil marriage. (5.4)
9. I believe that the General Authorities are inspired whenever they speak in their capacities, and that the substance of their remarks is binding upon the Church. (1.4)
10. I believe that tithing should be paid only by the more well-to-do members to keep the Church going. (8.4)
11. I believe that a couple should unquestionably marry in the temple when they first marry. (1.4)

12. Too much time is spent on theology and history in our meetings. (7.5)
13. I have a testimony of a sort about the divinity of the Church. (6.2)
14. I feel that the teachings of the Church have helped me to some extent in understanding life. (3.9)
15. I have strong doubts about the possibility of the reuniting of spirit and body. (9.4)
16. The Church asks its members for too much money. (8.6)
17. I would slightly prefer my child to marry in the Church. (5.3)
18. I feel that the Church has hindered me greatly from developing my personality. (10.2)
19. I believe that Joseph Smith actually saw the Father and the Son in a vision. (1.1)
20. On the whole, the Church members are happier people than they would be if they did not belong. (3.1)
21. My belief in God is quite strong, but sometimes I have doubts about His existence. (6.0)
22. I believe that tithing is necessary and that nearly everyone should pay some tithing. (2.5)
23. Our religion has some importance to me, but other things are more important. (7.2)
24. I believe all the teachings of the Church. (1.2)
25. I believe that marriage in the temple is little if any better than civil marriage. (9.6)
26. I would definitely prefer my child to marry in the Church. (2.1)
27. I have a fairly strong testimony of the divinity of the Church, but occasionally have my doubts. (4.7)
28. I believe that the Church is probably not justified in denying the Priesthood to the Negroes. (8.9)
29. I believe that tithing is a useless waste of money. (10.6)
30. I'm not against the Church, but I often can't agree with its leaders. (6.5)
31. I believe that Joseph Smith was a good man with some excellent ideas. (4.0)
32. I believe that a couple should regard temple marriage as a superfluous thing. (10.2)
33. I believe that the body we lay down at death is resurrected. (1.5)
34. I believe the plan of salvation in general, but find it hard to believe some details of the plan. (6.1)
35. Our religion may be important to some, but it is not particularly important to me. (7.6)
36. I am not sure what kind of body we will have when resurrected. (6.3)
37. We have too many sermons in our meetings. (7.7)
38. I believe that Joseph Smith led many people astray by his false doctrines. (10.8)
39. I feel that the Church has helped me to some extent in developing my personality. (4.1)
40. I believe that all eligible Mormon youth should marry in the temple. (1.3)
41. I believe that Joseph Smith's "vision" was simply a deliberate lie to further the ends of a desperate man. (10.9)
42. I have an unshakeable testimony of the divinity of the Church. (1.1)
43. I believe that the General Authorities are never inspired but pool their ideas in deciding the course of the Church. (10.0)
44. I believe wholeheartedly in the principle of tithing. (1.2)
45. I believe in only a few of the Church's teachings. (8.3)
46. I feel that the teachings of the Church have hindered me to some extent from understanding life. (8.7)
47. I believe that our religion is the most important thing in life. (1.1)
48. I believe that Joseph Smith was inspired by God at times and led a good life. (3.9)
49. I do not know whether or not the Church is justified in denying the Priesthood to the Negroes. (6.3)
50. About the only value of temple work is that it keeps some of the old folks occupied. (10.1)

Note: Scale values of each item are indicated in parentheses following that item and should not appear on the inventory when administered.

16.4
CONGREGATION CLIMATE SCALES
(Pargament, Silverman, Johnson, Echemendia, & Snyder, 1983)
Reviewed by Mark S. Rye, Tracey A. Jewell, and Curtis R. Brant

Variable: These scales measure the psychosocial climate of congregations. Congregation climate can be thought of as the "personality" of the church or synagogue (Silverman et al., 1983). More specifically, congregation climate is defined as "psychologically meaningful representations of the church/synagogue" (Pargament et al., 1983, p. 355). Climate theory assumes that climates vary with different settings, that climates are a product of environmental and individual characteristics, and that the relationships between climate, setting, and individuals are reciprocally influential (Pargament et al., 1983).

Description: The authors of the scales identified dimensions of congregation climate by visiting a variety of religious institutions, reviewing literature concerning organizational climate, and conducting structured interviews with clergy and members from Christian and Jewish religious institutions. The following 10 dimensions of congregation climate were identified: Autonomy, Sense of Community, Activity, Social Concern, Openness to Change, Stability, Expressiveness, Order/Clarity, Intrinsic Religious Orientation, and Extrinsic Religious Orientation. Initially, a scale consisting of 15 items was developed for each dimension. The revised scales measure five dimensions of congregation climate (i.e., Openness to Change, Activity, Stability, Organization and Clarity, and Sense of Community), and consist of 10 items each. Respondents are asked to consider how accurately various statements describe their congregation. Items are constructed on a 5-point Likert-type scale with response possibilities ranging from 1 (not at all descriptive) to 5 (completely descriptive). Scores for each dimension are computed by reverse coding negative items, and computing the mean score for each item (i.e., adding the scores of all congregation members on a particular

item and dividing by the number of responses). Item averages are then added together and divided by the total number of items in the scale.

Practical Considerations: The Congregation Climate Scales are easy to administer, score, and interpret. The instructions are straightforward and the items are clearly worded. Items are face valid, and the purpose of each scale is clear (i.e., to assess the climate of the congregation on a particular dimension). There is no ideal score on the CCS, and absolute scores from the questionnaire should be used for interpretation. Higher scores on the CCS indicate a positive congregation climate, whereas lower scores designate aspects of the congregational climate in need of improvement. Confidentiality of responses should be guaranteed in order to increase the chances that congregation members will respond honestly.

Norms/Standardization: The CCS was normed on 13 Christian congregations, but can also be used with synagogues. Five additional congregations (3 Jewish and 2 Protestant) declined to participate. The congregations were diverse in size (range 100 to 6,200), racial composition (4 black and 9 white congregations), denomination (e.g., Baptist, Roman Catholic, African Methodist Evangelical), and average length of membership (range 4–35 years). The sample consisted of 352 members and 13 clergy. Thirty-seven percent of the members were male, 22% were black, and 71% were married. The average member had belonged to the church for 18 years, had some college education, and was 44 years old. This sample was comparable to the total population of the 13 parishes on identifiable characteristics, but no information was available to compare the level of church involvement of the sample to the total population.

Reliability: The Cronbach's alpha coefficients were moderate to moderately high for all scales. The internal consistency estimates for the scales ranged from .69 (Intrinsic) to .83 (Sense of Community). A subsample of participants ($n = 25$) completed the CCS approximately 1 month after the initial administration. Test-retest reliabilities were all acceptable and ranged from .57 (Expressiveness and Autonomy) to .89 (Order/Clarity).

The intercorrelations among the scales were low to moderately high (range .02 to .58) and suggest some shared variance among the scales. The authors felt there was some theoretical overlap between the scales, and thus several revisions were made to the original scales. Five scales (Expressiveness, Social Concern, Autonomy, Intrinsic, and Extrinsic) were dropped, and some items were incorporated into the remaining five scales. The revision resulted in coefficient alphas that were moderately high: Openness to Change, .76; Order/Clarity, .72; Sense of Community, .78; Activity, .77; and Stability, .76. Taken together, these results show the CCS to be a fairly reliable measure.

Validity: Construct and predictive validity were examined by testing 3 hypotheses regarding congregational climate. First, climate scales related differently to different congregations. The CCS discriminated well among the members of the 13 churches, $F(120, 2470) = 6.67$, $p < .001$, and accounted for 97% of the variance in differences among members. Univariate F tests revealed that although all scales discriminated significantly among the churches, the Activity, Stability, Sense of Community, and Openness to Change scales were more discriminating. Homogeneity coefficients revealed that members within a particular congregation have similar perceptions of the climate of their church.

Second, the CCS related to several attributes of the congregations. A multivariate analysis was significant indicating that the

CCS did discriminate congregations based on racial composition, religious identification, and size of the congregation. Furthermore, the CCS explained a moderately high amount of variance ($\eta^2 = .81$) with respect to these attributes.

Finally, congregation climate related to the individual member's level of religiosity, congregation satisfaction, and competence. The CCS was a significant predictor of all three individual characteristics, particularly religiosity (R^2 range .22 to .37) and congregation satisfaction (R^2 range .10 to .39). Each of the scales of the CCS exhibited a different pattern of relationships with the member attributes. For instance, Stability and Openness to Change were positively related to member satisfaction, whereas Sense of Community was positively related to all three attributes.

In conclusion, the CCS seems to validly assess congregation climate. As it accurately distinguishes between congregations and is reasonably associated with institutional as well as individual characteristics, the CCS can be a valuable tool for use in religion research.

Location:
Pargament, K. I., Silverman, W., Johnson, S., Echemendia, R., & Snyder, S. (1983). The psychosocial climate of religious congregations. American *Journal of Community Psychology*, *11*, 351–381.
Scale items are not included in the article.

Subsequent Research:
Pargament, K. I., Echemendia, R. J., Johnson, S., Cook, P., McGath, C., Myers, J. G., & Brannick, M. (1987). The conservative church: Psychosocial advantages and disadvantages. *American Journal of Community Psychology*, *15*, 269–286.
Pargament, K. I., Falgout, K., Ensing, D. S., Reilly, B., Silverman, M., Van Haitsma, K., Olsen, H., & Warren, R. (1991). The congregation development program: Data-based consultation with churches and synagogues. *Professional Psychology: Research and Practice*, *22*, 393–404.
Pargament, K. I., Johnson, S. M., Echemendia, R. J., & Silverman, W. H. (1985). The limits of fit: Examining the implications of person-environment

congruence within different religious settings. *Journal of Community Psychology, 13,* 20–30.

References

Pargament, K. I., Silverman, W., Johnson, S., Echemendia, R., & Snyder, S. (1983). The psy-chosocial climate of religious congregations. *American Journal of Community Psychology, 11,* 351–381.

Silverman, M. K., Pargament, K. I., & Falgout, K. C. (1983). *The congregation development program manual.* Unpublished Manuscript, Bowling Green State University.

Appendix

Congregation Climate Scales

Instructions: The following statements have to do with the climate or unique personality of your church. Each statement may be more or less descriptive of your congregation. Please:

    A. Read each statement carefully.
    B. Think about how descriptive *you feel* the statement is of your church.
    C. Decide whether the statement is

        1 = not at all descriptive

        2 = somewhat descriptive
        3 = pretty much descriptive
        4 = very much descriptive
        5 = completely descriptive

    D. To the right of each statement is a row of five numbers. Please draw a circle around one of the five numbers to show how that statement describes your church.

Openness to Change
Think about how open the members, leaders, and ministers are to changes and new and different ideas in the church. Indicate how well each of the following statements describes *openness to change and different ideas* in your church.

(R)	1.	It is hard to change the church's rules.	1	2	3	4	5
(R)	2.	Members like to leave programs as they are rather than change them.	1	2	3	4	5
(R)	3.	Many members do not want to try new approaches and ideas in the church.	1	2	3	4	5
	4.	The educational programs in the church are often updated to meet changing needs.	1	2	3	4	5
	5.	The ministers often introduce changes to make the the religious services more interesting.	1	2	3	4	5
	6.	Members of this church are willing to change the way things are done to increase involvement in the church.	1	2	3	4	5
	7.	Members are open to differing ideas about religion.	1	2	3	4	5
	8.	Members are willing to share and listen to different points of view.	1	2	3	4	5
(R)	9.	Members of the church avoid discussing controversial topics.	1	2	3	4	5

(R) 10. Our church leaders seem to stay with old traditions   1   2   3   4   5
         rather than listen to new ideas.

Activity
Think about the variety of activities in the church and how much the members support these activities. Indicate how well each of the following statements describes the *activities* in your church.

(R) 11. During services the church is not very crowded.   1   2   3   4   5
    12. In this church, many kinds of educational programs   1   2   3   4   5
         are offered.
    13. In this church, members start new programs if their   1   2   3   4   5
         needs are not being met.
    14. This church has activities daily.   1   2   3   4   5
(R) 15. This church does not offer enough variety in   1   2   3   4   5
         activities to meet the needs of all members.
(R) 16. There are not enough activities (discussion groups,   1   2   3   4   5
         retreats) where members can get to know each
         other better.
    17. Our church offers courses that help members   1   2   3   4   5
         improve their family lives.
(R) 18. Social activities are not very well attended.   1   2   3   4   5
    19. In this church there are enough social activities to   1   2   3   4   5
         meet most members' needs.
(R) 20. Many of our members seldom participate in church   1   2   3   4   5
         activities other than the worship services.

Stability
Think about how secure and stable your church is as an organization. Indicate how well each of the following statements describes the *stability* in your church.

    21. It is usually not a problem finding teachers for   1   2   3   4   5
         religious education classes.
(R) 22. Some church programs have recently been dropped   1   2   3   4   5
         due to lack of interest.
    23. Over the years, our ministers have generally been   1   2   3   4   5
         happy to stay with this church.
    24. More and more members are coming to weekly   1   2   3   4   5
         services.
(R) 25. The members are more concerned with the survival   1   2   3   4   5
         of the church than its growth.
(R) 26. In the past few years, our church has had trouble   1   2   3   4   5
         attracting new members.
(R) 27. It is hard to find enough students to keep church   1   2   3   4   5
         education programs going.
(R) 28. This church has trouble keeping up its facilities   1   2   3   4   5
         due to lack of money.
    29. Enough members can usually be counted on to lead   1   2   3   4   5
         our church programs and activities.
    30. Once a program is begun (such as men's club,   1   2   3   4   5
         Bible study, etc.), it usually continues.

Organization and Clarity
Think about how well the church organizes its activities and decisions. Also, think about how clearly the church communicates to the members. Indicate how well each of the following statements describes the *organization and clarity* in your church.

31.	Our church offers a calendar of activities.	1	2	3	4	5
(R) 32.	Services are sometimes confusing and hard to follow.	1	2	3	4	5
(R) 33.	It is not always clear how decisions are made in this church.	1	2	3	4	5
34.	Our church has clearly stated goals for the future.	1	2	3	4	5
(R) 35.	Members often have trouble finding out what is going on in our church.	1	2	3	4	5
36.	If members are unhappy, there are ways to make complaints known.	1	2	3	4	5
(R) 37.	The religious education classes are not well planned.	1	2	3	4	5
38.	Church rules are easy to understand.	1	2	3	4	5
39.	There are clear steps to follow to become a member of this church.	1	2	3	4	5
(R) 40.	Members often do not understand why church leaders make the decisions the way they do.	1	2	3	4	5

Sense of Community
Think about the closeness, fellowship, and support that members of your church show for each other. Indicate how well each of the following statements describes the *sense of community* in your church.

41.	Members usually introduce themselves to new members.	1	2	3	4	5
42.	The clergy know most of the members by name.	1	2	3	4	5
(R) 43.	After services there is not enough time to talk with the ministers and other members.	1	2	3	4	5
44.	Members treat each other as family (for example, visiting the sick, celebrating anniversaries, etc.).	1	2	3	4	5
45.	Most members are close friends with each other.	1	2	3	4	5
(R) 46.	Members often do not notice the absence of other members.	1	2	3	4	5
47.	Activities make children feel like a part of this church.	1	2	3	4	5
(R) 48.	New members find it hard to be accepted by the congregation.	1	2	3	4	5
(R) 49.	Members have little one-to-one contact with the ministers.	1	2	3	4	5
(R) 50.	Members hardly see each other outside of church.	1	2	3	4	5

(R) = reverse code

Reprinted with permission of authors.

16.5
CONGREGATION SATISFACTION QUESTIONNAIRE
(Silverman, Pargament, Johnson, Echemendia, & Snyder, 1983)

Reviewed by Curtis R. Brant, Tracey A. Jewell, and Mark S. Rye

Variable: This scale measures church and synagogue members' satisfaction with the following dimensions of their religious institutions: religious services, fellow church/synagogue members, church/synagogue leaders, special programs and activities, religious education for children, and religious education for adults. The scale is useful for identifying the specific aspects of the church/synagogue that are not satisfying to members and can help to determine that changes would enable the church/synagogue to better meet the needs of the congregation.

Description: This scale was developed to measure member satisfaction with the church or synagogue. Several dimensions of member satisfaction were initially identified through interviews with clergy and congregation members from Christian and Jewish religious institutions. A content analysis of the tape-recorded interviews resulted in the following eight dimensions, which assessed satisfaction with leaders, members, facilities, services, education, policies, special programs and activities, and clergy. Approximately 20 words or short phrases were initially generated to describe each dimension. The revised scale contains seven dimensions (i.e., religious services, church members, church leaders, special programs and activities, religious education for children, religious education for adults and church facilities). For each dimension, respondents are asked to rate how accurately 10 words or short phrases describe their congregation. Questions are constructed on a 5-point Likert scale with response possibilities ranging from 1 (not at all descriptive) to 5 (completely descriptive). Items include both positive and negative descriptors. Scores for each dimension are computed by reverse coding the negative items, and computing a mean score for each item (i.e., adding the scores of all members on a particular item and dividing by the number of responses).

Item averages are then added together and divided by the total number of items in the scale.

Practical Considerations: The Likert-type item format and the short descriptors for each satisfaction dimension make this questionnaire relatively easy to complete. The instructions and the purpose of the scale (i.e., to measure member satisfaction on a variety of dimensions) are clear. The scale takes no special training to administer, score, or interpret. As there is no ideal score for each of the scales, interpretations can be made using the absolute scores from the questionnaire. Higher scores are indicative of greater satisfaction, whereas lower scores indicate areas in need of improvement to increase member satisfaction. Confidentiality of responses should be guaranteed to help ensure that the questions are answered in a forthright manner.

Norms/Standardization: The CSQ was normed on 13 Christian congregations, but is also applicable with synagogues. Five additional congregations (3 Jewish and 2 Protestant) declined to participate. The congregations were diverse in size (range 100 to 6,200), racial composition (4 black and 9 white congregations), denomination (e.g., Baptist, Roman Catholic, African Methodist Evangelical), and average length of membership (range 4 to 35 years). The sample consisted of 353 members (37% male; 79% white) with a mean age of 44 and average education of some college or trade school. This sample was comparable to the total population of the 13 congregations on identifiable characteristics, but no information was available to compare the level of involvement of the sample to the total population.

Reliability: Internal consistency estimates were moderately high for all scales except the Facilities Scale with an alpha coefficient of .67. Cronbach's alpha coefficients for the other seven scales ranged from .80 (Clergy) to .90 (Education). A subsample of participants ($n = 56$) completed the CSQ 4 weeks after the initial administration. Test-retest reliabilities were all acceptable and ranged from .62 (Clergy) to .82 (Policies).

Several revisions were made to the original scales: the Policies and Clergy Scales were dropped because they did not discriminate between congregations as well as the other scales; additional items were added to some scales (e.g., Facilities) to increase the internal consistency of the scale; the Education Scale was divided to assess the religious education of adults and children separately; and the response options were changed from a 3-point to a 5-point Likert scale to alleviate skewness. The revisions resulted in coefficient alphas that were moderately high: Religious Services, .85; Members, .85; Special Programs and Activities, .79; Child Education, .85; Adult Education, .88; Leaders, .82; and Facilities, .94. The CSQ seems to be reasonably reliable in assessing congregation satisfaction.

Validity: To examine how well the CSQ fits with existing theory and research, the authors investigated the scale's convergent and discriminant validity and how it correlates with demographic variables and other constructs. Along with the CSQ, the participants answered a single item that assessed each of the scale constructs. Correlation matrices were computed between the CSQ and its corresponding single item measure (heteromethod), between the individual CSQ scales (monomethod), and between the single item measures (monomethod).

Convergent validity was established using correlations between each of the scales and its single item counterpart. All correlations were significant ($p < .001$), and ranged from .32 (Facilities) to .43 (Leaders; Clergy).

Using criteria established by Campbell and Fiske (1959), divergent validity was examined by three criteria. (a) Correlations of the same satisfaction construct measured by the two different methods should be higher than the correlation between that

construct and any other construct (measured differently). In the analysis of the CSQ, this criterion was met in 95% of cases. (b) Correlations between the same satisfaction construct measured differently should be higher than the correlation between that construct and any other construct (measured in the same way). Little support was found using this criterion, as it was met only 31% of the time. (c) Kendall's coefficient of concordance was used to examine the pattern (rank order) of correlations in each of the monomethod and heteromethod correlation matrices. The Kendall's Coefficient (.77) was significant, indicating a comparable pattern of correlations between the two methods of assessing church satisfaction. Although the second criterion was not met, the first and third standards provide support for the divergent validity of the instrument.

Each of the scales was significantly correlated with at least one other demographic and/or religiosity measure (i.e., frequency of church activities, frequency of prayer, age, and number of church members known). For instance, satisfaction with religious services was positively related to frequency of church attendance and frequency of prayer outside of church. Furthermore, each of the scales had a relatively different pattern of correlations with other variables, suggesting that the scales measured distinct dimensions of church satisfaction. Social desirability had no influence on these correlations. Overall, the CSQ appears to validly assess congregation satisfaction.

Location:
Silverman, W. H., Pargament, K. I., Johnson, S. M., Echemendia, R. J., & Snyder, S. (1983). Measuring member satisfaction with the church. *Journal of Applied Psychology, 68*, 664–677.
Only sample items are found in the article.

Subsequent Research:
Pargament, K. I., Echemendia, R. J., Johnson, S., Cook, P., McGath, C., Myers, J. G., & Brannick, M. (1987). The conservative church: Psychosocial advantages and disadvantages. *American Journal of Community Psychology, 15*, 269–286.

Pargament, K. I., Falgout, K., Ensing, D. S.,

Reilly, B., Silverman, M., Van Haitsma, K., Olsen, H., & Warren, R. (1991). The congregation development program: Data-based consultation with churches and synagogues. *Professional Psychology: Research and Practice, 22*, 393–404.

Pargament, K. I., Johnson, S. M., Echemendia, R. J., & Silverman, W. H. (1985). The limits of fit: Examining the implications of person-environment congruence within different religious settings. *Journal of Community Psychology, 13*, 20–30.

References

Campbell, D. T., & Fiske, D. W. (1959). Convergence and discriminant validation by the multitrait-multimethod matrix. *Psychological Bulletin, 50*, 81–105.

Silverman, M. K., Pargament, K. I., Falgout, K. C. (1983). *The congregation development program manual.* Unpublished Manuscript, Bowling Green State University.

Appendix

Congregation Satisfaction Questionnaire

Listed below are several words and phrases that may or may not describe a specific area of your church. Please:

    A. Read each word and phrase
    B. Decide whether the word or phrase is
        1 = not at all descriptive
        2 = somewhat descriptive
        3 = pretty much descriptive
        4 = very much descriptive
        5 = completely descriptive
    C. Draw a circle around one of the five numbers before the word or phrase to show the answer you have selected.

Religious Services
Think of the *weekly* religious services at your church. Indicate how well each of the following words describes these services.

Church Members
Think of the majority of the people that you know at your church. Indicate how well each of the following words describes these church members.

Church Leaders
Think about the elected or appointed leaders of your church (do *not* consider each clergy as a leader in this section). Indicate how well each of the following words describes the church leaders.

Religious Services	Church Members	Church Leaders
1 2 3 4 5 Interesting	1 2 3 4 5 Close-minded (R)	1 2 3 4 5 Receptive to new ideas
1 2 3 4 5 Too long (R)	1 2 3 4 5 Uninvolved (R)	
1 2 3 4 5 Comforting	1 2 3 4 5 Supportive	1 2 3 4 5 Creative
1 2 3 4 5 Confusing (R)	1 2 3 4 5 Easy to get to know	1 2 3 4 5 Around when needed
1 2 3 4 5 Inspiring		
1 2 3 4 5 Dull (R)	1 2 3 4 5 Dedicated	1 2 3 4 5 Too set in their ways (R)
1 2 3 4 5 Useful in daily life	1 2 3 4 5 Willing to listen to problems	1 2 3 4 5 Inexperienced (R)
1 2 3 4 5 Not well planned (R)	1 2 3 4 5 Active	1 2 3 4 5 Dedicated
1 2 3 4 5 Not enough variety (R)	1 2 3 4 5 Hard to meet (R)	1 2 3 4 5 Slow to get things done (R)
1 2 3 4 5 Easy to understand	1 2 3 4 5 Prejudiced (R)	1 2 3 4 5 Well informed
	1 2 3 4 5 Complaining (R)	1 2 3 4 5 Not sensitive to members' needs (R)
(R) = reverse code		1 2 3 4 5 Cliquish (R)

*Special Programs
and Activities*

Think about the special programs and activities at your church, such as social events, fundraising activities, programs for helping needy groups, choir groups, etc. Indicate how well each of the following words describes the special programs and activities.

*Religious Education
For Children*

Think about the religious education and training offered by your church for children. Indicate how well each of the following words describes this education and training.

*Religious Education
For Adults*

Think about the religious education and training offered by your church for adults. Indicate how well each of the following words describes this education and training.

1 2 3 4 5 Inadequate (R)	1 2 3 4 5 Well organized
1 2 3 4 5 Hard to get involved in (R)	1 2 3 4 5 Qualified teachers

1 2 3 4 5   Inadequate (R)
1 2 3 4 5   Hard to get
           involved in (R)
1 2 3 4 5   Fun
1 2 3 4 5   Poorly planned
           (R)
1 2 3 4 5   Creative
1 2 3 4 5   Interesting
1 2 3 4 5   Not well
           publicized (R)
1 2 3 4 5   Something for
           everyone
1 2 3 4 5   Not well
           attended (R)
1 2 3 4 5   Well run

1 2 3 4 5   Well organized
1 2 3 4 5   Qualified teachers
1 2 3 4 5   Poorly taught (R)
1 2 3 4 5   Boring (R)
1 2 3 4 5   Interesting
1 2 3 4 5   Poorly attended
           (R)
1 2 3 4 5   Incomplete (R)
1 2 3 4 5   Misbehaving
           students (R)
1 2 3 4 5   Meaningful
1 2 3 4 5   Something for
           all ages

1 2 3 4 5   Qualified
           teachers
1 2 3 4 5   Boring (R)
1 2 3 4 5   Interesting
1 2 3 4 5   Weak (R)
1 2 3 4 5   Well organized
1 2 3 4 5   Poorly attended
           (R)
1 2 3 4 5   Meaningful
1 2 3 4 5   Incomplete (R)
1 2 3 4 5   Poorly taught
           (R)
1 2 3 4 5   Useful in daily
           life

Church Facilities

Think of the facilities of your church, such as the building, grounds, sanctuary, classrooms, etc. Indicate how well each of the following words describes these facilities.

1 2 3 4 5   Pleasant to be in
1 2 3 4 5   Enough parking
1 2 3 4 5   In need of repair (R)
1 2 3 4 5   Neat
1 2 3 4 5   Attractive
1 2 3 4 5   Poorly lit (R)
1 2 3 4 5   Well kept up
1 2 3 4 5   Not big enough (R)
1 2 3 4 5   Unsafe neighborhood (R)
1 2 3 4 5   Too hot or too cold(R)
1 2 3 4 5   Comfortable to be in
1 2 3 4 5   Services are hard to hear (R)

(R) = reverse code

Reprinted with permission of authors.

Chapter 17

Scales of Related Constructs

The scales included for review in this chapter are not, for the most part, measures of religion as much as they are measures that interest psychologists of religion. The scales have been and will continue to be useful measures of constructs that are crucial to the psychological study of religious experience. Certainly we cannot provide reviews of all scales that may be pertinent to the psychology of religion. Given the breadth of the religion variable, almost any psychological construct potentially could be a candidate for serious empirical investigation. Subsequent research will uncover the relationship of new variables with religion, making other measurement tools useful to the investigator of religious experience. What we can provide is a review of established measures that have proven useful in further understanding religious experience.

Clearly, a major construct of relevance to the psychology of religion is locus of control. Two measures of locus of control that appear particularly useful in the study of religious experience are reported here: Levenson's Multidimensional Locus of Control Scales (17.3) and the Religious Locus of Control Scale (17.6) developed by Gabbard and associates.

Two related constructs with clear implications for the scientific study of religion are dogmatism and authoritarianism. Each variable has been operationalized by a measure of immense value to psychologists of religion: Rokeach's Dogmatism Scale (17.1) and Altemeyer's Right-Wing Authoritarianism Scale (17.7).

Psychologists studying religion have thoroughly documented benefits from being religious, for example, a sense of meaning or purpose, a sense of control, and self-esteem. Measures tapping these constructs might include Crumbaugh's Purpose in Life Test (17.4) and the Short Index of Self-Actualization Scale (17.8) by Jones and Crandall.

We may begin to see the development of measures that are useful in studying the applied effects of religion or spirituality on, for example, social issues. One such already existing measure is the Transpersonal Orientation to Learning Scale (17.9) that assesses attitudes toward a transpersonal approach, with its emphasis on developing human spiritual potential, in the field of education.

The other two scales included in this chapter are admittedly hard to categorize, but, nevertheless, may be of value in future research. The Free Will-Determinism Scale (17.2) is self-explanatory as a measure of belief in one of these two philosophical positions. Embree's Religious Association Scale (17.5) is a creative attempt to measure religiosity by asking respondents to provide religious word associations with consonant-vowel-consonant letter combinations.

17.1
THE DOGMATISM SCALE (Rokeach, 1956)[1]
Reviewed by Peter C. Hill

Variable: The Dogmatism Scale measures individual's belief systems on the dimensions of their relative openness or closedness. According to this scale, people with closed belief systems are classified as dogmatic. They are characterized by viewing authority as absolute and the world as threatening (Rokeach, 1960). A person with a closed belief system is quick to reject any opinions or ideas that conflict with his or her accepted view. Such individuals tend to compartmentalize their beliefs in such a way that conflicting concepts from different sources of authority can exist in relative isolation from each other and therefore remain unscrutinized by the believer.

In contrast, an individual with an open belief system respects the power of authority but not to the extent of absolute acceptance. The open eye system is characterized by assessing information from authority in comparison to information from other sources. A person with an open system actively seeks out ideas from other perspectives. Conflicting concepts are not kept in isolation from one another but are tested through application to resolve descrepancies. The open person does not understand the world as threatening.

The fundamental differences between open and closed belief systems is the extent to which the individual relies on absolute authority. Other defining characteristics of openness-closedness are the degree to which conflicting ideas are kept in isolation, the degree of rejection of beliefs that conflict with one's own beliefs, and the extent to which the world is seen as a threatening place.

Description: This scale was developed to measure any type of dogmatism, not just

that of a religious nature. The items were devised in order to measure the general belief system of the respondent and not the specific content of his or her beliefs. The author maintains that the distinction between measuring the general belief orientation versus the specific belief content is the key in separating the Dogmatism Scale from the Authoritarianism, or F, Scale (Adorno et al., 1950). The Dogmatism Scale measures individual intolerance and general authoritarianism.

As originally designed, the Dogmatism Scale contained 57 items (Form A). After four successive revisions (Forms B through E) and the use of 89 different items, the final form (Form E) contains 40 items (see the Appendix). Though all forms are available for research, Form E has been most extensively used and, unless otherwise indicated, is the form discussed in this review. The test is scored on a 6-point scale ranging from +3 to –3, with the 0 point omitted. The respondent indicates relative agreement (to +3) or disagreement (to –3) with each item. For scoring purposes, the scale is converted to a +1 to +7 scale by adding the constant 4 to each item score. The total score on this scale is simply the sum of the scores obtained on all items, with a high score indicating a dogmatic or closed belief system. No items are negatively worded. The range of scores for Form E is 40 to 280. Rokeach maintains that this scale is equally valid for research in the Soviet Union and other Eastern European countries.

Practical Considerations: The test is self-administered and takes approximately 20 minutes to complete. Though the required reading level was not establised, normative data were collected not only from college students but also from British workers at an automotive plant and from a VA domiciliary. No other special instructions or administrator skills are necessary.

[1]Though not a direct measure of religious identity or experience, this scale taps a construct that may be of interest to researchers in the psychology of religion. A more complete analysis of the standardized normative data may be found in Robinson and Shaver (1973).

Norms/Standardization: Normative data (reported in Rokeach, 1960) for the first four versions of the scale included three separate samples from Michigan State University (one group for Form A; two groups for Form C), a sample from two New York City colleges (Form B), a group from Purdue University (Form C), and British students from University College in London and Birbeck College (Form D). Form E involved samples again from the University College in London and Birbeck College, five sample groups from Ohio State University, a sample from Michigan State University, and three samples of destitute veterans from a New York State VA domicilary. The normative data are thus based on a wide variety of respondents.

The total Form E sample consisted of 508 individuals. Mean scores for this version ranged from a low of 141.3 (one sample of Ohio State students) to a high of 183.2 (one sample of veterans). Among American college students only, the range was far more restricted (141.3 to 143.8). English students scored higher (152.8) than American students but this may be due, in part, to the existence of Communist students found in the British college sample who scored higher in dogmatism than other political groups (Rokeach, 1960, p. 91). Standard deviations for Form E were quite consistent among the sample groups, ranging from 22.1 to 28.2.

Reliability: One purpose of the scale's revisions was to increase reliablility (Rokeach, 1960). The highest reliability coefficient (.91) was found in Form D. Form E, the form used as the basis of review here, had reliability coefficients ranging from .68 to .93 among the various normative samples. Rokeach (1960) maintains that these reliabilities are satisfactory given the broad range of items, many apparently unrelated to each other, covered by the scale (p. 90).

Validity: The method of "Known Groups," a form of concurrent validity, was used to assess the validity of this scale. Two studies, which obtained apparently contradictory results, were conducted. In the first study graduate faculty in departments other than psychology at Michigan State University were asked to select nonpsychology graduate students whom they would describe as having either open or closed belief systems as defined by Rokeach. Sixteen subjects judged by their professors to be high in dogmatism and 13 subjects judged to be low were selected and paid for their participation. The students were administered the Dogmatism Scale along with the Opinionation Scale (Rokeach, 1956), the Authoritarian (F) Scale (Adorno et al., 1950), and the Ethnocentrism (E) Scale (Adorno et al., 1950). The results showed no difference between the two groups on any of the scales.

The second study was carried out in the same fashion as the first except psychology students selected the subjects from acquaintances of theirs who were not studying psychology. Ten subjects judged to be extremely high in dogmatism and ten that were judged to be extremely low in dogmatism were used. The results showed a highly significant difference between the two groups (p = .01) in the predicted direction.

The author, although admitting there may be other reasons, accounts for these different findings by suggesting that the student-professor relationship produces a "masking" effect on the professors' judgments. Students may be more guarded in their interactions with professors than with peers, mixing a respectful attitude with an enlightened facade.

Location:
   Rokeach, M. (1956). *The open and closed mind.* New York: BasicBooks.

Subsequent Research:
   Gilmore, S. K. (1969). Personality differences between high and low dogmatism groups of Pentecostal believers. *Journal for the Scientific Study of Religion, 8,* 161–166.
   Hoge, D. R., & Carroll, J. W. (1973). Religiosity and prejudice in northern and southern churches. *Journal for the Scientific Study of Religion, 12,* 181–197.
   Kilpatrick, D. G., Sutker, L. W., Sutker, P. B. (1970). Dogmatism, religion, and religiosity: A review and re-evaluation. *Psychological Reports, 26,* 15–22.
   Mangis, M. W. (1995). Religious beliefs, dogmatism, and attitudes toward women. *Journal of Psychology and Christianity, 14*(1), 13–25.

Stricklan, B. R., & Weddell, S. C. (1972). Religious orientation, radical prejudice, and dogmatism: A study of Baptists and Unitarians. *Journal for the Scientific Study of Religion, 11,* 395–400.

References

Adorno, T. W., Frenkel-Burnswik, E., Levinson, D. J., & Sanford, R. N. (1950). *The authoritarian personality.* New York: W. W. Norton.

Appendix

Dogmatism Scale (Form E)

Please indicate the degree to which you agree or disagree with each statement using the following rating scale.

−3 = strongly disagree	+1 = slightly agree
−2 = disagree	+2 = agree
−1 = slightly disagree	+3 = strongly agree
0 = neutral	

1. The United States and Russia have just about nothing in common.

2. The highest form of government is a democracy, and the highest form of democracy is a government run by those who are most intelligent.

3. Even though freedom of speech for all groups is a worthwhile goal, it is unfortunately necessary to restrict the freedom of certain political groups.

4. It is only natural that a person would have a much better acquaintance with ideas he believes in than with ideas he opposes.

5. Man on his own is a helpless and miserable creature.

6. Fundamentally, the world we live in is a pretty lonesome place.

7. Most people just don't give a "damn" for others.

8. I'd like it if I could find someone who would tell me how to solve my personal problems.

9. It is only natural for a person to be rather fearful of the future.

10. There is so much to be done and so little time to do it in.

11. Once I get wound up in a heated discussion, I just can't stop.

12. In a discussion I often find it necessary to repeat myself several times to make sure I am being understood.

13. In a heated discussion I generally become so absorbed in what I am going to say that I forget to listen to what the others are saying.

14. It is better to be a dead hero than a live coward.

15. While I don't even like to admit this even to myself, my secret ambition is to become a great man, like Einstein or Beethoven or Shakespeare.

16. The main thing in life is for a person to want to do something important.

17. If given the chance, I would do something of great benefit to the world.

18. In the history of mankind there have probably been just a handful of really great thinkers.

19. There are a number of people I have come to hate because of things they stand for.

20. A man who does not believe in some great cause has not really lived.

21. It is only when a person devotes himself to an ideal or cause that life becomes meaningful.

22. Of all the different philosophies that exist in this world there is probably only one that is correct.

23. A person who gets enthusiastic about too many causes is likely to be a pretty "wishy-washy" sort of person.

24. To compromise with our political opponents is dangerous because it usually leads to a betrayal of our own side.

25. When it comes to differences of opinion in religion, we must be careful not to compromise with those who believe differently from the way we do.

26. In times like these, a person must be pretty selfish if he considers primarily his own happiness.

27. The worst crime a person could commit is to attack publicly the people who believe the same things he does.

28. In times like these it is often necessary to be more on guard against ideas put out by people or groups in one's own camp than by those in the opposing camp.

29. A group which tolerates too many differences of opinion among its own members cannot exist for long.

30. There are two kinds of people in this world: those who are for the truth and those who are against the truth.

31. My blood boils whenever a person stubbornly refuses to admit he is wrong.

32. A person who thinks primarily of his own happiness is beneath contempt.

33. Most of the ideas that get printed nowadays aren't worth the paper they are printed on.

34. In this complicated world of ours the only way we can know what's going on is to rely on leaders or experts who can be trusted.

35. It is often desirable to reserve judgment about what's going on until one has had a chance to hear the opinions of those one respects.

36. In the long run the best way to live is to pick friends and associates whose tastes and beliefs are the same as one's own.

37. The present is all too often full of unhappiness. It is only the future that counts.

38. If a man is to accomplish his mission in life, it is sometimes necessary to gamble "all or nothing at all."

39. Unfortunately a good many people with whom I have discussed important social and moral problems don't really understand what's going on.

40. Most people just don't know what's good for them.

Rokeach, M. (1956). *The open and closed mind.* New York: BasicBooks. Copyright © 1956 by Basic-Books, Reprinted with permission of BasicBooks, a subsidiary of Perseus Books Goup, LLC.

17.2
FREE WILL-DETERMINISM SCALE (Stroessner & Green, 1990)
Reviewed by Randie L. Timpe

Variable: The Free Will-Determinism Scale measures the degree to which an individual believes in free will or determinism. Originally, philosophers and theologians held that free will and determinism were discrete categories of a dichotomy. Early social scientists modified it to be a unidimensional continuum with free will and determinism being opposite end anchors. Eventually social scientists recognized that the existence of free will or determinism was metaphysical and thus beyond empirical proof; however, they recognized that the degree to which an individual believes in free will or determinism affects the individual's actions, attitudes, and attributions. Several studies by Viney, Waldman, and colleagues (e.g., Viney, Waldman, & Barchilon, 1982) questioned the simplicity of the unidimensional nature of the belief system; they concluded that the free will-determinism belief system was multidimensional. The type of determinism may be conditioned by fundamental religious and philosophical factors or by operative psychosocial conditions.

The absence of determinism might suggest either free will or a nonlawful universe in which fate, chaos, or random forces operate to influence an individual's action. That is, determinism has preconditions of external control *and* order. Free-will has preconditions of internal control but no operative involvement of nonlawful entities as fate, luck, or chaos. In a capricious universe, neither free will nor determinism makes sense.

Description: The Free Will-Determinism Scale is a 19-item scale with some items adapted from earlier work by Viney, Waldman, and Barchilon (1982). The items are presented in a Likert-type format with responses ranging from (1) "strongly agree" to (9) "strongly disagree."

The scale yields three scores. Some items assess religious-philosophical determinism, "the belief that a force such as God or fate acts to control our behavior" (Stroessner & Green, 1990, p. 791). Others measure psychosocial determinism, "the belief that environmental factors determine our behavior" (Stroessner & Green, 1990, p. 791). The libertarianism items measure the role that free will and choice play in actions and outcomes.

Practical Considerations: The scale is an easy-to-administer paper-and-pencil instrument. The language is straightforward and simple. The scoring system utilizes numerical indicators of agreement-disagreement presented in a Likert format. The scale is appropriate for individuals of normal intelligence from the teen years on. The scale items do not address the issue of genetic or biological determinants of behaviors. This is a shortfall of the present scale.

Norms/Standardization: The original study was broad in that 507 students provided the data; the study was narrow in that the range of diversity was somewhat restricted: students attending a private liberal arts sponsored by a mainline Protestant denomination located in the midwestern United States.

Reliability: Stroessner and Green (1990) conducted a factor analysis (principal axes with varimax rotation) to determine the internal structure of the 19-item scale. Three primary factors were found, each conforming to one of the predicted dimensions. Each item loaded on only one factor; two items that contributed to no factor were not scored and were dropped from further consideration.

Stroessner and Green (1990) reported reliability in terms of internal consistency. The alpha coefficient for the six religious-philosophical determinism items was .87. The seven items relating to psychosocial determinism produced an alpha coefficient of .64. An alpha coefficient of .69 was reported for the four items regarding libertarianism.

No other measures of reliability were reported.

Test-retest reliability should be easy to establish with the type of items included in the scale.

Validity: The items are transparent and thus lack of face validity is of no problem to respondents.

No attribution bias was found in the study. Respondents judging self made the same type of judgment (i.e., punitiveness, rehabilitation, locus of control) as the respondents judging another. This represents a case or scale in which the fundamental attribution error was not reported. This in itself is unique.

The relationships between types of determinism and locus of control were interesting, yet unpredicted. Libertarians and religious-philosophical determinists exhibited more internal locus of control than did psychosocial determinists. Individuals endorsing a religious-philosophical deterministic belief exhibited more external locus of control than did those low in the belief. These findings hint for construct validity. The relationship to punitiveness for actions was mixed: individuals with extreme views in both directions were more punitive than individuals favoring a moderate belief.

Location:
Stroessner, S. J., & Green, C. W. (1990). Effects of belief in free will or determinism on attitudes toward punishment and locus of control. *Journal of Social Psychology*, *130*, 789–799.

Subsequent Research: The authors have not conducted further research using the scale, nor are they aware of other researchers who have employed the scale in their research. The scale and questions that the issue of free will determinism raises provide a potentially rich source of future research with issues relating to such diverse aspects of personality as religious experience, locus of control, attribution of responsibility and blame, and the limitations of self-control.

References

Stroessner, S. J., & Green, C. W. (1990). Effects of belief in free will or determinism on attitudes toward punishment and locus of control. *Journal of Social Psychology*, *130*, 789–799.

Viney, W., Waldman, D. A., & Barchilon, J. (1982). Attitudes toward punishment in relation to beliefs in free will and determinism. *Human Relations*, *35*, 939–950.

Appendix

Free Will-Determination Scale

Respondents are asked to rate their degree of agreement with each item on a 9-point Likert scale in which 1 denotes "strongly agree" and 9 denotes "strongly disagree."

1. My exercise of free will is limited by my upbringing.
2. Because of my background influences, I have no real free will.
3. I will have free will all of my life.
4. I have free will in life, regardless of group expectations or pressures.
5. My behaviors are determined by conditioning and life experiences.
6. My choices are limited by God's plan for my life.
7. My wealth, class, race, and gender determine my decisions and behavior.
8. My choices are constrained by God.
9. I am free to make choices in my life regardless of social conditions.
10. I have total free will.
11. My free will is limited by such social conditions as wealth, career, and class.
12. My decisions fit into and thus are limited by a larger plan.

13. My present behavior is totally a result of my childhood experiences.
14. God's will determines the choices I make.
15. God has my life planned out.
16. My behaviors are limited by my background.
17. When things are going well for me, I consider it due to a run of good luck.

Three subscales were constructed on the basis of loadings in a factor analysis. The score on "religious-philosophical determinism" is determined by summing the responses to items 6, 8, 12, 14, 15, and 17. The "libertarianism" score is determined by summing the responses to items 3, 4, 9, and 10. The score on "psychosocial determinism" is the sum of responses on items 1, 2, 5, 7, 11, 13, and 16. The score on the belief in determinism is calculated by reverse scoring and summing on items 3, 4, 9, and 10.

Stroessner, S. J., & Green, C. W. (1990). Effects of beliefs in free will or determinism on attitudes toward punishment and locus of control. *Journal of Social Psychology, 130,* 789–799. Reprinted with permission of the Helen Dwight Reid Educational Foundation. Published by Heldref Publications, 1319 Eighteenth St., N.W., Washington, D.C. 20036-1802. Copyright © 1990.

17.3
MULTIDIMENSIONAL LOCUS OF CONTROL SCALES
(Levenson, 1974, 1981; Levenson & Miller, 1976)
Reviewed by Gary L. Welton

Variable: The Multidimensional Locus of Control Scale addresses the generalized expectancy to perceive one's outcomes or reinforcements either as being contingent on one's own behaviors (internal control) or as the result of forces beyond one's control (external control). This multidimensional scale goes one step further by making a distinction between two types of external control. A chance Locus of Control (LOC) is the belief in the basic unordered and random nature of the world. A powerful others LOC is the belief that other people control one's reinforcers. Hence, this measure includes three scales: internal (I), powerful others (P), and chance (C) LOC.

Description: Rotter's (1966) Internal vs. External Control scale was the early standard in measuring LOC. There was concern, however, that Rotter's scale failed to distinguish between two distinct types of external control, which might be experienced very differently on a psychological level, and that to be external was not always undesirable or necessarily representative of maladjustment.

Levenson based the development of her items on Rotter's (1966) work, with four important distinctions. First, the items are presented with an agree-disagree response format, instead of a forced-choice format. This enables the three dimensions to be more statistically independent. Second, all items refer to one's own belief structure, rather than to the belief of people in general. Third, the three scales are constructed in such as way that there is a high degree of parallelism in every three-item set. Fourth, the items demonstrate negligible correlations with the Marlowe-Crowne Social Desirability Scale (.09, .04, and –.10, respectively [Levenson, 1981]; and .19, –.20, and –.09 [Walkey, 1979] for the I, P, and C scales).

According to the latest publication of the scale (Levenson, 1981), the test is scored on a six point scale ranging from +3 to –3 with the 0 point omitted. The respondent indicates relative agreement or disagreement with each item. The responses are summed, and a constant of 24 is added, to create a range of scores from 0 to 48 on each of the three scales.

Practical Considerations: The scales are brief and straight forward paper-and-pencil measures. Nevertheless, researchers have sometimes altered items to make the scales more appropriate for particular groups. For example, Levenson (1973) replaced one item in her research of psychiatric patients, and Wenzel (1993) altered or replaced seven items in her research of homelessness.

There have been frequent complaints with the measures of LOC for use with religious respondents. The measures tend to assume that a belief in God control is similar to an external belief, and generally do not allow a respondent to distinguish God control from other types of control. Recent research by Welton, Adkins, Ingle, and Dixon (1996) deals with these concerns by altering several of Levenson's items and adding a God control scale to the instrument. This revision is included in the appendix to this review.

Norms/Standardization: The Levenson scales have been used extensively. In her review of the literature (Levenson, 1981), Levenson listed 53 samples, testing 4510 subjects. For the internal LOC scale, the mean was 34.97 (using a possible range of 0 to 48). The 38 samples that reported standard deviations reported a range from 3.11 to 10.5, with a median of 6.76. For the powerful others LOC scale, the mean was 20.06. The standard deviations ranged from 4.67 to 13.1, with a median of 8.44. For the chance LOC scale, the mean was 19.54. The standard deviations ranged from 5.60 to 13.76, with a median of 8.52.

Reliability: Table 1 provides a summary of coefficient alpha results for the three scales. The data indicates adequate internal consistency for the powerful others and chance scales and marginal reliability for the internal scale.

Table 1
Internal Consistency of Levenson's Scales

Study	N	I	P	C
Hyman et al. (1991)	161	.63	.73	.69
Levenson (1973)	165	.67	.82	.79
Levenson (1974)	96	.64	.77	.78
Walkey (1979)	156	.60	.70	.72
Wallston et al. (1978)	115	.51	.72	.73

Walkey (1979) argues that items 4 and 9, both on the internal scale, do not correlate well with the other items of that scale. He suggests that they be removed or replaced. Removing the items would improve the coefficient alpha in his data from .60 to .69.

Test-retest reliability numbers have been similar to the above, with one exception. Levenson (1973) found reliabilities after five days of .08, .74, and .78, respectively. The reliability for the internal measure is, of course, problematic. However, it must be noted that the subjects were recent admissions to a psychiatric hospital, who may experience a major change in perceptions of control after a short adjustment period. Levenson (1974) found reliabilities after one week of .64, .74, and .78. Lee (1976) found reliabilities after seven weeks of .66, .62, and .73.

Validity: Research has demonstrated that the Internal Scale is unique from the other two. Correlations between the I scale and the others range from −.25 to .19. The two external scales, on the other hand, are related to each other, with correlations from .41 to .60 (Levenson, 1981). Levenson (1974) argues that although these two scales are correlated, they relate differently to other variables, and therefore they should not be grouped together as a unified measure of externality.

Factor analyses of the 24 items have been conducted by Levenson (1974), Walkey (1979), and Ward and Thomas (1985). They are unanimous in their conclusion that the three-factor structure is appropriate. Walkey, for example, found that seven of the P items loaded on Factor 1, six of the I items loaded on Factor 2, five of the C items loaded on Factor 3, and two of the C items loaded on both Factors 1 and 3 (reflecting the correlation between the P and C scales). The other six items did not load on any factor.

Because there has been extensive research with this measure, there is ample evidence about how the scales relate to other measures. The evidence is summarized in Table 2.

Table 2
Validity Data on the Levenson Scales

Measure	Correlations with		
Study and Scale	I	P	C
Faith Scale (Tipton et al., 1980)			
Faith in Technology			−.27
Faith in God			−.20
Faith in Self	.36		
Fear of Powerlessness Scale (Good et al., 1973)			
Royal & Rutherford (1994)	−.10	.45	.52
Internal vs. External Control (Rotter, 1966)			
Levenson (1972)	−.41	.25	.56
Donovan & O'Leary (1978)	−.15	.24	.44
Hall et al. (1977)	−.32	.22	.43
Multidimensional Health Locus of Control (Wallston et al., 1978)			
Internal Health LOC	.43		
Powerful Others Health LOC			.37
Chance Health LOC			.59
Multidimensional-Multiattributional Causality Scales (Lefcourt, 1981)			
Hyman et al. (1991)			
Achievement scale, internal attributions	.24	.08	.07
Achievement scale, external attributions	−.09	.25	.41
Affiliation scale, internal attributions	.27	.12	.04
Affiliation scale, external attributions	.00	.36	.56
Opinions about Mental Illness scale (Cohen & Struening, 1962)			
Morrison et al. (1994)			
Mental Hygiene Ideology factor	.37		
Benevolence factor		−.23	
Religious Problem-Solving Scales (Pargament et al., 1988)			
Self-directing	.33		.08
Deferring	−.44		.18
Collaborative	−.16		−.06
Trent Attributional Profile (Wong & Sproule, 1984)			
Hyman et al. (1991)			
Internal attributions	.28	−.09	−.13
External attributions	−.14	.28	.38

As a whole, these numbers show that the three scales relate to other variables in expected manners, although many of the correlations are only moderate in strength.

Location:

Levenson, H. (1974). Activism and powerful others: Distinctions within the concept of internal-external control. *Journal of Personality Assessment, 38,* 377–383.

Levenson, H. (1981). Differentiating among in-

ternality, powerful others, and chance. In H. M. Lefcourt (Ed.), *Research with the locus of control construct* (Vol. 1, pp. 15–63). New York: Academic Press.

Levenson, H., & Miller, J. (1976). Multidimensional locus of control in sociopolitical activists of conservative and liberal ideologies. *Journal of Personality and Social Psychology, 33,* 199–208.

Subsequent Research:

Degelman, D., & Lynn, D. (1995). The development and preliminary validation of the Belief in Divine Intervention Scale. *Journal of Psychology and Theology*, *23*, 37–44.

Pargament, K. I., Brannick, M. T., Adamakos, H., Ensing, D. S., Kelemen, M. L., Warren, R. K., Falgout, K., Cook, P., & Myers, J. (1987). Indiscriminate proreligiousness: Conceptualization and measurement. *Journal for the Scientific Study of Religion*, *26*, 182–200.

Pargament, K. I., & DeRosa, D. V. (1985). What was that sermon about? Predicting memory for religious messages from cognitive psychology theory. *Journal for the Scientific Study of Religion*, *24*, 180–193.

Pargament, K. I., Kennell, J., Hathaway, W., Grevengoed, N., Newman, J., & Jones, W. (1988). Religion and the problem-solving process: Three styles of coping. *Journal for the Scientific Study of Religion*, *27*, 90–104.

Richards, D. G. (1991). The phenomenology and psychological correlates of verbal prayer. *Journal of Psychology and Theology*, *19*, 354–363.

References

Cohen, J., & Struening, E. L. (1962) Opinions about mental illness in the personnel of two large mental hospitals. *Journal of Abnormal and Social Psychology*, *64*, 349–360.

Donovan, D. M., & O'Leary, M. R. (1978). The drinking related locus of control scale. *Journal of Studies in Alcohol*, *94*, 759–884.

Good, L. R., Good, K. C., & Golden, S. B., Jr. (1973). An objective measure of the motive to avoid powerlessness. *Psychological Reports*, *33*, 616–618.

Hall, E., Joesting, J., & Woods, M. J. (1977). Relationships among measures of locus of control for black and white students. *Psychological Reports*, *40*, 59–62.

Hyman, G. J., Stanley, R., & Burrows, G. D. (1991). The relationship between three multidimensional locus of control scales. *Educational and Psychological Measurement*, *51*, 403–412.

Lee, F. (1976). *A study of sex differences in locus of control, tennis, expectancy for success and tennis achievement.* Unpublished doctoral dissertation, University of Oregon.

Lefcourt, H. M. (1981). The construction and development of the multidimensional-multiattributional causality scales. In H. M. Lefcourt (Ed.), *Research with the locus of control construct* (Vol. 1). New York: Academic Press.

Levenson, H. (1972). Distinctions within the concept of internal-external control: Development of a new scale. *Proceedings of the 80th Annual Convention of the American Psychological Association*, 261–262.

Levenson, H. (1973). Multidimensional locus of control in psychiatric patients. *Journal of Consulting and Clinical Psychology*, *41*, 397–404.

Levenson, H. (1974). Activism and powerful others: Distinctions within the concept of internal–external control. *Journal of Personality Assessment*, *38*, 377–383.

Levenson, H. (1981). Differentiating among internality, powerful others, and chance. In H. M. Lefcourt (Ed.), *Research with the locus of control construct* (Vol. 1, pp. 15–63). New York: Academic Press.

Levenson, H., & Miller, J. (1976). Multidimensional locus of control in sociopolitical activists of conservative and liberal ideologies. *Journal of Personality and Social Psychology*, *33*, 199–208.

Morrison, M., de Man, A. F., & Drumheller, A. (1994). Multidimensional locus of control and attitudes toward mental illness. *Perceptual and Motor Skills*, *78*, 1281–1282.

Pargament, K. I., Kennell, J., Hathaway, W., Grevengoed, N., Newman, J., & Jones, W. (1988). Religion and the problem-solving process: Three styles of coping. *Journal for the Scientific Study of Religion*, *27*, 90–104.

Rotter, J. B. (1966). Generalized expectancies for internal versus external control of reinforcement. *Psychological Mongraphs*, *80* (Whole No. 609).

Royal, K. G., & Rutherford, D. (1994). Construct validation study of the fear of powerlessness scale. *Psychological Reports*, *75*, 1529–1530.

Tipton, R. M., Harrison, B. M., & Mahoney, J. (1980). Faith and locus of control. *Psychological Reports*, *46*, 1151–1154.

Walkey, F. H. (1979). Internal control, powerful others, and chance: A confirmation of Levenson's factor structure. *Journal of Personality Assessment*, *43*, 532–535.

Wallston, K. A., Wallston, B. S., & DeVellis, R. (1978). Development of the multidimensional health locus of control (MHLC) scales. *Health Education Monographs*, *6*, 160–170.

Ward, L. C., & Thomas, L. L. (1985). Interrelationships of locus of control content dimensions and hopelessness. *Journal of Clinical Psychology*, *41*, 517–520.

Welton, G. L., Adkins, A. G., Ingle, S. L., & Dixon, W. A. (1996). God control: The fourth dimension. *Journal of Psychology and Theology*, *24*, 13–25.

Wenzel, S. L. (1993). Gender, ethnic group, and

homelessness as predictors of locus of control among job training participants. *Journal of Social Psychology*, *133*, 495–505.

Wong, P. T. P., & Sproule, C. F. (1984). An attri-butional analysis of the locus of control construct and the Trent Attributional Profile (TAP). In H. M. Lefcourt (Ed.), *Research with the locus of control contruct* (Vol. 3). New York: Academic Press.

Appendix A

Multidimensional Locus of Control Scales: Original Version

Directions: Following is a series of attitude statements. Each represents a commonly held opinion. There are no right or wrong answers. You will probably agree with some items and disagree with others. We are interested in the extent to which you agree or disagree with such matters of opinion.

Read each statement carefully. Then indicate the extent to which you agree or disagree using the following responses:

If you agree strongly, respond +3
If you agree somewhat, respond +2
If you agree slightly, respond +1

If you disagree slightly, respond –1
If you disagree somewhat, respond –2
If you disagree strongly, respond –3

First impressions are usually best. Read each statement, decide if you agree or disagree and the strength of your opinion, and then respond accordingly. GIVE YOUR OPINION ON EVERY STATEMENT.

If you find that the numbers to be used in answering do not adequately reflect your own opinion, use the one that is closest to the way you feel. Thank you.

Scoring and Interpretation for the I, P, and C Scales

There are three separate scales used to measure one's locus of control: Internal Scale, Powerful Others Scale, and Chance Scale. There are eight items on each of the three scales, which are presented to the subject as one unified attitude scale of 24 items. The specific content areas mentioned in the items are counterbalanced so as to appear equally often for all three dimensions.

To score each scale, add up the points of the circled answers for the items appropriate for that scale. (The three scales are identified by the letters "I," "P," and "C.") Add to this sum +24. The possible range on each scale is from 0 to 48. Each subject receives three scores indicative of his or her locus of control on the three dimensions of I, P, and C. Empirically, a person could score high or low on all three dimensions.

1. (I) Whether or not I get to be a leader depends mostly on my ability.

2. (C) To a great extent my life is controlled by accidental happenings.

3. (P) I feel like what happens in my life is mostly determined by powerful people.

4. (I) Whether or not I get into a car accident depends mostly on how good a driver I am.

5. (I) When I make plans, I am almost certain to make them work.

6. (C) Often there is no chance of protecting my personal interests from bad luck happenings.

7. (C)   When I get what I want, it is usually because I'm lucky.

8. (P)   Although I might have good ability, I will not be given leadership responsibility without appealing to those in positions of power.

9. (I)   How many friends I have depends on how nice a person I am.

10. (C)   I have often found that what is going to happen will happen.

11. (P)   My life is chiefly controlled by powerful others.

12. (C)   Whether or not I get into a car accident is mostly a matter of luck.

13. (P)   People like myself have very little chance of protecting our personal interests when they conflict with those of strong pressure groups.

14. (C)   It's not always wise for me to plan too far ahead because many things turn out to be a matter of good or bad fortune.

15. (P)   Getting what I want requires pleasing those people above me.

16. (C)   Whether or not I get to be a leader depends on whether I'm lucky enough to be in the right place at the right time.

17. (P)   If important people were to decide they didn't like me, I probably wouldn't make many friends.

18. (I)   I can pretty much determine what will happen in my life.

19. (I)   I am usually able to protect my personal interests.

20. (P)   Whether or not I get into a car accident depends mostly on the other driver.

21. (I)   When I get what I want, it's usually because I worked hard for it.

22. (P)   In order to have my plans work, I make sure that they fit in with the desires of people who have power over me.

23. (I)   My life is determined by my own actions.

24. (C)   It's chiefly a matter of fate whether or not I have a few friends or many friends.

Appendix B

Multidimensional Locus of Control Scales: God Control Revision

The following revision (Welton et al., 1996) of Levenson's (1974) Multidimensional Locus of Control Scales includes two altered items (#10 and #15) and eight new items. The eight new items are indicated by a "G" and form the God Control Scale. Follow the directions for the original scale.

1. (I)   Whether or not I get to be a leader depends mostly on my ability.

2. (C)   To a great extent my life is controlled by accidental happenings.

3. (G)   What happens in my life is determined by God's purpose.

4. (P)   I feel like what happens in my life is mostly determined by powerful people.

5. (I)   Whether or not I get into a car accident depends mostly on how good a driver I am.

6. (I)   When I make plans, I am almost certain to make them work.

7. (G)   My life is primarily controlled by God.

8. (C)   Often there is no chance of protecting my personal interests from bad luck happenings.

9. (C)   When I get what I want, it is usually because I'm lucky.

10. (P) Although I might have good ability, I will not be given leadership responsibility without appealing to people in positions of power.

11. (G) When I am anxious, I rely on God for inner peace.

12. (I) How many friends I have depends on how nice a person I am.

13. (C) I have often found that what is going to happen will happen.

14. (G) Whether or not I get into a car accident depends on God's plans.

15. (P) My life is chiefly controlled by people who are more powerful than me.

16. (C) Whether or not I get into a car accident is mostly a matter of luck.

17. (P) People like myself have very little chance of protecting our personal interests when they conflict with those of strong pressure groups.

18. (G) In order to have my plans work, I make sure they fit in with the commands of God.

19. (C) It's not always wise for me to plan too far ahead because many things turn out to be a matter of good or bad fortune.

20. (P) Getting what I want requires pleasing those people above me.

21. (C) Whether or not I get to be a leader depends on whether I'm lucky enough to be in the right place at the right time.

22. (P) If important people were to decide they didn't like me, I probably wouldn't make many friends.

23. (I) I can pretty much determine what will happen in my life.

24. (G) When things don't go my way, I ought to pray.

25. (I) I am usually able to protect my personal interests.

26. (G) When faced with a difficult decision, I depend on God to guide my feelings and actions.

27. (P) Whether or not I get into a car accident depends mostly on the other driver.

28. (I) When I get what I want, it's usually because I worked hard for it.

29. (G) When good things happen to me it is because of God's blessing.

30. (P) In order to have my plans work, I make sure that they fit in with the desires of people who have power over me.

31. (I) My life is determined by my own actions.

32. (C) It's chiefly a matter of fate whether or not I have a few friends or many friends.

Levenson, H. (1974). Activism and powerful others: Distinctions within the concept of internal-external locus of control. *Journal of Personality Assessment, 38,* 377–383. Copyright © 1974 by the American Psychological Association. Reprinted with permission.

17.4
PURPOSE IN LIFE TEST (Crumbaugh & Maholick, 1964)
Reviewed by Daniel N. McIntosh

Variable: The Purpose in Life Test (PIL) was developed to assess the degree to which an individual possesses meaning, understood as the opposite of *existential frustration* or a lack of fulfillment of the *will to meaning* (e.g., Frankl, 1955, 1960). Higher scores on the PIL are taken to indicate less of a presence of *existential vacuum*, which is a state of emptiness, manifested chiefly by boredom (Crumbaugh & Henrion, 1988). Frankl viewed having meaning as a fundamental human motivation. Possession of a substantial degree of this is seen as a typical condition for normally functioning individuals, and one that may be absent in clinical populations. Note that the PIL is designed to measure the extent to which meaning has been found, not the motivation to find such purpose.

A theoretical connection between religion and purpose in life is made by Frankl (1955, 1958), as he indicates that this need can best be understood as spiritual, although it is not clear how the term "spiritual" is used. This association is empirically supported with findings reported by Crandall and Rasmussen (1975). Respondents who scored high on the PIL indicated that salvation was a relatively higher value on the Rokeach (1967) Value Survey than did individuals scoring lower on the PIL. Further, they found the PIL to be significantly correlated with having a more intrinsic orientation to religion, but independent of an extrinsic orientation (see, e.g., Allport & Ross, 1967, for discussion of these religious orientations).

The PIL has been the primary self-administered assessment of purpose and meaning in life (Chamberlain & Zika, 1988; Crumbaugh & Henrion, 1988; Dyck, 1987). New measures are being developed, but none yet has the empirical foundation of the PIL. In their evaluation of measures of meaning, Chamberlain and Zika (1987) concluded that the best general measure was the

PIL but that there are a number of components to meaning in life that should be more carefully evaluated. This is consistent with the view expressed by Crumbaugh and Henrion (1988) that as new measures are developed, it may become clear which tool is best suited for various purposes.

Description: The PIL has three parts. The objectively scored Part A (which is the part most frequently used for research and is the focus of this review) is composed of 20 items. Respondents indicate on seven point scales how much they experience the content described by the item. Each item has its own anchor points. For example, one item begins with the stem, "I am usually:" and subjects respond on a 1–7 scale, anchored by "completely bored" for 1 and "exuberant, enthusiastic" for 7. Four is labeled "neutral" on all scales. These responses are summed to determine the overall score.

Part B is 13 incomplete sentences to which the respondent provides completion. Part C has the individual write about his or her "life goals, ambitions, hopes, future plans, what has provided them meaning in the past, and what could motivate them in the future" (Crumbaugh & Henrion, 1988, p. 78).

Practical Considerations: This self-administered questionnaire requires a fifth-grade reading level ability. No time limit is typically given, but most respondents finish in less than 15 minutes (Crumbaugh & Henrion, 1988).

Because the Part A format has each item utilize different end points for the scale, it may be more confusing to respondents than a measure that repeatedly uses the same end points; this format also makes the test more awkward and bulky when used in group administrations (Harlow, Newcomb, & Bentler, 1987).

Parts B and C must be evaluated by a clinician and are ignored for most research purposes. Attempts to quantify these latter sections have added little to what is gained by part A (Crumbaugh & Henrion, 1988).

Norms/Standardization: The original study used five groups assumed to vary in life purpose to establish norms on the PIL (Crumbaugh & Maholick, 1964). Specifically, running from "high purpose" on down were (a) Junior League women and men from Frankl's Harvard seminar, (b) Harvard undergraduates, (c) outpatients of various psychologists and psychiatrists in Georgia, (d) outpatients of a nonprofit psychiatric clinic in Georgia, and (e) hospitalized alcoholic patients. Using these groups, Crumbaugh and Maholick (1964) reported means of 119 for nonpatients and 99 for patients. Combining these people with a large number of others, Crumbaugh (1968) reported the mean for normals as 112.4 (SD = 14.1) and for patients as 92.6 (SD = 21.3). Motivated business and professional people (M = 118.9) and trainees for a religious order (M = 119.3) score high on the PIL (Crumbaugh, Raphael, & Shrader, 1970). Prison inmates have twice been found to score, around 100 (Reker, 1977). Crumbaugh and Henrion (1988) give a "cutting score" of 102 between clinical and normal populations. The estimated standard deviation noted is 19. Scores at or above 113 indicate a definite presence of purpose and meaning, and scores at or below 91 indicate a lack of clear meaning or purpose.

The age of respondent should be considered when interpreting results. Adolescent scores (ages 13–19, M = 104.1) have been found to be lower than scores of older groups (25 and older, M = 111.5; Meier & Edwards, 1974), although associations with age are not always found (Crumbaugh & Henrion, 1988). Seldom have gender differences been statistically significant (Crumbaugh & Henrion, 1988; Meier & Edwards, 1974). Educational level is not clearly related to PIL scores.

Reliability: The original split-half reliability reported using the odd-even method was .81, Spearman-Brown corrected to .90 (Crumbaugh & Maholick, 1964). In a sample of inmates, Reker (1977) reported a solid split-half reliability of .85, corrected to .92; this was also found by Crumbaugh (1968) in a sample of 120 "active and leading Protestant parishioners" (p. 75). Test-retest correlations have been .68 (12 week; Reker, 1977), .79 (6 week; Reker & Cousins, 1979) and .83 (1 week; Meier & Edwards, 1974).

Validity: Though there is room for questions, the PIL appears to be a reasonably valid measure. That the PIL assesses something of psychological significance is supported by its ability to predict membership in clinical versus nonclinical populations. For example, it distinguishes between psychological patients and nonpatients (Crumbaugh, 1968; Crumbaugh & Maholick, 1964), and inmates and noninmates (Reker, 1977). It is also correlated with therapists' (r = .38) and clergy's (r = .47) ratings of individuals' possession of meaning or purpose in life (Crumbaugh, 1968). Further, a large number of studies have found it to be moderately associated with variables that the logotherapy suggests are tied to meaning.

The PIL is not identical to other constructs, as indicated by its low association with other measures. For example, Crumbaugh and Maholick (1964) report that scores on the PIL are not highly related to MMPI scores. It is also only moderately related to the desire to find meaning (Crumbaugh, 1977). In the original study, the highest association was with depression (r = .39); a follow-up study with normal and psychiatric patients found a higher association with depression (r = .65; Crumbaugh, 1968). The correlation between the PIL and depression is so consistent that Dyck (1987) views the PIL as primarily an indirect measure of depression. This connection may be what is responsible for its relation to clinical status.

There is some debate about the degree to which the PIL is contaminated by a socially desirable response bias. Crumbaugh and Henrion (1988) report several studies showing mixed results. As the PIL is self-administered, there is certainly the ability for individuals to manipulate their answers. They point out that more competitive situations may be more likely to bring out this association.

When the PIL is factor analyzed, it appears to be made up of a number of discernable components (e.g., Dyck, 1987; Reker & Cousins, 1979). This suggests a lack of conceptual coherence in the tool (Dyck, 1987). If used, it should be kept in mind that only a portion of the measure may be directly assessing purpose in life and that other components (e.g., depression) may be influencing the degree of association of the PIL to other variables of interest.

The PIL was developed using primarily white American respondents, and it is based on a culturally Western philosophical view. Thus there are questions about its validity among other populations. Researchers have begun the task of translating and modifying the instrument for such work, and the degree to which this can be successful likely will be known soon. This concern should be considered when using the specified cut-off scores. As one's sample diverges from the population used to create those such scores, the meaning of a particular score becomes more ambiguous.

In sum, the PIL is empirically associated with theoretically linked variables, and it is not identical to what is measured by other means. However, a more complete evaluation of the coherence and validity of the test is needed.

Location: The PIL was originally described in Crumbaugh and Maholick (1964). The PIL and manual are published by Psychometric Affiliates [P.O. Box 807, Murfreesboro, TN 37133], and can be ordered from them, or the Institute of Logotherapy in Berkeley, California. The version below was taken from Nackord and Fabry (1983).

Subsequent Research:
Florian, V. (1989–1990). Meaning and purpose in life of bereaved parents whose son fell during active military service. *Omega, 20*, 91–102.

Shek, D. T. L. (1994). Meaning in life and adjustment amongst midlife parents in Hong Kong. *The International Forum for Logotherapy, 17*, 102–107.

Waisberg, J. L. (1994). Purpose in life and outcome of treatment for alcohol dependence. *British Journal of Clinical Psychology, 33*, 49–63.

References

Allport, G. W., & Ross, J. M. (1967). Personal religious orientation and prejudice. *Journal of Personality and Social Psychology, 5*, 432–443.

Chamberlain, K., & Zika, S. (1988). Measuring meaning in life: An examination of three scales. *Personality and Individual Differences, 9*, 589–596.

Crandall, J. E., & Rasmussen, R. D. (1975). Purpose in life as related to specific values. *Journal of Clinical Psychology, 31*, 483–485.

Crumbaugh, J. C. (1968). Cross-validation of Purpose-in-Life test based on Frankl's concepts. *Journal of Individual Psychology, 24*, 74–81.

Crumbaugh, J. C. (1977). The seeking of noetic goals test (SONG): A complementary scale to the Purpose in Life Test (PIL). *Journal of Clinical Psychology, 33*, 900–907.

Crumbaugh, J. C., & Henrion, R. (1988). The PIL Test: Administration, interpretation, uses theory and critique. *The International Forum for Logotherapy, 11*, 76–88.

Crumbaugh, J. C., & Maholick, L. T. (1964). An experimental study in existentialism: The psychometric approach to Frankl's concept of noogenic neurosis. *Journal of Clinical Psychology, 20*, 200–207.

Crumbaugh, J. C., Raphael, S. M., & Shrader, R. R. (1970). Frankl's will to meaning in a religious order. *Journal of Clinical Psychology, 26*, 206–207.

Dyck, M. J. (1987). Assessing logotherapeutic constructs: Conceptual and psychometric status of the purpose in life and seeking of noetic goals tests. *Clinical Psychology Review, 7*, 439–447.

Frankl, V. E. (1955). *The doctor and the soul.* NY: Alfred A. Knopf.

Frankl, V. E. (1958). The will to meaning. *Journal of Pastoral Care, 12*, 82–88.

Frankl, V. E. (1960). Beyond self-actualization and self-expression. *Journal of Existential Psychiatry, 1*, 5–20.

Harlow, L. L., Newcomb, M. D., & Bentler, P. M. (1987). Purpose in Life Test assessment using latent variable methods. *Journal of Clinical Psychology, 26*, 235–236.

Meier, A., & Edwards, H. (1974). Purpose-in-Life Test: Age and sex differences. *Journal of Clinical Psychology, 30*, 384–386.

Nackord, E. J., Jr., & Fabry, J. (1983). A college test of logotherapeutic concepts. *The International Forum for Logotherapy, 6*, 117–122.

Reker, G. T. (1977). The Purpose-in-Life Test in an inmate population: An empirical investigation. *Journal of Clinical Psychology, 33*, 688–693.

Reker, G. T., & Cousins, J. B. (1979). Factor structure, construct validity and reliability of the Seeking of Noetic Goals (SONG) and Purpose in Life (PIL) Tests. *Journal of Clinical Psychology, 35*, 85–91.

Rokeach, M. (1967). *Value survey*. Sunnyvale, CA: Halgren Tests.

Appendix

Purpose in Life Test, Part A

Please complete each item by marking a single response.

1. I am usually:
   1   2   3   4   5   6   7
   completely   exuberant,
   bored   enthusiastic

2. Life to me seems:
   1   2   3   4   5   6   7
   completely   always
   routine   exciting

3. In life I have:
   1   2   3   4   5   6   7
   no goals or   very clear
   aims at all   goals and aims

4. My personal existence is:
   1   2   3   4   5   6   7
   utterly   very purposeful
   meaningless   and meaningful
   without purpose

5. Every day is:
   1   2   3   4   5   6   7
   exactly   constantly
   the same   new and different

6. If I could choose, I would:
   1   2   3   4   5   6   7
   prefer never   like nine more
   to have been   lives just like
   born   this one

7. After retiring, I would:
   1   2   3   4   5   6   7
   loaf   do some of the
   completely   exciting things
   the rest of my life   I have always
                                                                     wanted to do

8. In achieving life goals, I have:

    1   2   3   4   5   6   7
    made no   progressed to
    progress   complete
    whatsoever   fulfillment

9. My life is:

    1   2   3   4   5   6   7
    empty, filled   running over
    only with   with exciting
    despair   good things

10. If I should die today, I would feel that my life has been:

    1   2   3   4   5   6   7
    completely   very
    worthless   worthwhile

11. In thinking of my life; I:

    1   2   3   4   5   6   7
    often wonder   always see a
    why I exist   reason for my
                                                                     being here

12. As I view the world in relation to my life, the world:

    1   2   3   4   5   6   7
    completely   fits meaningfully
    confuses me   with my life

13. I am a:

    1   2   3   4   5   6   7
    very   very
    irresponsible   responsible
    person   person

14. Concerning man's freedom to make his own choices, I believe man is:

    1   2   3   4   5   6   7
    completely   absolutely free
    bound by   to make all life
    limitations of   choices
    heredity and
    environment

15. With regard to death, I am:

    1   2   3   4   5   6   7
    unprepared   prepared and
    and   unafraid
    frightened

16. With regard to suicide, I have:

    1   2   3   4   5   6   7
    thought of it   never given it
    seriously as   a second thought
    a way out

17. I regard my ability to find a meaning, purpose, or mission in life as:
    1   2   3   4   5   6   7
    practically   very great
    none

18. My life is:
    1   2   3   4   5   6   7
    out of my   in my hands and
    hands and   I am in control
    controlled by   of it
    external factors

19. Facing my daily tasks is:
    1   2   3   4   5   6   7
    a painful   a source of
    and boring   pleasure and
    experience   satisfaction

20. I have discovered:
    1   2   3   4   5   6   7
    no mission   clear-cut goals
    or purpose in   and a satisfying
    life   life purpose

Copyright © by Psychometric Affiliates, P.O. Box 807, Murfreesboro, TN 37133.

Reprinted with permission of the author and publisher.

17.5
RELIGIOUS ASSOCIATION SCALE (Embree, 1970, 1973)
Reviewed by Bernard Spilka and Kevin L. Ladd

Variable: The Religious Association Scale (RAS) measures religiosity as an "ability" rather than a personality predisposition. The stress is on performance: what a person does rather than who he or she is.

Description: The final version of this measure of individual religiosity is based on associations to 25 consonant-vowel-consonant (CVC) letter combinations or trigrams. Respondents are explicitly requested to give a religious word association to each of the CVCs and then to use that word in a sentence. Even when participants are unable to offer a religious association, they are instructed to provide any association that they can make. Associations were initially scored as 1 = nonreligious; 2 = religious; 3 =

clearly religious. This procedure was later modified to assign a score of 1 for religious content and a score of 0 if such was not present. A total religiosity score is thus computed.

Practical Considerations: Scoring requires only minor training, and this paper-and-pencil test is easily adminstered in group settings. It is recommended that this instrument be administered to participants prior to any other measures concerned with religion in order to obtain responses untainted by order effects.

Norms/Standardization: Embree (1970) initially scaled 280 CVCs for religious association value (RAV) and then selected 80 that elicited RAVs in more than 50% of the responses. The final short form version consisted of 25 trigrams with RAVs ranging from 50 to 64 percent in RAV. This was done to maximize response variance. The RAS was developed on undergraduate students and has not been employed with non-college populations. A total of 270 undergraduates served in the various development and validation studies.

Reliability: Internal consistency reliability coefficients range from .90 to 97; .96 and .97 are reported for the 80-item version, and .90 and .92 for the 25 item short form. Interscorer reliability yielded a coefficient of .93. Odd-even internal consistency for the associations for the 80-item scale was .97. Apparently the RAS can be objectively scored in a highly reliable manner.

Validity: A principal components analysis with varimax rotation of the RAS score with four other religious measures and an index of scholastic ability showed it loaded .38 and .58 on the two factors that resulted. On one of these factors, ability loaded very highly. Hence, there is the suggestion that intellectual capacity may influence the RAS. Correlationally, the 80-item RAS associates positively and significantly with a number of objective scales of religiosity. These coefficients tend to be low to moderate in strength, implying that the RAS

might be assessing an aspect of religiosity that is not found in most traditional measures of this phenomenon. The 25-item short form is independent of academic (intellectual) ability but correlates positively and significantly with a variety of scales of religious conservatism plus intrinsic religious motivation. Except for the latter, RAS scores are independent of the subscales in the Omnibus Personality Inventory, as well as the Edwards Social Desirability Scale.

That this instrument assesses some aspect of religious commitment is evident, but further work to more precisely define what is being measured is necessary. Unfortunately, little subsequent work has employed this scale.

Location:
Embree, R. A. (1970). The religious association scale as an "abilities" measure of the religious factor in personality. *Journal for the Scientific Study of Religion*, 9, 299–302

Embree, R. A. (1973). The religious association scale: A preliminary validation study. *Journal for the Scientific Study of Religion*, 12, 223–226.

Embree, R. A. (undated). *Religious Association Scale (Short form)*.

Embree, R. A. (undated). *An interpretation of the short form revision of the Religious Association Scale*. (The last two unpublished papers are available from Dr. R. A. Embree, 926 Third Ave. S. E., Le Mars, Iowa 51031.)

Subsequent Research: None.

Appendix

Religious Association Scale

Instructions. This Scale is designed to measure social attitudes. Look at each nonsense syllable and pronounce it to yourself silently. Is the nonsense syllable a word or does it sound like a word you associate with religion—a biblical character, place, idea, church or church teaching? Write that word in the small blank next to the syllable. Then use the word in a short complete sentence. If you do not associate the nonsense syllable with religion, then write the word you do associate with the nonsense syllable. Use that word in a short sentence. Leave no blanks.

Study the examples below, then turn the sheet over and begin.

Examples:
RAB *Rabbi* A Rabbi is a religious leader in the Jewish faith.
QAK *Quaker* The Quaker religion is mentioned in American history books.

TYR *Martyr* Paul was a Christian martyr.

(Below are given the full 80 nonsense syllables for the long form, along with their Religious Association Values. The final 25 in the short form are denoted by an (*).

CVC	RAV Value	CVC	RAV Value	CVC	RAV Value	CVC	RAV Value
RAB	91	SAR	78	LIB	58	VOW	84
MOS	92	SOR	63	WOM	85	ZEL	53
ZEK	77	MIR	76	PYR	63	SAQ	55
LUT	67	REQ	53	SEK	66	BEY*	51
RYT*	55	REN	56	LOF*	57	HYM	95
HEV	87	SEC	67	NAK*	50	SAH	86
JER	95	TYR	66	YEW*	64	LYZ	51
TYM*	52	WUN*	51	ZAC	74	CYR	65
JOL*	60	LUS*	64	LAS*	63	MUT	55
LUK	89	LUR*	58	RAL	55	SYP	56
MIZ*	51	GIB	51	MEC	73	VER*	64
GES*	59	NOH	93	GAV	68	CYP	59
NUW*	51	TOR*	55	LOH*	55	SYG	55
LAV*	58	LUZ	50	MER	90	LUF	65
BOD	71	GOL	84	CYN	79	BEM*	51
LYD	66	WIK*	50	MYR	74	KOW	55
DES	66	REY	57	DIV	76	LOR*	63
GEN	93	MIC*	57	FOL	71	HEB	78
COR*	61	MOH	71	SEM	71	PYL*	52
QAK	51	KOD	55	WAL	53	ROZ*	52

The RAVs assume a decimal. The CVCs are in random order as they appear on the scales. The values are for males and females combined.

General Setup (first 2 items)

	Word	Sentence
1.	RYT_____	_____
2.	TYM_____	_____

Embree, R. A. (1970). The religious association scale as an "abilities" measure of the religious factor in personality. *Journal for the Scientific Study of Religion, 9,* 299–302. Copyright © 1970, Journal for the Scientific Study of Religion. Reprinted with permission.

17.6
RELIGIOUS LOCUS OF CONTROL SCALE
(Gabbard, Howard, & Tageson, 1986)

Reviewed by Gary L. Welton

Variable: The Religious Locus of Control Scale is a revision of Rotter's (1966) Internal vs. External Control Scale that measures the extent to which people believe that control of their lives is in their own hands (internal) or that outcomes are beyond their own control (external). This particular revision addresses the concern that the strong chance, luck, and fate terminology of the Rotter scale may result in reduced appropriateness for strongly religious groups.

Table 1
Correlations among Various Measures of Locus of Control

	Original Version	Religious Revision	Neutral Revision
Levenson Chance LOC	.48	.37	.38
Levenson Powerful Others LOC	.33	.30	.32
Levenson Internal LOC	−.43	−.43	−.40
Dies Projective LOC	.00	−.07	.00
Nowicki-Duke LOC	.18	.16	.14

Note. High scores on all measures, except for the Levenson Internal LOC measure, indicate an external locus of control. Total number of subjects was 299.

Description: These two scales are revisions of Rotter's (1966) Internal vs. External Control Scale. Subjects are asked in a forced-choice format to indicate which of two statements (one of which reflects external control, the other, internal control) more closely represents their own thoughts. The complete instrument contains 29 items, including six distracters. Hence, only 23 of the items are scored. One's score is the number of external items selected. The location of the internal and external responses vary, such that 12 of the external options appear first in the pair, and 11 of the external options are last.

Eight of the original pairs of items included terminology on one or both statements relating to chance, using the words "accidental happenings," "chance," "fate," "flipping a coin," "luck," and "right breaks." The authors were concerned that religious individuals might be drawn to the internal items, not because they themselves are internal in beliefs but because they reject the notion of impersonal arbitrary control that is implied by such terms.

Hence, these items were rewritten to minimize such connotations. In the religious revision, the authors substituted references to God control, for the most part, in place of these references to chance. They inserted the terms "fortune," "God's help," "other powerful forces," "providence," "spiritual assistance," "spiritual guidance," "spiritual powers," "supernatural forces," and "supernatural happenings." The substitution of God words for the external control terms of chance and fate implies that God control has been interpreted as a type of external control.

In the neutral revision, they inserted alternatives for the same items, which largely exclude both the chance and fate connotation and the religious terminology. In the neutral version, they substitute using the words "fortune," "happenings which they can't understand," "no other forces," "powerful others," "providence," and "providential forces."

They argued that the religious revision produced a more valid measure for religious individuals than the original scale. In the end, however, they concluded that the neutral version could be used universally, for either religious or general populations.

Practical Considerations: The forced-choice format is sometimes difficult for subjects. When there are two items that describe oneself equally well (or equally poorly) it can become difficult and confusing for the respondent. Otherwise, this paper-and-pencil measure poses no particular problem. The face validity of the scored items is high. The inclusion of the six distracters is an attempt to disguise the nature of the instrument.

Norms/Standardization: Two samples were tested. The religious sample included 115 adults who belonged to two midwestern congregations of a Christian fundamentalist group. The general sample included 184 undergraduate students attending a state university in the same community. The two samples differed significantly in level of religiosity (p < .001), based on a brief religiosity measure. Subjects completed all three internal vs. external versions, as well as the Multidimensional Locus of Control Scales (Levenson, 1974), the Dies Projective Measure of Locus of Control (Dies, 1968), and the Nowicki-Duke Locus of Control Scale (Nowicki & Duke, 1974).

For the religious sample, the means for the original version, religious revision, and neutral revision were 7.23, 11.09, and 9.80 with standard deviations of 3.39, 3.05, and 3.63. For the general sample, the means were 10.40, 11.26, and 10.93 with standard deviations of 4.32, 4.08, and 4.17.

Reliability: No reliability information was reported.

Validity: Because the two revisions share 15 of 23 items with each other and with the original scale, it is not surprising that these three measures have high intercorrelations. The average correlations between the original and religious revision was .84; between the original and the neutral revision was .90; and between the two revisions was .91.

Of greater importance is the relationship between the revisions and other measures of locus of control. The average correlations for these relationships are listed in Table 1.

These numbers indicate moderate consistency with the frequently used Levenson (1974) scales. They also demonstrate a lack of correlation with the Dies (1968) and the Nowicki and Duke (1974) measures. These two measures, however, are used much less frequently and are probably not the best of standards themselves. Hence, overall, these numbers are encouraging.

The authors also included validity numbers based on a confirmatory factor analysis. This analysis, however, suffered from a failure to account for the artificial correlations between the original and revised scales, given the high item overlap. Hence, this approach was not very useful.

Location:
Gabbard, C. E., Howard, G. S., & Tageson, C. W. (1986). Assessing locus of control with religious populations. *Journal of Research in Personality*, *20*, 292–308. (For the complete original scale, see Rotter, J. B. (1966). Generalized expectancies for internal versus external control of reinforcement. *Psychological Monographs*, *80* (Whole No. 609).

Subsequent Research: None.

References

Dies, R. R. (1968). Development of a projective measure of perceived locus of control. *Journal of Projective Techniques and Personality Assessment*, *32*, 487–490.

Gabbard, C. E., Howard, G. S., & Tageson, C. W. (1986). Assessing locus of control with religious populations. *Journal of Research in Personality*, *20*, 292–308.

Levenson, H. (1974). Activism and powerful others: Distinctions within the concept of internal-external control. *Journal of Personality Assessment*, *38*, 377–383.

Nowicki, S., & Duke, M. P. (1974). A locus of control scale for noncollege as well as college students. *Journal of Personality Assessment*, *38*, 136–137.

Rotter, J. B. (1966). Generalized expectancies for internal versus external control of reinforcement. *Psychological Monographs*, *80* (Whole No. 609).

Appendix A

Internal vs. External Control
Religious Revision

The following revision of Rotter's (1966) measure of Internal vs. External Control includes eight altered items (Gabbard, Howard, & Tageson, 1986). Subjects are to select the statement with which they more strongly agree. One's score is the total number of underlined choices (i.e., external items) endorsed. The scale includes six filler items that are not scored (where neither option is underlined).

1. a.   Children get into trouble because their parents punish them too much.
   b.   The trouble with most children nowadays is that their parents are too easy with them.
2. *a.*   Many of the unhappy things in people's lives are partly due to forces of spiritual powers.
   b.   People's misfortunes result from the mistakes they make.
3. a.   One of the major reasons why we have wars is because people don't take enough interest in politics.
   b.   There will always be wars, no matter how hard people try to prevent them.
4. a.   In the long run people get the respect they deserve in this world.
   b.   Unfortunately, an individual's worth often passes unrecognized no matter how hard he tries.
5. a.   The idea that teachers are unfair to students is nonsense.
   b.   Most students don't realize the extent to which their grades are influenced by accidental happenings.
6. *a.*   Without God's help, one cannot be an effective leader.
   b.   Capable people who fail to become leaders have not taken advantage of their opportunities.
7. *a.*   No matter how hard you try, some people just don't like you.
   b.   People who can't get others to like them don't understand how to get along with others.
8. a.   Heredity plays the major role in determining one's personality.
   b.   It is one's experiences in life which determine what one is like.
9. *a.*   I have often found that what is going to happen will happen.
   b.*   Trusting to spiritual assistance has never turned out as well for me as making a decision to take a definite course of action.
10. a.   In the case of the well-prepared student there is rarely if ever such a thing as an unfair test.
    b.   Many times exam questions tend to be so unrelated to course work that studying is really useless.
11. a.*   Becoming a success is a matter of hard work; no other powerful forces are at work.
    b.   Getting a good job depends mainly on being in the right place at the right time.
12. a.   The average citizen can have an influence in government decisions.
    b.   This world is run by the few people in power, and there is not much the little guy can do about it.
13. a.   When I make plans, I am almost certain that I can make them work.
    b.   It is not always wise to plan too far ahead because many things turn out to be a matter of good or bad fortune anyhow.
14. a.   There are certain people who are just no good.
    b.   There is some good in everybody.
15. a.*   In my case getting what I want has little or nothing to do with spiritual guidance.
    b.*   Many times we might just as well decide what to do by relying on powerful others.
16. *a.*   Who gets to be the boss often depends on who was fortunate enough or was chosen to be in the right place first.
    b.*   Getting people to do the right thing depends on ability; powerful spiritual forces have little or nothing to do with it.

17. *a.* As far as world affairs are concerned, most of us are the victims of forces we can neither understand nor control.
    b. By taking an active part in political and social affairs, people can control world events.

18. *a.** Most people can't realize the extent to which their lives are controlled by supernatural happenings which man can't understand.
    b.* There really is no such thing as providence or fortune.

19. a. One should always be willing to admit mistakes.
    b. It is usually best to cover up one's mistakes.

20. *a.* It is hard to know whether or not a person really likes you.
    b. How many friends you have depends on how nice a person you are.

21. *a.* In the long run the bad things that happen to us are balanced by the good ones.
    b. Most misfortunes are the result of lack of ability, ignorance, laziness, or all three.

22. a. With enough effort we can wipe out political corruption.
    b. It is difficult for people to have much control over the things politicians do in office.

23. *a.* Sometimes I can't understand how teachers arrive at the grades they give.
    b. There is a direct connection between how hard I study and the grades I get.

24. a. A good leader expects people to decide for themselves what they should do.
    b. A good leader makes it clear to everybody what their jobs are.

25. *a.* Many times I feel that I have little influence over the things that happen to me.
    b.* It is impossible for me to believe that supernatural or spiritual forces play an important role in my life.

26. a. People are lonely because they don't try to be friendly.
    b. There's not much use in trying too hard to please people; if they like you, they like you.

27. a. There is too much emphasis on athletics in high school.
    b. Team sports are an excellent way to build character.

28. a. What happens to me is my own doing.
    b. Sometimes I feel that I don't have enough control over the direction my life is taking.

29. *a.* Most of the time I can't understand why politicians behave the way they do.
    b. In the long run the people are responsible for bad government on a national as well as on a local level.

    * These items have been revised from Rotter's (1966) original scale.

Appendix B

Internal vs. External Control
Neutral Revision

The following revision of Rotter's (1966) measure of Internal vs. External Control includes eight altered items (Gabbard, Howard, & Tageson, 1986). Subjects are to select the statement with which they more strongly agree. One's score is the total number of underlined choices (i.e., external items) endorsed. The scale includes six filler items that are not scored (where neither option is underlined).

1. a. Children get into trouble because their parents punish them too much.
   b. The trouble with most children nowadays is that their parents are too easy with them.

2. *a.** Many of the unhappy things in people's lives are partly due to powerful others.
   b. People's misfortunes result from the mistakes they make.

3. a. One of the major reasons why we have wars is because people don't take enough interest in politics.
   b. There will always be wars, no matter how hard people try to prevent them.

4. a. In the long run people get the respect they deserve in this world.
   b. Unfortunately, an individual's worth often passes unrecognized no matter how hard he tries.

5. a. The idea that teachers are unfair to students is nonsense.
   b. Most students don't realize the extent to which their grades are influenced by accidental happenings.

6. *a.** Without providential forces one cannot be an effective leader.
   b. Capable people who fail to become leaders have not taken advantage of their opportunities.

7. *a.* No matter how hard you try, some people just don't like you.
   b. People who can't get others to like them don't understand how to get along with others.

8. a. Heredity plays the major role in determining one's personality.
   b. It is one's experiences in life which determine what one is like.

9. *a.* I have often found that what is going to happen will happen.
   b.* Trusting providence has never turned out as well for me as making a decision to take a definite course of action.

10. a. In the case of the well-prepared student there is rarely if ever such a thing as an unfair test.
    b. Many times exam questions tend to be so unrelated to course work that studying is really useless.

11. a.* Becoming a success is a matter of hard work; no other forces are at work.
    b. Getting a good job depends mainly on being in the right place at the right time.

12. a. The average citizen can have an influence in government decisions.
    b. This world is run by the few people in power, and there is not much the little guy can do about it.

13. a. When I make plans, I am almost certain that I can make them work.
    b. It is not always wise to plan too far ahead because many things turn out to be a matter of good or bad fortune anyhow.

14. a. There are certain people who are just no good.
    b. There is some good in everybody.

15. a.* In my case getting what I want has little or nothing to do with other powerful forces.
    b.* Many times we might just as well decide what to do by relying on powerful others.

16. *a.** Who gets to be the boss often depends on who was fortunate enough to be in the right place first.
    *b.** Getting people to do the right thing depends on ability; powerful other forces have little or nothing to do with it.
17. *a.* As far as world affairs are concerned, most of us are the victims of forces we can neither understand nor control.
    b. By taking an active part in political and social affairs, the people can control world events.
18. *a.** Most people can't realize the extent to which their lives are controlled by happenings which they can't understand.
    *b.** There really is no such thing as providence or fortune.
19. a. One should always be willing to admit mistakes.
    b. It is usually best to cover up one's mistakes.
20. *a.* It is hard to know whether or not a person really likes you.
    b. How many friends you have depends on how nice a person you are.
21. *a.* In the long run the bad things that happen to us are balanced by the good ones.
    b. Most misfortunes are the result of lack of ability, ignorance, laziness, or all three.
22. a. With enough effort we can wipe out political corruption.
    b. It is difficult for people to have much control over the things politicians do in office.
23. *a.* Sometimes I can't understand how teachers arrive at the grades they give.
    b. There is a direct connection between how hard I study and the grades I get.
24. a. A good leader expects people to decide for themselves what they should do.
    b. A good leader makes it clear to everybody what their jobs are.
25. *a.* Many times I feel that I have little influence over the things that happen to me.
    *b.** It is impossible for me to believe that providence or the will of powerful others plays an important role in my life.
26. a. People are lonely because they don't try to be friendly.
    b. There's not much use in trying too hard to please people; if they like you, they like you.
27. a. There is too much emphasis on athletics in high school.
    b. Team sports are an excellent way to build character.
28. a. What happens to me is my own doing.
    b. Sometimes I feel that I don't have enough control over the direction my life is taking.
29. *a.* Most of the time I can't understand why politicians behave the way they do.
    b. In the long run the people are responsible for bad government on a national as well as on a local level.

* These items have been revised from Rotter's (1966) original scale.

Gabbard, C. E., Howard, G. S., & Tageson, C. W. (1986). Assessing locus of control with religious populations. *Journal of Research in Personality, 20,* 292–308. Copyright © 1986 by Academic Press, Inc. Reprinted with permission.

17.7
THE RIGHT-WING AUTHORITARIANISM SCALE (Altemeyer, 1996)
Reviewed by Raymond F. Paloutzian

Variable: The Right-Wing Authoritarianism (RWAS) Scale is intended to measure the trait of authoritarianism in the service of established authority. In Altemeyer's (1988, p. 2) own words, right-wing authoritarianism means the combination of the following three attitudinal clusters:

1. Authoritarian submission: a high degree of submission to the authorities, who are perceived to be established and legitimate in the society in which one lives.
2. Authoritarian aggression: a general aggressiveness, directed against various persons, that is perceived to be sanctioned by established authorities.
3. Conventionalism: a high degree of adherence to the social conventions that are perceived to be endorsed by society and its established authorities.

It should be emphasized that RWA is represented by the *combination* of these three attributes, not by one of them only. For example, someone who happens to hold conventional views is not automatically, necessarily authoritarian. But someone who shows conventionalism (in the sense given above) knit together with the other attitudes would be seen as right-wing authoritarian.

Description: The stimulus for the development of the RWA scale was the pioneering work on *The Authoritarian Personality* (Adorno, Frenkel-Brunswick, Levinson, & Sanford, 1950). Conceived in psychoanalytic terms, the high authoritarian was seen as being possessed of unconscious hostility and thus susceptible to fascist propaganda. This idea was a theoretical milestone because it was the first time that psychologists stated a compelling rationale for a possible link between personality and ideology. However, the F Scale, used to assess the authoritarian personality, contained methodological flaws, and by the 1960s much of the research centered on problems with the

scale rather than on the theory that underlay it.

Research on the topic waned until Altemeyer developed a simpler conceptualization of authoritarianism and a suitable scale to measure it. The RWA Scale, which, unlike the F Scale, is balanced against response sets, has been modified annually since its first publication in 1981. This review addresses the 1994 version.

It is often asked whether there is also an authoritarianism on the left. Altemeyer (1996) has recently advanced such a conceptualization and research bearing on it. Thus far, however, left-wing authoritarianism has proven unrelated to religious variables, whereas the right wing version has a rich history of connections.

The 1994 RWA Scale contains 34 statements but only the last 30 are scored. Each item is answered on a 9-point Likert scale for which the answer options range from –4 (very strongly disagree) to +4 (very strongly agree). A neutral answer is indicated by a 0. A final score is obtained by adding a constant of five to all answers. The individual scores are then summed to yield a total score. RWA scores can range from a low of 30 to a high of 270, with a theoretical midpoint of 150.

Practical Considerations: The scale takes approximately 20 minutes to complete. No special training or instructions are required. The instructions on the scale are clear and self-explanatory.

Norms/Standardization: While the initial standardization group consisted of University of Manitoba students in the early 1970s, cross-validating studies quickly extended the findings to many other North American student populations and even parents of university students. Tens of thousands of people have since completed the scale, resulting in a large volume of data collected from different samples and in different cultures and languages. The scale has shown robustness across its versions and the various samples, even internationally after being translated into Russian, German, and Spanish.

Means obtained with the 1994 scale tend to be somewhat lower than with earlier versions. On the present scale, student means tend to land in the 120s, whereas those of their parents place about 25 points higher. No appreciable sex differences are apparent in RWA scores, although women tend to score higher on items that tap conventionalism and men tend to score higher on items that tap authoritarian aggression.

Representing non-Christianized populations, Hunsberger (1996) reports data with the previous scale for a Toronto sample of 23 Hindus ($M = 157.2$, $SD = 22.0$), 21 Muslims ($M = 171.5$, $SD = 28.7$), and 32 Jews ($M = 110.8$, $SD = 41.0$).

Reliability: Altemeyer (1996) cites over 30 studies for which the internal consistency reliability ranged from .81 to .95. The only exception was a coefficient of .43 among 400 Xhosa-speaking students who answered the scale in English. Generally speaking, the reliability of the RWA Scale has increased to about the .90 level or better as a result of test improvements over the years. Test-retest reliability coefficients for students have ranged from .95 over a one-week interval to .85 for 28 weeks between testings.

Validity: The combined evidence suggests that the RWA Scale measures what it is intended to measure. High RWAs tend to adhere to traditional religious teachings more than low RWAs, suggesting that the scale is sensitive to the attribute of conventionalism. This finding occurs for samples of Christians, Palestinian Muslims, and Orthodox Jews. RWA is positively correlated with Christian orthodoxy and dogmatism. In several studies, RWA scores correlated between .66 and .75 with religious fundamentalism. Similar data show that high RWAs tend to be more prejudiced, more willing to use punitive measures, and more likely to inform established authorities of others who violate laws. People high in RWA also tend to endorse statements at Stage 2 (mythic-lit-

eral faith) and Stage 3 (synthetic-conventional faith) in Fowler's theory of faith development. Altemeyer (1996) has recently concluded that religious fundamentalism is largely the right-wing authoritarian's response to the religious impulse. Overall, the data fall into a pattern of what would be expected on theoretical grounds.

Location: The following book presents the 1994 RWA Scale. See Altemeyer's 1981 and 1988 books in the references below for earlier versions of the scale.

Altemeyer, B. (1996). *The authoritarian specter*. Cambridge, MA: Harvard University Press.

Subsequent Research:

Altemeyer, B., & Hunsberger, B. (1992). Authoritarianism, religious fundamentalism, quest, and prejudice. *The International Journal for the Psychology of Religion, 2*, 113–133.

Hunsberger, B. (1996). Religious fundamentalism, right-wing authoritarianism and hostility toward homosexuals in non-Christian religious groups. *The International Journal for the Psychology of Religion, 6*, 39–49.

Hunsberger, B., Pancer, M.S., Pratt, M., & Alisat, S. (1996). The transition to university: Is religion related to adjustment? In M. Lynn & D. Moberg (Eds.), *Research in the Social Scientific Study of Religion* (Vol. 7, pp. 181–199). Greenwich, CT: JAI Press.

Hunsberger, B., Pratt, M., & Pancer, S. M. (1994). Religious fundamentalism and integrative complexity of thought: A relationship for existential content only? *Journal for the Scientific Study of Religion, 33*, 335–346.

Leak, G. K., & Randall, B. A. (1995). Clarification of the link between right-wing authoritarianism and religiousness: The role of religious maturity. *Journal for the Scientific Study of Religion, 34*, 245–252.

References

Adorno, T. W., Frenkel-Brunswik, E., Levinson, D. J., & Sanford, R. N. (1950). *The authoritarian personality*. New York: Harper.

Altemeyer, B. (1981). *Right-wing authoritarianism*. Winnipeg: University of Manitoba Press.

Altemeyer, B. (1988). *Enemies of freedom: Understanding right-wing authoritarianism*. San Francisco: Jossey-Bass.

Appendix

Right-Wing Authoritarianism Scale (1994)

Instructions: This survey is part of an investigation of general public opinion concerning a variety of social issues. You will probably find that you *agree* with some of the statements, and *disagree* with others, to varying extents. Please indicate your reaction to each statement by marking your opinion next to the statement, according to the following scale:

- – 4 if you *very strongly disagree* with the statement
- – 3 if you *strongly disagree* with the statement
- – 2 if you *moderately disagree* with the statement
- – 1 if you *slightly disagree* with the statement
- + 1 if you *slightly agree* with the statement
- + 2 if you *moderately agree* with the statement
- + 3 if you *strongly agree* with the statement
- + 4 if you *very strongly agree* with the statement

If you feel exactly and precisely *neutral* about a statement, mark a "0" next to it.

You may find that you sometimes have different reactions to different parts of a statement. For example, you might very strongly disagree (–4) with one idea in a statement, but slightly agree (+1) with another idea in the same item. When this happens, please combine your reactions and write down how you feel "on balance" (that is, a –3 in this example).

1. Life imprisonment is justified for certain crimes.

2. Women should have to promise to obey their husbands when they get married.

3. The established authorities in our country are usually smarter, better informed, and more competent than others are, and the people can rely on them.

4. It is important to protect fully the rights of radicals and deviants.

5. Our country desperately needs a mighty leader who will do what has to be done to destroy the radical new ways and sinfulness that are ruining us.

6. Gays and lesbians are just as healthy and moral as anybody else.*

7. Our country will be great if we honor the ways of our forefathers, do what the authorities tell us to do, and get rid of the "rotten apples" who are ruining everything.

8. Atheists and others who have rebelled against established religion are no doubt every bit as good and virtuous as those who attend church regularly.*

9. The *real* keys to the "good life" are obedience, discipline, and sticking to the straight and narrow.

10. A lot of our rules regarding modesty and sexual behavior are just customs which are not necessarily any better or holier than those which other people follow.*

11. There are many radical, immoral people in our country today who are trying to ruin it for their own godless purposes, whom the authorities should put out of action.

12. It is always better to trust the judgment of the proper authorities in government and religion than to listen to the noisy rabble-rousers in our society who are trying to create doubt in people's minds.

13. There is absolutely nothing wrong with nudist camps.*

14. There is no "*one* right way" to live your life. Everybody has to create their *own* way.*

15. Our country will be destroyed someday if we do not smash the perversions eating away at our moral fiber and traditional beliefs.

16. It's a mistake to "stick strictly to the straight and narrow" in life, for you'll miss a lot of interesting people from quite different backgrounds who can change you, and some of the best experiences you can have.*

17. The situation in our country is getting so serious, the strongest methods would be justified if they eliminated the troublemakers and got us back to our true path.

18. It would be best for everyone if the proper authorities censored magazines so that people could not get their hands on trashy and disgusting material.

19. Everyone should have their own lifestyle, religious beliefs, and sexual preferences, even if it makes them different from everyone else.*

20. A "woman's place" should be wherever she wants to be. The days when women are submissive to their husbands and social conventions belong strictly in the past.*

21. What our country really needs is a strong, determined leader who will crush evil and take us back to our true path.

22. People should pay less attention to the Bible and the other old traditional forms of religious guidance and instead develop their own personal standards of what is moral and immoral.

23. Enough is enough! If the loafers, deviants, and troublemakers won't "shape up," then they should be severely disciplined and taught a lesson they'll never forget.

24. Our country *needs* freethinkers who will have the courage to defy traditional ways, even if this upsets many people.*

25. There is nothing wrong with premarital sexual intercourse.*

26. It may be considered old-fashioned by some, but having a normal, proper appearance is still the mark of a gentleman and, especially, a lady.

27. It is wonderful that young people today have greater freedom to protest against things they don't like and to make their own "rules" to govern their behavior.

28. What our country *really* needs, instead of more "civil rights," is a good stiff dose of law and order.

29. Government, judges, and the police should never be allowed to censor books.*

30. Obedience and respect for authority are the most important virtues children should learn.

31. We should treat protesters and radicals with open arms and open minds, since new ideas are the lifeblood of progressive change.*

32. Once our government leaders and the authorities condemn the dangerous elements in our society, it will be the duty of every patriotic citizen to help stomp out the rot that is poisoning our country from within.

33. Rules about being "well-behaved" and "respectable" should be changed in favor of greater freedom and new ways of living.*

34. The facts on crime, sexual immorality, and recent public disorders all show we have to crack down harder on deviant groups and troublemakers if we are going to save our moral standards and preserve law and order.

* Item is worded in the contrait direction, that is, the right-wing authoritarian response is to disagree.
Note 1. Only items 5–34 are scored.

Note 2. All items are scored on a 9-point basis. For protrait statements, "–4" is scored as 1, and "+4" is scored as 9. The keying is reversed for contrait items. For both kinds of items, the neutral answer ("0") is scored as 5. The lowest possible score is 30, and the highest is 270.

A –4 to +4 response scale has been used on the RWA Scale since 1980, rather than the usual –3 to +3, because experiments have shown it produces (marginally) higher reliability. Either a 9-point or a 7-point response scale appears to be superior to the 5-point scale Likert (1932) invented. A 3-point response scale ("disagree—?—agree") seems to damage appreciably a scale's psychometric properties among populations capable of making finer distinctions (Altemeyer, 1988, pp. 39–42).

(Emphasis in original.)

Reprinted by permission of the publisher from *The Authoritarian Specter* by Bob Altemeyer, Cambridge, Mass.: Harvard University Press, Copyright © 1996 by the President and Fellows of Harvard College.

17.8
SHORT INDEX OF SELF-ACTUALIZATION SCALE (Jones & Crandall, 1986)
Reviewed by Keith J. Edwards

Variable: The Short Index of Self-Actualization Scale (SISA) measures beliefs, attitudes, and behaviors that are assumed to indicate a level of self-actualization. Self-actualization is a dimension of personality derived from third-force, or humanistic, psychology. The best-known measure of self-actualization is the Personal Orientation Inventory (POI) (Shostrom, 1974). Research on the POI has found negative correlations between it and various measures of religiosity. Such data is taken as support for the conclusion that religious commitments interfere with self-actualization. Watson, Morris, and Hood (1990) argued that not all aspects of religiosity are inherently antiself. They observed that the negative correlation may be due to the antireligious nature of some of the items used to measure self-actualization. The authors postulate that there might be a form of self-actualization consistent with the Christian faith not captured by more humanistic measures such as the POI. The authors say,

deeper conflicts may exist in understanding the word "self" in the first place. Within humanistic frameworks, the "self" tends to be an unqualified "good," something to be accepted and nurtured toward its true realization, . . . [for believers the self is] ambivalently nuanced . . . . [However] to view the "self" as ambivalently nuanced is not to see it as wholly negative. . . . proreligious elements can also be iso-

lated within the POI and appear consistent with healthy self-functioning" (Watson et al., 1991, pp 41–41).

The Short Index of Self-Actualization (SISA, Jones & Crandall, 1986) was a preexisting scale selected by the authors to determine if a religiously sensitive measure of self-actualization could be derived from it. They intended to call the derived variable Religious Self-Actualization.

Description: The SISA is actually a measure of self-actualization, not a measure of a religious variable. However, since self-actualization deals with self-functioning, it has high relevance to religious research. The SISA was developed by Jones and Crandall (1986) as an alternative to the longer POI (150 items). It consists of 15 items, 7 positive and 8 negative, taken from the POI. Since the POI is a forced-choice inventory, the items selected for the SISA are the self-actualizing "half" of POI items. The items chosen had the highest item-total correlations with the POI total score. On the SISA, respondents react to each statement by indicating their agreement or disagreement on a four point scale (see scale).

Watson et al. (1990) submitted 14 items of the SISA to a methodology designed to determine whether they were pro or anti religious (omitted from their analysis was the SISA item, "I fear failure".) Items that could not be clearly classified as pro or anti religious were classified as neutral. Students in an introductory psychology class at a state university rated 7 positive and 7 negative items of the SISA on a 5-point scale ranging from "very consistent" to "very inconsistent" with personal religious beliefs. The students were "overwhelmingly" from Protestant backgrounds. The authors sought to identify items of the SISA that could be used to construct Religiously Pro, Neutral, and Anti "subscales." Their intended goal was to reverse the normal scoring of religiously anti statements and then to join them with the religiously pro items so to produce a Religious Self-Actualization Scale. They discovered that none of the SISA items were perceived as antireligious; 2 were determined to be religiously neutral and 12 were rated as proreligious. Proreligious and Neutral Self-Actualization subscales were created from the original SISA items.

Practical Considerations: This paper-and-pencil measure has no special scoring and requires about 10 minutes to complete.

Norms/Standardization: There are no known published norms. The instrument was intended to provide a short measure of self-actualization that could be used in research.

Reliability: No reliability data were reported by Watson et al. (1990). Jones and Crandall (1986) reported an internal consistency coefficient alpha of .65 and a test-retest reliability over a 12-day period of .69.

Validity: There are two aspects of validity relevant to the use of this instrument with religiously committed populations. The first has to do with the pro, anti, or neutral religious bias of the individual items. The authors' research concluded that the SISA was "overwhelmingly defined as 'proreligious'" and that the SISA may be a valuable tool in assessing the self-functioning of religious respondents.

The Proreligious and Neutral subscales demonstrated concurrent and discriminant validity when correlated with related measures of self functioning and with Intrinsic/Extrinsic religiosity. Both scales corre-lated significantly with self-esteem and self-acceptance, but only the Proreligious subscale correlated significantly with the Intrinsic scale.

Jones and Crandall (1986) report a correlation of .69 with the full-scale POI and significant correlations with self-esteem (.41), a measure of rational behavior and beliefs (.44), and a measure of neuroticism (−.30). They also conducted a principle components analysis with varimax rotation of factors with eigenvalues greater than one. This resulted in five components, four of which were objectively interpretable (using independent judges): autonomy or self-direction, self-acceptance and self-esteem, acceptance of emotions and freedom of expression of emotions, and trust and responsibility in interpersonal relations. Crandall (1991) summarizes several studies using the SISA and concludes that the evidence for the validity of the SISA is "overwhelming."

Location:

Jones, A., & Crandall, R. (1986). Validation of a short index of self-actualization. *Personality and Social Psychology Bulletin*, *12*, 63–73. (The original SISA)

Watson, P. J., Morris, R. J. & Hood, R. W. (1990). Intrinsicness, self-actualization, and the ideological surround. *Journal of Psychology and Theology*, *18*, 40–53. (Specifies the Proreligious and Neutral subscales of the SISA.)

Recent Research: Research using the SISA is summarized in Crandall (1991). While there is no research using the SISA as a measure of religious self-actualization, Watson, Morris, and Hood (1990) have reported numerous studies in which other psychological measures similar to the SISA are examined from a religious perspective. The interested reader can consult Watson et al. (1990) to get additional references.

Crandall, R. (1991). Issues in self-actualization measurement. *Journal of Social Behavior and Personality*, *6*(5), 339–344.

References

Shostrum, E. I. (1974). *Manual for the personal orientation inventory.* San Diego: Educational and Industrial Testing Service.

Appendix

Short Index of Self Actualization

Please respond to each item below using the following rating scale:

> 1 = agree   3 = somewhat disagree
> 2 = somewhat agree   4 = disagree

1. (P) I do not feel ashamed of any of my emotions.
2. (P) I feel I must do what others expect me to do.
3. (P) I believe that people are essentially good and can be trusted.
4. (P) It is always necessary that others approve of what I do.
5. (N) I feel free to be angry at those I love.
6. (P) I don't accept my own weaknesses.
7. (P) I can like people without having to approve of them.
8. (N) I avoid attempts to analyze and simplify complex domains.
9. (P) It is better to be yourself than to be popular.
10. (P) I have no mission in life to which I feel especially dedicated.
11. (P) I can express my feelings even when they may result in undesirable consequences.
12. (P) I do not feel responsible to help anybody.
13. (P) I am loved because I can give love.
14. (P) I am bothered by fears of being inadequate.
15.   I fear failure. (Original SISA item omitted from Watson et al., 1990)

P= Proreligious items, N= Neutral items

Jones, A., & Crandall, R. (1986). Validation of a short index of self-actualization. *Personality and Social Psychology Bulletin, 12,* 63–73, copyright © 1986 by Sage Publications, Inc. Reprinted with permission of Sage Publications.

17.9
TRANSPERSONAL ORIENTATION TO LEARNING SCALE
(Shapiro & Fitzgerald, 1989)

Reviewed by Beverly J. McCallister

Variable: The Transpersonal Orientation to Learning Scale (TOTL) measures attitudes toward using a transpersonal approach in education. According to Shapiro and Fitzgerald, a transpersonal approach to education would advocate the development of human spiritual potential. It would advance using intuitive and receptive modes of consciousness, such as fantasy techniques, meditation, and altered states of consciousness, in conjunction with the "cognitive, rational, logical and active modes" (Shapiro & Fitzgerald, 1989, p. 376).

Description: This 40-item scale uses a 5-point Likert format with the usual range of response options: "strongly agree" = 5 points, "agree" = 4 points, "uncertain" = 3 points, "disagree" = 2 points and "strongly disagree" = 1 point. All items were so worded that agreement to every item indicates greater support for the transpersonal approach to education. Four subscales of ten items each were identified: (a) Fantasy Techniques Applied in Schools, (b) Mysticism Preferred to Science as an Epistemology, (c) Mystical/Occult/ Paranormal Techniques Applied to Schools, and (d) Transcendent Consciousness. However, the authors caution that this scale may not measure four dimensions and instead measure only one dimension: a general orientation to the transpersonal approach; or possibly two: a theory-oriented dimension (subscales II & IV) and a practice-oriented dimension (subscales I & III).

The authors contend that the contents of their items are consistent and representative of contents in transpersonal psychology because they were developed from classic and current writings in the field. In describing what a transpersonal orientation professes, Shapiro and Fitzgerald (1989) write that "intuitive and receptive modes of consciousness are considered *equal* [emphasis mine] in importance to cognitive, rational, logical, and active modes" (p. 376). However, this inclusive description of the transpersonal approach does not seem reflected in TOTL items that decry the limits of science ("As a probe into the way things are, science is a powerful but strictly limited instrument." [Item 3]) while extolling the exclusivity of mystical states ("Mystical experience is the source of all true art and science" [Item 10]). If all modes are equal, why should the authors expect an advocate of transpersonal psychology to denigrate the cognitive/rational/logical modes in favor of intuitive and reflective modes?

Other apparent discrepancies exist between what Shapiro and Fitzgerald describe as this field's concern and what other representatives in the field have stated should not necessarily be this field's primary focus (ultimate, altered states and the paranormal). The authors state that transpersonal psychology concerns itself with "*ultimate human capacities and potentialities*" (p. 376), a view reflected in TOTL item 4: "Science can deal with instrumental values, but not with intrinsic (ultimate) values." In 1973, however, a mouthpiece for the field, *The Journal of Transpersonal Psychology*, decided to drop the term "ultimate" from its statement of purpose, acknowledging that much of the field does not focus on the ultimate (Walsh & Vaughan, 1993). Moreover, Wilber (1993) asserts that altered states, however valued by transpersonal psychology, should not necessarily be the field's dominant paradigm; yet TOTL items 13 and 14 privilege altered states. Finally, some au-

thors within transpersonal psychology would not include parapsychology as a subset (Boucouvalas, 1980) and so might question the references made to psychic phenomena used in items 17, 19, 20, 22, 31.

Practical Considerations: No special skills or instructions are needed to administer or score this paper-and-pencil measure of general orientation toward the transpersonal approach to education. The scale takes about 20 minutes to administer. TOTL scores and subscale scores equal the sum of the relevant item responses. Higher scores indicate greater endorsement of the transpersonal approach to education. In analyzing the scores, the researcher should consider that since the wording of every item supports the transpersonal approach and the same set of responses is used throughout, TOTL scores may be subject to response set bias.

Norms/Standardization: The pilot study for this measure used the responses of a total of 166 students from four different graduate programs in the School of Education at the University of California, Santa Barbara. The programs were the following: Confluent (Humanistic) Education, Counseling Psychology, Single Subject Teaching Credential, and Multiple Subject Teaching Credential. The size of the groups was unequal.

For the total TOTL, scores in the pilot study ranged from a low of 69 to a high of 198. Scores at the 90th, 50th and 10th percentiles were 165, 137 and 109, respectively.

Reliability: Analysis of the 40 items of the TOTL indicate a "reasonably high internal consistency" (Shapiro & Fitzgerald, 1989, p. 378) with a spilt-half reliability of .98 and a Cronbach alpha reliability of .96. For the subscales (factor), Cronbach alpha reliabilities were Factor I .83, Factor II .82, Factor III .93, and Factor IV .82.

Validity: The authors propose that the content validity of the TOTL's 40 items was built into the scale by basing item development on a content analysis of the writings of 25 noted transpersonal/humanistic authors in education and psychology. Then content validity was furthered by having the resulting 222 items independently judged by nine academics in Confluent (Humanistic) Education for relevance and clarity. On the basis of interjudge agreement and item variance from a pilot study, 67 items were retained. Based on an item analysis of these 67 statements, 40% of the items were eliminated. Nineteen items were eliminated because of "low item-total correlations and/or little response variance" (Shapiro & Fitzgerald, 1989, p. 378). Next, eight additional items were eliminated based on a preliminary factor analysis and the judgment of the authors about these items' substantive relevance. The remaining 40 items constitute the TOTL.

Criterion validity of the TOTL was supported in two ways: (a) use the TOTL to compare groups of students expected to have differing views on the transpersonal approach to education and (b) demonstrate the presence of positive correlations between TOTL and measures with similar constructs. First, it was anticipated and demonstrated that the mean score for the Confluent (Humanistic) Education students (152) would be significantly higher than mean score of Counseling students (139, F [3,61] = 14.08, $p < .001$). A post hoc test for comparisons between groups of unequal size reportedly supported these comparisons (Steel-Torrie extension of Tukey's HSD test [Lehman, 1995, p. 360]). It was further demonstrated that mean scores for the Confluent and Counseling groups would exceed both the Single Subject Credential mean score (127) and Multiple Subject Credential mean score (129). The two Teaching Credential groups did not differ significantly from each other.

To explore the relationship between the TOTL and measures designed to assess similar constructs, scores on the TOTL were correlated with four other scales. The significance level was set at .05. Responses to the TOTL correlated significantly (.46) with a measure of attitudes toward humanistic instructional values (Orientation to Learning scale; Shapiro, 1985). A second positive correlation (.38) was found between a mea-sure for a type of visionary seeker who might be expected to value the transpersonal (Intuitive-Feeling temperament scale of the Kiersey Temperament Sorter [Kiersey & Bates, 1978]) and the TOTL. Third, TOTL scores correlated (.22) with the Concrete Experience of the Learning Style Inventory (Kolb, 1976). However, TOTL did not correlate signficantly (.15) with the Divergent Learning Style subscale on the Learning Style Inventory (Concrete Experience Plus Reflective Observation).

Factorial validity was indecisive. One principal component analysis that used a varimax rotation (which attempts to minimize the number of variables that have high loadings on a factor, thereby enhancing the factor's interpretability) supports the unidimensionality of the TOTL. A second analysis using an equamax rotation (which attempts to simplify both variable and factors and divide the variance across factors) supported a four-factor solution. The four factors accounted for the overall variance (53%) as follows: Factor I, 16%; Factor II, 10%; Factor III, 15.5%, and Factor IV, 11%.

The TOTL appears to measure a general orientation toward a transpersonal orientation to education, although it may not match the transpersonal orientation as described by the authors or be representative of a field that has not yet agreed on how to define itself. The TOTL is unique in being a transpersonal measure related to educational research. For the psychology of religion, it may serve as a useful measure to compare with measures of spirituality and with measures of learning styles in religious education.

Location:

Stewart B. Shapiro, Department of Education, University of California, Santa Barbara, CA 93106-9490.

References

Boucouvalas, M. (1980). Transpersonal psychology: A working outline of the field. *The Journal of Transpersonal Psychology*, *12*, 37–46.

Chaudhuri, H. (1975). Psychology: Humanisitic and transpersonal. *Journal of Humanistic Psychology*, *15*, 7–15.

Kiersey, D., & Bates, M. (1978). *Please understand me*. Del Mar, CA: Prometheus Nemesis.

Kolb, D. A. (1976). *Learning style inventory*. Boston: McBer.

Lajoie, D. H., Shapiro, S. I., & Roberts, T. B. (1991). A historical analysis of the statement of purpose in *The Journal of Transpersonal Psychology*, *The Journal of Transpersonal Psychology*, *23*, 175–182.

Lehman, R. (1995). *Statistics in the behavioral sciences: A conceptual approach*. Pacific Grove, CA: Brooks/Cole.

MacDonald, D. A., LaClair, L., Alter, A., Friedman, H. L. (1995). A survey of measures of transpersonal constructs. *The Journal of Transpersonal Psychology*, *27*, 171–235.

Shapiro, S. B. (1987). The instructional values of humanistic educators: An expanded, empirical analysis. *Journal of Humanistic Education and Development*, *25*, 155–170.

Shapiro, S. B., & Fitzgerald, L. (1989). The development of an objective scale to measure a transpersonal orientation to learning. *Educational and Psychological Measurements*, *49*, 375–385.

Walsh, R., & Vaughan., F. (1993). On transpersonal definitions. *The Journal of Transpersonal Psychology*, *25*, 199–207.

Wilber, K. (1993). Paths beyond ego in the coming decade. In R. Walsh & F. Vaughan (Eds.), *Paths beyond ego: The transpersonal vision* (pp. 214–222). Los Angeles: J. P. Tarcher.

Appendix

Transpersonal Orientation to Learning Scale

Items should be responded to and scored by checking the following responses and using the following point scheme: strongly agree (5 points), agree (4 points), uncertain (3 points), disagree (2 points), and strongly disagree (1 point). The Roman numeral following each item indicates the item's subscale: I = Fantasy Techniques Applied In Schools, II = Mysticism Preferred to Science as an Epistemology, III = Mystical/Occult/Paranormal Techniques Applied to Schools, IV = Transcendent Consciousness.

1. Strictly speaking, a scientific worldview is impossible because it treats only a part of the world. (II)

2. As a probe into the way things are, science is a powerful but strictly limited instrument. (II)

3. Only a nonscientific approach to mankind and the world can give us meaning, purpose, and a vision in which everything coheres. (II)

4. Science can deal with instrumental values but not with intrinsic (ultimate) values. (II)

5. As a human being, a scientist may become engaged with questions of life meanings, but his science will not help him answer such questions. (II)

6. Scientific propositions leave the existential problems of life completely untouched. (II)

7. Reality far exceeds what science will ever register. (II)

8. People have a natural desire to experience altered states of consciousness. (IV)

9. We are on the verge of discovering and controlling a kind of biological energy that has to do with the occult, psychic phenomena, and other unusual occurrences. (IV)

10. Mystical experience is the source of all true art and science. (II)

11. Humankind's consciousness of self is approximately halfway between subconsciousness of nature and the superconsciousness of spirit. (IV)

12. Through transformative spiritual or mystical experience a realm of exquisite order, intelligence, and creative potential can be revealed to nearly everyone. (IV)

13. It is only through the traditions of spiritual or mystical direct knowing that the true nature of reality can be glimpsed. (II)

14. In mystical experience we see the way things "are," not how we wish them to be or analyze them to be. (II)

15. Bodily death does not end individual consciousness. (IV)

16. Death is not the final end, but rather the entrance to a new existence. (IV)

17. Psychic phenomena remind us that we have access to a source of higher knowing, a domain not limited by time and space. (IV)

18. Social transformation results from personal/individual transformation-change from the inside out. (IV)

19. Transcendence through altered states of consciousness, paranormal phenomena, and spiritual disciplines should be included in public school curricula where appropriate. (III)

20. Psychic phenomena, peak experiences, self-transcendence, spiritual growth, parapsychology, and Eastern psychologies all have their place in public education. (III)

21. Research has indicated that working with imagery often has a beneficial effect on physical, emotional, mental, and spiritual well-being. (I)

22. Children and youth in schools should be taught how to induce altered states of consciousness in themselves such as those states in psychic healing, parapsychological phenomena, yoga, biofeedback, and meditation. (III)

23. Effective methods of mind/body control have been practiced in yoga for thousands of years and should be taught in our schools and colleges. (III)

24. Directed fantasy trips and guided imagery have been practiced in yoga for thousands of years and should be taught in our schools and colleges. (III)

25. Teachers who use fantasy journeys and guided imagery have a vital key to improved instruction. (I)

26. Guided imagery and visualization techniques really work in improving instructional outcomes. (I)

27. The use of fantasy gives students an imaginary experience which they can relate to the verbal, logical material usually presented in class. (I)

28. Self-hypnosis should be used in public schools and universities to accelerate learning and to gain voluntary control over physiological functions. (III)

29. We cannot really understand the world that lies outside of us without understanding the deeper spiritual and mystical aspects of ourselves. (IV)

30. Contemporary physicists are now scientifically describing reality in almost identical terms with the views of mystics from many different religious traditions. (IV)

31. Dreamwork, fantasy, biofeedback, body awareness, psychic abilities, and meditation should all be implemented in the classroom. (IV)

32. Guided fantasy is a very useful learning tool. (I)

33. Teachers, parents, or counselors who are interested in opening up the world of fantasy for exploration by children should not overlook the fact that they too will benefit personally from the experience. (I)

34. Fantasy is a tool for human growth and development which is effective and rewarding at any age. (I)

35. Techniques like guided daydreams and sharing fantasies have very positive results in education. (I)

36. Classroom sharing through fantasy exercises is a very effective way for students to integrate inner experience with outer reality. (III)

37. Students in school should be taught that anyone can assert control over the healing process. (III)

38. Spiritual, transpersonal perspectives should be incorporated into all aspects of a graduate program in psychology. (III)

39. Various practices of meditation should be introduced into the public schools. (III)

40. Students in schools should be taught how to establish and maintain contact with their inner cores, where unity with all life energy occurs. (III)

Reprinted with permission of authors.

Contributors

Cay Anderson-Hanley
Glens Falls Hospital
Glens Falls, NY

Timothy J. Aycock
A New Start Counseling Center
Union City, GA

Rodney L. Bassett
Roberts Wesleyan College
Rochester, NY

Michael J. Boivin
Indiana Wesleyan University
Marion, IN

Curtis R. Brant
Bowling Green State University
Bowling Green, OH

Beth Fletcher Brokaw
Rosemead School of Psychology,
 Biola University
La Mirada, CA

Christopher T. Burris
University of St. Jerome's College
Waterloo, Ontario

Ronald J. Burwell
Messiah College
Grantham, PA

James Casebolt
Ohio University—Eastern Campus
St. Clairsville, OH

Caro E. Courtenay
College of William & Mary
Williamsburg, VA

James P. David
University of Iowa
Iowa City, IA

Keith J. Edwards
Rosemead School of Psychology,
 Biola University
La Mirada, CA

Leslie J. Francis
Trinity College Carmarthen and
 University of Wales Lampeter
Wales, United Kingdom

Richard L. Gorsuch
Graduate School of Psychology,
 Fuller Theological Seminary
Pasadena, CA

M. Elizabeth Lewis Hall
Rosemead School of Psychology,
 Biola University
La Mirada, CA

Todd W. Hall
Rosemead School of Psychology,
 Biola University
La Mirada, CA

Peter C. Hill
Grove City College
Grove City, PA

Laura Hinebaugh-Igoe
Wayne State University
Detroit, MI

Ralph W. Hood Jr.
University of Tennessee at Chattanooga
Chattanooga, TN

Bruce Hunsberger
Wilfred Laurier University
Waterloo, Ontario, Canada

Tracey A. Jewell
Bowling Green State University
Bowling Green, OH

W. Brad Johnson
United States Naval Academy
Annapolis, MD

Duane Kauffmann
Goshen College
Goshen, IN

Allison Kirby
Northeast Louisiana University
Monroe, LA

Lee A. Kirkpatrick
College of William & Mary
Williamsburg, VA

Kevin L. Ladd
Indiana University South Bend
South Bend, IN

Anne Lockow
University of Denver
Denver, CO

Beverly J. McCallister
San Francisco, CA

Michael E. McCullough
National Institute for Healthcare Research
Rockville, MD

Daniel N. McIntosh
University of Denver
Denver, CO

Mark R. McMinn
Wheaton College
Wheaton, IL

Roger C. Olson
George Fox University
Newberg, OR

Raymond F. Paloutzian
Westmont College
Santa Barbara, CA

Mark S. Rye
Bowling Green State University
Bowling Green, OH

Steven J. Sandage
Bethel Theological Seminary
St. Paul, MN

John D. Scanish
Wheaton College
Wheaton, IL

Kevin S. Seybold
Grove City College
Grove City, PA

Susan M. Sheffer
Loyola University of Chicago
Chicago, IL

Heather Silva
Spring Arbor College
Spring Arbor, MI

Randall Lehmann Sorenson
Rosemead School of Psychology,
   Biola University
La Mirada, CA

Bernard Spilka
University of Denver
Denver, CO

Daryl H. Stevenson
Houghton College
Houghton, NY

Nancy Stiehler Thurston
George Fox University
Newberg, OR

Randie L. Timpe
Mount Vernon Nazarene College
Mount Vernon, OH

Theresa Clement Tisdale
Boston University, The Danielsen Institute
Boston, MA

Laura Underwood
Prince Corporation
Holland, MI

Larry VandeCreek
Health Care Chaplaincy
New York, NY

P. J. Watson
University of Tennessee at Chattanooga
Chattanooga, TN

Gary Welton
Grove City College
Grove City, PA

David M. Wulff
Wheaton College
Norton, MA

Paul D. Young
Houghton College
Houghton, NY